W9-CAD-089

PROVENCE

A Country Almanac

PROVENCE

A Country Almanac

LOUISA JONES

Photographs by Louisa Jones, Vincent Motte,
Michel Barberousse, Philippe Giraud, and others

Stewart, Tabori & Chang

New York

To Bernard, my countryman

Text copyright © 1993 Louisa Jones

Due to limitations of space, photo credits appear on
page 171 and constitute an extension of this page.

Map by Oliver Williams

Published in 1993 by
Stewart, Tabori & Chang, Inc.
575 Broadway, New York, New York 10012

LIBRARY OF CONGRESS CATALOGING-IN-PUBLICATION DATA

Jones, Louisa E.
Provence : a country almanac / Louisa Jones.
p.   cm.
Includes bibliographical references and index.
ISBN 1-55670-278-7
1. Provence (France)—Guidebooks. 2. Seasons—France—
Provence—Alamancs. 3. Country life—France—Provence.
4. Provence (France)—Social life and customs. I. Title.
DC611.P961J66   1993
914.4'904839—dc20   92-40024
CIP

Distribution in the U.S. by Workman Publishing,
708 Broadway, New York, New York 10003
Distributed in Canada by Canadian Manda Group,
P.O. Box 920 Station U, Toronto, Ontario M8Z 5P9
Distributed in all other territories (except Central and
South America) by Melia Publishing Services,
P.O. Box 1639, Maidenhead, Berkshire SL6 6YZ England

Printed in Japan

10 9 8 7 6 5 4 3 2 1

Nyons

St.~Paul~
les~Trois~Châteaux

Rochegude

Bollène

Vaison~la~Romaine

Suze~la~Rousse

Cairanne

Malancène

Serignan

Bagnole

ORANGE

Crillon~le~Brave

Chateauneuf~du~Pape

Carpentras

VAUCLUSE MTS.

Tavel

Villeneuve

Isle~sur~la
Sorgue

Fontaine~de~Vaucluse

Gordes

Apt

AVIGNON

Barbantane

Bonnieux

LUBERON MTS.

Maillane

Saint Rémy

Tarascon

ALPILLES MTS.

Durance

Le
Paradou

Les Baux

Lunel

Salon

ARLES

Mausanne

MONT SAINTE VICTOIRE

P   R   O   V   E   N   C   E

C   A   M   A   R   G   U   E

Rhône

Aix~
en~Provence

Les~Saintes~
Maries~
de~la~Mer

MARSEILLES

Mediterranean Sea

Rhône

Gard

Contents

Printemps

Spring

Eté

Summer

Introduction

For centuries, country life and lore found expression in the farmer's almanac—a season-by-season guide that provided practical advice, quotations and proverbs, folklore, information about local festivals, recipe suggestions, curious bits of regional history, portraits of famous people, humor and entertainment for leisure moments. Benjamin Franklin created an internationally celebrated best-seller with *Poor Richard's Almanac*, published yearly between 1733 and 1758. Some 150 years later, southern French poet Frédéric Mistral tried to preserve the flavor of old-time Provence in a similar work.

Both Franklin and Mistral followed the usual pattern for almanacs: All items are short, pithy and amusing. Their only logic is that of the seasons, and surprising juxtapositions are part of their appeal. Almanacs aim to delight and instruct, supplying new background material, fresh insights and up-to-date information. *Provence: A Country Almanac* was inspired by this rural tradition. It is not, however, linked to a particular year, and it is designed for a far wider audience.

In recent years, people all over the world have been showing interest in Provençal country ways. The subject has almost become a media cliché. The present volume was not written, however, in response to a current fad; rather, it grew out of 20 years' experience teaching Provençal culture to American students in Avignon. Preparing these courses entailed exploring the region's history, geography, literature, arts and crafts, and even gastronomy, as fully as possible. Many portraits of this celebrated area touch only the surface; but its justifiably famous traditions of good living still hold many happy surprises, both delight and instruction for interested readers.

One popular misconception about Provence is that it has maintained its rich culture by living apart from the modern world, which is today threatening to spoil it. In fact, the Midi has drawn foreigners for millennia—starting with Greek traders 600 years before Christ. Always a major crossroads, invaded numerous times from the north and from the sea, it has nonetheless maintained its own strong identity. Indeed, outside influences have often enriched Provençal culture: For example, the brilliantly ornamental fabrics that are so popular today were originally printed on cottons imported from India; and salt cod, the basis of many a local dish in the remoter, inland areas, sometimes came all the way from New England. Even in the remote Middle Ages, small Provençal cities maintained active trade with distant places, thus bringing new wealth to a landed gentry whose rich valley farms later housed whole communities. The elegant way of life of this class, which reached its peak in the mid-nineteenth century, now evokes much nostalgia.

In the age of the European Community, when missile bases are built just steps away from famous truffle markets, can this vision still have meaning? The old ways embodied a certain *savoir vivre*, currently translated as "art of living"; it is this that makes Provence an inspiration for people today in many, far-flung places. At the same time, however, as food writer Leslie Forbes puts it, "The recent spotlight on Provence has had one beneficial result—an increase in regional pride."

Whatever the future may hold, Provence's rich heritage is clearly linked to the land. The town of Saint-Rémy-de-Provence, for example, has been famous for centuries for its spring vegetable market. Now it is attracting many jet-set personalities, from rock stars to royalty, as a summer retreat. One local woman, a farmer's daughter who is also the descendant of a great poet and the wife of a successful painter, judges that her community still has about an equal number of working farms and cosmopolitan vacation homes. As long as that proportion can be maintained, she believes, the old values can survive.

Max-Phillipe Delavouet, another southern poet (one of many), concludes that "art in Provence, in its best manifestations, is always peasant art. It never forgets the earth from which it springs and its finest works, even those born in cities, always keep that refined and rustic air which confers nobility on our countryside. . . ."

Provence country life is all about "that refined and rustic air," some of which, I hope, has found its way into these pages.

Louisa Jones
Avignon, July 1992

The theatrical unveilings of flowering orchards among

 the silver and somber greens of olive and

cypress: almonds followed by apricots and

plums, cherries, peaches, apples, pears and quinces.

Fires among the fruit trees for frost protection. Small

Spring in

lambs and kids taking their first stumbling steps in

open fields and, within the hour, racing around mer-

rily; the shearing of the sheep and their departure for

the summer pastureland of the pre-Alps.

Pounding rains and spring floods . . . and

still frost. Delicate bulbs completing their growth cycle

in preparation for summer dormancy . . .

sheets of wild narcissus and iris on the

hillsides of the Luberon and Mont Ventoux.

The first swallows and then the nightingales. The first

Provence is . . .

of May, considered to be the first day of summer in

Provence. Numerous flower festivals celebrating young

lovers. All the delights of the market gardens: the first

asparagus, strawberries, cherries, melons, apricots.

Pentecost, the first harvest festival.

Spring

*Gardens in Provence mingle aromatics such as fennel, lavender, hyssop
and rosemary with similar perennials (here the yellow swirls of phlomis) for
exuberant scenes where shapes and texture count as much as bloom.*

A Glorious Spring Garden:
Giverny in Provence

[Joseph Bayol, Quartier Plantier Major, 13210 Saint-Rémy-de-Provence.
Tel: 90 92 11 97. Leaving Saint-Rémy-de-Provence on the road to Maillane,
watch for the Bayols' name on the right, just after the city limits sign.
Open Fridays, Saturdays and Sundays.]

Spring had really come.

The south opened like a mouth. It blew one long breath, humid and warm, and flowers quivered inside the seeds, and the round earth began to ripen like a fruit.

Jean Giono, REGAIN

Tucked among the lush farms that surround the market-gardening center of Saint-Rémy lie many old properties that now serve other creative purposes. Indeed, this area supports more artists per square foot than any other part of provincial France. For many, it is the landscape that inspires them; but for Joseph Bayol, it is also the rich garden that his wife tends at their doorstep.

In the late 1960s, the couple bought a property that had once grown vegetables, a rectangle of about 1,000 square yards, separated from neighbors, as is customary in this countryside, by thick cypress hedging. The house they built on this land is now adorned with traditional trelliswork along its south side. Here vines and wisteria climb and intermingle. Next door is a small gallery, where Monsieur Bayol's artistic efforts as well as those of many friends—painters, sculptors, jewelry makers, furniture designers—are on display. In front of both house and gallery lies the garden.

Cherry trees, planted by former owners, are flanked by a pink-flowering horse chestnut and three redbuds. Closer to the house is a persimmon tree, which is draped with golden fruit in autumn. Paths wind through densely packed flowers—perennials from poppies to delphiniums to Japanese anemones, and annuals that thrive in the rich soil. Madame Bayol's columbines are twice the size of any others in the

Painter Joseph Bayol of Saint-Rémy lovingly paints the garden that his wife cultivates for his pleasure and inspiration.

ABOVE: *Early, spring-flowering photinia frames the bird-man statue in the garden of the Auberge de Noves near Avignon.* OPPOSITE: *Iris and redbud together enhance the Mas de la Pyramide near Saint-Rémy-de-Provence.*

Alpilles, and her husband loves to paint them.

Such floral abundance suggests an English cottage garden, or the riot of color at Monet's beloved Giverny, more readily than a Mediterranean setting. But farm gardens are also traditional in Provence: Van Gogh admired—and painted—their brilliance in 1888, citing dahlias, pomegranates, figs and red roses.

Monsieur Bayol's paintings capture the strong contrasts of sun and shade, throughout the day and year, that only a Mediterranean climate can produce. Although his work has been exhibited in Paris, Washington and San Francisco and been seen by an ever wider audience, he remains a homebody. He and his wife are deeply rooted in the soil of Saint-Rémy.

The Miracle of Tarascon

This charming small town on the Rhone's left bank was long beset by a water dragon of frightful appearance called a *Tarasque.* Somewhat resembling a giant porcupine, every year it devoured a good proportion of the local young people. Luckily Saint Martha, one of Provence's most popular saints, was able to tame the beast, a miracle that was commemorated for centuries by a public festival in May. A model of the Tarasque was paraded around the town, followed by joyful crowds. As rowdy as Carnival, this holiday used to be considered a failure if no one broke an arm during the day.

If the first four days of April are windy, forty more like them will follow.

Si les quatre premiers jours d'avril sont venteux, il y en aura pour quarante jours.

Si l'abrihando es venousa, n'ia pèr quaranto jour.

Cold in April means bread and wine, but a cold May destroys the harvest.

Avril froid donne pain et vin, si mai est froid, il moissonne tout.

Abrieou fres pan et vin douno, S mai es fres l'y va meissouno.

Among the professional corporations that always took part in the long parade were the Gardeners, mounted on a flower-bedecked float, carrying vases of rare blossoms and herbs. With great delicacy, before the eyes of an admiring public, they planted out a most agreeable garden. A local troubadour, Desanat, quoted by nineteenth-century poet Frédéric Mistral, described what would usually happen next:

While the plants line up
And measures are made
Near the girls to court
Three lads start to turn
Then, without warning
Throw into their bosoms
Seeds which tickle . . .
If the beauties allow
While they are scratching
The lads take advantage
And plant a kiss.

But as every good gardener knows, seeds must be watered, and so the gardeners naturally gave the girls—and the laughing crowd—a good soaking with the watering cans. Then a shower of bonbons and bouquets was thrown, and more than once, according to the poet, marriages would follow soon after.

The entrance to an elegant manor house in the Alpilles reveals the splendid, carefully pruned canopy of ancient plane trees within.

Today, the Fête de la Tarasque has been replaced by a wonderful flower festival, which takes place on Whitsun weekend (late May or early June). Dealers in rare plants display their wares for gardeners who come from far and wide.

L'Ourteto Herb Soup

▲▲▲▲▲▲▲

The name of this simple herb soup means "little garden." The recipe has been adapted from Réné Jouveau's *La Cuisine provençale de tradition populaire.* Serves 4.

2 pounds fresh spinach
Handful of young celery leaves
1 pound sorrel leaves
1 medium leek, white part and small section of the green
Salt
1 small onion, sliced
2 cloves garlic, minced
4 thin slices dense country bread
4 tablespoons olive oil
4 fresh eggs

Wash and drain the spinach, celery, sorrel and leek; coarsely chop each vegetable. Place the vegetables in a pot, cover with water and bring to a boil. Add salt, the onion and garlic. Simmer the mixture for about 30 minutes. Place the slices of bread in a soup tureen (or place a slice in individual soup bowls) and

Manguin Fruit Liqueurs and Brandies

[*Manguin, Ile de la Barthelasse, 84000 Avignon. Tel: 90 82 62 29 and 90 86 56 60. Visits by appointment.*]

Hidden between two channels of the Rhone, just beyond Avignon's picturesque medieval bridge, lies the Island of Barthelasse—rich vineyards and orchards only minutes from the city center. Down its winding back lanes can be found a number of elaborate old properties, some of which were originally built in the fourteenth century as hunting lodges. One of the most impressive belongs to the Manguin family, producers of fine fruit brandies and liqueurs.

Agricultural engineer Claude Manguin, son of early Fauve painter Henri Manguin, began to farm here during World War II while his father continued to paint in his studio in Avignon. It was not long before Claude decided to specialize in the production of luxury pears and peaches. These choice fresh fruits are now sold in local markets, bearing a dab of red wax on each stem to preserve freshness; they are even more widely appreciated in alcoholic form. Today, grandsons Jean-Pierre and Henri, like many heirs to family businesses in Provence, combine traditional methods requiring a great deal of individual attention with the most modern machinery and techniques. They have also become leaders in the crusade for organic production of fruits and vegetables.

British novelist Ford Madox Ford described the Island of Barthelasse as an earthly paradise. And after a recent visit to the Manguins, U.S. Department of Agriculture specialists had to agree. The soil has been enriched by centuries of flooding, controlled and directed (most of the

sprinkle them generously with the olive oil. When the vegetables are tender, add the eggs to the broth, partially cover the pot and poach the eggs lightly for about 3 minutes. Pour the entire mixture over the bread in the tureen and serve immediately.

time!) by a system of ducts and dikes. Both the poplars bordering the island and the ivy that grows at their feet provide shelter for more than 15 different insects that help to combat fruit pests. The ecological balance in these orchards is indeed harmonious. For example, while most local fruit growers spray their trees three times a year against red-spider mites, the Manguins have not treated theirs in ten years—and in some sections, not for 17 years! The fruit they produce are beautiful to the eye and to the palate . . . and are healthy as well!

Creativity and enterprise are family hallmarks. In the 1940s, when Jean-Pierre was a boy, he wanted to buy one of his grandfather's paintings. First, he cut down a tree to sell for firewood, but the proceeds did not amount to the "family price" of 3,000 francs required to purchase it. To earn the rest, Jean-Pierre patiently grew and sold vegetables. Today, reproductions of Grandpapa's paintings are used to advertise the produce of the estate.

The range of brandies and liqueurs (and related items, such as alcohol-filled candies) has been deliberately limited so that distillation can follow immediately after natural fermentation, in season. (Companies that treat many different fruits often block the first fermentation by the introduction of an acid; this intervention allows distillation to be postponed to a more convenient time.) Best known is the Manguins' *eau de vie de poire,* or white pear alcohol, made from the excellent Williams pear (known in the United States as the Bartlett). Available in bottles of 350 milliliters, 700 milliliters and 1.5 liters, aged a minimum of two years, this brew is smooth and mellow. Grandfather's taste for warm colors and light has found a successful new expression.

Early Fauve artist Henri Manguin painted fruit lovingly; his descendants distill the fruits of Provence into a variety of delicious nectars.

23

Visited by the Nightingale

Weatherworn stone statues around the Roman basin at the bucolic Château de Roussan have been listening to nightingales in the nearby thickets for more than two centuries.

In the first half of April, one of the Provençal gardener's favorite companions, the nightingale, makes its presence felt. The mellifluous voice of *Luscinia megarhynchos* emerges from thickets and glades ("verdurous glooms and winding mossy ways," says Keats), from marshlands as well as dry areas, on moonlit nights and on cool mornings. Plainly dressed, this bird is a wonder to hear but difficult to see—so much so that the Greeks invented a powerful myth to explain its shyness. They portrayed the nightingale as Philomel, sister-in-law to the king of Thrace who, having done violence to her, cut out her tongue. The gods turned her into the bird, a victory for voice much celebrated by poets, such as T. S. Eliot in *The Waste Land*:

The change of Philomel, by the barbarous king
So rudely forced; yet there the nightingale
Filled all the desert with inviolable voice

Nightingales are less common in the south of France today than they once were. In a description of Tarascon in the 1930s, British novelist Ford Madox Ford remarked that "upon that wall—and at noon—I have known the nightingale voices to be as loud and extended as were those of the starlings on the cornices of the National Gallery." He added that in the heart of town you could not sleep for the abundance of their music.

Southerners often take a less romantic view of the bird than Anglo-Saxon poets, and consider it a nuisance. Transcriptions of its song are hardly appealing: "Jug jug," "chooc, chooc," "a crescendo based on 'pioo,' with many guttural and froglike noises," "hweet," "tacc, tacc," a "scolding 'krr' and a grating 'tchaaa'." Not really a love song, moreover, this virtuosity is intended for the defense of territory!

March wore out its rainy gusts, April its rainbows and May arrived, gently wet, bringing the wild thyme and the sainfoin into flower. Among the beehives one could see, between ten in the morning and noon, huge bursting suns—the first flights of young bees getting their bearings at the home base, a sure sign that the births were continuing on schedule and that the swarms would not be long in emerging.
Marcel Scipion, MEMOIRS OF A BEE SHEPHERD

Still, for John Keats, in his "Ode to a Nightingale," this song conjures up visions of southern wine, "tasting of Flora and the country green, dance, and Provencal song, and sunburnt mirth. . . ." F. Scott Fitzgerald was so moved by these romantic sentiments that when writing about southern French landscapes in *Tender Is the Night*, he borrowed his title from Keats's poetic homage to the nocturnal bird.

Luscinia megarhynchos is related to chats, wheatears, thrushes, robins and redstarts. In Provence, one of the latter species, *Phoenicurus phoenicurus*, is also known as a nightingale (*rossignol des murailles*) and is very active and sociable.

LEFT: *Earthenware urns and jars, like this one containing a hosta at the Bayol garden, are for sale at the shop Jardins de Provence.* ABOVE: *Cherry orchards bloom behind the lavender fields and medieval well, opposite the farmstead of the Mas de la Pyramide.*

Country Decor: Jardins de Provence

[*Aux Jardins de Provence, route d'Avignon, 13210 Saint-Rémy-de-Provence. Tel: 90 92 01 57. Owners: Monsieur et Madame Gérin.*]

Just outside Saint-Rémy-de-Provence, on the road to Avignon, a discreet sign points to a nursery specializing in Mediterranean plants (perennials, shrubs, climbers, topiary, fragrant flowering and large subjects). Indoors, a display room contains unusual items of garden furniture, light fixtures, fountains, pottery and sculpture. Under the same ownership is a shop for smaller objects, such as vases and candles. La Boutique du Jardin, 1, cours Mirabeau, in the center of town. Telephone: 90 92 11 60.

A Provençal Folk Song

Recorded by Provençal poet Frédéric Mistral, who
learned it from a plowman named Jan Roussière.
Translated into English by George Wickes.

"Welcome, wild nightingale so free,
Now that you've arrived safely.
I thought you had come to harm
In Gibraltar's mighty storm.
But from the moment I heard you,
My heart was glad.

"Sir, you have a good memory
To have remembered me so long.
It will always be my wish
To spend summers here with you.
To your love I will respond,
Warbling sweetly;
Day and night I shall sing
Here around you.

"I shall give you all the freedom
And enjoyment of my garden.
The gardener has my orders
Not to cause you any grief.
For your nest you'll find a place
Among the leaves;
For your nestlings you will find
Enough to eat.

"I can tell, sir, by your look
That you love all little birds.
I shall bring the goldfinch here,
Who will sing new songs to you.
The goldfinch has a pretty song
When he's alone;
He can sing you charming airs
In plain song.

"Till the month of September
We'll be your neighbors.
You'll enjoy hearing me
In the night as well as day.
But when it's time to fly away,
What sadness!
All the trees will be in mourning
At our flight.

"Goodbye, sir, we're on our way.
For that, you know, is our sad fate.
You may be sure we're sorry
When it's time to leave Provence.
Every year we must go winter
In the Indies.
The swallows go there too;
We leave together.

"Don't go near America,
For the air is full of lead.
Over there by Martinique
They are firing cannonades.
For a long time the King of Spain
Has been besieged:
If you don't want to be stopped,
Keep far away."

*The purplish flowering of
Judas trees or redbuds overlaps
the feathery salmon bloom of
the tamarisks in a typical
rustic scene.*

A Family Bird-Whistle Factory

[Raymond et fils, avenue Pierre-de-Coubertin, 84200 Carpentras.
Tel: 90 63 18 09. Visits are by appointment only.]

A typical vertical village house in Gordes shelters a private patio garden.

In a suburb of the town of Carpentras stands a modern stuccoed "villa," with its typical small front garden. From the street, one can glimpse plastic greenhouses behind, without suspecting that they contain not tender plants but pigeons! For this house belongs to the Raymond family, bird lovers and makers of bird whistles. Ancestor Théodore Raymond, a careful observer of local wildlife, with a musical ear and a genius for invention, began the company in 1868. Still in family hands, it produces more than 120,000 whistles a year. Its catalog offers 68 items, notably whistles for songbirds, ducks and geese, and all variety of game birds.

Everything is still made, packaged and mailed from a backyard workshop, where a handful of skilled employees can be seen bending over the old machines. There is a small museum in the storage room containing a nineteenth-century collection of stuffed specimens.

Who buys bird whistles in Provence today? Hunters certainly constitute a large part of the family's clientele, though Madame Raymond protests energetically that "real" hunters love and respect wildlife. Nevertheless, some people claim that there are more guns than songbirds in modern-day Provence. Not surprisingly, the protection of wildlife has become an active local political issue.

Madame Raymond insists, however, that her family's products are of equal use to ornithologists and even to schoolchildren. Thanks to these whistles, youngsters have learned to recognize local bird calls. A visitor to the premises can leave with the sound of a nightingale tucked away in his or

Provençal garden fountains appeal to all five senses, blending pleasure with necessity.

her pocket. One just needs to learn how to turn the metal handle of the whistle's small wooden plug to produce the right kind of friction. Formerly composed of such varied materials as cherry, peach and apricot stones, as well as goose or chicken feathers, today whistles are made with tin or nickled iron and molded rubber. Leather has proved too expensive and time-consuming to work with; as for the wooden parts, boxwood has now been replaced by beech or ash.

Each whistle is tested as it is made, and special orders are not unknown. A friend in Africa requested a crocodile lure; the Raymonds agreed, on the condition that good sample recordings could be provided.

A Cocktail rose bursts into brilliant spring color against an old castle wall.

A Striking Site: The Open-Air Terrace Museum at Goult

[North of the N100 road from Avignon to Apt, through Lumière, up through the medieval hilltown of Goult, beyond the ramparts, to a small parking lot next to a stone tower (an abandoned windmill). A footpath to the conservatory leads off past the tower and is marked with explanatory panels and arrows. If one walks at a comfortable pace, while admiring views on both sides, it will take about 15 minutes to reach the site.]

Hundreds of miles of terracing still punctuate the steep slopes of Mediterranean France. Their beauty lies not only in the lines they create on the hillside but in their considerable detailing: steps from one level to another, constructed most frequently parallel to the wall itself; tall stones to indicate special passages or ends of vine rows on the outer edge. There is a whole language to the stonework of these landscapes. Unfortunately, intensive farming of the fertile land; a diminished labor force (especially after World War I); the mechanization of agriculture; specific calamities, such as the phylloxera epidemic; and, in general, the rural exodus have all contributed to their abandonment. Dry stone walls are hard to maintain and few people today know how. Some terraces are now used to pasture sheep and goats, whose activity quickly causes walls to deteriorate. And, if the quick drainage of heavy rains is impeded in any way, the walls soon develop "bellies" and give way.

Attempts are now being made to conserve these hillsides for specialized crops. Despite the need for intensive labor, these plants benefit from the terraces' microclimates, deeper soil and resistance to erosion and even fire. Dried flowers, herbs and aromatics; luxury potatoes, such as the famous

OPPOSITE: *Stone huts called* bories *can be found on many terraced hillsides around Gordes, including those of the Open-Air Terrace Museum.*
ABOVE: *Hillside terracing involves intricate designs and constructions, such as these upright stones topping a solid wall at the museum.*

ratte beloved by Parisian chefs; Japanese artichokes (*Stachys tuberifera Naud*); kiwis; raspberries and other bush fruits are now being cultivated there. In addition, peach, almond, apricot, fig and olive trees, which have always been grown here, are being irrigated to increase their production. Plantations of other varieties have been added or extended: walnuts and chestnuts on the northern or higher slopes; truffle oaks, pistachios, caper bushes and pomegranates facing south. With the use of solar greenhouses set against the back retaining walls, avocados and Brazilian passionflowers are flourishing.

APARE, a cultural association based in Avignon (41, cours Jean Jaurès, 84000 Avignon, telephone: 90 85 51 15), began the restoration of this village site near Goult in 1982. First, the group organized a workshop similar to others it has set up to preserve various historical monuments reflecting the rural heritage of Provence. One can now see traditional shelters, beehives and cisterns, either made from dry-set stone or dug directly in the rock. And, thanks to the Luberon National Park and the Botanical Conservatory of Porquerolles, a plant museum has been established containing local essences typical of this microclimate: old fruit varieties (notably olive and almonds) that once grew abundantly on such terraces. It is a little-known and strikingly beautiful place to visit.

Soft young grass bending in the breeze, fresh foliage and bloom on fruit trees, new light on old stone and roof tiles—warm spring days in Provence can be a real enchantment.

An April landscape, discovered at dawn from a moving train:

Then, as I watched, the sun rose, and with it the whole panorama ceased looking like an underexposed photograph and came literally to light—the cabin roofs shone orange, the fields turned out to be scattered with poppies the color of new blood, the long green grass was streaked with yellow flowers and cobalt flowers and round scabious flowers that were a hard, firm mauve. Over the distant crimson hills the sky was already blue, and the few people in the fields were a very dark walnut brown. Nothing I had expected of Provence had equaled the harsh and yet mysterious quality of this flying landscape.
James Pope-Hennessy,
ASPECTS OF PROVENCE

The Fountain of Vaucluse

[The village and site are east of Avignon, north of the main N100 road to Apt, near Isle-sur-la-Sorgue, on the D25.]

The emerald water of the Sorgue flows by the Petrarch Museum, underneath the castle ruins that dominate the village of Fontaine de Vaucluse.

By the age of 37, the fourteenth-century poet Petrarch was the most famous private citizen of Europe. He spent his early years in Avignon, where the Popes then resided, as did his muse and inspiration, the divine Laura. But finding public life oppressive at times, and Laura's presence a source of pain, he took refuge at the Fountain of Vaucluse, a village that had enchanted him as a child.

The actual spring was considered a natural wonder in Roman times and remains haunting, not only for its dramatic landscape but for its geological mysteries as well. Indeed, the technical term "Vauclusian spring" (inverse-siphon type), which refers to the seepage of water through miles and miles of limestone filters and underground grottoes to sudden emergence, derives from the Fountain of Vaucluse. Jacques Cousteau's research teams have been unable to plumb its depths: They sent a robot down more than 1,000 feet without touching bottom. The fountain's output can range from roughly 1,000 to 33,000 gallons per second, and the temperature remains a constant 53.6 to 55.4° F.

Botanically, too, the site is an enigma. The spring owes its emerald color to the water parsnip (*Sium officinalis*), which was

Colette, traveling south on the famous "Blue Train" from Paris, describes a Provençal spring:

We just passed Avignon and I might have thought, yesterday, after sleeping only two hours, that I had slept two months: Spring had come to meet me, a fairytale spring, the exuberant, brief, irresistible spring of the South, rich, fresh, with its spurts of sudden greenery, its grasses already high, which sway and ripple in the wind, its mauve Judas trees, its paulownias the color of gray periwinkles, its laburnums, wisteria, and roses. . . . My head has been spinning since Avignon. The northern mists have melted over there, behind the cypress hedges bent by the force of the mistral. The silky murmur of tall reeds came through the open train window that day, along with the scent of honey,

used as a fertilizer for olive trees in the nineteenth century. The moss of the spillway, *Hedwigie acquatica*, is a rare species, growing only in one other valley, near Geneva. Since the output of the spring varies greatly, parts of the spillway are sometimes dry and exposed. At those times, the moss dries up completely, but then turns green again at the slightest rain or increased flow. As for animal life, the river trout are famous, and a few families of beaver still live downstream.

A museum, known as Petrarch's House (his actual house has long since disappeared), is situated across the river from the path leading to the grotto. It contains many portraits of Laura. High above the site stand the ruins of a medieval castle that once belonged to the poet's friend the Bishop of Cavaillon, who would invite Petrarch there to dine. Around the house are several flat spaces, supported by rocky dams, planted out with flowers that beckon colorfully to the pilgrims on the other side. Although not Petrarch's original garden, it nicely evokes the difficulties encountered by the poet in his battle, as he put it, with "the nymphs of the Spring."

In the summer of 1340, Petrarch began to clear a small, stony field with his own hands; he brought in new turf and created a meadow. The nymphs, however, protested by flooding it out and undoing all his work. Undaunted, he started over, but once more a summer storm got the best of him.

After many trials and tribulations, Petrarch tried to make a garden once more. In 1346, he hired peasants, shepherds and fishermen to sink large rocks at the river's edge, forming a breakwater. A stone walk led to a viewpoint, and in the middle of the garden stood a shrine to the Muses. This time it was the winter storms that did the damage to the garden. Petrarch yielded, keeping for himself and the Muses only one rocky nook, strongly fortified.

of pine, of varnished buds, of lilac about to bloom, that bitter smell of lilac before it flowers, a blend of turpentine and almond. The cherry trees cast violet shadows on the reddish earth, already parched with thirst.
Colette, THE VAGABOND

Later generations flocked to the spring because of its romantic associations with Petrarch and Laura, and the fountain became a favorite spot for just-marrieds. When Henry James visited in the 1880s, he remarked on its popularity with honeymooners and "Sunday trippers." James also admired the water's magnificent color and was overwhelmed by its beauty: "You find yourself at the foot of the enormous straight cliff

Early spring rains are much desired in the country. And so it is said that:

April has thirty days /
    If it rained for thirty-
    one / It wouldn't hurt
    a soul.
Avril a trente jours, /
    S'il pleuvait trente
    et un jours / Cela
    ne ferait de mal
    è personne.
Abriéu es de trento /
    maie quand plourié
    tren'un / Farié mau
    en degun.

out of which the river gushes. It rears itself to an extraordinary height—a huge forehead of bare stone. . . . The little valley, seeing it there, at a bend, stops suddenly and receives in its arms the magical spring. . . . The setting of the phenomenon struck me as so simple and so fine—the vast sad cliff, covered with the afternoon light, still and solid forever, while the liquid element rages and roars at its base—that I had no difficulty in understanding the celebrity of Vaucluse."

Provençal farm domains often have twin-pillared stone entries, as here at Estoublon in the Alpilles.

Here where it is still hilly but not yet mountainous, we have April storms that are as brutal as bulls.
Jean Giono,
RONDEUR DES JOURS

ABOVE: *Village houses sport carefully trained trellises, which leaf out slowly as the season progresses.* RIGHT: *The many-layered geometries of Provençal hilltown design inspired Cézanne, then Picasso and Cubist painters.* OPPOSITE: *The soft tones of climbing roses set off the ocher washes of old buildings. The overhanging tile roof is designed to protect the walls from the infiltration of heavy rains.*

The Muses, from their exile now released,
Share my retreat, but visitors are few
Save those who come to see the famous Fount.
Petrarch, Epistolae metrica, c. 1340, quoted in
Life of Petrarch by Ernest Hatch Wilkins

Here I have the Fountain of the Sorgue, a stream that
must be numbered among the fairest and coolest,
remarkable for its crystal waters and its emerald channel.
No other stream is like it; none other is so noted for its
varying moods, now raging like a torrent, now quiet as a
pool. . . . The hills cast a grateful shadow in the morning
and in the evening hours; and at noon many a nook and
corner of the vale gleams in the sunlight. Round about,
the woods lie still and tranquil, woods in which the
tracks of wild animals are far more numerous than those
of men. Everywhere a deep and unbroken stillness, except
for the babbling of running waters, or the lowing of the
oxen browsing lazily among the banks, or the singing of
birds. I would speak of this more at length, were it not
that the rare beauties of this secluded dale have already
become familiar far and wide through my verses.
Petrarch, Epistolae variae XLII, 1347, quoted in
Petrarch, An Anthology, edited by David Thompson

Skies fill and empty like great sails with the breath of the rogue wind . . . it supples out the cypresses like fur, rushes to explode the spring blossom of almond and plum like a discharge of artillery.
Lawrence Durrell,
MONSIEUR

An ocher-tinted manor house near Apt has a succession of sheltered courtyards.

A Provençal Vegetable Classic: AïOLI

This feast of fish and a rich array of fresh vegetables can be served at any time of year, with whatever produce is in season—for example, fennel and cauliflower or broccoli can be substituted for tomatoes and zucchini in winter. But to be authentic, it must contain potatoes, chick-peas and the thick garlic sauce that gives the dish its name.

The amount of garlic may seem intimidating, but it is good for the heart and the lungs . . . and there are those who crave *aïoli* as others yearn for chocolate!

Note that the fish must be set to soak two days before the meal, and the chick-peas, the night before.

Serves 6

2 pounds dry codfish	12 cloves garlic, peeled
1 bay leaf	(2 per person is the rule!)
½ pound dry chick-peas	Salt
About 2 cups, plus 1 tablespoon,	Pepper
extra-virgin olive oil	2 cooked beets
Sprigs of fresh thyme or savory	1 celery heart
12 carrots	½ pound fresh mushrooms
12 small potatoes	1 lemon
6 small zucchini	6–12 small tomatoes
½ pound green beans	1 pound of black olives
8 eggs	(optional)

Place the codfish in a large bowl and cover with cold water. Soak the fish for two days, changing the water several times. Remove any bones and skin from the fish and cut into 3-inch squares. Place them in a saucepan and cover with water. Add a bay leaf and poach the fish for about 10 minutes, depending upon thickness. Drain and refrigerate.

Put the chick-peas in a bowl and cover with water. Soak them overnight. Drain, then pour them into a saucepan and cover with water. Add a tablespoon of olive oil and a branch of thyme, and cook for 30 to 40 minutes. Drain and set aside.

Pare the carrots and the potatoes, then clean and trim the zucchini and green beans. Steam the carrots and potatoes for 20 minutes, if winter varieties; for 10 minutes, if young spring ones, adding thyme to the cooking water. Arrange the green beans on top of the carrots and potatoes during the last 5 minutes of steaming, testing until the vegetables are just done. The zucchini take from 5 to 15 minutes to cook and may be steamed with the other vegetables or poached separately.

Hard boil 6 eggs and set aside. Keep the yolks of the remaining two eggs at room temperature, to make a garlic mayonnaise. Using a large mortar and pestle (or a blender or food processor) crush the 12 garlic cloves finely, then add the two yolks and begin to beat the ingredients together. Add the 2 cups of olive oil very slowly, drop by drop, and continue beating. When the emulsion begins to "take," increase the flow of oil to a thin stream. If the mixture should separate, start afresh with another yolk in a clean bowl, adding the curdled mixture gradually. Season to taste with salt and pepper. The sauce should be thick and yellow.

Reheat the cooked codfish briefly.

Peel and slice the beets, cut the celery heart into strips and clean and slice the mushrooms, rubbing them with lemon juice. Arrange all the vegetables, the hard-boiled eggs and the olives attractively around the fish on a large platter. Serve the sauce separately.

Portrait of a Provençal Gardener: Jean Lafont, Rancher

The spring mistral can play havoc with flowerpots on balconies, as here in Sérignan-du-Comtat.

How many gardeners can give advice about which plants best frame a pasture of grazing bulls? Jean Lafont is just such a person, and he has had to consider the question for his own garden in the Rhone delta—that flat marshland, known as the Camargue, which belongs as much to the western province of Languedoc as to Provence. His main activity in life is the raising of bulls on some thousand acres of ranchland, an occupation that combines harmoniously, but surprisingly, with his collector's passion for rare trees and shrubs. Both interests depend on an intimate knowledge of the locality's most unusual microclimate and terrain: The land around the ranch often floods in winter, but can support summer pastures and, closer to the house, a wealth of garden plantings quite unlike those found in the drier hinterland. Monsieur Lafont has decided that olive trees and cypresses would look out of place with bulls behind. Instead, he has chosen stands of tall grasses and reeds, such as tiffa and papyrus, the local tamarisk and cornus, with its bright red stems in winter. The reliable evergreens of the area—cistus, laurustinus, juniper and laurel—are used as hedging throughout the property. His collection, nonetheless, contains 15-odd varieties of cypress in the arboretum in addition to many other rarities. Wooden fences, picturesquely irregular in their double spans, keep the two parts of Monsieur Lafont's life separate.

The rancher owns about 300 bulls, and he knows all of those old enough to fight in the arena by name. He and they will remain friends for many years—for in the Provençal

OLD-FASHIONED SOAPS

[Rampal-Patou, 71, rue Félix-Pyat, 13300 Salon-de-Provence.
Tel: 90 56 07 28;
FAX: 90 56 52 18.
Owner: Monsieur Rampal.
Visits for small groups are by appointment only.]

Although soap has been made in Marseilles and the surrounding area since the fourteenth century, it was not until the seventeenth century that the French finance minister, Jean Colbert, turned its manufacture into a model industry. With the arrival of modern detergents, unfortunately, soapmaking went into a decline. Current interest in protecting the environment and ensuring good health, however, have contributed to the growing popularity of Marseilles soap, which is 100 percent biodegradable and good for one's skin. The Rampal family, which has been producing it in Salon since 1910, survived in the 1950s by putting out a line of pure bath soaps containing only vegetable oils (olive, almond, palm or copra) and light washing sodas. It is still popular and is exported worldwide. The washing soap goes through numerous stages — rinsing, cooking, purifying and compressing — before being set out to dry in huge cakes. Later, these are cut into small cubes and stamped with their maker's mark. The smaller versions are individually molded. In addition, verbena, lime and other essences, notably a lavender scent so powerful that a single cake will perfume an entire room, have been successfully added to part of the production line.

course libre, or *course à la cocarde*, the bulls are not killed. The crowd, which knows the animals and is often on their side, watches as each one confronts about 20 young men, who try to remove ribbons (*cocarde*) from the animal's sharp horns. Prize money is offered by local businesses, and the amount increases as the suspense mounts. About 25 such herds, known as *manades*, exist today. Although Jean Lafont's has been in existence since 1851, he did not purchase it until after World War II. The bulls participate in more than a hundred events yearly, one to six animals at a time, and they are treated more like racehorses than are their Spanish cousins. Outsiders are often unaware of the humane way the animals are handled. In fact, some years ago, when the British Queen Mother was to tour Provence, a visit to the Lafont ranch was planned. Her chief of protocol objected, saying that the English public might well misconstrue her appearance there as indicating approval of bull-fighting.

The mid-nineteenth-century ranch buildings reflect the owner's strong personal style. One wall now extends out into a semicircular veranda to let light in during the winter. In the summer, dense shade over this "winter garden" is provided by two ancient plane trees, allowed to soar into the blue. The subtle beiges, grays and greens of their trunks are the dominant tones in the house and the surrounding landscape. Textures play an important role here; they are provided by a wealth of ground covers, under and beyond the planes and other trees, such as the rare *Arbutus andrachne*,

Rancher Jean Lafont has created an unusual arboretum and garden around his farmstead in the northern Camargue. Bulls come and graze just beyond the fence that protects his exotic collection of trees.

THE CAMARGUE
MUSEUM

[*Musée Camarguais, Mas du Pont
de Rousty, 13200 Arles. Nine miles
southwest of Arles on the D570
road to Les-Saintes-Maries-de-
la-Mer. Tel: 90 97 10 82.
Open all year, except January 1,
May 1, and December 25, and
Tuesdays in winter.*]

On opening in 1979, this
vast restored sheepfold received the European Prize
for museums. The imagina-
tive exhibits present every
aspect of life in the cowboy
country of the Camargue,
the marshy delta of the
Rhone so different from
the rest of Provence. Its
whitewashed, thatch-roofed

with its peeling bark. And there are colorful accents, too. In
winter, besides the more common plants, such as forsythia,
there are the laurustinus, loquats, shrubby honeysuckle
(*Lonicera fragrantissima*), *freylinea cestroides* from South Africa,
and a dark green hedge of *saracocca ruscifolia*, with its wonderful scent. A country garden, well-set in its landscape and
adjusted to the seasons, but one of great refinement.

Country Decor:
A Troglodyte Hilltown Gallery

[*Anna Bonde (creator of original furniture) and Arne Tengblad (painter
and sculptor), L'Aire d'été, 13, rue de la République, 84480 Bonnieux.
Tel: 90 75 88 70; FAX: 90 75 88 59. Open 9:00 A.M. to 12 M (noon)
and 2:00 P.M. to 7:00 P.M. daily, except for Sundays.
A house built into the cliff on the upper side of the village's main street,
not far from the Bakers' Museum.*]

These two creative individuals have successfully married local traditions and resources with cosmopolitan
inspiration. Their efforts, along with numerous others', have brought new life to remote villages that might otherwise have been abandoned. Bonnieux, like nearby Luberon
hilltowns, now houses artists and craftspeople who initially
rented summer homes here, then found local life so appealing that they settled in year round. Anna and husband Arne
bought a wonderful house in the village, which is steeped in
history—they claim that a Roman road runs through their
bathroom. Transformed into an elegant residence in the
fourteenth century, when the ennobled but inadmissible offspring of Avignon popes lived in these communities, the

cottages; industries (salt
extraction, rice culture,
sand wines); wildlife (major bird-migration routes
pass over it, and there is
a sanctuary in its heart);
vegetation (tough, wind-
bent tamarisks, and the
famous SALADELLE, a wild
flower); centuries-old
traditions of raising
stocky, pearl gray horses
and small-scaled, feisty
bulls; folklore and
festivals, including the
biennial pilgrimage to Les-
Saintes-Maries-de-la-Mer,
for gypsies as well as for
the Provençaux . . . all
these aspects, along with
the region's geology and
history, are recounted with
the help of slides, recon-
structions, illuminated
displays, maquettes and
models, fine old tools and
furniture. Outside one can
see the other buildings
of this typical ranch and
walk on a two-mile trail
through the national park
in which it lies.

house acquired an impressive stone staircase around 1610. Today, this addition looks out onto an inner, well-like courtyard that lights the surrounding rooms. These and the vaulted caves on the first floor provide fascinating spaces for the display of Arne's painting and sculpture, Anna's collections of old and new garden furniture (the latter of her own making) and original decorative objects. Anna has kept to Scandinavian simplicity in her designs, but adorns her furniture with unusual fabrics made in southern France. Bonde furniture can be seen in Paris at the Hôtel du Grand Veneur, owned by the Baker company, which, in turn, shows its creations in Bonnieux at Anna's gallery. Arne exhibits his work in Tokyo, New York, and Paris. Both artists have met with wide international acclaim, but feel deeply rooted in their adopted land.

OPPOSITE: *A charming Renaissance well stands in the courtyard of the Tour Cardinal, near Les Baux.*

Earthenware pots and jars, essential to traditional Provençal décor, can be purchased at many garden centers, such as Appy, in Roussillon.

West Meets West in Provence

Around the turn of the century, a surprising number of exchanges took place between the cowboys (*gardiens*) of the Camargue and their American counterparts—and with several Native Americans. In fact, the decline of the latter group drew much sympathy from Provençal poets such as Alphonse Daudet and Frédéric Mistral, who felt that their own culture was doomed to a similar fate. But it is a Parisian, Joë Hamman, who stands as the key figure in these encounters, which were a mix of life and legend, history, theater and cinema.

Hamman was born into a wealthy Parisian family in 1883. As an adolescent, Joë accompanied his father on a trip to the United States. While there, he happened to strike up a conversation with a factory cleaner, an Indian who had left his reservation. As a result of this chance meeting, Hamman traveled to Montana, where he met the famous chief Red Cloud, now old, blind and in despair. The latter's lieutenant, Spotted Weasel (who was to become the Frenchman's friend for life) gave Hamman his own war costume to take back to France, as well as an Indian name that paid homage to the young man's gentle humor: Mocking bird.

Back in Paris, Hamman later became an actor in the growing movie industry, then a screenplay writer and

One of the most spectacular spring flowerings is provided by fragrant shrubby coronillas, here used as a dazzling hedge under the soaring branches of a well-established hackberry tree.

I worked [a canvas] to death yesterday, a cherry tree against a blue sky, the young leaf shoots were gold and orange, the clusters of flowers white, and that against the green-blue of the sky made a glorious show. Today alas there's rain, which prevents my going to have another shot at it.
Van Gogh, DEAR THEO

producer. He first went to Provence to play a role in the film version of Mistral's epic poem *Mireille*, and eventually returned to create a whole series of pseudo-American westerns. He invented the character of "Arizona Bill," whom he portrayed in some 200 tales. The hero was famous for his horsemanship, and it is said that at least one Provençal rancher was taught to ride by Hamman, who was active well into his eighties. Hamman also wrote two books, founded a satirical newspaper, and became an expert on Indian affairs. He died in 1974.

Another legendary cowboy, somewhat older than Hamman

The medieval and nineteenth-century battlements of the Château de Barben, near Salon, protect elaborate collections of paintings and furniture which can be visited by the public.

MARIE LEPOITEVIN'S GOAT'S-CHEESE TART

▲▲▲▲▲▲▲▲

When the young kids have been weaned from their mothers, goats' milk is turned into fresh cheeses, which are available in Provençal markets throughout the summer. The filling for this tart can also be used, uncooked, to stuff tomatoes. The recipe serves four as an entrée, two as a light supper dish.

and a native Provençal, was the Marquis Folco de Baroncelli-Javon. Both a friend and a follower of Mistral, he led the life of a gardien in the Camargue (the so-called "Wild West of France") for 60 years while trying to protect its traditions and its threatened minority groups, such as the gypsies. In 1905, he went to Paris to see a popular new entertainment that had just arrived from the United States—Buffalo Bill's Wild West Show. And there he was introduced to Joë Hamman, who served as interpreter for the American Indians accompanying Buffalo Bill Cody.

Thus began a new chapter in the great romance linking Provence and the American West. The traveling show came south, and Baroncelli offered the Indians, Iron Tail and Lone Bear, champagne as they watched a lasso competition between the gardiens of the Camargue and Buffalo Bill's experts. Beaded bags, which the Indians left as gifts for the Marquis, can still be seen in the Provençal folklore museum in Avignon, located in the Baroncelli townhouse.

Frédéric Mistral and Buffalo Bill, who curiously looked much alike, met in Provence. The American offered the poet his dog, and the animal is now buried next to Mistral in the cemetery of Maillane.

All that remains of these friendships are some much-loved relics in museums and private collections. After Hamman's death, his Indian artifacts were handed down to another actor, Jacques Nissou, born in Montmartre and now living in Provence, whom Hamman met in the early 1960s. The younger man certainly shares the elder's sense of the great romance, and, in 1991, made a pilgrimage to the United States to find the tomb of Sitting Bull. As he stood there, thinking of generations of sympathetic exchanges linking the American West and the Camargue, an eagle circled overhead.

Pastry for a 9-inch pie
3 fresh goat's cheeses,
    just barely solid (about
    3 ounces each)
1 tablespoon prepared mustard
Sprinkling of chopped fresh
    chives, parsley or basil
½ cup heavy cream

Preheat the oven to 350° F. Line a pie dish with the pastry.

In a bowl, beat together the goat's cheeses, mustard, chives and cream with a wooden spoon. Pour the cheese mixture into the pie crust and spread evenly. Bake the tart for 45 minutes, with the source of heat from below if possible. (Otherwise, prebake the pastry in a 400° F. oven for 10 minutes before filling.) The filling should be just barely golden color, not brown. The absence of eggs in the mixture preserves the goat's-cheese flavor but prevents the filling from setting like a quiche. Serve the tart with a fresh green salad, preferably seasoned with garlic.

Châteauneuf-du-Pape, Provence's Best-Known Wine

[Paul Coulon et fils, Domaine de Beauregard, avenue Pierre-de-Luxembourg, 84230 Châteauneuf-du-Pape. Tel: 90 83 71 79; FAX: 90 83 78 06; ordering service 90 83 51 20.

Château Mont-Redon, 84230 Châteauneuf-du-Pape. Tel: 90 83 72 75; FAX: 90 83 77 20. Owners: Monsieur Fabre and Monsieur Abeille.]

Covering some 7,000 acres on the Rhone's left bank, the Châteauneuf-du-Pape wine country produces majestic, full-bodied red wines from an unusual clay soil studded with large, round river pebbles deposited years ago by passing glaciers. Used as mulch, these store heat during the day and increase the grape's sugar, and therefore the alcohol content of the finished product.

The wine's name evokes a fourteenth-century papal castle, now a picturesque ruin overlooking the village of Châteauneuf-du-Pape ("the little town with the big name," says writer Peter Mayle). Pope John XXII constructed this impressive building as a summer residence while living in Avignon. But the vineyards entitled to this controlled appellation label may also belong to the communities of Bédarrides, Courthézon, Orange and Sorgues. In 1923, the vintners of this area founded the first association to set standards for fine wine. And from their efforts emerged the government-controlled rating system used today.

Famous for its varietal mixtures (as many as 13 for one wine; some, like Syrah and le Viognier, were grown by the

In spring begins again the steady, careful nurturing of vines which will produce, if the weather obliges with the right dosage of sun and rain (without hailstones), fine grapes like these.

The vineyards of Châteauneuf-du-Pape are famous for their mulch of large, river-polished pebbles. These store up the heat of the strong Provençal sun and help produce grapes rich in sugar, for wines high in alcoholic content.

Romans); celebrated also for the high degree of alcohol of its wines (up to 15%) and for its small production per acre, Châteauneuf-du-Pape produces wines far better known abroad than a number of its equally deserving neighbors. Many producers offer tastings, in the center of the village or in outlying châteaux.

The Domaine de Beauregard, belonging to the Coulon family, is located on the southern edge of town, close to the

Avignon road. Both Monsieur and Madame Coulon come from old wine-making families, and their two sons, who represent the seventh generation, are actively involved in the production of Châteauneuf-du-Pape—one trained as a vintner, the other in computer science and business management. Their business is a fascinating mixture of earthiness and sophistication, millennia-old methods of cultivation and the most refined contemporary technology. Madame Coulon explains

PEACH-LEAF CORDIAL

▲▲▲▲▲▲▲

In Provence, many people make their own aperitif wines from walnuts, oranges and spices, as well as from gentian roots and many other plants. This unusual, fruity version is easy to prepare, provided there is a nearby peach tree.
Makes one quart

120 fresh, young peach leaves
25 sugar cubes
1¼ bottles good-quality wine
   (red, rosé or white)
1 cup white fruit brandy
   (eau de vie) or kirsch

Place the leaves and sugar cubes in a large pan. Add the wine, cover, and either refrigerate or store the mixture in a cool cellar for four or five days. Strain the wine, then add the brandy to it. Bottle the liqueur and cork, but wait at least a week before serving.

its operation with obvious pride, her face both weatherworn and elegant, her clothes chosen to resist outdoor exposure and hard work, yet cut in the latest fashion. Throughout the various stages, beginning with the grapes ripening on sunny slopes to their final bottling and labeling, the same piquant contrast between the old and new persists.

This small village cave employs 14 salaried employees and four very hard-working family members. All the processing is done on the premises. The meticulous care needed at every stage is impressive. A sorting of the grapes by quality is obligatory to obtain the Châteauneuf label. At the Domaine de Beauregard, each person carries two baskets and sorts while picking (the grapes of lesser quality will be turned into Côtes du Rhône). This task requires considerable skill and training—some workers have been harvesting here for 25 years. Although there are producers who do the sorting once the grapes have been delivered to the cave, Madame Coulon believes that there has been too much intermingling by then.

Once the grapes are crushed, they are stored in tall, gleaming, stainless steel vats for 18 to 21 days. The temperature is crucial, for the grapes arrive from the vineyards gorged with sun and need to be cooled. In the old days, they would have been stored underground (at a later stage, longer storage at Beauregard also takes place some 23 feet below ground level). For the initial period, however, the Coulons have invested in equipment that can be gently cooled (or heated, in a cold year) by water circuits spiraling around the vats. And when the wine has been strained and purified, it moves into a vaulted room, similar to a modern cathedral nave, full of equally immaculate steel vats. The temperature of each vat can be checked immediately at the central computer perched on a balcony above.

Thunder in March means
   good almonds.
Quant il tonne en mars,
   l'amande est bonne.
Quan mars tona, l'amendo
   est bona.

49

For two days now, the wind of the flowers has been blowing, . . . except for the joyful greenery of young wheat fields, the whole countryside is white. The air smells good, trees bend under the weight of this fragrant snow, fallen petals whirl about in the perfumed light like so many white butterflies.
Paul Arène

Flowering almond trees contrast beautifully with dark cypress pillars near the ruins of a Renaissance château north of Aix.

Thus the wines move, under loving supervision, toward their nine-month storage in oak casks. Advanced technology and constant, practical surveillance do not preclude ritual. A collection of wines of the property, some more than 100 years old, is reverently checked every 25 years, before being resealed.

The Coulons have a comfortable and welcoming tasting room, open all year round. In addition, they have opened a fascinating vintners' museum in a nearby village, Rasteau. Their wines (both Châteauneuf-du-Pape and Côtes du Rhône) are imported by most European countries (handled by Grant of Saint James in England and by Park Wines in California), and soon they will also be available on the East Coast of the United States. Unfortunately, the small but delicious production of white Châteauneufs is rarely exported.

In complete contrast to the village cave, the Château-de-Mont-Redon is a country property set to the north of the village, among wild, rolling hills, where the Rhone pebbles among the vines are not only gold but also bleached white. This domain once belonged to the Mathieu family: One famous member was the romantic nineteenth-century poet Anselme Mathieu. Purchased in 1923 by the present family, today the vineyard is run by first cousins, the Abeilles and the Fabres. As with the Coulons, pride and care determine the production of the Mont-Redon wines. Both families have, indeed, won innumerable medals. Mont-Redon wines are imported into the United States by the Kobrand Corporation in New York and are widely available in England at such centers of gastronomy as Harrods and Fortnum and Masons. The family motto, not surprisingly, is "Tradition and Progress."

The sequence of ripening fruits, from cherries and

apricots to peaches, apples, pears and

grapes. Garlands of garlic and onions hung

on the rafters to dry. Fresh almonds with their furry

green skins. Wheat harvesting and haymaking. Cicadas

Summer in

by day and frogs by night. Swimming pools, siestas,

pastis (the legendary licorice-flavored aperitif). Carry-

ing endless cans of water in spite of

what was supposed to be an automatic

watering system. Examining the sky

anxiously for storm clouds that always bring rain to the

next valley, or that ram water into the

ground for just ten minutes, along with

hailstones the size of large marbles. For

many temperate-climate plants, a second period of

Provence is...

dormancy that is similar to hibernation. Forest fires,

and still more forest fires. Theater, opera and film

festivals. The filtered shade of cool afternoon rooms,

of patios under trellises. Dragonflies, praying mantises

and grasshoppers.

Summer

Summer living in Provence means dining in cool, refreshing shade, half indoors, half out.
Traditional, rustic settings make use of a vine-and-wisteria-laden trellis along the front of the farmhouse.
This particularly elegant patio, a separate wing with one wall open onto the garden, adjoins a château.

A Great Naturalist's Workshop: The Harmas of Jean-Henri Fabre

[Five miles northeast of Orange on the D976 road to Nyons, just outside Sérignan-du-Comtat. Tel: 90 70 00 44. Phone ahead to check opening hours. Caretaker: Monsieur Teocchi.]

North of Orange, in front of the nineteenth-century farmstead of scientist and writer Jean-Henri Fabre, a botanical garden displays carefully labeled local plants.

On the outskirts of a quiet village lies a nineteenth-century farmstead, built by a well-known naturalist of the time, Jean-Henri Fabre, as a haven from the storms of his professional life. Its name, *harmas*, means uncultivated ground, and it proved to be an ideal place for him to observe his beloved insects. The large garden remained wild until after Fabre's death. Since then, it has been transformed into a collection of local plants and wildflowers, all carefully labeled in several languages, but not completely tamed. Visitors can find many corners and paths that have the intense fragrances of the unkempt *garrigue* landscapes.

Fabre's life was a tale of fortitude and perseverance. Born in 1823 to poor café owners, he obtained his education as a scholarship student, but there were long gaps in his studies. He began his first botanical writings in Corsica while teaching mathematics in a high school, and continued them in Avignon after obtaining a teaching position at the Imperial College in 1853. During his tenure there, he became friends with Frédéric Mistral, John Stuart Mill and Stéphane Mallarmé. A popular teacher for 17 years, he, nonetheless, was forced to resign after giving evening classes in natural history: The topic of flower fertilization offended parents of his female students. Jobless, with five children, he accepted a loan from John Stuart Mill that allowed him to settle in Orange and concentrate on writing. Between 1870 and 1879,

Instinctively these days I keep remembering what I have seen of Cézanne, because he has exactly caught the harsh side of Provence. It has become very different from what it was in spring, and yet I certainly have no less love for this countryside burnt up as it begins to be from now on. Everywhere is old gold, bronze-copper, one might say—and this with the green azure of the sky blanched with heat: a delicious color, extraordinarily harmonious, with the blended tones of Delacroix.

Van Gogh, DEAR THEO

he published more than 80 school texts. At the end of this period, he began his famous work, *Souvenirs entomologiques*, which has been reprinted in countless languages. In 1879, he purchased the property in Sérignan.

A traditional Provençal farmstead, the house faces south, but is shaded by ancient plane trees that spread their canopies over the usual terrace and a stone well. A low wall marks the edge of this space, beyond which lies the garden.

Indoors, a small museum displays Fabre's beautiful watercolors of local mushrooms (soon to be reproduced in a special book), editions of his works and samples of his correspondence—including a chatty note from Charles Darwin. Upstairs, his study has been maintained intact, with his writing table and parts of his vast collection of fossils, birds' nests, and archaeological artifacts.

Although tended by a devoted caretaker and his family, this site has been somewhat neglected— despite such an enthusiastic following in Japan that a plan once evolved to purchase and remove the entire property to the Far East! Local authorities recently agreed that a reception center should be built on nearby land, along with a small museum, so that Fabre's admirers may visit in comfort, without disturbing the tranquillity of the old domain. More and more people are making the pilgrimage to the home of the man who has often been called the "Homer" or "Virgil" of the insect world. Who better than Fabre illustrates Virgil's maxim: *Felix qui potuit rerum cotnoscere causae* ("Happy is the man able to penetrate the secrets of nature").

Wheat was once grown much more widely in Provence than it is now. The first harvest, coinciding with the summer solstice, was celebrated by many elaborate festivals and rituals.

In June, the wheat harvest begins, in July it is in full swing.

Au mois de juin on moisonne un peu de blé, au mois de juillet on moisonne à pleines mains.

Au mes de Jun s'en meissouno quaucun, au mes de Juliet se meissouna à plen dèt.

In August, in our region, just before evening, a powerful heat sets the fields ablaze. . . . One could hardly hear the buzzing of a fly drunk on the ray of sunshine that filtered through a crack. Outside the air was burning in columns of fire and, by the threshing floor, between the haystacks, rose up an odor of wheat, fiery as a furnace. The whitewashed, beaten soil radiated against the low wall of the abandoned sheepfold. . . . From there, no noise, not any more than from the barnyard where the animals were dozing. . . .

The heart of the house remained cool, however. . . . There remained in this retreat some reserves of shade and freshness that were fed at night and which, during the heat of the day, were a great resource.
Henri Bosco,
Le Mas Théotime

Country Decor:
Dick Dumas's Sun House

[La Guelardière, 1, route d'Apt, 84800 L'Isle-sur-la-Sorgue. Tel: 90 38 24 77; FAX: 90 20 87 02. Open: 9:00 A.M. to 12 M (noon); 2:00 P.M. to 6:00 P.M. every day but Sunday.]

In recent years, the town of L'Isle-sur-la-Sorgue, east of Avignon on the way to Apt, has become a highly fashionable center for the antiques business. Professionals and amateurs from all over Europe flock to its weekend fairs. Designer and interior decorator Dick Dumas has opened a shop in a corner house just on the edge of town, next door to the prestigious dealers' collective, the Espace Béchard, on the road to Apt. Based in Provence for more than 20 years, he has owned three homes there that have been the subject of admiring articles in *Vogue, Elle Décoration,* and *Maison et Jardin.*

Monsieur Dumas specializes in garden furniture of simple, classic design; each piece is made as much for comfort as for visual appeal. Various tables and chairs, as well as glassware and other accessories, all bearing the mark of his personal taste and style, have won him many prizes. One of his particularly successful items is a doorstop, which proves most useful in Provence on days of the full mistral. Most of his production is custom-made in the region, and then is shipped all over the world.

As a decorator, Monsieur Dumas redesigned the interior of the Château de Castille near Uzès, and created furniture to complement the Picasso frescoes that line its patio. More recently, he helped to renovate the château-hôtel at Crillon-le-Brave. He enjoys mixing antiques with modern furnishings in ways that are always distinctive.

ABOVE: *Plants in pots and jars grace all summer gardens in Provence.* OPPOSITE TOP: *Dick Dumas's garden terrace in a Luberon village shows off furniture of his own creation, the whole composition in tones of white and green.* OPPOSITE BOTTOM: *An ancient, flower-decked well embellishes the farmstead garden of couturier Bernard Perris.*

Eating figs in the morning is gold, at noon, silver and
  in the evening, lead.
Figues du matin sont de l'or, à midi sont de l'argent,
  et le soir sont de plomb.
Le figo lou matin soun d'or, à miejour soun d'argènt,
  e lou sèr soun de ploumb.

Tavel Wines:
The Château d'Aquéria

[Château d'Aquéria, 30126 Tavel. Tel: 66 50 04 56; FAX: 66 50 18 46. Open: 9:00 A.M. to 12 M (noon); 2:00 P.M. to 6:00 P.M. every day but Sunday. Owners: the de Bez family. Located north of Avignon, toward Bagnols-sur-Cèze (N580), on the smaller D177 west.]

Although the rosé wines of Provence have the reputation of being light, summer vacation beverages, best sipped on shaded terraces before siesta time, the Tavel region produces a different rosé, with a wide following and a rich history. The early-eighteenth-century Château d'Aquéria, visible from the Bagnols–Avignon road, sits imposingly among its 130-odd acres of vineyards. A family tradition begun in the 1920s is carried on by two brothers, one who handles the business transactions, the other the winemaking.

They produce Tavel, a dry, full-bodied rosé, from a mixture of Grenache, Cinsault, Clairette, Mourvèdre and Bourboulenc grapes. Before blending, each type is treated separately. Tavel also differs from lesser rosés in its higher alcohol content. So be advised that it packs an unexpected punch on a hot day.

The rosé of Aquéria is consumed all over the world. In fact, a customer once complained that he had to pay more for it at the Carleton Hôtel in Cannes than at New York's Waldorf Astoria. The latter hotel has been a good customer since the 1930s.

Next to Tavel lies the community of Lirac, and at Aquéria one vineyard is split between the two municipalities. Since Lirac also produces fine reds and whites, small amounts of both wines are also available at the château.

LEFT: *On the terrace at the Château d'Aquéria, Anduze jars frame the surrounding countryside.* ABOVE: *The parterre beyond is a green garden in the Italian style.*

A Roman Quarry with Character

[*Mas de la Pyramide, quartier Saint-Paul, 13210 Saint-Rémy-de-Provence. Tel: 90 92 00 81. Open in summer 9:00 A.M. to 12 M (noon); 2:00 P.M. to 7:00 P.M. In winter, 9:00 A.M. to 12 M (noon); 2:00 P.M. to 5:00 P.M. Owner: Monsieur Mauron. Just off the D5, as one leaves the center of Saint-Rémy, heading south toward Les Baux.*]

South of Saint-Rémy-de-Provence stand two of the region's finest Roman monuments, which are known as *Les Antiques*. They consist of a cenotaph and a partially destroyed municipal arch. These once indicated the entry to the bustling commercial community of Glanum, whose digs may be visited in the valley nearby. A few hundred yards off lies a former Benedictine monastery, Saint-Paul-de-Mausole, that was converted into a mental hospital in the nineteenth century. It is where Van Gogh spent his last year in Provence. Just behind the cloister, near swaths of lavender that bring out the harmonies of its twelfth-century bell tower, is a parking lot. Here, a sign directs visitors to the most curious site of all.

A small path leads downhill, through a gate, and opens onto a vast oval area, surrounded by low, wooded hills: This spot was quarried by the Romans, who cut out from its slopes the stones used

The ancient quarry of Saint-Rémy-de-Provence, magically lit with snowy cherry trees in spring, will sport intense blue spikes of lavender in summer. An old stone well still supplies the nearby farmstead.

MADAME BOURG'S EGGPLANT MOUSSE

▲▲▲▲▲▲▲▲▲

In his *Almanach*, Frédéric Mistral recounts a dialogue in which Provençaux from different regions compare recipes for eggplant, always so plentiful at the height of summer. In Sérignan, for example, it is stewed in oil, but in Carpentras, it is baked au gratin. In Le Thor, however, it is sautéed with garlic, onion and "love apples" (tomatoes), while in Maillane, it is prepared as fritters. In Saint-Savournin, eggplant slices are dried in the summer sun and served with sausages in winter. In Apt, they are turned into jam! In Pertuis, eggplants are cooked whole in the embers of a wood fire, then opened, salted, peppered and drizzled with olive oil. Some add a crushed anchovy. The following recipe was invented by a cheese seller in the Avignon public market. Serves 6

to build not only the ancient town of Glanum but also most of the monuments in Arles. A tall, irregular stone column in its center marks the original height of the land before excavation; its apex corresponds still to the level of the surrounding hills. This strange ruin was mistakenly called a pyramid in medieval times—hence the name of the site.

Today, a cherry orchard fills one end of the former quarry, while lavender fields extend around an ancient stone well at the other. And built into the northern slopes is a troglodyte farmstead—the Mas de la Pyramide.

The present owner, Monsieur Mauron, claims his ancestors have lived here since the days of Charlemagne. He conducts tours of both the quarry caves and his house. In the former, he has arranged an impressive display of old agricultural equipment. There are also huge stone Roman vats for storage of provisions, an aqueduct fragment and a wall that slaves scraped at to make gravel for roadbeds. Within the house, rustic furniture (some made from stone) and faded family photographs are grouped as they must have been in the late nineteenth century. Monsieur Mauron lives very simply: In his kitchen, a few potatoes are kept in an earthenware bowl; outside, his dishes are laid out on a slab of rock to dry. At one end of the property, however, he has installed two comfortable guest rooms that may be rented by tourists.

In front of the farmstead, lilacs and redbuds bloom in the spring along with irises that edge the path—very like those painted by Van Gogh, a stone's throw away. The site has unusual character, much like its owner, who lives here happily with his dogs and cats and pet rook, welcoming all those who are interested in the place's unusual beauty and strange history.

3 shallots or mild onions, chopped fine

3 tablespoons olive oil

3 pounds eggplant, peeled and diced

Salt

Pepper

2 cloves garlic, chopped

2 tablespoons chopped parsley (and basil, if you wish)

7 large eggs

2 cups fresh tomato sauce

Preheat the oven to 350° F. In a large skillet, sauté the shallots in the olive oil until they are translucent. Add the eggplant and cook until tender, over very low heat, turning often. Halfway through the cooking, add salt, pepper, garlic and herbs. Put the mixture in a food processor or blender, and purée, or put it through a sieve. In a separate bowl, beat the eggs, then add them to the eggplant mixture. Pour the eggplant mixture into a 2-quart greased loaf pan set in a pan of hot water, and bake for about an hour. Serve the mousse hot or lukewarm with the tomato sauce.

Saint John's Day: Herbal Lore of the Summer Solstice

An olive for Saint John
(June 24), thousands
more to come.

Une olive déjà pour la
Saint-Jean, mille pour
tous les autres.

Une óulivo pèr Sant-Jan,
milo pèr touti li Sant.

Medieval land rotation was triennial in northern France, biennial in the south, where milder winters made autumn sowing possible. The wheat was then ready for the following summer solstice, associated with Saint John's Day (June 24), and celebrated as a harvest festival. In the valleys, extra hands were needed from May onward, and workers would come from the northern hills in teams of three—two men cut and a woman collected. Starting in the vicinity of Arles, they would follow the ripening fields north as the season progressed, moving across the land like a tide, arriving home just in time to harvest their own crops.

Around this major event of the agricultural year, ancient pagan rituals became linked to Christian symbolism. Its popular folklore came to permeate the smallest details of everyday life. Saint John's Eve was the time for gathering medicinal herbs such as catnip, sage, some thymes, southernwood, hyssop, and wild hypericum, which is more commonly referred to as St.-John's-wort. Some market centers, such as Marseilles, still hold herb fairs in late June. Old-fashioned gardens in which aromatics are grown together with fruit and flowers are often called St. John's gardens.

In Provence, ladybugs are known as "St. John's hens"; early ripening pears and apples are called *poires et pommes de la Saint-Jean.* When someone sneezes, there are Provençaux who still say, "May Saint John make you grow!" Bills used to be due on June 24; it was also the date that farm workers' contracts were established or renewed, until Toussaint, or November 1.

Two plumbers, "rough characters," broke the garden tap, a rather fancy one with a sort of key-shaped handle that could be removed in order to foil marauders. (In the summer, a good deal of water pinching from the neighbor's well is quite fashionable. You wait until your neighbor goes out and then swiftly water your geraniums.)
Lawrence Durrell, SPIRIT OF PLACE

Common wild aromatics (rosemary, sage, box, cistus, lavender) make wonderful garden plants: at the Bergerie du Bosquet (opposite), and in a Luberon village (above). Edibles can also be beautiful: zucchini mixed with roses in a farmer's vegetable garden (right).

One afternoon, in the valley of Refresquières, Manon was sitting in the dry grass, watching the yellow carapace of a small prehistoric monster that had planted its claws on a sprig of Queen Anne's Lace. The large insect remained perfectly immobile, but something was happening inside, for suddenly its back split along almost its entire length, and a pale green creature worked hard to extract itself from this prison. It was wrapped in damp, crumpled wings and it climbed slowly and clumsily to the top of the plant, where it stayed motionless in the burning July sun. It was a cicada. Its body turned brown in a matter of minutes, its wings unfolded, grew hard and transparent, like mica veined with gold.

Marcel Pagnol,
MANON OF THE SPRINGS

Fires are lit on hilltops in Provence, as they are all over Europe, to celebrate Saint John's Day. The proverb *Sant Jan fai fue, Sant Pèire l'abro* ("Saint John lights the fire, Saint Peter stokes it") may allude both to this ancient custom and to the growing heat of summer. Southerners also claimed that anyone who could jump over the St. John's fire without getting burned would be protected against fleas for the coming year.

Today, the northern Provençal town of Valréas maintains its own harvest traditions that began five centuries ago: On the evening of June 23, a five-year-old boy is crowned king for a year and draped in a white sheepskin. He is carried triumphantly through the charming village, accompanied by a torchlight procession of 300 people in period dress, as bowsmen and pages, soldiers and herders with carts of oxen.

Harvest festivities take place in other towns throughout the summer: Some communities celebrate Saint Eloi (June 25), patron of blacksmiths and protector of all farm animals and agriculture. And every village in the northern Alpilles, for example, has a parade featuring a harvest cart, heavily laden with produce and flowers, pulled by about twenty horses decked out with multicolored ribbons, pompons and feathers. Saint Roch merits similar homage. Many of these celebrations are further enchanced by competitions of lawn bowling (*boules*), mass banquets outdoors (usually involving huge quantities of *aïoli*), and Provençal bull running. Often, there is folk and street dancing, which is prolonged late into the evening, accompanied by fireworks. Barbantane, Eyragues, Châteaurenard, Rognonas and Maillane are among the villages holding such festivals.

A Mountain Inn: Crillon-le-Brave

[*Hostellerie de Crillon-le-Brave, place de l'Eglise, 84410 Crillon-le-Brave, Tel: 90 65 61 61; FAX: 90 65 62 86. Northeast of Avignon and Carpentras, just south of Malaucène, on the D974, heading toward Vaison-la-Romaine.*]

ABOVE: *Crillon-le-Brave, a charming hilltown named for a Renaissance hero, rises north of Carpentras. Its château has been tastefully transformed into an elegant hotel.* RIGHT: *The terrace at Crillon-le-Brave gives onto the Roman-tiled roofs of village houses below, and the nearby Mont Ventoux beyond.*

American novelist Edith Wharton remembers driving into northern Provence: "Ahead of us, all the way from Avignon to Orange, the Mont Ventoux lifted into the pure light its denuded flanks and wrinkled silvery-lilac summit. But at Orange we turned about its base, and bore away north-eastward through a broken country rimmed with hills. . . . " Today, she might have been heading for the Hostellerie de Crillon-le-Brave, a country inn closer to Carpentras than Orange, in a picturesque hilltown named after a Renaissance hero, whose statue stands in the village square. Peter Chittick, an enterprising Canadian, has converted the town's medieval château into a comfortable and elegant hotel. Its bright cotton fabrics and ocher-colored walls; its welcoming sitting rooms furnished with antiques and splendid books about Provence; its chamber-music concerts and chatty newsletter, with tips on local sites and crafts; its terraced garden, where the swimming pool affords a spectacular view of the valley below—all these features lead its many regular guests to consider it as a second home rather than a hotel. Others come mainly to eat local specialties . . . in the garden.

August rain gives oil
and wine.
Pluie d'août donne de
l'huile et du vin.
Pluio d'aous douno
d'ooulivo eme de mous.

Crillon-le-Brave's Olive Mousse

Serves 4

1¼ cups medium-sized black olives
   (preferably Nyons)
1¼ cups heavy cream
½ teaspoon powdered (unflavored) gelatin
1 tablespoon finely chopped chervil
Salt
Pepper
¼ pound fresh escarole, washed and dried
1 tablespoon balsamic vinegar
1 shallot, chopped fine
4 tablespoons good-quality olive oil

Pit the olives, setting aside four halves for garnish. Chop the rest to a fine texture, or purée it in a food processor or blender.

In a saucepan, gently heat ¼ cup of cream, then sprinkle the gelatin over it. Stir the mixture until the granules are completely dissolved. In a bowl, whip the remaining cream, fold in the olive pulp, then the gelatin mixture. Add the chervil, salt and pepper. Pour the mixture gently into four individual molds and refrigerate for at least two hours.

Dip the bottom of each mold very quickly into hot water and unmold each onto individual plates. Place half an olive in the center of each mousse. Surround with escarole leaves.

Pour the vinegar in a bowl and season with salt and pepper. Add the finely chopped shallot, then beat in the olive oil until well blended. Dribble the dressing over the salad and serve.

One after one the Rhone bestowed upon us its historic sites and little drunken towns, snuggled among vines, bathed in the insouciance of drowsy days and drowsy silences broken only by the snip-snop of the secateurs among the vines—the holy circumcision that ends the elegiac summers of Provence.
Lawrence Durrell, LIVIA

The Cuckoo and the Cicada

A popular fable taken from Frédéric Mistral's *Almanach* of 1890.

Now one day the Cuckoo, well-fed and fat, observed while calling "Cuckoo! cuckoo!" that the meadows that year were thickly grown; and that for the May mowing, the local farm workers were making good money . . . and believe it or not, he hired out to mow. And to collect the hay, he took on the Cicada.

But the Cuckoo is an idler, so much so as you know that he lays his eggs in the nests of others . . . and when the summer heat struck, this lazy creature stopped all the time to sharpen his scythe, yawning in the face of the hard work to be done. But the Cicada, thin and light, thrived on the heat and sang out to him petulantly, "Cut! cut! cut! cut!" Then the Cuckoo began again; but after only a few steps, dropped his scythe once more to go have a drink, while the hardworking Cicada exclaimed, "Fat loafer!" and cried, "Cut! cut! cut! cut!" And thus the Cicada continued the livelong day, always scolding the Cuckoo, telling him constantly to cut, cut, cut. . . .

So much so that the plump bird, when the great heat came which ripens the wheat, could stand it no longer and, from laziness, found himself a clump of grass, lay down and stayed silent.

But the good Cicada, gladdened by the sun, hired out to bind the sheaves of the harvesters who were cutting the wheat, and all during the harvest, as long as it lasted, she cried out, "Cut! cut! cut!"

This is why in May, the Cuckoo can be heard, but as soon as it gets hot, he hides and keeps still, while the Cicada sings loud. . . .

The cicada, known as *cigale* in French, is frequently misnamed "grasshopper" in English. In La Fontaine's famous fable *Le Cigale et le fourmi*, it is the cicada who is lazy, dancing away the summer while the industrious ant stores up food for winter. Mistral's Provençal tale, which also contrasts laziness with hard work, portrays the cicada as a hard-working farm woman whose man lets her down.

The poet John Keats also admired the insect's summer song (he also used the term "grasshopper"). In his Romantic English version, however, no one works at all! Just as in the Provençal fable, however, the birds dislike the heat of summer:

> When all the birds are faint with the hot sun,
> And hide in cooling trees, a voice will run
> From hedge to hedge about the new-mown mead;
> That is the Grasshopper's—he takes the lead
> In summer luxury,—and he has never done
> With his delights; for when tired out with fun
> He rests at ease beneath some pleasant weed.

For Keats, both the cicada's summer song and that of the cricket on the hearth in winter simply show that "the poetry of earth is never dead."

Celebrated in antiquity as a symbol of music, the cicada remains a special favorite in Provence today. Ceramic effigies of this creature can be purchased in most souvenir shops.

Olive-Wood Crafts

A. Parodi et famille. The shop is on the main street of Mirabel-aux-Baronnies, between Vaison-la-Romaine and Nyons, northeast of Avignon on the D938. Tel: 75 27 12 07. Open: 9:00 A.M. to 12 M (noon); 2:00 P.M. to 6:00 P.M., every day but Sunday.

O n display here are many different objects made from elegantly veined hard olive wood. Among them are classic salad bowls as well as mortars and pestles, which are used in the preparation of many traditional Provençal dishes, such as aïoli, or the "rouille" that accompanies bouillabaisse. Since the hard April frosts of 1956 that destroyed so many old orchards, craftsmen have also had olive tree roots at their disposal. Many of these gnarled forms have been transformed into original lamps bases. The Parodis' work can also be found in shops all over Provence, but it is worth seeing at the source, in the heart of the rich olive country around Nyons. Their workshops are situated a mile from the town center and can also be visited.

Orchards of century-old olive trees have an imposing presence. Besides the bounty of their fruit and oil, they provide a dense wood much prized for both carving and burning.

Portrait of a Provençal Gardener: A "Sun Queen"

A ix-en-Provence is one of Europe's most distinguished and cultured cities. From the fifteenth century until the French Revolution (1789), a powerful parliament convened here, governing Provence on behalf of French monarchs. The surrounding countryside still contains hundreds of elegant residences built by the town's nobility, called *bastides* or *pavillons*. One of the best

ROGER VERGÉ'S COOL SUMMER SALAD

▲▲▲▲▲▲▲▲▲

Serves 4

20 medium-sized black olives
  (preferably Nyons)
2 lemons
3 young, very fresh zucchini
  (no more than an inch
  in diameter)
3 tomatoes, still a bit green
Sea salt
4 sprigs coriander,
  chopped finely
20 fresh mint leaves,
  chopped finely
4 tablespoons good-quality
  olive oil

Pit the olives. In a salad bowl, squeeze the juice of one lemon. Peel the other lemon, cut it into quarters and add them to the bowl. Wash and trim off the ends of the zucchini. Slice the zucchini thinly and add them to the bowl.

Wash the tomatoes and remove the stem ends. Cut the tomatoes in half crosswise, then cut them into ½-inch cubes. Add them to the bowl. Sprinkle the vegetables with sea salt

preserved of these, Bidaine, has recently been restored by an American enthusiast, Lillian Williams.

This passionate archivist of eighteenth-century life beautifully maintains its rococo buildings, encircled by elaborate fountains and gardens. Years ago, in San Francisco, she used to attend opera openings and balls dressed in period gowns, driven in a Louis XVI carriage and accompanied by coachmen in livery. She now owns a museum-quality collection of eighteenth-century French costumes. Her husband collects seventeenth- and eighteenth-century keyboard instruments, including a spinet by Pascal Taskin, made for Marie Antoinette. The couple has renovated the property at Bidaine with such attention to period detail that it could serve as the perfect setting for *The Marriage of Figaro.*

Bidaine has many unusual features. Below the house lies an original water garden, with its island plantings bordered by canals. Opening onto the west terrace is an astonishing, rococo-style grotto, lined with seashells in intricate patterns. It was designed and installed by Mr. and Mrs. Williams as a summer project just a few years ago. Most of the domain is tranquil throughout the seasons, lulled by the trickling of the fountains and the occasional gliding of the family swan. As soon as one approaches the walk leading to the outdoor theater, however, furious barking usually erupts: This avenue is overlooked by a majestic *tapis vert* ("extensive lawn"), where reside some 25 King Charles spaniels. The dogs sleep in their two miniature châteaux and drink fresh spring water from their private Louis XIV-style fountain. Only the royal members of this canine family are admitted to the house itself, where the dowager queen, Manon Lescaut, is allowed to sleep in a miniature eighteenth-century canopied bed.

and let them macerate for 20 minutes.

Add the olives and the herbs. Sprinkle with olive oil and toss. Serve immediately, so that the tomatoes and zucchini do not get mushy.

Reprinted with permission from *Les Legumes de Mon Moulin,* by Roger Vergé, published by Editions Flammarion in 1992. Translated by Louisa Jones.

Tumbling tamarisk and a stone nymph overlook the unique water parterre at Bidaine, keeping watch by the wrought-iron gate.

Lillian Williams, now based in New York and Paris, is also restoring another marvelous eighteenth-century *folie* château in Normandy. She feels she was born in France in that era, and is in the midst of writing a book on the charms of its daily life. She concentrates not on great furniture but on such simple objects as frivolities, ribbons and powder boxes.

A specialist in the exoticism of the eighteenth century, Lillian Williams has revived a tradition of extravagance and refinement that perfectly suits both Bidaine and the cultural heritage from which it sprang. No wonder this estate has recently been called "The Pavillon of the Sun Queen."

In the Provençal garden at Val Joanis, cool, filtered shade, fragrant potted plants and comfortable armchairs offer an invitation to repose.

Authentic Traditional Fabrics: The Olivades

[Les Olivades, avenue Barberin, Saint-Etienne-du-Grès, 13150 Tarascon. Tel: 90 49 16 68. Near the traffic circle southeast of Tarascon, on the D99, heading toward Saint-Rémy-de-Provence. A shop selling "seconds" is open Monday to Fridays from 9:00 A.M. to 12 M (noon); 2:00 P.M. to 6:00 P.M. Visits to the factory, for groups of ten (minimum), are by appointment only.]

Provençal fabrics with their intricate designs and compelling colors have become much more fashionable in recent years. But their popularity dates back to the Renaissance when the Compagnie des Indes began importing printed cottons from India. By the second half of the seventeenth century, local workshops that produced imitations of these successful imports had sprung up all over Europe. As a result, from 1686 onward, successive kings of France forbade them entirely. Provence, on the outer edge of this interdiction, became a center of contraband, continuing production on the Papal territories, which included Avignon. One hundred years passed before this prohibition was lifted. It had only served to increase the popularity of these beautiful fabrics.

The inimitable designs of Provençal fabrics were first inspired by Indian cottons in the eighteenth century. Now several companies produce them, each with its own style.

The ancestor of today's best-known companies was founded near Tarascon following the troubled period of the Revolution. In 1976, cousins within the family branched out to found the Olivades, now the only manufacturer to maintain traditional means of production in Provence. The original business, Souleiado, has achieved wide international recognition and has moved toward brighter, gayer, sunstruck colors. The Olivades still sells most of its production to Provençal customers, and has retained both the subtler tones and printing processes of earlier times (flat frame rather than rotating drums). Indeed, in Saint-Etienne the entire sequence of production is laid out on tables some 75 yards long. The cottons are cleaned and dried, printed one color at a time, steamed for color fastness, cleaned and dried again, and finally stretched. All of these steps take place in one large building, where about 20 people are employed.

Although the making of these "Indian" fabrics has been a major industry in Provence for centuries, involving many families and whole towns, there has invariably been a highly cosmopolitan dimension to it. For instance, the cottons have always been imported from Louisiana or Calcutta, even in the seventeenth century. Jean-François Boudin, in partnership with his brother and sister, runs the Olivades business. According to him, what characterizes the Provençal style today is the manner of interpreting certain traditional patterns, such as the geometric, nonspecific floral designs, the cashmere swirl, the Imperial bee from Napoleonic times, and the Pompadour bouquet. His generation is the first to have learned English rather than the local Provençal dialect.

Tradition and innovation: Century-old models serve as inspirations for the latest fashions. About 20 percent of the Olivades' fabrics are newly designed every year, in line with current trends. They are sold both as yard goods and ready-to-wear items. The Olivades factory lies among some of the loveliest countryside of the Alpilles, and the patterns seem like a concentration of the subtle beauties of this landscape. The fabrics can easily be slipped onto a patio table, transformed into cushions for a chaise-longue or turned into curtains, shirts or headscarves. (The California company

The village of Aurons, north of Aix, keeps up a floral display even in the summer heat.

ZUCCHINI FANS

Serves 4

4 medium zucchini, washed and trimmed
4 medium tomatoes
2 tablespoons chopped parsley
3 tablespoons grated Swiss cheese
Salt
Pepper
2 tablespoons olive oil

Preheat oven to 375° F. Steam or poach the zucchini for 5 to 7 minutes, or until just barely cooked but still quite firm. Create fans by making two lengthwise cuts almost to the end of each zucchini. Cut the tomatoes into slices and insert them between the layers of zucchini.

Grease a baking dish just large enough to hold the vegetables, and then arrange them gently in it. Sprinkle with parsley, grated cheese, salt, pepper and olive oil. Bake for 15 to 20 minutes, or until lightly browned.

Smith and Hawkins has already made all these adaptations).
They also nicely lend themselves to a variety of decors
and clothing styles. Bags and *pochettes,* fabric-covered boxes,
umbrellas, even bracelets are also available in the company's
shops, which can be found in every town in Provence.

ABOVE: *Lotus seed pods,*
emerging from a fountain,
surround a particularly
elaborate terra-cotta garden
ornament. RIGHT: *The hilltown*
of Roussillon is famous for its
ocher quarries. Its houses all
sport tones of orange, flame
and yellow.

Field Patterns in Provence

There are gardens of
beans, orchards with
apples, pears and peaches,
cherry trees that catch
your eye, fig trees that
offer you their ripe figs,
round-bellied melons that
beg to be eaten, and beautiful vines with bunches
of golden grapes—ah,
I can almost see them!
THE MEMOIRS OF
FRÉDÉRIC MISTRAL,
trans. George Wickes

Historians of rural France love to discuss the lay-
out of its cultivated fields in an attempt to
explain why there are such radical regional variations, especially between north and south. The hedged
and stone-walled patchwork of the northwest and the long,
narrow "open-field" system of the northeast both stand in
striking contrast to the Mediterranean design. It is thought
that some of these differences are the result of two separate, prehistoric migrations by nomads, one from the
Danube valley and the other from the inland sea, who
moved into the territory that is now France.

It was the Romans, however, who gave the southern
countryside its modern gridlike configuration. They sur-
veyed the entire region and cut it into squares of land that
they called "centuries." Some 415 stone fragments recording
the results of their planning, the oldest dating from about
77 B.C., can be seen in the municipal museum in Orange.
When whole, each of these tablets measured at least 23 feet
by 20 feet; they were all meant to be posted for public
viewing. Thus the Romans, through this division of land
called "centuriation," created a grid pattern for the rural
landscape comparable to the typical Roman town plan, fix-
ing dimensions of holdings at about 375 square feet, a size
still surprisingly common today. In addition, southern
fields also remained small because of Roman inheritance
laws, which gave equal shares to each son rather than the
whole estate to the eldest. It has also been said that southern plowmen appreciated square fields because the water
gourd that waited at the end of each row of plantings could
be reached that much more quickly! However that may be,

*The custom of planting fruit
trees among vineyards dates
from Roman times. Shade trees
in cultivated fields provide a
place to rest and store the
water gourd while working in
hot weather.*

THE MIDSUMMER GARLIC FAIR IN MARSEILLES

It hangs in short braids, or loops in long heavy cables from all the stands that spring up in a few hours. It spills from the backs of parked trucks and wagons. It lies in piles on canvas spread on the sidewalks, and there are nutlike sacks of it as tall as a man. Housewives pinch and sniff and fill their baskets for storage; buyers for big hotels and restaurants in Provence sample freely as they make out their orders; wholesalers from half of Europe compare lots and bargain with the farmers. It is exciting, and a handsome scene, with the silky glistening garlic everywhere, to look at and to breathe. Some men in Provence say their women are beautiful because of garlic, and some women

aerial photographs confirm the persistence of this type of Roman patterning in today's countryside.

Another factor that helped determine the country's field patterns was the tool chosen to work the land. Since Roman times, southern fields were tilled with the *araire*, an instrument that differed radically from the northern plow, or *charrue*. The latter, much heavier, needed a team of animals to pull it and hence more turning room at the end of each row. It worked well, therefore, in larger, more regular spaces. The lighter araire, on the other hand, opened the earth without turning it over, and suited sandy, stony soil. It was easier to manipulate on slopes and could be drawn by one animal. The farmer who used it had to plow each field twice, once up and down and once crosswise, to prepare it for sowing. (Many of these araires are on display in country museums today, at the Mas de la Pyramide in Saint-Rémy, for example, and at the wine cooperative in Laudun, near Avignon).

The southern rural landscape is also characterized by its absence of walls between fields. Once again, it is the Romans who are responsible for this. The force of the Roman legal code was such that physical barriers were not necessary to mark the limits of private property. The general survey and a few stones, even clods of earth, sufficed to demarcate holdings. Walls in the traditional Provençal countryside support earth or mark bridges and canals. Both walls and hedges are becoming more common in the modern countryside, however. Although rights of passage for sheep and goats still form part of many property deeds, vacation and retirement home owners have now enclosed large tracts of rural land.

say their babies are healthy because of it, and their men stronger than other men.
M. F. K. Fisher,
TWO TOWNS IN PROVENCE

The Romans loved trees in groves, which had sacred significance in their gardens. Often, they planted these wooded clusters in the middle of fields. Thus began another ancient custom in Provence that was to last for 2,000 years and that was to leave its mark on the rural scenery: the mingling of fruit trees, vines and cultivated strips, called *ouillères.* Typically, three to five yards of wheat would

The intricate Provençal patchwork of agricultural and grazing land changes character from season to season, each with its own colors, textures and light.

be cultivated with four or five vine rows on each side, among which, in turn, stood olive or fruit trees. If modern mechanical and specialized farming has made this mixture impractical, there are vestiges of it everywhere. Even now, it is not unusual to find trees standing in the middle of many fields, providing fruit, or shade when it is time to quench one's thirst from the water gourd.

An Elegant Country Retreat:
Le Prieuré

[*7, place du Chapitre, 30400 Villeneuve-lez-Avignon, across the Rhone from Avignon. Tel: 90 25 46 28; FAX: 90 25 45 39. Owner: Madame Marie-France Mille; Chef: Serge Chenet. Next door to the hotel, a pastry and candy shop is run by their pastry chef, Monsieur Lorensot. Tel: 90 25 84 95; FAX: 90 25 86 77.*]

In 1322, Cardinal Arnaud de Via, nephew of reigning Avignon Pope Jean XXII, built a fine residence in Villeneuve. Feeling the approach of death, he set up a priory with a chapter of 12 canons, 12 priests and two deacons, ruled over by a dean, to pray for his soul. Part of this original property became Villeneuve's parish church, and the rest became a private residence. First transformed into a comfortable modern hotel by the late Monsieur Mille's parents in the 1930s, renovated again in recent years, it is one of Provence's "best addresses" for both restful stays and good food. In summer, a formal garden edged with an ancient pergola brims over with colorful blooms, visible from the dining terrace. Chef Serge Chenet has been using a wide variety of local ingredients since 1988. Light, sweet olive oil seasons many of the most refined dishes. Vegetables served here come largely from the plots of nearby neighbors, located beyond the tennis court and the cutting garden, from which Madame Mille collects fresh flowers to make up bouquets for the dining tables.

ABOVE: *Rough-hewn stone wells often turn into planters for heat-loving flowers as here, in a garden in Fontvieille.* OPPOSITE: *The colorful gardens of the Prieuré hotel in Villeneuve combine the traditional lines of box-edged parterres with a riot of summer color—a careful blending of annual and perennial bloom.* FOLLOWING PAGE: *Monkfish cocoons, in a simple, olive oil—based dressing, provide rustic but refined fare, here enhanced by old-fashioned Provençal pottery.*

Monkfish Cocoons with Eggplant

Serves 4

1 monkfish, weighing 3½ pounds

3 medium-sized eggplants

1½ cups extra-virgin olive oil (first cold pressing)

4 ripe tomatoes

1 shallot

1 clove garlic

Salt

Pepper

2 anchovy fillets in oil

S A U C E

1 hard-boiled egg

1 lemon

1 tablespoon salmon roe

½ tablespoon lumpfish caviar

2 tablespoons chopped chives

1 tablespoon chopped parsley

Preheat the oven to 350° F. Grease a baking pan or cookie sheet.

Clean the fish and remove the fillets. Refrigerate them.

Halve the eggplants lengthwise. Make several slits in the flesh with a knife and place the halves, cut side up, in a baking dish. Salt them lightly and drizzle 1 tablespoon of olive oil over them. Bake for about 35 minutes, or until just soft.

Plunge the tomatoes into boiling water for 30 seconds, then peel them. Cut each tomato in half, squeeze gently to remove the seeds and chop the flesh into small cubes. Reserve half for the garnish.

Mince the shallot and the garlic. In a frying pan, heat 1 tablespoon of the olive oil. Add the shallot and cook, without browning, until soft. Add the garlic, then the cubed tomatoes. Season with salt and pepper, and simmer the mixture for 5 minutes, or until soft.

Remove the eggplants from the oven and spoon out the pulp. Chop it coarsely. Heat another tablespoon of olive oil in a large saucepan and add the anchovy fillet. Add the eggplant pulp and the tomato mixture. Simmer, uncovered, until the mixture is reduced. Add more salt and pepper, if necessary.

Prepare the monkfish: Cut each fillet crosswise into 20 thin slices. Arrange 20 of these slices in the prepared baking pan or on the cookie sheet. Spoon some of the eggplant mixture onto each slice, then cover this layer of fish slices with the remaining slices. Tuck the edges of the slices under to make individual fish packages. Bake them for 2 minutes on each side.

Meanwhile, prepare the sauce. Separate the yolk and white of the hard-boiled egg. Squeeze the lemon juice into a bowl, add salt, pepper and the remaining olive oil. Add both types of fish eggs, half of the white and half of the yolk of the egg, the chives and the parsley, and combine.

Arrange 5 fish cocoons, like the petals of a flower, on each plate. In the center put 1 teaspoon of the tomato mixture. Spoon over the sauce. Crumble the remaining yolk and white of the egg and decorate. Garnish with the reserved cubed tomatoes.

Between Tarascon and the Alpilles lies "a little territory of an extreme fertility where the Tarasconnais garden in the evenings and erect the little huts that serve them for weekend cottages. For the Tarasconnais, like the Parisian and like myself, is an inveterate kitchen gardener . . . the moment the shades of evening begin to fall he is up and away from desk or counter and wading amongst the profusions of his melon-patch, his pumpkins, his gourdes, pimenti and his tomatoes. . . ." Ford Madox Ford, PROVENCE, 1935

ABOVE: *Lavender and its commercial variety,* lavandin, *produce some of Provence's headiest and best-loved fragrances.* LEFT: *Old-fashioned, single-flowered hollyhocks will self-sow in any crack between two stones, and spring up in every Provençal village.*

Provençal Fragrance

A seasonal evocation contributed by Anne Simonet, co-author of *Le Nez de la Drome* and a fine Provençal "nose."

In Provence, intensive farming turns the whole countryside into a garden, and yet wild corners persist along every roadside, on every hilltop. Fragrance is always present, from season to season, a gauge of continuing rustic authenticity. It is often discrete—dog roses in a hedge, thyme crushed underfoot in the *garrique*. And often heady—the anise perfume of a whole field of fennel, the dense shade of a linden tree in full flower when the air is so thick, so rich with scent as to be almost edible. Mixed fragrances of a summer market—herbal, floral, fruity, animal. As complex and seductive as music where perfume provides the counterpoint: from peach to lavender, back to melon and basil.

In Provence, one must be led by the nose, remain still, and sniff. Each season, each landscape has its aromas.

In winter: truffles, olives and wine.

In spring: flowers and aromatic herbs. Wild lily-of-the-valley and a beech forest in northern Provence, pinewoods, with their hot resinous smells, farther south. Rosemary still in flower as the season opens, thyme and sage as it moves onward.

In summer: commercially grown lavender; the wild odor of savory; green basil, almost anise flavored. The divine peach with its contained power, fresh from the tree, abundant in the village markets.

In autumn: wild mushrooms, and the delicate aromas of the *primeur* wines: strawberry, raspberry, gooseberry . . . and even banana—a cornucopia of delights!

The terraced Italian garden at the wine château of Val Joanis, north of Aix, beautifully combines tones of grey, green and blue. Many aromatic plants contribute to the effect.

Jenny Fajardo's Almond Cake

[*Mas la Burlande, 13520 Le Paradou, Madame Jenny Fajardo de Livry,
Tel: 90 54 32 32. Private road off the D78F, southwest of Les Baux,
between Le Paradou and Arles.*]

At the southern entrance to the valley of Les Baux, with its grotesque rock formations that are thought to have inspired descriptions in Dante's *Inferno*, lies a secluded farmstead. Here at the Mas Burlande, Jenny Fajardo and her husband welcome travelers to their home, which has received the highest classification in several guides as a *gite rurale* ("bed and breakfast lodging in a private home"). A separate wing contains six bedrooms with modern baths, while outside, the garden beckons with patios and swimming pool. But the dining room is the heart of the house. Madame Fajardo prepares excellent seasonal cuisine, based on local tradition and market availability, but always with her personal touch.

continue beating until the mixture is lemon colored, then add the butter. In a separate bowl, combine the cornstarch and baking powder, then add to the egg-yolk mixture. Add the crushed almonds.

In another bowl, beat the egg whites until they are frothy. Add salt and continue beating until stiff peaks form. Gently fold the egg whites into the egg-yolk mixture, just enough to incorporate.

Spoon the batter into the prepared pan and spread evenly. Bake for about 40 minutes, or until a toothpick inserted in the center of the cake comes out dry. Let the cake cool in the pan.

Prepare the frosting: Preheat the oven to 375° F. Coarsely crush or blend the remaining almonds. Place them on an ungreased baking sheet and toast for 5 to 10 minutes until slightly browned, or in a small, heavy skillet over medium-high heat, shaking frequently, for 5 to 10 minutes until golden brown.

Remove the cake from the pan and split in half horizontally with a long serrated knife; or place a long piece of thread around the middle of the cake and pull the two ends in opposite directions (someone else must hold the cake while you split it). Spread half the jam evenly over the bottom layer, not quite to the outside edge, then top with the second layer. In a bowl, beat the confectioners' sugar with the remainder of the jam and the rum so that the mixture is just spreadable. Frost the sides and top of the cake. Decorate with the crushed almonds.

CAKE

1 cup almonds

4 eggs, separated

1 cup granulated sugar

*1 stick (4 ounces) butter,
   softened to room
   temperature*

*2 tablespoons of cornstarch or
   potato starch*

2 teaspoons baking powder

Pinch of salt

FROSTING

*1¼ cups berry jam
   (berries go best with
   almonds, says Madame
   Fajardo, and in summer
   fresh purée may be
   substituted)*

*1 cup sifted confectioners'
   sugar*

*1 tablespoon rum or
   orange liqueur*

Preheat the oven to 350° F. Grease and flour an 8- or 9-inch round pan.

Using a mortar and pestle or a food processor or blender, crush or blend half the almonds into powder. In a large bowl, beat the egg yolks. Gradually add the granulated sugar and

Lizards in Life and Literature

As far as the eye could see, the torrid white road covered with its powdery dust the gardens of olive trees and little oaks, under a round sun of burnished silver that seemed to fill up the sky. Not a speck of shade, not a breath of wind. Nothing but the quivering of the hot air and the strident cry of the cicada's mad music, deafening, urgent, which seemed to embody this immense, vibrating radiance.
Alphonse Daudet,
LETTERS FROM MY MILL

In his novel about the wild shepherdess Manon of the Springs, Marcel Pagnol imagines the young girl taming a lizard—not one of the tiny, friendly creatures that dart in and out of dry stone walls, but the much more imposing *limbert* (sometimes called *lambert*). Manon sets out goat's milk on a tin plate and plays a few notes on her mouth organ. The lizard springs out from a distant bramble thicket, and "like a streak of light, ran towards the music and plunged its horny snout into the bluish milk of the garrigue." Ugolin, the peasant in love with Manon, watches this reenactment of beauty and the beast from behind a bush and wonders if she is a witch . . . or perhaps a fairy?

Lacerta lepida, characterized by its astonishing emerald green back and turquoise throat, is often more than two feet long and is the largest lizard in Europe. Living in the dry brushland of the garrigue, it seeks out underground springs and other spots of moisture. It feeds on big insects, smaller lizards, birds and mice, and is a ferocious hunter that never relinquishes its prey.

The limbert is not, however, averse to human company. Colette once saved such a dragon from her favorite cat and nursed it back to health. Colette and her lizard lunched together daily; the animal developed a passion for fresh cream. But, at that point, afraid of ruining its health altogether, Colette took it back to the vineyard and stroked its head in farewell while the lizard's throat pulsed appreciatively. She then withdrew her hand, barely glimpsed a green comet, then found the spot suddenly, glaringly empty. She pictured the limbert carrying off the traces of her human solicitude, "which imagined itself disinterested. . . ."

The great green lizard of Provence, with its turquoise throat, becomes the friendly companion and helper of many Provençal gardeners.

A second spring, with a new season of growth through

October, first frosts usually late November.

Fall sowing of wheat, oats, rye and barley.

Tree planting: "On Saint Catherine's Day

(November 25), all trees take root." The season when

Autumn in

Bacchus comes into his own again, for each year's grape

harvest. Fall colors in vineyards and orchards, each

variety of vine and fruit tree turning a different tone

of brilliant red, or rust, or gold. Wisps of wild clem-

atis over old walls. Quince paste and quince rolls, a

Provençal bread specialty. Jelly from the hips of wild

roses. Hanging fruit: catalpas, Judas trees, "snail trees"

(*Gleditsias*). Fields of fat, shiny cabbage

rows sheltered by cypresses, and in drier

soil, golden asparagus feathers mixed with vineyards

Provence is . . .

and orchards. Fruitwood still bright red and gold when

the leaves have gone. Colorful pyracantha hedges on

dull days, left arching or pruned into

flat bands, sometimes mixing yellow,

orange and red berries. The finest weather of the year.

Autumn

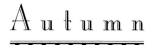

A bent wooden pitchfork leans casually against the stone wall of the farmhouse at the Mas de Curebourg, an antique store at Isle-sur-la-Sorgue.

The Charterhouse of Bonpas: From Charlemagne to Côtes du Rhône

[Chartreuse de Bonpas, 84510 Caumont. Southeast of Avignon. Tel: 90 23 09 59. Owners: Monsieur and Madame Casalis. Open: 9:00 A.M. to 6:30 P.M. Wine tasting is possible every day but Sunday.]

One of the most ancient roads in Europe, a drover's trail in Neolithic times, leads east from the Rhone valley toward the Alps. It crosses the mighty Durance River north of the market town of Cavaillon. For the Romans, this point on the Via Domitia was a ford of vital importance; they policed it well and guaranteed its safety. But once they left, it became a favorite spot for highway robbers.

In 751, nearby Avignon fell into the hands of the Saracens, invaders from North Africa, and subsequently, a great battle took place at just this spot. In 805, no less a general than Charlemagne collected the bones of the dead for burial, built a chapel and founded a monastery on the steep cliff overlooking the river, in order to shelter travelers and protect this ford. The brigands receded and traffic was successfully regulated. This stretch of the Durance, known until then as *maupas*, or "evil passage," now took the name of Bonpas.

The chapel and buildings have undergone many changes since they were first constructed. Monks of the Chartreuse order took over the premises in the fourteenth century, erecting the battlements that still remain. Although the monastery was partially destroyed during the Revolution, it was restored in the nineteenth century by ancestors of the

At the Charterhouse of Bonpas:
OPPOSITE, *steps leading to the
upper garden;* LEFT, *Virginia
creeper on the upper terrace by
the entrance to the yew parterre;*
LEFT BELOW, *the thick walls of
medieval battlements encircle the
domain; and* ABOVE, *a delicate
faun's head fountain in the
lower courtyard.*

After the feast of Saint Maurice (September 22), the
   days walk backward like a crayfish.
Le lendemain de la Saint-Maurice, le jour fait des
   pas d'écrivisses (marche à l'envers).
Lou lendeman de Sant-Maurice, lou jou fais
   pas d'escarabisso.

By Saint Michael's day (September 29), rain spoils the figs.
Pour la Saint-Michel, la pluie gâte les figues.
Pèr Sant Miquèu, li figo soun pèr li pichot aucèu.

present owners. Today, the property also includes an elegant terraced garden. Cut out of three steep levels, it comprises a large main courtyard, a formal parterre above, and a wild garden farther up. The chapel, rebuilt in the twelfth century, stands below the courtyard, on the outer edge of the ramparts.

The formal parterre, with its topiary cones, splendid statuary and sculpted basins, is the heart of the garden: It is laid out where monastic buildings once stood. The luminous, golden stone contrasts warmly with the somber greens of trimmed yew and box, and the soaring shapes of old, windbent stone pines. But this austere decor is enhanced by seasonal color: spring wisteria and redbuds bringing forth their mauve display against black wood; and the serpentine flames of virginia creeper in the fall. In addition, Monsieur and Madame Casalis are underplanting the severely pruned shapes with blue leadwort, Corsican rosemary, pink dianthus, and silvery bush convolvulus.

A modest sign points the way to this domain, north off the main Avignon–Apt road, just after the Avignon–Sud autoroute exit. Gracious stone pillars topped with urns mark the property. An avenue leads to a double-gated fortress entrance decorated with frescoes on its inner walls. In an office installed in an ancient guardhouse, information can be obtained about the owners' excellent Côtes du Rhône wines.

The Chartreuse de Bonpas dominates the surrounding landscape. It is visible from three sides, particularly from the autoroute at its foot. The ancient river ford it guards now serves modern traffic as well. And before long, the secret garden may be further invaded by the passage of the bullet train from Paris.

OPPOSITE: *Vineyards at Bonpas, with the fortress rising majestically beyond.* ABOVE: *The main courtyard entrance, near which wine tastings of the family vintages are held.*

A University for Wine

[Université du Vin, Le Château, 26790 Suze-la-Rousse. Tel: 75 04 86 09, FAX: 75 98 24 20. Just east of the autoroute exit for Bollène, on the D94 toward Nyons. Château visits every day but Tuesday and during the month of November.]

The imposing Renaissance château of Suze-la-Rousse has now become a well-known university for the study of wines.

S cattered along the entire length of the narrow funnel of the Rhone valley is a series of châteaux. Some of these are picturesque strongholds dominating the road below, while others have been transformed throughout the centuries into elegant residences. In the past, the Château at Suze has been the site of heroic deeds and legends, but in 1978, thanks to the efforts of a farsighted group of professional vintners, agricultural researchers, businessmen and chambers of commerce, it became the Wine University of Suze-la-Rousse. They are responsible for the recent restoration of its distinguished medieval and Renaissance buildings.

The château is surrounded by a wonderfully wild oak wood and a garden displaying different types of vinestocks. Inside is one of the most beautiful and scientifically up-to-date tasting rooms, which, along with an equally modern laboratory and an extensive library, lies at the heart of the university's comprehensive training program. It is for professionals concerned with all phases of wine production, as well as for groups of amateurs who wish to perfect their knowledge of wine in general and of the Côtes du Rhône appellation in particular. Diploma programs include advanced technology, management and marketing, specialized law and training for sommeliers; also available are workshops of a half day to a week in regional wines, vinification, bottling, commercialization and distribution. Scientific efficiency has found a most romantic setting.

Saint Michael's day rains never stay in heaven.

Les pluies de la Saint-Michel ne restent jamais au ciel.

Li pluèio de Sant-Miquèu reston jamais au cèu.

Wine Festivals
of the Côtes du Rhône

Pierre Joseph Garidel, a doctor in Aix who published a treatise on botany in 1715, praised wine as "that liquor as precious as it is delicious, which offers us both medicinal nourishment and nourishing medicine, whose benefits affect the spirit as much as the body. . . ." The organizers and participants of Provence's many wine festivals would certainly agree. Most of the following *fêtes* incorporate a variety of other activities, such as parades in which the townspeople dress in local costumes.

Fall color and light in Provence create breathtaking compositions, with the taut lines of vineyards and orchards set against the scrubby evergreen hillsides called garrigue.

ABOVE: *The lavish and extensive gardens of the wine estate Val Joanis, north of Aix; in the kitchen garden vegetables are mingled with flowers for cutting.* RIGHT: *Grape harvesting in progress on the terraced slopes of northern Provence, in the Dentelles de Montmirail.*

MARCH	Vinsobres, local fête
APRIL	*April 20:* Villeneuve-lez-Avignon, Festival of Saint Marc
MAY	*May 1:* Bagnols-sur-Cèze, local fête
	Whitsun weekend (April or May): la Baume-de-Transit, competition of Tricastin wines
JUNE	*about June 15:* Saint-Victor-la-Coste, local fête
JULY	*first week:* Violès, local fête
	mid-July: Gordes (Côtes du Ventoux), Bourg-St-Andéol (local fête), Carpentras (Côtes du Ventoux), Buisson (local fête), Mondragon (local fête), Visan (local fête), Vacqueyras (festival for the local Côtes du Rhône appellation wines)
	late July: Pont-Saint-Esprit (local fête), Cairanne (local fête), Gordes (local fête), Caromb (festival for Côtes du Ventoux, in a different village each year)
AUGUST	*first half:* Valréas in combination with the lavender parade, Bédoin (local fête), Saint-Maurice-sur-Eygues (local fête), Ruoms (local fête), Mazan (local fête with a banquet), Vinsobres (festival of Côtes du Rhône–Villages appellations, in a different village each year)
	mid-month: Mirabel-aux-Baronnies, Séguret, Bédoin, Rasteau
SEPTEMBER	beginning, Visan (local fête)
NOVEMBER	*mid-month:* Wine and Food Fair at Vaison-la-Romaine
	late: Avignon Fête des Primeurs
	November 20: Sainte-Cécile-les-Vignes (wine and music festival), Tulette (Provençal mass)

For further information, contact the Maison du Vin, 6, rue des Trois Faucons, 84000 Avignon, Tel: 90 27 24 14, FAX: 90 27 24 13; or the "Vins en fête," BP 5, 84110 Séguret.

The grapes are magnificent this year because of the fine autumn days. The vines I have just painted are green, purple and yellow, with violet bunches and branches of black and orange. On the horizon are some willows, the winepress a long, long way off, and the lilac silhouette of the distant town. In the vineyard there are little figures of women with red parasols, and other little figures of men working at the vintage with their cart.
Van Gogh, DEAR THEO

Château de Rochegude

[Hotel and restaurant, in the village of Rochegude, 26700.
North of Orange, at the intersection of several country roads.
Tel: 75 04 81 88; FAX: 75 04 89 87.]

The winding streets of this typical medieval village lead up to the castle at its summit, restored several times in past centuries and transformed into a luxury hotel in the 1960s. There are only 25 bedrooms in this immense property, each decorated in a distinctive style, with a sumptuous bathroom. Some have terraces looking onto the battlements; many offer spectacular views of the wine country all around. Across the castle's moat is an adjoining park. Here, a swimming pool has been placed in a sunny spot beyond century-old pines, once underplanted with saffron, now run wild. At the top of a nearby hill (an easy walk) stands a picturesque ruin.

Chef Pascal Alonso presides in the mock-medieval dining room of the château. Young, but having already served apprenticeships to some of the most celebrated names in France, he makes the most of local resources, including fine pigeons from nearby Grignan. His brother has also settled in the area as a fruit farmer, and both appreciate the delicate white peaches that are called for in the following recipe. Of course, yellow ones can be used as a substitute, and will provide a more colorful contrast with the pale ice cream. In recent years many chefs have been experimenting with traditional herbs: they have discovered that lemon verbena, usually served as a tea at the end of a heavy meal, makes a delicious complement to fruit.

The medieval castle of Rochegude, now a luxury hotel, sits above the town surrounded by high battlements. To enter, you must pass over the old moat.

For Saint Martin's day (November 11), chestnuts and new wine.
Pour la Saint-Martin, la chataigne et le vin nouveau.
A sant Martin, la castagne et liu nouvèu vin.

For Saint Catherine's day (November 25), the oil is in the olive.
Pour la Sainte-Catherine, l'huile est dans l'olive.
Pèr Santo-Caterino, l'oli es dins l'oulivo.

WHITE PEACHES WITH LEMON VERBENA ICE CREAM

▲▲▲▲▲▲▲▲▲

Make the ice cream the day before it is eaten.

Serves 5

6 egg yolks
5 tablespoons sugar
2 cups whole milk
1 ounce dried lemon verbena
   leaves or another herb, such
   as mint
2 teaspoons grated lime peel

Beat the yolks and sugar together in a heatproof bowl. Pour the milk into the top of a double boiler. Add the lemon verbena and heat gently until the milk comes to a boil. Strain the milk, then pour it gradually over the yolk mixture, stirring constantly. Pour the mixture back into the top of the double boiler and cook over medium-high heat, stirring, until a custard forms. Stir in the lime peel and let the mixture cool. Pour the custard into an an ice-cream maker and freeze according to the manufacturer's directions.

The inner courtyard of Rochegude castle is full of niches, basins and fountains, set off by sculpture and simple local plants: santolinas and Virginia creepers.

The fruit should not be cooked until just before serving:

5 large, ripe white peaches
1 tablespoon butter
1 teaspoon sugar
½ cup sweet, fruity wine,
   such as Muscat de
   Beaumes-de-Venise or
   other Muscat wine
Juice of 1 lemon
Juice of 2 oranges

Peel the peaches: If they are just ripe, the skin will come off easily. Otherwise, dip them into boiling water for 20 seconds. Cut each one in half.

Melt the butter in a sauté pan, and add the sugar and the peaches. Cook gently over medium heat until the fruit is golden. Remove the peaches to a serving dish and pour the wine into the pan with the juice of the lemon and the oranges. Let the liquid reduce and thicken, stirring constantly.

Spoon the ice cream onto individual plates. Arrange the warm peaches around the ice cream and spoon the sauce over all.

Transhumance:
Age-Old Migration of Sheep

Transhumance is the name given to the seasonal migration of sheep over long distances: up to mountain pastures in summer, down into valleys in winter. The trails followed were established in the dawn of history. Some historians believe that it was the mountain dwellers who first started the practice of moving their charges to the lowlands for the winter. Others suggest that the animals themselves may have naturally begun the practice in search of food.

In Provence, by the mid-nineteenth century, as many as 400,000 animals would travel along the various routes, or *draios*. Such numbers could not migrate twice yearly without inflicting some damage: in fact, records of litigation between shepherds and farmers exist dating back to the Middle Ages. Certainly the herds' overuse of pasturelands led to vegetal impoverishment and loss of topsoil. Since sheep and goats eat almost everything in sight, except for some prickly, strong-tasting plants, their migration, unfortunately, has played a major role in creating the barren *garrigue* of today.

Transhumance constituted an important part of traditional rural life. French historian Fernand Braudel describes it as "the typical opening onto the outside world of primitive communities." Over the years, specific customs, costumes, even festivals became associated with this age-old practice. And until the early part of this century, the passage of the animals was an extraordinary spectacle to behold. The sheep were classed by sex, age and variety, with the weakest leading the way. Each category was further subdi-

ABOVE: *The luminous yellow autumn foliage of the mulberry tree. Its leaves were traditionally gathered in spring by farm women to feed to silk worms.*
RIGHT: *Migrating flocks of sheep are still a common sight throughout the Midi.*

BELOW: *Vineyards on the north slopes of the Luberon hills look toward the Mont Ventoux. The Calavon river valley possesses a particularly rich rural patchwork, spread out at the foot of its fashionable hilltowns.*

OPPOSITE: *Traveling to and from mountain pastures during transhumance, the famous biennial migration, sheep are marked for identification with ocher and colorful pompoms.*

vided into groups of 1,600 to 2,400 head, with one shepherd and one dog assigned to watch over 400 animals. The dogs were enormous and supposedly tough enough to fight a wolf. Long-haired donkeys wearing bells carried the supplies. The rams, too, were bedecked with headdresses, and the sheep were marked with different colors of ocher to show ownership. Alphonse Daudet has left one of the most vivid descriptions of the returning flocks in his *Letters from My Mill.* He observes them coming along the ancient Roman Aurelian Way, through Eyguières, then Le Paradou. "The road itself seemed on the march . . . the old rams first, leading with their horns, with a wild look to them; behind came the bulk of the sheep, the mothers somewhat weary with their suckling lambs underfoot; the mules, with red pompons, carried the newborn in baskets on their backs that rocked like cradles by the slow rhythm of the march; then the dogs, all in a sweat, their tongues hanging to the ground, and two shepherds, great rogues draped in homespun russet coats that reached to their feet like great capes."

Even in Daudet's time, transhumance met with opposition from agronomists, who feared for the forest land of the Alps, or who were interested in selecting varieties of sheep for qualities other than their road hardiness. The defenders of transhumance, however, insisted that the sheep remained healthier if they migrated, and objected to the cost of fodder in areas where summer drought was inevitable. Today, of course, the automobile has provided both the obstacle and

Meal shared by a land owner and his shepherd in a stone shelter, when the flocks come down from the mountains in November:

Arnaviel offered me a ripe ewe's cheese wrapped in fresh leaves. We lit a fire between two stones. I had some late September figs, already a bit dry, but sweet, rich with honey. The bread was hard but smelled of the wheat. The spring water was light on the tongue, with its sweet, pure taste of the rock.

As the weather was very clear, the air stayed calm and the smoke of our fire rose straight up through the chimney of our stone shelter.

Henri Bosco,
LE MAS THEOTIME

the solution to the practice: transhumance, insofar as it persists, is generally done by truck.

Flocks of sheep can still be seen throughout the Midi, even near villages transformed by the wealthy, the artistic, and the cosmopolitan. The average motorist has every chance of encountering the animals on small country roads

in the Alpilles or the Luberon. One friendly shepherd guards his charges on the high pastures overlooking the dramatic village of Saignon, near a road that might seem remote, but along which toot cars with surprising regularity. Almost every driver knows him, and stops to chat, whether antiques dealer, painter or café owner. It seems as if the shepherd, living on the outskirts of a highly sophisticated and touristic community, has discovered his own outdoor café.

Botanical Trails
in Historic Mountains

[Notre-Dame-de-Groseau: a mountain lake off the road between Carpentras and Vaison-la-Romaine, leading northeast toward the white cone of Mont Ventoux. Just over one mile outside Malaucène on the D974.]

Backed by the southwest flanks of Mont Ventoux, about 1,300 feet high, lies a famous spring, a deep turquoise pool that spreads its cool waters amidst rocky outcrops. This spot was much appreciated by the Romans as a summer resort, and became the site of a monastery in the seventh century. Clement v, the first pope to settle in Avignon, built his summer residence here in the early fourteenth century, around an older chapel. Fragments of these structures, with elegant sculptural detailing, still stand by the approach road. Even more strikingly poised on the steep slope above is an immaculate, ruined plaster works, erected in 1919 and abandoned in 1950, presiding over a gypsum quarry that had already been exploited in Roman times.

In high summer, Notre-Dame-de-Groseau is crowded with swimmers and families picnicking on stone slab tables under the spreading canopies of old plane trees. Off season, it has a peaceful mood. The addition of two botanical trails leading through the nearby hills, one of which takes about half an hour to walk, the other taking more than an hour, has added to its appeal. Even the shorter one reveals a wealth of plants: wild clematis, junipers, viburnums, the brilliant blue stars of aphyllanthes in May, wild aromatics, brooms, three kinds of oaks, as well as two different pines, and much more. Orientation tables explain the evolution

In September, if the water-willow flowers, the grapes ripen well and the peasant is all smiles.

En septembre, si l'osier fleurit, le raisin mûrit et le paysan rit.

En setèmbre, se lou vege flouris, lou rain s'ama-duro et lou paisan ris.

OPPOSITE AND RIGHT: *The mountain spring at Notre Dame de Groseau near Malaucène, where first Romans, then a fourteenth-century Pope, once bathed, remains a popular watering place today.*

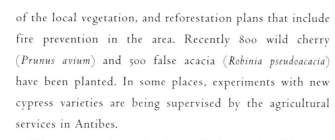

of the local vegetation, and reforestation plans that include fire prevention in the area. Recently 800 wild cherry (*Prunus avium*) and 500 false acacia (*Robinia pseudoacacia*) have been planted. In some places, experiments with new cypress varieties are being supervised by the agricultural services in Antibes.

The geology of the site is equally impressive. The gypsum dates from at least 27,000,000 years ago, while the stone fragments may be Roman or Renaissance . . . or possibly modern cement imitation. The pool itself has a rough, grottolike setting, with natural stone eruptions creating cool reflections in the multitoned water.

The old plaster works and their wild surroundings (an area of about 55 acres) have been purchased by the General Council of the Vaucluse. Plans are afoot to make it a center for nature study: it is already a stopping point for hikers and horseback riders.

A simple restaurant across the road from the spring serves a Ventoux salad, composed of mountain ham and cheese, curly, crisp escarole and local olive oil. The autumn air is fresh and sweetly scented. Sometimes a dog may be heard barking in the distance, or a donkey hee-hawing, but otherwise all is tranquil. This is a place—in the off-season—for enjoyment of all the senses.

Splendidly patterned vineyards with poplar and cypress hedging spread out against the rocky hillside beyond. In view of such glorious fall landscapes, many people consider autumn the most beautiful season in Provence.

Country Decor:
The Vernin Faience Factory

[Etablissements Vernin, Les Carreaux d'Apt, Le Pont Julien,
84480 Bonnieux. Tel: 90 74 16 80. Open: 9:00 A.M. to 12 M (noon);
2:00 P.M. to 6:00 P.M.]

This cheerful sundial decorates the ocher-washed wall of the Vernin tile factory, west of Apt.

This strange structure of brick and glazed, multi-colored tiles standing north of the main road between Avignon and Apt is not the studio of a modern sculptor but the Vernin Factory: a busy workshop, with a display room and offices. In a large double barn, some 20 employees produce a wide variety of ceramic and earthenware tiles from clay brought from Apt. The tiles are individually molded by hand, dried in the air, baked 24 hours and formed into squares, rectangles, diamonds, cloverleafs. Many are enameled with rich colors and designs. The Vernin family has been in the business since 1868, and now ships its production all over the world. Close by is a genuine Roman bridge, the Pont Julien.

Family Cooking,
Southern Style

[Le Domaine de Saint-Luc, la Baume-de-Transit, 26700 Saint-Paul-les-
Trois-Châteaux (about 17 miles northeast of Orange). Tel: 75 98 11 51;
FAX: 75 98 19 22. Evening meal provided only for guests, by reservation.
Closed Saturday.]

Set in some of the most beautiful wine country of France, this guesthouse has been created from an eighteenth-century farmstead by Eliane and Ludovic

PORK FILLET
WITH CHESTNUTS

Serves 4

1 tablespoon butter
2 tablespoons vegetable oil
1 pound peeled, cooked whole chestnuts (unsweetened)
Sprig of fresh sage, or 1 teaspoon dried
Salt
Pepper
1½ pounds pork tenderloin
1 teaspoon prepared mustard
1 cup white Tricastin wine or other fruity white wine

1 tablespoon crème fraîche or heavy cream

In a casserole dish, melt the butter in 1 tablespoon oil over medium heat. Add the chestnuts and the sage. Turn them well to coat; season with salt and pepper, and cook over low heat while preparing the pork.

Cut the meat into ½-inch-thick slices. In a frying pan, heat the remaining 1 tablespoon oil and add the meat. Brown lightly, season and turn the slices to color the other side. Cook for about 5 minutes. Transfer the pork slices to a serving platter and keep them warm in the oven. Add the mustard to the juices in the pan, cook over medium heat, stirring well. Pour in the wine, stirring up all the browned bits in the pan, and blend well. Let the sauce reduce for about 5 minutes, then add the cream. Stir well, bring the sauce just to a boil, then pour over the meat. Serve very hot.

Cornillon, as a complement to their production of Château de Tricastin wines (red and rosé). By 1980, they had created five charming, comfortable rooms, for a maximum of 12 visitors. Guests have the privilege of eating Eliane's cuisine, Provençal but personal, based on homegrown vegetables, or her finds in the nearby markets of Pierrelatte and Valréas. Chestnuts are plentiful in the northern hills of Provence in the fall, and so she often pairs them with pork, as in the recipe opposite. Perhaps an endive salad with melted goat's cheese (seasoned with olive oil and a little thyme) will precede the main course, and a mixed fruit compote of apples and prunes with cinnamon will be offered as dessert. Eliane suggests a white Tricastin St. Luc wine to begin the meal, and a red Syrah St. Luc 1989 with the main dish. The latter is a fruity wine, with mild tannins, the type that ages well in young wood casks. Both selections are produced on the property.

The old farmyard of the Domaine de Saint Luc has been transformed into a welcoming garden, full of flowers in spring, brightened by the red foliage of a climbing creeper in fall.

The Olive Harvest

For millennia, farmers all over the Mediterranean have been picking olives—green ones in October, brown ones in November, black and oily ones in December. Mentioned in both the Bible and the *Odyssey*, olives were dedicated to Athena by the Greeks (who used the oil in wrestling matches), and to Minerva by the Romans. Hercules fought his monsters—in southern Provence among other places—with a club of olive wood. And while the wild variety of the tree (*Olea europea oleaster*) grew naturally in Provence, it produced spiny, sour fruit with little oil. Not until the Greeks arrived around 600 B.C. did the native population learn the art of grafting.

Today, an olive tree that has been grafted and cultivated and is in full production can yield 65 pounds of olives a year (giving roughly six quarts of oil). Although olive trees can survive almost anywhere, and are nearly indestructible except when hit by hard, late frosts, those grown for fruit or oil need a lot of attention. A Provençal proverb imagines the olive tree saying to the farmer: "Feed my feet and I'll wet your whistle!" Sheep manure works wonders, as does good pruning. It is said that the silvery branches of the olive tree must be kept open enough so that a swallow can fly through without touching its wings. With such loving care, an olive tree can be expected to enter into full production at the age of . . . 35 years.

Olive culture is declining in France, like so many other old customs: Of the 16,000,000 trees thought to be growing there in the early part of the century, only 5,000,000 remain. But the commune of Mouries alone, in the southern Alpilles, has more than 80,000 olive-producing trees, a

ABOVE: *Olives that are allowed to ripen on the tree turn black and wizened, thick with the oil that pressing at the local mill will soon extract. Cold pressing produces the finest oil.*
OPPOSITE: *The olive harvest marks the year's end. Still often carried out by hand today, it requires considerable attention and skill.*

The olive harvest—an epic event. From the steel gray branch to the clay jar, the olive pours through a hundred hands, rushing on in torrents, piling up the weight of its black waters in attics where old beams complain in the night. On the edge of this great river of ripe fruit that streams through the villages, all our people sing together. Jean Giono, POEM OF THE OLIVE

world record. Most Provençal chefs, however, prefer to get their oil in Maussane, or Fontvieille, towns located in the Alpilles between Avignon and Arles.

Generations ago, trees reached as high as 50 feet, but new varieties and present-day pruning practices restrict their growth to about 15 feet. As a result, harvesting olives is much easier today. The old practice of using long rods to beat high branches proved detrimental to the trees, which produce only on new, soft wood. But even now, in many areas, some harvesters of ripe olives climb into the trees to shake the branches while others (usually the women) collect the fruit that falls on nets spread directly on the ground below. To harvest the crop mechanically, with shakers, vibrators and aspirators, the orchards must be specially planted and spaced from the start.

Green olives must be picked off the trees by hand, as they will not readily shake down and will bruise easily. A skilled harvester can collect up to 30 pounds an hour from heavily laden trees bearing a variety that detaches easily. Labor costs obviously count high in the production of oil.

Traditionally, olive picking is a family activity, sometimes extending to neighbors from the same village. Naturally enough, there is time for festivity—usually in the form of that favorite banquet food in Provence: a massive *aïoli*.

Olives are picked first green, then brown, then black as they ripen on the tree. They are then cured to remove bitterness and blended with various herbs and condiments. The resulting variety can be found in any country market, as here at Saint-Rémy-de-Provence.

Curing Olives at Home

Olives change in color from green to brown to black on the tree as they ripen, but at no time during this process are they edible, because of their bitterness. To dispel this unpleasant taste, they are "cured," usually with potassium obtained from wood ashes (either from vine or olive wood, never cypress). Traditionally, an equal amount of olives and ashes were mixed in a bowl with enough water to make a paste, which was then stirred several times a day for two days. When the flesh of the fruit came off easily under pressure from a nail, the olives were carefully washed and soaked in clear water that was changed twice daily, for another week. At

the end of that time, the fruit were ready for their final salt bath: Two pounds of sea salt were added to ten quarts of water, then the mixture was boiled for 15 minutes along with fennel, orange peel, coriander, bay leaf or sage . . . whatever fancy preferred. The olives were added once the mixture cooled and then were put into storage for at least a week. Removed with the characteristic perforated dipping spoon (made with olive wood, of course) so as not to disturb the brew, they could be expected to last until Easter.

As the days passed, the bloodied wound of the maple spread, the roads were edged with two streaks of blood. A secret inflammation swelled up within the earth. The poplars were lit with a cold flame, more sparkling than that of the sun. Orange embers snaked among the hedges. The wounded fields turned blue along the streams. A heavy dust of autumn crocuses stifled the fields under its yellow vapor. The forest remained, it remained with its thick, solid pines. We envied the men of the forest, for our weak trees in the

The "Bistrot à Michel"

[Bistrot à Michel, Grand Rue, 84220 Cabrières d'Avignon. Tel: 90 76 82 08. Owner: Michel Bosc. Chef: Ian Bosc.]

Discovered by artists even before World War II, the hilltown of Gordes has become one of the most chic vacation spots in the world. How does rural life survive in this rarefied atmosphere? This restaurant provides one answer: Here celebrities and millionaires rub shoulders with antiques dealers, tourists . . . and local farmers, all providing part of the show for each other. Famous chef Georges Blanc lunched at the bistrot when visiting the local truffle markets. Writer Peter Mayle made this café the focus for his essay on *pastis*, the local anise-flavored drink. To the right as you go in, owner Michel Bosc stands at the bar, discussing seasonal topics, such as hunting or truffle digging with villagers, while his wife presides at the cash register opposite.

Monsieur Bosc apprenticed as a chef at several famous establishments before deciding to return to his native village to open his own place. Now his son Ian, equally well-trained, produces succulent and original dishes, served by his sister to cosmopolitan customers at ten marble-topped tables. The bistrot style has been carefully maintained: The walls are packed with framed movie posters featuring Pagnol and Raimu, cartoons about life in the Luberon, original oils wih bullfight themes and a poster from the Museum of Modern Art in New York. In the center stands the classic buffet, laden with assorted bottles of aperitifs, brandies and liqueurs. Each table has a colorful bouquet: squash and mountain flowers for autumn. The wine list is handwritten and a bit smudged. The *patron* may come by as

meadows, our copses, the poplars of our fountains, all that was now aflame. And with each passing day, the burning trees grew less rust-colored, more yellow, slighter. . . . One could feel that all that was about to be extinguished.
Jean Giono,
RONDEUR DES JOURS

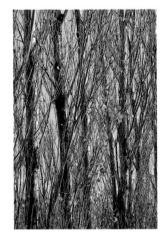

Poplar pillars grow as windbreak hedges along many country roads in Provence, making a delicate fretwork against a mistral-blue sky.

you dine, reverently carrying a huge sausage to show the men at the bar.

The Bosc cuisine presents the same mix of sophistication and country origins as does its decor. In the fall, stuffed pheasant may be offered, with onion marmalade, vanilla-flavored quince and potato pancakes. Or, the menu may feature an entrée of wild duck neck stuffed with chickpeas, served with pigs' feet cracklings and mixed greens. The main dish might be lamb petals, with garlic prepared in three different ways (as custard, as fritters and simply fried), followed by a small filler of quince paste covered with lukewarm chocolate. A Côte du Lubéron Val Joanis wine would nicely complement the meal, which might conclude with this light but flavorful fruit dessert.

Village fountains, many beautifully carved, often stand near communal washing basins at town entrances as here, at Mallemort du Comtat.

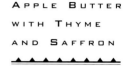

APPLE BUTTER
WITH THYME
AND SAFFRON
▲▲▲▲▲▲▲▲

Serves 6

2½ pounds Jonathan, winesap, or other flavorful apples
Juice of 1 lemon
1¼ pounds sugar
1 teaspoon thyme flowers or leaves
⅓ teaspoon saffron

Peel and dice the apples. Put them in a glass or pottery bowl and sprinkle with lemon juice. Add the sugar and mix with a wooden spoon. Pour the apple mixture into a thick-bottomed pan and simmer, covered, for 45 minutes, checking regularly, until a syrup forms. Remove the cover and continue simmering for an additional hour, stirring frequently, until the "butter" thickens. Remove the mixture from the heat and add the thyme and saffron. Cover the pan again and let the mixture cool. Serve cold.

Evergreens, trees and shrubs—
often cypresses, box and
laurustinus—protect farm-
houses from winter winds and
anchor them to the landscape.

Scourtins: An Unusual Craft

[La Scourtinerie: 86, la Maladrerie, 26110 Nyons.
Tel: 75 26 33 52. Owner: J. Fert. Visits by appointment.]

For many people, the northern boundary of Provence is determined by the range of the olive tree's successful growth, and the town of Nyons lies close to this edge. Because of the configuration of surrounding mountains and narrow valleys, Nyons enjoys a favorable microclimate that permits even palm trees to survive. Its extensive olive orchards have produced oil that has been praised for centuries; indeed, it is the only area to have a controlled appellation for this product.

As part of the process of pressing, the numerous local mills long used a filtering system of woven, flattened baskets, called *scourtins*. One family factory still makes them. Situated in an elegant seventeenth-century domain, shaded by majestic plane trees, its vast workshop is full of revolving metal drums with spokes. This largely nineteenth-century machinery produces mats, like flattened berets, that are about 15 inches wide, densely woven and prickly.

The first scourtins were of straw, fabric or alfalfa fiber. But with the advent of the Industrial Revolution, wooden equipment was replaced with steel in the mills, and more resistant material was called for. In 1882, Ferdinand Fert, a weaver and locksmith in Nyons, devised the modern scourtin, using sisal, or coconut fiber. He also invented the machinery to manufacture it, and founded the family business that still operates on the same site today.

Hidden in a remote part of an out-of-the-way town, this activity might seem purely local. But, typically, in Provence, which has always allied mountain and sea, the production

I have done another canvas, An Autumn Garden, with two cypresses, bottle-green, shaped like bottles, and three little chestnut trees, a little yew with pale lemon foliage, two bushes blood red with scarlet-purple leaves; some sand, some grass, and some blue sky. . . . The falling of leaves is beginning; you can see the trees turning yellow, and the yellow increasing every day. It is at least as beautiful as the orchards in bloom.
Van Gogh, Dear Theo

Old Provençal farmhouses, like this one at the foot of the Luberon, expanded piece by piece over centuries, sometimes turning into entire hamlets.

of these sisal mats depends on Mediterranean commerce: The raw materials come from the Malabar coast of India. For it is there that the best quality of coconut fiber can be found. During the monsoon period, which lasts several months, it undergoes a long soaking process, ending with pure rainwater. The final result is sisal that resists rot, takes dyes better and does not rust the machinery.

By the mid-1950s, there were several scourtin factories still operating in the south, and the Fert family decided to invest in improved equipment. Then came the terrible frosts of 1956, which destroyed so many ancient olive orchards in Provence. In addition, almost an entire year's production of scourtins already shipped to North Africa was lost at the outbreak of the Algerian War. Monsieur Fert, son of the founder, decided not to despair; instead, he diversified, concentrating on the fabrication of doormats and rugs, tinting them in a wide range of bright colors. He also began to import Indian crafts, which he sells alongside Provençal products in the family shop. In the 1970s, when drought in India threatened to cut off his supply of sisal, Monsieur Fert bypassed his British middleman and went to see his supplier for himself. The result was a surprising tale of country cunning on an international scale, which might well have happened a hundred years ago.

Arriving in India, Monsieur Fert discovered a convent where young women from remote country villages were

The famous Mas du Juge, the farmstead where Nobel prize-winning poet Frédéric Mistral spent an idyllic childhood, described in his memoirs.

Southwest wind, dry one minute, wet the next.
Vent du sud-ouest, sec une minute, le bain après.
Labechado une seco, uno bagnado.

sent for three years of schooling by parents who could not afford to give them dowries. The nuns, in conjunction with the Institut Catholique, willingly trained their charges in the production of sisal as part of their education, thus providing the Fert factory with its raw materials and the women with savings toward their dowries, as well as equipment and a craft that they could pursue in later life. The school has since expanded from 8 to 600 pupils.

Monsieur Fert relishes these international exchanges between country villages on different continents, and the continuity of an ancient local tradition. In his office, a stained glass panel depicts olive pressing using scourtins; it was copied from a Roman mosaic. The founding ancestor viewed his craft as a harmony between man, the tree and the earth, and his descendants still feel this very strongly.

The premises of the factory are vast: They occupy three levels. A showroom has been installed on the first floor, where the temperature remains constant in all seasons, and a lively videotape explains the history of the business and the evolution of its techniques. At one end can be seen remnants of an old mill wheel, and outdoors, a neglected formal garden from the days when the house was a noble residence. Today, with the new techniques employing centripetal pressure, the need for scourtins is disappearing in olive oil mills. But Monsieur Fert has plans for the future. He proudly shows drums of sisal netting that he has just imported: These can be used by gardeners for planting on difficult slopes, or for delicate sowings during dry spells to encourage germination. Discovery and innovation are themselves this family's richest heritage. The owner's daughter is now in charge of most of the current production.

But in my native Provence, pinewoods and olive groves turn yellow only when they die, and the first rains of September, which wash anew the green branches, bring back the month of April. On the barren hillsides, the thyme, rosemary, juniper and kermes oak keep their green foliage forever, while the wild lavender stays everblue. It is in the depths of the silent valleys that furtive autumn sneaks in; he takes advantage of rain at night to turn the little vineyard yellow, or the four peach trees, which then look sick, and in order to hide his arrival all the better he brings a blush to the naive arbutus, which begins to flower anew even as its berries turn red.

Marcel Pagnol,
MY MOTHER'S CASTLE

ZUCCHINI AND FENNEL SOUP

▲▲▲▲▲▲▲

Serves 4

4 small or 2 medium zucchini
1 fennel bulb, with a few leaves
1 leek
1 tablespoon butter
4 cups good chicken broth
1 teaspoon cornstarch
1 egg yolk
½ cup heavy cream

Wash, trim and cut the zucchini into thin rounds. Remove the outer leaves of the fennel and leek. Wash the vegetables carefully and chop them finely; include a small green section of the leek. Reserve the fennel leaves.

Melt the butter in a thick-bottomed pan, add the vegetables, and cook them gently, without browning (add 1 tablespoon of water, if necessary), for 15 to 20 minutes.

Set aside some zucchini rounds for decoration. Put the remainder of the vegetables through a food mill or food processor. Return them to the pan with the chicken broth. Bring the mixture gently to a boil and simmer for 5 minutes.

Cairanne Vintners' Cooperative

[*Cave des Coteaux, 84290 Cairanne. Tel: 90 30 82 05; FAX: 90 30 74 03. On the D8, northeast of Orange. Open: 9:00 A.M. to 12M (noon); 2:00 P.M. to 7:00 P.M.*]

The hilltown of Cairanne stands silhouetted against the dramatic shapes of Mont Ventoux and the Dentelles de Montmirail, dominating vast stretches of surrounding vineyards. Highest of the Rhone wine villages, with about 800 inhabitants today, it is known to have existed in 739, when it was called Queroana. Its wine cooperative, started in 1929, counts among the most active and appreciated of the region. Some 300 vintners sell three-quarters of their wine to the French market, and export the rest (much is sold by correspondence, in lovely gift packages). Three categories are produced: "vin de pays," labeled Principauté d'Orange; Côtes du Rhône; and the Côtes du Rhône–Villages wines, labeled Cairanne. The reds are the best known, with their ruby or dark carmine color, and their characteristic echo of strawberry and raspberry flavors. They are a blend of Grenache, Cinsault, Syrah, Mourvèdre and Carignan grapes, while Clairette, white Grenache and Bourboulenc are used for the whites. Also produced here are floral and peppery rosés, and a natural sweet aperitif wine called Cairador. The modern cave situated in the lower village displays many medals won by its wines all over Europe. The prestigious gastronomic guide *Gault et Millau* regularly commends it.

In a small bowl, beat together the cornstarch, the egg yolk and the cream in that order. Add a small amount of hot soup to the egg-yolk mixture, stirring constantly. Then pour the egg-yolk mixture into the soup and keep stirring until it thickens. Pour the soup into four bowls and garnish each with some zucchini rounds and fennel leaves.

The village of Cairanne stands dramatically silhouetted against the cloud-topped Mont Ventoux, above its colorful vineyards. Its vintners' co-operative is much appreciated for Côtes du Rhône wines.

Vineyards like script on the slopes, or the designs of

Persian carpets, always variation within formal patterns.

Lunch on the patio in warm sunshine, followed by snow

the next day. Persimmon trees with multicolored foli-

age; once the leaves have fallen, brilliant orange

Winter in

globes, like Christmas tree ornaments, against black

wood and a deep blue sky. Bell ring-

ing on February 5 in Mistral's village,

Maillane, so that Saint Agatha will ward off storms.

New Year's Day, when traditionally a stewed rooster is

served, accompanied by twelve partridges, thirty truf-

fles ("blacker than the soul of the damned") and thirty

fried eggs . . . to represent months, nights

and days. Fragrant, fluffy, tiny yellow balls

of mimosa, like a promise of summer sun, dotting the

Provence is . . .

landscape, followed by the almond blossoms of late

February. The killing of the family pig, traditionally

part of the "fat" side of Carnival, which

ends with Mardi Gras. The mistral, the

mistral and again the mistral. . . .

Winter

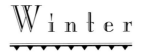

*An elegant portal at the Château de la Nerthe at Châteauneuf-du-Pape separates
the stately manor house and park from the wintry vineyards that surround it on all sides.*

The Magnificent Saint Andrew Abbey Garden of Villeneuve

*[Abbaye de Saint-André. 30400 Villeneuve-lez-Avignon. Tel: 90 25 55 95.
Open daily, April 1 to October 1: 9:00 A.M. to 12:30 P.M.; 1:30 P.M. to
7:00 P.M.; in winter, 10:00 A.M. to 12 M (noon); 2:30 P.M. to 5:00 P.M.
Owner: Mademoiselle Roseline Bacou. Take the* Montée du Fort *road
from the center of town up the hill to the fortress on top.
The abbey is inside, on the right.]*

O pposite the city of Avignon, overlooking the
Rhone, an impressive white limestone crenellated
wall crowns the hilltop at Villeneuve. These
fourteenth-century ramparts protect the much older village
of Saint Andrew, which originally sprang up around the
dwelling of a sixth-century hermit, Sainte Césarie. Today,
only a picturesque ghost town remains within the walls,
along with the abbey originally founded around the saint's
shrine. Unexpected behind its forbidding gate, this magnificent property with its terraced gardens is open to the public, and has become a favorite place for local people to have
their wedding pictures taken.

The imposing buildings were formerly part of the
twelfth- to seventeenth-century premises of a Benedictine
community. But they are just a vestige of the original domain, which was dismantled at the time of the French Revolution—indeed, around 1910, much of modern Villeneuve
was built with stones from the abbey, which was then used
as a convenient quarry. A succession of post-Revolutionary
owners made the most varied uses of this site: One man
built an observatory in an attempt to see the island of Elba.
An impoverished religious community lived here without

Winter is no bastard, if it
doesn't come sooner,
it comes later.
L'hiver n'est pas bâtard,
s'il ne vient pas de
bonne heure, il vient
plus tard.
L'ivèr es pas bastard, se
noun vèn d'ouro, vèn
plus tard.

OPPOSITE: *A Romanesque chapel at the summit of the steep Saint Andrew Abbey garden in Villeneuve-lez-Avignon.* ABOVE AND LEFT: *The stone pergola of the Abbey garden, underplanted with iris; in the foreground, a low basin, one of a pair framing the parterre of roses and santolina.*

water, sustained by wild herbs and dandelions. And then, in the early twentieth century, an art collector began its restoration. His friend Emile Bernard (companion also of Van Gogh and, especially, Cézanne) decorated the interior with a set of frescoes. Another friend, poet Paul Claudel, stayed at the abbey when visiting his poor sister, the misunderstood sculptress, who was condemned to the asylum in Avignon. By 1916, two talented women, a poet and a painter, had begun redesigning the gardens.

Their main achievement was the rose parterre, which has recently received an award for period gardens. Fan-shaped, it extends between elegant rococo stone basins, and is best seen from the terrace above, where the main buildings once stood. This acknowledgment of an architectural axis long since disappeared lends magic to a garden that is full of echoes and ghosts. The present owner, Mademoiselle Bacou, a distinguished art-historian, had the courage to dig into the hillside to uncover two ruined chapels with the sanctuary of Sainte Césarie. Banked by fragrant yellow coronilla in March, and encircled with cypresses, these are the most important ruins but not the only ones. A series of steps and paths leads uphill, past iris-lined olive orchards (some trees are more than 400 years old) to a twelfth-century chapel at the top.

This fine old Provençal garden is an ideal place to discover local styles and vegetation. Intimate yet elegant, enclosed and protected from the wind but with marvelous views of the Rhone valley south and east, it is always varied, never fussy. The subtle, luminous grays of the stone itself set the tone, for which dark vegetation provides the foil. The garden's lines, levels and perspectives are emphasized by the different greens of its olive trees, cypresses,

The sanctuary of Sainte Césarie, a ruined chapel with remnants of tombs, is a dramatic feature of the garden's middle levels. It is backed by the fourteenth-century ramparts which still encircle the old town.

laurustines and box, highlighted with color in all seasons: Redbuds overhang the rococo basins, cascades of white banksia roses cover a stone-pillared arbor, and white doves often circle above. Wisteria, lavenders, oleanders, centranthus all play their part as each season unfolds. Even in the heart of winter, strong design and evergreen plantings make it a place of great and calm beauty. And if snow should fall, it adds just the right emphasis.

SANTONS of Provence: The Fair in Arles

In 1223, Saint Francis of Assisi celebrated Christmas by re-enacting the Nativity with live actors. The Christ child alone was carved out of wood, but even he miraculously drew breath when touched by the saint. Thereafter, Nativity scenes, using life-sized statues, became common in churches all over Europe. In the eighteenth century, wealthy families enjoyed small-sized crèches at home, sometimes made of Venetian glass. The fashion for cribs became widespread in Provence when the Revolution closed down the churches after 1793, and the region remained faithful to its religious heritage. At the same time, a craftsman named Jean-Louis Lagnel began to produce crib figurines made of clay, which he sold for pennies. Thus every family could have its *santons*, or little saints, on a tabletop at home, and their manufacture became one of Provence's most appreciated popular arts. The first santon fair took place in Marseilles in 1803,

At Christmastime in Provence, miniature wintry hilltowns spring up on table tops in every home, re-creating the Nativity scene with figurines called san-tons. This Provençal tradition dates to the eighteenth century and remains active today through the work of craftspeople who continue to invent new themes and characters.

SANTON Addresses

Always call ahead for an appointment:

Danièle Camargue, 10, rue de Bouillargues, 30128 Garons, Tel: 66 70 14 57.

Elizabeth Ferriol, 4, rue du 4 septembre, 13200 Arles, Tel: 90 93 37 60.

Paul Fouque (Meilleur Ouvrier de France), 65, cours Gambetta, 13100 Aix-en-Provence, Tel: 42 26 33 38.

Laurent Bourges, route de Maillane, Saint-Rémy-de-Provence, Tel: 90 92 20 45.

Colette and Julien Dévouassoux, Puyvert, 84160 Cadenet, Tel: 90 68 02 12.

and still continues today. M. F. K. Fisher described it as "jammed with people, pushing and gaping and joking with the vitality that I believe is peculiar to Marseilles."

The story that the santons depict is always the same. It is as if the Nativity took place in a Provençal hilltown. All the village characters bring as offerings to the Christ child whatever they produce: the garlic seller, his garlic; the poultry raiser, her hens; the shepherd, his lambs. Today, most of the figurines are still made of clay, and may be left in their natural earth colors, or be brightly painted or clothed like little dolls. Some, however, are of papier-maché, wood, and even bread dough. Children often make santons for their parents, adding new ones each year. But all over the southern countryside, professionals have evolved personal styles, based on the old traditions.

Every December, a santon fair is held in the medieval cloister of the cathedral of Saint-Trophime in Arles. Its richly sculpted capitals already include three renderings of the Nativity, which are considered among the finest in Europe. Vaulted rooms lend themselves beautifully to the presentation of these colorful folk. One is devoted to amateurs, whose originality frequently provides some surprises. For example, an entire village produces santons using plastic dolls, clothed in fabrics rescued from the public dump! Others use olive wood for their figurines, choose gypsy themes or offer futuristic renditions. Another room is reserved for the Christmas crafts of a guest country. But

Stone and vegetation are ever mingling in Provence, even in winter, where the tracery of a vine growing up a wall repeats the patterns of a sculpted coat of arms.

On Saint Lucy's day
(December 13), the
days lengthen by a
flea's leap.

A la Sainte-Luce, les jours
augmentent d'un saut
de puce.

A Santo-Lucio, li jour
aumenton d'un saut
de clusso.

the heart of the exhibit remains the professional show, which every season pays homage to a different master santon maker.

Each fair celebrates a different type of santon: musicians, for example. Today it is fashionable to create village settings for the figurines, much like those crafted for old model-train sets. Indeed, an enormous display of this sort is open year round in Arles, next to the tourist office and the Hôtel Jules César. Taped music, poetry and commentary explain each scene as it is highlighted.

Santons are a wonderful introduction to Christmas in Provence, combining the color, the humor, the love of storytelling with a deep appreciation for rural tradition and for work well done. The scene they depict is still enacted live in the village *pastourales*. Among the many village types represented, a young girl appears, decorated with fine jewelry (in reality, she wears olive-leaf eardrops and grass rings on her fingers). The other villagers mock her, but she replies that the child is far more beautiful than she, and that her ornaments will be her offering. They comment with the typical skepticism of Provençal folk humor: "That's a surer sign than the star! If he can make coquettes sacrifice their finery, he really must be a savior!"

Unfortunately, the santons do not speak. But as one poet commented, in their rich array they constitute the flowers of the winter season.

LEFT: *An eerie, rocky landscape, inhabited since prehistoric times, surrounds the medieval castle and hilltown of Les Baux.* OPPOSITE: *Cypresses, like soldiers, guard tiny oak-leaf lettuce on a winter morning.*

Oustau de Baumanière

[Oustau de Baumanière, Restaurant and hôtel, Les Baux, 13520 Maussane.
Tel: 90 54 33 07; FAX: 90 54 40 46. Owners and chefs:
Raymond Thuilier and his grandson, Jean-André Charial;
chef de cuisine: Alain Burnel.]

In 1884, Henry James visited Les Baux and admired "the crags of Provence; they are beautifully modeled, as painters say, and they have a delightful silvery color. The road winds round the foot of the hills on the top of which Les Baux is planted . . . the pleasure of climbing into this queerest of cities on foot is not the least part of the entertainment of going there. Then you appreciate its extraordinary position, its picturesqueness, its steepness, its desolation and decay. It hangs—that is, what remains of it—to the slanting summit of the mountain." The writer concluded sadly that "the empty shells of a considerable number of old houses, many of which must have been superb, the lines of certain steep little streets, the foundations of a castle, and ever so many splendid views, are all that remain today. . . ."

Before falling into such ruin and neglect, this famous hilltown had known many brilliant destinies: Once inhabited by cave dwellers, it housed a great lineage of medieval robber barons before being given, as a recompense for loyal services, to the Grimaldi family (the Prince of Monaco still holds the title of Marquis des Baux) by Louis XIV. But its advanced decay was dramatically reversed just after World War II by a new great "lord" of Les Baux, Raymond Thuilier, who transformed an old olive mill at the foot of the hills into the restaurant that has since become a gastronomical mecca. The village above sprung to life again, and

LEFT: *Symbols of permanence and change, sundials are a familiar presence on the façades and terraces of Provençal domains.*
BELOW: *Terraced orchards, fresh-tilled, stand out against the evergreen* garrigue, *topped by the medieval keep at Suzette.*

Thuilier has served as its mayor for many years. He has even won fame as an artist—all the china and linens used at Baumanière are of his design. The menu cover, however, is the work of a colleague—Jean Cocteau, who dedicated it "To my friend Thuilier, 1959."

Many famous guests, including the Queen of England, have enjoyed the subtle flavors, smooth service and old Provençal decor of this haven, protected by its narrow valley and dominated by the rugged cliffs of the town. One summer, when forest fires from the surrounding slopes threatened the restaurant, French national radio announced the danger to the entire country, which held its breath. Luckily, Baumanière was spared.

Today, although over 90, the patriarch still receives his guests with gracious dignity. But Jean-André Charial, Thuilier's grandson and successor, has developed new areas of interest—including Baumanière's extensive vegetable gardens. These produce, for example, the tiniest and most succulent of green beans, which even the famous wholesale market gardens of the area cannot supply. Monsieur Charial has captured the spirit of the gardens in his published collection of recipes and quotations entitled *A Bouquet from Provence* (Pavillon Books). The restaurant offers a tempting, meatless garden menu that is based on its own produce. A typical example might be:

Winter vegetables and fruits— persimmons, leeks, broccoli and many kinds of greens for salads—add color both to the landscape and the table. Shrubby rosemary flowers all winter long.

Vegetable soup of the day
Wild mushrooms in puff pastry
Artichoke mousse
Charlotte of eggplant with sweet pepper sauce
Pear delight and local-fruit tart

As the days increase,
    so does the cold.

A mesure que les jours
    croissent, le froid
    augmente.

Janvié creissènt,
    fre couiènt.

Baumanière's regular winter menu may well feature the following chicken dish. It is often preceded by a salad of artichoke hearts with cod fritters or truffle ravioli with leeks. Either a white Châteauneuf-du-Pape wine or a Château Simone, powerful and supple enough to accommodate the strong flavors of the main course, would make an excellent accompaniment. Afterward, dessert can be chosen from the restaurant's fabulously laden cart, or, if something hot, such as a tart of spiced pears, is preferred, it can be ordered at the beginning of the meal.

On clear days, the Mont Ventoux, with its observatory tower, can be seen dominating even highly perched villages such as Methamis.

Chicken Breast with Rosemary and Anchovy

▲▲▲▲▲▲▲▲▲▲▲▲▲▲▲

Serves 2

3½-pound chicken

3 anchovy fillets in oil (unsalted)

STOCK

Chicken carcass

2 teaspoons butter

¼ pound mushrooms, cleaned and chopped

2 carrots, scraped and sliced

2 onions, peeled and chopped

1 celery stalk, cleaned and chopped

*1 small leek, cleaned and chopped (the white part and a small section
    of the green)*

1 clove garlic, peeled and chopped

1 cup white wine

2 cups cold water (or enough to cover the carcass in the pan)

SAUCE

2½ cups chicken stock

2 cups heavy cream

Branch of rosemary, fresh if possible, or 1 teaspoon dried rosemary

Salt

Pepper

1 tablespoon butter

Prepare the chicken: Remove the wings and skin with a sharp boning knife. Make two deep cuts next to the backbone, on either side, to loosen the breasts. They should come off easily with two further incisions at the point where the wings were removed. Cut off the rest of the meat from the chicken and reserve for another purpose. Only the carcass will be needed to prepare the stock.

This dish can also be made with chicken breasts (about ½ pound each) if you have bones left over from another meal for making the stock.

Make 3 small incisions in each chicken breast, then insert half an anchovy fillet into each. Cover the breasts and refrigerate while making the stock.

Prepare the chicken stock: Break the carcass into pieces and flatten with a cleaver. Melt the butter in a large pot, then add the carcass pieces and brown. Add the vegetables and stir. Pour in the white wine and the water. Bring the mixture to a boil and simmer, uncovered, for an hour. Skim off any particles that have risen to the surface and strain. There will be enough stock left for another recipe.

Prepare the sauce: Pour 2 cups of the stock into a saucepan with the cream and the branch of rosemary. Reduce the liquid, uncovered, simmering for about 40 minutes, or until thick. Remove the rosemary branch (or strain if dried rosemary is used). Season to taste.

For the final preparation: In a sauté pan, melt the butter, then add the chicken breasts. Brown lightly on both sides. Add the remaining ½ cup stock and simmer gently for 15 minutes.

Arrange the chicken breasts in the center of a platter, ladle some sauce over them and surround with steamed broccoli or other colorful vegetable.

Ancient Music

[*Jean-Pierre Magnan, 8b, rue de Mazeau, 84100 Orange.*
Tel: 90 34 25 62. Situated in back of the municipal museum in
Orange, with a separate entrance. The antiques shop is open 8:00 A.M. to
12 M (noon); 2:00 P.M. to 7:00 P.M. and Saturday mornings. To visit the
furniture and instrument workshops, an appointment is necessary.]

ABOVE: Tambourins *(drums)*
are among the traditional
Provençal instruments made
by Jean-Pierre Magnan.
OPPOSITE: *Frosty winter light*
magically highlights an aban-
doned shed and orchard.

The Magnans have been makers of fine furniture for four generations. Jean-Pierre, however, creates musical instruments in precious woods and ivory. Naturally, he concentrates on the local specialties, the *galoubet* (similar to a fife or a recorder) and the *tambourin* (a long drum). But eight other old instruments are also available.

A galoubet is made of boxwood, tropical woods or ebony. A drum, which can be beautifully sculpted, consists of a hollow walnut cylinder with the skin of a stillborn calf stretched over the top end, and deerskin over the bottom. Decoration, which might include a coat of arms and floral motifs (similar to that of Louis XVI furniture) can take 40 hours to complete.

Traditionally, one man would play both instruments, using one hand for each, as he walked in a parade or accompanied a folk dance. First made in Provence between the tenth and twelfth centuries, these instruments most likely did not originate in the Midi. It is known that they were once used to play folk music in countries as far apart as Argentina and Belgium. Imported into Mexico by Spaniards, they later became popular during the American Revolution. Antique Provençal versions can be seen in the Arlatan Museum in Arles and the Château d'Ambert, near Marseilles.

Monsieur Magnan's main customers are lovers of ancient music, folk groups and curious musicians. Their interest is

not, he insists, a mere survival of folklore, but the active continuity of a lively tradition of popular music.

The manufacture of musical instruments and furniture is housed in the vaults of an old priory (the workshop was once the kitchen). Monsieur Magnan produces bedsteads, wardrobes, even grandfather clocks with the same elaborately sculpted motifs that were fashionable in the eighteenth century. There is always an apprentice at the Magnan workshop, as the craft can be learned only through practical experience. The time involved, however, makes production too costly to attract too many new devotees. Fortunately, there is a young Magnan willing to take on the family business in the next generation.

Vines in winter create intricate and unexpected patterns that foliage hides for most of the year. Often used for trellising because they leaf out late, they provide shade only when the weather has turned hot.

Storytelling for Winter Evenings

Telling tall tales has long been a favorite southern sport, in cafés, over meals, or around the fire. In the preface to his famous book *Letters from My Mill*, Alphonse Daudet described how he collected his stories from the shepherds, tinkers and blacksmiths who stood around the fire of the Château de Montauban after supper. Long winter evenings certainly lend themselves to this form of entertainment. Called *veillées* (literally "watches"), they helped friends pass the time after dark. Gathering at one person's home, everyone helped out with some common, tedious task, such as the peeling of chestnuts for preserves, while exercising their fertile imaginations.

Taletelling, legends . . . this oral literature survives today with surprising strength, and has often been admired by such foreign authors as Lawrence Durrell and Ford Madox Ford. Its resilience owes much to the efforts of the late nineteenth-century Provençal revivalist group, the Félibrige. Their most famous representative, Nobel-prize-winning poet Frédéric Mistral, called his personal memoirs *Moun Espelido: Memori et Raconte* (My Beginnings: Memoirs and Tales), to stress what his growth as a writer owed to the "land of glorious deeds and legends" from which he sprang. Mistral and his friends collected as much of the old folklore as they could, for fear of its disappearance in an increasingly industrial age.

Many Provençaux now complain that television has killed the veillée, but Mistral, even in 1900, lamented the effects of outside influences: "In our village nowadays the peasants go to the café after supper to play a round of billiards, of cards, of what you will. And all that remains of the old evening gatherings is a vague semblance among a few crafts-men who work by lamplight, such as cabinetmakers or shoe-makers." It would seem that in spite of these fears, the people of Provence remain a sociable lot, whether in the café or at home. And in describing a local fair, Mistral proudly stated that "in the cabaret you had no end of story-telling and bragging and lies as big as Mount Ventoux."

Today, the town of Barbentane holds a public veillée every December, at which storytellers, singers and musicians per-form. And some professional taletellers can be invited, for a reasonable fee, to introduce any interested parties to the de-lights of Provençal legends—these are always a mixture of

February snows last as long as water in a basket. February snows, poor man's manure.

Neige de février ne tient pas plus que l'eau dans un panier. Neige de février, fumier du pauvre.

Nèu de febrié tèn pas mai que l'aigo dins un panié. Nèu de febrié fumié.

Old Provençal farmhouses show the irregularities of handmade constructions: some parts higher than others, open-ings not quite symmetrical, the lines of their tile roofs some-what wavering. All this is more visible in winter.

A Chick-Pea Fable

Two Marseilles sailors promised during a storm at sea to climb the hundreds of steps leading to Notre-Dame-de-la-Garde, high above the city, with chick-peas in their shoes. They were spared.

But chick-peas are hard, and have pointed little beaks like donkey horns. Walking half an hour uphill with them in your shoes can be hard on the feet.

One of the sailors was straining, limping and lamenting, while the other remained serene. So much so that in the end, his friend asked him how he managed. Easy, replied the other, I cooked them first.
Frédéric Mistral,
ALMANACH 1872

magic, vivid observation and the humorous realism that expects little of people but enjoys their foibles. After all, taletelling was once the very fabric of social identity in country villages. A form of elaborated gossip, it testifies, according to art critic John Berger, "to the always slightly surprising range of the possible." This gossip neither idealizes nor condemns. In our time, it gave rise to the mastery of Marcel Pagnol, who never lost sight of these rural roots, even as a French academician, and whose *Jean de Florette*, *Manon of the Springs* and *Memories of Childhood* have been made into highly successful movies.

One professional storyteller working in Provence today is Sara de Neyman (4, rue de la Moutette, 84600 Valréas, Tel: 90 37 33 41). Her family came from Riga just after World War II, where her grandfather was an established *conteur*. Sara did not begin this career until she was in her 40s, feeling that a certain maturity is needed for the job. Intrigued by the cultural crossroads that Provence has always been, she finds strong Moorish influence even in the ancient tales, and has made a specialty of the rich Jewish lore of the region.

Classical Elegance: The Château de Barbentane

[Château de Barbentane, 13570 Barbentane. Tel: 90 95 51 07. Open: Easter to November 1, daily except Wednesday: 10:00 A.M. to 12 M (noon); 2:00 P.M. to 6:00 P.M. In winter, Sundays only. Gardens may be seen only as part of the château visit. Owner: Henri de Puget de Barbentane.]

Southwest of Avignon lies the charming town of Barbentane, where a typical maze of medieval streets settles against a cliff topped by a public promenade.

That year winter was hard, the ice had never been so thick on the stream. Never had we felt such cold, so bitter that it froze the wind in the depths of the sky. The whole country shivered in silence. The grazing slopes above the village were all silvered over. There was not a cloud in the sky. Every morning, a rusty ball rose in silence, took three careless giant steps across the heavens and disappeared. Night heaped up the stars like grain.
Jean Giono, REGAIN

ABOVE: *The long north terrace of the château of Barbentane has a rococco balustrade, sheltered under canopies of redbud trees and century-old planes.*
ABOVE RIGHT: *The tight pinkish-red buds of laurustinus are highly decorative; when the* flowers open to pinkish-white in mid-winter, their fragrance carries some distance. RIGHT: *At Barbegal, the Romans constructed a sophisticated hydraulic plant, the ruins of which now look down on the geometries of winter fields below.*

On a back road stands one of the few extant windmills of Provence that has kept its sails. A ruined tower in the old town can be seen from all sides; it is where an Avignon pope took refuge in the fourteenth century, during the plague.

In 1443, the Good King René ennobled a local family, ancestors of today's château owners. In 1654, Jean de Puget bought land on the edge of town, and his grandson began construction of the château 20 years later. An eighteenth-century descendant returned after years as ambassador to Tuscany to complete the interior decoration, which is ornate and reflects both Parisian and Italian influences. This mini-Versailles has remained undamaged throughout all the vagaries of history, keeping its original furniture, and has stayed in the original family's possession. No doubt the ancestor who served as a general in the Revolutionary army did his part to preserve the family heritage.

Inside, Florentine marble decors and Venetian chandeliers complement a series of flat-vaulted stone ceilings, which were the specialty of a gifted local architect. Family portraits; pirate chests; hand-painted eighteenth-century wallpapers, with matching fabrics; and rare enameled commodes are among the priceless treasures displayed. One reception room has its own, specially ordered Louis XV furniture, including a pair of matching, asymmetrical couches. Each piece is covered with embroidered tapestries depicting La Fontaine fables. Their woodwork is painted black, probably as a sign of mourning after the beheading of Louis XVI. Photographed countless times, the château interior served also as decor for a television serial based on the popular novels called *Les Gens de Mogador*.

Outside, little remains of the château's original neo-classical gardens, relandscaped in the nineteenth century.

On New Year's Day, the days lengthen by a cock's meal.
Au jours de l'an, les jours croissent du repas d'un coq.
Oou jou de l'an, lei jou creissoun doou repas d'un can.

Winter vineyards against the austere, windswept slopes of the Alpilles hills look like some mysterious script on the landscape.

Outside the mistral purred. In the slowly thawing gardens were the memorable flaccid palms in their circles of molting grass. There was still snow-rime in the flowerbeds.
Lawrence Durrell,
MONSIEUR

When the mistral blows here, the countryside is anything but welcoming for this wind is extremely irritating. But, on the other hand, how wonderful when it stops, what intensity of color, what pure air, what supreme luminosity.
Vincent Van Gogh,
COLLECTED LETTERS

The oriental planes, which now soar high above the southern esplanade, were grown from seeds brought back from Italy by the ambassador ancestor. Also from the past is a unique series of garden sculptures; those on the balustrade combine eighteenth-century elegance and wit in a most appealing manner.

Visitors are welcome at Barbentane and are shown around by efficient, trained guides every half hour. But there is never, even at the height of the season, a hurried atmosphere. And, occasionally, those waiting their turn may come upon the Marquis pruning his roses.

The "Mud-Eater" Mistral

One of the popular *santons* of Provence is an angel with puffed, round cheeks, who hangs above the manger scene, blowing for all he is worth. This is the angel *Boufarèu*, or "mud-eater," who is also represented in stone above the monumental stairwell of the Château de Barbentane. The cold north blast he blows with such force is the famous mistral, a term derived from the Latin word *magister*, meaning "force," and which quite independently gave rise also to the family name Mistral.

The mistral does, indeed, dry up mud, clearing skies almost instantly—qualities so appreciated by the philosopher Nietzsche that he composed a song in its praise. For him, it becomes a symbol of all that chases gloom away: "Mistral wind, hunter of clouds, death of grief, purity of heaven, How I love your roaring. . . . On slippery, rocky paths, I run, dancing, to greet you. . . ." His sentiments are

God give us joy, god give
us joy,
Christmas is coming,
May God's grace ensure,
in the coming year
That if we are not more,
we may not be fewer.

Chant recited together by
the oldest and youngest
members of the family
during the Christmas
Eve ceremony of the
CACHO-FIO, when an olive
branch which has been
dipped in mulled wine is
used to anoint the yule
log. Thus human growth
and that of the land are
linked in prayer.

not generally shared by the local populace, however. The mistral has the reputation of getting on one's nerves. Marie Mauron, a writer of the Alpilles region, records her mixed feelings about "the blue wind, the drunken wind which intoxicates people with its drunkenness, enervates animals, maddens flowers, plants, trees, the very sky even as it sand-papers it to a hardness. It sings strong and loud, with hoarse throaty noises of excitement at the game . . . Aerial Rhone which is the river of our sky. . . . The Provençaux say that you do too much ill to speak well of you and too much good to speak ill. But this judgement says nothing of the virile beauty of your song."

Mistral-swept skies set off almond blossoms near the picturesque Romanesque chapel of Eygalières in the Alpilles.

This dry north or northwest wind builds force in the funnel of the Rhone Valley whenever pressure mounts over the mountains on either side. Folklore claims that it blows in cycles of three days, at least if it starts up by daylight. Rising by night, it may last only "the time it takes to bake bread," according to a regional proverb.

Recently, a group of Provençal schoolchildren participated in a survey. Asked what they would put on a poster to represent Provence, they all suggested landscapes: the wild *garrigue*, with its thyme, lavender and rosemary, cicadas, green oaks, pines and olive trees. Some mentioned cultivated orchards and old habitations—farmhouses, villages and the vaulted stone dwellings called *bories*—under an eternally blue sky. But they all agreed that it would be best not to mention the mistral!

Generations of Candy Making:
The Jouvaud Family

[*Jouvaud, rue de l'Evêché, 84200 Carpentras. Open: 9:00 A.M. to
12 M (noon); 2:00 P.M. to 6:00 P.M. daily, except Sunday.
Tel: 90 63 15 38; FAX: 90 63 21 62.*]

Candied fruit and delicate pastries are prepared in small batches with the best ingredients by the Jouvaud family in Carpentras.

In the medieval center of the town of Carpentras, near the public market, not far from the cathedral of Saint-Siffrein, one shop window is so beautifully arranged, so colorful in its array, that it seems almost like a gallery. And so it is, although most of its wares are edible: Here, the Jouvaud family—parents and children—sells candy and pastries of great elegance and refinement. On the walls hang watercolors by Monsieur Jouvaud senior, representing local rural landscapes at different seasons.

The older Monsieur Jouvaud apprenticed in the candy business with a descendant of the man who, in 1850, invented the famous Carpentras specialty, the *berlingot,* a mint-flavored sweet reputed to cure all ills. Now the younger generation has transformed the shop into a small tearoom, decorated with local fabrics and carefully chosen pottery, much of which is also for sale.

Candied fruit was once a regional specialty in Carpentras, as it still is in Apt, where, however, most of the candy makers have become industrialized (heavily polluting the local rivers). In their factories, fruit is stored in vats of chemical solutions until there is enough to process it in large batches. Jouvaud, on the other hand, makes very small quantities at a time, always with fresh

fruit that is just ripe—pears, melons, prunes, cherries. As for apricots, he uses an old-fashioned variety called "rose de Provence," which a local farmer grows solely for him. For chocolate-covered cherries, he seeks out the sour variety that is rarely seen in the public markets because of its modest appearance. For quince buns, a local specialty in which the fruit is baked in bread dough, he selects quinces from unwatered hedges, because their flavor is much more intense. Aware of his customers' preference for confections that are less sweet than formerly, Jouvaud uses only half the amount of pure cane sugar that his father did 20 years ago. He takes great care with his methods, explaining, "You can't really cheat even if you wanted to, the old ones are always watching."

Christmas breads and deep-fried oreillettes *are featured during the festive season; but the Jouvauds imagine new creations every month for celebrations all year round.*

So are the young, it would seem. There is now a six-year-old Jouvaud who, at this tender age, is undecided about his future. The elder Monsieur Jouvaud took his grandson to Flassans last fall, where they planted a patch of wheat. Grandfather and grandchild tended it through the growing season, harvested it in June, threshed it and ground about two pounds of flour. With this, they made tea cakes (*madeleines*), much to the boy's delight. And so the family looks to its future. . . .

No child nor adult can resist the subtle flavors of the Jouvaud specialties: the Saint Siffrein, for example, with its caramelized walnuts and its blend of soft and crackly chocolate; the lemon cake, with its hidden layer of praline; or the chocolate truffles, with three kinds of chocolate. The Jouvauds invent one new cake a month for the pleasure of their regular customers, and also furnish chocolates to such fine hotels as the Hostellerie de Crillon-le-Brave.

Although the Jouvauds mail their confections all over the world, it is worth visiting the shop for its beautiful displays and happy atmosphere.

CURNONSKY'S STEWED TRUFFLES

Watching wily truffle dealers on winter mornings at the Friday market of Carpentras (northeast of Avignon) is one of the best local sports.

"Proust conjures up Combray," says the great chef Curnonsky, "its panorama and its good people, from a teacake dipped in a cup of herb tea. An exiled citizen of Carpentras could call into being his native town, with its monuments and all the resources of its countryside, as in a dream, from a truffle stew.

"You must find local truffles the size of an honest potato. Brush them. Peel them. Crush the peelings with a little olive oil in a mortar and strain the mixture through a sieve. Slice your truffles into scallops and put them to cook gently in an earthenware pot, with a carrot, the white part of one leek,

Country Decor:
Antiques in an Ocher Mill

[Sud Restauration, La Ribière, 84570 Mormoiron. Tel: 90 61 85 01. East of Carpentras, on the D942 to Sault. Open every afternoon except Sunday. Owner: Anouk Lautier.]

Many parts of Provence have pockets of brightly colored ocher pigments—ranging from yellow to burnt orange to flame to a luminous pale gold. For many years they were processed in Apt, until cheaper synthetics were discovered. This building at Mormoiron, not far from the white cone of Mont Ventoux, was once a mill for refining the multicolored ores. Its broad spaces, on two levels, provide a wonderful setting for the wealth of objects that Anouk Lautier has been displaying here since 1988. Although Provence has legions of dealers in fine luxury antiques, Madame Lautier specializes in more modest items: pine furniture rather than oak, which is often brightly painted, as well as building elements, storefronts, staircases, fireplaces, floor tiles. Old ironwork bedsteads are ingeniously converted into garden furniture, adorned with gay, new cushions. She also sells new ceramics, both as tiles and pottery, which she brings back from regular forays to Spain and Portugal. This is a place where imagination runs rampant—who else would transform the wooden and canvas frames used by market gardeners to protect their winter sowings into elegant room dividers or paravents, decorated with stencilled designs? And in the off-season, when it is not too crowded, Madame Lautier offers tea and biscuits around 5:00 in the afternoon.

an onion, thyme, bayleaf, all chopped very fine; add also your puréed peelings and some thickened veal broth. During the cooking, lengthen with a glass of Châteauneuf-du-Pape, and serve up, placing each slice on a triangle of fried bread."

OPPOSITE: *A terra-cotta fisherman is displayed among the many treasures at Sud Restauration, east of Carpentras.* ABOVE: *A young enthusiast presents a fine selection of truffles at the Friday-morning market in Carpentras.*

PUMPKIN SOUP WITH LEEK GARNISH

▲▲▲▲▲▲▲▲▲▲

Serves 6

2 large leeks, white and small
  section of green, cleaned
  and minced
4 tablespoons butter
1 large onion, peeled and minced
1 clove garlic, peeled and minced
2 pounds pumpkin or winter
  squash, peeled and cubed
Pinch of grated nutmeg
2 cups heavy cream
2 tablespoons vegetable oil
1 clove unpeeled garlic
5 slices fresh white bread,
  crusts removed, cubed
2 tablespoons flat parsley
  or chervil

Place one of the minced leeks in a bowl of cold water and set aside for use as garnish. In a large saucepan, melt 2 tablespoons butter over high heat, and when foaming, add the remaining leek, the onion and minced garlic. Lower the heat and cook gently, without browning, for 5 minutes, or until just barely soft. Add the cubed pumpkin and nutmeg, and turn well to coat with butter. Cover the pan and simmer the mixture for about

Christian Etienne: A City Chef Who Loves Vegetables

[Christian Etienne, 10, rue de Mons, 84000 Avignon. Tel: 90 86 16 50; FAX: 90 86 67 09. Closed Saturday noon and Sundays. Chef and owner: Christian Etienne.]

Christian Etienne belongs to Avignon, and, nowadays, Avignon to Christian Etienne. Few local sons have won such a strong and loyal following; his is due primarily to the rigor and originality of his cuisine, but also, perhaps, to the extraordinary setting of his restaurant—it is housed in the only private dwelling to be linked by a stone arch to the massive fourteenth-century Papal Palace for which Avignon is famous. Period frescoes and a painted ceiling were discovered during extensive restoration work, and provide an incomparable decor.

A city man, Christian Etienne spent some years working in Paris, notably at the Ritz. But when his car was impounded for illegal parking twice in one day, he began to think longingly of his native Avignon. He returned to open a tiny bistrot, and it did not take long for the avid local clientele to discover him. One of his customers mentioned that an abandoned property in the center of town was for sale. Strangely, Monsieur Etienne's mother remembers taking her son to the public gardens on a nearby hill when he was only four years old, and swears that, even at such a tender age, he pointed out this very building to her, saying, "Someday I will buy that house, Maman."

So his prediction has come true; his restaurant opened in 1990. But in Provence, city and country are inextricably linked, and no one knows better than Monsieur Etienne how

30 minutes, turning often.

Provençal pumpkin gives off quite a bit of liquid, whereas American squash, of a denser texture, may need a few tablespoons of water added. Continue simmering (uncovered, if very liquid) for about 20 minutes longer, or until evenly cooked through. Stir in the cream and simmer for another 20 minutes. Pour the soup into a food processor or blender and process to a smooth consistency. Return to the saucepan and keep hot.

Prepare the croutons: In a sauté pan, melt 1 tablespoon of butter with 1 tablespoon of oil and the unpeeled garlic. Add the bread cubes and cook, turning often, until the croutons are evenly golden. Set them aside.

Prepare the leek garnish: Remove the minced leek from the water and drain well. In a sauté pan, melt 1 tablespoon of butter with 1 tablespoon of oil and cook the minced leek until the shreds become just crispy and brown.

Serve the soup hot, garnished with the leek shreds, croutons and a sprinkling of parsley.

Monsieur Pitot's faience draws on the craft traditions of Apt, but his tableware is recognizable all over the region as distinctively his own.

COUNTRY DECOR: THE FAIENCE OF APT

[A. Pitot, Quartier de Ponty, 84200 Goult. Tel: 90 72 22 79. Located on the south side of the main road (N 100) to Apt. Visit by appointment.]

Monsieur Pitot has made quite a reputation for himself as a successful creator of the glazed earthenware

to follow the seasons to ensure the absolute freshness of all his food. Simplicity is his hallmark; he always seeks to bring out the best flavors of the natural ingredients he uses, without the elaborate and mysterious mixtures that once characterized sophisticated cooking. His cuisine reflects his concern for precision with what he calls "feeling," or individual inspiration; in this respect, he is like a musician. As chef, he is both composer and interpreter, and he claims that his exchanges with customers always affect his performance. Many who eat in his restaurant simply leave the menu to his discretion. Sometimes clients will feel like drinking a certain wine, and he will confer with his excellent sommelier, Monsieur Reboul, about creating a menu around this choice. Monsieur Etienne and his staff like to welcome guests as they would to their own homes. Although many owners may make such a claim, the easy and happy mood of those working here ensures that it rings true.

Christian Etienne regularly offers a meatless menu based entirely on seasonal produce. Here, you might encounter a fennel sherbet with saffron sauce or the hard Provençal mountain wheat known as *épeautre.* The recipe, opposite, for pumpkin soup is an excellent example of the chef's inspiration. No dish could be more traditionally Provençal, and yet his version has a subtle refinement all its own. It remains simple, and each ingredient (Monsieur Etienne likes to quote Brillat-Savarin on this score) keeps the taste of what it is.

known as FAIENCE. He draws on the country traditions surrounding Apt, where the familiar ocher tones and greens of Provençal pottery elsewhere were further enriched by a special marbling effect called JASPAGE, which catches the light most decoratively. Monsieur Pitot's colors are obtained by using white clay tinted in the mass with copper oxides. Enameled without lead, his tableware can be used every day—and is much sought after by those who seek to create Provence country decors. The elaborate cakes produced at the Pâtisserie in Villeneuve-lez-Avignon are displayed on his crockery. Reasonably priced, it ranges from small cups and butter dishes to elaborate assemblages of brightly colored fruit on platters to baskets with fretwork as fine as lace.

BARIGOULE OF ARTICHOKE HEARTS WITH FENNEL RAVIOLI AND ROSEMARY

▲▲▲▲▲▲▲▲

Serves 6

ARTICHOKES BARIGOULE

6 tablespoons olive oil

8 medium-sized artichoke
  hearts, cut in quarters

2 large carrots, pared
  and minced

20 cloves garlic, peeled

20 very small white onions,
  peeled

6 ounces salt pork, cut into
  small dice

1½ cups fruity white
  Provençal wine

Salt

Pepper

RAVIOLI STUFFING

2 tablespoons olive oil

1 pound fennel, washed, tough
  outer parts removed, hearts
  chopped into fine dice

3 ounces anchovies preserved in
  oil, drained and puréed

RAVIOLI

1 pound flour

Large pinch salt

3 whole eggs plus 2 egg yolks

Few drops natural green
  food coloring

DRESSING

¼ cup heated olive oil
½ cup grated Parmesan cheese
1 teaspoon powdered thyme
Sprigs of rosemary

Prepare the artichokes barigoule: In a large saucepan, heat 2 tablespoons of olive oil and add the other ingredients, in order, except for the wine. Turn them until they are coated with the oil. Cook the vegetables gently for about 30 minutes, stirring frequently, until they are golden. Add the wine and boil the mixture over high heat until the liquid is reduced by half. Season, then blend in the remaining olive oil and simmer over very low heat for about 15 minutes. Set the mixture aside but do not refrigerate.

Prepare the ravioli stuffing: In a pan, heat the olive oil and add the fennel dice. Cook the vegetable over low heat for about 45 minutes, or until all juices have evaporated. Stir in the anchovy purée until well blended and set the mixture aside but do not refrigerate.

Prepare the ravioli: Place the flour with the large pinch of salt in a bowl. Make a well in the center

Clos de la Violette

[*Clos de la Violette, 10, avenue de la Violette, Aix-en-Provence. Tel: 42 23 30 71; FAX: 42 21 93 03. Closed November, March, Monday noon and Sundays. Owner and chef: Jean-Marc Banzo.*]

On the northern edge of Aix-en-Provence, halfway between Cézanne's studio and the cathedral, a private house and garden have been converted into a quiet restaurant, which is obviously much appreciated by local connoisseurs. This is the Clos de la Violette, where chef Jean-Marc Banzo has officiated since 1986. Provençal by birth, he is a committed purist about local ingredients, and would like to see more of them, such as asparagus, sporting official labels of origin. Southern cuisine, he explains, has always been characterized by intense flavors (due to the sunshine) but has never been heavy, since it is based on olive oil. He rarely uses anything imported, and constantly looks to seasonal rhythms to renew his repertoire. Provence has many culinary riches, often created by poor but ingenious country people. Monsieur Banzo values this heritage; he works to preserve it unspoiled in his cuisine, while adding his own personal note of inspiration. The following dish, Artichokes à la Barigoule, is a perfect example: Based on a favorite old recipe, it is here transformed in his inimitable style. It might be followed by a roast of monkfish with shallot, pepper and red wine sauce, and an unusual garnish of bone marrow; or by spring lamb wrapped in pastry with herbs and garlic. For dessert, he may offer a rosemary meringue served with honey, almond and orange iced nougat. Choosing an appropriate wine for this first course poses a problem because of the artichokes' astringency. But Monsieur Banzo suggests a Côtes du Luberon, Château La Verrerie 1988, from nearby Lauris.

and break the eggs and yolks into it. Add the food coloring. Mix these ingredients together with a wooden spoon, then with the fingers until dough can be handled easily. Shape into a ball, wrap in waxed paper and refrigerate for an hour. On a floured board or table, roll out the dough to a ⅛-inch thickness. Using a floured 2-inch-round cookie cutter, cut out rounds. Place a teaspoon of stuffing in the center of each round, wet the outer edges and fold over the tops to make the ravioli. Press the edges together carefully to seal.

Heat the artichoke mixture gently. In a large pot of boiling, salted water, poach the ravioli for about 5 minutes, until they come to the surface, turning once. Drain.

On each plate, spread the barigoule in such a way that the artichoke hearts are in the middle and can serve as supports for the ravioli. Arrange the ravioli on them. Sprinkle everything with warm olive oil, grated Parmesan and powdered thyme, then garnish with rosemary sprigs.

Herbal Remedies
for Colds and Flus

The almond, a fine tree, offers the bees their second flowering after the boxwood. In our mountainous country of the Haute-Provence, it starts flowering in late February. At that time, it lights up the entire countryside with its pink or white bouquets. I love to sit beneath an almond tree, with my back against its trunk. A perfumed music envelops me—the hum of the honeybees hard at work, mingled with the gently wafted scent of the flowers.
Marcel Scipion, MEMOIRS OF A BEE SHEPHERD

Provence has long been celebrated for its pungent aromatics, whose essences concentrate within themselves the intensity of the southern sun. Many of the most famous herbs are evergreen—sage, rosemary, the entire group of thymes and savories—while others take the bulbous form, such as garlic, onions, leeks.

The people of Provence are indeed fortunate to have such a wide range of herbs and vegetables to help them combat the ills of winter. Each plant has its traditional claims to health-giving properties, but none more so than garlic (*Allium sativum*). Modern medicine has confirmed its capacity to stimulate circulation and digestive secretions, as well as to protect the respiratory system.

Garlic is also an acknowledged antiseptic. It contains a sulfur oil that releases its vapor when a clove is crushed. If the smell pleases, it can be used to disinfect the air and clear the lungs and the bronchial tubes. One source recommends macerating peeled, crushed cloves in alcohol, then mixing them with milk to mask the taste. Thirty to fifty drops a day of this elixir are said to cure the worst case of bronchitis.

Brilliant persimmons hang from bare branches— precious color in the winter landscape, and fruit for the table that is rich in vitamin C.

AIGO BOLLIDO

▲▲▲▲▲▲▲

Serves 2

1 tablespoon olive oil
1 small leek (the white part
    and the tender green section),
    cleaned and minced
2 cloves garlic, peeled
    and minced
Sprigs of sage and thyme
Branch of fennel
Bay leaf
3 cups freshly boiled water
Salt
Pepper

In a small pan, heat the
olive oil. Add the leek
and garlic, and cook, without browning, until limp.
Add the herbs, then pour
the simmering water over
the mixture. Season,
cover and let sit for about
10 minutes. Remove the
herbs. Reheat the mixture,

There are those with whom garlic disagrees, of course.
But for them, it is probably a matter of infrequent consumption rather than disposition. Digestive systems only
gradually become accustomed to the strong essence if not
born and bred to it. As for its effect on one's breath, garlic
seems to linger longer among the uninitiated. Chewing on
a fresh coffee bean is thought to help.

A Provençal proverb states that he who has sage in his
garden does not need doctors. Antiseptic, like garlic, sage
is also reputed to calm the nerves and spasms of coughing
or asthma. It can be taken as an infusion, or herb tea,
sweetened with honey (steep half an ounce in a quart of
water; proportions vary, depending on the freshness of the
plant). Or, it can be made into a wine. (Macerate three
ounces in a bottle of Port or similar wine for a week, then
strain. Take one to three soupspoons after each meal.)

The many thymes and related savories of Provence also
provide valuable protection against respiratory infections.
When thyme is made into an herb tea, its tannins are effective against coughs. Thyme has long been used to combat
infection and encourage the digestive juices. It is also reputed to be aphrodisiac. Its essence "thymol" is highly valued in both the perfume and pharmaceutical industries, and,
furthermore, is essential in the production of banknotes!

The most famous and enjoyable winter remedy in Provence is the broth known as "Boiled Water," or *Aigo bollido*
(which, according to a local proverb, can save your life!). A
cross between a soup and an herb tea, it comes in many
versions, varying in complexity from the simplest infusion
of sage and garlic, to a vegetable broth, which, with the
addition of a poached egg and grated cheese, can become a
meal in itself.

but do not boil. Serve
warm, inhaling the brew
before swallowing.

Variations: Any of the
following ingredients
can be added to the
basic recipe:

A chopped onion can be
cooked with the leek and
the garlic.

A peeled tomato can
be cooked with the leek
and garlic, or a tablespoon
of tomato sauce added
before reheating.

Cooked pasta can be
added before reheating.

A poached egg can be
added to each person's
bowl, before the soup is
poured in.

A pinch of saffron can
be stirred into the mixture
just before serving.

Grated Gruyère cheese
can be sprinkled over each
person's serving.

Bibliography

Benoit, Fernand. *La Provence et le Comtat Venaissin: arts et traditions populaires.* Avignon: Aubanel, 1975.

Bosco, Henri. *Le Trestoulas.* Paris: Gallimard, 1935.

____. *Le Mas Théotime.* Paris: Gallimard, 1952.

Braudel, Fernand. *L'Identité de la France.* 4 vols. Paris: Arthaud-Flammarion, 1986.

Cameron, Roderick. *The Golden Riviera.* Honolulu: Editions Limited, 1975.

Clébert, Jean Paul. *Almanach Provençal 1984.* Paris: Rivages, 1984.

Colette. *La Vagabonde.* Paris: Albin Michel, 1973.

____. *Prisons et paradis.* Paris: Fayard, 1986.

Daudet, Alphonse. *Lettres de mon moulin.* Paris: Fasquelle, 1970.

Doran, P. M., ed. *Conversations avec Cézanne.* Paris: Editions Macula, 1978.

Durrell, Lawrence. *Monsieur.* Harmondsworth: Penguin, 1984.

____. *Livia.* Harmondsworth: Penguin, 1984.

____. *Spirit of Place.* New Haven, Connecticut: Leete's Island Books, 1969.

____. *Caesar's Vast Ghost.* London: Faber and Faber, 1990.

Fisher, M. F. K. *Two Towns in Provence.* New York: Vintage Books, 1983.

Forbes, Leslie. *A Taste of Provence.* Boston: Little Brown and Co., 1988.

Ford, Ford Madox. *Provence.* New York: Ecco Press, 1979.

Giono, Jean. *Rondeur des Jours.* Paris: Gallimard, 1969.

____. *Le Chant de la Terre.* Paris: Gallimard, 1969.

____. *Manosque-des-Plateaux suivi de Poème de l'olive.* Paris: Gallimard, 1986.

____. *Regain.* Paris: Gallimard, 1969.

Harant, Hervé and Daniel Jarry. *Guide du naturaliste dans le Midi de la France.* Neuchâtel, Switzerland: Delachaux and Niestlé, 1967.

Jacobs, Michael. *A Guide to Provence.* London: Viking Penguin, 1988.

James, Henry. *A Little Tour in France.* Oxford: Oxford University Press, 1984.

Jouveau, René. *La Cuisine provençal de tradition populaire.* Nîmes, France: Imprimerie Bene, 1976.

Lequenne, Fernand. *Olivier de Serres: agronome et soldat de Dieu.* Paris: Berger-Levrault, 1983.

Levron, Jacques. *Le Bon Roi René.* Paris: Arthaud, 1972.

Mauron, Marie. *Le printemps de la Saint Martin.* Paris: Atelier Marcel Julian, 1979.

Mayle, Peter, *A Year in Provence.* London: Hamish Hamilton, 1989.

____. *Toujours Provence.* London: Hamish Hamilton, 1991.

Mistral, Frédéric. *Dernières proses d'alamanch.* Paris: Bernard Grasset, 1930.

____. *Memoirs.* Translated by George Wickes. New York: Directions, 1988.

Mouriès, Nathalie. *Almanach Provençal 1991.* Paris: Rivages, 1991.

Office Régional de la Culture. P.A.C.A. et Conseil Régional des Bouches-du-Rhône de la ville de Marseille. *Semanié provenç au è di païs d'o pèr 1991.* Marseille: Racussel, 1991.

Pagnol, Marcel. *Le Château de ma mère.* Paris: Press Pocket, 1972.

____. *Jean de Florette.* Paris: Editions de Fallois, 1989.

____. *La Gloire de mon père.* Paris: Editions de Fallois, 1988.

____. *Manon des Sources.* Paris: Presse Pocket, 1976.

Pickvance, Ronald. *Van Gogh in Arles.* New York: Metropolitan Museum of Art, 1984.

Pope-Hennessy, James. *Aspects of Provence.* London: Penguin Travel Library, 1988.

Riche, August, ed. *La Provence en Poésie.* Paris: Gallimard Folio Junior, 1986.

Romilly, Jacqueline de. *Sur les Chemins de Sainte Victoire.* Paris: Julliard, 1987.

Roskill, Mark. *The Letters of Vincent Van Gogh.* New York: Atheneum, 1963.

Scipion, Marcel. *L'homme qui courait après les fleurs: mémoires d'un berger d'abeilles.* Paris: Seghers, 1984.

Stone, Irving, ed. *Dear Theo: The Autobiography of Vincent Van Gogh.* New York: Signet, 1987.

Thompson, David. *Petrarch: An Anthology.* New York: Harper & Row, 1971.

Tournier, Michel. *Pétites proses.* Paris: Gallimard Folio, 1986.

Van Gogh, Vincent. *Lettres à Théo.* Paris: Gallimard, 1988.

Wentinck, Charles. *Provence: Mythes et réalités.* Arles, France: Editions Bernard Coutaz, 1989.

Wentick, Charles and Lucien Clergue. *Arles Van Gogh.* Arles, France: Editions Bernard Coutaz, 1989.

Wickes, George, ed. "Readings for Innocents Abroad." Anthology of photocopied literary excerpts, Avignon, Spring 1985.

Wilkins, Ernest Hatch. *Life of Petrarch.* Chicago and London: Phoenix Books, 1962.

Wylie, Lawrence. *Village in the Vaucluse.* Cambridge: Harvard University Press, 1974.

Yapp, Peter, ed. *The Travellers' Dictionary of Quotations.* London: Routledge and Kegan Paul, 1983.

Zola, Emile. *Le Docteur Pascal.* Paris: Fasquelle, 1984.

Photo Credits

LOUISA JONES: Back cover (bottom left), 7 (top), 12 (top and bottom), 13, 14, 18–20 (all), 22–24 (all), 25 (left), 26, 28 (left), 29, 32, 33, 35, 36 (left), 37 (right), 38, 40–45 (all), 54–56 (all), 58, 60, 61 (bottom), 62–63 (all), 66–69 (all), 74, 76, 78, 79 (left), 84, 88 (bottom), 89, 94–99 (all), 102, 104 (top and left), 106–08 (all), 110, 112–13 (all), 116 (left), 117, 122, 123 (both), 125 (right), 126–28, 130–31 (all), 134, 135 (bottom), 138, 139 (bottom), 140–42 (all), 145, 146 (left), 147, 152, 155 (bottom), 156–57, 159, 162, 165.

VINCENT MOTTE: Front cover, back cover (top left and bottom right), 2, 6 (both), 10–11, 25 (right), 31, 36–37, 50–51, 52–53, 59, 61 (top), 64, 72–73, 80–81, 83, 84–85, 88–89, 92–93, 100, 101, 103, 104–05, 108–09, 114–15, 118, 120–21, 121 (right), 124, 132–33, 135 (top), 136, 143, 144, 146 (right), 148, 150–51, 153, 154–55, 155 (top), 168.

PHILIPPE GIRAUD: 3, 7 (bottom), 47, 48, 86, 88 (left), 119, 121 (left), 150 (left), 160–61 (all), 163.

MICHEL BARBEROUSSE: 21, 39, 46, 70, 90, 116 (right), 166.

RAOUL BUSSY: 28 (right), 139 (top).

CONSTANTINE CHRISTOFIDES: Back cover (top right), 79 (right).

BERNARD DUPONT, SR.: 91.

BERNARD DUPONT, JR.: Author portrait.

HEATHER WILLINGS: 111.

Painting on page 17 © Joseph Bayol.

Cloth patterns on page 77 are reproduced courtesy of Olivades Fabrics.

Acknowledgments

The author would like to express warm thanks to the many people whose helpful cooperation made this book possible: to the garden owners, Mademoiselle Bacou, Monsieur de Barbentane, Madame Casalis, Madame Bayol, Monsieur Lafont and Mrs. Williams; to the many diligent men and women who perpetuate the traditions of country crafts; to the chefs, particularly Christian Etienne and Jean-André Charial for their patient advice; to Jacques Avril at the Wine University in Suze-la-Rousse; to Nicole Arbroireau in Frejus for sharing her vast knowledge of plant lore; to George Wickes and Molly Westling for his wonderful translation of Mistral, and their common support; to Marie Lepoitevin for her friendly listening ear; to Monsieur and Madame Jacques Martin-Raget for their good advice; to Monsieur and Madame Michel Barberousse for their good company on restaurant outings.

And, not least, to my publishers: Leslie Stoker, for her enthusiasm, efficiency and willingness to experiment; Andrea Danese, for her quick responses to my queries; Barbara Sturman, for setting the type and making it all fit; and freelance designer Adriane Stark, for her imaginative design.

Addresses

ABBAYE DE SAINT-ANDRÉ, 30400 Villeneuve-lez-Avignon. Tel: 90 25 55 95

L'AIRE D'ÉTÉ, 13, rue de la République, 84480 Bonnieux. Tel: 90 75 88 70; FAX: 90 75 88 59

APARE, 41, cours Jean Jaurès, 84000 Avignon. Tel: 90 85 51 15

AUX JARDINS DE PROVENCE, route d'Avignon, 13210 Saint-Rémy-de-Provence. Tel: 90 92 01 57

JOSEPH BAYOL, Quartier Plantier Major, 13210 Saint-Rémy-de-Provence. Tel: 90 92 11 97

BISTROT À MICHEL, Grand Rue, 84220 Cabrières d'Avignon. Tel: 90 76 82 08

ANNA BONDE, L'Aire d'été, 13, rue de la République, 84480 Bonnieux. Tel: 90 75 88 70; FAX: 90 75 88 59

LAURENT BOURGES, route de Maillane, Saint-Rémy-de-Provence. Tel: 90 92 20 45

LA BOUTIQUE DU JARDIN, I, cours Mirabeau, in the center of Mirabeau. Tel: 90 92 11 60

DANIÈLE CAMARGUE, 10, rue de Bouillargues, 30128 Garons. Tel: 66 70 14 57

CHARTREUSE DE BONPAS, 84510 Caumont. Southeast of Avignon. Tel: 90 23 09 59

CHÂTEAU DE BARBENTANE, 13570 Barbentane. Tel: 90 95 51 07

CHÂTEAU DE ROCHEGUDE, in the village of Rochegude, 26700. North of Orange, at the intersection of several country roads. Tel: 75 04 81 88; FAX: 75 04 89 87

CHÂTEAU D'AQUÉRIA, 30126 Tavel. Tel: 66 50 04 56; FAX: 66 50 18 46

CHÂTEAU MONT-REDON, 84230 Châteauneuf-du-Pape. Tel: 90 83 72 75; FAX: 90 83 77 20

CLOS DE LA VIOLETTE, 10, avenue de la Violette, Aix-en-Provence. Tel: 42 23 30 71; FAX: 42 21 93 03

PAUL COULON ET FILS, Domaine de Beauregard, avenue Pierre-de-Luxembourg, 84230 Châteauneuf-du-Pape. Tel: 90 83 71 79; FAX: 90 83 78 06; ordering service: 90 83 51 20

COLETTE AND JULIEN DÉVOUASSOUX, Puyvert, 84160 Cadenet. Tel: 90 68 02 12

DOMAINE DE BEAUREGARD, avenue Pierre-de-Luxembourg, 84230 Châteauneuf-du-Pape. Tel: 90 83 71 79; FAX: 90 83 78 06; ordering service: 90 83 51 20

LE DOMAINE DE SAINT-LUC, LA BAUME-DE-TRANSIT, 26700 Saint-Paul-les-Trois-Château (about 17 miles northeast of Orange). Tel: 75 98 11 51; FAX: 75 98 19 22

CHRISTIAN ETIENNE, 10, rue de Mons, 84000 Avignon. Tel: 90 86 16 50; FAX: 90 86 67 09

ELIZABETH FERRIOL, 4, rue du 4 septembre, 13200 Arles. Tel: 90 93 37 60

PAUL FOUQUE, Meilleur Ouvrier de France, 65, cours Gambetta, 13100 Aix-en-Provence. Tel: 42 26 33 38

LA GUELARDIÈRE, I, route d'Apt, 84800 L'Isle-sur-la-Sorgue. Tel: 90 38 24 77; FAX: 90 20 87 02

HARMAS OF JEAN-HENRI FABRE, five miles northeast of Orange on the D976 road to Nyons, just outside Sérignan-du-Comtat. Tel: 90 70 00 44

HOSTELLERIE DE CRILLON-LE-BRAVE, place de l'Eglise, 84410 Crillon-le-Brave. Tel: 90 65 61 61; FAX: 90 65 62 86

JOUVAUD, RUE DE L'EVÊCHÉ, 84200 Carpentras. Tel: 90 63 15 38; FAX: 90 63 21 62

JEAN-PIERRE MAGNAN, 8b, rue de Mazeau, 84100 Orange. Tel: 90 34 25 62

MAISON DU VIN, 6, rue des Trois Faucons, 84000 Avignon. Tel: 90 27 24 14; FAX: 90 27 24 13

MANGUIN, Ile de la Barthelasse, 84000 Avignon. Tel: 90 82 62 29 and 90 86 56 60

MAS DE LA PYRAMIDE, quartier Saint-Paul, 13210 Saint-Rémy-de-Provence. Tel: 90 92 00 81

MAS LA BURLANDE, 13520 Le Paradou, Madame Jenny Fajardo de Livry. Private road off the D78F, southwest of Les Baux, between Le Paradou and Arles. Tel: 90 54 32 32

SARA DE NEYMAN, 4, rue de la Moutette, 84600 Valréas. Tel: 90 37 33 41

LES OLIVADES, avenue Barberin, Saint-Etienne-du-Grès, 13150 Tarascon. Tel: 90 49 16 68

OUSTAU DE BAUMANIÈRE, Restaurant and hôtel, Les Baux, 13520 Maussane. Tel: 90 54 33 07; FAX: 90 54 40 46

A. PARODI ET FAMILLE, main street of Mirabel-aux-Baronnies, between Vaison-la-Romaine and Nyons, northeast of Avignon on the D938. Tel: 75 27 12 07

LE PRIEURÉ, 7, place du Chapitre, 30400 Villeneuve-lez-Avignon, across the Rhone from Avignon. Tel: 90 25 46 28; FAX: 90 25 45 39
Le Prieuré pastry and candy shop, Tel: 90 25 84 95; FAX: 90 25 86 77

RAMPAL-PATOU, 71, rue Félix-Pyat, 13300 Salon-de-Provence. Tel: 90 56 07 28; FAX: 90 56 52 18

RAYMOND ET FILS, Pierre-de-Coubertin, 84200 Carpentras. Tel: 90 63 18 09

LA SCOURTINERIE, 86, la Maladrerie, 26110 Nyons. Tel: 75 26 33 52

SUD RESTAURATION, La Ribière, 84570 Mormoiron. East of Carpentras, on the D942 to Sault. Tel: 90 61 85 01

ARNE TENGBLAD, L'Aire d'été, 13, rue de la République, 84480 Bonnieux. Tel: 90 75 88 70; FAX: 90 75 88 59

UNIVERSITÉ DU VIN, Le Château, 26790 Suze-la-Rousse. Tel: 75 04 86 09; FAX: 75 98 24 20

VERNIN, Les Carreaux d'Apt, Le Pont Julien, 84480 Bonnieux. Tel: 90 74 16 80

"VINS EN FÊTE," BP 5, 84110 Séguret

Index

Designed by Adriane Stark

Composed with QuarkXpress 3.1 on a Macintosh IIsi in Centaur, Mona Lisa Recut and Bank Gothic at Stewart, Tabori & Chang, New York, New York. Output on a Lintronic 1300 at Typogram, Inc., New York, New York.

Printed and bound by Toppan Printing Company, Ltd., Tokyo, Japan.

Political Struggle, Ideology, and State Building

JEFFREY C. MOSHER

Political Struggle, Ideology, and State Building

Pernambuco and the Construction
of Brazil, 1817–1850

University of Nebraska Press | Lincoln & London

Portions of chapter 3, "Liberal Reforms
and the Resort to Arms, 1831–35," previously appeared in *Luso-Brazilian Review* 37 no. 2 (2000) and are used by permission of the University of Wisconsin
Press. Portions of chapter 6, "The Centralized State and Political Polarization,
1844–47," and chapter 8, "The Praieira
Revolution, 1848–50," originally appeared in *Luso-Brazilian Review* 42, no. 2
(2005) and are used by permission of the
University of Wisconsin Press. Portions
of chapter 7, "Political Parties, Popular
Mobilization, and the Portuguese," previously appeared in *Hispanic American
Historical Review* 80, no. 4 (2000).

Mosher, Jeffrey C.
Political struggle, ideology, and
state building : Pernambuco and the
construction of Brazil, 1817–1850 /
Jeffrey C. Mosher.
p. cm.
Includes bibliographical references
and index.
ISBN 978-0-8032-3247-1 (cloth : alk.
paper)
1. Pernambuco (Brazil)—Politics and
government—19th century. 2. Revolutions—Brazil—Pernambuco—History—19th century. I. Title.
JL2499.P62M67 2008
981'.3404—dc22
2007049779

For Carl and Anne Mosher
and
For Talia and Miriam Mosher

Contents

Maps

Acknowledgments

The debts I have accumulated in the course of this project are substantial. I cannot hope to recognize everyone who contributed to it, but I do want to acknowledge at least some of them. At the University of Florida, I was extremely fortunate to have a dissertation committee of excellent scholars and wonderful individuals. While their scholarly strengths may have contributed most obviously to this publication, it has been their kindness and generosity that have touched me even more. I have worked most closely with Jeffrey Needell, whose wise guidance I have greatly benefited from. He has been unfailingly supportive and vastly more giving of his time than anyone could reasonably ask. If I can offer a fraction as much to my students as he has to me, I will know I have done well. It was a great pleasure to work with David Bushnell and Murdo MacLeod. I enjoyed working with Steven Sanderson and Harry Paul in their respective fields. Among other historians at the University of Florida, I'd like to acknowledge Thomas Gallant. I would also like to thank Betty Corwine.

Many historians of Latin America have provided helpful critiques of my work and assisted me in other ways as well. Judy Bieber and Hendrik Kraay deserve special mention for their excellent, detailed (and timely!) responses to my work. This book is much better as a result of their suggestions. It will come as no surprise to Brazilianists that Roderick Barman has been generous and encouraging. Bert J. Barickman and Timothy Anna have offered valuable feedback. Anonymous readers at the *Hispanic American Historical Review* and the *Luso-Brazilian Review* gave useful suggestions. Of course, any problems with the book are my responsibility alone.

Commenting on manuscripts and offering questions and suggestions at conferences are not the only ways that scholars can be supportive of their colleagues. I would like to offer deeply sincere thanks to Timothy Anna, Christon Archer, Roderick Barman, Judy Bieber, Dain Borges, Marshal Eakin, Jeffrey Lesser, Ron Rainger, and William Sater for their confidence and support.

This project would not have been possible without the work of archivists in Brazil at the Arquivo Público Estadual Jordão Emerenciano, the Instituto Arqueológico, Histórico e Geográfico Pernambucano, the Arquivo Nacional, the Biblioteca Nacional, the Instituto Histórico e Geográfico do Brasil, and at the Arquivo Nacional da Torre do Tombo in Portugal. I would especially like to acknowledge Hildo Leal da Rosa, whose support at the Arquivo Público Estadual Jordão Emerenciano was more valuable than he will ever know. I would also like to thank José Antônio Gonsalves de Mello and the various members of the Instituto Arqueológico, Histórico e Geográfico Pernambucano who made it possible to work there.

Marcus Joaquim Maciel de Carvalho has been extremely helpful. His body of work on nineteenth-century Pernambuco is of considerable importance; even more impressive is the generosity and good will he has so often demonstrated. Thank you. Also in Pernambuco, Marc Hoffnagel was of assistance. In Alagoas, I enjoyed the hospitality and good cheer of Luiz Sávio de Almeida.

I am grateful for financial support from the Tinker Foundation, the Fulbright Commission, the National Science Foundation, the University of Florida, and Texas Tech University. I am aware of the work individuals must do to decide on funding research proposals and my gratitude extends to those unnamed individuals.

Peter Stern, as head of the Latin American Collection at the University of Florida, acquired a microfilm collection of newspapers from Pernambuco that was quite valuable for this project. Richard Phillips was director of that collection during most of my time in Gainesville and was my supervisor when I worked in the library. I would be remiss not to also mention a co-worker at the library, Justino Llanque-Chana. They made working in the Latin American Collection fun. I wish the best for Justino, including all the Hare Krishna lunches he might want.

At Texas Tech University, Ed Steinhart, David Troyansky, and above all, Catherine Miller, offered valuable comments on various papers and articles. Many others offered insightful questions and comments during a faculty colloquium. Such occasions make it easy to appreciate the high quality of so many of my colleagues at Texas Tech. A scholar of colonial Latin America, Allan Kuethe, facilitated research and travel funds in his capacity as department chair. I am, and always will be, profoundly grateful to the dean of the College of Arts and Sciences, Jane Winer, for her support. Life is immeasurably enriched by good friends. I especially appreciate and value several individuals at Texas Tech or in Lubbock whom I would like to name—Patricia Pelley, Stefano D'Amico, Aliza Wong, Paul Deslandes (now at the University of Vermont), Hafid Gafaiti, Catherine Miller, Jonathan Miller, Ron Rainger, and Judy Rainger.

At the University of Nebraska Press, Heather Lundine and Ann Baker have made the somewhat daunting task of publishing a first book easier. I also appreciate the careful efforts of Sandra Crump.

I would like to thank Alice Martin for her valuable support during my years in Gainesville and also all of those who extended their concern and a helping hand after my daughter Talia suffered an accident. I would also like to acknowledge Thomas Flynn of Emory University's Philosophy Department for the example he offered many years ago of a scholar/teacher.

Finally, and most important, I would like to acknowledge people closer to home. Whatever words I might type would be inadequate, so I will simply offer my gratitude to my parents, Carl and Anne Mosher, to Dina Mosher, whom my children are fortunate to have as their mother, and to Talia and Miriam Mosher, whom I love with all my heart.

Political Struggle, Ideology, and State Building

Introduction

I n the first half of the nineteenth century a series of revolts erupted in Pernambuco, a large slave-holding, sugar-producing province in northeastern Brazil. An unsuccessful republican, secessionist uprising in 1817 and the achievement of independence in 1822 were followed not by peace but by violent upheavals in 1824, 1831, 1832–35, and 1848. These challenges to the emerging sociopolitical order exposed tensions generated by state- and nation-building. The conflicts were not simple battles among a few elite families; rather, they included the active participation of subaltern groups. Diverse actors with distinct political projects struggled throughout this period. This study explores the intertwined dynamics of local social and political struggles in Pernambuco and the construction of the state and nation in postcolonial Brazil between 1817 and 1850.

Building the State and Nation

Historians of Brazil have shared in the renewed interest among scholars in the construction of states and nations and in teasing out the ways in which diverse social groups have participated in these processes. Scholars have reconsidered, for example, equating political emancipation from Portugal with the founding of a new nation, Brazil. Such new views are clearly revisionist. From early on, narratives of independence accorded a heroic role to Emperor Pedro I, the monarchy more generally, and the elites that supported it, in securing national independence from Portugal, and in establishing a regime that could maintain social order. Cultural institutions such as the Historical and Geographical Institute of Brazil gave institutional support to create and celebrate such narratives. The lure of nationalistic assumptions has proved so strong that in the second half of the twentieth century as prominent a historian of Brazil as José Honório Rodrigues wrote of the independence period, "From the beginning, unity was an aspiration shared by everyone."[1]

The new revisionism includes voices questioning the existence of a national consciousness before political emancipation from Portugal, although only recently has the question drawn sustained scholarly attention. The early voices, though few, have been impressive. Sérgio Buarque de Holanda and Maria Odila Silva Dias both emphasized at the outset of their widely read essays that political emancipation from Portugal was separate from the construction of national unity.[2] In 1988 Roderick Barman explored the issue, examining the material circumstances of the relative isolation of the various captaincies of Portuguese America and the primacy of the local *pátria* in political identities. The *pátria* was the "visible, physical community in which an individual was born" and lived; its range varied but often corresponded to a captaincy. The name "Brazil," in contrast, while in use, did not imply a cohesive political identity that drew on basic loyalties. Rather than an independence struggle that pitted Brazilians against the Portuguese, Barman saw a contest between regimes in Lisbon and Rio de Janeiro to secure the loyalty of diverse *pátrias* in Portuguese America, *pátrias* that sought in turn to secure their autonomy. A key implication of these analyses is that instead of assuming a teleological subtext, in which the nation-state of Brazil was seemingly inevitable, they draw attention to the contingent nature of the relevant political processes.[3]

In recent years scholars across the globe have explored the relationship between state building and nation building. Of special relevance here are the cases in which the state preceded the nation and played an important role in creating and shaping nationalism.[4] State building and nation building are interrelated but distinct projects. The heart of this book is state building, but the construction of a national consciousness, a sense of belonging to the same nation, and the meaning ascribed to such national bonds also play a role. The period chosen for study, from 1817 to the mid-nineteenth century, encompasses political separation from Portugal and the creation and consolidation of the imperial state. In principle, of course, state building continues indefinitely, as the institutions of the state change, but my interest here is in the competing political projects at play during the construction of a stable system of governance under the monarchy.

Integrating the Court and the Provinces

Much attention has been given to state and nation building at the center of the empire (above all to events in Rio de Janeiro), and recent contributions have greatly enriched the historiography of the independence and post-independence era. For the independence era alone, serious attention has been given to the changing understanding of the Bragança monarchy with the transfer of the royal court to Rio de Janeiro, the meanings contemporaries attached to the Luso-Brazilian empire, the construction of an autonomous Brazilian identity and the image of a royal sovereign ordering and legitimating that society, the ways in which political actors worked to define the meaning of their struggles, the significance of republican political projects in a period in which legitimate rule was so strongly associated with monarchy, and the ways in which the newly uncensored press played a prominent role in structuring political struggles.[5] This book complements such work by focusing on a major province far from the imperial court and how the social and political struggles there influenced and were influenced by the larger system.

Whether in early modern Europe, former European colonies after the Second World War, or nineteenth-century Latin America, state making has often been characterized by violent local resistance to centralization. Cohen, Brown, and Organski have argued that violence is an integral part of the accumulation of power by the new national state.[6] Charles Tilly's work exemplifies a considerable body of literature that explores the institutional consequences of struggles between state makers seeking to extract resources and populations striving to maintain local control.[7] Recent studies, however, demonstrate that state making is not a one-directional process.[8]

Consider in Brazil, for example, the successful push from 1817 to the early 1830s for provincial autonomy by regional elites in Pernambuco and much of Brazil that ultimately contributed to the definitive consolidation in the 1840s of a highly centralized regime that could establish and maintain the social and political order. The elites in Pernambuco and across Brazil, like others throughout Latin America, were profoundly concerned with order. In a society deeply divided by class, slavery, and race, much political discourse revolved around the theme of establishing and maintaining institutions that could ensure order.

The presence of the state was tenuous in much of the country, especially in rural areas. Political competition turned violent at times, and when elite groups mobilized the lower classes, the latter sometimes broke free of upper-class control. Various groups traditionally marginalized from political power sought to act in the public arena, a phenomenon legitimated by liberal notions such as popular sovereignty. In a period in which the old order had collapsed and the shape of a new one was contested, diverse groups resorted to violence to achieve their ends.

Following Pedro I's abdication in 1831, a barracks revolt by forcibly recruited, lower class soldiers rocked Pernambuco's capital city, Recife, in September; in November, military officers seized a fort in the city and issued demands; and a restorationist revolt seeking Pedro's return to the throne erupted the following year. When the urban leaders of this movement put down their arms, a rural rebellion continued for three years. Upheavals plagued Brazil in this period, and for the men who led the Regresso (return) movement, much of the blame lay in the reforms of the 1830s that shifted authority from the imperial court to the provinces and increased citizen participation. As a consequence, many of the same regional elites that had succeeded in achieving autonomy, when subsequently threatened from below, became important proponents of centralization.

Politics and the Party System

Analysis that integrates local, provincial, and national politics is necessary to advance our understanding of political processes in general and parties in particular. In Pernambuco, by the early 1820s, distinct, competing factions of the elite can be observed. By the early 1840s, as centralization of the political system allowed leaders in the imperial court to hand over considerable power to their provincial allies, linkages between parties in the province and the court are clear. Political polarization continued throughout the decade, culminating in the last of the great regional rebellions, the Praieira Revolution. Reconstruction of politics in Pernambuco in the 1830s and 1840s allows insight into both party dynamics in Pernambuco and the relationship between provincial parties and their national allies. Even at the national level, the party system and its role in the politics of the empire is not well understood.[9] Lack of agreement on such basic questions as when political parties emerged and even what names were in common use at the time suggests that much work remains. The relationship between provincial and national parties and between provincial leaders and provincial supporters remains largely unexplored. Fundamental questions remain about the functions of the party system itself. Were parties simply vehicles for spoils, without any significant programmatic content? Did party competition express the struggles of competing interests over public policy? Were parties and the political system as a whole principally means of legitimating the social and political order?

In reconstructing and analyzing the social and political struggles of the late 1830s and the 1840s, focusing on the interaction between a major province and the imperial court in Rio de Janeiro, we can recover the specificity needed to understand how the party system emerged and functioned. Very little research at the provincial level has been done. Judy Bieber's pioneering analysis of the impact of state centralization on municipal politics in the *sertão* of northern Minas Gerais over the course of the empire is a notable exception.[10] Recovering the specificities that provincial case studies can provide is essential for more fine-grained analyses that can build on seminal works on imperial politics by Roderick Barman, José Murilo de Carvalho, Emilia Viotti da Costa, Thomas Flory, Ilmar Rohloff de Mattos, and others.[11]

One reason for the relative lack of research on these issues may be the longstanding emphasis on the importance of informal structures based on kinship and patron-client networks.[12] Analyses that emphasize the importance of family and patron-client networks over formal political institutions have typically seen political parties as personalistic groups formed to capture the spoils of government. Many authors have assumed similarity in their class composition, outlook, and interests and have paid little attention to whatever differences may have existed in their political ideas. Richard Graham has provided the most powerful argument for viewing parties as devoid of ideological content and any significant differentiation. Graham believes that emphasizing struggles over policies is to misunderstand nineteenth-century politics. Politics was not fundamentally about government policies; rather, politicians were concerned with patronage above all else. In its focus on patronage, politics was most fundamentally about reinforcing values that undergirded stability.[13]

By depicting parties as primarily patronage systems, the focus on kinship and patronage networks tends to understate the complexity of human motivations and ignore the role of political ideas and ideology. This analysis recovers the importance of formal political institutions and ideas and links them to broader social and political conflicts. Pernambuco provides considerable evidence that differences existed among the parties at three levels: in the programs they espoused, in the socioeconomic composition of their support, and in their degree of willingness to mobilize the lower classes. Liberals in the province, for example, distinguished themselves both in championing a decentralized, democratic liberalism and in promoting a nationalistic economic model. Liberals mobilized the lower and middle classes through anti-Portuguese appeals that harnessed discontent over continuing Portuguese economic and political strength. Opponents of the Portuguese expressed their social, economic, and racial resentments in formal party politics, in newspapers, and even in violent confrontations in the streets. When subalterns employed violence against the Portuguese, they sometimes openly asserted their right to do so, employing the language and symbols of the nation and political legitimacy in defense of their own vision of society; at times, they even went so far that they brought themselves into conflict with party leaders.[14]

The Age of Revolution aptly suggests the remarkable changes of the late eighteenth and early nineteenth centuries around the Atlantic. In the Portuguese world, a great empire ceased to be. The ideas that had legitimated the old order were in some cases repudiated, in others modified, and in still others largely unchanged. The first half of the nineteenth century was a period of tremendous fluidity; the old order had collapsed, new possibilities could be imagined, and social groups that were previously marginalized from having a meaningful say in the public sphere were now asserting themselves. The language of liberalism could be used in support of many different political projects. A central issue of dispute was the extent to which previously excluded groups would be acknowledged as citizens with the right to participate in public affairs.

In this study I reconstruct the interplay of these various groups in the construction of the Brazilian state and nation. I specify the mutual influence between provincial social and political struggles on the one hand and politics in the national capital on the other. I am far from the first to explore the revolts and politics of the era in Pernambuco or the empire as a whole; there are serious studies of specific revolts and varied political issues and I have learned from them all.[15] However, none of them takes the period as a whole and benefits from seeing how events at one moment conditioned those that followed. In this, much is lost. The fluidity of the period cannot be stressed too much. As people struggled to improve their lot, seized weapons and risked their lives, followed the orders of others, asserted themselves publicly for the first time, felt the sting of punishment when defeated, or assimilated new ideas, they acquired experience that might suggest new options in the future or close off others. One of the principal contributions I attempt here is to capture the dynamic quality of the period, tying together the local, provincial, and national events and ideas, and showing their change over time.

The Portuguese Empire in the Age of Revolution: Pernambuco, 1817

In 1807, with French troops marching on Portugal, João VI made the remarkable decision to transfer the Portuguese royal court to Rio de Janeiro. Soon the ports of Portuguese America were opened to international commerce, and Portuguese mercantilism was largely abandoned. The elite in Rio de Janeiro benefited greatly from these developments, and many of the thousands of Portuguese who accompanied João across the Atlantic set roots in Brazil. Across Portuguese America, people welcomed the changes.

Opening the ports to international commerce dramatically accelerated the penetration of new ideas from the North Atlantic world. Increased commercial contact and an influx of migrants to port cities were particularly important in spreading ideas of constitutional, even republican, government. Of course, notions of popular sovereignty and representative government could mean different things to different people. In the captaincies distant from Rio de Janeiro, the elite doubtless saw these notions as the basis of a social and political order that they could run largely free of excessive outside intervention, while people of more limited means and influence hoped for greater social mobility. Despite such crucial differences, large numbers of people were coming to share anti-absolutist assumptions.

Masonic lodges served as important vehicles for the spread of enlightened political ideas such as constitutional government and republican-ism. By 1817, in Pernambuco, authorities were becoming increasingly suspicious of these organizations. In March a crackdown on the lodges sparked the first large-scale challenge to Portuguese rule in America. Ini-tially a military revolt, it quickly became a movement with broad support among planters, local merchants, petty officials, the clergy, free skilled individuals, and men of lesser means. A provisional government was se-lected, with five leaders drawn from key sectors of the elite. The provi-sional government declared itself to be a republic and made plans for a constitutional assembly to write a charter.

The movement found common ground in the notion of popular sover-eignty as the basis of authority, in contrast to royal tyranny, and on rejec-tion of excessive taxation from Rio de Janeiro, which was seen as an ex-pression of tyranny. Yet the extent of popular participation would surely have been a contentious issue, one that was never worked out, as mili-tary defeat put an end to the movement. Certainly the potential aboli-tion of slavery was a divisive issue. The provisional government hinted at broader popular mobilization on the basis of a gradual abolition, but it quickly backtracked in the face of elite objections. The depth of com-mitment to republican institutions is also open to question. The use of the term "patriot" for supporters of the movement and the rejection of certain traditional practices that reinforced hierarchy, as seen in the new linguistic convention in which the informal *vós* was to be used in all situ-ations, were clearly suggestive of French republicanism. Indeed, if Per-nambuco and nearby captaincies were to break away from the rest of Portuguese America, was there any alternative to a republic? What mon-archy could have been formed?

The royal defeat of the 1817 revolt was accomplished without great difficulty. The armed forces stitched together by the rebels lacked suffi-cient weapons, ships, and experienced military leaders. In contrast, the Count of Arcos in Salvador, Bahia, acted decisively, seizing an emissary sent south to draw adherents to the revolt, blockading Recife's port, send-ing a force of eight hundred men north to Pernambuco by land, and en-gaging in a propaganda campaign. When more ships and men arrived from Rio de Janeiro, the rebels were handily defeated.

Yet while the movement was quickly defeated on the field of battle, it would have long-lasting repercussions. The exemplary punishments meted out—executions, mass imprisonments, and seizures of property— embittered many. More importantly, a new political education was under way. In a period of dramatic change, in which absolutism was on its last legs and a lengthy period of struggle over what would take its place was beginning, people of diverse social groups had seized arms and contested political authority. The experience of once having taken up arms would make future recourse to armed action that much easier to imagine. New possibilities were opening up.

The Setting: Pernambuco
Since early colonial days, the bulk of Pernambuco's population had lived in the coastal *zona da mata*, or forest area. This humid region, with its rich black *massapê* soils, rivers, and rainy and dry seasons, was early recognized as ideal for cultivating sugar cane. The coastal region south of Recife, the capital city and principal port, was particularly favored because of its greater rainfall and large rivers that were important for transportation. By the nineteenth century, the greatest estates were located around Cabo, between the Jaboatão and the Serinhaem rivers. In the drier *mata* north of Recife, landholdings were not as large. In drier areas, squatters or slaves planted beans, manioc, or fruit. In some places sugar cane shared the landscape with cotton, although the latter crop was more important in the transitional *agreste*, to which the zona da mata gives way within 90 kilometers of the coast north of Recife and 160 kilometers in places to the south.[1]

The agreste lay between the coastal forest area and the harsh, dry scrublands of the *sertão*, or backlands. Drier than the zona da mata, the agreste supported a sparser population, although scattered elevated areas, with cooler temperatures and moist winds, allowed for pockets of denser settlement. The majority of Pernambuco's cotton was produced in the agreste, in operations ranging from large landholdings worked by numerous slaves to small plots worked by renters and sharecroppers. The small labor and capital requirements, the short growing cycle, and the practice of planting beans and maize alongside the cotton made small-scale farms feasible. Cattle raising was also important. Commercial centers such as Caruaru, a key point in the cattle route from the backlands

MAP 1. Brazil

BRAZIL

MAP 2. Pernambuco

to the coast, and Bom Jardim, important in the cotton trade, developed in the region as well.[2]

The hot, dry *sertão*, an enormous area often struck by drought, was thinly populated. The region's settlers spread over the area, grazing cattle for the coastal sugar industry, which needed beasts of burden for mill work and transportation as well as meat. Extensive grazing and massive ranches, only vaguely demarcated, were the norm; ten hectares were needed for each head of cattle.[3] Cowboys were central figures in the "leather civilization" that developed, as hides were put to multiple and ingenious uses. Great cattle drives were common sights as cattle were

Sertão

Agreste

Zona da Mata

MAP 3. Pernambuco after 1817

transported to commercial hubs in the agreste and on to the coast, or to more humid areas in the *sertão* during the driest times.[4] Rivers provided relief from the region's dry spells, as did the elevated areas touched by moisture-laden winds.[5]

Since the pioneering efforts of the 1530s, growing and processing cane and transporting and exporting sugar had overshadowed other activities in Pernambuco. Sugar supplied the foundation for the planter elite, which controlled the land and rural labor, and sugar was likewise the basis for fortunes made in Recife by merchants, often Portuguese born, who loaned capital to planters, exported their sugar, and imported goods and captive African laborers for their use.[6]

By the nineteenth century the zona da mata was mostly occupied. The bulk of the best lands were controlled by a relatively small number of families, many of whom had acquired land through the generous land grants made by the crown in the colonial period. Smaller estates spread across the countryside as well. Boundaries between landholdings were often vague, and many people held land without formal title. De facto control of land was ensured by the threat or the use of force and through political influence.[7]

Male heads of wealthy families controlled the great estates of Pernambuco's rich littoral and their dependent populations. Not surprisingly, wealthy landowners exercised considerable political influence. Consider the leading family, the Cavalcanti de Albuquerques. Captain-Major Francisco de Paula de Holanda Cavalcanti de Albuquerque, suspected as an organizer of a turn-of-the-century conspiracy against Portuguese rule and a significant figure in the failed struggle for an independent Pernambucan republic in 1817, claimed descent, in typical fashion for elites seeking to justify their power, from four powerful families—the Coelhos, Cavalcantis, Albuquerques, and Holandas—who settled early in Portuguese America, three of them in the sixteenth century. He in turn fathered four sons who were ennobled during the empire (1822–89), three of whom became significant political leaders in their own right—the liberal leader Antônio Francisco de Paula de Holanda Cavalcanti de Albuquerque (the Viscount of Albuquerque) and the conservatives Francisco de Paula Cavalcanti de Albuquerque (the Viscount of Suassuna) and Pedro Francisco de Paula Cavalcanti de Albuquerque (the Viscount of Camaragibe). Over the course of the empire, the Cavalcanti de Albuquerques and their cousins received fifteen titles, more than any other family in Brazil.[8]

Planters typically owned around 50 slaves (or even 150 on the larger plantations) to carry out the arduous and labor-intensive work of cane growing, harvesting, processing, and transporting.[9] The cane was processed much as it was in other sugar-growing regions of the world. It was crushed in rollers to extract juice; water was evaporated from the juice in boiling kettles; the remaining juice was strained and cooled and put into a form with a hole from which water was purged; and the crystallizing sugar was left in the form in the sun to dry, yielding the final product, dry loaves of sugar.[10] The loaves were most cheaply transported along rivers or the coast on *barcaças*, sailing vessels capable of carrying loads of twenty-five to fifty tons, or even on small and accident-prone *jangadas*.[11] The English traveler Maria Graham described the latter craft as "six or eight logs made fast together by two transverse beams . . . with a sort of rudder . . . an upright pole . . . and a large triangular sail . . . the waves constantly washing over it."[12] For those without access to water transport, oxcarts loaded with a ton to a ton and a half of sugar and drawn by six to twelve oxen made a plodding substitute.[13]

Sugar loaves and cotton were brought to warehouses in the Bairro do Recife. This commercial district, the oldest of Recife's three sections, housed the customs house and sugar inspection buildings. Here ships were loaded and unloaded, protected from rough seas outside the harbor by the wall of reef (*recife*) that gave the city its name. A traveler commenting on the "marvelous natural break-water" wrote, "We heard the surf dashing without, and saw the spray, but we ourselves were sailing along smoothly and calmly, as if in a mill-pond. . . . The reef is certainly one of the wonders of the world." Old brick and tile-roofed three- and four-story buildings lined narrow, twisting streets and housed larger commercial establishments and their warehouses, insurance companies, foreign consuls, small shops, bars, and the coffee houses in which merchants carried out transactions. People resided in smaller structures along these paved streets as well. A crowded hustle and bustle continued from morning until late afternoon. A French observer noted the "continuous movement of blacks coming and going, carrying bundles, picking up their spirits with simple, monotonous song," into which were mixed cries of Afro-Brazilian women selling cloth and other wares that they carried in baskets on their heads.[14]

Three miles to the north of the Bairro do Recife sat Olinda, the first European settlement in the area, which was built on hills that allowed a spectacular view. One of the country's two law schools that trained many members of the political elite was located here until the 1850s, when it was reestablished in Recife. A thin sandy isthmus, upon which the Brum and Buraco forts were built, linked Olinda and Recife. Canoes were commonly used to traverse the distance. In the other direction, one could leave the commercial district by crossing a bridge over the Beberibe River into the Bairro de Santo Antônio. This island neighborhood between the Bairro do Recife and Boa Vista was the site of the principal government buildings, such as the presidential palace, the treasury building, and the prison. There was also much commercial activity in Santo Antônio, but it consisted of retail sales, not the large-scale merchant activities of the Bairro do Recife. Crossing a bridge over the Capibaribe River to Boa Vista, one stepped onto the landmass. While the oldest section, near the river, housed some retail commerce, by and large Boa Vista was a residential area. In the nineteenth century it quickly gave way to the countryside, with country homes surrounded by gardens.[15]

Recife's population was rapidly growing in the period between 1817 and 1850. A systematic study published in 1852 estimated the population of the city at between 60,000 and 70,000, out of a provincial population of 644,000. Sixty-five percent of Pernambuco's population was of at least partly African descent, and the proportion was nearly 70 percent in Recife. In the province as a whole, some 23 percent of the inhabitants were slaves, while in Recife the proportion was 26 percent.[16] The residents of the capital thus comprised only a fraction of the entire provincial population, but they exercised greater influence on politics than their numbers alone would suggest.

Brazil and the Portuguese Empire

In the sixteenth century, Duarte Coelho established the first successful sugar cane cultivation in Portuguese America in what became the captaincy of Pernambuco. Planters and merchants prospered, and Recife became a regular stop for ships in the Portuguese fleet system. With the discovery of gold in the 1690s and diamonds in the 1720s in the center-south of the colony, revenues from its American possessions took on central importance for the Portuguese government, particularly in light of its trade deficits with Great Britain. A variety of policies were implemented to increase metropolitan control, above all in the mining districts. The crown created new administrative and judicial units, sent more armed men to the mining region, diminished a degree of the autonomy of the *câmaras municipais* (municipal councils), and increased taxes.

In the mid-eighteenth century, enlightened reformer Sebastião José de Carvalho e Melo, the Marquis of Pombal, implemented a wide-ranging reform project to enable Portugal to better exploit its far-flung empire. The Marquis of Pombal was particularly concerned with the British penetration of the Portuguese economy, which enabled Portugal's long-time ally to capture many of the benefits of trade with the American colony. Through a series of monopoly companies, taxation policies, and subsidies, enlightened reformers encouraged agricultural production in Brazil. Likewise, large Portuguese merchant houses were favored in an effort to strengthen metropolitan merchants who would then be better able to compete with their British counterparts.

As in Spanish America, greater metropolitan control and extraction of revenue from the colonies provoked tensions. Portuguese efforts to co-opt the American-born elite, through access to positions in the Portuguese bureaucracy, no doubt eased the tensions between the colonial elite and the metropolis, as did the significant growth of agricultural production late in the century and the advantages for social control that a stable monarchy offered those who sat atop a multiracial slave society.[17]

Nonetheless, Portuguese authorities did uproot several conspiracies—most notably, the Inconfidência Mineira in 1788–89 and the 1798 Tailors' Conspiracy in Salvador, Bahia. The former was an elite affair in which heavy taxation played a large role. The subsequent investigation also revealed some resonance with the ideals of the American Revolution among the conspirators. The Tailors' Conspiracy in Salvador was more quickly repressed, although the prospect of slaves, freedmen, and mulatto artisans invoking slogans of the French Revolution and calling for independence and equality must have been particularly distressing to royal officials, especially in light of the slave rebellion and upheaval in the French Caribbean colony of Saint Domingue. In 1801 the so-called Conspiracy of the Suassunas in Pernambuco suggested some elite interest in the French Revolution, although this was a minor event and perhaps not too much should be read into it. While the Age of Revolution around the North Atlantic did offer examples of challenges to imperial powers and established institutions, the Terror of the French Revolution and the slave rebellion in the French colony of Saint Domingue served clear notice to the elites of the dangerous possibilities of social upheaval if political institutions were threatened.[18]

The Transfer of the Royal Court

What made the Brazilian path to independence truly distinctive was Portugal's transfer of the seat of its empire to its American colony in 1807. Napoleon sought to tighten his Continental System, more effectively excluding Great Britain from the European landmass, by seizing control of Iberia. In response to the invasion of Portugal in November, João VI, the royal family, leading government figures, and perhaps eight thousand to fifteen thousand others set sail for the Americas in forty-seven ships and reestablished the royal court in Rio de Janeiro. The British navy ensured a safe crossing and British commercial interests were quickly rewarded.

Opening its ports to international trade dismantled much of the mercantilist system that Portugal had used to monopolize trade with its colonies. A "tropical Versailles" emerged in Rio de Janeiro, as the empire's governing institutions were reestablished (and transformed) and a cultural ambience appropriate to a European empire was created. The dynamics of the new system were brought to their logical conclusion when João VI raised Portugal's American possessions to coequal status with Portugal as a separate Kingdom of Brazil under the Bragança crown in 1815. The major sources of friction between the former colony and metropolis were thus substantially diminished.[19]

The transfer of the royal court to Rio de Janeiro and the dramatic changes introduced did not, however, mean that the entire colonial mercantilist system, the interests it served, and the beliefs developed over centuries disappeared overnight. When Napoleon's army drove the royal court from Portugal, the thousands of Portuguese who crossed the Atlantic with João fully expected to maintain the privileges that proximity to the king allowed them. The monarch did not disappoint them. He surrounded himself with advisors who had made the passage with him and extended patronage and favors disproportionately to such individuals. This did not, of course, negate the great benefits that accrued to members of Rio de Janeiro's elite who were now in close proximity to the royal court. Likewise, people born in Portuguese America but far from Rio de Janeiro also benefited from no longer being ruled by a metropolis across the Atlantic Ocean, despite the fact that, compared to those near Rio, they were at a disadvantage in seeking influence with and patronage from João.

The opening of the ports to international trade in 1808 appeared to end mercantilist policy (although the decree that established this policy was explicitly provisional in nature). At the same time that liberalizing measures opened Brazil to direct access to international trade without going through Iberian middlemen and removed a variety of restrictions on economic activities in the colony, João was busy enacting a series of decrees that favored the crown and the Iberian-born Portuguese. Royal monopolies were exempted from liberalizing measures and textiles, and a variety of other products manufactured in Portugal were exempted from tariffs, as were goods from Asia that were imported by Portuguese merchants. Only Portuguese ships were allowed to unload goods from Asia or anywhere beyond the Cape of Good Hope. Such measures continued some of the practices associated with mercantilism and upset not only foreign merchants but also Brazilian-born traders who had to contend with advantages for the Portuguese-born. Likewise, de facto control of important sectors of trade by small numbers of Portuguese-born merchants, such as the eight individuals who controlled the cotton trade in Pernambuco, was a source of resentment for American-born producers and merchants. Thus, while the conflicts of interest between the Portuguese-born and the American-born were vastly diminished by the liberalizing measures, they nonetheless persisted to some degree. Indeed, after Napoleon's defeat, Portuguese mercantile interests struggled to reassert their pre-1808 privileges, ultimately pushing for the virtual recolonization of Brazil.[20]

At the same time, taxes increased. Establishing and maintaining a royal court in the tropics was an expensive proposition. New fiscal measures ensured the flow of resources to Rio de Janeiro. Not surprisingly, the taxation required to support the court quickly became a source of discontent. Governor and Captain-General of Pernambuco Caetano Pinto de Miranda Montenegro's correspondence with the central government demonstrated his concern with the burden of taxation and the possibility that it might prompt challenges to royal authority.[21]

Questioning Absolutism

Clearly there were multiple reasons for tension between the people of Pernambuco and the Portuguese royal court in Rio de Janeiro. Yet discontent is one thing, and an active challenge to royal authority quite another. A key element that helped bridge the distance from dissatisfaction to revolt was the increasing penetration of anti-absolutist ideas from Europe and the United States.

Enlightened ideas from the Age of Revolution were sufficiently widespread that they were even entering Portuguese America through official channels. Eighteenth-century reforms of colonial policy and the curriculum at the University of Coimbra implemented by the Marquis of Pombal, for example, were clearly influenced by enlightened thought and attitudes. Like other European monarchies, the Portuguese crown hoped to control change as new ideas were introduced. The case of José Joaquim de Azeredo Coutinho, however, demonstrates the difficulty inherent in efforts to compartmentalize and limit change. This respected, Brazilian-born intellectual, whose best-known work, *Economic Essay on the Commerce between Portugal and Her Colonies* (1794), clearly reflected up-to-date Enlightenment economic thought in its criticism of monopolies and government controls, founded the Seminary of Olinda in 1796. This institution subsequently played a crucial role in disseminating enlightened thought among priests, who in turn would play a substantial role in the revolt in 1817. Enlightened thought, especially the aspects of enlightened thought that challenged monarchical authority, had been conspicuous in the principal conspiracies against Portuguese rule in Minas Gerais in 1789 and in Salvador, Bahia, in 1798.[22]

By the second decade of the nineteenth century, ideas that challenged Portuguese absolutism, not only the works of eighteenth-century encyclopedists and their intellectual brethren but also republican ideas from revolutionary France and the increasingly successful United States, were penetrating Brazil far more deeply. In addition to the long tradition of students crossing the Atlantic to pursue education and travel, Brazilian-born merchants had increasing opportunities for European experience after the opening of the ports to international commerce. Books from Europe were more readily available after 1808. Printing presses were established in the royal court in 1808, in Bahia in 1811, and in Pernambuco in 1817. Particularly important was the influx of foreigners into Brazil after the transfer of the Portuguese royal court to Rio de Janeiro in 1808, an influx that accelerated again after the defeat of Napoleon in 1814. From 1808 to 1822, more than four thousand foreigners, largely professional men and artisans, registered in Rio de Janeiro alone. That number does not include their families or servants or the twenty-four thousand people that arrived from Portugal. In the port cities above all, a new intellectual climate was coming into being in which anti-absolutist assumptions were common currency and republicanism was not infrequent.[23]

Secret societies modeled on the Masonic lodges of Europe facilitated the spread of republican ideas. Early in the nineteenth century, "academies" sprang up in the major urban centers of Brazil. Masonic lodges linked to European, usually Portuguese, lodges spread especially rapidly after the opening of the ports in 1808. Both the informal groups and the Masonic lodges with their secrecy, rites, and ritual provided the space in which new ideas could be discussed and in which contacts could be made with like-minded people within one's own captaincy and across Brazil, as well as with the masons in Europe who were working to undermine absolutism.[24]

The first secret society in Pernambuco, the Areópago de Itambé, seems to have been formed in 1798 by Miguel Arruda da Câmara, a Carmelite friar, upon his return from studies in Europe. Members included Father João Ribeiro, Francisco de Paula Cavalcanti de Albuquerque, and his brother Luís Francisco de Paula Cavalcanti de Albuquerque. The latter two belonged to one of the most powerful families in the captaincy and in 1801 were arrested for the so-called Conspiracy of the Suassunas, an apparent conspiracy aimed at independence under French protection. After being cleared in 1802, the two formed a secret society, the Academy of Suassuna, on the estate of Francisco de Paula Cavalcanti de Albuquerque. Other founders of secret societies, all of whom also participated in the 1817 revolt, were Antônio Carlos Ribeiro de Andrada Machado a Silva (the Democratic University), Father João Ribeiro (Paradise Academy), Antônio Gonçalves da Cruz (Pernambuco of the Orient), and Domingos José Martins, a merchant with experience and Masonic contacts in Europe (Pernambuco of the Occident). Members of such societies were typically from the middle and upper sectors of society, priests, teachers, doctors, public employees, merchants, and planters. A French merchant in Recife at the time, Louis-François de Tollenare, wrote in his diary of the banquets at which lodge members ostentatiously disdained food and wine from Europe and offered toasts against royal tyranny and in favor of independence.[25]

The Frenchman's depiction illustrates the penetration of liberal European ideas into at least some sectors of Brazil. Such men often visited Tollenare, eager to discuss politics and learn of developments in French art, science, and philosophy. The Frenchman noted that one, João Ribeiro, was carried away with his readings of Marie Jean Antoine Nicolas Cartitat, Marquis de Condorcet, and demonstrated great confidence in the progress of the human spirit. Ribeiro was indignant at arbitrary actions and spoke of individual rights and the sovereignty of the people. He always took extreme positions, such as the necessity of passing through anarchy in order to achieve order. He began a private library to help spread the new ideas. To Tollenare, Ribeiro had lost his head over eighteenth-century French philosophers and was far ahead of his time in Brazil. Tollenare clearly distinguished Ribeiro from people like Domingos José Martins, whom the Frenchman believed to be cynical and opportunistic in his adoption of Jacobin manners and speech during the revolt of 1817.[26]

Pernambuco 1817: Challenging the Luso-Brazilian Empire

In March of 1817 a royal effort to crack down on political dissidents organizing in Masonic lodges in Pernambuco sparked the greatest challenge to Portuguese rule before independence. For some years Governor and Captain-General Caetano Pinto, like other governors, had tolerated secret lodges. He became concerned, however, when an officer of the black Henriques militia regiment beat a Portuguese-born individual for insulting Brazilians. Caetano Pinto alluded to tensions between Portuguese-born and Brazilian-born individuals in an order to the army on March 4. It is telling that the conflict occurred at a festival for Our Lady of Estança, which celebrated the defeat of the Dutch in the seventeenth century. This conflict was remembered as a demonstration of the self-assertion and glory of Pernambucans and would later be interpreted by some as the first stirrings of a national consciousness.[27]

In the first days of March rumors of a conspiracy against the government surfaced and Caetano Pinto issued arrest orders for five civilians and five military officers. On March 6 the Portuguese Brig. Gen. Manuel Joaquim Barbosa called a meeting of army officers and attempted to arrest one of the suspects, José de Barros Lima. The latter responded by drawing his sword and, with the assistance of another Brazilian-born officer, killed the Portuguese general. Caetano Pinto immediately sent his aide-de-camp, Alexandre Tomás de Aquino, to gather troops and arrest the two officers who had killed the general. Capt. Pedro da Silva Pedroso, however, when he saw Alexandre Tomás de Aquino, shouted, "Comrades! There is the enemy of Pernambuco and the cause of our misfortune; fire." Tomás fell dead and the troops were now in open rebellion. The French merchant Tollenare recorded in his diary three days after the

events that on March 3 rumors were spreading of a government crackdown on dissent. Noting the speed with which the revolt spread, the di-
arist speculated that word of the coming arrests was leaked to the conspirators, who then planned the uprising. José Carlos Mayrink da Silva
Ferrão, secretary of the government before, during, and after the revolt,
largely confirms this account in the detailed reconstruction of the events
he subsequently offered in defense of his actions.[28]

Governor Caetano Pinto and his family quickly went to the Brum
Fortress for safety, and he withdrew loyal troops from their posting and
gathered between 200 and 250 men inside the fortress. Some Portuguese
sought protection aboard ships anchored in the harbor. Meanwhile rebels
opened the prisons and released all the prisoners. Various prisoners proceeded to rampage through Santo Antônio and, joined by members of the
lower classes, both slave and free, attack the Portuguese. Shouts of "Mata
marinheiro!" (Kill the sailors! [i.e., the Portuguese]) were heard. About
fifty or sixty persons were killed, mainly Portuguese. Three Frenchmen
apparently mistaken for Portuguese also were killed. In contrast to the
prisoners, the rebels themselves, who soon controlled the city, appear
not to have engaged in indiscriminate violence.[29]

The rebels easily secured control of the entire city, with the exception
of the Brum Fortress, which the governor and his troops occupied. The
artillery officer Pedro Pedroso played an important role in the fighting,
defeating the men who were attempting to destroy the bridge that linked
Santo Antônio with the Bairro do Recife, where the remaining troops
loyal to the Portuguese authorities were gathered. That evening, rebel officers met with leading civilians and planned the attack on the governor's
position. In the morning eight hundred soldiers marched to the fortress.
A bloody battle was avoided, however, as an agreement was reached that
Caetano Pinto would turn over the fortress and that, in return, he and
his supporters would be sent on a ship to Rio de Janeiro.[30]

The Provisional Government
Large numbers of people soon gathered in the Campo do Erário and
cheered the leaders of the rebellion. Inside the treasury building, the leaders set to work creating a provisional government. At midday on March 7
a proclamation informed the population that a five-man provisional gov-

ernment had been established, composed of representatives from key sectors of elite society. The church was represented by João Ribeiro Pessoa de Melo Montenegro, the military by Capt. Domingos Teotônio Jorge Martins Pessoa, the judiciary by José Luiz de Mendonça, agriculture by Colonel Manuel Correia de Araújo, and commerce by Domingos José Martins. Among those signing the proclamation were Luís Francisco de Paula Cavalcanti and Francisco de Paula Cavalcanti, two brothers of the wealthy, prominent Cavalcanti family.[31]

Almost immediately conflict emerged within the provisional government. José Luiz de Mendonça raised the possibility of adopting a conciliatory attitude toward the royal government in Rio de Janeiro, one that would ensure continued loyalty to the monarch while communicating the reasons for the rebellion and requesting tax relief and new laws that would reduce the arbitrary actions of captains-general. Capt. Pedroso promptly drew his sword and threatened Mendonça's life. Accused of treason, the new representative of the judiciary backtracked. The following day he issued a statement of principles for the junta, which harshly denounced royal tyranny.[32]

Mendonça's initial indecisiveness and vacillation, followed the next day by his authorship of a repudiation of royal authority, raises the question of how to interpret the new government's declaration of a republic. One historian, Evaldo Cabral de Melo, has suggested that Mendonça was working with Antônio Carlos Ribeiro de Andrada and that they were left out of the initial conspiracy because of their preference for a constitutional monarchy. In any event, the rhetoric of the republican provisional government harshly attacked the despotism of the monarch. Oppressive taxation was one piece of evidence. This was all the more galling in that it ran roughshod over the special relationship Pernambuco was thought to have with the Bragança royal family by virtue of having expelled the Dutch from Portuguese America, with no assistance from Portugal, in the seventeenth century. Indeed, official documents from the provisional government routinely referred to the "Second Restoration of Pernambuco."

In opposition to despotism, supporters of the new regime referred to themselves as patriots. More than simply lovers of the *pátria*, they used the term of address to suggest associations with the French Revolution.

As in France the word evoked the unity of the French people in support of revolutionary principles, so in Pernambuco the term suggested support for a republic based on popular sovereignty, in opposition to royal tyranny. Royal symbols were torn from uniforms and from church facades. (Domingos José Martins went further, encouraging the systematic destruction of all the symbols of tyranny to erase them completely from memory.) As French revolutionaries had done, the patriots prohibited traditional forms of address that reinforced hierarchy and privilege and allowed only the use of the informal *vós*. New symbols of a republic, such as a flag, were established.[33]

The revolt can be seen in considerable part as a response to increasing control and taxation from Rio de Janeiro. A long list of new taxes had been imposed since 1808, affecting all sectors of the population. The rebels' first proclamation declared that people would be "free of the weight of enormous tribute that burdens you." The provisional government quickly declared its intention to abolish certain "taxes of manifest injustice." Among the earliest measures taken by the newly installed leaders was to reduce taxes on small shops and on sales of meat. An English traveler observed afterward that Pernambucans "were disgusted at the payments of taxes and contributions, by which they never profited, and which only served to enrich the creatures of the court." A participant in the revolt, Francisco Muniz Tavares, years later wrote of the heavy burden of taxation by alluding to the bad taste that was left from being "subject to sating the hunger of a mendicant Court." The new government quickly implemented several other popular measures, providing significant relief from interest payments on debts dating back to the era of Pombaline monopoly companies, increasing military salaries substantially, and approving a large number of promotions for military officers.[34]

Prominent figures served as advisors to the provisional government: Antônio Carlos Ribeiro de Andrada, a crown judge in Olinda at the time and a figure on the national stage for some years after independence, Antônio de Morais, whose intellectual accomplishments brought him a measure of fame in both Brazil and Portugal, the merchant Gervásio Pires Ferreira, who would play a leading role in Pernambucan political struggles in the independence and the immediate post-independence era, and Deacon and General Vicar Bernardo Luiz Ferreira Portugal, the highest church author in the region.[35]

The church provided strong support for the new government. A French traveler noted that it was common to see priests speaking with officials of the new government. Liberal tendencies had long been pronounced among the clergy, and pastoral letters forcefully supported the new regime. The vicar of Santo Antônio arranged for a Te Deum, with all the appropriate pomp and ritual, to demonstrate church adhesion to the new order. A proclamation from Deacon and General Vicar Bernardo Luiz Ferriera Portugal in Olinda asserted that it was a dogma of the holy religion that people should obey the constituted authorities and that failure to do was one of the most serious crimes that one could commit against God and the fatherland. Supportive priests were a valuable resource. The vicar of Itamaracá, Pedro de Sousa Tenório, for example, was encouraged by the government to keep an eye on a judge in Goiana whose loyalty was doubted. The priest ended up arming himself and a group of men to arrest the judge after his behavior aroused their suspicions. Tenório was hardly alone in his support for the provisional government; when royal authority was restored, forty-four priests were arrested for their support of the rebels.[36]

Given the animosity toward Portuguese-born individuals, the provisional government moved to reassure Portuguese merchants about their safety and the security of their property. The government thus hoped to avoid capital flight by the Portuguese, who held a commanding presence in commerce. A new judicial appointee in late March, for example, was instructed to "work without ceasing to inform yourself of people that . . . raise voices or in any way try to excite the people for any acts of violence against the persons or property of our compatriots born in Portugal." The bishopric issued a proclamation lamenting the "fatal indisposition" between Europeans and Brazilians and appealing to shared Christian faith for the "fraternity of all men."[37]

The Movement Spreads

Priests played an important role in extending the movement. In the two captaincies immediately to the north of Pernambuco, provisional governments in support of the rebels were quickly established. In the interior of Paraíba, for example, clergymen who had been exposed to liberal ideas as students in the Olinda seminary played a key role. In Rio Grande do Norte, a priest's energetic encouragement prompted a wealthy land-owner to arrest the governor who opposed the movement and to establish a provisional government. Another priest, José Martiniano de Alencar, carried news of the events farther north to Ceará. A native of Crato, Alencar hoped to use his ties of kinship and friendship in the area to win support for the secessionist bid. He was cheered with vivas when he rose to the pulpit during the festivities of a saint's day and read a proclamation from the provisional government in Recife. The crowds quickly dispersed, however, when word came of the imminent arrival of armed men who were coming to squash the movement. Alencar was quickly arrested. In the absence of any movement in support of the revolt in the interior of Ceará, the captaincy stayed secure in loyalist hands throughout the revolt in 1817.[38]

The provisional government entrusted José Ignácio Ribeiro de Abreu e Lima with the task of securing support to the south, in Alagoas and Bahia. Commonly known as Father Roma, by virtue of his having studied and been ordained in Rome, Ribeiro de Abreu e Lima was from a wealthy Pernambucan family. By 1807 he had left the priesthood, and he subsequently developed a well-respected legal practice. Father Roma embraced the revolt and was among those who participated in the selection of the provisional government.

Success in Bahia might have had a tremendous impact, substantially enlarging the scope of the challenge to royal authority. However, the royal government was vastly stronger in Bahia than in the captaincies to the north and was headed by the very able Governor-General Marcos de Noronha de Brito, the Count of Arcos, a former viceroy. Moreover, the authorities in Bahia had news of events in Recife and of Father Roma's imminent arrival, reportedly on a *jangada*.

The Count of Arcos took preventive measures. He had a proclamation distributed in Pernambuco denouncing the revolt. He began preparations for a military assault on the rebels. He had leading masons in Bahia under surveillance. Men were posted along the coast with instructions to search every vessel from Pernambuco. The distinctive cut of the sail common in Pernambuco made the *jangada* on which Father Roma arrived all the more conspicuous, and he was easily captured. The Count of Arcos immediately convoked a military tribunal, circumventing normal legal protections, and before any instructions could arrive from the royal court, he had Father Roma executed. Father Roma's son, José Ignácio de Abreu e Lima, imprisoned in Bahia at the time, was forced to witness the execution. (One might speculate about the impact this may have had on the son, who later fought for Spanish American independence under Bolívar, wrote as a liberal journalist in Pernambuco in the 1840s, and in the 1850s published one of the first books on socialism to appear in Brazil.) With Padre Roma's execution, the hopes of bringing Bahia into the breakaway republic died.[39]

The provisional government also sought support overseas. Antônio Gonçalves da Cruz, a wealthy Pernambucan with experience in Europe, traveled to the United States to buy arms and secure diplomatic recognition for the new government. In exchange, he offered twenty years of exemption from import and export duties to American merchants. Nothing came of the trip. The provisional government wrote to Hipólito José da Costa, the London-based editor of the influential newspaper *Correio Braziliense*, which circulated around Portugal and its empire. The rebel leaders hoped that with his support the movement might secure diplomatic recognition from Great Britain. This effort too was a failure. Hipólito José da Costa rejected the movement because of the threat he believed it posed to the unity of the Brazilian nation.[40]

Despite Father Roma's disastrous failure to bring Bahia into the secessionist movement and the rebuff of efforts to gain diplomatic support and military supplies overseas, the rapidity with which the movement had spread throughout Pernambuco and into several nearby captaincies must have encouraged those struggling for an independent republic. The crucial task at hand was to construct a fighting force that could withstand the royal armies that would be sent to crush the movement.

Mobilization for War

To have any hope of success, the provisional government would have to mobilize considerable popular support. This, inevitably, would bring the issue of slavery to the fore. Large numbers of slaves could potentially be mobilized for the republican cause. British Consul General Henry Chamberlain in Rio de Janeiro, presumably reflecting opinions expressed there, reported that if the blacks of the region were to join the struggle it would be pointless to estimate the magnitude of the ruin that would inevitably follow. Such mobilization, however, would surely alienate slave owners, who would see it as a threat to their ownership of human property. It also raised the specter of social conflagration and perhaps a "race war" if the mobilization were to escape elite control. The provisional government addressed these concerns in a provisional constitutional project that it circulated to the municipal councils. The proposed law's reference to legal equality nonetheless set off rumors of an impending abolition of slavery. The government promptly issued a proclamation affirming its support of both the equality of free men and the inviolability of property. The proclamation was meant to reassure slave owners that there would be no general abolition of slavery. Instead, the government suggested a slow, legal process to gradually eliminate slavery, which would include compensation for slave owners.

Another example of the government trying to mobilize resources without alienating slaveholders can be seen in its assurances that there would be no general mobilization of slaves, but that freedom from bondage would be offered to slaves who would enlist. Their owners were promised that a future indemnification would be paid. Even this limited effort provoked a backlash. One consul reported to his home government that the freeing of slaves to fight for the patriot cause was one of the sources of discontent with the provisional government. There was only limited mobilization of slaves, as few men followed the examples of Francisco de Paula Cavalcanti de Albuquerque and Domingos José Martins in leading armed slaves.

A similar tension between broad mobilization of support and elite discomfort with potentially upsetting the social and racial hierarchy can be observed in the issue of political representation. The French traveler Tollenare observed that government leaders were drawn to the French constitutions of 1791, 1793, and especially 1795. He noted, however, that the issue of political representation was problematic. The leaders were uncomfortable with a broad franchise that would give representation to men of color and preferred property qualifications based on property ownership to restrict the suffrage.[41]

Forming a credible fighting force was a considerable challenge. There were only two regiments of first-line troops in the captaincy, and the militia forces were generally ill equipped and poorly trained. Arms were in short supply. The provisional government requested that individuals owning weapons sell them at a fair price to the public authorities, but few responded to this call. Forming a naval force was not much more successful. A total of three ships, only one of which was armed, were enlisted, but there were no experienced naval officers to direct even that meager sea presence.

The patriot military efforts did not benefit from capable leadership that could mobilize resources and effectively deploy them. Immediately following the outbreak of the movement, for example, landowners from Igarassu, Pau d'Alho, and Limoeiro mobilized their clients and marched to Olinda to fight for the republic. Yet the government instructed them to return home. The poor decision may be explained by the chaos of the situation—or by the fact that the breakaway republic did not have many army officers to lead its men under arms. Most of the men directing the patriot forces were members of the elite who did not have military experience. Not surprisingly, their lack of training in the military arts led to poor decisions on the field of battle.[42]

Armed Struggle

The provisional government's effort to reinforce its southern territory of Alagoas is another example of poor leadership that damaged the republican cause. The government named José Mariano Cavalcanti the Military and Civilian Governor of the District of Alagoas and prepared to send him sixty infantry soldiers, twenty artillery men, and four pieces of artillery to strengthen the patriot presence there. The new district commander seemed irresolute and fearful of engaging the enemy. At Porto de Pedras his subordinate officers had to convince him of the strategic importance of holding the position. In battle José Mariano Cavalcanti appeared to panic, and he proved unable to maintain discipline among his men. He soon abandoned his troops and returned to Recife on a *jangada*. In the ensuing confusion, others also returned to Recife by boat and still others fled into the countryside where they were captured by royalist forces. Artillery pieces were simply abandoned. News of this defeat soon spread, further encouraging the counterrevolution in Alagoas, which had been fueled by royalist proclamations originating in Bahia.

After the royalists in the south seized the initiative at Porto de Pedras, they never relinquished it.

Meanwhile, before José Mariano Cavalcanti arrived back in Recife, the provisional government sent Capt. João do Rego Dantas south with eighty men to help counter the royalist actions in Alagoas. But by the time Capt. Rego Dantas had traveled the thirty miles to Ipojuca, people were unwilling to assist his troops. Royalist propaganda and the humiliating disaster at Porto de Pedras had undermined support for the rebels. He came to the conclusion that he had reached hostile, pro-royalist territory, opted not to advance further, and set up camp at a well-defended position in Barra Grande.[43]

In contrast, the governor-general of Bahia, the Count of Arcos, acted decisively. The former viceroy contained the revolt and pushed it back before additional troops and ships arrived from Rio de Janeiro. The governor-general sent several ships to blockade the port of Recife and sent an expedition of eight hundred men north by foot under the command of Marshal Joaquim de Melo Cogominho, augmented by a militia regiment from Sergipe. The governor-general also engaged in a propaganda campaign to encourage resistance to the revolt, issuing proclamations that appealed to the loyalty of the king's subjects. He attacked the character of the leaders of the revolt, proclaimed that Bahia was firmly royalist, and threatened severe punitive action against anyone siding with the revolt. Meanwhile, a military force was being formed in Rio de Janeiro. On April 2 Vice-Admiral Rodrigo Lôbo set sail from Rio de Janeiro, bound for Recife, with a frigate, two corvettes, and a schooner. He reinforced the blockade of the port and awaited the arrival of the invasion force from the royal court, which took longer to prepare. Rodrigo Lôbo then sent ships to patrol the coasts and spread more proclamations designed to drive a wedge between the population and the leaders of the revolt.[44]

The areas farthest from Recife were the first to restore royal government. In Rio Grande do Norte the provisional government, even at its inception, had not inspired the degree of popular enthusiasm witnessed in Recife. Faced with precarious finances, it instituted few changes that might have garnered it more support. In the end, a member of the provisional government turned against the patriot cause and led its overthrow.

Supporters of the republic did establish a new provisional government in the interior, in the Serra do Martins, but this proved short-lived.

In Paraíba defenders of the provisional government were more forceful in confronting challenges from royalists. Supporters of the royalist cause in the interior impeded the movement of cattle and foodstuffs to the capital and to Pernambuco, seriously disrupting food supplies. The French merchant Tollenare noted in mid-April that food was more expensive every day; in early May, he wrote that with roads from the interior cut off, there would soon be starvation. The provisional government of Paraíba was determined to reopen access to supplies from the interior. Believing the capital to be safe, Colonel Amaro Gomes Coutinho led the first-line troops into the interior of Paraíba. Pro-royalist crowds then took advantage of the light defense of the city and overran the government palace. Royalists quickly seized power. When Col. Gomes Coutinho approached the city, he saw that many of his men responded favorably to the restoration of royal authority. Fearful that they might rise against him, he opted to flee.[45]

While Alagoas, Rio Grande do Norte, and Paraíba had all fallen to the royalists, Recife and the nearby towns were still in republican hands. The provisional government in Recife named Francisco de Paula Cavalcanti as head of a force of four hundred men to aid the besieged forces of Capt. Rego Dantas in the south. "General Paula," as he was now called by virtue of receiving the title general, was a captain-major of the militia but had no military training or experience. His lack of military experience was soon obvious. Although known for strict discipline as a planter, he was unable to maintain firm control over his troops and was at times openly disobeyed. He nonetheless managed a victory in a five-hour battle at the Utinga estate, although he was later criticized for not pursuing the retreating enemy to inflict a more decisive defeat.[46]

By then, most of Pernambuco had been recovered by royalist forces. Only Recife and the nearby towns of Cabo, Igarassu, Itamaracá, and Goiana still held out. Although the provisional government still had four thousand men under arms, it sought in vain to win over more people to actively support the movement. Luís Francisco de Paula Cavalcanti had no more success than his brother General Paula in encouraging militia commanders to mobilize their men to fight against the royalist restoration. Domingos José Martins, the wealthy merchant and member of the provisional government, took men to reinforce General Paula, but Martins could not easily accept a subordinate position and taking orders, and he withdrew with his men. He in turn fell victim to an ambush and was captured. In the last battle of any significance, General Paula's three hundred men faced a force four times as large and were outmaneuvered by the royalist Marshal Joaquim de Melo Cogominho, whose scouts were effectively communicating enemy movements. Francisco de Paula managed to escape, but most of his troops were captured.[47]

With the end clearly near, the patriot leaders maneuvered to protect themselves. Only two of the members of the provisional government, Father João Ribeiro and Domingos Teotônio, continued in that capacity. Domingos José Martins had been captured, and the other two, José Luiz de Mendonça and Col. Manuel Correia de Araújo, feigned illness and stayed in their homes. This strategy was also employed by three of the advisors to the government: Antônio de Morais, Gervásio Pires, and Bernardo Luiz Ferriera Portugal. Soon an offer of surrender was sent to Vice-Admiral Rodrigo Lôbo, on the condition that the rebels receive a general amnesty. On May 18 his response made clear that he would not tolerate the conditions. "I have in my favor reason, the law, and armed forces on the land and sea to be able to enter Recife with a sword in my hand in order to punish . . . any patriot or unfaithful vassal, which are synonyms, for they have trampled on the sacred law of the King . . . [T]herefore, I can not accept any unworthy conditions."[48]

The governor of arms, Domingos Teotônio, immediately replied to Vice-Admiral Lôbo's letter with a threat to kill all the prisoners and then all the European-born, and then to burn down the city if an amnesty was not guaranteed. The desperation in such a threat is evident, all the more so considering that Domingos Teotônio did not even wait for a response but fled north of the city on May 19 with the government treasury and his troops, including the freed slaves who fought for him. Within five days all his troops had dispersed. On May 20 one thousand soldiers landed from the ships in the harbor. Patriot leaders who remained in the city pinned their hopes on a possible pardon. Luís Francisco de Paula Cavalcanti, for example, who was in charge of the Cinco Pontas fortress, released the royalist prisoners and opened the gates to the fortress when a crowd carrying the Portuguese flag approached. The revolt was effectively over. On May 23 thousands more soldiers arrived from Bahia.[49]

Several days of disorder followed, as the released prisoners celebrated their freedom by drinking, shooting guns, and shouting vivas. Rewards were publicized for the capture of the rebel leaders, all of whom were captured in short order, with the exception of João Ribeiro, who committed suicide. To the end, João Ribeiro acted consistently with his beliefs, sending a note to the French merchant Tollenare that he could rest assured that he (Ribeiro) would know how to die a free man. The Frenchman noted in his diary that Ribeiro was an honest man, "but one hallucinating with the reading of our [France's] eighteenth-century philosophers."[50]

Reprisals

The idealistic former priest may have died free, but his body was used to illustrate the cost of rebellion. His cadaver was dug up, the head and hands severed and publicly displayed. The property of leading patriots, including perhaps as many as forty-four sugar plantations, was seized. Likewise, an example was made of slaves who temporarily earned their freedom by fighting for the patriot cause. Before they were returned to their owners they were publicly whipped two hundred to three hundred times, often until the flesh of their buttocks was ripped open, in what a French observer labeled a "pungent spectacle" that attracted many spectators. Likewise, the authorities undertook a general reestablishing of the racial order. The future governor-general of the captaincy, Luiz do Rego Barreto, later referred to the Haitian Revolution to evoke the fear and horror among the elites. He explained that some "men of color embraced the rebel cause in an excessive and insulting manner and reminded the inhabitants of this captaincy of the scenes of Saint Domingue. The men of this abject class, the same beggars who insulted their gentlemen and lady benefactors and promised, utterly shamelessly, to soon possess a lady. . . . This degree of arrogance was formidable." He could hardly have been clearer, invoking a racialized sexual threat, in condemning the challenge to the established hierarchies. He noted with satisfaction that the interim governor promptly had such men whipped, a practice Luiz do Rego Barreto continued.[51]

Hundreds of people were soon arrested for their support of the republican cause. As the cells in the Cinco Pontas fort filled, new arrivals were held in ships and then shipped off to Bahia. Prisoners were paraded through town to the accompaniment of military music. Antônio Carlos, Pedroso, José Mariano, and Friar Joaquim Caneca were singled out for especially humiliating treatment, having heavy metal weights attached around their necks. Domingos José Martins, José Luiz de Mendonça, and one other were hanged shortly after they arrived in Salvador.[52]

On June 29, 1817, Luiz do Rego Barreto arrived in Recife. He officially took office as governor-general in a ceremony witnessed by five thousand men under arms, including the first-line forces of Pernambuco and the militia, the military forces of Bahia that had yet to return there, and the units that arrived with the new governor. The first group, composed of men who had been on duty during the revolt, was gathered to watch the execution of Antônio Henriques and then promptly loaded on ships to leave the captaincy. The new governor established and presided over a military commission to try the prisoners. In short order, three more leaders were executed, including Father Pedro de Sousa Tenório and Domingos Teotônio. Like João Ribeiro before them, their heads were severed and publicly displayed and left to decompose. On August 21 and September 6 five leaders of the republican movement in Paraíba mounted the gallows. After being severed, their heads and hands were taken back to Paraíba for public display. Scores of prisoners, meanwhile, had their property seized.[53]

Display of the mutilated body parts was only one aspect of the public demonstration of royal power. There was a lengthy public ritual that involved a procession to take the condemned, with ropes around their necks, from the prison to the gallows. The governor-general, dressed in red and carrying a candle, rode in front, accompanied by soldiers, brotherhoods with their flags flying, a judge dressed in the black of mourning and carrying a copy of the judgment and death sentence, and long lines of priests reciting prayers. The procession stopped for mass at five altars along the way. The entire spectacle was witnessed by large crowds in the streets and people watching from their balconies.[54]

Soon a court with civilian judges was established to try the remainder of the cases. Although the court heard only witnesses for the prosecution, it still moved slowly. In 1819 it released a few prisoners, but several hundred others were sent to Bahia. There another court gathered evidence and heard cases. Justice continued to proceed slowly, although a few more men were pardoned each month. The large majority regained their freedom only in 1821, when the governor of the captaincy was overthrown in support of the liberal regency in Lisbon. The only two to face further punishment were Pedroso and José Mariano, who were sentenced to lifelong banishment in the Portuguese prisons of Asia for having murdered a military officer in the first hours of the revolt.[55]

The 1817 revolt was the first time that a broad section of society had openly defied the Bragança monarchy. Neither the Inconfidência Mineira (1788–89) nor the Tailors' Conspiracy in Bahia (1798) nor the dubious possible conspiracies in Rio de Janeiro (1794) and Pernambuco (1801) had mounted any serious challenge to Portuguese rule. Profound changes had occurred by 1817. Governor and Captain-General Caetano Pinto's efforts on March 6 to crack down on a military conspiracy led to a military revolt that quickly found support among the planter elite, the Brazilian-born merchant community, the clergy, petty officials, and large numbers of the free, often mixed race, skilled artisans and literate persons of limited means.

Motives among such socially heterogeneous groups were no doubt quite mixed (although everyone was burdened by heavy taxation.) Enlightenment thought, and specifically republicanism, had been strengthened by the influx of Europeans after the transfer of the royal court in 1808. The possibilities of greater social mobility suggested by the new ideas must have appealed greatly to many skilled people of modest means. Among merchants the "ostentatious republicanism" of Domingos José Martins might not have been typical, but the threats to their interests posed by continuing metropolitan restrictions provided reason to hope for severing the imperial tie. Prominent planters—men as powerful and prestigious as Francisco Paes Barreto, the future Marquis of Recife, and Francisco de Paula Cavalcanti de Albuquerque—may have been particularly concerned about royal threats to their autonomy and control over affairs in Pernambuco.[56] Like their counterparts around the North Atlantic world, they saw in notions of popular sovereignty and representative government a viable basis for an elite project that would ensure their prominence while diminishing outside interference from the royal court in Rio de Janeiro. Clearly, they expected to leave unrealized the leveling potential that such ideas offered to free men of more limited means, especially free men of color. The tension between broad mobilization and maintaining the social order was most clear in the issue of arming slaves. While the provisional government made tentative steps in this direction, offering freedom to slaves who enlisted and future compensation to owners, it immediately backtracked and guaranteed slave owners support for their property rights. Broad mobilization for military victory gave way to the defense of the racial order and rights to human property.

It would be a mistake to only highlight the innovations of 1817. The calls for "*Pátria*, Religion, and Liberty," for example, clearly suggest traditionalist elements in the movement. The church blessed the new government and saw forty-four of its priests arrested when it was defeated. The prominence of the church suggests the transitional nature of the movement, a fusion of old and new. The church itself was a mixture of old and new—traditionalist in some respects, yet a vehicle for enlightened thought. (Indeed, among the papers of the Deacon and General Vicar Bernardo Luiz Ferreira Portugal is evidence suggesting that the vicar intended to urge the king to accept a constitution.)

Repudiation of royal despotism was accompanied by emphasis on popular sovereignty. Based on this concept, the new government prepared a provisional constitutional project for consideration by the municipal councils, the centerpiece of which was a call for a Constituent Assembly to write a constitutional charter.[57]

In hindsight, the call for constitutional government in 1817 appears simply to have been premature, but only barely. Across the Atlantic that same year, a subversive movement for constitutional government, the Gomes Freire Andrade conspiracy, took hold in the Portuguese military. In 1820 a constitutional movement within the military would prevail and force a reformulation of the monarchy along constitutional lines. But what of the efforts to create an independent republic? This seems less deeply rooted. In an armed struggle against a royal government seen as tyrannical, proponents of republicanism and secession came to the fore. What were the realistic alternatives to such a platform? The rebels in Porto in 1820 could threaten João with the loss of his throne in Portugal, but the

1817 rebels in Pernambuco had no such leverage. Perhaps for lack of any viable alternative, supporters of a republic were well positioned to carry the day. Likewise, what of independence? Regional elites clearly sought autonomy, which would allow them to enjoy a dominant position, and everyone suffered from the heavy hand of the royal court in Rio de Janeiro when it demanded tax revenue. But was there strong commitment to outright independence? Again, it seems that once an armed movement erupted, the goal of secession was nearly inevitable. One could hardly risk life and limb (and a severed head) in the hope that an absolute monarch would willingly negotiate a new distribution of power that would codify the loss of some of his power. A movement for independence, moreover, was far from arbitrary, as it drew on a commitment to the pátria.[58] A proclamation from the provisional government clearly communicated the importance of the *pátria* at the same time that it acknowledged multiple identities. "The *pátria* is our common mother, you are her sons, descendents of valorous Lusitanians, you are Portuguese, you are Americans, you are Brazilians, you are Pernambucans."[59] Appealing to the *pátria* of Pernambuco seemed a viable strategy.

José Luiz de Mendonça, a member of the provisional government, hesitated at the prospect of armed rebellion and suggested recourse to the time-tested stratagem of resistance not to the king but to his agents. But that smacked of surrender and could not serve as the basis of a movement. Tollenare notes that in the first days the leaders only whispered among themselves of a republic, for fear of alienating support for the movement.[60] It seems that independence and a republic, while they had some support, were ultimately adopted out of strategic necessity. If the king was to be rejected, then a republic could be built on the solid ground of commitment to the *pátria*. A federation with like-minded neighboring *pátrias* would provide strength.

The crown crushed the republican, secessionist attempt in 1817. Yet the ground was quickly shifting beneath the feet of the Portuguese authorities. Military conspirators in Portugal and the boldness of rebels in Pernambuco, Paraíba, Rio Grande do Norte, and Ceará who were willing to repudiate monarchy altogether must have been deeply disturbing, regardless of the relative ease with which these subversive movements were repressed. The limited social mobilization, the small number of captaincies involved, and the largely autonomous movements (each based on separate, although allied, *pátrias*) all worked against the success of the challenge to royal authority. Were any of these limitations to change, a far greater challenge to Portuguese rule might be mounted. Moreover, the experience of having seized arms and challenged royal authority once might well have made the resort to armed actions easier to imagine in the future.

The crown response to the republican movement for independence was harsh. The international context, in which Spain was struggling against independence movements in its American empire, must have been much on the minds of leading government figures. Nonetheless, Luiz do Rego Barreto, the Portuguese governor-general of Pernambuco, recognized the dangers of excessively broad repression. In his memoirs he described the state of Pernambuco upon his arrival as "a theater of vengeance" and a "system of terrorism" guided by the "incontestable principal that the total destruction of all the accomplices and adherents of the republican party was a meritorious act before God and the King." The governor-general was sharply critical of the tribunal established in Pernambuco and accused the presiding judge, Bernardo Teixeira, of aiming to "reduce the town of Recife to ashes" in order to "crush once and for all the seed of discord." In a letter he wrote that Bernardo Teixeira's error was to "look at everyone as a rebel." Luiz do Rego Barreto argued for more selective punishment and efforts at reconciliation; despite this, many critics still accused him of despotism and tyranny. The repression, shutting down of secret societies and lodges, and stationing additional troops from Portugal in Pernambuco (as well as Bahia and Rio de Janeiro) did little to quell discontent. Nor were reforms introduced to minimize sources of conflict. The inflexibility of Tomás Antônio de Vilanova Portugal, King João VI's chief minister, has led one historian to judge him the most reactionary of all of Dom João's ministers. Nonetheless, despite the discontent, it would take dramatic events in Europe to set in motion the events that would lead to a political separation from Portugal.[61]

2

Independence, Regional Rebellion, and the Struggle over the State, 1820–31

By 1820 the foundations of Portuguese absolutism had been greatly weakened. Sustained economic difficulties provided fertile soil for an explicit challenge to the absolutist traditions of the Bragança monarchy. The military took the lead, allied with powerful mercantile interests, in threatening João with a loss of his throne if he failed to return to Portugal and cooperate with the creation of a constitutional regime. The Revolution of 1820, or the "Regeneration," was a period of reform to update the institutions of the monarchy along constitutional lines and, its supporters hoped, lead to the recovery of prosperity.

In Portuguese America, the Revolution of 1820 was widely embraced. The impact was dramatic—the abandonment of absolutism shattered long-established political assumptions and ushered in struggles over new "rules of the game." Within two years the political ties that bound together Portugal and Portuguese America were severed, although that was probably not a common goal in Brazil in 1820. Political conflict that lasted until mid-century can be seen as a working out of new rules, along with attendant institutions, and the formation of new identities that reflected the political communities that were being forged.

In early 1821 provincial juntas that claimed popular support began emerging across Brazil. Elections were held to select representatives to the Portuguese Cortes to participate in writing the new constitution. In

Pernambuco the municipal councils selected figures sympathetic to the 1817 revolt. Meanwhile, in the northern city of Goiana, opponents of Captain-General Luiz do Rego Barreto established a governing junta that declared itself the legitimate government. The Junta of Goiana promptly demonstrated its superiority in force of arms. Luiz do Rego Barreto soon received instructions to organize elections for a new provincial junta and to subsequently return to Portugal. In late October, an 1817 rebel, Gervásio Pires Ferreira, won the election. The captain-general's return to Portugal along with many Portuguese troops marked the end of the Lisbon Cortes's ability to impose its will in Pernambuco.

In many captaincies across Brazil there was a strong commitment to avoiding domination by any distant center of power. In Pernambuco, as the ability of Portugal to control affairs had sharply declined, the captaincy enjoyed a high degree of autonomy. That freedom of action, however, was potentially threatened both by the Cortes's increasingly clear intention to reassert control over Portuguese America and by Prince Pedro's government. In Rio de Janeiro, José Bonifácio de Andrada e Silva led the defiance of the Portuguese Cortes. A wide range of planters, merchants, government employees, and professional men in Rio de Janeiro, São Paulo, and Minas Gerais supported José Bonifácio in his efforts to maintain a strong seat of government authority in Brazil (even if not all supported his vision of a strongly centralized system.) There was, in effect, a competition between Pedro's government in Rio de Janeiro and the Lisbon Cortes; whichever of the two offered the prospect of greater autonomy was likely to secure the support of the far-flung provinces. Across Brazil, buoyed by the prospect of a constitutional regime based in Rio de Janeiro, most provinces sided with Pedro when the prince regent called for Brazilian independence on September 7, 1822.

There were considerable debates over the contours of a new political system and the appropriate extent of popular participation. Yet the political struggles in this period were not only intra-elite affairs. In the court and in capital cities across Brazil, popular mobilizations were becoming a common tactic to pressure governments. Lower-class men had been mobilized for armed struggle in Pernambuco in 1817 and in diverse areas of Brazil from 1821 to 1823. Rioting and looting that victimized Portuguese businesses and Portuguese-born persons had erupted in various cities. Such experiences must have made it easier to imagine seizing arms to pursue one's goals. In February of 1823 the military governor of Pernambuco, Pedro da Silva Pedroso, led a revolt of black and mulatto military men and seized control of Recife. White elites fled the city as their long-standing fears of a race war along the lines of the Haitian Revolution seemed nearer fulfillment. The revolt was put down in a little over a week, and in hindsight it was probably not nearly the radical assault on the social order that the elites and others feared. Nonetheless, the "Pedrosada" illustrates the unpredictable possibilities opened up by political struggle, increasing popular political participation, and mobilization of men for armed conflict.

In May 1823 representatives from across Brazil gathered in Rio de Janeiro to write a constitutional charter. At issue was the locus of authority. Would representative institutions express popular sovereignty or did the emperor, as the direct embodiment of the nation, have final authority? Would provincial governments have ample authority or would the central government exert decisive influence across the country? In the end, the deliberations of the Constituent Assembly came to naught, as Emperor Pedro forcibly closed the assembly and chose his own Council of State to write the new constitution. It was a course of action that left Pedro the target of bitterness and suspicion that he would never overcome.

Alienation from Pedro and his project of a centralized empire, a project that for many was all too reminiscent of Portuguese absolutism, was so great that the governing junta in Pernambuco, along with neighboring provinces, attempted a republican secessionist movement (the Confederation of the Equator). Military suppression of the 1824 Confederation of the Equator, however, was fairly rapid. The consequences of defeat were predictable—exemplary punishment for leaders and the handing over of power across the province to Pedro's allies. Also noteworthy in this period was the clear evidence of a significant split between the Pernambucan elites to the north and the south of Recife, a split that is essential to understanding provincial politics up to mid-century.

Pedro's constitution, the 1824 Constitution, named both the emperor and the General Assembly (the Senate and the Chamber of Deputies) representatives of the Brazilian nation; in practice, however, the substantial "moderating power" that the emperor enjoyed gave him the decisive role in the political system. He could dismiss the Chamber of Deputies and call for new elections, choose and dismiss cabinet members, select members of the Senate from lists of the three candidates with the most votes in provincial elections, suspend judges, and veto legislation. He was virtually unchecked by the judiciary. Despite his strong position, however, the emperor still needed the cooperation of the General Assembly. This he did not receive. The arbitrary manner in which he had dismissed the Constituent Assembly, and the suspicions it aroused across Brazil among men who sought to avoid domination from Rio de Janeiro, set the tone for Pedro's reign.

The key institutional conflict revolved around the role of cabinet members. The emperor named ministers, but were they accountable to the Chamber? With Pedro unwilling to acquiesce in greater power sharing, and with no store of good faith on which to draw, he was unable to push through his programs. Even powerful figures who had benefited from Pedro's support, men such as the Pernambucan Holanda Cavalcanti, proved obstructionist. By the late 1820s, radical liberals in Pernambuco were emboldened to attempt an overthrow of the provincial government. The loss of the Cisplatine province, harsh attacks on the ministers who had suspended the constitution in their rush to punish the rebels in Pernambuco, an apparent incompetence in handling public finances, and perhaps, to some small degree, the inspiration derived from the 1830 July Revolution in France all contributed to the final crisis. In the end, Pedro, raised in the absolutist traditions of the Bragança monarchy, was unwilling to continue a fight that he perhaps thought beneath him, a fight he was unlikely to win as even his military officers deserted him. If so many Brazilians would not accept his leadership, he would abdicate and return to Portugal to fight for his daughter's claim to the Portuguese throne.

The Porto Revolution

In 1820 economic conditions were depressed in Portugal. Part of the difficulty stemmed from an inability to compensate for the loss of control over trade with Brazil in 1808. The weak state of the economy was reflected in poor government finances, which in turn led to military salaries eight months in arrears. In the midst of such difficulties, and despite the defeat of Napoleon and the withdrawal of his occupying army, the king and the seat of royal government remained in the Americas. In August of 1820 the military rose in revolt in Porto, the second largest city in Portugal and one whose economy was heavily oriented toward overseas trade. Soon the military in Lisbon rose as well. Mercantile interests played a leading role in what became known as the Porto Revolution. By the end of the year leaders of the liberal Regeneration of 1820 movement were ruling Portugal through a provisional junta, demanding the return of Dom João VI from Brazil, and preparing to establish a new basis for the monarchy. A constituent assembly (the Cortes Gerais Extraordinárias e Constituintes, or Cortes), composed of elected representatives from around the Portuguese world, would write a constitution.[1]

Many in Brazil welcomed the Porto Revolution and the liberal, constitutional regime it offered. Faced with royal equivocation, often it was military troops, and especially Portuguese troops, that took the initiative to push for the new order. On January 1, 1821, Portuguese soldiers in Belém, Pará, mounted an uprising and established a liberal governing junta that would organize elections to the Cortes in Lisbon. On February 10 it was Brazilian artillery officers who first took up arms in opposition to the old absolutist order in Bahia. The governor-general was overthrown and a governing junta took his place. An uprising of Portuguese military troops in Rio de Janeiro on February 26 prompted Dom João to call for provincial juntas to organize elections to the Cortes. This demonstration by military troops was noteworthy not only because it secured João's commitment to the constitution that was to be written but also because it established the streets of the court as a public place from which to pressure the government. Moreover, the king's son Pedro had played a role in resolving the conflict, an act that suggested his possible importance as a political actor and ally.

Although the military took the initiative in each of these cases, support for the liberal constitutionalism of the Porto Revolution was far broader than just among the men in arms. João's approval of the new arrangements eased the way for elections to be organized across Brazil. After much intrigue among supporters and opponents of the king's return to Portugal, the monarch soon acceded to demands from the Cortes. The risk of losing Portugal was too great for him; leaving Pedro in Rio de Janeiro to rule as the prince regent during his absence, Dom João set sail for Lisbon on April 26, 1821. The king was well aware of the likelihood of grave conflict if the government in Lisbon attempted to reassert control over Brazil. Indeed, reflecting on a possible bid for independence, he gave the remarkable advice to his son before leaving, "Pedro, if Brazil breaks away, let it rather do so for you who will respect me than for one of those adventurers."[2]

Pernambuco and the Revolution of 1820: Captain-General Luiz do Rego Barreto

The Revolution of 1820 undermined the traditional, absolutist basis of royal authority. A period of great fluidity ensued in which the old rules no longer applied and broader sections of society seized opportunities to participate in the political system. Across Brazil, political competition sharpened in this period of unprecedented openness, as the Revolution of 1820 moved toward establishing the basis for liberal constitutionalism. In Pernambuco, Captain-General Luiz do Rego Barreto warily adapted to these changing circumstances with strong determination to maintain the integrity of Portuguese America. When word arrived of the military action in Bahia, he declared support for the Cortes regime in Lisbon. On March 26, 1821, news reached Pernambuco that the monarch had sworn loyalty to the constitution to be written. Within five days the captain-general named a junta constitucional governista (constitutional governing junta) to bolster the legitimacy of his position. On May 29 Luiz do Rego, like leaders in other captaincies, swore to uphold the constitution that was to be written. On June 7, 1821, seven deputies and two alternates were selected to represent Pernambuco in the Cortes. They soon embarked and were the first representatives from Brazil to arrive in Lisbon. Most had been supportive of the rebellion in 1817; indeed, Francisco Muniz Tavares, who had spent several years in prison in Bahia for his role in the failed independence bid, was among those selected. Another participant in 1817, Antônio Carlos Ribeiro de Andrada, was selected from São Paulo. Cipriano Barata, a conspirator in Bahia in 1798 who supported the 1817 prisoners incarcerated in Bahia, was chosen from Bahia.[3]

The captain-general navigated these novel and uncertain conditions backed by the powerful Algarves Battalion, which was led by Portuguese-born officers. Yet he knew that force alone was insufficient. Luiz do Rego made concerted efforts to reconcile with the rebels of 1817, paying many of them back salaries and offering a return to the positions they had held previously. These efforts were to no avail in diminishing hostility toward the official who had carried out harsh sentences in the aftermath of the 1817 rebellion. In his memoirs Luiz do Rego made his frustration clear; the prisoners of 1817, upon their return from Bahia, were hailed as victims and martyrs of liberty. Their arrival emboldened opponents of the administration. Disturbances in the streets at night, attacks on people who had testified against participants in the 1817 rebellion, and constant denunciations of Luiz do Rego's actions as despotic all undermined his authority. He complained that members of the governing constitutional junta were depicted as "timid slaves before me, their tyrant." In this context of open hostility, conspirators plotted the assassination of the captain-general.[4]

On July 21 several would-be assassins waited beneath bridges where they expected the captain-general to pass. João de Souto Maior, who along with several of his brothers had served time in prison in Bahia for fighting for the rebels in 1817, fired on Luiz do Rego at nearly point-blank range. The captain-general survived the attack; forty-two suspects were deported to Lisbon and another thirteen were sent to the island prison of Fernando de Noronha.[5]

While Luiz do Rego recovered from his gunshot wounds, plotters were organizing an effort to drive him from power. On August 29, 1821, members of the municipal council of Goiana selected a provisional government known as the Junta of Goiana. This junta immediately dismissed Portuguese-born military officers. The main initiative appears to have come from the planter elite, principally from the regions north of Recife. The president of the junta, Francisco de Paula dos Santos, and the secretary, Filipe Mena Calado da Fonseca, both had served time in prison in Bahia for their participation in the 1817 republican independence bid. Captain-General Luiz do Rego responded to this challenge to his authority by calling a meeting of the municipal council of Recife, leading officers of the militia, and high government authorities. This group, in the hopes of winning support for the government, selected a new governing junta and named Luiz do Rego as its president.[6]

In the ensuing struggle for power the Junta of Goiana successfully mobilized support across the captaincy, while Captain-General Luiz do Rego's forces suffered continual defections. In a strong position, the junta refused Luiz do Rego's September 4 offer of peace and his promises to convoke a congress to select a new government. Indeed, taking the title of the Governo Constitucional Temporário (Temporary Constitutional Government), the Junta of Goiana proceeded to act as the legitimate government, claiming to operate in accordance with instructions from the king and the Cortes in Lisbon that governing juntas be formed in the captaincies until the constitution was completed. In its first meeting on September 2 it shrewdly granted pay raises for soldiers and offered positions in its armed forces to any officers who deserted Luiz do Rego's forces.[7]

The largest battle was fought on September 21, 1821. A northern column attacked Olinda as a southern column came under canon fire from the Cinco Pontas fort as it attacked Recife. Despite the arrival of three hundred men from Bahia who reinforced Luiz do Rego, the Junta of Goiana was in a strong position, with two thousand men under arms and desertions weakening their opponents. Finally, following a battle in Afogados, Recife was surrounded and cut off.[8]

On October 5 Captain-General Luiz do Rego acknowledged his difficult position and signed an armistice. The agreement, the Beberibe Convention, provided for two separate governments, one for Recife and Olinda, loyal to Luiz do Rego, and the other led by the Junta of Goiana and the municipalities that followed its lead. Soon instructions from the Cortes arrived and Luiz do Rego was directed to hand power over to the new junta when it was selected and to return to Portugal. The elections were held on October 26 and Gervásio Pires Ferreira, a rebel in 1817, was voted president. Captain-General Luiz do Rego sailed for Portugal the same day, accompanied by many of the Portuguese troops stationed in Pernambuco. In January the Algarves Battalion returned to Portugal as well. By the time the Cortes regime rethought the wisdom of removing so many soldiers from Pernambuco it was too late. When reinforcements of Portuguese troops arrived, Gervásio Pires and the junta denied them permission to come ashore, arguing that the presence of Portuguese troops would lead to disturbances and upset public order. Portuguese control of Pernambuco had been dealt a serious blow, one from which it would never recover. When the English traveler Maria Graham left Recife on October 14, 1821, she accurately sized up what had transpired. She wrote, "We leave Pernambuco, with a firm persuasion that this part of Brazil at least will never again tamely submit to Portugal. Where the firmness and conduct of Do Rego have failed to hold the captaincy in obedience, it will be in vain for other governors to attempt it."[9]

The conflict between the captain-general and the Junta of Goiana is also of considerable interest in revealing an emerging fault line between Pernambucan elites. In 1817 there had been differences over the extent of social mobilization, especially over the wisdom of mobilizing slaves, for the war effort in support of the patriot cause. There were not, however, distinct elite factions struggling with each other to impose their particular political vision. On the whole, the elites acted fairly cohesively in challenging royal authority. In contrast, in 1821, and in the 1824 Confederation of the Equator, a key fissure opened up among the elite. This split would be of signal importance to politics in Pernambuco in the three decades after independence.

Marcus Carvalho has demonstrated that the politically significant division that was emerging was between the coastal elites north of Recife and those in the richer coastal area south of the capital city. The northern coast was an area of more recent settlement. Drier conditions there allowed cotton and sugar cane cultivation. The region first prospered during the cotton boom of the late eighteenth century. In contrast, the more humid coastal zone to the south of Recife was superior for sugar cane and was among the first regions of Portuguese America to see sugar cultivation in the early colonial period. Here planters took advantage of the superior soil and rainfall to enrich themselves by growing cane. A wealthy elite emerged that was well connected to the government.

Although the split between the northern and southern elites is not perfectly clear-cut, the usefulness of viewing the north and the south as politically distinct is apparent when one observes the continuity in the composition of the rival political groupings over time. Individuals associated with these two groups contested state power from the independence struggles of 1821 and 1822 to the Praieira Revolution near mid-century. By the time of the 1824 Confederation of the Equator, the split in the Pernambucan elites was clear. Francisco Paes Barreto and the Cavalcantis, wealthy and prestigious landowners in Cabo, south of Recife, led one elite fraction. Gervásio Pires Ferreira provided leadership for the northern elite during the Junta of Goiana period, and Manuel de Carvalho Paes de Andrade led during the Confederation of the Equator. In 1817 large numbers of the Pernambucan elites had acted to throw off rule from afar; indeed, all the leaders just named took up arms. By 1824 the wealthier, well-connected elites of the south saw the utility in calling on imperial authorities to shore up their threatened positions in Pernambuco. They were unable to defeat the government of Manuel de Carvalho on their own. With troops from Rio de Janeiro, however, the Confederation of the Equator was crushed. As much as they desired autonomy for themselves, it was a lesson they would not forget.[10]

Rio de Janeiro and the Revolution of 1820

Between May and September of 1821 elections to the Cortes were held across Portuguese America. The majority of the men selected had been born in Brazil and three had fought in the 1817 republican independence bid in Pernambuco. Although in hindsight historians of Brazil have seen the significance of the Cortes in its efforts to re-subordinate Brazil to the status of a Portuguese colony, that objective was not immediately apparent to contemporaries. Indeed, the undermining of royal power in Rio de Janeiro by the Cortes in Lisbon offered greater autonomy to the provisional juntas that had emerged in the wake of the constitutionalist uprising in Bahia in February 1821. Of course, sending representatives to contribute to writing the new constitution also offered the prospect of political participation. The deputies sailed for Lisbon with the hopes of helping to negotiate a new social contract, one that would both allow them to remain part of the Luso-Brazilian empire and create the institutional basis for a reasonable degree of autonomy.

Roderick Barman argues against teleological interpretations that view the emergence of a Brazilian nation-state as the inevitable outcome of this process. He has emphasized that for local elites the main focus of political loyalty was the *pátria*, the community with which one most closely identified and which typically encompassed a captaincy or province (or an even smaller area), not the nascent nation-state of Brazil. Barman sees it as a mistake to conceptualize the independence struggle as simply a battle between Portugal, working through the Lisbon Cortes, and Brazil, defended by the prince regent and government in Rio de Janeiro. Rather, there was a struggle between these two governments to secure the backing of the many *pátrias*, which by June 1821 enjoyed significant autonomy. Whichever government offered greater autonomy would have the upper hand.[11]

It is not easy to confirm exactly when a broad movement emerged with the clear goal of achieving political independence. Complicating any assessment are the conflicting agendas of those who sought to construct a centralized monarchy ruled by Pedro in Rio de Janeiro and those who prized autonomy and consequently sought a federalist foundation for any new political system. The demand from the Cortes that Dom João VI return to Lisbon provoked a wide-ranging opposition and marked an important step in the alienation from Portugal. The landed elite had little interest in seeing the Lisbon regime reestablish dominance over Brazil. Planters from the expanding economy of Rio de Janeiro, many of whom benefited from political influence in the nearby court, had even more to lose if Brazil were to be subordinated to Portugal. Powerful mercantile interests in Rio de Janeiro had prospered over the previous decades, especially with the transfer of the court. The growth of Rio de Janeiro, Minas Gerais, and São Paulo allowed both large-scale merchants who did well in the trans-Atlantic trade, especially trade in humans from Africa, and smaller merchants who did well in linking the court with the interior to prosper and to rise socially. Many successful figures in the former group secured status and influence within ruling circles as they received royal appointments and honors. Joined by Portuguese merchants who had prospered in Brazil, they were a powerful force that would resist any effort to reestablish a privileged position for Portugal. Brazilian-born government employees were joined by many of the Portuguese-born, whether judges, bureaucrats, or other government employees (some as high-ranking as the statesman Tomás Antônio de Vilanova Portugal), court hangers-on, teachers, or professionals who had established roots in Brazil and now saw their interests in this side of the Atlantic and did not want the seat of government to be reestablished in Europe. Facing the imminent return of João VI to Portugal, radicals and well-connected figures in the court attempted a coup on April 21–22, 1821, to try to keep João in Brazil. The disparate groups had different long-term goals, but they shared a common interest in the king remaining in Rio de Janeiro. The plotters' effort to seize control of a meeting of Rio de Janeiro's electors to choose deputies to the Lisbon Cortes and pressure João was easily defeated. Four days later, on April 26, João set sail for Portugal, leaving Pedro, as regent, in charge of the Brazilian kingdom. Those who had sought João's permanence in Rio immediately transferred their hopes to the prince-regent Pedro.

In early December 1821 news arrived from Lisbon that pushed many individuals to the point of open defiance of Portuguese authority. The Cortes had decreed the dismantling of the governing institutions established in Rio de Janeiro in 1808. It further created the post of *governador das armas* (military governor) in the captaincies, which created authorities that were directly responsible to Lisbon. In addition, Prince Regent Pedro was ordered to return to Lisbon immediately.

Diverse groups in Rio de Janeiro and São Paulo pressured Pedro to ignore the order to return as the best means to retain their autonomy from rule across the ocean. Politicians, elite figures, the press, and a petition drive that garnered eight thousand signatures joined together in an effort to convince Pedro to stay. On January 9, 1822, their efforts were rewarded when Pedro announced his intention to remain, an act that nationalist historiography has celebrated as the Dia do Fico (from the Portuguese word *ficar*, meaning "to remain or stay"). Although some still hoped for autonomy within the Portuguese nation, and a formal declaration of independence would not come for nine months, in hindsight the prince regent's clear defiance of the authority of the Cortes regime stands out as a milestone on the path to independence.[12]

A week later a long-time crown employee, the Brazilian-born José Bonifácio de Andrada e Silva, was named to head the prince regent's cabinet ministry. An experienced and capable administrator, José Bonifácio quickly emerged as the leading politician in Brazil and the single greatest influence on Pedro. Although remarkably progressive on the issue of slavery (his support for the gradual abolition of slavery was far ahead of its time), he had rather conservative instincts when it came to political participation. Thus, while José Bonifácio played a key role in the eventual achievement of independence from Portugal, he simultaneously worked to ensure a central role for Pedro in any new political arrangement and to impede the efforts of radical liberals to establish representative institutions based on popular sovereignty.

Through much of the first half of 1822, José Bonifácio and others may have held out hope for an independent Kingdom of Brazil retaining a connection with Portugal, but by May the intention of the Cortes to reduce Brazil to something like colonial status was clear, as was the willingness of the government in Rio de Janeiro to defy the Cortes regime. The outcome would be, in significant measure, determined in the provinces across Brazil, where many of the provisional juntas, particularly in the north, were determined to maintain the level of autonomy they enjoyed since the Cortes had undermined absolutist rule from Rio de Janeiro.[13]

Rio de Janeiro, Lisbon, Provincial Autonomy, and Brazilian Independence

In late October of 1821 the Portuguese Captain-General Luiz do Rego left Pernambuco after handing over power to the provisional junta. The remaining Portuguese military troops left in January. Subsequent Portuguese efforts to land troops failed because Gervásio Pires and the provisional junta denied the troops permission to disembark. The ability of the Cortes to exercise power in the region had been checked, and the government in Rio de Janeiro was unable to enforce its will there. The junta largely ceased to send tax revenue to the court. If, as Richelieu famously observed, finances are the sinews of the state, Pedro's government was barely being held together. Government coffers were empty. João had taken the wealth in the royal treasury with him when he returned to Portugal, and as in Pernambuco, most provinces had largely ceased to send revenue to Rio de Janeiro.

In the first half of 1822 the Pernambucan provisional junta was effectively autonomous. José Bonifácio, however, had sent agents to Pernambuco to agitate in support of Pedro in his conflict with the Cortes. These efforts came to fruition on June 1, 1822. A combination of civilian disturbances in the streets and threats from lieutenant Wenceslau Miguel

Soares to unleash the firepower of his artillery battalion effectively pressured the provisional junta into signing a statement asserting that it would only obey the Cortes when its decrees did not contradict the wishes of Prince Regent Pedro. Although making some gestures of respect for the Lisbon Cortes, the junta, led by Gervásio Pires Ferreira and joined by representatives of the military and the church, openly defied the Cortes and came out in favor of Brazilian independence under Pedro.[14] The 1817 revolt had already demonstrated the penetration of enlightened ideas into the region and also that the common people, and not only regional elites, were willing to challenge Portuguese authority.

Within a month, Gervásio Pires Ferreira and the junta were backtracking on their commitment to Pedro, suggesting popular consultation through a plebiscite. Yielding to pressure to support Pedro had distanced one menace, that of domination from across the Atlantic, but it also allowed another danger to approach, that of control by the regency in Rio de Janeiro, which might live up to its absolutist origins. The church's representative on the junta warned that Pedro was usurping "executive power over the province, without our [the members of the junta] having conferred it on him." Would domination from across the Atlantic simply be replaced by domination from Rio de Janeiro?

The president of the provisional junta had impeded the landing of new Portuguese troops and welcomed the Fico, Pedro's decision to defy the Cortes's orders to return to Portugal. Yet he also resisted efforts by emissaries of the regency in Rio de Janeiro to secure a commitment to Pedro's cause. Likewise, he would not enact the decrees for elections to the Conselho dos Procuradores (Council of Delegates) that José Bonifácio was organizing for fear that it might become a tool of a powerful central government that would threaten local autonomy. He also found excuses to delay the selection of representatives to the Constituent Assembly in Rio de Janeiro, yet he had his hand forced by popular demonstrations and the military on August 3.[15]

The prince regent's government meanwhile was deeply disturbed at the possibility of a vote for autonomy. Not only were events in Pernambuco likely to influence surrounding provinces, but as a major province north of Bahia (at that time in a state of civil war), Pernambuco had considerable strategic importance. José Bonifácio's two agents kept Rio de Janeiro in touch with events in Pernambuco. Antônio de Menezes Vasconcelos Drummond, who had played a leading role in securing Gervásio Pires and the junta's statement of support for Pedro on June 1, made clear to José Bonifácio the depth of the fear of absolutism among the leaders of the junta. Bernardo José da Gama, meanwhile, led a campaign against Gervásio Pires in the press. The two were also involved in conspiracies to overthrow the provisional junta, plans that bore fruit on September 16, 1822, when a military coup removed the provisional government. The military, acting to ensure loyalty to a constitutional monarchy led by Pedro, brought to power a government dominated by the planter elite in the region south of Recife. The new government was so thoroughly dominated by this rural elite that it became known as the Governo dos Matutos (the Hick or Hillbilly Government).[16]

On the other hand, the willingness of the new Governo dos Matutos to throw in its lot with Pedro illustrates another crucial dynamic. The leaders of the government, Afonso de Albuquerque, Francisco de Paula Cavalcanti de Albuquerque, and Francisco Paes Barreto, represented the wealthiest planters in the province, those with estates in the coastal forest zone south of Recife. Powerful, well-connected men of the long-established, wealthy families south of Recife would, over the subsequent decades, seek the support of the government in Rio de Janeiro when trying to bolster their position in the province. Once they were secure in the province, however, they would often zealously guard their independence from the central government.

Events in Pernambuco show the local elite's commitment to autonomy. The greatest threat seemed to come from Lisbon. This was especially clear after the prince regent's June 3 decree that called for a Constituent Assembly to write a constitution for Brazil. The call for a constitutional charter written by representatives from across Brazil suggested a commitment to the principle of popular sovereignty. Leaders in the many provinces of Brazil were being assured a voice in the new political order. The contrast with what the Cortes offered was clear. Although in principle the Cortes regime was likewise allowing input by Brazilian representatives, in practice the Cortes's intentions to re-colonize Brazil and the Brazilian representatives' inability to stop that effort were clear. Given the apparent choice between subordination to Lisbon or at least a voice in a con-

MAP 4. Brazil in 1822

stitutional system based in Rio de Janeiro, most provinces quickly opted
to support the regency of Pedro against the Cortes regime.[17]

The definitive break with Portugal came on September 7, 1822. On the
banks of the Ipiranga River, upon receiving the latest orders that coun-
termanded his decrees and demanded his return to Lisbon, Pedro reportedly squashed the correspondence and declared Brazil independent.
"Friends, the Portuguese Cortes has wished to enslave and persecute us.
From today forward our relations are broken." He is said to have dramatically drawn his sword and shouted, "Independence or death!" Most
provinces quickly supported Pedro's new government; the only resistance
of note was in Bahia, Pará, Maranhão, and Montevideo. The most significant resistance came from Salvador, Bahia, where Portuguese troops

held out until July of 1823, when, facing a naval force under the British mercenary Lord Cochrane, they sailed for Lisbon. For all practical purposes, the political independence of Portuguese America was now a fact. Scattered resistance in the north ended in July and August. In November the last Portuguese troops left Montevideo.[18]

The Battle for Local Control: The Pedrosada

The struggle against Portuguese rule was also a contest for authority within Portuguese America. The aspect of this internal struggle that has drawn the most attention from historians was the intra-elite struggle over the distribution of power. Yet Brazil was deeply divided by class, race, and slavery. Political instability, especially with the overthrow of absolutism and the innovations introduced by the Cortes regime, opened up space for challenges from groups previously excluded from formal politics. Across Brazil, and especially in Pernambuco, which had experienced the 1817 battle for secession and a republic, the challenge to traditional political authority created opportunities for the lower classes to assert themselves.

Events in Pernambuco in February 1823 illustrate how the upheavals of the period created possibilities for lower-class challenges to elite rule. In all likelihood, the warfare of 1817 in Pernambuco and of 1821–22 in Pernambuco and elsewhere made the recourse to arms easier to imagine. In February 1823, Military Governor Capt. Pedro da Silva Pedroso, who had been singled out for imprisonment in Portugal for his role in the 1817 uprising, led an uprising of black and mulatto military men as well as some civilians. Accounts from the period refer to him as mulatto and almost without exception make clear his identification with blacks and mulattoes in the military, groups he referred to as "my men." He socialized with them and is reported to have attempted to secure membership in a black sodality.[19]

The conflict began when Military Governor Capt. Pedroso ordered the arrest of Manuel Alexandre Taveira, a second lieutenant in the artillery service, on February 21. The junta instructed Taveira not to leave the government building, as he had been ordered to do, and the members of the junta then wrote Pedroso of their opposition to the arrest order. The military governor left and quickly returned with three pieces of artillery. He then threatened the junta that if they did not hand over the prisoner, he would bring down the building. Several contemporary accounts consider this arrest order a mere pretext for an uprising that Pedroso had already planned.[20]

On the morning of February 22, Pedroso's men seized the artillery headquarters. When government forces tried to subdue Pedroso's men, the latter fled to the Afogados neighborhood, where large numbers of deserters joined them. Shouts of "Viva Pedroso, our military governor" rang out. An additional uprising of supporters broke out, and more soldiers marched to Afogados to support Pedroso. Soon Capt. Pedroso and men loyal to him returned to the center of Santo Antônio, encouraged by shouts in support of Pedroso, the "Father of the *Pátria*." Pedroso arrived dramatically, riding on an artillery piece, only to find that all but one of the members of the junta had fled south to Cabo, where junta members and prominent planters Francisco de Paula Cavalcanti de Albuquerque and Francisco Paes Barreto had estates. That day an uprising in support of Pedroso in the Brum Fort allowed his supporters there to seize control of the fort.[21]

Captain Pedroso and his men controlled the city for a week. Commerce shut down and many wealthy families fled to the city outskirts. Contemporary accounts emphasize the upsetting of the racial order. Blacks and mulattoes were released from the jails, but whites were not. One contemporary reported, "The riff raff and the majority of the blacks and mulattoes, especially those in uniform, looked at whites like contemptible objects." Portuguese-born residents seem to have been particular targets of hostility, as the majority of the 160—180 individuals arrested by Pedroso's men were born in Europe. A ditty sung in the streets, in contrast, aimed at all whites, regardless of place of birth:

> Portuguese and Brazilian whites
> All of them will disappear
> Because only pardos and blacks
> will inhabit the country.

Such lines must have triggered deep anxiety among whites, raising the specter of a race war. Indeed, many of the witnesses cited by the police reported that the desire to recreate the uprising and race war of Saint

Domingue in the 1790s was one of the goals of the rebels. The ditty also challenged whites' claim to racial superiority; as Marcus Carvalho has pointed out, the Portuguese term *caiados*, translated here as "Brazilian whites," might more literally be rendered as "whitewashed," suggesting that Brazilian whites were not really of entirely European ancestry. The challenge to the racial order also contained a sexual component. One witness alluded to "constant and notorious petulant expressions directed at white women."[22]

By February 28 the junta had gathered enough forces to attempt to retake the city. The municipal council of Recife distributed a proclamation calling on citizens to gather to restore order. In anticipation of the battle, Capt. Pedroso distributed arms widely. Blacks and mulattoes, slaves and free alike, received weapons and ammunition. The bulk of these forces took positions in the Campo do Erário, while others spread throughout the city.

At this point the municipal council of Recife stepped in and mediated between Pedroso and the junta. Pedroso had already spoken with Cipriano Barata, the noted radical liberal from Bahia (who settled in Recife upon his return from the Lisbon Cortes); Barata had encouraged him to step down as military governor in the interest of maintaining order. The members of the municipal council made the same plea, and on the brink of a large battle, Capt. Pedroso relented. He agreed to end the rebellion and went out into the Campo do Erário with members of the municipal council to communicate to his supporters the end of hostilities. Despite Pedroso's stepping down, when the armed men from Cabo arrived, many of his supporters engaged in a fierce half-hour battle with them, firing artillery shells from the Campo do Erário. Pedroso clearly did not have complete control over them. Over the next week sixteen of them would die in battle. Nonetheless, the Pedrosada was over and Capt. Pedroso was shipped off to prison in Rio de Janeiro. Pedroso's backing down exemplified the limits that radical liberals faced when broad mobilization appeared to endanger the social order. The fact that some of his supporters followed his instructions to put down their arms raises the possibility that they too perceived that the rebellion was becoming unacceptably threatening to the social order. For although a vast gap separated them from the elite, they nonetheless had achieved a position in society that they did not want to see threatened.[23]

The witnesses cited in the judicial records emphasized three themes in explaining the motives of the rebels. Most common was the challenge to the racial order. Nearly all of the witnesses (most of whom were white) emphasized the insults directed at whites. Allusions to the use of the term *caiados* (Brazilian whites) were nearly universal. A few invoked the dangers to white women posed by assertive Afro-Brazilians. A more extreme form of challenge to the racial order was the charge that the rebels hoped to recreate the "lamentable scenes" that had occurred in Saint Domingue. This charge, although not universal like the charges of insulting terms against whites, was cited by many witnesses. Another common theme was that Capt. Pedroso was planning to allow the Portuguese to return and reconquer the area. This charge seems utterly inconsistent both with Pedroso's behavior in 1817 and with his mobilization of the black and mulatto lower classes. One wonders if the charge might have been floated by the authorities in an attempt to discredit Pedroso. The final charge that was frequently cited by the witnesses was that the challenge to the racial order was an effort by Pedroso to stay in power.[24]

The uprising, known as the Pedrosada, showed the lower-class and middling black and mulatto population asserting itself. The armed conflicts of 1817 and the independence struggle had entailed broad mobilization. Now those darker-skinned lower and middling classes were resorting to arms to further their interests. There is little evidence for the notion that a Haitian-like race war was on the minds of the rebels. There was no widespread violence against whites, nor were there significant incidents of theft and looting.[25] The concern about recreating Saint Domingue tells us more about the fears of whites than the plans of the rebels. The rebels' goal appears to have been to secure a government more attentive to their needs.

These men were not acting on their own, however. They were led by the military governor, who cultivated their support. Pedroso in turn was supported by others, including one member of the provisional junta, Francisco de Paula Gomes dos Santos. Paula, as he was often called, was reported to have been involved in plotting the movement. He also wrote letters trying to mobilize support in Goiana for the movement after the uprising had broken out, and he was heard affirming that Pedroso was right in not submitting to the authority of the junta. José Fernandes Gama, a customs judge, was another plotter. He had been incensed when he failed to win the presidency of the junta at the meeting of the electoral college in Olinda. He insisted that as the biggest opponent of Luiz do Rego he was entitled to the post. He further asserted that the new government needed to admit blacks and mulattoes. His nephew, magistrate Bernardo José da Gama, was reported to have been involved in the conspiracy as well.[26]

Considerable testimony suggests that it was the imminent replacement of Capt. Pedroso as the military governor that precipitated the rebels' movement. The testimony of 2nd Lt. Taveira, whose arrest prompted the movement's outbreak, illustrates the rebels' concern about the arrival of a new military governor. En route to Recife from his previous post he was questioned about the soon-to-arrive military governor and the possibility that the new figure would be independent of the provisional junta and would be an instrument of those seeking a centralized monarchy. During the uprising there were repeated incidents in which the rebellious soldiers shouted their support for Capt. Pedroso. One witness succinctly summed up the attitudes of the rebels when he reported that a second lieutenant working closely with Pedroso asserted that they did not want anyone except Pedroso as military governor, that they did not have to accept the replacement the emperor sent, and that the provisional government should be done away with. Pedroso himself was reported to have expressed similar sentiments in his assertion that people were free to elect and bring down governments as they wanted and that the emperor, in sending a new military governor, was seeking the surrender of the province.[27]

For many witnesses the Pedrosada was a challenge to the racial order and for some it raised the specter of a race war. Yet the lack of widespread looting or random violence belies the notion of a movement inspired by the Haitian Revolution. Indeed, the participation of a member of the governing junta and a judge, and the concern over the imminent removal of Capt. Pedroso as the military governor, suggests (in hindsight) that the events of that February should be seen not as a radical assault on the entire social order but as a continuation of the political struggle of the period. The "rules of the game" were in flux. Independence from Portugal had been achieved, but the new political system was not yet defined. There had been broad mobilizations for armed struggle in 1817 and 1821–22. The appeal to Afro-Brazilians seemed a viable strategy to Pedroso and his fellow conspirators. The response, however, in which the elites came together to repress the Pedrosada, showed the limits to what elite opinion would tolerate—racially based appeals that mobilized the lower classes were beyond the pale. In the face of a potential threat to the social order, even radical liberal leaders like Pedroso backed down. Of equal importance, even if it can only be inferred, is that many of Pedroso's supporters appear to have concurred with his estimate of the risk of continued struggle. Thus, with white fears, a lack of control, and the potential for social revolution threatening their own interests, the radical liberals abandoned their attempt to strengthen provincial autonomy by calling on racial solidarity among freemen.[28]

The Battle over the Rules of the Game: The Constituent Assembly

Struggles over political power also took center stage in Rio de Janeiro. The Constituent Assembly opened on May 3, 1823. Divergent views of the nature and proper distribution of political authority quickly emerged among the eighty-eight elected deputies who gathered to write a constitution. The central issue was the locus of power. Would authority reside primarily in representative institutions, or did the emperor, as the direct embodiment of the nation and the fullest expression of legitimate authority, have final say on all political issues? In practice this central issue also raised another source of contention, the relationship between provincial governments and the central government in Rio de Janeiro. Would popular sovereignty, expressed through representative institutions, allow the provinces considerable autonomy from the government in Rio de Janeiro, or would the central government be able to direct provincial affairs?[29]

The contest over the institutional structure of the new government was the central political issue of the First Reign, the 1822–31 period of Pedro I's rule. This struggle was often expressed as a dispute over the role of Portuguese-born citizens in the new nation. Across Brazil anger over the predominance of Portuguese advisors in Pedro I's court would heighten opposition to the first emperor. The availability of a prince of the House of Bragança to head the new country had eased the path to independence, yet it also meant that a clean break with Portugal had not yet occurred.[30] As early as 1823 charges were leveled in the press about undue Portuguese influence with the emperor, officially through "Portuguese cabinets" and informally through "secret cabinets." *O Tamoyo*, a Rio de Janeiro newspaper whose name referred to an indigenous people who had fiercely resisted Portuguese occupation, depicted politics as a contest between the Portuguese party surrounding the emperor and the large, patriotic Brazilian party. Proponents of a decentralized system would come to cast Pedro's centralism as essentially a continuation of Portuguese absolutism, now based in Rio de Janeiro. One veteran of the 1817 revolt and a Pernambucan deputy to the Constituent Assembly, for example, asked, "How can we assure our constituents that we are incorruptible in the defense of their interests? . . . [B]y sending them . . . those same abuses . . . a governor with his name changed to president, an independent commander of arms, a secretary who is identical to that of the old Captain General; and all sent from Rio de Janeiro, the presumed source of Despotism?"[31]

The emperor's assumption of supremacy was clear in his Speech from the Throne that opened the Constituent Assembly. He swore to defend the constitution "if it be worthy of Brazil and me." He rejected liberal constitutions that were based on the French charters of 1791 and 1792, claiming they were "totally theoretical and metaphysical and so impractical, as France, Spain, and most recently Portugal have demonstrated." Such constitutions lead to "licentious liberty" and ultimately to despotism.[32] The legacy of the French Revolution was clearly much on the minds of Pedro and his advisors. A strong executive was needed to avoid the dangers of elected legislatures that might fall under the influence of demagogues. Yet Pedro's desire for a powerful monarch, who could check the dangers of radicalism and democracy, was incompatible with the vision of the deputies, who sought to limit royal power through parliamentary supremacy. Tension further heightened in late July 1823 when news reached the court of a coup in Portugal that ended the constitutionalist regime there and restored absolutism. Events in Portugal raised the possibility of a re-colonizing effort, which the Portuguese in Brazil might support, or military action against the Constituent Assembly. Journalistic attacks on the Portuguese increased; newspapers like *O Tamoyo* questioned the loyalty of the Portuguese. In September the Constituent Assembly produced a draft of a constitution clearly at odds with Pedro's vision of a strongly centralized system in which sovereignty ultimately resided in the monarch. The document named both the emperor and an elected general assembly as representatives of the nation and granted the general assembly considerable power, including the power to override vetoes by the emperor. The efforts to limit his power and the heightening conflicts over the loyalty and role of Portuguese-born Brazilians finally exhausted the emperor's patience.

The catalyst for shutting down the Constituent Assembly was the controversy over an incident in which two Portuguese-born army officers had roughed up an apothecary on November 5, mistakenly believing him to be the author of an article critical of Portuguese-born officers in the armed forces. The victims appealed to the Constituent Assembly, where politicians critical of the emperor's pretensions took up their cause. On November 12 the emperor acted. Military troops closed the Constituent Assembly and the six members were arrested. The emperor announced that he would produce a constitution "twice as liberal" as the draft the assembly had written. The 1824 Constitution would not be written by elected representatives of the nation; it would be imposed by the emperor.[33]

News of the forcible closing of the assembly confirmed the worst fears of radical liberals and raised the specter of a new absolutism. In Salvador, Bahia, anti-Portuguese disturbances were already taking place. The largely Afro-Brazilian lower classes controlled the streets and were beating Portuguese residents. These riots intensified when word of the closing of the assembly arrived on November 12, 1823. The provincial government reported that the city was "on the brink of anarchy," and only promises to expel all the Portuguese pacified the Lusophobic crowds.[34]

Pernambuco and the Rules of the Game
When word reached Recife that the Constituent Assembly had been dissolved, the province was already in a state of high political tension. On September 15, 1823, first-line soldiers and an artillery brigade attempted

to overthrow the provincial government. Civilians led by Cipriano Barata and Manuel de Carvalho were also involved. The coming together of civilians and the military illustrates the influence that radical liberals like Cipriano Barata exerted in the barracks. A large gathering of people presented a document, with 115 signatures, to the municipal council; the document accused the military governor of conspiring with his counterparts in other provinces to make Pedro an absolute monarch. The document also noted the potential for despotism if the military governor independently controlled the military in the province, and it called for subordinating the military leader to provincial civilian authorities. This request by soldiers for provincial civilian leaders to have authority over military leaders is understandable if one bears in mind the high percentage of Portuguese-born officers in the armed forces and the association that radical liberals made between the Portuguese-born authorities, absolutism, centralism, and despotism.[35]

Tensions in the province were ratcheting up. On November 17 the popular radical liberal Cipriano Barata was arrested. Barata, a former representative to the Cortes in Lisbon, was elected to the Constituent Assembly in Rio de Janeiro, but he never took his seat because he feared for his life. He stayed in Pernambuco and continued agitating in the streets and publishing *A Sentinela da Liberdade*. Outrage over his arrest spurred sharp protests. The municipal council of Goiana demanded that the governing junta step down and threatened a rebellion. Barata himself wrote to the junta from jail, accusing it of working through the Clube do Apostolado (Club of the Apostles) in Recife, with the government in Rio de Janeiro and Portuguese-born residents, to persecute Brazilians, oppress the *pátria*, and exercise violence.[36]

On December 12 the Pernambucan soldiers that had fought in Bahia against the Portuguese arrived back in Recife. They were greeted with celebratory canon blasts and treated to parades and three days of festivities. They were led by Col. José de Barros Falcão Lacerda, who had earned the nickname Barros Vulcão, or Volcano. This military officer had fought for independence in 1817, for the Junta of Goiana in its confrontation with Luiz do Rego, and against the Governo dos Matutos the following year. Coinciding with the arrival of the troops was the return to Pernambuco of the deputies to the Constituent Assembly. The news they brought of the dissolution of the assembly seemed to confirm the fears of those who suspected Pedro of absolutist tendencies. On December 13 the deputies published a manifesto denouncing Pedro's dissolution of the Constituent Assembly, which further inflamed popular sentiment.[37]

With the province on the verge of civil war and with their opponents bolstered by the arrival of more troops, the governing junta resigned on December 13. Francisco de Paula Cavalcanti de Albuquerque, speaking for junta president Francisco Paes Barreto, cited the convulsed state of the province, the gathering of armed men in Goiana against the government, and the junta's loss of moral authority in justifying their stepping down. The Grande Conselho (Great Council) voted overwhelmingly to accept the resignation and then selected an interim government, with Manuel de Carvalho Paes de Andrade as president, José Natividade Saldanha as secretary, and Col. José de Barros Falcão as military governor.[38]

Elections were immediately organized to select a caretaker government on a firmer foundation that would hold office until an imperial selection of a provincial president arrived. In organizing elections for a junta, the provincial electors were returning to a practice that had begun with the provisional junta in Bahia in February of 1821. On October 11, 1823, a law, intended as a temporary measure until the new constitution came into effect, had been passed, which ended provincial elections for governing juntas and dramatically shifted the locus of political power from the local elites to the central government. Reverting to the older practice was thus implicitly a challenge to the central government.

On January 8, 319 electors gathered in a meeting of the Great Council. Word had already reached Pernambuco that in Rio de Janeiro the *Diário Fluminense* had published Francisco Paes Barreto's name in the list of new provincial presidents appointed by the emperor (although the official notification had not yet arrived). Nonetheless, the electors again chose Manuel de Carvalho as president, José de Natividade Saldanha as secretary, and Col. José de Barros Falcão as military governor. With 110 votes Manuel de Carvalho easily outdistanced the candidate in second place, Luís Francisco de Paula Cavalcanti de Albuquerque, who had 19 votes. The implicit challenge to the emperor was now quite open.

The electors sent the emperor an explanation of why they had rejected his choice, and the letter went even further, challenging the emperor's right to select provincial presidents, the secretary, and commanders of arms. The letter pointedly indicated the "not inconsiderable lack of trust" in the province because of "the extraordinary event of November 12" (the dissolving of the Constituent Assembly). It went on to note the fear of "re-establishing the old and always detestable despotism which we are willing to oppose courageously."[39] Clearly, a significant element of the elite was willing to defy the emperor.

With the emperor's support, Paes Barreto was willing to make a new bid for power. On February 2, 1824, he passed on to Manuel de Carvalho the emperor's letter appointing him (Paes Barreto) president of the province. The acting president responded by calling for the municipal councils to send representatives to a meeting on February 21 to decide the issue. At that meeting, representatives from Recife, Olinda, Igarassu, Pau d'Alho, Cabo, and Limoeiro maintained that Francisco Paes Barreto had alienated the responsible men of the province, especially with the imprisonment of Cipriano Barata. They unanimously chose Manuel de Carvalho to continue in the presidency.

Francisco Paes Barreto then turned to the army. He appealed to the military governor, Col. José de Barros Falcão, to help restore him to power. The military governor called a meeting of high-ranking military officers, and they unanimously agreed not to intervene in the political dispute. Moreover, they decided to send between one hundred and two hundred soldiers to reinforce the troops in Cabo, Francisco Paes Barreto's hometown and center of support, to arrest deserters from the army. The political impact of this was another blow to Paes Barreto because the deserters were his own supporters who had been involved in a brief and failed uprising on January 12 and then fled to Cabo. Although the military officers couched their actions in terms of non-involvement in politics and pursuing military deserters, the political effects of these measures were obvious.[40]

The military governor struggled to maintain the unity of his forces in a society rife with political conflicts. The importance of the armed forces made this virtually impossible, given that any actions in support of the established authorities, or any failure to act in support of them, had potential political consequences. With the rules of the game still in flux, the appeal to the army, or factions in the army, for support must have been an attractive option.

When the municipal councils received instructions from the court to swear loyalty to the new constitution, once again Col. José de Barros Falcão faced a challenge. Some army officers proposed that they too should swear their loyalty to the charter. In Rio de Janeiro, Pedro and his advisors hoped that the swearing of loyalty to the new constitution would diminish concern over the dissolving of the Constituent Assembly. Provinces in the south had done so, but there was resistance in some northern provinces. On March 4 the military governor convened a meeting of high-ranking officials to discuss whether the military should swear loyalty to the constitution that would soon be promulgated. At the end of lengthy discussions the issue was essentially avoided; the officials decided that such a political issue should be decided by the municipal councils, not the military. Yet some officers, such as battalion commanders Maj. Antônio Correia Seara and Maj. Bento José Lamenha Lins, were strongly in favor of swearing loyalty to the constitution; divisions within the army were apparent.[41]

On March 25, 1824, the tensions within the army burst into outright rebellion. Battalions led by Majors Correia Seara and Lamenha Lins surrounded the Palácio do Governo and, with bayonets unsheathed, seized Manuel de Carvalho and took him to the Brum Fortress. Huge numbers of soldiers from Recife and Olinda forces were quickly mobilized to free the president. They were joined by armed civilians. Then the soldiers inside the Brum Fortress itself rebelled and the president was freed. Manuel de Carvalho was then escorted triumphantly to the municipal council. The leaders of the rebel movement, accompanied by two hundred loyal soldiers, fled to the plantation of Francisco Paes Barreto in Cabo, where they joined the cavalry troops that had deserted in January.[42]

The former president had gathered a considerable number of men in Cabo, including such prominent persons as Dr. Tomás Xavier Garcia de Almeida, a judge in Recife, Dr. Bernardo Luís Ferreira, the deacon of the cathedral in Recife, and Col. José Carlos Mayrink da Silva Ferrão. Paes Barreto formed a provisional governing junta, which included, in addition to Paes Barreto as president, fellow prominent landowners in the Cabo area, vice-president Luís Francisco de Paula Cavalcanti de Albuquerque, and, as an advisor, Francisco de Paula Cavalcanti de Albuquerque. This provisional government, however, did not have sufficient forces to hold off the troops sent from Recife, so Paes Barreto moved his base to Barra Grande on the province's southern border with Alagoas.[43]

At the end of March a naval force of two frigates arrived from Rio de Janeiro under the command of John Taylor. Taylor informed the commander of arms that if Francisco Paes Barreto were not installed as president, he (Taylor) would carry out a naval blockade of the port of Recife. On April 7, 319 members of the Great Council deliberated and voted to maintain Manuel de Carvalho in the presidency. They also authorized three representatives to travel to the court and explain their position to the emperor. Taylor, for his part, initiated a blockade of the port of Recife.[44]

The blockade lasted for nearly three months. In addition to the hardships brought about by shutting down the principal port for the whole region, tensions were further exacerbated when naval forces under Commander Taylor attacked a register ship in the port of Recife, resulting in several deaths. In this tense atmosphere, a number of Portuguese-born citizens were attacked and several were killed. A larger death toll was averted when Major Emiliano Felipe Benício Mundurucu's efforts to mobilize the mulatto battalion and civilians to attack the Portuguese-dominated commercial district of the Bairro do Recife were frustrated by Agostinho Bezerra Cavalcanti de Sousa, the commander of the black battalion. Hostility toward the Portuguese-born may well have been exacerbated by official policies. Junta president Manuel de Carvalho had earlier enacted policies that targeted the Portuguese. On December 17, 1823, he issued a proclamation that any Portuguese person who had not sworn loyalty to the cause of independence had ten days to leave the province or his possessions would be confiscated. On February 11 of the following year he issued a similar edict. On February 5 he had several Portuguese sent to prison on the island of Fernando de Noronha as suspected enemies of the cause of independence. A week later he prohibited the importation of any Portuguese goods. During the blockade, his instructions to arrest anyone aiding the naval forces—for example, by distributing proclamations from John Taylor—specifically mentioned that the Portuguese might behave treasonously. Attacks on Portuguese-born people could only aggravate tensions with the court, where a Portuguese-born emperor was surrounded by many Portuguese-born advisors.[45]

By early May 1824, events seemed to be moving inexorably toward armed conflict. On May 6 the Great Council authorized an attack on the province of Alagoas in response to their support of the troops that had deserted and crossed into Alagoas. Francisco Paes Barreto now had his base of operations just across Pernambuco's southern border, on property he owned there. Two weeks later the emperor attempted to slow the escalation toward civil war. He withdrew his nomination of Francisco Paes Barreto in favor of Paes Barreto's ally José Carlos Mayrink da Silva Ferrão. However, he remarked to one of the three Pernambucans that the junta had sent to speak with the emperor, "I regret that the Pernambucans have been traitors to me." There would be no more conciliatory efforts; after this point, there was a march to war.[46]

On June 6 the municipal council of Recife gathered and discussed whether to swear support for the new constitution that the Council of State had drafted after the dissolution of the Constituent Assembly. The dissolution of the Constituent Assembly in November of 1823 and the arrest and exile of several members of the assembly had seemed to fulfill the fears of absolutism. Many saw the November 1823 creation of the Council of State as further evidence of the revival of absolutism. Friar Caneca pointed out in the pages of *O Typhis Pernambucano* that the council was largely composed of men who had long served Portuguese absolutism. The ongoing disputes over the emperor's appointment of provincial presidents exacerbated these concerns. Indeed, Pernambucan deputies had been prominent in the battle against the October 11, 1823, bill that shifted the locus of power to the court. Even among the deputies elsewhere who accepted the law, many assumed that provinces would still have indirect influence on national policy through representative institutions in the court. The dissolution of the Constituent Assembly, however, seemed to belie expectations that effective representation would be institutionalized. A Pernambucan deputy warned that "the chains of the former and most justly detested despotism are being readied for [the people]; and that gilded shackles under the alluring name of Independence are about to be put on them."[47]

Nothing in the meantime had lessened those concerns; conflicts over the nomination of Francisco Paes Barreto as president only worsened them. Friar Caneca outlined a coherent explanation for the rejection of the constitution, based on the notion that the proposed constitution did "not come from a legitimate source." Sovereignty resided in the people, he affirmed. The people decide their form of government and the distribution of power within it; the way they do this is through drafting a constitution. He elaborated that the emperor was not the nation and did not possess sovereignty, and neither did his commission to write the constitution. Moreover, the emperor was attempting to impose the constitution forcibly, through a blockade, whereas the people's representatives must act in clear liberty. Friar Caneca argued that the proposed constitution did not safeguard the independence of Brazil. The Great Council proceeded to reject the proposed constitution as "contrary to the liberty, independence, and rights of Brazil" and presented by a power that did not have the right to create a constitution. Likewise, on June 17 the municipal council of Olinda declined to swear loyalty to the constitution.[48]

On June 10 the emperor issued a proclamation to be circulated to all the provinces. He warned of an imminent Portuguese attack in an effort to re-colonize Brazil. He instructed that all ships from across the empire should return to Rio de Janeiro to defend the capital. The provinces would need to defend themselves with their own resources. In the proclamation to Pernambuco, he specifically denied the accusation that a faction was sold out to Portugal and was facilitating a Portuguese conquest of Brazil.[49]

The Confederation of the Equator

On July 1 the ships blockading the harbor of Recife sailed for Rio de Janeiro. The next day, Manuel de Carvalho issued the "Proclamation of the Confederation of the Equator." Addressing the "inhabitants of the provinces of the north of Brazil," he declared that the brazen, despotic dissolution of the Constituent Assembly was an attack on the sovereignty of the Brazilian nation. He asserted that in trying to divide Brazilians, the emperor was encouraging the King of Portugal to attack their homes. With the tone of indignation rising, Manuel de Carvalho went on to declare that now that they were exposed to Portuguese bayonets and cannons, the emperor has abandoned the provinces. The proclamation ended with an appeal to join together for mutual defense and to establish a truly constitutional government. A second proclamation addressed to Brazilians further developed the themes of the emperor's betrayal of the nation, his violation of the sovereignty of the people, and his leaving the provinces exposed to Portuguese attack after having drained the provinces of resources. Manuel de Carvalho argued that constitutions, laws, and institutions in general are made for the good of the people. He called for the creation of an up-to-date "American system" and disdained the oligarchical institutions of Europe. He concluded with a call for the others to join the six provinces that were forming the Confederation of the Equator. Manuel de Carvalho made clear the federative quality of the representative government that was being formed. Electors in each province would vote on a capital and the capital of each province would join together in a great, invincible ring.[50]

The Confederation of the Equator marked the second major challenge to Pedro's plans for a centralized system that he could dominate. When the Constituent Assembly prepared to approve a constitution that Pedro judged inadequate in securing his royal prerogatives, he called on the army to shut it down. Pedro proceeded to issue a constitution on March 25, 1824, that established the authority of the central government, in which he played the central role, to control policy in all the provinces across the empire. In the North, Pernambuco, Paraíba, Rio Grande do Norte, and Ceará were unwilling to acquiesce to this system, a system that seemed all too analogous to the absolutism only recently thrown off and that appeared to offer domination from a distant center of power—probably Rio de Janeiro, but possibly Portugal if it managed a reconquest. Asserting their need to defend their liberty and ensure their independence, the struggle would be decided in open warfare over the Confederation of the Equator.[51]

Manuel de Carvalho organized a provisional government to prepare for the possible attack by Portugal and the certain offensive by imperial forces. He further requested that all the juntas, municipal councils, and governors of arms send representatives to the Great Council that was to meet on August 17. This body would then establish the new government on a firmer basis and would install a Constituent Assembly. Manuel de Carvalho went on to propose several principles. Provinces in northern Brazil would form a union known as the Confederation of the Equator. The constitution of the United States of Colombia would serve as the model for the new constitution. Proclamations were quickly sent to other provinces in the North, denouncing the emperor's illiberal assaults on the sovereignty of Brazil and the need for the northern provinces to join together to and protect themselves from domination by Portugal and Rio de Janeiro.

To mobilize resources for the upcoming military confrontation, guerilla companies were organized, militia forces activated, a draft instituted, and deserters pardoned. A naval force composed of two brigs and two schooners was organized, sailors' pay was raised, and efforts were made to purchase two ships from the United Kingdom and six from the United States. Men, supplies, proclamations, and salaries for the soldiers were sent to the Pernambuco/Alagoas border to reinforce the so-called Constitutional Division of the South and to win support in Alagoas.[52]

The imperial regime responded to the challenge by sending a naval division of a corvette, a brig, and two supply ships under the command of Lord Cochrane to blockade the ports of Pernambuco. En route they unloaded twelve hundred soldiers under the command of Brig. Gen. Francisco de Lima e Silva, along with artillery and cavalry, at the Alagoan port of Jaragua. Lord Cochrane reached Recife on August 18 and began a blockade of Recife and the coast. He reported to Pedro that the revolution had "vigorous roots and [that] the democratic spirit of Pernambucans is not something to be played with." He wrote of the high level of support for the confederation, saying that "the population is indifferent to the imperial cause." He noted that propaganda, such as copies of the constitution of Colombia and two issues of *O Typhis Pernambucano*, which contained a piece by Friar Caneca ("Bases for the Formation of the Social Pact") on the need for a liberal constitution, had been spread in other provinces. Such works were consistent with journalism in *A Sentinela da Liberdade*, which for some time had been critical of the seemingly absolutist tendencies of the emperor, his manipulation by a Portuguese faction, and the domination of the provinces of the North by those of the South. Such positions were apparently widely held, as the Confederation of the Equator had solid backing in Paraíba, Rio Grande do Norte, and Ceará and some support in Piauí and Pará.

On August 19 Lord Cochrane sent a proclamation, followed by another one four days later, warning that without a surrender, bombardment of Recife would begin on August 28. One last effort at negotiation was attempted when the English traveler Maria Graham, who was on board an English ship in Recife at the time of Cochrane's arrival, acted as an intermediary, communicating Cochrane's message that Manuel de Carvalho's position was hopeless and that he should surrender. The president responded that he would only agree to put down arms if the Constituent Assembly was reseated in a location distant from Rio de Janeiro and the imperial troops stationed there.[53]

With military action imminent, many wealthy families fled the city. At midnight on August 28, a schooner under Lord Cochrane began shelling Recife and continued for two and a half hours. With tensions elevated, on September 3 latent hostilities among Afro-Brazilians and Portuguese-born Brazilians burst into the open. A Portuguese-born tavern owner killed a mulatto soldier. In response, a group of soldiers then knifed and bayoneted the tavern owner. The group proceeded to kill thirteen other Portuguese-born individuals. One of the attackers reportedly brandished a knife as he threatened the Portuguese in the presence of officers who did nothing. Hostilities against the Portuguese were also vented on September 15, when the chaos of fighting in the city allowed Afro-Brazilians, and the lower classes generally, to loot Portuguese-owned stores.[54]

Even before the arrival of more imperial soldiers, the confederation's Constitutional Division of the South, reinforced by additional troops from Recife, had been unable to defeat the armed men gathered by Francisco Paes Barreto on the Alagoan border. With word that the brig and schooner sent south from Recife had been captured by imperial forces and that the mission to secure support in Alagoas had failed, the Constitutional Division of the South started retreating to the north.[55]

On September 11 Gen. Lima e Silva sent a demand to Manuel de Carvalho that he surrender. The leader of the Confederation of the Equator ignored the order and helped organize the defense that was concentrated at two key points, one at Carvalhos Bridge on the Jaboatão River and the other at Jaboatão. The next day, after a feint at the bulk of the enemy troops at the Carvalhos Bridge, Lima e Silva quickly moved his forces, named the "Army Cooperating with Good Order," on an attack on the capital. Entering through Afogados, his forces faced considerable opposition in Boa Vista, and both sides suffered serious losses. The imperial forces managed to occupy Boa Vista and Santo Antônio but were stymied in their efforts to enter the Bairro do Recife. Three artillery pieces helped the confederation forces defend the bridges connecting Santo Antônio with the Bairro do Recife. For two days the Brum and Buraco forts shelled Lima e Silva's troops, as did a schooner at the port. Some of the urban lower classes took advantage of the opportunity to loot Portuguese-owned businesses. On September 13 Confederation President Manuel de Carvalho fled on a *jangada*, boarded the English corvette *Tweed*, and went into exile. On September 17, Lima e Silva's men seized Olinda. The victory clearly belonged to the imperial forces, but some of the defending troops fled to the north and joined confederation forces still resisting. Scattered resistance in the countryside in provinces further to the north was not definitively put down until November.[56]

The army and navy of the empire easily defeated the forces of the Confederation of the Equator. Yet the principles espoused by confederation leaders were still a potential danger. Victory would not be complete until exemplary punishments were meted out to the rebels. Indeed, in July a royal proclamation to the troops had warned of the consequences of challenging the emperor's power. "What do such insults demand? . . . Surely a punishment, and such a punishment, that it will serve as an example for posterity." On December 20, 1824, a military commission gathered with orders to summarily try rebel leaders. The first round of trials included the most prominent leader, Friar Caneca, who, between his various activities as a priest, writer, and newspaper publisher, was a popular and well-known critic of the imperial government. His articles and the paper he published, *O Typhis Pernambucano*, provided some of the most coherent and hard-hitting attacks on the imperial government.[57]

After militarily defeating the Confederation of the Equator, Brig. Gen. (and interim provincial president) Francisco de Lima e Silva headed the military commission. Two of the commission's judges were colonels who had seen action defeating the confederation. The prosecutor was Tomás Xavier Garcia de Almeida, a judge who had supported Francisco Paes Barreto. With a royal commitment to harsh punishments, despite Lima e Silva's arguing for prudence and caution, the outcome of the prosecution was never in doubt. Friar Caneca was executed. Over the following months, fifteen others would be executed as well. As exemplary punishments often do, however, and as Lima e Silva had feared, the executions generated considerable resentment. The military commission in effect made martyrs of those they executed. Friar Caneca became a symbol of resistance to tyranny. (Indeed, the heroic image of Friar Caneca as a martyr to the cause of liberty still can be found in school books in the twenty-first century.)[58]

Nonetheless, the armed forces of the empire had efficiently crushed the challenge from the North that contested Pedro's design for a highly centralized system. There was little prospect that disputes over the nature and distribution of power would soon take the form of armed secessionist struggles. Critics continued to question the order created by the 1824 Constitution; indeed, there were still radical liberals who favored republican institutions, even if they were on the margins of the official world and were not generally acknowledged in mainstream political discourse. It is noteworthy that the propaganda and rhetoric of the confederation did not emphasize the republican nature of the proposed regime. Was a strategic judgment made that an emphasis on republican repudiation of the monarchy would alienate potential supporters? More likely, the deeper commitment was not to a republican form of government but to a constitutional regime with decentralized institutions. As in 1817, a secessionist struggle had little choice but to adopt a republican form. What monarchy could they propose if they were to break away?

Another radical feature of the confederation was Manuel de Carvalho's ending the importation of slaves into Pernambuco the day after the creation of the confederation.[59] One can speculate that such a measure, while expressed in humanitarian terms, might have been an effort to mobilize Afro-Brazilians for the struggle the confederation faced. If it was a tactic for mobilization, it proved no more effective than the freeing of slaves to fight for the rebel movement in 1817. It no doubt alienated many wealthy and influential men. In putting the issue of slavery on the table for discussion, Manuel de Carvalho raised a potentially significant challenge to the current institutions. However, as with republicanism, one may question whether abolishing the slave trade was a central aspect of the confederation and its appeal. Other issues were more significant, and they persisted. Dramatic challenges such as republicanism and serious questioning of slavery did not emerge in a significant way in the years immediately following the defeat of the Confederation of the Equator. Rather, struggle over the institutional structure established by the 1824 Constitution characterized the remaining years of the First Reign. This conflict was largely fought within mainstream institutions.

By 1824 the Pernambucan elites were sharply divided. The relative cohesion of 1817 was a thing of the past. The north/south split among the elites now marked crucial contours in provincial politics. To cope with the armed seizure of power by Manuel de Carvalho Paes de Andrade and the northern elite that he led, the rich, well-connected elites of the South relied on imperial troops from Rio de Janeiro. The Confederation of the Equator was no match for these forces and was easily smashed. As much as rich, powerful planters and political leaders like Francisco Paes Barreto, Francisco de Paula Cavalcanti de Albuquerque, and his brother Luís Francisco de Paula Cavalcanti desired freedom from imperial control, the value of Rio de Janeiro in buttressing their dominance in Pernambuco was incontestable. Indeed, with order restored, the imperial government rewarded its supporters, handing over state authority in Pernambuco to the southern elite and their allies.

A Centralized Political System

On March 25, 1824, Pedro issued the Constitution of 1824 and swore to uphold it. On December 1 in Pernambuco, ceremonies were held to swear loyalty to the constitution. A Te Deum was held and celebrations were organized. Municipal councils throughout the province held similar rituals to affirm their commitment to uphold the constitution.[60] The 1824 Constitution that people swore to uphold established Brazil as a unitary state. The central government appointed and removed presidents to administer the provinces. Voters in each province elected members to provincial general councils, but the authority of these bodies was extremely circumscribed. In Rio, an upper house, the Senate, in which members enjoyed lifetime tenure, and a lower house, the Chamber of Deputies, to which deputies were elected at least every four years, together made up the General Assembly. Both the General Assembly and the emperor were the "representatives of the Brazilian nation" to whom

77

political powers were delegated. Independent male citizens (excluding slaves, who were neither citizens nor independent, and men under the control or authority of others, such as servants and sons living in their fathers' houses) with an annual income of one hundred *mil-réis* were entitled to vote in parish elections. This made for a rather broad suffrage for its day, but the impact of participation was limited by a two-tier electoral system. Parish voters chose electors, who in turn selected members of the General Council, the Chamber of Deputies in the imperial court, and lists of candidates for the Senate. Income qualification doubled to be an elector, doubled again to be a deputy in the Chamber of Deputies, and doubled again to eight hundred *mil-réis* to serve in the Senate.[61]

The emperor played a fundamental role in the system, not only as the executive but also by virtue of exercising the "moderating power." The constitution asserted this fourth branch of government to be "the key to the entire political organization." It affirmed that "the person of the Emperor is inviolable and sacred; he is not subject to any accountability." The emperor consulted with the Council of State, whose members he chose. (The council facilitated his efforts; it did not check his power in any significant way.) The emperor was to use the moderating power to "oversee the independence, equilibrium, and harmony of the other political powers." Thus, he could dismiss the Chamber of Deputies when he thought it appropriate, choose and dismiss cabinet ministers as he wished, nominate members of the Senate from lists of the three candidates with the most votes, suspend judges, and grant pardons. The emperor sanctioned legislation and exercised a power of veto that was extremely difficult for legislators to override. The assertion in the constitution that the General Assembly and the emperor together were representatives of the nation to whom powers were delegated was clearly belied by the dominant role he was assigned. Nor did the judiciary check royal power, for it had a relatively limited role, which did not include judicial review of executive or legislative (much less moderating) power. Bearing in mind the reach of the power of appointment—that is, ministers chosen by the emperor appointed their subordinates in the provinces, who in turn chose their subordinates—it is not hard to understand why the rebels of the Confederation of the Equator, who feared absolutism in a new guise, objected so strongly to the new institutional structure that threatened a loss of provincial and local control over public policy.[62]

The Empire and Foreign Relations

Having won independence by force of arms, issued a constitution that assigned a central role to the monarch, and easily suppressed a secessionist attempt by rebels distraught at the loss of provincial and local control of policy, Emperor Pedro I in the mid-1820s focused on solidifying the new nation-state in its foreign relations. These efforts were primarily exerted toward two ends: securing diplomatic recognition from the European powers and battling the United Provinces of the Rio de la Plata (the region that would become Argentina) for control over the Cisplatine province, the former Banda Oriental (present-day Uruguay), which Brazil claimed as national territory.

Diplomatic recognition by foreign powers would greatly enhance the legitimacy of the new regime. To achieve that end, the Portuguese government would need to acknowledge the independence of Brazil. Great Britain played a key role in the negotiations. A long-time ally of Portugal, Britain had substantial commercial interests in Brazil; indeed, Brazil was among the largest markets for its exports. Moreover, Great Britain's 1810 commercial treaty with Portugal, which Brazil was respecting, would expire in 1825. Great Britain had both an interest in the resolution of the issue and the diplomatic weight to help bring it about. The British would, of course, expect favors from Brazil in exchange for its support in securing international recognition. With British diplomats actively involved in the negotiations, Brazil and Portugal signed a treaty on August 29, 1825, that secured Portuguese recognition of the independence of Brazil. In short order Great Britain and other European powers recognized the independence of Brazil. This considerable success came at a heavy cost, however. Not only was Brazil obligated to pay two million British pounds to Portugal in compensation, but British diplomats would soon employ their leverage on two other issues.[63]

For years Great Britain had been attempting to shut down the trans-Atlantic trade in slaves. For two and a half centuries large numbers of enslaved Africans had been brought to Brazil. The commitment to slavery was strong and widespread. Given the high death rates and low birth rates among slaves, Brazilians who were enriching themselves on the labor of captives and merchants who were profiting in the trade of humans could not be pleased with the prospect of an end to the slave trade.

Nonetheless, on November 23, 1826, Brazil signed a treaty with Great Britain committing to end the trade within three years.[64]

British diplomats also pressed to ensure access to Brazilian markets on favorable terms. The 1810 commercial treaty between Portugal and Britain was set to expire in 1825. The 15 percent tariff ceiling on British goods that was established in the treaty limited the revenue that the government could obtain from one of its basic revenue-raising instruments. Moreover, through most-favored nation practices, this ceiling applied to many other trading partners as well. The expiration of the treaty thus offered Brazilian statesmen a significant opportunity. Nonetheless, on August 17, 1827, the imperial government signed a new commercial treaty with Great Britain that continued the 15 percent maximum tariff and other preferential features for British merchants.[65]

The concessions that such agreements codified were substantial. Their political impact was magnified, however, because they were not simply the result of diplomatic weakness following the struggle for independence. Pedro was also reliant on the British to support the struggle of his daughter, D. Maria da Glória, for the Portuguese throne. With British troops still stationed in Portugal, Pedro's brother, Dom Miguel, would have difficulties claiming the throne as an absolute monarch. Thus, despite constitutional prohibitions on any union of the Portuguese and Brazilian crowns, Pedro was still heavily involved in struggles over the Portuguese throne. (Indeed, the 1825 treaty that recognized Brazilian independence preserved Pedro's rights to the Portuguese throne.) His large concessions to the British were widely seen as sacrificing Brazilian interests to pursue his own dynastic ambitions in Portugal.[66]

Pedro's handling of the negotiations over independence damaged his reputation. The results not only were costly, they also raised the specter of a monarch possibly more committed to dynastic ambitions in Europe than Brazilian interests. The confrontation over the Cisplatine province further undermined his political position. The confrontation might not even have been necessary, because while Dom João VI had secured control over the province and claimed it, the inhabitants of the former Banda Oriental did not, on the whole, see themselves as part of the Luso-Brazilian world. Nonetheless, Pedro's commitment to maintaining sovereignty in the area led him into a costly war, which resulted in perhaps eight thousand deaths. Impressments of soldiers raised tensions and resentment. The cost of the war damaged already weak government finances, resulting in the issuing of more currency and more inflation. In June of 1828 foreign mercenaries contracted to help fight the war revolted in the court. With the promises that had lured them to Brazil unfulfilled, and facing harsh conditions and corporal punishment, they rose up in revolt in the very capital of the empire. Although they were put down within several days, it was a damaging episode. The emperor quickly moved to disentangle the country from the war. British diplomats arranged for a solution that both Brazil and the United Provinces could live with, an independent Uruguay. Pedro's prestige and the perception of his leadership abilities had suffered another blow.[67]

The Emperor and the General Assembly

In May of 1826 the General Assembly, composed of the Chamber of Deputies (the lower house) and the Senate (the upper house), opened for the first time. Over the next five years the emperor and the Chamber of Deputies would clash on numerous occasions. At the heart of the conflict was the same issue that had set the emperor and the Constituent Assembly at odds: the distribution of power between the General Assembly and the emperor. The Constitution of 1824 established both the emperor and the General Assembly as representatives of the nation. At issue was whether in practice the emperor, embodying the nation on the basis of inherited authority, would play the central role in the political system, a role in which he was not ultimately accountable to the General Assembly. A key issue over which the conflict played out was the role of the cabinet ministers. The constitution allotted the emperor the right to freely name the ministers he wished, but could the deputies expect the ministers to be accountable to the Chamber of Deputies?

Given the role that the constitutional arrangements assigned to the emperor, one might expect that the emperor could simply bully the Chamber, but in practice this was not the case. The emperor could not force the Chamber to adopt any particular policy, even if he could dissolve it and call for new elections. Fiscal policy illustrates the limitations that constricted the emperor. The independence struggles and the conflicts in the North that culminated in armed struggle over the Confederation of the Equator had disrupted several regional economies and damaged overseas trade. A drought in the North further damaged production there. The war in the Rio de la Plata inflated government expenditures and disrupted labor supply. These problems led the government to issue more money, thereby increasing inflation. Effective fiscal policy was needed to turn the tide on these difficulties. It was not an easy task; the commercial treaty with Great Britain limited the revenue that could be raised through tariffs on imports. Clearly, the General Assembly, which was solely responsible for initiating legislation and thus exerted considerable influence on government finances, had an important role to play. If government finances were to be put on a sounder footing, the emperor would have to work with, not against, the legislative power. The General Assembly could hardly implement policies without Pedro's acquiescence, but neither could he ignore the legislators. In practical terms, the Chamber of Deputies, in which the concern to protect legislative prerogatives in the name of safeguarding the liberal constitutional system was the greatest, could check the emperor's initiatives if they disapproved of them, thereby creating a deadlock in which pressing issues were not resolved.[68]

Many deputies in the Chamber were suspicious of Pedro. The dissolution of the Constituent Assembly had raised fundamental doubts about the emperor's intentions. The execution of sixteen rebels from the Confederation of the Equator—men who took up arms over concerns that many of the deputies shared—did nothing to diminish those doubts. The emperor's continuing role in the dynastic struggles in Portugal and his subservience to Great Britain in matters of diplomacy, apparently motivated at least in part by a desire for British support in Portugal, solidified the notion that Pedro was more interested in Portugal than in defending Brazilian interests.

With the Senate and the Council of State packed with close allies of the emperor, and with informal influence exerted by the "secret cabinets" of his Portuguese-born friends, confidants, and members of his entourage, as well as by his mistress, D. Domitila de Castro, it was left to the Chamber of Deputies to protect a liberal, constitutional order. Yet Pedro and the ministers he chose showed little sign of accepting the notion of ministerial accountability to the Chamber of Deputies. The General

Assembly did manage to pass legislation on abuse of power and dereliction of duty by ministers and counselors of state that established slight limits on executive power. The legislators also strengthened the new office of the justice of the peace, which included locally elected officials who were taking over functions traditionally performed by centrally appointed magistrates. On the whole, however, they were frustrated in their efforts to move Pedro toward accepting the ministers' accountability to the Chamber and the fundamental issue embodied in the dispute: parliamentary supremacy as the expression of the will of the people. The emperor was also frustrated. By the middle of 1828, with repeated friction in the halls of the General Assembly, with a revolt in the capital city by foreign mercenaries and the subsequent admission of defeat in an expensive and unpopular war, and with economic difficulties that showed little hope of resolution, the emperor's ability to lead was significantly undermined.[69]

From Mutual Suspicion to Rupture

By the late 1820s, across Brazil concern was increasing over centralized government and Pedro's seeming impulses toward absolutism, or at least his domination of policymaking and control over who could hold office. Radical liberals played prominent roles in challenging Pedro. Such men, *exaltados*, tended to come from somewhat lower class backgrounds than other politicians and found support among artisans, clerks, lower-ranking bureaucrats, teachers, lesser professionals, and people on the fringes of the official world. These men wanted more egalitarian institutions and greater social mobility. It was only among radical liberals that one found significant support for republican institutions. In Pernambuco, the liberal club the Sociedade Jardineira (or Carpinteiros de São José) included various radical liberals. A prominent radical liberal in the province was Antônio Borges da Fonseca. A journalist and newspaper publisher, he became known nationwide for engaging in street agitation and political proselytizing in army barracks and through the many newspapers he published over the years, not only in Pernambuco but at times in the court as well.[70]

In the late 1820s Pedro was increasingly on the defensive. The shift in political fortunes was especially clear in Pernambuco where radical liberals felt sufficiently emboldened to attempt an uprising to overthrow the provincial president and military governor. Following the defeat of the Confederation of the Equator, Pedro had rewarded members of the elite in Pernambuco who had supported the crown. Francisco Paes Barreto was named the Viscount of Recife in 1824, the first Pernambucan to receive a title of nobility from the emperor. The military victor of 1824, Gen. Lima e Silva, now the Baron of Barra Grande, stayed on as provincial president, while allies of Francisco Paes Barreto were named to staff positions across the province. In the south of the province in particular, where Paes Barreto's forces had spent six months, his supporters nearly monopolized government posts. The provincial president, taking advantage of an 1825 law that allowed him to organize militia forces from the reserve army, appointed many of these men militia officers. These posts granted authority over armed men and limited access to state resources. The new, locally selected justices of the peace not only carried out police work and adjudicated minor cases but also played a key role in recruiting men for the army. Impressing men into the army for seven years was a coercive power that was particularly valuable for rewarding friends and punishing enemies. Even before the judicial reforms, large numbers of men who fought for the losing side in 1824 were drafted into the army and later sent off to fight in the Rio de la Plata.[71]

Opponents of Pedro's centralism especially hated Provincial President Tomás Xavier Garcia de Almeida. He had not only supported the winning faction in 1824 but had served on the military commission that ordered the execution of Friar Caneca and other leaders of the Confederation of the Equator. Leading up to elections on February 1, 1829, there were sharp partisan attacks in the press. The simple fact that a lively and critical press had appeared was a sign of the increasingly open politicization and polarization. In Pernambuco, the press attacks led to six journalists being arrested, including the radical liberal Antônio Borges da Fonseca.[72]

An uprising known as the "Republic of Afogados" was initiated on election day, when partisan fever was at a pitch. About twenty men gathered in Afogados, near Recife, led by João Roma (the son of Padre Roma, executed for his participation in the 1817 revolt) and a number of other military veterans of the Confederation of the Equator. They moved on to Vitória de Santo Antão, where they claimed to establish a provisional government and reportedly called for a republic. The rebels had circulated pamphlets beforehand, but they were unable to gather enough support to seriously threaten the provincial government. They did attract a few people along the way and numbered seventy to eighty men by the time they reached Brejo da Madre de Deos in the *sertão*. There, a few veterans of the 1824 campaign who were in hiding joined the rebels, most prominently the military leader in 1824, Col. José de Barros Falcão Lacerda. Recognizing that the expected support had failed to coalesce around their movement, and being pursued by government troops, the rebels soon disbanded and fled. When troops arrived they found fifty rifles that the rebels had abandoned.[73]

The República de Afogados episode is significant not only as an indication of dissatisfaction, polarization, and an increased willingness among radical liberals to openly challenge the government but even more because of the emperor's response to these events. As soon as word from Provincial President Tomás Xavier Garcia de Almeida reached Rio de Janeiro, the imperial government swiftly took action. The minister of justice suspended constitutional guarantees in Pernambuco, later explaining that "in a province where two times already they had tried to establish the democratic system, [the revolt] could have great ramifications." The minister of war established a military commission to try the rebels. In a special session of the Chamber of Deputies held to deal with the fiscal crisis, however, Bernardo Pereira de Vasconcelos and Holanda Cavalcanti both lambasted the government for violating the constitution. On April 24, 1829, on the floor of the Chamber, Holanda Cavalcanti called for the impeachment of the ministers of justice and war. By July the two ministers were cleared of criminal wrong doing, the minister of justice by a 41-29 vote and the minister of war by a narrower 39-32 vote. Despite surviving the votes, the debates revealed the depth of distrust and the Chamber's loss of confidence in the constitutional inclinations of the emperor. Vasconcelos played a prominent role in defending the prerogatives of the Chamber, accusing the ministers of criminal behavior and linking it to the "criminal [and] violent" dissolution of the Constituent Assembly in 1823 and the arrests and deportations that followed. The future regent, Diogo Antônio Feijó, voting to impeach the minister of war, declared, "Without doubt this is Brazil's first constitutional day. Until today our Constitution has been nothing but an empty name."[74] The entire episode made clear the immense chasm between the Chamber's expectation of appropriate constitutional arrangements and the emperor's conception of his own role.

The opposition to Pedro's centralism clearly extended well beyond radical liberal circles. In Pernambuco, one element of this opposition came from what might seem like an unlikely source. As a representative in the Chamber of Deputies, Holanda Cavalcanti, a leader of the most powerful family in the province and an ally of the crown in 1824, was outspoken in his opposition to centralism. Indeed, in 1828 he had eschewed customary subtlety when he challenged the emperor with an amendment to the Chamber of Deputies' response to the Speech from the Throne. The Pernambucan statesman explicitly objected to the emperor's entering treaties with foreign powers without the General Assembly's knowledge. As a wealthy, prestigious, and powerful member of the Pernambucan elite, Holanda Cavalcanti objected to a strong centralist government that would impinge on his freedom of action in Pernambuco. In this objection one can understand the reason for his participation in the 1817 independence bid. At the time of independence, however, he was challenged by the Junta of Goiana and the members of the northern elite; he and the Governo dos Matutos (Government of the Hicks) looked to the court for support. Again in 1824 he allied with the court. There is a clear logic to his shifting positions: When the faction of the elite he represented, largely the southern elite, was secure in Pernambuco, it did not want interference from Rio de Janeiro. When it was challenged in the province, however, it turned to the imperial government for support.[75]

The efforts by prominent deputies in mid-1829 to impeach two ministers for violating the constitution, and the denunciations of the hollowness of claims to constitutional government, illustrate the crisis in the relationship between the Chamber of Deputies and the emperor. Moreover, the repudiation of the emperor's unconstitutional behavior that the attacks on the ministers implied came in the context of an attack on the ministers' ability—and by implication, Pedro's ability—to manage government finances. The special session that opened on April 1, 1829, during which the accusations of impeachable offenses were made, was called to deal with the fiscal crisis of the government. The session was the scene for mutual recriminations between deputies and Pedro's ministers. Nothing concrete was achieved and the Chamber never managed to approve a budget. The costs of the lost war in the south, the financial liabilities to Portugal for the independence agreement, and the limits on tariffs in the commercial treaty with Great Britain seemed to have hemmed in the government. Only politically painful budget cuts, which surely would be unacceptable to the emperor, would be able to make up the 50 percent shortfall in government revenues. To many deputies, Pedro's government suggested not only dangerous absolutist tendencies but also ineptitude in handling the challenges of the day.[76]

There was one brief period of compromise (after Pedro turned his back on his unpopular mistress and made an acceptable marriage). He appointed a compromise cabinet on December 4, 1829, but it was too late. In such a polarized atmosphere, the cabinet could not find solid political support. The new Chamber of Deputies that was seated in 1830 had more opposition deputies, and they proved more confrontational and insistent on asserting parliamentary power. (In Pernambuco, Francisco de Carvalho Paes de Andrade, the brother of the president of the Confederation of the Equator, had been elected.) Celebrations in the streets of major cities across Brazil at news of the July Revolution in France, in which a popular uprising overthrew Charles X in favor of a more liberal government, indicated the extent of the alienation from the emperor. The increasing polarization, with absolutist and radical liberal clubs agitating, with both groups seeking to influence the men in arms in the barracks, and with a popular press hurling invective (especially at the Portuguese), made for ever greater frustrations for Pedro.[77]

The emperor undertook a trip to Minas Gerais, much like he had done in 1822, when he successfully gathered support for an independence bid under his leadership. This time, however, while he was traveling, radical liberals like Antônio Borges da Fonseca were organizing gangs for street fighting and intimidation and building support in the barracks. On March 13–15, clashes in the street with Pedro's supporters—an episode known as the "nights of breaking bottles"—raised tensions and led to the arrests of army officers who stepped in to protect the radical liberals. Pedro responded with a new cabinet of opposition figures, but the time had long passed for such a measure. The quick dismissal of this cabinet on April 5 in favor of a new ministry of close allies prompted the final crisis. In response to demands that he recall the dismissed ministry, Pedro reportedly commented that he "would do everything for the people, but nothing by the people," succinctly affirming a policy that had brought him into irresolvable conflict with the Chamber of Deputies.

Thousands of soldiers and civilians gathered in the Campo de Santa Ana. The mobilization made clear that Pedro could not count on the backing of the military in a showdown. Without military support, the situation was untenable for him. On April 7, 1831, Pedro abdicated to pursue dynastic ambition in Portugal, supporting the cause of his daughter, Maria da Glória, for the Portuguese crown. In Brazil he left his crown to his five-year old son Pedro.[78]

The 1820 Porto Revolution and the Regeneration swept aside the absolutist traditions of the Bragança monarchy. The prospect of greater political participation in a constitutional monarchy was widely embraced in Brazil. In 1821 juntas emerged across Brazil, and they governed with a degree of popular representation. By May 1821 provinces had begun selecting representatives to participate in writing a constitutional charter. In Pernambuco an unauthorized junta in Goiana emerged to challenge Portuguese Captain-General Luiz do Rego Barreto and quickly proved its broader support in an armed contest with him. The captain-general and the Portuguese army units supporting him were recalled; the Portuguese Cortes never recovered its influence in the region.

In Rio de Janeiro a movement emerged to oppose the transfer of the seat of government back to Portugal. Landowners and merchants who had prospered from the growth of Rio de Janeiro, São Paulo, and Minas Gerais, royal officials who saw their future in Brazil, and a variety of professionals and court hangers-on all shared the desire to avoid the return of the seat of royal government to Iberia. Failing that, they hoped that at least the government in Rio de Janeiro could maintain a considerable degree of authority. In April 1821, João succumbed to pressure from Lisbon and returned to Portugal. In December the Cortes ordered that the governing institutions created in Rio de Janeiro with the transfer of the court in 1808 be dismantled. The intention of the Cortes to re-subordinate Brazil was becoming increasingly clear. On January 9, 1822, Prince Regent Pedro defied the Cortes, announcing his intention to remain in Brazil. José Bonifácio de Andrada e Silva guided Pedro in his defiance of the Cortes and, in time, became the architect of plans to create a powerful centralized monarchy based in Rio de Janeiro, one in which the monarch would have the upper hand over any representative bodies. On September 7 Pedro declared Brazil independent of Portugal. With the Lisbon Cortes clearly attempting to re-subordinate Brazil to something like colonial status, and with the hope that a constitutional monarchy based in Rio de Janeiro offered greater autonomy to the diverse *pátrias* across Brazil, Pedro's movement quickly gained the adherence of most provinces. Portuguese arms were defeated in short order.

The overthrow of absolutist institutions had created unprecedented possibilities for broader political participation in fashioning a new political system. Moreover, without agreement on rules of the game, the ability to mobilize armed men was proving important. This was not a game that only the elites could play. The February 1823 Pedrosada in Pernambuco showed that the black and mulatto middling and lower classes might seize the opportunity to press for their interests. The mobilization of such men for armed action in 1817 and 1821 no doubt made the decision to take up arms once again easier.

The central issue in writing the new constitution was whether Pedro had final authority in political matters, as the direct embodiment of the nation, or if representative institutions expressed the will of the sovereign people of Brazil. Flustered at the direction in which the Constituent Assembly was headed, Pedro forcibly dismissed the assembly and issued a constitution written by allies who shared his vision of a centralized monarchy in which the emperor played the decisive role. Although Pedro was able to impose the Constitution of 1824, he was never able to reconcile with opponents who sought something closer to the British system of parliamentary predominance.

The most overt challenge to Pedro was the Confederation of the Equator, the 1824 secessionist republic centered on Pernambuco. This breakaway effort was militarily defeated rather easily, but it revealed the depth of alienation and resentment that Pedro's arbitrary actions had generated. (On the other hand, it also showed practical benefits for those who supported the crown, as Pedro's armed forces won the day and the elite members who supported him were rewarded with government posts.) For the remainder of the First Reign the locus of opposition to Pedro was in the Chamber of Deputies. A solid bloc of deputies proved obstructionist, hoping to force Pedro to yield some power to representative bodies. Even Pernambucan beneficiaries of Pedro's support, such as Holanda Cavalcanti, pressed him for ministerial responsibility in the Chamber of Deputies. By 1831 disenchantment with Pedro was so great that he was unable to maintain what he saw as his rightful role as Brazil's emperor. In April 1831 he abdicated, leaving his young son to rule one day. For the immediate future, however, his parliamentary opposition would have its opportunity to govern.

3

Liberal Reforms and the
Resort to Arms, 1831–35

Pedro's abdication came as a shock.[1] Politically active Brazilians were, like the citizens of any newly independent country, abruptly forced to confront basic political questions. In an emergency meeting, senators and deputies established a provisional regency. To the great disappointment of many radical liberals who had opposed Pedro through their street actions, the fiery language of their newspapers, and their nativism, the dream of a republic went unrealized.[2] When the General Assembly met in May, it reaffirmed its commitment to the monarchy and appointed a three-man regency to rule until the six-year-old heir to the throne, Pedro II, came of age. Throughout this regency (1831–40) intense struggles occurred over the nature of political authority and the appropriate institutional structures to ensure stability and progress.[3]

Far-reaching liberal reforms restructured political authority in this formative period. The early years of the regency saw dramatic institutional changes. Key liberal reforms decentralized power from the imperial court to the provinces and assigned citizens a more active role in the political process. The 1832 Criminal Procedure Code established locally elected justices of the peace as key figures in the criminal justice system. These judges enjoyed broad powers, including both judicial and police functions, and displaced the professional magistrates appointed by the court. The 1834 Additional Act deepened the decentralization of power, replacing the weak provincial general councils with provincial assemblies that enjoyed considerable prerogatives. Also noteworthy was the creation in 1831 of a national guard that replaced the militia inherited from the colonial period. Not only was the new force independent of the centrally controlled army, but election of its officers was a democratic innovation. In part, these reforms, especially the Additional Act, were a strategic response to the fear of a restoration attempt by Pedro and his Brazilian allies, the *caramurus*—or the *colunas*, as they were commonly referred to in Pernambuco (after the restorationist society Coluna do Trono e Altar, or Column of the Throne and Altar).[4] More fundamental, however, was an earnest commitment to institutional change based on localism as the means of securing a stable, progressive nation in which individuals could freely pursue their own goals.[5]

A series of revolts erupted in Pernambuco early in the regency. In September 1831 enlisted men in the army rose up in revolt, and military and civilian authorities promptly fled Recife. The military rebels, mostly victims of forced recruitment, cried out against corporal punishment, against the Portuguese, and against proponents of the restoration of Pedro I. The elites, in contrast, feared the collapse of social order in an overwhelming wave of anarchy. They quickly recovered control of Recife and killed perhaps several hundred men in the brutal repression that followed the revolt known as the Setembrizada. In November, extreme liberal military officers seized control of the Cinco Pontas fort in Recife and issued demands that Portuguese-born officials and their Brazilian—born restorationist allies be dismissed from military and judicial posts and that many of them be deported. With much of the army in Recife incarcerated, dismissed, or sent to other provinces following the events of September, militia members and other civilians gathered at the fort. These impromptu forces soon made clear, however, that they would not fire on the rebellious officers, whom they saw as fellow propertied citizens. This incident would be settled without any bloodshed.

If military revolts in September and November illustrated the strength of anti-Portuguese sentiments among both the enlisted men and officers of the army, in April of 1832 Portuguese-born military officers, urban shopkeepers and artisans, and their Brazilian-born planter allies demonstrated their willingness to take up arms. Leaders of the Abrilada, as their revolt came to be called, sought to restore Pedro to the throne and to recover positions they had lost since his abdication. They further mobilized a rural rebellion to complement the urban effort. Restorationist planters mobilized peasants who were also uneasy with the innovation, turbulence, and land encroachment of the period. The elite component of this alliance soon backtracked, but the lower classes carried on for three years, mounting the first significant peasant rebellion in Brazil.

In the unsettled conditions of the early regency, diverse groups were willing to press their agendas with arms in hand. Together with other revolts that broke out across Brazil, these upheavals raised doubts about the optimistic assumptions that intellectually undergirded the liberal reform efforts. Many of the elite would conclude that without traditional, centralized political authority, the social order could be profoundly threatened.

Judicial Reform: The Criminal Procedure Code of 1832

Portugal had exercised colonial rule in large part through its legal system, with judges defending the interests of the crown throughout the realm.[6] Criticism of the legal system, which, after independence, served the emperor in Rio de Janeiro, was widespread. Routine complaints concerned cost, inefficiency, and delays. Many voices denounced corruption and a corporate spirit among the magistracy. It was this system to which reformers first turned their attention.

Liberal, decentralizing reform actually had a modest beginning in the First Reign, with the passage in 1827 of a law establishing locally elected justices of the peace. Although the 1824 Constitution had called for this institution (indeed, there was a history of elected justices, with extremely limited powers, in the Portuguese empire), the law passed in 1827 was very much a product of the conflict between Pedro and the moderate and radical liberals. Although the institution of locally elected judges was certainly seen as a means to improve a judiciary associated with Portuguese absolutism, inefficiency, and corruption, its political importance lay in its establishment of "independent" judges—that is, judges not under the control of the central government. The responsibilities of these unpaid justices, for whom there was no requirement of legal training, were somewhat vague. They included encouraging out-of-court settlements of potential lawsuits, trying minor cases in which a negotiated settlement could not be reached, keeping the peace locally with limited police powers, assembling evidence for the prosecution of crimes, and enforcing municipal regulations. Three years later, another significant reform to the judicial system, the 1830 Criminal Code, was passed. This code replaced the body of Portuguese laws defining crimes and setting punishments. Significantly, legislators anxious to reduce the emperor's power reduced the scope of what qualified as political crimes and what punishments could be meted out. More profound changes would be crafted after Pedro's abdication.[7]

Of course, institutional changes that redistributed political power were not implemented without struggle. At the beginning of the regency, the Senate and the Chamber of Deputies battled for three years, debating fundamental reforms to overhaul the political system through modification of the 1824 Constitution. The Senate consistently attempted to block the far-reaching reforms proposed by the moderate and radical liberals to reduce the emperor's prerogatives, eliminate the Senate (or, failing that, to end its lifetime appointments), and shift power to the provinces. In July 1832 the frustrated minister of justice, Diogo Antônio Feijó, led a coup attempt with the support of the regents, the ministry, and the majority of the Chamber. The minister expected that, with the armed backing of the national guard, the Chamber of Deputies would declare itself a national convention in order to write a new constitution (the so-called Pouso Alegre Constitution) and pass sweeping reforms. A dramatic and powerful appeal to constitutional process by *mineiro* representative Honório Hermeto Carneiro Leão on the floor of the Chamber, however, rallied opposition to the effort and weakened the plotters' will. The coup attempt failed, with significant long-term consequences. Feijó's willingness to dismiss legality raised an ugly specter for men who prized order. It encouraged the drift of many *moderados* toward more conservative stances. It also increased personal bitterness and animosity toward Feijó, which later weakened him when he served as regent.

In the short run, however, even a failed coup attempt revealed the depth of desire for reform. The following day, the Senate approved a measure to allow the next legislature to reform the constitution. Within several months legislators passed the Criminal Procedure Code of 1832, over-hauling the judicial system inherited from the Portuguese empire.[8]

The Criminal Procedure Code of 1832 was based on the notion that localism would facilitate a more democratic and responsive system. Elections at the county level would bring to office men who enjoyed local support, had an interest in local stability, and, crucially, would not be agents of the government in Rio de Janeiro. Judicial independence from central control would strike the sharpest blow against the legal system founded on colonial rule.[9]

The 1832 Criminal Procedure Code greatly strengthened the elected justices of the peace, making them the linchpin of the criminal justice system and displacing centrally appointed, professional magistrates. The new position, which did not require a law degree, combined judicial and police functions. A justice of the peace could order arrests, a function previously limited to the police. Crucially, justices of the peace were entrusted with the *formação da culpa*—gathering the facts of the case, explaining the circumstances, citing which laws were broken, and justifying charges with statements and evidence. They tried lesser crimes themselves. A justice of the peace also exerted great influence over local elections. He served, with the parish priest and president of the municipal council, on the electoral boards that judged individuals' credentials to vote and counted the votes once cast. A justice of the peace could also influence voters directly through his right to authorize conscription and his ability to dispense favors.[10]

Localism also informed changes such as assigning municipal councils the role of presenting triplicate lists of nominees to the provincial president for the new position of county judge (who did not need a law degree and was largely an assistant to the district judge), for district attorneys, and for judges of orphans. Again, the central government was losing the power to make local appointments.[11]

The 1832 Criminal Procedure Code also instituted citizen juries. From the lists of electors (free men with an annual income of at least two hundred mil-réis), sixty jurors were randomly chosen. Twice a year, or up to six times a year in large cities such as Recife, grand juries and juries were assembled to hear cases. Centrally appointed, professional district judges were thus reduced to presiding over trials and deciding only the punishments for those found guilty by the juries. Individual liberties were further protected by the right of *habeas corpus*.[12]

The localism that underlay the 1832 Criminal Procedure Code can also be seen in the creation of the national guard in 1831. The commitment to decentralization is evident both in the basic concept of a local armed force that is independent of the centrally controlled army and, particularly, in the election of national guard officers. Income requirements for membership equaled those for voting, except in the empire's four largest cities, where the income requirement for national guard membership was double the requirement for voting. Thus, a local armed force of propertied (if sometimes rather modestly propertied) men was to help maintain order. Although its effectiveness in that central charge was often undermined by inadequate training and equipment, it was still of considerable importance, and all the more so in areas with only a limited military presence. The upheavals associated with barracks revolts and other disturbances by poor men drafted into the army in Pernambuco and across Brazil made reducing the size of the army, and partially replacing it with a national guard, all the more attractive to legislators. Membership in the guard in turn had an important reward; it offered a prized benefit to members: exemption from military recruitment.[13]

The Additional Act of 1834

In 1834 Pedro triumphed in securing the Portuguese crown for his daughter, increasing the expectation in Brazil of a restorationist attempt. This strengthened the hand of those Brazilians who sought to decentralize power in order to avoid the possibility of a coup in Rio de Janeiro that might seize the locus of institutional power. With this added threat, a legislative compromise was reached and the Additional Act of 1834 passed.[14]

Although they were successful in passing the Additional Act, liberals struggling against the legacy of absolutism failed in their attempts to abolish the Senate, a bulwark of royal authority, or its lifetime appointments, and provincial presidents continued to be appointed from Rio de Janeiro. Nor did the reformers manage to eliminate the emperor's extensive prerogatives under the constitution's "moderating power," which Friar Caneca, the eloquent leader shot for his role in Pernambuco's separatist rebellion in 1824, termed the "master key for oppression of the Brazilian nation and the strongest garrote of peoples' liberty" (playing off the constitutional affirmation that "the moderating power is the key to the entire political organization").[15] The Additional Act did, however, suspend this power during the regency period (1831–40). Liberals also succeeded in abolishing the Council of State, the influential policy-making and advisory body that assisted the emperor in his exercise of the moderating power and was a bastion of support for the absolutist tradition. Liberals firmed up the position of regent, replacing the three-man regency with a single regent, now chosen by the provincial electors. The *moderado* leader Diogo Antônio Feijó was elected to the post in 1835. The decisive victory, however, was obtained in delegating considerable powers to the provincial assemblies that replaced the weak provincial general councils.[16]

Provincial assemblies were authorized to legislate concerning the civil, judicial, and ecclesiastical structure of the provinces; public education; expropriations for the public good; municipal police; county and provincial taxes and expenditures; the creation and elimination of, and appointment to, provincial and county posts; public works; charitable organizations; and the provincial president's authority to appoint and dismiss provincial employees. The Additional Act at the same time established limits to the province's broad powers. Collection of provincial and county taxes was not to interfere with the ability of the national government to collect tax revenue. Import taxes were not allowed. Provinces could not legislate to the detriment of the interests of other provinces. Provincial presidents continued to be named by the imperial court. In Pernambuco the new provincial assembly, the Legislative Assembly of Pernambuco, would meet for the first time on April 1, 1835.[17]

Liberal reforms succeeded in undermining rule from Rio de Janeiro, rule that was associated with absolutism and colonial subjugation. The dependent magistracy that Portuguese rulers, and subsequently Pedro, had relied on saw its power significantly weakened as locally elected judicial officials gained new powers. The locus of state power shifted decisively toward the provinces, where provincial assemblies exercised broad authority.[18] Yet would greater provincial power, localism, and increased citizen participation succeed in Brazil? There were high expectations that liberal institutions that succeeded in Europe and the United States would bring about progressive changes in Brazil. Popular handbooks and newspaper articles explained the new institutions and suggested paths to responsible citizenship. Optimistic images of Brazil, emphasizing its vast potential and common interests in progress, offered an intellectual foundation for liberal reforms. Yet there were doubters from the start. Those who dissented tended not to see harmony in Brazilian social relations but instead to see diversity, conflict, and danger.[19]

The Regency and Political Order: The Setembrizada

Brazilian elites were deeply concerned with maintaining order. They were keenly aware of the profound divisions of class and race that structured their society, a society in which slavery played a prominent role. Thus, restructuring political institutions offered not only promise but risks as well. The crucial test of any reform effort would be if the promised improvements could be attained without upsetting social and political stability. Over time, a series of revolts and rebellions erupted in Pernambuco and elsewhere in Brazil. Along with the perception of a crime wave (discussed in chapter 4), such disruptions opened the way for a conservative critique of the liberal reforms that would have a profound and enduring impact.

Disorder and conflict marked the regency from its inception. It was the sight of several thousand people gathered in the national capital, including most of the military units there, and the prospect of violence that had prompted Pedro to abdicate. When word of events in the imperial court reached the provinces, uprisings erupted in various locales.[20] On May 4, news of the abdication reached Recife, where it was greeted with celebrations, fireworks, and frequent *vivas*. Seizing the opportunity, Capt. Francisco Ignácio Roma led forty to fifty military men to Olinda, where they were joined by other soldiers, officers, and law school students. They sent a petition requesting the dismissal of fourteen army officers and public employees "well known for their anti-national and openly absolutist behavior and opinions."[21] The list of Portuguese and their Brazilian-born absolutist allies to be dismissed included the commander of arms, Bento José Lamenha Lins; the military commander, Lt. Col. Francisco José Martins; and Captain Major Domingo Lourenço Tôrres

Galindo—all of whom had played prominent roles in putting down the 1824 Confederation of the Equator. The list also included two magistrates on the High Court of Appeals and commanders of the Eighteenth and Nineteenth Army Battalions. Two days of riots in Recife strengthened the bargaining position of those making demands in Olinda. The general council acted with urgency, accepting the demands and thus defusing the tense situation.[22] Far more dramatic, however, would be the events in September 1831.

Military troops provided the most significant armed force in the province. Paradoxically, however, these forces, crucial for social control, were themselves a source of considerable turmoil. Soldiers were forcibly recruited for lengthy terms of service, generally from the Afro-Brazilian poor, who lacked powerful patrons to protect them. Poorly paid and subject to harsh discipline, soldiers were quick to desert or rebel, and their rebellion reflected not only problems specific to military service but also a broader discontent among the poor.[23]

Brig. Gen. Francisco de Paula Vasconcelos, the commander of arms in charge of the military in the province, was keenly aware of the unreliability of the troops. Salaries were a particularly sore point with the soldiers. At 126 réis a day, the salary not only was quite small but, just as elsewhere in Brazil, it was routinely late, often many months in arrears. Compounding matters was the widespread counterfeiting of copper coins, the currency in which soldiers were paid, which led many merchants to refuse to accept them. Indeed, in September alone the government discovered two counterfeiting operations, which prompted the authorities to prohibit the sale of sheets of copper. The commander of arms pushed for prompt payment of salaries, but the issue was outside his control. He also tried to reduce wasteful use of military funds, terminating contracts of suppliers who failed to adequately meet their obligations and eliminating payments to officers who were no longer on active duty.[24]

At the same time, Brig. Gen. Vasconcelos insisted on strict discipline and was willing to use the common practice of corporal punishment to enforce it. Officers commonly whipped or beat soldiers. The beatings could be so brutal that an 1823 decree required that a doctor be present when corporal punishment was administered. On the night of September 14, 1831, the commander of arms's effort to impose discipline sparked a military rebellion. At issue was Brig. Gen. Vasconcelos's recent order to lock the gates to the barracks and carry out inspection of the troops at eight o'clock at night, the same time as the curfew imposed on slaves a month before. This additional indignity, together with indignation over the corporal punishments inflicted on several soldiers that afternoon, made the situation unbearable. (A few years earlier, a critic of the recruitment system, Gen. Cunha Mattos, compared the status of the conscripted soldier to that of slaves. On the floor of the Chamber of Deputies he said, "The worst disgrace in all the universe is to be a recruit in Brazil. It is a real punishment; a common soldier is considered a miserable slave.")[25]

At nine o'clock, soldiers of the Fourteenth Battalion from Rio de Janeiro, stationed in Santo Antônio, began shouting about the commander of arms, who quickly arrived at the barracks, only to be met with gunshots. The rebellion spread rapidly to the Campo do Erário, where artillery troops joined the rebels, bringing artillery pieces with them. Rebellious troops broke into the Laboratório, an arms deposit, seized more weapons and ammunition, and then set fire to the building. Soon troops across the Bairro de Santo Antônio were in rebellion, shooting their guns, looting stores and taverns, clamoring for an end to corporal punishment, for the death of the commander of arms, and against the Portuguese. Rebels freed prisoners from jails. Some slaves and some of the urban poor joined in the looting. By eleven o'clock, another arms deposit, the Trem, was broken into and its arms distributed. The elite's ever-present fear of anarchy, so often a subtext in the political discourse of the period, was being realized.[26]

That evening, the commander of arms went to the Cinco Pontas fort to gather troops and exhort civilians to arm themselves and help regain control of the city. The next day, September 15, Commander Vasconcelos returned to the Cinco Pontas fort with the military, militia, and civilian forces he had gathered on the city's outskirts. Rebellious soldiers left the fort and fraternized with Vasconcelos's men. With cries of "traitors" and "death to the colunas" (restorationists), Vasconcelos's troops turned on him and on the other officers and the civilians who supported him, chasing them from the city.[27] The brigadier general sent messengers to gather militia troops from the interior of the province. Francisco

Ignácio Ribeiro Roma was sent to Cabo and his brother, João Ignácio Ribeiro Roma, to Casa Forte to gather army battalions. Not until midday on September 16 would the commander of arms be ready to enter the fray again.[28]

Meanwhile, the intendant of the navy, Lt. Capt. Antônio Pedro de Carvalho, attempted to halt the spread of the rebellion to the Bairro do Recife. When the rebellion broke out in Bairro do Santo Antônio, Carvalho was worried about the large crowd that gathered at the Arco da Conceição. He went to the arsenal, gathered a few troops, and had the justice of the peace gather civilians and instruct them to chop down (and make impassible) a section of the bridge that linked the Bairro de Santo Antônio with the Arco da Conceição in the Bairro do Recife, the heavily Portuguese business district. The civilians strongly opposed this, however, and prevailed by claiming that the disturbances were simply arguments among soldiers and were not serious. Despite the intendant's requests, the civilians simply dispersed.[29]

On September 15 looting had spread to the Bairro do Recife, and the intendant gathered civilians from Fora de Portas. Seventy volunteers from Olinda, including fifty students from the law school there, joined the police and Arsenal Guard. After setting out to stop the looting, however, about forty of the police and Arsenal Guard mutinied. The remainder of the intendant's force quickly dispersed under fire. The law students regrouped and went to the Fortaleza do Brum, only to discover that the soldiers there also had rebelled when their officers began firing on rioters on the bridge to the Bairro do Recife. Led by the intendant, the law students managed to take back the fort when the rebellious soldiers abandoned it to join the rebel assault on the arsenal to seize more artillery pieces. On September 16 the intendant ordered the war schooner *Rio da Prata* to fire on the barricades in the Arco da Conceição, near the bridge linking the Bairro do Recife with Santo Antônio. Once the barricades were demolished, order was soon reestablished in the Bairro do Recife.[30]

By the afternoon of September 16 the bulk of the rebels and their artillery pieces were concentrated in Santo Antônio, near the Palácio Velho. The various groups attempting to reestablish order converged there. The eighty to a hundred men whom João Ignácio Ribeiro Roma had gathered in Casa Forte joined the three hundred to four hundred men that militia Col. Francisco Jacinto Pereira had brought from Olinda. Students and other civilians in the Fortaleza do Brum joined in, as did various civilians from the Bairro do Recife. When the rebels opened fire at two o'clock, Col. Francisco Jacinto's men and the civilians from Recife led the attack and the rebels were soon defeated. The revolt was over.[31]

This rebellion, called the Setembrizada, demonstrated the precarious nature of social and political order. Even the most important repressive force, the military, was itself a source of instability. Contemporary observers were quick to point out the inherent risks in forced recruiting of the poor. The Sociedade Patriótica Harmonizadora (Patriotic Harmonizing Society), a moderate liberal group, noted the dangers of relying on "those cohorts of mercenaries often pulled from prisons to which they had been sent for their immoral acts."[32] A letter to a newspaper characterized forced recruits as "extracted from the most vile and most corrupt class of society . . . (with) all the attendant vices and crimes of an entirely brutal education and without the slightest honor or virtue."[33] Forcibly seized, poorly fed and clothed, paid little and late, and punished severely, the armed men of the marginal poor had proven unreliable.

In the aftermath of the rebellion, Pernambucan authorities called in troops from other provinces to guard the large number of prisoners. Law students consented to manning forts for several months. The ranks of the municipal guards were raised to five hundred.[34] Other measures taken by the justice of the peace of Santo Antônio revealed great anxiety. He prohibited dancing in the streets by slaves during the festival of Our Lady of the Rosary, sponsored by an Afro-Brazilian brotherhood. He instructed police to prohibit gatherings of any kind, shouting in the streets, *batuques* (gatherings at which Afro-Brazilians, especially slaves, drank and danced, accompanied by percussion instruments), and any incidents in which individuals incited others to anger, whether by showing a lack of respect, by drunken behavior, or by throwing stones.[35] Efforts to retrieve the arms stolen or distributed to civilians who helped put down the rebellion met with little success.[36]

The newspaper *Diário de Pernambuco* suggested reducing the size of the conscript army by dispersing soldiers to the countryside to perform agricultural labor and replacing them with a small, well-paid militia recruited from property-owning citizens. The newspaper thus anticipated similar reforms that had recently passed in the imperial court (but news of which had not yet reached Pernambuco), which reduced the size of the army and created the national guard. In Rio de Janeiro, soldiers also had played a prominent role in upheavals that followed Pedro's abdication. Based on a recently passed French law establishing a national guard, the moderate liberal cabinet in power in the court placed its hopes on a national guard made up of propertied citizens and led by elected officers, which would maintain order and carry out certain police functions. In the wake of the Setembrizada, the *Diário de Pernambuco*'s suggestion that a citizens' militia take over some functions from a reduced army reflected widespread lack of confidence among moderate liberals in an army that was all too prone to revolts (and that drained the national treasury).[37]

Reports by the provincial president, the commander of arms, and several military leaders, as well as journalistic accounts, emphasized the spontaneous nature of the uprising, denying it any political motivation.[38] The provincial president declared to the minister of the empire that it had "no political character." He reported that "it was not possible to deal with rebels, who, armed, and spread across the entire city in groups, demanded nothing and did not have a leader." He also noted that no attempt was made to seize the presidential palace, nor had any attempt been made on his life.[39] Little effort was made to organize an effective rebel defense.[40] Indeed, many of the rebels abandoned themselves to drinking and frequenting houses of prostitution. Many of the stolen goods were subsequently found in brothels.[41] Nor did any officers incite the men to riot. Numerous reports had soldiers consistently expelling officers from their midst. The commander of the Thirteenth Battalion, for example, reported that his troops were furious in their insistence that they would not accept orders from him or any other officers.[42]

Although most accounts blamed harsh discipline for provoking the uprising, the *Diário de Pernambuco* suggested afterward that the rebellion may have been the result of a restorationist conspiracy that sought the return of Pedro I to the Brazilian throne. The newspaper noted that a few witnesses had asserted that fireworks had gone off just before the outburst, possibly as a signal to begin the rebellion. Presenting no evidence, the newspaper asked rhetorically why the restorationists would not sow disorder to open the way for Pedro's return and suggested that troop rebellions in Rio de Janeiro and Salvador, Bahia, may have been similarly motivated.[43] Yet leading officials and military officers, even the commander of arms, a noted sympathizer of the radical liberals and a proponent of federalism, all failed to report evidence of such a conspiracy. In fact, the greatest losses in the uprising were suffered by the small businesses dominated by the Portuguese—the thirty-three stores and twenty-one taverns looted in Santo Antônio, the nine stores and four taverns looted in the Bairro do Recife, and the three taverns looted in Boa Vista.[44] The *Diário de Pernambuco*'s suggestion seems to have been part of the jostling for partisan advantage as it debated with the extreme liberal newspaper *Bússola da Liberdade* (Compass of Liberty) over who deserved more credit in putting down the rebellion. Restorationists maneuvered for political advantage as well, making an appeal to people of color and trying to drive a wedge between them and the restorationists' political opponents.[45]

The anarchy that gripped Recife was clearly not in the interests of any of the politically active groups of propertied men. Faced with the breakdown of order, the elites of the region, of all political descriptions, came together. Militia units, civilian volunteers rounded up by the justices of the peace, and law students from Olinda were mobilized to restore order.[46] Assistance from the interior of the province was crucial. Regaining control of the city was achieved at no small cost; contemporary estimates placed the number of rebels killed between one hundred and three hundred, with about thirty deaths among their opponents. About one thousand rebels were arrested, including more than eight hundred soldiers. Most of those arrested were sent immediately to ships in the harbor, and many were subsequently banished to the distant island of Fernando de Noronha for imprisonment.[47]

A reference in the official narration of the events to abuses during the reestablishment of order, as well as a proclamation circulated by the provincial president and the provincial general council warning against excesses in searches and in arrests of criminals, raises the question of the severity of acts of vengeance. Given the low number of casualties among those repressing the rebellion, it seems possible that many of the deaths of the defeated may have come not in pitched battles but from retaliatory acts. Mário Márcio de Almeida Santos has gone so far as to argue that most of the rebels were massacred, as those repressing the rebellion responded to their fear of anarchy with acts of utter savagery. Almeida Santos judges the repression as thoroughly excessive and contrasts the repression with the lack of killing by the rebels, noting that there were no rapes reported and that only one house was burned down by the rebels.[48]

Statements and testimony of the rebels have not survived, but the attitudes of the rebels can be inferred. There were various reports of shouts against the commander of arms, against corporal punishment, and against the Portuguese. One cry, sounded repeatedly during wild shooting of firearms, summed up the complaint: "Out with the *colunas* (restorationists)! Out with the *castigo de espada* [being struck with the flat of the sword]! Out with the Brigadier [Commander of Arms Vasconcelos]! Out with the *marinheiros* [sailors, i.e., Portuguese]! Long live Pedro II, Long live Brazilians!"[49] Such protests clearly contradict the various assertions that the disturbances were apolitical in nature. Appointed officials, military leaders, and most journalistic reports may have been accurate in describing the outbreak as spontaneous, but divorcing events from their political context distorts them. True, the rebels did not, for example, engage in negotiations with representatives of formal political institutions. Yet they protested their conscription in political terms—their shouts invoked the emperor, attacked restorationists, railed against the Portuguese, and demanded changes in the military institution into which they had been forcibly conscripted by the state.[50]

The fusion of outrage against the commander of arms and outrage against the Portuguese points to an important element of the political context. Portuguese-born officers were numerous in the Brazilian army. At the time of independence the number of Brazilian-born officers was small enough that it was imperative that the army allow many Portuguese-born officers to remain in the institution; indeed, at the rank of general they outnumbered Brazilian-born officers in 1831.[51] This presumably accounted for some of the cries against Brig. Gen. Vasconcelos that identified him as a restorationist—for example, "Out with Vasconcelos, who's a *coluna*, death to the *colunas!*"[52] The commander's political orientation was far different, however. He had played a key role in exerting military pressure against Pedro, helping to force his abdication.[53] After arriving in Pernambuco in late June, he proceeded to reintegrate some officers who had been expelled after the suppression of the 1824 Confederation of the Equator, and he removed a number of officers considered to be absolutists and of questionable loyalty to the national cause.[54] Vasconcelos had even been elected the first vice-president of the radical liberal Federalist Society, which formed in October.[55] In the course of military reforms he had angered various restorationists when he terminated their contracts as suppliers to the military.[56] Yet in the minds of many of the aggrieved soldiers, the commander, hated for his efforts to impose discipline, was equated with the evils of the Portuguese and their restorationist Brazilian allies.

The anger the soldiers felt for the Portuguese exposes an important issue. Because Portuguese-born naturalized citizens made up a large percentage of the upper ranks of the army officer corps, outrage at corporal punishment and other military issues might be directed at Portuguese-born officers (or, as in the case of Brig. Gen. Vasconcelos, someone confused with their restorationist allies) and fused with other resentments toward the Portuguese. Anti-Portuguese hatred (or Lusophobia), however, encompassed far more than resentment of the military. Hatred of the Portuguese and of Portuguese-born naturalized citizens (also known as *adotivos*, those who acquired Brazilian citizenship after independence) was widespread.

The continued political influence and economic importance of the Portuguese and Portuguese-born citizens after independence seemed to frustrate expectations for change. The anti-colonial discourse of the independence era of course blamed the Portuguese for many of the ills afflicting Brazil. That Portuguese-born officials, especially ministers and advisors to Pedro, continued to exert political influence was a source of tension throughout the First Reign and was linked to the struggle over Pedro's efforts to maintain a centralized political system, a system that to Pedro's critics was reminiscent of Portuguese absolutism. The strong presence of the Portuguese in retail commerce also was deeply resented. On the one hand, the Portuguese appeared to be monopolizing job opportunities, with Portuguese shop owners seemingly colluding to hire only their own countrymen rather than Brazilians. On the other hand, the heavy Portuguese presence in retail commerce put a Portuguese face on the rising prices of the period and on the common refusal to accept the easily counterfeited copper coins of the era. There was also an element of racial tension because the Brazilian lower classes had a very large Afro-Brazilian component. Thus, the Setembrizada rebels' intense anti-Portuguese hatred, which burst forth propelled by specifically military issues, was no doubt fed by a deeper well of Lusophobia.[57]

The Novembrada

The Setembrizada demonstrated that the elite's doubts about social stability and their ever-present fear of anarchy were indeed well founded. Then, just two months after the violent eruption of poor, forcibly conscripted soldiers in September, a different type of challenge arose. Radical liberals took control of Cinco Pontas fort, the principal fort in the city. The Novembrada, as the revolt came to be known, contrasted sharply with events in September. Military officers and propertied citizens, with clear leadership and well-defined political goals, staged the second revolt. These men insisted that they were exercising their right to petition the government. They engaged in no random violence or looting and killed no one.

The radical liberal demands centered on displacing the Portuguese and their Brazilian allies from their government posts. A list was prepared of thirty-three people who were to be dismissed from judicial, military, and other posts and deported, including prominent restorationists such as Manuel Pedro de Moraes Mayer, Domingo Lourenço Tôrres Galindo, Col. Bento José Lamenha Lins, and even the Marquis of Recife, Francisco Paes Barreto. Another list named eight others who were simply to be dismissed from their posts. All the Portuguese-born officials who had become naturalized Brazilians after independence were to be fired from their public posts as well, except those who had distinguished themselves in service to Brazil. All Portuguese with less than two million réis (a large majority of Portuguese residents) were to be deported, as were those who were single or "enemies of liberty." Government weapons that had been distributed to the Portuguese, including militia members, were to be confiscated. Finally, the ban on foreign societies and political groups was to be enforced. The rebels' petition railed against the restoration-ist political society Coluna do Trono e Altar and warned against an attempted military invasion by the "despot" Pedro.[58] Once again we see the centrality of Lusophobia, although in the case of officers and propertied citizens the focus was specifically on displacing the Portuguese-born officers and their allies from their posts and thus opening up access to their government positions.

The revolt seems to have been set off by the dismissal of Brig. Gen. Vasconcelos from his position as commander of arms. In the first days of November, Pernambuco received word that the minister of war had replaced Vasconcelos after receiving news of the Setembrizada.[59] Both the radical liberal newspaper *Bússola da Liberdade* and the more moderate *Diário de Pernambuco* criticized the move.[60] A petition to rescind the measure was circulated by the radical liberals.[61] Apparently the loss of a powerful supporter prompted the radicals to resort to dramatic means to press their nativist agenda.[62]

On the night of November 15, a group overpowered those guarding the Cinco Pontas fort in the Santo Antônio district of Recife. Provincial President Francisco de Carvalho Paes de Andrade immediately sent a justice of the peace from Santo Antônio to disperse them, but they refused to leave the fort. The rebels argued that they were not an illegal gathering of armed men; rather, they were peaceably gathered citizens and they insisted on their constitutional right to petition the government.[63] Without sufficient force to overwhelm the fort, the provincial government bided its time. On November 16 emissaries from the government were told to wait, that a petition would be issued. The rebels were gaining strength as people entered the fort to join them. Even some of the soldiers instructed to impede the action went over to the rebel side. Meanwhile, some inhabitants of the city, with memories of the Setembrizada still fresh in their minds, abandoned Recife for the safety of ships in the harbor, carrying what possessions they could.[64]

With much of the army incarcerated or dismissed after the Setembrizada, the government amassed some eight hundred militiamen and civilians who were gathered by the justices of the peace. Yet the efforts to use force to rout the radicals were undermined when the citizens refused to fire on the rebels. After all, unlike the lower-class soldiers of the

Setembrizada, these rebels included military officers and were of similar background to the propertied militiamen and citizens. The newspaper *Olindense* reported that the militia and citizens argued that "those in the fort are Brazilians, . . . they have not yet acted aggressively, is there any need to spill blood?"[65] The *Diário de Pernambuco* later criticized their insistent claim that "we will not fire on our countrymen."[66]

On November 17 the rebels finally issued their petition, which was promptly rejected.[67] The provincial president then instructed troops not to fire unless fired on first, to "avoid insults and demonstrations of enthusiasm for the triumph . . . (and proceed) carefully, so that not even one drop of blood is spilled."[68] He also allowed the Federalist Society to send a commission to the fort to convince the rebels to put down their arms. The Federalist Society shared many of the rebels' goals, and the commission was greeted enthusiastically. It failed, however, to convince the rebels to abandon the fort. The Federalist Society sent a second commission the following day, which was joined by Francisco Carneiro Machado Rios and several members of the law school faculty, including future statesmen João Lins Vieira da Cançação and José Tomás Nabuco de Araújo. The rebels issued a reduced, although still considerable, list of demands to the commission—that the Portuguese be disarmed, that Portuguese without two million réis be deported, and that the government not treat the rebels as if they were engaged in a criminal act.[69]

Although by this time the government had assembled more forces, it did not attack. One historian has seen this as evidence of the provincial president's indecisiveness, yet the restraint was consistent with the president's manifest desire to avoid bloodshed; and it was tactically sound, as the rebels would only weaken over time. They were trapped in the fort, without supplies, while the government accumulated forces from the interior of the province.[70] Indeed, the weakness of their position was becoming clear, and on November 18 some rebels abandoned the fort. The next morning, nearly all the rebels left the fort, and it was taken without resistance.[71]

The Novembrada demonstrated key characteristics of Pernambuco's rough-and-tumble political struggle during this period of fluidity. After Pedro's abdication, there was no royal figure on the throne to symbolize the unity of Brazil and the stability of its institutions. The regency that ruled in place of Pedro's son could not embody authority and stability as fully as an emperor exercising his powers. Political institutions and practice were open to challenge. In Pernambuco, radical liberals, repressed since the defeat of the 1824 Confederation of the Equator, had become newly active since Pedro's abdication, resorting to violence in order to pressure the government to carry out their favored policies. The government's tenuous control of armed force, particularly after the imprisoning of eight hundred soldiers following the Setembrizada, made such a tactic feasible. The government possessed no monopoly over the instruments of coercion. Various groups could mobilize armed men.

In this particular instance, the radicals' armed efforts failed. The government dismissed a few restorationist army officers, but otherwise the demands for action against the Portuguese and their allies went unsatisfied. Indeed, Col. Pereira dos Santos, an ally of the dismissed commander of arms, Brig. Gen. Vasconcelos, was briefly jailed, and the two radical liberal officers who led the rebellion were jailed for several months.[72] Moreover, the rift between the moderates and the radical liberals, who had been allies during the struggle against Pedro (and potential allies against any restorationist attempt), was significantly exacerbated.[73] Nonetheless, the government's conciliatory efforts and pursuit of a peaceful resolution even in the face of an armed challenge to its authority, as well as the refusal of the militia and citizenry to fire on the rebellious officers and citizens, made clear that the resort to arms could be a viable tactic in political struggle.

The Abrilada

The next month, December 1831, a restorationist rebellion led by Joaquim Pinto Madeira erupted in the interior of Ceará and spread quickly to the backlands of nearby provinces.[74] Fearful of a broader conspiracy to facilitate Pedro's return to the Brazilian throne, and worried by rumors of an uprising in Pernambuco to support Pinto Madeira, the government tightened security measures. Influential restorationists Domingos Lourenço Tôrres Galindo and Bento José Lamenha Lins were ordered to appear in Recife for questioning, and authorities searched many Portuguese houses for arms. The effect, however, was to prompt, earlier than planned, the rebellion known as the Abrilada.[75]

This time the conspirators were mainly restorationists—both Portuguese-born citizens and their Brazilian-born allies. In a period of ferment of liberal ideas from abroad and turbulent challenges to traditional
authority, restorationists sought a retreat from unsettling change. They
hoped the return of Pedro would allow them to recover the positions and
privileges lost or threatened in recent years. Portuguese-born military
officers, for example, were deeply resented by Brazilian-born officers. In
Pernambuco, some officers had been expelled or threatened with expulsion after the riots in May 1831 (when news arrived of Pedro's abdication) and after the Novembrada.[76] The Portuguese-born officers played
a prominent role in the Abrilada. Likewise, planters in the interior who
had lost their positions as colonial militia officers when that militia was
eliminated were fearful of persecution by their local enemies, and they
conspired with restorationists in Recife to open a second front in the interior of the province. Portuguese shop owners, clerks, and artisans in
Recife, victims of the heightening nativism of the times (as in the recent
Setembrizada) and no doubt resentful of calls for their expulsion, were
active in the Fifty-third Militia Battalion that was central to the rebellion. In addition, wealthy Portuguese merchants were a significant force
in the restorationist milieu. With large loans extended to Brazilian landowners and valuable merchandise warehoused in Recife, they had much
to lose if nativism spread dramatically.[77]

The prominent Cavalcanti family provided another source of support,
including hosting some of the conspiratorial meetings on their property. The Cavalcantis, along with Francisco Paes Barreto (the Viscount,
and future Marquis, of Recife), did not show great interest in restoration. They did, however, want a chance to topple the provincial government of Francisco de Carvalho so that one of their own, Provincial Vice-
President Francisco de Paula Cavalcanti de Albuquerque, could assume
the presidency. When the urban rebellion failed, however, they quickly
withdrew their support.[78]

The conspirators counted on the relative weakness of the government's
armed support. Not only had the Setembrizada left many of the military
troops imprisoned or dismissed, but the Novembrada had opened a rift
between the government and the radical liberals, whose combativeness
made them especially valuable beyond their numerical importance and

significant presence in the army. With the government relying on the volunteer municipal guard and the militia, many of whom were Portuguese and favorable to the restorationist cause, the conspirators' plan to launch a simultaneous rebellion in Recife and in the countryside posed a formidable threat.[79]

On the night of April 14, 1832, the Fifty-third Militia Battalion, composed largely of Portuguese-born men and stationed in the Bairro do Recife, the commercial district with a heavy Portuguese presence, rose in rebellion. Some Portuguese-born men in the militia in Santo Antônio crossed over to the Bairro do Recife in support of the movement. The rebels damaged the bridge linking the Bairro do Recife with Santo Antônio, built barricades from the customs building to the Arco da Conceição (next to the bridge connecting the Bairro do Recife with Santo Antônio), and placed an artillery piece near the bridge as well. Through the Brum and Buraco forts, where lack of resistance indicated connivance on the part of the commanders, the rebels commanded control of the isthmus to Olinda that provided the only other access to the peninsula on which the Bairro do Recife was built. With the Bairro secure, they planned to await news of the uprisings in the interior.[80]

Deprived of significant military troops, the government relied on the Fifty-fourth Militia Battalion, the permanent municipal guards, the national guards from nearby towns, Olinda law students, and volunteers. Col. José Joaquim Coelho led these forces.[81] On April 15 the schooner *Rio da Prata* began firing on the Arco da Conceição and 400 to 450 men attempted to enter the Bairro do Recife. This initial assault failed because they could not cross the damaged bridge and artillery fire forced the ship to withdraw. In the meantime, the students from Olinda, led by the commander of arms, Major Joaquim Jose da Silva Santiago, crossed the isthmus from Olinda, took the Buraco fort, and fired artillery shots at the Brum fort for the rest of the day. On April 15 the fort fell to the students. On the next day, Coelho's forces from Santo Antônio, carrying large wooden boards to pass over the damaged areas of the bridge, successfully passed into the Bairro do Recife.[82]

The rebels, already in flight, put up no resistance to the forces from Santo Antônio. Up until this point, casualties had been relatively low (one source cites sixteen dead), but now the killing began in earnest. An eyewitness subsequently wrote of a massacre. Rebels who surrendered were murdered. Some were marched off the damaged bridge to drown. Others were shot on *jangadas* as they tried to reach ships in the harbor. Some sought refuge in churches, but those in the Madre de Deus Convent found no succor. A contemporary reported that amidst angry screams and the echo of repeated gunfire, rebels were systematically killed. Others, however, escaped the Bairro do Recife; among them, the leaders of the rebellion, Col. Francisco José Martins and Sgt. Maj. José Gabriel de Morais Maier.[83]

The Guerra dos Cabanos

In the meantime, a rural uprising erupted that became known as the Guerra dos Cabanos (named after *cabanos*, the rural people who dwelled in shacks or shanties, called *cabanas*). Men who had participated in the repression of the 1824 Confederation of the Equator, and who were rewarded by the provincial administrations that followed until Pedro's abdication in 1831, planned and led the insurrection. Captain Major Domingo Lourenço Tôrres Galindo, a cotton planter in Vitória who was dismissed after the events of May 1831, was active not only in plotting against Francisco de Carvalho's government in Pernambuco but also in aiding Pinto Madeira's restorationist rebellion with men and supplies. Supporters in the south of the province were led by Sgt. Maj. Manuel Afonso de Melo. From Barra Grande, Lt. Col. João Batista de Araújo mobilized support, including financial support from the local Portuguese community. Considerable support was forthcoming for the rebellion in the south of the province, where landowners who were rewarded for their efforts against the 1824 Confederation of the Equator rebels were increasingly marginalized after Pedro's abdication. Across the province, former captain majors and sergeant majors of the extinguished colonial militias played leading roles in the rebellion.[84]

The rural rebellion proved to be far longer lasting than the barracks uprising in Recife. Forests and mountains impeded rapid movement of forces and facilitated ambushes by the rebels. The government's shortage of arms and ammunition, as well as the habitually late payment of salaries, continued to damage troop morale and effectiveness. The rebel forces were substantially enlarged when Antônio Timóteo, a small property owner from Panelas de Miranda, mobilized hundreds of Indians from Jacuípe for the struggles. The rebels then numbered more than one thousand. Abuses by soldiers, such as theft and rape, helped alienate the rural population, many of whom were already sympathetic to the rebel cause. Nevertheless, over the course of 1832, local opponents of the rebels, armed by the provincial government and aided by the five hundred members of the municipal guard of the capital and the newly organized national guards of various towns, managed some victories. Tôrres Galindo fled the province in September; Manuel Afonso de Melo and João Batista de Araújo were arrested in October. The following month in Ceará, the militia and army troops sent from Rio de Janeiro succeeded in capturing Pinto Madeira. Much of the leadership of the restorationist rebellion had been eliminated.[85]

The rebellion did not end when the bulk of the leadership failed, however. Restorationist conspirators had expected a quick victory, and when the urban rebellion failed, they shifted to a guerrilla strategy. In light of the considerable elite preoccupations with social control, this was a dramatic decision. Mobilizing the lower classes for intra-elite conflict and engaging in prolonged violence would be fraught with risks. Indeed, even as most of the remaining restorationist leaders fled, were captured, or simply abandoned arms, the rebellion did not end. Rather, the struggle was transformed into the first major peasant rebellion in Brazil.

Restorationist planters had, in time-tested fashion, mobilized their retainers to supply the bulk of the rebel forces. In the south of the province, especially in the Jacuípe Valley and Panelas, this involved mobilizing Indians. There was nothing new about this. As early as the seventeenth century, Indians had fought against the Dutch and against the runaway slaves of the Palmares *quilombo*. Indians had fought in the independence struggles. Although they lived in their own communities and possessed land grants, and although they had a greater degree of independence than did personal retainers on landed estates, their leaders were still subordinate to the locally powerful and were incorporated into clientelistic networks. Exercise of their rights might have depended de facto on understandings with the locally powerful.[86]

If many Indians were mobilized through clientelistic ties, others joined the rebel cause due to the hardship that the government imposed on them during the rebellion itself. The provincial government authorized large-scale forced recruitment in the areas of the struggle. In Panelas, attempts to draft all men between eighteen and twenty-five years of age set off a rebellion and brought large numbers of Indians into the battle against the provincial government. Land encroachment accelerated during the course of the war, as area landlords who sided with the government seized the opportunity to expel Indians from their lands. Indians and other rural poor persons, many of them recently evicted from their lands, continued the struggle the restorationists had begun for three more years.[87]

By the end of 1832, when the upper-class leaders of the rebellion had been eliminated, Vicente de Paula emerged as the undisputed leader of the peasant rebellion. This former army sergeant and deserter, son of a priest from Goiana, proved to be a charismatic figure who effectively led the cabanos throughout the rest of the war.[88] From Indians, the rural poor, and runaway slaves, he molded a fighting force that for three years used guerilla tactics to stymie the government. Vicente de Paula organized his forces in accordance with his military experience, and he took the title of General of the Royalist Force.[89]

Vicente de Paula's calls for the restoration of Pedro responded to the upheaval of recent years. He crystallized the discontent of the rural poor, blaming the various crises that befell them on the liberals who had overthrown the emperor. Legal protection of the forests as a government monopoly was repealed after Pedro's abdication, facilitating the seizure of lands by powerful landowners. Land encroachment increased. Inflation hit the poor very hard. Over the course of the rebellion, liberal reforms that shifted the locus of political power to provinces and municipalities made the locally prominent even more powerful, diminishing the mediating role the state had played previously. Vicente articulated a belief that the problems afflicting the rural poor were the handiwork of irreligious jacobins, liberals who respected neither property nor tradition nor God. His proclamations and letters urged the return of an absolutist regime in which Pedro would not be restrained by a constitution.[90]

Under Vicente de Paula's leadership, the cabanos were composed almost entirely of the rural poor. Yet they attracted the support of restorationists elsewhere. They periodically received aid from Recife. Ammunition was occasionally supplied from Maceió, the capital of Alagoas.

Indecision on the part of the provincial president and army in Alagoas was of such benefit to rebels operating in that province that one historian has speculated that the authorities might have been sympathizers.[91] Even prominent Pernambucan restorationists in Rio de Janeiro maintained hopes for their cause. Gen. José Ignácio Abreu e Lima wrote from the imperial court to his brothers Luís and João, both of whom were also involved in the restorationist cause, urging Luís to go to the battlefield in Jacuípe and assume leadership of the movement. "Do not delay one moment, apart from the *cabanos*, I do not see any solution for Brazil." He assured his brother that with a prominent victory and his own subsequent public incorporation into the movement, a widespread restorationist movement would erupt.[92]

Outside support, however, was never enough to greatly aid the cabanos. Still, for the provincial government, with its limited resources, it was no easy task to easily impose itself in the countryside against an often hostile population. Indeed, the government's difficulties in suppressing the cabanos created new problems when radical liberals sought to exploit the government's weakness on three separate occasions in 1834 and 1835. Brothers Antônio Carneiro Machado Rios and Francisco Carneiro Machado Rios led these efforts and the incidents came to be named after them. In the first "Carneirada," in January 1834, the brothers mobilized large numbers of national guardsmen and gathered in Recife, insisting on more energetic action against the restorationist cabanos. The guardsmen's refusal to disperse showed the fragility of Provincial President Francisco de Paula de Almeida e Albuquerque's position. He promptly resigned and was replaced as provincial president by Manuel de Carvalho Paes de Andrade, the rebel of 1817 and leader of the Confederation of the Equator. A stronger figure, Manuel de Carvalho offered assurances that everything possible would be done against the cabanos, and he gathered a sufficiently large number of armed men to intimidate the guardsmen and prompt them to disperse.

The second and third Carneiradas encompassed several episodes about a year later. During a December 2, 1834, parade in honor of the emperor's birthday, Francisco Carneiro Machado Rios attempted to gather enough armed force to overthrow the provincial president. After this attempt failed, he drew up a plan to coordinate a march and urban uprising in Recife by supporters in the south, in Alagoas dos Gatos. On January 11 two hundred guardsmen in Alagoas dos Gatos imprisoned their officers and set off on a march to Recife with a piece of artillery in tow. The urban plotters, meanwhile, issued proclamations and writings to mobilize support in Recife. On December 20, Antônio Carneiro Machado Rios issued a proclamation in which he attacked the government in Rio de Janeiro. He claimed that the government bribed people throughout the provinces to gain support for its persecution of liberals. Antônio Carneiro Machado Rios denounced the government's "paltry reform," which did not even allow voters to select a group of three citizens from among whom the government could select one as provincial president. He further denounced Manuel Carvalho de Andrade as a "false republican" who was about to be selected as a senator of the empire. His efforts did mobilize support, but the plotters, who were to coordinate their uprising with the arrival of their allies from Alagoas dos Gatos, grew impatient and rose up before the guardsmen from the south arrived. With considerable support behind them, at one point they threatened to overrun the government palace. After about twenty hours, however, government forces managed to recover control of the city. The third Carneirada began in late January, in the aftermath of this defeat, as 160 rebels who had retreated north of Recife gained enough adherents to bring their number to 300. They successfully seized control of Goiana but failed to take Recife. Government forces of about equal number pursued them, and the rebels dispersed, retreating to the safety of the Catucá forest. By late March the rebels abandoned any further resistance.[93]

Despite these uprisings, 1834 saw the turning of the tide in the struggle against the cabanos. A scorched-earth policy, in which everyone in the theater of operations was warned to leave the area or be treated as cabanos, proved decisive, and a fierce campaign by the government followed. Offers of amnesty separated many rebels from their cause. In 1835 the Bishop of Pernambuco toured the region, preaching among the rebels and convincing most to lay down their arms. Vicente de Paula and a small number of followers, mostly escaped slaves who feared bondage and punishment, refused. They founded a community, Riacho do Mato, where, protected by difficult access in mountainous forests, they were not captured. However, the Guerra dos Cabanos was over.[94]

Despite finally putting down the rebellion, the government revealed its weakness. Undermined by conflict among its supporters, a lack of supplies for its troops, and the inability to control the excesses of its soldiers or avoid their desertion, the government had needed three years to win the war. Much of the fighting had been carried out by local planters and their retainers, supplied and funded from by the provincial government in Recife.[95] The government's authority in the countryside was still, to a considerable degree, delegated to the locally powerful. All of this pointed to a significant political reality: preservation and retention of power depended on local elites' social control; conflict among the elite could threaten social stability.

Moreover, if powerful planters had been accustomed to thinking of the poor as resources to be mobilized for their own purposes, the Guerra dos Cabanos showed another possibility. The rural poor, led by a shrewd and charismatic leader, carried on their own struggle long after the restorationist planters had abandoned the battle field. Actively intervening in politics in the most direct of ways—by waging war—they stymied the government for several years. In demonstrating the possibility of their independent action, they added a new element to future calculations of political struggle.

The upheavals in Pernambuco were by no means unique. The mobilization of soldiers and civilians in the streets of the imperial court, which had pressured Pedro, did not end with his abdication. On the contrary, the absence of a reigning monarch opened up previously unknown possibilities and enabled diverse groups, some of whom had never had political influence, to think that the time was at hand to push for their agendas. Starting in late April 1831, agitation in the streets of the court occurred periodically. On July 12 radical liberals and the military rose up; the municipal guard saw little prospect of controlling the situation and returned to their quarters, leaving the streets unpoliced. The initial elite fear of anarchy passed when written demands were issued. The rebels demanded the deportation of eighty-nine, mostly Portuguese-born, individuals, the dismissal of many more from government offices, and a ten-year suspension of new Portuguese immigration to Brazil. More than a week passed before the government secured control of the city and the rebellious troops.

The government and public order were fragile in the capital of the empire and even more so in some of the provinces. In April militia officers and civilians in Salvador, Bahia, seized a fort and demanded the expulsion of Portuguese-born officers; rumors soon sparked violent riots against the Portuguese. In May and September military rebels issued more demands for dismissals and expulsions of Portuguese-born officers and citizens. In October a federalist rebellion broke out, and another erupted in the town of Cachoeira in February of 1832. In April of 1833 political prisoners rose up and seized a fort in their struggle for federalism. Muslim slaves in Salvador rebelled in 1835. Although authorities needed only a few hours to suppress the movement, elites across Brazil took notice. Even four decades after the Haitian Revolution, the thought of that Caribbean uprising and slaughter of the white elite still provoked anxiety among the Brazilian upper classes.

The disturbances, riots, and revolts were of various sorts. Lusophobia figured in many uprisings, occasionally leading to unrestrained violence against Portuguese-born citizens—most notably in Mato Grosso in May 1834. Very different was an elite-led separatist struggle that brought civil war to Rio Grande do Sul from 1835 to 1845. One theme that was common to many of the upheavals was intra-elite conflict spinning out of control into a larger upheaval. In Pará, fierce struggles among the elites led to civil war in January 1835; by August a general conflagration had erupted in which Indians and *caboclos* (people of mixed Indian and European ancestry) slaughtered the wealthy. Not until 1840 was the Cabanagem, as this rebellion was called, repressed, and the cost was startling: a fifth of the population, about thirty thousand people, perished. In Salvador, resistance to perceived efforts to "re-colonize" Bahia, this time in subservience to the court in Rio de Janeiro, led to the Sabinada. Intra-elite conflict quickly spilled over to a mass movement. Rebels seized Salvador, and only after four months and eighteen hundred deaths did government troops defeat them. Maranhão likewise saw elite conflict spread to a mass movement, the Balaiada, in 1838–41.

Across Brazil, time and again, violent upheavals erupted as slaves, Indians, and the urban and rural poor (in uniform or not), largely people of color, in different combinations and at different times and places, seized the opportunity presented by intra-elite conflicts. Moreover, intra-elite conflict was on the rise as liberal reforms that decentralized state power raised the stakes of local and provincial elections. In time, many in the elite would conclude that a strongly centralized, authoritarian regime was needed to secure the fragile social order.[96]

4

Social Control and the Construction
of a Centralized State, 1836–43

Writing after the fall of the monarchy, Joaquim Nabuco argued that Pedro's shocking abdication on April 7, 1831, ushered in, de facto, a decade-long republic, and with it, a threat to the nation's integrity and order.[1] Without the stabilizing influence of a centralized monarchy with a reigning monarch, there had been considerable rebellion, crime, and at times even anarchy. Order was tenuously maintained in the best of circumstances. The state presence across much of the vast empire was nominal. Administrative agents and repressive forces had few resources and the bureaucratic capacity of the state was limited. The elites were constantly concerned with maintaining social control. The first part of this chapter addresses the institutions that contributed to social control.

Pedro's abdication unleashed intense political struggle. Liberal political reforms decentralized power and provided for greater popular participation. A wide range of revolts, barracks uprisings, Lusophobic violence, slave and peasant uprisings, and a major secessionist struggle seemed to confirm long-standing elite fears of the breakdown of hierarchy and social order. The tumultuous years of the regency discredited political innovation. With authority and order undermined, increasing numbers of politically active Brazilians accepted a conservative critique of liberal reformism. When elected justices of the peace were introduced, they seemed to offer the prospect of improved justice through independent judges well-informed of local conditions. But in practice, many appeared incompetent. Citizen juries were easily intimidated and reluctant to convict the accused. Liberal judicial reforms, although crucial to restructuring political power, seemed to set off waves of crime, leading to complaints of criminals acting with impunity. Leading critics of the reforms argued that the innovations were not applicable to Brazil, that Brazil lacked the level of civilization required for such institutions.

The movement to reverse the regency reforms and return to a centralized system with a strong emperor was called the Regresso (return). It was closely associated with the province of Rio de Janeiro, but it also drew support from across the empire, especially from moderate liberals, who had reevaluated their earlier calls for decentralization, and from former restorationists, who gained respectability once Pedro's death nullified the possibility of a restoration. The *regressistas* passed the Interpretation of the Additional Act in 1840, which reduced the authority of the provincial assemblies in favor of the central government. The decisive victory was the approval of the Reform of the Criminal Procedure Code on December 3, 1841. This law laid the institutional basis for the cabinet to control networks of police and professional judges that would span the entire country. Supporters of the changes expected that a centralized system would improve the criminal justice system and ensure political stability. The new system would also create vast possibilities for patronage, which would allow the cabinet to reward allies for their support. Centralization also augmented the prestige of the emperor; court rituals and ceremonies were consciously structured to this end.

Institutions of Social Control

The upper classes and the government in Pernambuco had always been deeply concerned with maintaining order. Vast stretches of thinly populated lands, in which people could easily hide, were difficult to police. In the more populated *zona da mata*, concentrations of slaves and free poor on plantations presented other problems. With very limited government presence, slow communications, and widespread ownership of guns, many regions, though long settled, bore a certain resemblance to frontier zones.[2]

Even in times with no rebellion, the provincial government and representatives of the imperial government in Recife found considerable obstacles in working their will throughout the province. Bureaucratic capacity was sharply limited. Indeed, in 1838 the provincial president of Pernambuco, Francisco do Rego Barros, explained to the provincial assembly that he was unable to report crime statistics or the number of national guardsmen in the province, as the district judges (*juízes de direito*) and national guard leaders had failed to provide such information, despite requests that they do so.[3] A similar situation prevailed in other provinces; in 1838 the minister of justice reported the same inability to present crime statistics because many provincial presidents could not supply the relevant information.[4]

Across Brazil police forces suffered from poor organization, and Pernambuco was no exception.[5] In 1842 discipline difficulties were so pervasive that most police units employed national guardsmen to supplement their numbers. Using guards from the unit's own region was also problematic, presumably because they were subject to the same local influences, prompting the use of national guards from other regions.[6] Because of the poor condition of their horses, the police cavalry was ineffective, so much so that the provincial president recommended that if new horses were not purchased, the cavalry should be disbanded. More generally, effective police work depended on diligent and competent work by the justice of the peace, who by virtue of the 1832 Criminal Procedure Code exercised key police functions.[7] Unpaid police officials, *subprefeitos* (subprefects), and *comissários de policia* (police commissioners), created in 1836, generally did not devote sufficient time to their official duties, a complaint that continued even after the reorganization of 1841 that reduced the functions of the justice of the peace and created unpaid *delegados* (police commissioners) and *subdelegados* (deputy police commissioners) who were responsible to the centrally appointed provincial chief of police.[8]

The national guard was the largest force in the province.[9] In theory it consisted of nineteen thousand members, but the number of men actually available, trained, and armed was far less.[10] As in other provinces, Pernambuco's national guard was poorly organized and generally poorly led, although the problems were less severe in urban areas such as Recife and Olinda.[11] There were insufficient arms, as demonstrated by the frequent, almost routine, requests for weapons. Many of the arms available were defective, often being leftovers from the extinct colonial militias.[12] Training and discipline were poor. Many of the leaders had no knowledge of military organization and tactics. Leaders often resided far from their units because there was no requirement that the officer live in the same district or county. Consequently, rapid mobilization was undermined.[13] Often men sought positions as officers only for the associated honors, and once they received the position, they evaded their responsibilities. A common tactic was to resign on the pretext of illness; the law allowed one to continue to enjoy the honors.[14] Because turnover among officers was rapid, they had little incentive to make improvements; the fruits of one's efforts might be enjoyed by someone else. Registration boards, composed of the justices of the peace and the electors, determined the men's eligibility to serve in the national guard. Leaders of the guard often became embroiled in disputes because of their considerable partiality; they provided troops for units led by allies and impeded the filling of positions in units commanded by rivals. Yet, despite all of its problems, the national guard was crucial. In areas with little military presence, the guard was the only significant force available to repress political disputes that erupted into violence, to capture criminals, and to guard prisoners.[15]

The military provided the most reliable troops, although troop riots in the 1830s and desertion throughout the first half of the nineteenth century caution against overestimating their reliability. Soldiers were forcibly recruited for extended military duty, during which they received meager (and often late) salaries and harsh discipline. Recruitment was a common tactic to deal with troublemakers, vagrants, and those among the poor who lacked the protection of a powerful patron.[16] Along with the national guard, they were the linchpin of repressive strategies for responding to major disturbances.

The police, the national guard, and the army could put down major disorders, but they were not capable of ensuring order on a daily basis. In the countryside, the maintenance of order depended largely on the efforts of planters, whose groups of armed retainers provided the force to impose their will. A planter's power depended in part on his ability to mobilize armed followers to defend his interests.[17] Planters allowed various free poor people to squat on their land in exchange for labor and loyalty, including armed service when needed. The effectiveness of such a system had limits, for while planters controlled their own lands, conflicts with other planters could arise, pitting one armed group against another. There were also bands of outlaws who roamed the countryside and whose mobility enabled them to escape the forces of the large land owners as well as the government. Such bands often made use of provincial borders, crossing from one province to another to elude capture.[18]

Crime, Insecurity, and a Critique

In 1841 the minister of justice, Paulino José Soares de Sousa, the future Viscount of Uruguai who was one of the chief spokesmen for the political grouping that would evolve into the Conservative Party, explained the rise of powerful bosses, surrounded by numerous armed retainers, as a consequence of the backwardness of the interior. There, he reported, the inhabitants lived in isolation, out of the reach of governmental authorities, without morality, religion, or the benefits of civilization. They were characterized by barbarous customs, ferocious behavior, and horrible crimes, constituting a distinct society from that of the littoral.[19]

The minister of justice explained the predominance of powerful *senhores*, who protected large groups of men in exchange for their loyalty, in terms of an adaptation to the severe conditions in the interior, which he conceived of as outside the coastal society. "Even the notables that inhabit those places are forced, in self defense, to oppress in order not to be oppressed themselves; they create small centers of power, to which the persecuted agglomerate . . . each one attempting to achieve greater preponderance and become feared in order to be respected seeks to protect the largest number of villainous criminals and turbulent individuals."[20]

This description might also apply to *senhores de engenho* in the *zona da mata*, yet the minister invoked the barbarous condition of the interior as his explanation. Perhaps openly recognizing the predominance of such a system across the entire province might have admitted too great a contradiction between the ideals of a constitutional system, in which free citizens respect the rule of law, and the everyday reality.[21]

Incidents like the human sacrifices that had occurred in Pernambuco's *sertão* might have been in the back of the minister's mind as he characterized the countryside. In 1838 a woman by the name of Pedra Bonita convinced her neighbors that an enchanted kingdom existed but was about to lose its enchantment. A follower of hers preached that human sacrifice was needed to restore the enchanted kingdom and that people should be burned and the soil irrigated with their blood. All the victims would be resuscitated and would be rich, powerful, and happy. The provincial president reported that ignorant and superstitious fathers handed over their children in good faith. In all, forty-two people were sacrificed. The nearest police unit subsequently carried out an attack, killing twenty-nine, arresting others, and losing five of their own forces.[22]

Government leaders were greatly distressed by the high incidence of crime. In 1841 the same minister, Paulino José Soares de Sousa, blamed Brazil's "state of civilization" on its sparsely populated large territory and the government's lack of resources; in 1843 he lamented the spread of immorality.[23] In a similar vein, Provincial President Francisco do Rego Barros invoked backwardness in customs and civilization, as well as the apathy of eyewitnesses, when he explained the increasing number of crimes, their gravity, and the boldness of criminals.[24] Even in the provincial capital, in plain day, people were not safe. On June 28, 1841, the provincial president reported, a man was murdered and witnesses were too fearful to point out the perpetrator. Likewise, at midday on January 25, 1842, two men, described as blacks dressed in mourning, knifed a man to death on the Rua da Cadeia, "the busiest street" in the center of Recife. Again, witnesses failed to intervene or even to shout to alert the police. Subsequent investigation revealed that it was an act of vengeance and that the victim had been warned, but he failed to believe he was in danger in the capital. Again, no witnesses identified the perpetrators.[25]

Wealth did not provide sure protection from crime. In July 1842 the interim police commissioner of Rio Formoso, Pedro Cavalcanti de Albuquerque Uchoa, was murdered near the Genipapo estate. In response, a group of armed men surrounded the plantation and killed a man they thought to be the murderer. On October 19, 1842, a group again surrounded the estate and proceeded to kill two individuals. On January 6, 1843, the owner, Antônio Francisco do Rego Barros, arrived from Ceará, where he had earlier fled to protect his life. Although he returned backed up by armed men, a local police official convinced him to disband the armed men. Once disarmed, however, Antônio Francisco was murdered, just as he had feared.[26]

The reality of unpunished criminality was exacerbated by the violence and terror associated with slavery. Slave owners ran risks by employing coerced labor. Antônio Rabello da Silva Pereira, for example, long feared an attempt on his life by his enemies. When he was murdered on the evening of March 27, 1843, suspicion immediately fell on one of his slaves. The police speculated that the slave may have been hired by an enemy of Antônio's.[27] In another case, Manuel Xavier de Vasconcelos fell asleep drunk, only to be shot at midnight by his slave, Isabel, who had been aided and taught to use the gun by another slave, José.[28]

Critics endlessly denounced liberal reforms for exacerbating the difficulties of maintaining order in such a society. Liberal reforms were judged "theoretical," uninformed by Brazilian realities, the result of an excessive reaction against Portuguese colonial rule and based on doctrines of exaggerated and impractical liberty. As a result, it was claimed, the reforms undermined what little security there was in the country. In particular, critics attacked the jury system and the extensive powers of the justice of the peace. Indeed, minister of justice reports of this period can be read as salvos in the intellectual assault on liberal reforms. Bernardo Pereira de Vasconcelos, who from 1835 to 1837 was the key figure in marshalling parliamentary support for the assault on Feijó and the decentralizing reforms the latter had championed, and Paulino José Soares de Sousa, the brilliant jurist who wrote the 1838 and 1841 ministerial reports cited above that decried Brazil's "state of civilization," were the principal authors of the laws that would overturn the liberal reforms.[29]

Central to the attack on the reforms were repeated denunciations of the alleged impunity that criminals enjoyed. The term *impunity* implied not only high frequency of crime with little chance of being punished but also an upsetting of the moral order. Disorderly criminal elements brazenly attacked, offended, and disrupted the decent, law-abiding portion of society. In 1841 Paulino José Soares de Sousa noted that nearly all provincial presidents complained that impunity prevailed. A number of causes were cited, chief among them the organization of the judiciary that placed excessive power in the hands of ill-prepared, elected justices of the peace and the jury system.[30]

As we have seen, justices of the peace were entrusted with considerable responsibility. They gathered the facts of cases, ordered arrests, explained the circumstances of the alleged criminality, cited which laws were broken, and justified the charges with statements and evidence. These elected judges were not required to have legal training. Reports of the ministers of justice denounced the incompetent, ignorant, sometimes dishonest justices of the peace. They were criticized as unprepared professionally for their responsibilities and for routinely failing to successfully prosecute individuals whose guilt was hardly in doubt. District judges, the nominal police chiefs, were unable to achieve much if the justice of the peace, who actually wielded considerable police powers, was not effective. In 1838 Minister of Justice Bernardo Pereira de Vasconcelos lamented the fact that the police could not carry out their functions as long as power rested with inexperienced justices of the peace and county judges (the latter selected by the municipal councils); in such circumstances, he argued, the police chief's authority was "ridiculous, nominal and illusory." The minister of justice argued that to ensure the selection of competent individuals, the central government should nominate police authorities and the police should be granted wider jurisdiction.[31]

Critics were scathing in their denunciation of another liberal reform—the jury system. Above all, they attacked the institution for routinely absolving individuals despite considerable proof of guilt. Detractors condemned the selection of individuals who would be subject to the influence of the locally powerful (and thus unlikely to risk retribution for having voted in favor of conviction). They also criticized the routine administration of the jury system, noting the failure to convene juries at appropriate intervals.[32] In decrying the low rate of convictions, Pernambucan Provincial President Francisco do Rego Barros noted that only three of the twenty-six individuals brought before juries in the district of Santo Amaro in 1837 were convicted, sarcastically suggesting that this might have been due to the bonhomie of the jury. He further lamented the demoralization and associated atmosphere of impunity that resulted from juries absolving criminals.[33] Several years later he addressed the same issue, blaming it for the spread of immorality in Brazil.[34]

The unwillingness of witnesses to testify increased the difficulty of arresting and convicting criminals. Impunity ensured that powerful figures were likely to escape punishment, making witnesses fearful of retaliatory acts by the accused. An official in Recife complained about the apathy of witnesses to a murder who failed to help the victim or even alert the police. In frustration, he declared that if only witnesses would testify, it would be easy to get convictions or at least to publicly accuse the guilty.[35] In 1841 Paulino José Soares de Sousa insisted on surrounding those who were making accusations and protecting them with force. In 1843 this same minister of justice reported the comments of a police chief frustrated by the intimidation of witnesses. The latter observed that his jurisdiction did not seem to be part of a constitutional empire of free citizens; rather, it was a complex of fiefs with lords and vassals on whom the police authorities and criminals were completely dependent.[36] Even in the case of the murders at the Genipapo estate, a case in which there were various witnesses and a lengthy investigation, no one could be found who was willing to testify.[37]

If arrests and convictions were demanding tasks, keeping prisoners jailed was even more so. Police records are full of reports of jailbreaks. Prisons were often in woeful condition, leading provincial presidents to call repeatedly for improved penitentiaries. Moreover, there was a shortage of guards, and those who were available were sometimes bribed.[38]

The Regresso

By the latter 1830s, the conservative critique found much resonance in public opinion. The optimistic images of Brazil that liberals had earlier favored, emphasizing common interests and the possibility of significant improvement through institutional reforms, seemed out of touch with the disorder and violence that marked the regency. Elected justices of the peace seemed to offer not improved justice administered by people who were intimately familiar with local conditions, but incompetent judicial practice that undermined effective police work and that was performed by people chosen through coercion of the electorate. Citizen juries, susceptible to intimidation by those they judged, seemed to ensure impunity for lawbreakers. Even the most prominent of liberals, statesmen like

Diogo Antônio Feijó and the influential editor of the *Aurora Fluminense*, Evaristo da Veiga, were conceding failure with the reforms.[39]

For many people, a pessimistic interpretation of Brazil had displaced the seemingly ill-founded optimism of First Reign and regency liberalism. Brazilian civilization was depicted as in an early state of development. Brazilians, especially the lower classes, were seen as not yet sufficiently civilized to participate in the modern liberal institutions derived from Europe and North America. Foreign models, many now thought, might work in their lands of origin, but only impractical theorists, out of touch with local realities, could still have hopes for them in Brazil. This argument and variations on it would provide a long-lasting foundation for conservative thought.[40]

Leading the reevaluation was a group of politicians opposed to the liberal leader Regent Diogo Antônio Feijó. All of them had figured among the *moderado* leadership. Honório Hermeto Carneiro Leão and Bernardo Pereira de Vasconcelos, two Coimbra-trained magistrates who were well-versed in liberal constitutionalism and had earlier broken with Pedro I over his absolutist tendencies, were the key figures of the Regresso. Supporting them were three astute politicians known as the *saquaremas*—Paulino José Soares de Sousa, Eusébio de Queirós Coutinho Matoso Câmara, and Joaquim José Rodrigues Tôrres, whose estate near Saquarema supplied the nickname for the three. These men, who formed the core of what would become the leadership of the Conservative Party, marshaled the opposition to Feijó from 1835 to 1837.[41]

The bitter experience of the regency prompted many to abandon reformist liberalism and to embrace the Regresso. Vasconcelos epitomized this shift in attitude. On the floor of the Chamber of Deputies, speaking of the First Reign, he declared:

> I was a liberal. Then liberty was new in the country; it was in everyone's aspirations, but not in the laws, not in practical ideas. [State] power was everything; I was a liberal. Now, however, society has changed. Democratic principles have prevailed everywhere and have proved prejudicial. Society, which was then threatened by [state] power, is now threatened by disorganization and anarchy. Today, I want, as I wanted then, to serve society, and save it, and therefore

I am a *regressista*. I am not a turncoat. I do not abandon the cause I defend in its time of peril and weakness. I abandon it when it is so secure in its triumph that its excesses damage it.[42]

Like Vasconcelos, many other moderates split from their allies. This was made much easier by Pedro's death in 1834, which ended any chance of restoration. Former restorationists, no longer discredited by association with the cause of restoring an autocratic, Portuguese-born monarch, joined former moderate liberals in a formidable parliamentary majority in opposition to Regent Feijó. Utterly blocked in the Chamber of Deputies, and weakened by both the lack of success in the war against the secessionist movement of the *farrapos* in Rio Grande do Sul and the split with the extremely influential journalist Evaristo da Veiga, Feijó resigned in 1837. The new regent, the Pernambucan Pedro de Araújo Lima, named Bernardo Pereira de Vasconcelos minister of justice and minister of the empire. He rounded out the cabinet with other regressistas of considerable talent—two Pernambucans, Antônio Peregrino Maciel Monterio and Sebastião do Rego Barros (a brother of the Pernambucan Provincial President Francisco do Rego Barros); a saquarema, Joaquim José Rodrigues Tôrres; and, from Bahia, Miguel Calmon du Pin e Almeida, the Marquis of Abrantes. The cabinet came to be known as the Ministry of the Capable. Its task was to dismantle the liberal reforms.[43]

In 1838 Minister of Justice Vasconcelos asserted, "Unhappiness will always be excited, clamor will always be produced, grave inconveniences will always follow legislative changes which are rapidly introduced, when they are not in complete harmony with the country's habits and customs."[44] The fundamental regressista verdict on the liberal reforms was thus declared. Liberal reforms inspired by European and North American success were not always attacked frontally as inherently mistaken; rather, they were judged inapplicable to the particular circumstances of Brazil. In 1841 Minister of Justice Paulino José Soares de Sousa declared that "having recently left the colonial regime, too mistrustful and fearful of arbitrariness, we avidly embraced vague doctrines of exaggerated liberty, putting aside . . . the facts, whose observation, analysis and study, pours immense light on the applicability of legislative, political and moral questions of a country."[45]

Radical innovations had resulted in "calamity," "anarchy," and "sad lessons."[46] Paulino, as minister of justice in 1843, affirmed that "nothing is more fatal and demoralizing for a country than weak (government) power."[47] Regressistas thus sought a return to strong centralized rule. Above all, by insulating power from local influences and by making government officials in the provinces dependent on, and agents of, the central government, firm rule could be reestablished and crime and political instability reduced. Much of the struggle to shift power from the provinces to the imperial court would be fought in the Chamber of Deputies, with key battles over undoing the localism of liberal judicial reforms.[48]

The initial blows of this battle actually had already been delivered several years earlier. By virtue of the Additional Act, which granted provincial assemblies the right to legislate concerning all provincial and municipal employees, some provinces in the mid-1830s had already started counteracting the decentralizing liberal reforms that called for greater popular participation. Pernambuco went the farthest in this direction and served as a model for other, mainly northern, provinces wracked by instability. Police officials called prefects and subprefects assumed the police and criminal functions of justices of the peace. In Pernambuco the income requirement for serving on a jury was increased by 300 percent. Moreover, in Pernambuco, São Paulo, and several other provinces, elections for national guard offices were abolished, and provincial presidents were given the authority to name the officers. Such reforms responded to social upheaval by reducing popular participation and by linking local offices to a central (provincial) source of authority.

The Regresso would take this logic farther, creating centrally controlled networks of judicial and police power that endowed the cabinet in Rio de Janeiro, through the power of appointment, with command over judicial and police posts throughout the empire. First, provincial assemblies were denied any role in legislating on these matters by the Interpretation of the Additional Act passed in May 1840. The decisive act was the Reform of the Criminal Procedure Code, commonly referred to as the December 3, 1841, Law. This legislation allowed the minister of justice to appoint judges and prosecutors to judicial courts across the empire from among the graduates of Brazil's two law schools. Law judges (*juízes de direito*) were the key figures, supervising municipal judges and officials below them. The December 3, 1841, Law also created a network of local police commissioners and deputy police commissioners (*delegados* and *subdelegados*) appointed by the provincial chiefs of police, who were themselves named by the minister of justice. Police commissioners both carried out police functions and took over some judicial functions from justices of the peace in criminal cases. Justices of the peace, having lost most of their functions to the newly created judges and police commissioners, were reduced to mere conciliators in minor civil disputes. The ministry in Rio de Janeiro thus secured control over judicial and police officials in every parish, municipality, and province of the empire. The utter reversal of the liberal reforms' decentralization and greater popular participation was not just an abstract question of political philosophy, of course. The opposition objected vociferously. In the Senate, Pernambucan Holanda Cavalcanti indignantly exclaimed that "everyone else is excluded and the [dependent, centrally-controlled] magistrates are the provincial presidents, members of the Parliament and chiefs of police. In short, they are everything."[49]

Reestablishing the prestige and authority of the monarch was an essential element of strong central rule. In part, this process involved institutional changes such as the November 23, 1841, reestablishment of the Council of State, which offered the emperor support and advice on exercising the moderating power, thus influencing cabinets and legislative programs. Yet an effective centralized monarchy required more than a particular machinery of government and corresponding legislation. It required integrating the institution into the traditions and habits of society to create what Walter Bagehot later described as the British monarchy's "dignified" aspect, in contrast to its efficient aspect (the actual making and implementing of public policy). The achievement of this dignified element required a theatrical show of prominent persons identified with the government, one that would reinforce public acceptance and the colonial traditions of the monarchy.[50] Even in 1843 the leading conservative journalist in Brazil, Justiano José da Rocha, wrote, "Public spirit is clearly tending towards monarchy, yet that tendency, born of reason, inspired by love of order, is not aided by our laws, nor by our customs, nor by our habits: the throne does not have a foundation."[51]

Strengthening the emotional, intuitive embrace of the monarchy was an important aspect of creating a strong, stable, centralized monarchy. To this end, the trappings of the monarchy were quite carefully refurbished. Traditional rituals of court ceremony were reintroduced. In 1837 the new regent, Pedro de Araújo Lima, complemented the legislative battle for the Regresso by kneeling before the eleven-year-old emperor in a public street and humbly kissing the child's hand. This ritual, revived by the regent, emphasized hierarchy and obedience and was known as the *beija mão* (hand kiss). Portraits of the emperor were distributed to bring his image to presidential palaces, provincial assemblies, and town halls in all the provinces. On the emperor's birthday in 1840, a three-hour ceremony, also referred to as a *beija mão*, was held in Recife's presidential palace. Prominent individuals of the province, elegantly dressed, filed one by one in front of a large portrait of the emperor that was flanked by the provincial president and the bishop. Pernambuco's leading citizens each bowed to the portrait, which was symbolically supported by church and state, and paid their respects.[52]

Although it found broad support, the Regresso was most closely associated with one province, Rio de Janeiro. Sugar in Rio de Janeiro's hinterland, commerce (in humans and other goods), and employment by the crown made for an elite that favored a strong imperial government. Moreover, by the 1830s a relatively new crop, coffee, had overtaken sugar as Brazil's leading export. Coffee exports initially came largely from Rio de Janeiro's Paraíba Valley and subsequently spread to the provinces of São Paulo and Minas Gerais. Historians have long associated the Regresso with these coffee interests. Jeffrey Needell has revised this longstanding assumption, however, by demonstrating that in the 1830s coffee interests were still a junior partner in Rio de Janeiro, largely playing a supporting role for their allies who occupied positions of political leadership. The tremendous boom in coffee exports, and the revenues that taxes on increased imports and exports allowed the state, facilitated a mutually beneficial relationship between a strong monarchy and the wealthy *fluminense* (i.e., natives of the province of Rio de Janeiro) planters and merchants.[53]

Coffee planters in particular needed a stable government with considerable authority. Slaves, the majority of whom were African-born (and thus more likely to rebel), provided the bulk of the labor pool. The fear of rebellion, even the dreaded possibility of a race war like the Haitian Revolution, was ever present, and the dramatic increase of the trade in humans that provided the labor for the rapidly growing coffee sector only increased this fear. Particularly worrisome were unstable political conditions, because upheavals of any nature might create divisions and openings that rebellious slaves could seize upon. A strong and stable government, with an effective army and national guard, was the surest guarantor of order. Stability was also important to ensuring Brazil's creditworthiness in foreign financial markets where it sought long-term loans. A strong national government also had a role to play in providing basic infrastructure for an expanding export economy.[54]

Conservative *fluminense* planters of sugar and coffee and allied merchants shared their interest in a strong state with large-scale exporters elsewhere, particularly in the sugar, tobacco, and cotton areas of Pernambuco and Bahia. But there was an important distinction. Rooted in the port and province of Rio de Janeiro, the *fluminense* were best positioned to establish connections at the imperial court and to influence politics there. The prominent politicians that led the Regresso were well connected with the closely knit Portuguese and *fluminense* merchant and planter elite of the court and its hinterland. Consider, for example, the saquaremas. Paulino José Soares de Sousa, who came from a prominent family in Minas Gerais whose members married into various *fluminense* families, himself married a woman from a prominent planter clan of the province. His wife's sister married Joaquim José Rodrigues Tôrres. Rodrigues Tôrres, born in Itaboraí to a prominent local Portuguese man and his *fluminense* wife, himself headed an extended family of planters with relations throughout the old plantation region of the *baixada fluminense* (Rio de Janeiro's provincial lowlands). Eusébio de Queirós, a Portuguese man born in Angola, son of a prominent crown magistrate who had set down Brazilian roots, married into a prominent Portuguese merchant family in Rio de Janeiro; his mother-in-law, after the death of her first husband, married José Clemente Pereira, an important Portuguese-born statesman of the First Reign. Likewise, the strong-willed conservative leader Honório Hermeto Carneiro Leão, who had roots in Minas Gerais, married the daughter of a prominent Rio merchant and in time became a *fluminense* planter. Thus, this elite, with interests ranging from the crown magistracy to Portuguese commerce and provincial planting, had especially strong reasons to see its future and fortune identified with the monarchy, and they provided the monarchy with solid political support and, via taxes on its exports and imports, a strong revenue base for the state.[55]

Maintaining order was a constant concern of the Brazilian elite. The immense and thinly populated interior was difficult to police, and coastal plantation regions had large concentrations of slaves and the free poor. Communications were slow and the government's bureaucratic capacity was limited. Police and national guard units were ill-trained and often poorly equipped and led. The military provided the most reliable repressive force, although troop riots and desertion suggest that one should not overstate their dependability.

The intense political struggles of the regency, along with diverse revolts and military uprisings, Lusophobic violence, and high crime rates, gave substance to elite fears of a threat to the social order. Restoring security and maintaining order was of paramount priority.

The upheavals during the regency discredited liberal reforms that decentralized power and provided for greater popular participation. Large numbers of politically active Brazilians came to accept a conservative critique of liberal reformism that diagnosed the ills of political instability and criminal impunity as the result of an excessive reaction against Portuguese colonial rule. According to this view, Brazil lacked the level of civilization required for European institutions such as powerful, locally elected justices of the peace and the jury system.

Regressistas believed a centralized system could reestablish firm rule and maintain order. The key was to insulate power from local influences and establish government officials in the provinces as agents of the central government. In 1840 the Interpretation of the Additional Act reduced the authority of the provincial assemblies in favor of the central government. The December, 3, 1841, Reform of the Criminal Procedure Code was decisive, establishing networks of police and professional judges throughout the country that were controlled by the cabinet in Rio de Janeiro. The political advantages for the cabinet of dispensing vast amounts of patronage were lost on no one. Proponents of the Regresso also structured court ritual and ceremony to enhance the prestige of the emperor.

Across Brazil, support for the Regresso came from moderate liberals who reversed their earlier support of decentralization and from former restorationists who became newly respectable after Pedro I's death eliminated any possibility of restoration. Yet the movement was most strongly associated with the port and province of Rio de Janeiro, where planters of sugar and coffee and allied merchants shared an interest in a strong state. The politicians who led the Regresso were intimately connected with this Portuguese and fluminense merchant and planter elite of the court and its hinterland. The regressista triumph they engineered ultimately gave significance to the regency by drawing the conclusions that led to the strengthened state that emerged in the 1840s. For this reason, Joaquim Nabuco would later write about the regency that "the agitation of those ten years produced the peace of the fifty years that followed."[56]

5

Political Organization by Pernambuco's Southern Elite and Its Rivals, 1836–43

Although Joaquim Nabuco looked upon the instability of the 1830s as the key to understanding the empire, the implications of the regency were not fully worked out until the following decade. The issue of political order, the distribution of power it maintained, and the conceptualizations of society it implied were central not only to the Regresso but also throughout the years up to mid-century. It was in this period that the two-party system emerged. Indeed, the historiography of Brazil commonly cites the Liberal and Conservative parties as coming into being during the regency, with the 1837 defeat of Regent Feijó as the starting point. This is misleading. Roderick Barman has pointed out that contemporaries did not use this party terminology during the regency, even if some subsequent historians have. Barman maintains that the parties of the 1830s were more groups of deputies than cohesive political movements. He pushes back the date of distinct Liberal and Conservative parties to 1844, with an identifiable Conservative Party associated with the elections of 1842. Jeffrey Needell dates the emergence of parties to the 1830s, earlier than Barman, but notes (based on work in parliamentary records, correspondence of leading statesmen, newspapers, and memoirs) that the term *Conservative Party* was not in common usage until the early 1850s; the Party of Order, or after 1844 the *saquaremas*, was the usual term.[1] Given these issues, in this text the terms

Liberal Party and *Conservative Party* are applied beginning in the early to mid 1840s. Further research might prove that such usage is anachronistic for the mid-1840s. The difficulties of timing and nomenclature speak to the substantial work that remains to be done to reconstruct the emergence, functioning, and meaning of political parties in this period. Moreover, in speaking of parties, one needs to be careful not to assume a degree of coherence that skirts the key issues of the relationship between leaders in the imperial court and provincial parties and the relationship of individuals in the provinces to party leadership at the provincial and national levels.

Regresso legislation, especially the modifications of the Additional Act and the Criminal Code, created a centralized political system in which partisan leaders in the court would wield great influence throughout the country through their power of appointment. With the stakes high, political organization accelerated. We have seen a split in the Pernambucan elites dating back to 1821. By the early 1840s these political groupings were becoming more cohesive.

Francisco do Rego Barros, the Baron of Boa Vista, was the leading Pernambucan political figure of this period. He came to power in 1837 and over the next seven years he, the Cavalcantis, and their allies among the wealthy elite south of Recife would entrench themselves in positions of power. Rego Barros undertook a program of urban improvement and beautification following European, especially French, models. Although such reforms were designed to overcome "backwardness," the preference for foreign models and foreign engineers and artisans prompted considerable criticism. Indeed, such criticism belies the view that provincial politics in this period were largely harmonious. In fact, political conflict among local rivals continued and even conflicts among allies occurred, as they jostled for position and sometimes ran against each other in elections.

By 1842 a strong opposition emerged. The Partido Nacional de Pernambuco (National Party of Pernambuco), commonly known as the Praieiros or Praia after the street where the party newspaper was published, brought together the varied opposition to Francisco do Rego Barros. It was a diverse group committed to battling the provincial president and the Rego Barros–Cavalcanti alliance he headed. Praieiro rhetoric emphasized the theme of order. Praieiros asserted that the administration of the Baron of Boa Vista dangerously undermined order by abuse of power, political violence by its partisans, and a lack of morality in public affairs that encouraged private criminal violence. These various accusations coalesced in the charge of despotism and dovetailed with the classic liberal defense of decentralization. Praieiro rhetoric insisted that the corrupt and oppressive administration of Francisco do Rego Barros in Pernambuco was made possible by a despotic, highly centralized political system at the national level. Complicating matters was the tactic of the Cavalcantis to oppose centralization when their political power was secure in Pernambuco but to welcome imperial intervention when threatened in the province.

Elite Connections, Elite Conflict

The Cavalcanti de Albuquerque and Rego Barros families played leading roles in provincial politics in the 1830s and 1840s. Along with a handful of other families, such as the Sá Albuquerques and the Paes Barretos in Cabo, the Lins in Escada, the Sousa Leãos in Jaboatão, and the Wanderleys, this relatively small elite group occupied commanding economic and political positions and enjoyed great prestige. The elite families were closely knit. Consider, for example, the most powerful family of all—the Cavalcanti de Albuquerques. Joaquim Nabuco, a noted abolitionist, diplomat, and the monarchy's historian, noted that the Cavalcanti family was not, strictly speaking, one family; rather, it was "diverse circles, formed by the old families" who controlled a large portion of the land in the province. The four ennobled Cavalcanti de Albuquerque brothers—Antônio Francisco de Paula de Holanda Cavalcanti de Albuquerque (commonly referred to as Holanda Cavalcanti, the future Viscount of Albuquerque), Francisco de Paula Cavalcanti de Albuquerque (the future Viscount of Suassuna), Pedro Francisco de Paula Cavalcanti de Albuquerque (the future Viscount of Camaragibe), and Manuel Francisco de Paula Cavalcanti (the future Baron of Moribeca)—were cousins of Francisco do Rego Barros (the Baron of Boa Vista), the provincial president from 1837 to 1844 and leader of the Rego Barros family. One of the four Cavalcanti brothers, Manuel Francisco de Paula Cavalcanti, was also a son-in-law of Francisco do Rego Barros. The Baron of Boa Vista's brothers, Sebastião and João, were also active politically and, of course, related to the Cavalcantis. Holanda Cavalcanti was a son-in-law of an imperial senator from Pernambuco, Manuel Caetano de Almeida e Albuquerque. He thus served in the Senate both with his brother, the Viscount of Suassuna, and with his father-in-law.[2]

Powerful as the Cavalcantis and their allies were, their predominance did not go uncontested. From the early 1820s, opposition coalesced around elite families, largely of more recent origin, of the littoral north of Recife. The Cavalcantis and their allies, however, scored a significant victory when they placed one of their own, Francisco de Paula Cavalcanti de Albuquerque (the future Viscount of Suassuna), into the provincial presidency in 1835. They managed this, ironically enough, by supporting a radical liberal barracks revolt against Provincial President Manuel de Carvalho Paes de Andrade, a leader of the opposing faction.[3] In 1837 their relative and ally, Francisco do Rego Barros, the future Conservative leader and Baron of Boa Vista, replaced Francisco. He served as provincial president, with some interruptions, for the unusually long period of seven years. Under his leadership, the so-called Rego Barros–Cavalcanti oligarchy became thoroughly entrenched in government positions. The baron was thus a central figure of the era.

Francisco do Rego Barros, the Baron of Boa Vista

Like many members of the elite, Francisco do Rego Barros had undertaken university studies in Europe. Arriving in Paris in 1823, Rego Barros must have felt the same admiration for European civilization that so many of his contemporaries did. Across Latin America, many of the educated in the newly independent countries felt a degree of cultural inferiority in relation to Europe. Their countries had suffered from colonial rule that had retarded their progress. In the eyes of some, even the Iberian colonial powers that had bequeathed them many of the European elements of their culture and population lagged behind in the changes associated with the Enlightenment.[4]

In Brazil, as in some other parts of Latin America, these feelings were compounded by the contradictions of living in a society with profoundly racist assumptions, in the midst of a population in which people of color predominated and in which African-born slaves were present in large numbers. Padre Lopes Gama summed up an attitude common among the elite when he wrote, "We, unfortunately born in the midst of African slaves, are mainly and almost inevitably, poorly raised. The crude and brutal ways, the vices of that unfortunate race, have been inoculated in our people, and that is the seed of our general immorality."[5] The view that Brazil was less civilized than the more advanced countries of Europe was powerfully reinforced by the perceived failures of the liberal reforms of the regency.

If Brazil was lacking in civilization, Europe was the idealized model to which many looked. French and British literati exerted considerable influence, and not only among those who devoted serious attention to their works. Serialized versions of their work appeared in newspapers, making it available to the broad range of the politically active population. Newspapers provided regular coverage of European politics. One Pernambucan newspaper explicitly stated that it was reprinting an article on the July Revolution of 1830 in France and its consequences because of the applicability of its lessons to Brazil.[6]

It is easy to understand how Francisco do Rego Barros was swept up in the ambience of Paris. In subsequent years his opponents often noted that he had acquired in Europe the manners of a *grand seigneur*. Immersion in French culture had not simply spurred vanity, however. After his experience in Paris, he was convinced that beautifying Recife and enriching the cultural life of the capital could play an important role in avoiding the flight of talented men and in advancing the province.[7] He further decided on the necessity of improving the economic infrastructure of the province. Public-works projects were crucial to achieving these goals.

The president lamented the difficulty of carrying out these projects. He cited the "lack of intelligent workers . . . [and] engineers to direct them" and deplored the absence of people capable of making maps, establishing budgets, and directing the construction of roads, bridges, sidewalks, and public buildings. He wanted to establish a school of architecture to train people and insisted on the need to hire competent professionals, wherever they might be found. In 1838 he addressed the shortage of skilled labor by recruiting artisans from Europe. The following year the Company of Workers brought 105 German artisans, masons, carpenters, and blacksmiths. They added considerably to the skilled labor available in the province, working on the construction of roads, bridges, wharves, and buildings until the company was disbanded in 1843. Their contribution was notable in the two most dramatic architectural achievements of the period—the Santa Isabel Theater and the Caxangá suspension bridge over the Capibaribe River.[8]

In 1838 the French engineer Júlio Boyer was hired to direct port improvements and build the Quay do Colégio. However, Rego Barros relied mainly on another French engineer, Louis Léger Vauthier, who had trained at the renowned École Polytechnique in Paris. Hired in 1840, he was granted considerable authority to increase the scope of public works. Vauthier and his team of foreign engineers subsequently oversaw all public works under Rego Barros.

The French engineer met resistance from various quarters. Rego Barros was determined, however, to see his plans through. He reorganized the department of public works and placed it directly under the orders of the provincial president, avoiding bureaucratic entanglements that could delay projects. Vauthier was given complete responsibility for the preparation and execution of all public works projects, including preparing their technical and administrative aspects, acquiring materials, handling the accounting, and supervising the work performed. The French engineer only needed to submit his plans to Rego Barros and receive his approval. Vauthier's freedom of action was guaranteed.[9]

Seeking foreign technical experts was not a novelty. As early as 1825, Provincial President Francisco de Paula Cavalcanti de Albuquerque had written to Holland, seeking a hydraulic engineer to direct port improvements. In 1830 the municipal council of Recife hired the German engineer João Bloem as chief architect for the city. Bloem helped develop plans to improve Recife along European lines. The narrow, twisting streets were to be replaced with wider ones that would be straight, of uniform sizes, and divided into blocks. Building codes were to ensure greater uniformity. Contiguous buildings were to be of the same height. The height of new homes, as well as the number and size of windows and doors, were regulated; cornices were made mandatory; and stone sidewalks of determined width were specified.[10]

Although acquiring access to foreign technical expertise was not new, the scale of the reforms undertaken was indeed unprecedented. Under the provincial president's leadership, old structures were improved and new ones were constructed, including an impressive presidential palace. Most striking, however, was the Santa Isabel Theater. During his 1823–25 residence in Paris, Francisco do Rego Barros had been taken with French theater and had seen the openings of impressive theaters—the Gymnase, Gaîté and Porte Saint-Martin—as well as the rebuilding of the Odéon. As president, Rego Barros sought a new theater that, with the "advantages that result for civilization and morality," would play an important role in enriching the capital's cultural life.[11]

Rego Barros discussed his ideas for a new theater with Vauthier, who then drew up plans for an appropriately sumptuous theater. The project was thoroughly foreign in inspiration and architectural models. A Frenchman directed its construction, employing many foreign artisans, using new construction techniques, and using various materials imported from abroad—stone blocks from Lisbon, iron from France, copper nails from England, and cement from Sweden.[12]

Beautification of the provincial capital was only part of Rego Barros's plans. His immediate concern upon entering office was to improve the economic infrastructure of the province. In his first report to the provincial assembly in March 1838, he wrote:

> [P]ersuaded, Senhores, of how beneficial it would be for the province to establish the means of easy transportation of goods to the market of this city, thus shortening the distance between places, diminishing the risk of travelers and avoiding the increase in costs of production, it was my first and principal care to find out exact information on works in progress . . . I arrived at the conclusion that . . . very little has been done for the material improvement of our land.[13]

Road construction figured prominently in the president's plans. During his administration, considerable progress was made on four trunk roads from Recife to Goiana in the north, Limoeiro in the northwest, Vitória de Santo Antão in the west, and Escada in the southwest. Likewise, his annual reports to the provincial assembly were filled with details on the progress of repairs to bridges and the earthen embankments around them. Citing the extraordinary costs of continual repair of wooden bridges, Rego Barros ordered that the Recife and Boa Vista bridges be rebuilt with iron. He also noted that new iron bridges would beautify the city and conserve labor. In 1843 work began on a startling innovation in the province, a suspension bridge over the Beberibe River near Caxangá.[14]

Political Consensus?

The historiography of the period has depicted a politically calm backdrop for the Baron of Boa Vista as he initiated his reform projects. He often has been presented as conciliating his opponents and achieving a consensus in the early years of his administration. Barbosa Lima Sobrinho, for example, wrote of the moderate policies of the provincial president and the understandings he arrived at with provincial liberals. Izabel Andrade Marson considers the 1835–42 period as one of moderation among the property-owning elite and of tenuous party differences. Like Marson, José da Costa Porto noted a "harmony ticket" that prevailed in the elections for the 1838–41 Chamber of Deputies. The ticket joined elements of the most diverse tendencies, including two future leaders of the Praieiros—Nunes Machado and Urbano Sabino Pessoa de Melo.[15] Indeed, the *Diário Novo*, the press organ of the Praieira opposition to Francisco do Rego Barros, later stated that Rego Barros had entered office at a time of low political passions, when people were tired of battle.[16]

It is possible, however, to overstate the consensus or conciliation of the 1837–42 period. Partisan struggle certainly continued in some of the localities around the province. The district of Limoeiro, fifty-four miles northwest of Recife, for example, was the scene of frequent conflict. Groups led by João Maurício Cavalcanti da Rocha Wanderley, a landowner aligned with the Baron of Boa Vista and a representative in the provincial assembly and the Chamber of Deputies, were engaged in seemingly endless hostilities with opponents led by national guard Col. Henrique Pereira de Lucena, who years later would fight on the rebel side in the Praieira Revolution. Official documents and newspapers were full of reports on the struggles.

In January of 1840, for example, Lucena complained that João Maurício was abusing his police powers. His agents were intimidating the local national guard, openly insulting its members in view of other authorities and threatening them with beatings and murder if they obeyed their officers. These tactics prompted insubordination among guard members and unwillingness to carry out their duties.[17] Later that month João Maurício was brought up on libel charges for pamphlets he had distributed denouncing Lucena.[18] Even after he was removed from office, charges were made that his loyalists forcibly released two military recruits.[19] In January of 1841 João Maurício was named district judge, prompting a series of vehement protests by people who feared a renewal of hostilities and abuse of power.[20] Likewise, in the *sertão* district of Pajeú de Flores the partisans of Leonardo Bezerra da Siquiera Cavalcanti, supporters of the provincial president, were in frequent conflict with Francisco Barbosa Nogueira Paes and his allies, who were aligned with opponents of the Baron of Boa Vista. They too defended their actions with appeals to newspapers readers.[21]

Personal correspondence by Francisco Anselmo Peretti, a magistrate and politician from Goiana, forty-five miles northwest of Recife, also reveals an agitated and partisan political environment in the late 1830s. Felipe Lopes Neto, a political ally of Peretti's and a future liberal participant in the Praieira Revolution, wrote in July of 1838 that Francisco de Paula Cavalcanti de Albuquerque (the future Viscount of Suassuna) had substituted the daggers of 1836 (when Francisco was provincial president) with infernal criminal charges. "The intention of that infamous scum is to throw aside, by means of just or unjust sentences, anyone with enough prestige and courage to face him in the next elections."[22] The previous month Lopes Neto had written of how Francisco de Paula, José Tomás Nabuco de Araújo, and Félix Peixoto de Brito e Melo were working together. Francisco de Paula criticized Antônio Joaquim de Melo; Nabuco, as prosecutor, immediately charged him, and Félix Peixoto, as judge, condemned him.[23]

The Cavalcantis were well established in the provincial assembly. In frustration, Lopes Neto described this body as "stupid and detestable," adding that it "entirely ignores the obligations that link it to our unhappy population, mocks morality and public opinion to bow down infamously to an ignorant and presumptuous family, indecorously sanctioning its brutal whims."[24] Still, such men recognized that the struggle to gain seats in the assembly would be crucial in this era. Lopes Neto advised Peretti that, in light of the grave criminal charges, they must pretend moderation, reach the elections whole, and only then wage a fierce war.[25]

Political conflict was not only drawn along lines of future Conservatives and Liberals. Although the historiography has depicted the early years of Francisco do Rego Barros's presidency as one of consensus, there was tension and competition, even among those who generally supported his leadership. In February 1839 Lopes Neto wrote Peretti that their opponents were divided and that Francisco de Paula Cavalcanti de Albuquerque (the future Viscount of Suassuna) and the provincial president would lead separate tickets in the election. News had spread of Francisco de Paula promoting an obstinate opposition to the president in the next assembly. Rego Barros responded to this threat by shuffling nominations to judicial positions, placing key judges in Recife whom he expected would be grateful for their appointments and therefore loyal to him.[26] The Cavalcantis split from Rego Barros and ran competing tickets against him, as did their opponents, the radical liberals.[27] By 1844 another Cavalcanti—Pedro Francisco de Paula Cavalcanti de Albuquerque (the future Viscount of Camaragibe)—was emerging as the key Conservative leader, challenging Rego Barros for leadership of the party.[28]

In 1837 Antônio Francisco de Paula de Holanda Cavalcanti de Albuquerque (Holanda Cavalcanti) was associated with the opposition to the Ministry of the Capable, the September 19, 1837, ministry led by regressista Bernardo Pereira de Vasconcelos. As a prominent defender of provincial autonomy, Holanda Cavalcanti enjoyed prestige nationally. Yet his position was complex. His brother, Pedro Francisco, was an influential leader in Pernambuco who, in contrast, enjoyed support in the imperial court among the backers of the September 19 ministry. In the 1840s he would be an important Conservative leader. Although the Cavalcantis had their political differences, their political struggles were limited. When the family faced serious threats, it united in self-defense. Thus in the 1840s Holanda Cavalcanti consistently used his influence in the court to oppose the nomination of any Liberal who might aggressively battle his Conservative family members. In Pernambuco he rejected any harsh opposition to Provincial President Rego Barros.

The Opposition: The Praieiros

With the Cavalcantis in commanding positions in both political factions (and, in time, in both the Liberal and Conservative parties), and therefore able to promote their interests in the imperial court regardless of which party was in power, those opposed to the Cavalcantis formed a separate party. The Partido Nacional de Pernambuco (National Party of Pernambuco), like Holanda Cavalcanti, was allied with the Liberals in Rio de Janeiro. Thus, throughout the 1840s in Pernambuco there were two adherents to the Liberal Party, although the Partido Nacional was by far the larger. The latter party became known as the Praieiro Party (after the street, the Rua da Praia, where its party organ, the *Diário Novo*, was printed). The Praieiros were a diverse lot. Many well-off families whose opposition to the Cavalcantis can be dated at least to the Governo dos Matutos in 1822 were affiliated with the party. The Praia Party also had success in appealing to individuals lower in the social order. Considerable numbers of small merchants and artisans also supported the party, particularly in the latter 1840s when its leaders called for taxes on commercial establishments that had more than one foreign clerk, nationalization of retail commerce, and protectionist measures to ease the burden of foreign competition on artisans. Many members of liberal professions supported the Praieiros. With a broad appeal (Pedro Francisco de Paula Cavalcanti de Albuquerque, the Viscount of Camaragibe, claimed years later that nine-tenths of the population supported the Praieiros), the party was vulnerable to attacks that labeled it as a party of the lower class.[29] The pejorative connotation of such a description was well understood. Politically active, lower-class members of the party were considered potentially disorderly, unreliable, ambitious (in the negative sense of seeking advancement over people more deserving than themselves), and above all, violent. Joaquim Nabuco later described the party in similar terms, although his general analysis is more subtle and sophisticated than the analyses put forth by contemporary anti-Praieiro polemicists. Nabuco saw "in the Praieiro movement the force of a popular whirlwind. Violent, indifferent to laws and principles . . . drunk in its excesses of authority . . . But the truth is that the Praia was the majority, it was almost the entire Pernambuco *povo*. . . . More than a political movement, it was a social movement."[30]

Descriptions that emphasize the lower-class nature of the Praieiro movement have the drawback of diverting attention from its character as a coalition that included wealthy sugar planters as well as artisans and shop clerks. In the early 1840s the party adopted doctrinaire liberal positions such as calling for greater provincial autonomy. Subsequently, the party adopted more radical positions, attacking land monopoly by "Cavalcanti feudalism" and calling for nationalization of retail commerce. Yet even as the party approached a violent break with constitutional norms—indeed, in the midst of an armed revolt—some elements opposed the tendency toward radicalization.

In contrast to Holanda Cavalcanti's allies, the far larger Partido Nacional de Pernambuco emphasized its opposition to Provincial President Rego Barros and his supporters. The Praieiros party organ, the *Diário Novo*, spearheaded opposition to Rego Barros. Many of the Praieiro criticisms of the baronistas or *guabirus* (supporters of Rego Barros, the Baron of Boa Vista, were often called baronistas; the Praieiros routinely used the pejorative term *guabiru*, a reference to alley rats) revolved around the theme of order—criminal violence rampant in the province, politically motivated violence of the governing party and its supporters, and an absence of morality, with baleful consequences on public order.

The *Diário Novo* often reported on the prevalence of crime and violence, lamenting the impunity that reigned under the Conservative government. In its first issue, the paper denounced the murder of a lawyer in Recife by a man mounted on a horse. The *Diário Novo* made frequent reference to this and other well-known murders, such as the murder of planter and politician Lt. Col. Pedro Cavalcanti Uchoa.[31] The paper provided even more extensive coverage of the revenge murder in January of 1843 of Antônio Francisco do Rego Barros, the man believed responsible for Uchoa's murder.

Antônio Francisco do Rego Barros had returned from hiding in Ceará backed by armed men. In his absence his sugar plantation had been overrun several times, his crops burned and two of his nephews killed and another wounded. Antônio Francisco and his men were surrounded for twelve hours, until a local police official convinced them to accept an offer of reconciliation. When his armed men disbanded, Antônio Francisco's house was broken into and he was chased out a window, shot on the roof, and after he fell to the ground, repeatedly shot in the stomach. The attackers mutilated the ears and cut the face of the corpse. The victim left a widow and ten children, including a baby born only two days before his murder. The *Diário Novo* denounced the failure of the government to take adequate and timely preventive measures against a predictable crime.[32] The paper also pointed out the contrast of this failure with the abundance of government will at election time, when its agents could seemingly do anything. The party organ charged that "the government is the primary cause" of our problems, arguing that the murder of Antônio Francisco do Rego Barros either was caused by the lack of government will to arrest and punish people or, even worse, might actually have been committed by a government agent.[33]

The opposition paper periodically ran cumulative lists, naming each individual murdered that year. The paper explicitly rejected the regressista critique that blamed the customs of the people, weak laws, and judicial organization for the homicides. It countered with the argument that Brazil's population was increasing, its backlands were becoming more populated, and there were more frequent relations and interactions among people. Despite these conditions, which were favorable to "improving civilization," murders increased.[34] Nor was the problem to be blamed on elected judicial officials, the opposition organ argued; the paper cited various cases in which government-appointed county judges and district judges released criminals. Rather, the *Diário Novo* placed the blame for crime and disorder squarely on the provincial government. The problem was the administration's lack of moral authority as well as its absence of will to confront the problem.[35]

From the opposition's perspective, the administration undermined its moral authority in various ways. Violence by the governing party and its allies was one way, and this was a constant theme in the Praieiro press. Typical of such attacks was the charge that "a few assassins, skilled in wielding daggers and muskets, [prepared] to attack certain opposition members, who have dared denounce the monstrous crimes of Sr. Barao da Boa-Vista and the infamous sycophants who surround him."[36] Accusations were particularly frequent at election time.

Violence of baronistas in Pernambuco was depicted as a regional manifestation of such acts by Conservatives across Brazil. "Do you want to create victims in our province, as your fellow party members did in Minas, Paraíba, Ceará, Rio Grande do Sul, São Paulo?!"[37] At various times the opposition denounced conservative repression of the 1842 rebellions in São Paulo and Minas Gerais as excessive. Instead of employing means proportional to the needs, constitutional guarantees were revoked; terror was employed; people were dismissed from their jobs, deported, and arbitrarily imprisoned; property was confiscated; and hundreds of widows and orphans were created.[38] The paper charged that the repression was worse than the rebellions.[39]

The liberal paper maintained that arbitrary use of government power was complemented by selfishness and immorality. Instead of providing positive examples, the Conservatives carried out illegal contraband trade in African slaves and counterfeit money.[40] The administration misused government funds.[41] Its agents arrested people without legal cause.[42] The Conservatives engaged in widespread electoral fraud, intimidating voters, falsifying electoral documents, and gerrymandering parishes (the basic electoral district).[43] The opposition depicted the Conservatives' motivations as purely self-interested, without any genuine principles. The Conservatives' willingness to place opposition figures on the government electoral ticket when it suited its purposes was presented as one more example of the absence of principles.[44] As a consequence of such behavior, the government suffered from an absence of prestige and support.[45] Unable to provide firm, respected rule, the province suffered from disorder. "[All the problems] today are due to the provincial government and its lack of prestige . . . Look at all the districts, and there we will see disorder and intrigue, impunity, and consequently lack of respect for the law and authority."[46]

The opposition was not satisfied with criticizing the administration on the issue of order; it also attacked the public works projects, programs that defenders of the administration saw as some of its greatest accomplishments. Conservatives trumpeted these projects as marking significant progress for the province and its capital. In contrast, the opposition was harsh in its condemnation. A strong xenophobic element ran throughout the attacks.

The *Diário Novo* lamented that foreign engineers, technicians, and artisans were paid high wages, while Brazilians of equal capacities were without jobs. Father Lopes Gama attacked the provincial president for *estrangerismo*, a preference for foreigners. While foreigners received jobs, the lack of employment for Brazilians increased vice, crime, hunger, and prostitution.[47] Arguments like these had a broad and powerful appeal in the face of insufficient employment opportunities.

The supposed superior quality of the foreigners was doubted. The French engineer Boyer, for example, was mocked when the wharves whose construction he had supervised collapsed after three years. Condemnations of the administration routinely included this project as one of its dismal failure, in an effort to undermine any sense of achievement on the part of Rego Barros.[48] A critic questioned why engineers and artisans of high quality would undertake the rigors of ocean voyages and work in a foreign country, asserting that, of course, they would not and that only those with inferior skills and prospects came to Brazil. Foreigners' use of new techniques also raised questions. One critic noted that Brazilians had long succeeded in constructing tall, straight buildings, even on marshy soils. Why use new techniques and materials, such as those in the foundation of the Santa Isabel Theater, when proven methods were already in use?[49]

The *Diário Novo* appealed to Brazilians' resentments over having to accept orders from foreigners. Much was made of the dismissal of the Inspector General Firmino Herculano de Moraes Âncora. He was depicted as a venerable man of intelligence, unquestioned honesty, and long service, who was fired to free Vauthier from outside inspection. "It is unpardonable, the contempt that is shown to a deserving man, only because it is suspected that he won't humble himself to the command of a foreigner." Similarly, all public employees "were obligated to stoop down to receive blindly the orders of that *senhor* (Vauthier) and his partners!!"[50]

The expenses of the public works projects were routinely attacked. The *Diário Novo* accused the president of nepotism in patronage. Conservatives and foreigners were enriching themselves while public finances suffered. One critic complained, "Sr. Vauthier, who knows so much about art, doesn't he know that frugality is also an art and very useful?"[51] The *Diário Novo* lamented the priorities of the president, complaining that huge sums of money were spent on superfluous projects while essential needs were ignored. Expensive, unproductive projects, such the presidential palace, the Boyer Quay (the failed Cais do Colégio, which collapsed after three years), and the Santa Isabel Theater made public works "one of the greatest whirlpools [of money lost] of the withered Provincial Treasury."[52] Yet essentials such as revenue collection, public education, police, religious worship, and public relief were underfunded. Public employees had not been paid in eight or nine months. The *Diário Novo* lamented that in their suffering, some of these employees might abuse their positions. Consequently, "the ties of subordination and obedience were relaxed."[53]

The *Diário Novo* stated that all public works projects and major expenditures of public money that the president proposed would have constituencies that supported them. Combined with the president's disregard of the government's fiscal possibilities and the chaotic state of fiscal policy, deficits were guaranteed. Recourse likely would be made to the "monstrous" policy of printing paper money; otherwise, faced with the necessity of providing truly necessary services that had not been budgeted for, taxes would have to be raised. New taxes would slow capital formation and lower consumption, reducing public revenues. The deficits might paralyze the very public works projects that caused them.[54]

The Praieiro organ attacked the reorganization of the public works department as granting arbitrary power to the provincial president and undermining accounting and control of expenditures. The reorganization eliminated the requirement that all expenditures on specific projects be made public so they could be voted on by the legislature. Even under the old system, Boyer had been criticized for dictatorial ways of resisting examination of his accounts. The new regulations allowed the president to appoint his clientele to positions. Eased reimbursement requirements would make it easier to file false claims, thus allowing, for example, vacations at public expense.[55]

The Praia opposition also consistently leveled charges of despotism against the administration of Francisco do Rego Barros. Many of these were accusations of specific abuses by the provincial administration, its agents, and supporters, which, according to the Praieiros, resulted from the development of a highly centralized national political system—a fundamental issue of the period.

Centralization and Federalism

The Regresso project was centered on reversing the regency's experiments with provincial autonomy and establishing firm rule from the imperial court. The struggle over centralization marked a dividing line between the political factions that would soon be organized as Conservatives and Liberals, as the former embraced the new laws and the latter denounced them as tending toward despotism. The Praia press, like Praiero allies elsewhere, objected to the concentration of power and railed against the potential for abuse that a centralized system facilitated.

Beginning with its inaugural issue on August 1, 1842, the Praieiro press organ the *Diário Novo* consistently and harshly criticized the centralizing laws that were the key achievement of the Regresso.[56] The last of these laws, the December 3, 1841, Reform of the Criminal Procedure Code, was a special target of criticism. The paper noted that despite the new code, violence continued in the province.[57] The December 3 law was attacked as unconstitutional and as a violation of the separation of powers. It was further denounced for nullifying juries, thereby abolishing the last remaining bit of judicial independence. For the liberal opposition of the period, the charge of ending judicial independence meant excessively centralizing power, making judges political agents of the ruling party in the court, and creating the conditions for wholesale violation of rights, thus leading to despotism. This imbalance in the distribution of power, one that would facilitate abuses by the court, contrasted with the paper's proclamation in its inaugural edition that "our political dogma [is] that the extensive territory of Brazil should always constitute a moderate and representative monarchy. The ideas of order are based on this moderate approach to the aggrandizement of all the provinces."[58]

Despite the clearly and consistently enunciated party position, the position of several prominent figures in the party is unclear with regard to the issue of centralization. In 1841 several members of the Chamber of Deputies who would subsequently be among the leaders of the Praia Party voted for the centralizing laws of November 20 and December 3, which restored the Council of State and reformed the Criminal Procedure Code. Joaquim Nabuco's explanation for this contradictory position was that the future Praieiro leaders of the Chamber, being interested primarily in ruling in Pernambuco and willing to make deals in the court to increase their provincial power, traded support for the centralizing laws in exchange for advantages in Pernambuco. Nabuco does not specify what these advantages were. Closely following Nabuco's analysis, Paula Beiguelman argued that Paulino José Soares de Sousa, the minister of justice in the March 23, 1841, cabinet, went against members of his own party and made an alliance with the Praieiros in order to remove obstacles to the passage of the Regresso laws.[59] Nabuco notes the paradoxically close relationship between the Praieiros and Paulino José Soares de Sousa, who, on the face of it, ought to be opponents. The argument for such an alliance is supported by the fact that the March 23 ministry quickly replaced the Baron of Boa Vista with Manuel de Sousa Teixeira, an opponent of the baronistas, as provincial president, yet returned the baron on December 7, just days after the passage of the December 3 Reform of the Criminal Procedure Code, the last major centralizing law of the Regresso.[60]

Other future Praieiros were adamant in their opposition to the centralizing laws. Felipe Lopes Neto, for example, introduced several proposals to the provincial assembly, rejecting the laws of November 20 and December 3, 1841, as unconstitutional. Opponents of the Reform of the Criminal Procedure Code charged that the reform created a dependent magistracy for the purpose of repressing citizens. They further argued that the reform, which they labeled a "blood law," would end the inviolability of one's home. They also claimed that the laws were passed in tumultuous sessions without proper discussion.[61] Although Urbano Sabino Pessoa de Melo, a member of the opposition and a future Praia leader, voted against the proposal, other Praieiros such as Peixoto de Brito e Melo and Lourenco Bizzera voted with Lopes Neto. Creation of the Council of State was the less controversial measure of the two. Many who opposed the Reform of the Criminal Procedure Code did not vote against restoring the Council of State. In any case, the proposals were both voted down in the assembly—the objection to the Reform of the Criminal Procedure Code by a vote of eighteen to thirteen and the objection to the creation of the Council of State by a vote of twenty-four to seven.[62]

In sum, in late 1841 promoters of the centralizing laws were able to secure the support of several future Praieiros for passage of the laws, but once the thoroughly centralized system was in place and its implications were clear, the Praieiros were united in opposition to centralization. Indeed, the Praia Party itself was formed in 1842 in a context of heightened political conflict and organizing efforts, when the high stakes in the battle for control of the newly centralized system were increasingly clear. The fight for the classic liberal position of federalism was a key component of their platform.

Voting with Lopes Neto in favor of the petitions were the Cavalcanti brothers—Pedro Francisco de Paula Cavalcanti de Albuquerque and Francisco de Paula Cavalcanti de Albuquerque—both future Conservative leaders. Likewise, their brother Holanda Cavalcanti, the future Liberal leader, had opposed the 1840 Interpretation of the Additional Act on the floor of the imperial Senate.[63] In opposing the centralizing laws, Holanda Cavalcanti was consistent with liberals elsewhere in the empire, for whom provincial autonomy was a key plank.

Holanda Cavalcanti's opposition in the Senate, along with Pedro Francisco's and Francisco de Paula's opposition in the provincial assembly, was consistent with positions these representatives of the Cavalcanti de Albuquerques had taken since independence. As we have seen, the Cavalcantis were well ensconced in Pernambuco and exercised considerable authority. They had little interest in seeing strong rule by a distant center of power. Indeed, in 1801 Col. Suassuna, the father of the Cavalcanti brothers, might have flirted with the idea of a conspiracy to achieve independence from Portugal under the tutelage of Napoleon. In 1817, along with much of the landholding elite of Pernambuco, Suassuna and the Cavalcanti brothers supported the struggle for an independent republic. Yet in 1822 they supported a coup against the provisional government established by Gervásio Pires and other provincial rivals, who had declared independence from the Portuguese crown. In doing so, the Cavalcantis established a leading role for their family in the so-called Government of the Matutos (Government of the Hicks), which was controlled by the Cavalcantis and their southern planter allies. In a choice between independence under local rivals and loyalty to the emperor in Rio de Janeiro, this Cavalcanti-dominated provincial government supported national unity under Pedro I. In 1824, again the Cavalcantis opposed an attempt at an independent republic, the Confederation of the Equator, led by the opposing faction of landowners. Throughout the latter 1820s they supported the local governments appointed by the emperor, and in so doing they opposed both the faction of lesser families that had supported the confederation and their sometime allies, the radical liberals. Yet, at the same time, in Rio de Janeiro they joined the opposition in the Chamber of Deputies that struggled to limit the emperor's power. In 1829 Holanda Cavalcanti prompted a government crisis when he objected to the emperor's heavy-handed repression of a radical liberal coup attempt in Pernambuco, demanding the resignation of the ministers of war and justice. Maneuvering to improve their position in the province, in 1832 the Cavalcantis initially supported the Abrilada restorationist coup, and in 1834 they supported a radical liberal coup attempt.

Again, this seemingly curious mix of positions yields a clear pattern on examination. The Cavalcantis, as extraordinarily powerful members of the local elite, were ill-disposed to the crown increasing its authority in Pernambuco, particularly when the Cavalcantis and their allies controlled the key posts of provincial resident and commander of arms. When the Cavalcantis' provincial influence was threatened by local opposition, however, their attitude toward imperial power was quite different. The 1822 provisional government of Gervásio Pires, the 1824 Confederation of the Equator, the Francisco de Carvalho administration in 1832, and the Manuel de Carvalho Paes de Andrade administration in 1834 all challenged Cavalcanti supremacy in the province. In each case the Cavalcantis sought to topple the Pernambucan government. When they needed help against their opponents, they appealed to the crown for assistance.[64]

The Cavalcantis' somewhat ambiguous position exemplifies the conundrum facing far-flung regional elites across Brazil. Other things being equal, the logic of federalism had an obvious appeal for regional elites. But other things were not equal. Threats, or potential threats, to social and political stability suggested the need for a strong central government that could enforce order. When this side of the equation was weighted heavily, as it was during the upheavals of the regency, the need for security in an unstable world prevailed. In the maneuverings of the Cavalcantis we see a significant elite group still grappling with how to maximize autonomy when secure, yet rely on a strong central government when threatened.

In Pernambuco, Francisco do Rego Barros, the Baron of Boa Vista, led a coalition of elite planters concentrated along the rich lands of the *zona da mata* south of Recife. From 1835 to 1844 leaders of this group directed the provincial government; Rego Barros himself served as provincial president for most of the period. Rego Barros carried out a modernization program to beautify Recife and strengthen the economic infrastructure of the region, especially through road building. He hired European experts, who implemented European models, used techniques and even materials from across the ocean, and hired not only engineers but artisans from Europe as well.

The Regresso movement created a strongly centralized state. The party in power in the court could control the levers of power at every level of government throughout the country. With so much power concentrated in the hands of those who controlled the state, political organization accelerated. By 1842 opposition to the movement led by the Rego Barros–Cavalcanti elites had coalesced around the Praieiro Party. Opponents labeled the Praieiros a dangerous, lower-class movement, but in reality it was a broad coalition that included planters, merchants, clerks, liberal professions, and artisans.

From its beginning the party appealed to nativism, criticizing the provincial government's reliance on foreign models, engineers, and artisans. The Praieiros also raised the liberal banner of federalism, sharply criticizing the centralization of the Regresso. They linked a despotic national political system with despotism in Pernambuco, highlighting what they claimed was the harmful effect on public order of pervasive partisan violence, abuse of power, and immorality by the government of Francisco do Rego Barros. The Praieiros were harsh in their denunciation of the December 3 law, the Reform of the Criminal Procedure Code, arguing that it institutionalized abuse by eliminating judicial independence and making centrally appointed judges agents of partisan politics.

Political organization was solidifying a two-party system. With the centralization of the state, the benefits of like-minded leaders joining efforts to secure control of that state were apparent. Conflicts around the province, in the city of Goiana, in the town of Limoeiro, and in the *sertão* district of Pajeú de Flores revealed factions that by 1842 were joined in clearly defined provincial political groups. During this period links also were being formed with other groups across Brazil. Consider, for example, the Praieiro newspaper article that asked, "Do you want to create victims in our province, as your fellow party members did in Minas, Paraíba, Ceará, Rio Grande do Sul, São Paulo?!" The outlines of what would become the Conservative and Liberal parties were already evident.

In Pernambuco, it was not simply a story of the elite led by Francisco do Rego Barros struggling against another elite faction for the spoils the state could supply. Rather, there were real differences in party programs, composition, and the willingness of the parties to mobilize the lower classes. Moreover, the picture of an emerging two-party system was complicated by the prominent leader Holanda Cavalcanti, who was a member of the dominant elite faction but who associated with the same political groups as the Praieiros. That is, both Holanda Cavalcanti and the Praieiros, although provincial rivals, would be associated with Liberals nationally. Holanda Cavalcanti's position exemplified the paradox that many provincial elites across the empire faced—they benefited from autonomy in their province when they dominated it, but when challenged, they wanted the support of a strong central state.

6

The Centralized State and Political Polarization, 1844–47

O n July 23, 1840, the fourteen-year-old son of the first emperor took full authority as Emperor Pedro II. The constitution had specified eighteen as the age of majority, but the continuing crisis of authority, as well as the self-interested calculations of politicians who hoped to benefit from being champions of the early rise to power, allowed for an early majority that few opposed with any vigor. By the time of his eighteenth birthday, the emperor's confidence was growing. Pedro's willingness to assert himself was evident in his handling of a conflict that led the Conservative heavyweight Hermeto Honório Carneiro Leão to resign from his post as minister of justice; the January 23, 1843, cabinet he led soon collapsed.

Pedro sought a political reconciliation that would leave behind the bitterness that followed the defeat and punishment of the leaders of the unsuccessful rebellions in São Paulo and Minas Gerais in 1842 against the centralization of the Regresso. His efforts were frustrated, however, because neither Conservative nor Liberal leaders were willing to set aside their partisan interests. When a Conservative leader rejected Pedro's offer to head a ministry that would grant amnesty to the rebels of 1842, Pedro turned to José Carlos Pereira de Almeida Torres, the Viscount of Macaé, a trusted figure who was independent of the two parties. Macaé's cabinet was made up of individuals who would soon be identified as Liberals, and they shifted further away from the Conservatives with the selection of Aureliano de Sousa e Oliveira Coutinho, the Viscount of Sepetiba, as the provincial president of Rio de Janeiro, a post Aureliano Coutinho was sure to use to contest the power of the Conservative *saquaremas*.

Liberals differed on the degree of partisan battling to pursue; Pernambuco was a case in point. Minister of the Navy Holanda Cavalcanti was opposed to the confrontational politics of the Praieiros in Pernambuco that challenged his family and their allies in the Rego Barros-Cavalcanti–led elites. Holanda Cavalcanti exerted his influence in the imperial court in favor of provincial presidents for Pernambuco who would not challenge his family, but Praieiro electoral strength necessitated that some provincial posts be turned over to them. In May 1845 Holanda Cavalcanti apparently miscalculated, acquiescing in the choice of Antônio Pinto Chichorro da Gama as the new provincial leader. Even before he arrived, his vice-president began massive dismissals of Conservative baronists from police positions and selected Praieiros to replace them.

Under Provincial President Chichorro da Gama the Praieiros forcefully challenged the power of Pernambucan Conservatives. The most confrontational tactic was to search the estates of baronist planters for evidence of crimes. The victims of this policy were infuriated to see their homes "invaded" by their enemies in the name of policing crime. These conflicts revealed a basic dilemma of the Conservative centralizing project. The Conservative judge and polemicist Tomás Nabuco de Araújo recognized the validity of imposing law in the countryside, but he criticized the partisan way in which it was done. Yet the system was designed to have local and provincial positions in the hands of partisan actors. The implied alternative of a nonpartisan imposition of order might have been desirable, but such a notion was irrelevant to the way the political system actually functioned.

When the Praieiros sought to consolidate their power by placing two loyalists in the imperial Senate, they became embroiled in a national controversy. Conservatives in the Senate twice nullified the results of electoral victories with charges of fraud. These unprecedented nullifications provoked a crisis in which Liberals threatened to implement reforms to curtail the power of the Senate. This battle led directly to the highly partisan, confrontational ministry of May 22, 1847. At both the national and provincial levels political competition was becoming increasingly polarized.

Baronist planters in Pernambuco took to armed action in resisting Praieiro authorities. At first individually and then in large-scale coordinated actions, they challenged Praieiro provincial authorities. At the same time, Conservative politicians in Recife introduced a new practice to deepen their mobilization during the electoral campaign for the Senate in late 1847. In urban "meetings" speakers atop platforms addressed crowds, denouncing their opponents and rallying support for their candidates. The Praieiros soon followed suit. A key theme in this campaign was Lusophobia. Praieiros sought to harness resentment toward the Portuguese for electoral purposes, and Conservatives denounced them as dangerous and irresponsible for using such tactics.

The increasing polarization, nationally and in Pernambuco, is explicable in terms of the tight linkages between local, provincial, and national politics that the centralization of the Regresso had established. The party in power in the court could, through the power of appointment, fill official posts with its partisans in every district, municipality, town, city, and province throughout the empire. It was the interwoven nature of the institutions at these various levels that led to heightened conflict. With a thoroughly centralized system, conflict anywhere could reverberate to the other levels.

An Emperor Comes of Age

On December 2, 1843, Pedro II turned eighteen, the constitutional age of majority. For some time, tension between Conservative leaders and the emperor's favorite, Aureliano de Sousa e Oliveira Coutinho (the Viscount of Sepetiba, commonly referred to as Aureliano), had been heightening. An earlier clash between them had precipitated the fall of the Conservative March 23, 1841, ministry in which Aureliano had served with Minister of Justice Paulino José Soares de Sousa and José Clemente Pereira. The subsequent January 23, 1843, Conservative ministry, which was formed by Honório Hermeto Carneiro Leão, excluded Aureliano. When Aureliano's brother Saturnino de Sousa e Oliveira opposed the Conservative leaders' ticket in provincial elections in Rio de Janeiro to occupy a Senate seat, Honório responded by asking the emperor for Saturnino's dismissal as inspector of customs in Rio de Janeiro. The emperor refused, later noting, "I understood such a dismissal to be unjust, and by the way in which Carneiro Leão insisted, I understood that if I yielded I would be thought weak."[1] Honório's unacceptable, demanding manner in dealing with the emperor, and Pedro's refusal to acquiesce, left Honório little choice but to resign. The January 23, 1843, ministry he led immediately collapsed. The incident suggests that the emperor, upon reaching eighteen years of age, was more determined to assert himself and defend his prerogatives.[2]

Pedro did not simply turn over power to leading Liberals. Rather, he first offered a Conservative leader, José da Costa Carvalho, the Viscount of Monte Alegre, the opportunity to form a ministry, with the understanding that the 1842 rebels of São Paulo and Minas Gerais would be amnestied. When Monte Alegre declined, the emperor turned to José Carlos Pereira de Almeida Torres, the Viscount of Macaé, who was a Bahian close to the emperor and not clearly identified with either political party. Almeida Torres formed the February 2, 1844, ministry amidst talk of conciliation. A conciliatory ministry would reduce excessive partisanship and factionalism, especially in Bahia, Pernambuco, and elsewhere in the North. The rebels of 1842 were to be amnestied. No longer would there be what future Liberal leader Paula Sousa had denounced as party ministries, rather than national ministries, in reference particularly to the January 23, 1843, cabinet.[3]

Implementing the idea of conciliation in a highly partisan atmosphere proved extremely difficult. Conservative opposition to the ministerial change and the notion of conciliation was interpreted by the emperor as a continuation of the practice of the previous ministry denounced by Paula Sousa, acting for the good of a political party, instead of the nation. A Liberal paper denounced the "declaration of war" on the conciliation ministry by Conservative newspapers *Sentinella da Monarchia* (Sentinel of the Monarchy, directed by Vasconcelos) and *Echo*, and lauded the ministry's attempt to convince the opposition of the need to "finish with the fatal designation of winners and losers."[4] Amnesty of the *paulista* and *mineiro* rebels was a sine qua non for reconciliation, yet when the emperor decreed the amnesty on March 14, 1844, Conservatives in the Chamber of Deputies and Senate were adamant in criticizing it. The Praia press reprinted Liberal journalism from the imperial court that attacked Conservative opposition to the amnesty, labeled the right to grant amnesty "the most beautiful of royalty's prerogatives," and implied that to criticize the amnesty was tantamount to criticizing the emperor.[5]

Opposition to the amnesty contradicted the common practice of leniency after a rebellion's leaders had been punished, the dangers had passed, and peace had been restored.[6] The leading Pernambucan Conservative newspaper, rather than supporting conciliation, argued for the record of achievement of the Conservative ministries since 1837, including the suppression of the 1842 rebellions.[7] The Conservative organ blamed Aureliano's palace faction for the ministerial change, implying that it did not reflect the will of the people. The Pernambucan Conservative Sebastião do Rego Barros, brother of the provincial president, turned down an offer of a ministerial post, opting instead for solidarity with other Conservatives in opposition.[8]

Many Liberals likewise sought not conciliation but a complete reversal of political fortunes. Liberals had been through a period of ostracism in which centralizing laws had undermined provincial rights that Liberals held dear. Many Liberals who had participated in the 1842 rebellions in Minas Gerais and São Paulo against the centralizing measures still suffered from exile, arrest, and loss of political rights. Moreover, the usual desire to seize patronage prompted many to shy away from conciliation. Liberal newspapers such as *Novo Tempo* argued that the March 23, 1841, Conservative ministry had dismissed officeholders appointed by the Liberal majority ministry and had tried to annihilate the Liberal Party after the 1842 rebellions, and that now it was the Liberals' turn. The Praieiro paper *Diário Novo* reprinted such articles.[9]

Liberal papers also called for the dissolution of the Chamber of Deputies elected under the influence of the March 23, 1841, ministry. The *Diário Novo* argued that the violence and fraud that marked the elections made for an unrepresentative Chamber, and it reprinted articles from Liberal papers elsewhere that made similar arguments.[10] One paper argued that the ostensible reason for the Conservatives' opposition to the current cabinet, disagreement with the amnesty, was not the real motive for their stance. Rather, the goal of the leaders of the oligarchy was to annul the emperor's liberty of action and, by limiting his prerog-

atives, better maintain their own power.[11] The *Diário Novo* also continued its criticisms of Provincial President Rego Barros, airing the standard charges of electoral abuse, such as falsifying the electoral list of
Igarassu to exclude Antônio Joaquim de Melo from the provincial assembly, and violence by Conservative police or their allied thugs.[12] The
paper charged, for example, that in the parish of Goitá alone, five murders and six serious injuries occurred, yet the known perpetrators were
not arrested. The Praieiro organ explained such impunity by charging
that the provincial president's nominations to police posts were motivated by electoral concerns, not justice and the public interest.[13] The paper also charged Conservative leaders in the court with ordering allies
in the provinces to crack down on the Liberal press. It was in this context that the paper explained charges against the publisher of the *Diário
Novo*, João Ignácio Ribeiro Roma, for slander and libel in defaming the
Chamber of Deputies.[14]

Support for the February 2, 1844, ministry initially came from some
dissident Conservatives in the North, such as Cansanção de Sinimbu in
Alagoas and Bernardo Sousa Franco in Pará, from Pernambucan Praieiros, such as Urbano Sabino and Nunes Machado, and from various Bahian deputies. This so-called Northern League was insufficient to govern,
however. Facing a larger Conservative opposition, the ministry tilted toward the Liberals. An important step in this direction was taken on April
1, 1844, when Aureliano de Sousa e Oliveira Coutinho was selected as
provincial president of Rio de Janeiro.[15]

Aureliano de Sousa e Oliveira Coutinho

Joaquim Nabuco considered Aureliano's influence in the 1840s to be an
enigma of Brazilian constitutional history. Nabuco wrote of him as an
"erratic element outside of party classification."[16] Aureliano served both
in the Majority ministry of July 24, 1840, with several future Liberal
leaders, and in the succeeding March 23, 1841 ministry, this time with
future Conservative figures. He also provided crucial support for various Liberal ministries from 1844 to 1848 as provincial president of Rio
de Janeiro. His independence from the political parties was noteworthy.
In 1842 a French diplomat reported to Paris that Aureliano had not acquired obligations to any political party, while another reported in 1844

that ministers took no action without consulting him first.[17] His influence was based on his closeness to the emperor and the widely held belief that he represented Pedro's political preferences.[18] The emperor's moderating power, for practical purposes, enabled Pedro to decide when to alternate parties in power. The electoral system ensured that the ministry at the time the elections were called (and whom the emperor had chosen) had sufficient influence to emerge victorious. Thus, those who influenced Pedro could themselves exert considerable influence.[19] Aureliano's influence dated from the regency. He shared it, to a lesser degree, with his ally Paulo Barbosa da Silva, the palace chief of protocol, who in the 1830s had chosen the individuals who would educate the child prince. They led the informal political group nicknamed the Joana Club, after the official residence of the chief of protocol. They were also known the palace faction, or *palacianos*.[20]

Although Aureliano had served as foreign affairs minister in the Conservative March 23, 1841, ministry that passed crucial centralizing measures, the influence of the palace faction was deeply resented by Conservative leaders such as Rodrigues Torres, Paulino José Soares de Sousa, and Honório Hermeto Carneiro Leão. Conflicts between Aureliano and Minister of Justice Paulino José Soares de Sousa and Rodrigues Torres had led to the fall of the March 23 ministry, and the January 20, 1843 ministry that replaced it fell over a dispute involving Aureliano's brother Saturnino, which forced Honório's confrontation with the emperor. Conservative organs such as the *Sentinella da Monarchia*, led by Vasconcelos, and *O Brasil*, directed by the premier Conservative journalist Justiano José da Rocha, denounced the influence of the palace group. In February 1844 the *Sentinella da Monarchia* complained, "Now we do not have an emperor; Aureliano, Paulo Barbosa and Saturnino give the orders."[21] Likewise, the *Diário de Pernambuco* blamed the Joana Club for the fall of the Conservative January 23, 1843, ministry led by Honório, lamenting that palace intrigues, not parliamentary struggles, would determine the future. The paper saw the hidden maneuvers of an "impure black trinity" of Aureliano, Saturnino, and Paulo Barbosa behind the rise and fall of political leaders and parties.[22]

Named provincial president of Rio de Janeiro by the February 2, 1844, ministry, Aureliano decisively challenged the Conservatives at the very base of their power, the *fluminense* bailiwicks of the coffee planters. There, he could undercut their electoral support through patronage, fraud, and violence. Joaquim Nabuco considered Aureliano's support of the Liberal ministries of 1844 to 1848 as their principal support because of Aureliano's alleged favor with the emperor. Thus the Praieiros were shrewd enough to gain influence in the imperial court through an alliance with Aureliano.[23]

Liberals in Power, Liberals Divided

In May 1844 two Liberals, Holanda Cavalcanti and Manuel Galvão, joined the ministry, shifting its composition further to the Liberals. The emperor dissolved the Chamber of Deputies and new elections were called, just as partisan Liberals had hoped. Electoral fraud and violence by the ruling party, which were norms of electoral practice, ensured that Liberals would control the Chamber. In the province of Rio de Janeiro, where saquarema power was the greatest, violence was particularly widespread. In Alagoas, a significant rebellion erupted. Nonetheless, the elections returned a huge Liberal majority to the Chamber. In Pernambuco, only Francisco do Rego Barros and Pedro Francisco de Paula Cavalcanti de Albuquerque managed to win seats for the Conservatives, and they declined to occupy their seats. Across Brazil, Conservatives were forced to adjust to the prospect of a lengthy exclusion from office. Pernambuco's Conservatives reacted by forming closer ties with saquarema leaders in the Senate.[24]

Even with Liberals ensconced in the cabinet there was tension over the political line to pursue. Minister of Justice Manuel Alves Branco (the second Viscount of Caravellas) and Foreign Affairs Minister Ernesto Ferreira França favored partisan conflict with the Conservatives at the national and provincial levels. Holanda Cavalcanti, while supporting struggle at the national level, was an advocate of moderation within Pernambuco. Many of his relatives were Conservatives who had close links with the Conservative administration there; indeed, his brother, Pedro Francisco (the future Viscount of Camaragibe), was rapidly rising to prominence within the party. Accordingly, Holanda Cavalcanti wanted a moderate policy in the province that would minimize the challenge to his relatives' interests. In contrast, the Praieiros were bitter enemies of the Conservative administration and engaged in all-out conflict in Pernambuco. They sought alliances and deals in the court that would further their provincial interests, and they were willing to take a more moderate stance nationally when it favored their position in the province.[25]

Conflict within Pernambuco was intense. The powerful Cavalcanti oligarchy had prompted a determined opposition. The curious party alignment, with competing Liberal groups—one seeking accommodation in the province and the other full-scale conflict—can be explained as an adaptation to the oligarchy's control of both parties. With Cavalcantis prominently represented in both the Liberal and Conservative parties, they were assured of political influence in whichever party was in power in the court. The emergence of the Praieiro Party gave expression, within a party affiliated with Liberals in the court, to the oligarchy's opponents. Thus, the national two-party system, which generally was deemed to be controlled by a small oligarchy, was in fact sufficiently flexible to allow representation for some opponents of the dominant groups, at least at the provincial level.

Holanda Cavalcanti's prestige and influence in the court, where in May he became the minister of the navy, was sufficient to enable him to influence the choice of a new Pernambucan provincial president. Presumably to ensure the continued support of the minister of the navy, an ally of Holanda Cavalcanti, Joaquim Marcelino de Brito, was sent to Recife in June 1844 to replace the Conservative president, Rego Barros. Ironically, the *Diário Novo* in its response to these events invoked the Praia attacks on feudalism and oligarchical control. The newspaper rejoiced that the February 2 ministry had "recognized that [the province] is not the entail of Sr. Rego, who believed he had the right to control its destiny, as if it were his estate!"[26]

Their nemesis departed, the Praieiros hoped for dramatic gains. As they had earlier argued the necessity of a provincial president compatible with the Liberal cabinet in Rio, so they sought widespread dismissals and the appointment of Praia partisans to police, national guard, judicial, and military positions of leadership. A *Diário Novo* article made the case that "one of the most indispensable conditions [for any government] for carrying out its tasks is the uniformity of its views and sentiments and those of its functionaries."[27] The new cabinet would be unable to implement its policies if key positions were occupied by Conservative loyalists to the former president. The *Diário Novo* argued that such sweeping changes in personnel were normal practice in constitutional governments.[28]

Praieiro hopes for an "inversion," as sweeping reversals of officeholders along party lines were called, were soon dashed. A Praieiro police chief was named, but the provincial president did not authorize widespread substitutions among officeholders.[29] The *Diário Novo* subsequently lamented that Provincial President Marcelino de Brito left in place the partisan Conservative officialdom that Francisco do Rego Barros had constructed over many years, substituting only five police commissionerss.[30] Indeed, relations between the Praieiros and the provincial president deteriorated to the point that Marcelino de Brito, in correspondence with the court, declared that a decent man like himself would not join with a party composed of such insignificant people. The meaning of "insignificant" in this context is clear—lower class and potentially dangerous. The president unsuccessfully requested the dismissal of the Praieiro police chief, arguing that his recommendations of such lowly, useless people for police posts were clearly unacceptable.[31]

Despite the lack of an inversion, the weakening of the political and administrative apparatus constructed by former President Rego Barros was sufficient that the Praieiros were able to win sweeping victories in elections for justices of the peace and municipal councilmen in August and September 1844.[32] The political climate was extremely tense. The U.S. consul wrote of rumors of a disturbance planned for September 7, the anniversary of independence (as well as election day in the interior of the province), during which a national guard battalion would demand changes in local authorities. He reported that "politics and party spirit [were] daily becoming more violent, as the time approached for the elections."[33]

The rumored national guard rebellion did not erupt, but the elections did involve considerable violence. Violence in elections was not an aberration, but the reported incidents in Afogados, a suburb of Recife, were unusually grave. Richard Graham has clarified the important role that violence or the threat of violence played in elections. There were various points in the electoral process at which violence might break out. When each bloc of voters went to the polling place at the parish church, battles might erupt. Inside the polling place, the proceedings of the electoral board might be interrupted by violence. The board played the key role of making final decisions on who could vote, ensuring that the identities of the individuals present matched those on the electoral roles. Disputes over these points could lead to physical confrontations. As votes were cast, or afterward, violence could flare if a faction that feared losing the election attempted to steal the ballot box in order to invalidate the election. The mere threat of violence might also be effective if it scared off one's opponents. Intimidation was an important element in electoral battles. It must have been an unsettling experience when twenty Conservative voters at one polling place on September 22 faced three hundred Praia voters, accompanied by a huge number of supporters who lined the other side of the church where the elections were held. (The variety of tactics used to intimidate voters is suggested by the actions of a justice of the peace in an election in 1847. First he attempted to pressure voters by spreading rumors of the likelihood of much bloodshed on election day; then he had his father prohibit access to wells on his land from which people had always drawn water. The father went on to threaten a ward inspector with expulsion from his land.) Even if an opponent's control of the electoral board allowed little chance of winning the election, a significant display of force might demonstrate sufficient strength so that the board would record complaints concerning the validity of the electoral process. The very recording of such objections, in demonstrating a degree of power by a challenger, could constitute a partial victory.[34]

The violence in Afogados on September 7, 8, and 9 was unusual in its proportions. Conservatives claimed that the Praieiros would be unable to win if there were a free expression of public opinion and that the Praieiros had therefore resorted to fraud and, when fraud failed, violence. The baronists argued that Praia leaders Nunes Machado and Vilella Tavares harangued crowds on election day, following the Praia principle of inciting popular passions.[35] The Praieiro police chief, Antônio Afonso Ferreira, tried to convince the justice of the peace to continue with the elections, but the Conservative judge refused, claiming that the crowds of Praia partisans whom Afonso Ferreira had dispersed were milling around town, ready to return and disrupt events. The *Diário de Pernam-*

buco claimed that when Manuel Joaquim de Rego e Albuquerque arrived on horseback with armed men to restore order, he was surrounded by a thousand men armed with clubs and knives and subjected to cries of "Out with the despot, out with the *cabano* Baronist."[36] The police chief provided no support to Manuel Joaquim, who was saved by two cavalry detachments. Conservative newspapers further charged that the crowds unleashed anarchy, beating people and sacking stores. Reports of violence against merchants led to American, Sardinian, French, and Portuguese ships being sent to Recife from Bahia. The *Diário de Pernambuco* also leveled the charge that Nunes Machado, Vilella Tavares, and the police chief returned to Recife from Afogados that night with three hundred men marching in close order and continued their work of intimidation, this time at a church in Santo Antônio.[37]

Praia journalists, in contrast, played down violence and illegality. They depicted events in Afogados as the actions of people who were fed up with being excluded from political influence through violence and arbitrary acts. Two thousand people peacefully gathered on election day to protest electoral abuses and to make their presence felt, but they did not break the law.[38] They dispersed at six o'clock in the evening at the urging of Nunes Machado. The *Diário Novo* also argued that part of the crowd had gathered out of curiosity to see why troops had been called to assemble; the newspaper insisted on the illegality of the calling of the troops by Conservative Capt. Mathias de Albuquerque.[39] The paper argued that the Praieiros had no motive to disrupt the election, which they handily won. It also insisted on the beneficial effects of the Praia leaders' efforts to disperse the crowds. The Praia organ also assured readers that the city and suburbs were calm and denied Conservative claims of widespread violence, noting that customs receipts were not down, even when anarchy had supposedly reigned and commercial houses had purportedly been sacked.[40]

Praia gains made life increasingly difficult for President Marcelino de Brito. In October 1844 the U.S. consul reported that "owing to the excited state of the Province," the government had replaced Marcelino de Brito with Conselheiro Tomás Xavier Garcia de Almeida. The consul further noted that the new president was to be supported by additional troops sent from Rio de Janeiro.[41] Holanda Cavalcanti's influence was felt again in the selection of this new president. Equally telling, Tomás Xavier Garcia de Almeida was also a friend of the Conservative Baron of Boa Vista and had substituted for Rego Barros as provincial president in 1838.[42]

The Praieiros did not immediately attack the newly appointed president. The *Lidador*, the newspaper directed by leading Conservatives such as Jerônimo Martiniano Figueira de Melo and José Tomás Nabuco de Araújo, noted that the Praieiros exhibited a pattern of welcoming new presidents, in the hope of controlling them, and then stridently opposing those whom they were unable to dominate.[43] Indeed, the Praieiros welcomed Xavier Garcia de Almeida's reduction of revenues for public works.[44] It was soon clear, however, that Holanda Cavalcanti's choice as president would not go far toward satisfying the Praieiros.

In working against the new president the Praieiros managed a victory in the Senate elections of January 1845. Allying with the *paulista* Liberals (*luzias*) and with the palace faction, the Praia successfully ran the prominent politician Antônio Carlos Ribeiro de Andrada Machado e Silva.[45] The Conservatives attempted to sway opinion in the court, despite such Praia influence. They argued that of the two Liberal parties supporting the ministry, one (Holanda Cavalcanti's) was orderly, with a history of principled opposition to Conservative ministries and policies, while the other was merely opportunistic and therefore undeserving of ministerial support. Nonetheless, the Praieiros' strength could not be ignored indefinitely.[46]

Indeed, Holanda Cavalcanti, minister of the navy and war since May 1845, finally yielded in allowing the appointment of a provincial president more acceptable to the Praieiros. He apparently expected that Antônio Pinto Chichorro da Gama would exercise restraint and that the Praia could be contained.[47] On June 4, 1845, the steamship *O Imperador* arrived in Recife with the news that Antônio Pinto Chichorro da Gama had been appointed provincial president and that, until his arrival, Vice-President Manuel de Sousa Teixeira would serve.[48] Contrary to Holanda Cavalcanti's expectations, Sousa Teixeira, as the interim executive authority, immediately made clear his intentions of presiding over a fundamental change in the balance of power in the province. On his first day on the job, he replaced the provincial police chief and the director of the municipal police. In short order, three hundred police commissioners, deputy police commissioners, alternates for these posts, officers of the municipal police and national guard, and district attorneys were dismissed, and Praia partisans took their places.[49] When the new provincial president, Chichorro da Gama, arrived, he set to dismissing another 340 officeholders.[50]

The U.S. consul reported on the charged political atmosphere, stating that "party spirit runs higher than I have known it during any of the revolutions of the last twenty-one years" and that "political intrigues have led to violent animosities and I have serious cause for fearing some outbreak [and] . . . much bloodshed and destruction of property."[51]

Whose Order?

Debate over the reversal of power was centered on the issue of order. Conservatives argued that the changes undermined the "legitimate influence" of prestigious, influential families, "citizens distinctive for their merit, for their services and social importance" in favor of "proletarians, agitators, and the disorderly."[52] The Conservative organ *Lidador* lamented the "immense abundance of principles of conflagration . . . that every day accumulate and ferment in the middle of certain classes of society."[53] The paper elaborated on this depiction of the beneficiaries of the changes with charges that they were hostile to the monarchy and a threat to national unity, and that they would soon raise the banner of 1824—that is, seek an independent republic.[54] Conservative journalists deplored the "exterminating instinct of the disorderly party" and warned that "Pernambuco is on the crater of a volcano, ready to explode." The U.S. consul echoed these views, informing Washington that many police authorities had been "replaced by men who are . . . known to be anything but friendly to the preservation of good order, in fact, the mob are now in power."[55]

The Praieiros also focused on the theme of order, depicting the changes in police posts as the necessary step for ending the unpunished murders, theft, embezzlement of public funds, and bandits that characterized the Conservatives' "reign of the dagger and musket."[56] The *Diário Novo* claimed that the police force was ineffective, staffed by people chosen on the basis of political favor, some of whom behaved irregularly, facilitated prisoner escapes, or were alcoholics or even murderers.[57] Scandalous police behavior included electoral fraud and arbitrary acts of personal vengeance.[58] The police needed to be reorganized to prevent crime and arrest those who broke the law, instead of protecting criminals.[59]

Once their partisans had replaced Conservatives in official posts, the Praieiros were ready to further the assault on Conservative power. The central contention in Praia polemics was the need to impose the law on the unrestrained, corrupt, personal power of the Cavalcantis and their Conservative allies. This power was depicted as feudal (complete with images of Cavalcanti castles) and immune to public authority. The Praieiros, in control of the provincial government, would bring law to the feudal redoubts of the Conservatives.

The principal charges to justify police action were illegal slave trafficking and slave theft, murder, harboring (or even leading) criminal gangs, and illegal possession of large stores of weapons. On the basis of such charges, legal action was taken against Conservative *senhores*, and police searches of their properties were conducted.[60] José Maria Paes Barreto's Pindoba and Crusahy estates, for example, were "invaded," as Conservatives termed it, several times. At Pindoba police found slaves who had been stolen in Recife for resale in the *sertão*. Finds like this provided valuable material for Praia newspapers, which printed the statements of the slaves over the course of January 1846. The *Diário Novo* mocked recent Conservative defenses of José Maria, who had claimed that Praia police were harassing him. The paper sarcastically claimed that José Maria could not lay eyes on a slave without stealing him.[61]

Later that year the Praia police entered José Severino Cavalcanti de Albuquerque's Cacimbas estate and located the buried remains of a man. A slave and several others on the estate confessed that they had committed the murder and then buried the corpse in a cave on the property.[62] The victim, known as Alexander the Great, had been receiving the affection of José's mistress and wanted to marry her, prompting José to order the murder.[63]

In September, it was José Maria Paes Barreto's turn again, as his Crusahy plantation was searched for the fifth time. The *Lidador* indignantly reported that the police "witnessed with a smile the tears and discomfort of his family; and insulted them . . . in the presence of the riffraff. . . .

José Maria saw his house invaded by his personal enemies, invested with public authority, accompanied by the curious riffraff and over a hundred armed men."[64] The humiliation to which the planter's family was subjected was no small matter. A *senhor's* power depended in part on his prestige and reputation as an effective patron and protector. These characteristics helped earn planters the loyalty of their clients and contributed to their ability to marshal armed men when needed. Yet even the poor had seen him unable to protect himself, his family, or his property in the face of his enemies.[65]

Curiously, even as the Conservative politician and polemicist Nabuco de Araújo denounced the partisan manner in which the police carried out these searches, he also affirmed the principle of imposing law on rural planters.[66]

> That feudalism . . . that haughty and arrogant spirit that seeks to undermine public authority, or dominate or despise it, is it exclusive to the Cavalcantis? No, a thousand times no; that anti-social, absurd and dangerous spirit is a vice rooted in the property owners in the interior of Pernambuco, and perhaps [all] the Empire.[67]

Nabuco de Araújo further characterized the Praieiro discourse against the feudalism of the planters as an important service to the country, which, if it had been carried out honestly, would have earned glory that even Conservatives whose immediate interests were prejudiced would have conceded.[68] Nabuco de Araújo lamented, however, that the Praieiros only manipulated these ideas; their implementation was thoroughly partisan and unjust—only Conservatives felt the force of the law.[69]

Nabuco de Araújo's comments reflect a degree of ambiguity inherent in the Conservatives' centralizing project. From the colonial period, rural elites had been accustomed to a very small state. The government largely ruled through local elites, and only in larger cities were the crown's agents particularly visible. As long as peace was maintained and revenues collected, there was generally little need for a greater state presence than the church, periodic appearances of circuit judges, and perhaps occasional demonstrations of strength. In independent Brazil, however, Conservatives concluded from the experience of the regency that only a strongly centralized system could maintain order. Though conflict among local elites appeared to require the state to play a significant mediating role, the practical difficulties of exercising that role were formidable.

Centralizing reforms in the early 1840s did establish a substantial role for professional magistrates appointed by the imperial court (and routinely rotated among various locations to reduce local influences upon them), yet the most common contact with state authority continued to be with police commissioners and deputy police commissioners. These posts were staffed by prominent individuals on the winning side of political struggles. The *Lidador*'s objections to the search of José Maria Paes Barreto's property illustrate the problem. José Maria "saw his house invaded by his personal enemies, invested with public authority."[70] Nabuco de Araújo objected to the partisan nature of the Praia police activities, but what else could one expect? The state did not have the resources or bureaucratic capacity to staff a professional police force across the vast country in order to rule directly. Elections may have kept the court somewhat in touch with the balance of power across the empire, thus helping maintain stability, but the paradox of playing a mediating role while delegating considerable powers to local partisan actors continued.[71]

Compare this to crown judges, who were, of course, political appointees. Nabuco de Araújo, for example, was both a Conservative polemicist and a professional magistrate assigned to Pernambuco in the 1840s. Partisanship no doubt often prevailed, but there was at least some room for a mediating role. While professional judges were agents of the central government, they were not immune to local influences. Thomas Flory and José Murilo de Carvalho have emphasized the integrative role they played not only in enforcing the will of the court but also in tempering actions so as to suit local interests and in representing those interests to the court. Astute magistrates could sometimes manipulate this role to personal benefit, such as marriage into a powerful family. Nabuco de Araújo, for example, married a niece of Francisco Paes Barreto, the future Marquis of Recife, and thereby strengthened his political standing. In this crosscurrent of influences, there were possibilities for brokerage. Centrally appointed judges were selected by a partisan minister of justice and were expected to both promote partisan interests and help keep the peace; they were also subject to local influences. Although the case of Nabuco de Araújo provides an example of local influences reinforcing the partisan role of a centrally appointed judge, in other cases a role for political mediation might emerge.[72]

Struggle for the Senate

The Praieiros not only exercised authority delegated from the court, they also attempted to consolidate their position in the institutions housed there. Their struggle to place Antônio Pinto Chichorro da Gama and Ernesto Ferreira da França, Pernambuco's provincial president and police chief, in vacant seats in the imperial Senate became a cause célèbre that was debated in newspapers across the country. Twice the Praieiros won elections to nominate the six candidates from whom the emperor would choose two to occupy the most coveted positions in the empire, lifetime appointments to the imperial Senate. In each instance, the emperor chose the leading candidates of the Praia party. In unprecedented and never again repeated maneuvers, Conservatives in the Senate rejected the imperial choices, invoking the senators' authority to verify election results and declaring that fraud and irregularities rendered the elections invalid.[73]

The dispute over the Pernambucan elections took on special significance nationally because of the ongoing struggle between the Chamber of Deputies and the Conservative-dominated Senate. The Senate, long a Conservative bulwark, had survived Liberal attempts to eliminate its lifetime appointments during the regency. During the "liberal quinquennium," a five-year period of Liberal ministries in the court from 1844 to 1848, tensions mounted between the two representative bodies. In 1845 *paulista* Liberals in the Chamber led a battle against Senate Conservatives in seeking an electoral reform law. The southern Liberals called for a joint session of the Senate and Chamber to handle the issue, invoking Article 61 of the Constitution. The Senate, in turn, asserted its right to block a fusion of the two institutions. Tensions between the two bodies rose any time Liberals in the Chamber of Deputies saw their efforts impeded by the Senate.

Cristiano Otoni, a prominent Liberal from Minas Gerais, succinctly expressed the Liberal view of excessive senatorial power when he asserted that "life-time appointments were a public danger, modified only by two correctives: the gradual recomposition brought about by death and (sub-sequent) admission of new senators and by fusion (with the Chamber)." If the Senate insisted on annulling elections like those in Pernambuco and refused fusion, there would be no choice but to reform the Senate, diminishing its powers.[74]

The first election in Pernambuco was held in 1846. In May of the following year, when the emperor chose the new senators from the list of the six candidates receiving the most votes, he disregarded Holanda Cavalcanti's lobbying against the Praia candidates. Holanda Cavalcanti had little choice but to resign his post as minister of treasury, and the May 2, 1846, ministry quickly fell. This ministry was known as a "conciliation" ministry because, although it was headed by the Liberal Holanda Cavalcanti, it had the support of the saquaremas. (This "conciliation" ministry should not be confused with the better-known Conciliação of the mid-1850s.) These Conservative leaders were bitter enemies of Aureliano, the valued Praieiro ally in the court. The ministry also enjoyed the support of Praia opponents in Pernambuco.[75] The saquarema Paulino José Soares de Sousa cooperated with this ministry as the lesser of evils and to avoid a "violent coalition of Alencar, Aureliano, [and] the Praieiros." He observed that "a ministry that seeks to live with everyone (which is impossible) and that fears everyone, is ready to do favors for us, to nominate a vicar, a county judge."[76]

The May 22, 1847, ministry that replaced the conciliation ministry was composed of staunch, partisan Liberals such as Manuel Alves Branco and Nicoláu de Campos Vergueiro, who, like their Praia allies, were interested in battle with the Conservatives. The saquaremas were incensed with Aureliano, whom they blamed for the nomination of the Praieiros for the Senate and whose support for the new ministry was clear in his brother Saturnino's membership in the cabinet as minister of foreign affairs.[77] The Senate's June 1, 1847, annulment of the Pernambucan senatorial elections thus was not only a rejection of membership for partisan Liberals but also partly a reprisal against Aureliano.[78]

Conservative leaders saw themselves as the great champions of the monarchy. They had struggled against Liberal efforts to reduce the crown's influence during the regency and then led the Regresso movement's consolidation of centralized authority and refurbishing of the trappings of monarchy.[79] This made Aureliano's influence on the emperor all the more galling. In their minds, the emperor was forsaking his real supporters and bestowing favors on Aureliano and his Praieiro allies. The Conservative Pernambucan *Lidador*, lamenting the selection of the Praieiro candidates for the Senate, noted that they could only hope "that one day, the clamor of the people could reach the crown, across Aureliano's trenches that obstruct the road." Several days later the paper asserted that

> one day when He [the Emperor] remembers His Father, His minority . . . He will remember us, we who are dedicated to the real monarchy, we who have defended the monarchy, against which the dominant faction [the Praieiros], the Palace, . . . have conspired; we will be in favor, in defense of the Son of the Founder of the Empire, the Orphan of 1831, whom we saved from the perils of July 30, from the insidiousness of December 1832 plotted by the new senator Chichorro and by the omnipotent Aureliano, and from the extermination against him proposed by Sr. França aided by his son and new senator Ernesto. We exposed ourselves to the danger and confronted the revolutionary waves to save Him from your [Praieiro] claws.

No effort was made to hide the sting of the perceived injustice at the hands of the monarch. "As for His Royal Majesty, we have nothing to do but adore him, and respectfully kiss his august hand for this slap in the face."[80]

The Conservative nullification of the Senate elections placed these stalwart defenders of royal prerogatives in the awkward position of committing an unprecedented act of open defiance of the emperor. The Liberal press made much of this. Liberal papers in the court warned that "an oligarchical faction entrenched in the life-term Chamber [i.e., the Senate] intends to dictate the law to him who is above the laws [the emperor]." Under the plan, the papers argued, "the moderating power will no longer be the key to our political organization, because *another power raises itself higher*—the irresistible power of the *saquaremas* in the life-term Chamber [i.e., the Senate]."[81] Another paper declared that "the *saquarema* faction judges itself [was] born with the right to perennially govern not only the country, but the very Crown." It asserted that "since the elevation of the meritorious cabinet of February 2 [1844] those proud oligarchs nourish profound resentments against the crown."[82]

The Liberals' argument that they had the emperor's support was a strong one; the emperor twice chose Praia candidates when either time he could have chosen the Baron of Boa Vista, who also appeared, although with fewer votes, on the list of Senatorial candidates from which the emperor chose. The Praieiros' alliance with Aureliano further deepened their confidence in the emperor's support. The Liberals' unusual open invocation of the emperor's support nonetheless infuriated Conservatives.[83]

Much as the Conservatives attempted to justify their actions as something other than an infringement on the emperor's power, in the end it was clear that, in defending the Senate's prerogatives, they were willing to challenge the crown's authority. The elder Conservative statesman and senator from Pernambuco, the Viscount of Olinda, spelled it out explicitly on the floor of the Senate: "The descendants of those who knew how to resist the King in order to better serve the King will also know how to resist the oppression of the ministers to better serve the emperor."[84]

Born of the annulment of the Senate election, the combative May 22, 1847, Liberal ministry was unlikely to prove any more accommodating than their enemies, the Conservatives in the Senate. The cabinet's leader, Manuel Alves Branco, did not disappoint his Praia allies and other Liberal partisans with his letters that declared the obligation of all public employees to provide political support during the November elections to the Chamber of Deputies. These instructions, tantamount to an invitation to abuse official positions, have been interpreted by some historians as an attempt to rally Liberals and avoid intra-party dissension.[85]

Conservative Resistance and Mobilization

In Pernambuco the spirit of the new ministry was mirrored in the polarized atmosphere of provincial politics. Contributing to the heightening tension in the province were the numerous incidents of Conservative *senhores* openly defying Praia police in the countryside. By 1847 many baronist planters had had enough of their enemies, who were invested with police authority, invading their estates. The police reported that there were individual cases of overt resistance, that Conservative planters were coordinating their activities in the countryside, and that criminal bands led by *guabirus* were roaming the countryside. Police commissioners blamed the Conservative press for inciting resistance when the press declared, for example, that Praia police actions against Conservative estates would be defeated through armed responses.[86]

In March 1847 a group of a hundred men impeded the execution of an arrest order by a civil judge in Caruaru, eighty-seven miles southwest of Recife, in the transitional zone of the *agreste*, and proceeded to chase local judicial officials and fifty soldiers out of town. The police reported that although the incident appeared to have originated in a private squabble, in fact it was a rehearsal for a larger uprising and a means of testing public support for the government. The president responded by sending over four hundred armed men, but they found only barricades and trenches because the rebels had abandoned the town.[87]

As early as August 1846, police authorities in Limoeiro, fifty-four miles northwest Recife, warned of gatherings of armed men. Sebastião Lins de Araújo was reported to be planning a revolt with Vicente Ferreira de Paula, the leader of the Guerra dos Cabanos in the 1830s.[88] In December Sebastião reportedly led a gang of fourteen well-armed men who committed various thefts and murders. Maintaining order in Limoeiro proved difficult because Sebastião and his ally João Maurício Cavalcanti da Rocha Wanderley, when pursued, took shelter on the Natuba estate in the neighboring province of Paraíba.[89] In July 1847 police authorities reported that Limoeiro, and especially Sebastião Lins de Araújo's parish of Taquaratinga, was the site of some of the most horrible incidents in the province. In the next two months Sebastião's band was cited for brutal murders.[90]

José Pedro Veloso da Silveira, the wealthy owner of the Lages estate, organized Conservative resistance in the parish of Escada, located thirty-six miles southwest of Recife. In June 1847, various Conservative planters gathered there with their followers. Police reported efforts to organize a rural rebellion that would mobilize Indians and peasants of Jacuípe and Panelas against the provincial government.[91]

João Guilherme and Lt. Col. Eustáquio José Veloso da Silveira, a brother-in-law of José Pedro, were both residents on José Pedro's estate. Both played prominent roles in seeking an alliance with Vicente Ferreira de Paula for an uprising among the Indians and peasants of Jacuípe and Panelas. Conservatives reportedly paid off Vicente to cement the alliance. In June and July police officials sent various reports on these efforts to organize a rural rebellion against the provincial government, as well as numerous requests for more troops, weapons, and ammunition.[92] Perhaps the baronists were hoping to capitalize on the peasants' discontent, which had been triggered by recent government actions. The police commissioner of Água Preta informed the chief of police that he had sent the local military commander to calm people down, people who had been upset by recent government orders.[93]

João do Rego Barros's Buranhaem estate served as another gathering place for Conservatives determined to resist the Praia administration. João, the Baron of Boa Vista's brother, and José Severino Cavalcanti de Albuquerque led a gathering of two hundred armed men in November 1847. When a police force supplemented by twenty national guardsmen arrived to seize armaments and munitions and disperse the gathering, they were surrounded by the two hundred men. The national guard promptly fled. After reinforcements brought their number up to sixty, discretion perhaps was the better part of valor and the strengthened force still did not attack. The police chief explained that with elections near, this was not the time for an armed confrontation. The provincial president immediately wrote the minister of justice for more army troops to confront the forces gathered by João do Rego Barros.[94]

Confrontations were not limited to the *zona da mata*, as Liberal authorities in the *sertão* made clear. Serrafim de Sousa Ferraz, the police commissioner of Flores, 327 miles southwest of the capital, warned of a plan hatched by Conservatives in Buique and Pesqueira to attack Flores. Rumors had it that with a successful rebellion there, the area could serve as a base for infiltrating other areas. He gathered two hundred men, fearing that his opponents might be able to marshal even more. The police commissioner requested more arms and ammunition from Recife and noted the need for a larger permanent force at his disposal. He argued that it took time to gather the national guard and there were limits on how long they would serve.[95]

Against this conflictive backdrop, elections were held in September and October to again vote for two new senators, and November elections were held for the Chamber of Deputies in Rio de Janeiro. In the midst of intense electoral competition a significant campaign innovation appeared. In an attempt to broaden their appeal and effectiveness, Conservatives initiated the practice of holding electoral "meetings." At these events, which were referred to by the English term "meetings," prominent politicians stood atop platforms making speeches and appealing to crowds for their votes. Leaders as prominent as the Baron of Boa Vista and his brother Sebastião do Rego Barros, for example, addressed gatherings and denounced the Bahian-born Praieiro candidates for the Senate as unacceptable to represent Pernambuco. The *Diário do Rio* reported that the initial "meeting" was the first of its kind in Brazil. The Baron of Boa Vista also spoke at bars to gather electoral support, and he offered the presidential residence for a dance for master artisans.[96]

The Praieiros made even bolder appeals to the middle and lower classes. In August, Praia leader Joaquim Nunes Machado, speaking in a shoemaker's shop, called for nationalization of retail commerce.[97] Praieiro candidates used the new campaign technique of electoral meetings to make a naked appeal to resentment of the large Portuguese presence. Conservative journalists denounced Praia abuses, gathering "the most ignorant part of the population for night-time meetings, in which they sought, by means of the most incredible calumnies and absurd stories, to excite popular hatred."[98] In the increasingly polarized province, resentment of the Portuguese would remain a staple of Praieiro politics.

The electoral meetings are also significant in showing how politicians worked crowds to gather electoral support. Although this phenomenon is unremarkable in the twentieth century, nineteenth-century campaigning in Brazil has been depicted as a gentleman's affair in which candidates gathered support among the politically influential, especially through letter writing. In this view, politicking among the masses of voters, in the sense of trying to convince voters on the basis of salient issues, was nearly absent. The development of this new campaign technique in Pernambuco can probably be explained by the unusually high degree of polarization there.[99]

As a result of the Regresso centralization, local, provincial, and national institutions were tightly linked, and whoever ruled from the court could thoroughly dominate government offices throughout Brazil. With such rewards available, political organization accelerated. We can speak of Conservative and Liberal parties as having emerged by the early to mid-1840s. Although political discourse centered on maintaining order, political competition constantly threatened disorder. Not only was violence routine in the electoral process, but Pernambuco's highly polarized atmosphere undermined elite restraint motivated by fear of unleashing social and political instability. Conflict over Praieiro partisans taking coveted seats in the imperial Senate escalated tensions between Conservatives and Liberals nationally and contributed, by mid-1847, to a combative Liberal ministry that supported the Praieiros. The aggressive police actions of these Pernambucan Liberals prompted Conservative baronist planters to band together in armed resistance. Conservative innovation in urban electoral politics, with political meetings in which leaders made direct appeals in speeches to crowds, was matched by Liberals. Praieiro speakers, however, were prepared to escalate tensions further, mobilizing the middle and lower classes with nativist appeals against a Portuguese presence that purportedly monopolized economic opportunities and denigrated the native-born.

7

Political Parties, Popular Mobilization, and the Portuguese

Conceptualizations of nineteenth-century Brazilian political organization have long emphasized informal structures, such as kinship and patronage networks, over formal political institutions. Political parties, for example, often have been perceived both as façades for personalistic groups formed to capture the spoils of government and as devoid of ideological content and significant differentiation. One influential work concisely reflects the assumptions of the Liberal and Conservative parties' similarity in class composition, interests, and political ideas, affirming that Liberal and Conservative governments had different labels "without that variety of nomenclature having the slightest significance."[1] Such generalizations have hardly been tested at the provincial level, however.[2] Evidence from Pernambuco suggests the need to reexamine such perspectives. The Praieiros made democratic and nationalistic appeals to the middle and lower classes through Lusophobia.[3] As in many newly independent countries, the continued economic and social presence of the former colonial power's subjects appeared to frustrate expectations for change in nineteenth-century Brazil. Not surprisingly, politicians shared and spoke to such strongly held views. In newspapers, in electoral gatherings, and on the floor of the Chamber of Deputies, Praieiro leaders proposed policies to limit the Portuguese role in the economy. The challenge to classic liberal economic principles posed by their program of Lusophobic, nationalistic development and their promotion of decentralized, democratic liberalism marked clear ideological and programmatic differences from the Conservatives. Likewise, liberal Lusophobia helps explain differences in the socioeconomic composition of the Liberals' political support and their willingness to use violence. All of this suggests the need to examine anew the role of ideology and formal political institutions in the era of early Brazilian state formation.[4]

Lusophobia in Post-Independence Brazil

In nineteenth-century Brazil, resentment of the Portuguese and the Portuguese-born was just below the surface.[5] The reasons for this bitterness were varied. Although the anti-colonial discourse of the independence era had blamed the metropolis for the ills afflicting Brazil, continued Portuguese political influence after independence was a far greater issue.[6] Throughout the First Reign, anger over the influence of Portuguese-born advisors in Pedro I's court fueled opposition to Pedro. Many of those struggling for a decentralized system perceived Pedro's centralism as essentially a continuation of Portuguese absolutism, now based in Rio de Janeiro.

Economic competition and resentment, however, were the greatest sources of conflict. Two complaints—omnipresence in the economy and exclusiveness among the Portuguese—were staples of Lusophobia. One analyst has noted that in Bahia the terms "Portuguese" and "merchant" were largely synonymous.[7] Accusations of Portuguese monopoly were commonplace. Portuguese merchants did not, of course, monopolize trans-Atlantic trade; in fact, the British dominated it.[8] Nonetheless, for many of native-born citizens, it was the seemingly pervasive presence of the Portuguese that made for, as Praieiro leader Joaquim Nunes Machado expressed it, "that terrible anomaly of Brazilians being true foreigners, guests in their own country."[9] The Portuguese, who had access to capital gained in international commerce as well as lengthy experience in the country, controlled a large percentage of the retail commerce in many Brazilian cities, including Recife. Moderate liberals such as Joaquim Nunes Machado and radical liberals such as Antônio Borges da Fonseca both decried the large number of jobs lost to the Portuguese. Nor was it simply a matter of competition. There were constant accusations that the Portuguese kept to themselves, always aiding each other and hiring other Portuguese. Portuguese insularity seemed a nearly insurmountable barrier for Brazilians seeking employment.[10]

Racial tension could strain relations with the Portuguese as well. The majority of poorer Brazilians, who for the most part bore the brunt of exploitation by and economic competition from foreign shopkeepers, small retailers, and artisans, were people of color. When day-to-day contact led to confrontations, the Portuguese were quick to hurl racial epithets at Afro-Brazilians.[11]

Tension and conflicts with the Portuguese were no small matter. Lusophobic violence erupted in the streets of Pernambuco and Bahia in 1824 and in the national capital in the weeks before Pedro's abdication. Following Pedro's return to Portugal there were anti-Portuguese actions in the streets of nearly all of Brazil's larger cities, most often demanding dismissal of Portuguese-born officials from public office and the military and often deportation as well. Rio de Janeiro was the scene of four Lusophobic uprisings in the months after the abdication, and Bahia witnessed a half-dozen over the next two years. Violence between nativists and the Portuguese resulted in nearly one hundred deaths in Belém, Pará, in April 1833, and an anti-Portuguese riot left thirty *adotivos* (naturalized Brazilians born in Portugal) dead in Mato Grosso in May 1834. Lusophobia was central in some of the major rebellions of the regency, such as the awful carnage of the Cabanagem, in Pará, and in the Balaiada in Maranhão, and to a lesser extent in Bahia's Sabinada.[12]

Lusophobia in Pernambuco

Liberal newspapers appealed to these deep currents of resentment and in turn intensified them.[13] Radical liberal newspapers went beyond the political and economic influence that were the focus of the moderate papers and hammered away at the supposed insolence, crimes, and moral depravity of the former colonizers, calling for action against them. There was even one paper, the *Voz do Brasil* (Voice of Brazil), which was dedicated exclusively to attacking foreign influence in Brazil.[14] Only rarely, however, did the Lusophobic press direct much of its ire at foreigners other than the Portuguese.[15] The Portuguese consul in Pernambuco was very clear about the impact of the Lusophobic press. Explaining an outburst of violence against the Portuguese, he noted, "The editors of several incendiary newspapers have for some time spread extravagant ideas and occasionally distributed flyers with [Lusophobic] doctrines . . . such that they have predisposed the riffraff [to violence]."[16]

It was easy to stoke resentment of the economic success of the Portuguese, who seemingly prospered in the midst of Brazilians suffering poverty. A supposed Portuguese "monopoly" controlled the sugar trade, and it was charged that the Portuguese dominated warehousing as well.[17] The most common accusation was that Portuguese domination of retail commerce sharply limited job opportunities for Brazilians. Indeed, it was common practice for Portuguese businessmen to hire immigrants from Portugal, lending credence to accusations that Portuguese shippers, warehousers, and retailers colluded, routinely hiring other Portuguese, rather than Brazilians, as clerks, *O Regenerador Brazileiro* (the Brazilian Regenerator) claimed that six thousand Portuguese-owned retail commerce houses in Pernambuco employed twelve thousand Portuguese clerks, depriving Brazilians of eighteen thousand jobs.[18]

Lusophobic newspapers also claimed that competition from imported goods and from Portuguese artisans working in Brazil ruined opportunities for native-born artisans. One newspaper asked the rhetorical question of how Brazilians were to find work in commerce or as artisans when "our cities are overflowing with goldsmiths, tailors, masons, cabinet makers, coopers, even barbers from all over the world?" Particularly galling was the employment of Portuguese in government projects, such as the fifty carpenters employed in 1848 in the naval arsenal in Rio de Janeiro, when there were qualified Brazilians available.[19]

Although the greatest tension with the Portuguese was at the popular level of commercial transactions and employment, Brazilians of greater wealth might also resent the role of the Portuguese. For example, the Praieiro press lashed out at the public works projects undertaken by the Baron of Boa Vista in the latter 1830s and early 1840s. Some of the complaints were about hiring foreign artisans, such as the 105 European artisans brought to Pernambuco in the Baron of Boa Vista's administration, but the hiring of foreign engineers also provoked sharp attacks in the press. Resentment over politically connected foreigners obtaining access to government contracts might have been behind the attacks on new construction techniques. The use of new construction materials threatened suppliers of the traditional materials. The building of iron bridges was defended as a means of reducing the substantial cost of repairing wooden bridges, yet this also hurt those with contracts to carry out repairs.[20]

There was also potential for conflict between Brazilian planters and Portuguese merchants. Even planters with vast estates routinely lacked ready capital. The common practice was to use urban middlemen to sell plantation products, supply goods from the city and abroad, and provide the all-important slaves and working capital. These middlemen, known as *comissários* or *correspondentes*, were often Portuguese. The high rates of interest charged allowed Portuguese *correspondentes* to prosper at the expense of native-born *senhores de engenho*.[21] Gilberto Freyre, the noted scholar of the northeastern sugar plantation and its civilization, described the figure of the middleman as "a city aristocrat, with a gold chain about his neck, silk hat, a tiled mansion, a luxurious carriage, eating imported delicacies, raisins, figs, prunes, drinking Port wine, his daughters ravishingly attired in dresses copied from Parisian fashion books when they attended the *premières* of Italian divas at the opera house."[22] Clearly, such a figure, who enriched himself through seemingly usurious rates of interest, could provoke resentment.

The Portuguese role, of course, was not invariably exploitative, especially for the elite. After all, marital alliances might be struck, allowing capital-rich, Portuguese *comissários*, or their offspring, to enter the prestigious world of planters, while the latter gained access to much needed capital. Moreover, while interest rates were elevated, the middlemen did provide a crucial service that entailed risk. The uncertainty of sugar cane crops, as well as the difficulty of collecting debts when harvests failed, made loans to planters something of a gamble.[23] Lusophobic newspapers, however, seized on the risk for Brazilians in the relationship, claiming that once Brazilians were entrapped in debt, the Portuguese raised the rate of interest or demanded that the debtors support political candidates who favored Portuguese interests.[24] This was a variation on the common theme of the Portuguese controlling politics behind the scenes, corrupting and buying influence with elected representatives and newspapers.[25]

A frequent charge in Lusophobic journalism was that Portuguese political influence made a mockery of Brazilian independence. Defeated on the field of battle, the Portuguese used their influence over Pedro I to achieve their goals despite independence. The newspaper *A Voz do Beberibi* declared, "We were independent, but subject to a foreign prince."[26] Pedro violently shut down the Constituent Assembly and imposed a Constitution that contained "the seed of all the evils that have brought us to the edge of the abyss"—a clause that granted Brazilian citizenship to Portuguese residents in Brazil at the time of independence.[27]

The imperial court in Rio de Janeiro was supposedly flooded with Portuguese.[28] One newspaper asserted that since the reign of the Portuguese-born Pedro I, a Portuguese plan had been in effect to occupy public posts, expand influence, and limit access to public posts to individuals of pro-Lusitanian persuasion.[29] The active promotion of a more centralized political system gave the Portuguese dominating the court greater control over the entire country. The government supposedly overlooked the provinces, choosing ministers from the court. "Infernal centralization" made for despotic rule by provincial presidents comparable to colonial captains-general.[30]

Radical liberal newspapers appealed to the offended honor of Brazilians, depicting the Portuguese as untrustworthy, depraved, and abusive. They were accused of selling poor-quality goods at inflated prices. The Iberians reportedly used a variety of tricks to cheat Brazilians, such as giving the wrong weight of goods, introducing counterfeit money, and mixing water into the milk they sold. Lusophobic newspapers reported Portuguese thefts, even by administrators of church and brotherhood funds.[31] Tales of Portuguese men abusing Brazilian women—luring them with promises of marriage, only to abandon them after compromising their virtue; prostituting young girls; raping women, even with the assistance of slaves—were not unusual. The *Voz do Brasil* accused the Portuguese of intentionally sowing the seeds of depravity by encouraging gambling, dances, and sexual license.[32] The Portuguese were routinely depicted as insolent toward the native-born citizens—flaunting their wealth, riding in rich carriages, splattering mud on humble Brazilians.[33]

Lusophobic journalism sometimes appealed to race. The Portuguese were accused of holding the belief that Brazilian people of color were anarchic, always waiting for the opportunity to rise in rebellion, thus suggesting racial contempt and fear of Brazilians.[34] As a consequence, it was charged, the Portuguese sought to increase the immigration of their white countrymen and to encourage war and violence in Brazil, which would cause the deaths of Brazilian soldiers, largely people of color.[35] This charge was a particularly strong formulation of the common accusation that the Portuguese employed a divide-and-conquer strategy with Brazilians.[36]

Lusophobic newspapers at times exhorted their readers to action against the Portuguese. Praieiro journalists tried to generate support for legal restrictions on Portuguese economic activities. *O Liberal*, in the September electoral season of 1847, hinted at possible violence, reminding the Portuguese that they had been victims of violence in the past and advising them to stay out of politics.[37] The *Voz do Brasil*, like the Praieiros, also proposed severe restrictions on Portuguese immigration, naturalization, and employment opportunities, especially in commerce.[38] The radical liberal paper, however, also openly made clear, unmistakable threats. In April 1847 the paper declared that the Portuguese had left only two alternatives: Brazilians could accept being enslaved by the Portuguese, or they could demand their rights, with a high cost in blood and war.[39] On May 2, 1848, the paper praised France's 1848 Revolution as the overthrow of tyranny and lamented that shouts of "liberty or death" were not heard in Brazil. Accusing the Portuguese consul of offering two thousand Portuguese to help put down any similar uprisings by native-born citizens, it encouraged Pernambucans not to retreat, assuring them that with two hundred canes and *ponteiras de Pasmado* (artistically worked knives from Pasmado, Pernambuco), they could reduce the Portuguese presence to zero.[40]

These attitudes toward the Portuguese clearly resonate with depictions of other groups that have been termed "middlemen minority" groups— Jews in Europe, Asians in East Africa, Chinese in Southeast Asia, for example. The classic middleman function is commercial, but others, such as lending money, are frequent as well. Common characteristics are that they remain attached to their homelands and that they form a distinct community within the host society, one with strong ethnic or national ties. Their commercial operations are typically family operated, facilitating great thrift and lower costs; and when they incorporate people, typically extended family members, people from their homelands, or individuals of the same ethnic group, strong bonds of loyalty comparable to family ties are formed. Such groups are frequently stereotyped as shrewd, ambitious, unethical, parasitical, and composed of people who take from the host country but return little. Perceptions of clannishness, disloyalty, and economic strength that increase their capacity for corruption coalesce to suggest dangerous outsiders prepared to take over the society. Such groups have often been the targets of legal discrimination, riots, and deportation.[41]

The Praia and Lusophobia

The Liberal *Diário Novo* and the Praieiro representatives in the court were not so reckless as to exhort people to Lusophobic violence. As political leaders working within a legal system, they could not afford to call openly for violence. Nonetheless, they were quite forceful in their denunciations of Portuguese influence, and they proposed a range of restrictions on immigration and the economic roles permitted to foreigners. Indeed, Lusophobia was often the medium through which the Praieiros raised issues of economic nationalism and democratic participation.

Joaquim Nunes Machado, for example, addressed the Chamber of Deputies in Rio on June 28, 1848, and railed against Portuguese insolence and involvement in Brazilian politics. His speech, however, focused on the baleful effects of the large Portuguese presence in the economy and the need for the state to reduce that presence. He forcefully denounced the importations of finished products that destroyed Brazilian production of goods such as clothing, shoes, furniture, and leather and silver goods. He criticized Brazil's export of raw materials that foreigners then processed and sold back to Brazil as finished goods.[42]

The circumstances of independence, Nunes Machado lamented, in which Brazil needed foreign support, had forced an open-door policy, allowing foreign goods and immigrants to enter without restrictions. The influx of foreigners, with their exclusiveness, impeded native commerce, industry, and the development of a spirit of national solidarity. That Brazilian artisans, not up-to-date with the latest techniques, and Brazilian merchants, lacking capital, were competing with foreigners who worked together was indicative of the national peril. Nunes Machado invoked revolutionary events in Europe (the revolutions of 1848), affirming that chronic problems must not be put off. "First of all, we should assure our countrymen of reliable means of subsistence," he declared.[43] Nunes Machado thus outlined the rationale for strong corrective action.

Challenging the universality of basic liberal economic thought, the Praieiro leader argued that statesmen needed to apply economic principles according to the circumstances of each country. In the young country of Brazil people were "still learning all of the artisanal skills and kinds of work." Only recently emerged from a colonial regime, they were behind in knowledge and could not effectively compete with foreigners.[44] On June 3 Praia representatives Joaquim Nunes Machado, Felipe Lopes Neto, José Francisco de Arruda Câmara, Joaquim Francisco de Faria, and Jerônimo Vilella Tavares, as well as a deputy from Rio Grande do Sul, Casimiro José de Moraes Sarmento, proposed the nationalization of retail commerce. On June 28, speaking on the floor of the Chamber of Deputies, Nunes Machado defended this idea. Foreigners would be allowed a short time to liquidate their holdings; subsequently, only native-born merchants would work in this sector of the economy.[45] He further proposed selectivity in whom Brazil accepted as immigrants. Instead of Portuguese "adventurers," who were immediately offered good jobs in the cities by their Portuguese countrymen, Brazil should welcome only those who would work uncultivated rural lands. In defense of his proposals, he offered examples of European countries restricting the economic activities of foreigners.[46]

Liberal Lusophobia, of course, was not limited to Portuguese economic domination. As noted earlier, the Portuguese were accused of exploiting their economic power to influence voting. More significantly, wealthy Portuguese merchants had long found entrée into prominent social (and thus political) circles in Pernambuco. Many merchants managed this by fulfilling their aspirations to enter the prestigious and influential world of the province's planters.

Moreover, as Praieiros and other Liberals made clear, the political position of the Portuguese was not a problem exclusive to Pernambuco. Portuguese merchants were well established at the nation's center in socially and politically prominent families in the court and the province of Rio de Janeiro. By the latter 1840s, the Portuguese-born emperor, Pedro I, was no longer on the scene; nor was his Brazilian-born son, Pedro II, surrounded by a completely Portuguese circle of advisors, as his father had been. Nonetheless, Portuguese who had settled in Brazil and become naturalized Brazilians still dominated, in many ways, the court in Rio de Janeiro. There were important links between various Portuguese bureaucrat and merchant families, the provincial planters of Rio de Janeiro, and the Conservative politicians who rose to power in the Regresso of 1836–41.[47] This could only sharpen the liberal nativism felt by those in Pernambuco and other provinces who resented the Portuguese influence and the authoritarian centralization that the Regresso ushered in. More than simple xenophobia, these factors help explain the Praieiro conflation of Liberal hatred of authoritarian centralism and Lusophobia, as well as the willingness to incite Lusophobia among the discontented urban middle and lower classes. The domination of state institutions was a key subtext.

The Praia, Lusophobia, and Popular Mobilization

At least in this era of political debate, Liberals and Conservatives were far from being ideologically identical or nearly interchangeable. On the issue of Lusophobia and the other issues that the Praieiros linked to it, the parties were sharply distinguished, as they were over the issues of mobilization of mass support and decentralization of political institutions. Given the depth of feeling about the Portuguese, it is hardly surprising that Liberals saw the usefulness of Lusophobia as a means of mobilizing support. Acknowledging the instrumental value of Lusophobia, however, is not to deny its ideological quality or to reduce ideology to nothing more than partisan manipulation. Readers might recall the ways that the ideology of anticommunism in the post-war United States, for example, independent of the merits of the ideology in its own right, was useful as a political weapon with which to bludgeon one's opponents in electoral contests. Few analysts would deny the ideological quality of anticommunism simply because it also served partisan interests.

Appeals to anti-Portuguese sentiments were clearly part of the Liberal strategy. One contemporary noted in his diary that stirring up hostilities with the Portuguese "attracted the people to the Liberals' side."[48] Joaquim Nunes Machado, while campaigning for his party's nominees to the imperial Senate in 1847, gave a speech in a shoemaker's shop in which he called for the nationalization of retail commerce. Mobilization of aggrieved artisans, clerks, and individuals who aspired to positions that Portuguese immigrants occupied, as well as others who harbored resentment toward the Portuguese, marked a major difference with the Conservatives.

The Conservative press in Pernambuco, in sharp contrast to the *Diário Novo*, defended the Portuguese presence. The *Lidador* noted Portuguese contributions to commerce that stimulated the economy generally and raised customs duties in particular, as well as the benefits Portuguese artisans conferred on industry in Brazil. The *Lidador* further argued for the beneficial effects of immigration of industrious white Europeans "in preference to that African race that . . . every day . . . demoralizes and barbarizes our land."[49] The prominent organ of the Conservative Party thus insulted Afro-Brazilians, to whom the Praieiros were successfully appealing.[50]

The Praieiro mobilization against the post-1836 status quo was especially daring because order was a fundamental, common political value.[51] Lusophobia, in contrast, appealed to a potent tradition of violence against the Portuguese. There were veritable outpourings of violent Lusophobia in Pernambuco in the First Reign and early in the regency. In the period of the Regresso, however, the province, under the presidency of Francisco do Rego Barros, had enjoyed a respite from Lusophobic violence. Order prevailed.[52] The return of a Liberal ministry to power at the court in 1844, however, and the subsequent appointment of a Praieiro ally as provincial president, set the stage for renewed challenges to the social stability the Conservatives had achieved and dominated. Indeed, in Pernambuco the willingness of the Praia to attack an order they identified with the Portuguese and the Conservative Party, and their willingness to do so by popular mobilization, significantly shaped the identity of their party, in contrast to their enemies. In fact, contemporary accounts by their enemies defined the Praieiros as a party of the lower classes.

In Pernambuco, Conservative journalists of the period denounced this Praia involvement with the lower classes using a traditional appeal to an ordered, hierarchical society. Following the September 1844 elections, for example, the *Diário de Pernambuco* denounced the tactics of the Praia leaders in the suburb of Afogados. The newspaper claimed that three hundred men armed with clubs had marched to Afogados to steal ballot boxes and invalidate the election.[53] Praia parliamentary leader Joaquim Nunes Machado, the newspaper announced, had incited the "heterogeneous masses" to "throw themselves like wild beasts, with clubs and knives, against an unarmed people."[54] Such behavior followed the principle of "flattering the passions and inflating popular excesses."[55]

The response of the Praieiros is revealing. In defending Praia actions in the September elections, the *Diário Novo* in turn attempted to undermine and reverse the assumptions of the Conservative attack. On September 13, 1844, the Praia organ rebutted the Conservative depiction of Nunes Machado as "in the middle of the rabble, corrupting it." Challenging the Conservatives' view of the social hierarchy, the paper declared that in Brazil "there is no rabble, because among us there are only the people and slaves, and the people are all of us, from the most elevated category to the artisan or peasant."[56] Thus the Praia organ explicitly declared its justification of widespread political mobilization in terms of a democratic, leveling vision of society. The basic division in society was between the free (all of whom ought to enjoy full rights of political participation) and the un-free.

The Conservative *Lidador*, in contrast, viewed the lower classes as lacking the requisites for responsible political participation. Conservative discourse routinely reinforced this notion. Denouncing Praia electoral meetings in 1847, for example, the *Lidador* declared that "the masses do not have the necessary time or means to form personal opinions on the questions of the day, by reading the indispensable books and documents, and if they had them they would always lack the prior intellectual preparation."[57] Thus it was logical for the Conservatives to charge that the Praieiros abused electoral meetings by failing to inform and wisely guide the benighted masses. Conservatives argued that Praieiro deputy police commissioners intentionally gathered the most ignorant part of the population for meetings in which raging, furious speakers excited mob hatreds with incredible fables and calumnies.[58]

After attacks on the Portuguese in the streets in December 1847, the *Lidador* denounced the Praieiros along similar lines, again arguing that they undermined the prestige of rightful authority when they lowered themselves to court the lower classes. The Conservative newspaper railed against Praia journalism, which "excite[d] all the low passions of the riff-raff against those who . . . apply themselves to industry, and obtain some fortune." Among the tactics the article criticized were the promotion of the 1844 Artisans' Manifesto, which called for expelling foreign artisans from the country, and electoral meetings in which Praia orators promised to lead artisans to a new society of economic abundance.[59]

The Praia, Its Ideology, and Violence

The linkage the Conservatives sought to establish between the Praia and anarchic, popular violence points to basic distinctions between the parties. We have already seen part of Joaquim Nabuco's description of the lower-class character of the Praia Party, in which he reflected the views of his father, a leading Conservative figure of the 1840s. His full statement is as follows: "One cannot help but recognize in the Praia movement the force of a popular whirlwind. Violent, indifferent to laws and principles, incapable of permitting within itself the slightest discord, always employing means far more energetic than resistance requires, drunk in its excesses of authority: all of this is exactly the domain of the *Praia*, and those are the very characteristics of democracy."[60] The reference to democracy is particularly telling. As used in this passage, it is clearly pejorative, implying that the lower classes were unprepared for civic responsibilities, yet nonetheless were exercising broad rights. This Conservative depiction is, of course, misleading. The Praia was not exclusively made up of urban radicals and the lower classes. The Praieiros gathered support from various sectors of society; rural planters and educated urban groups also identified with the party.[61]

Nonetheless, urban radicals and masses among the Praieiros and the policies they pursued do point to fundamental differences in party membership, program, and ideology between the Praia and the Conservatives. Despite the claim in much of traditional and contemporary historiography that there was no fundamental difference between the monarchy's two parties, the Praieiros of Pernambuco demonstrate otherwise. For one thing, they were willing to use popular violence.

The Praia cultivated Lusophobia; by doing so, they also encouraged violence. This significance of the Praieiro Lusophobic appeal to the urban radicals and poor is clear in the events of the latter 1840s. An important consequence of the Liberals' willingness to mobilize the lower classes was to increase violence and agitation in an already unstable setting. When, as the governing party in the province, moderate Praieiros appealed to xenophobic currents in popular thought, more extreme factions were inevitably prepared to go further to incite people against the Portuguese. While officeholders and other prominent Praieiros could not publicly endorse violence, the potential for violence was inherent in the Lusophobic policies they pursued.

If resentment of the Portuguese was always just below the surface, it only took political agitation to stir it up. The Portuguese consul in Pernambuco made exactly this point, commenting on the disturbances in the September 1844 elections. He informed his government that "[the situation] of Your Majesty's subjects [is] always risky, in case of any disturbance of public order due to the incitements of the agitators of the common people."[62] Elections, when partisan animus was greatest, provided ideal settings for xenophobic outbursts.[63] One sees this in September 1847, when hotly contested elections for two new senators were held in Pernambuco.[64] Praieiro orators, seeking to harness urban discontent for electoral purposes, made direct appeals to Lusophobia in electoral meetings. Joaquim Nabuco had recently called for nationalization of retail commerce. On September 22, just three days after the vote was held, several Portuguese were beaten. The Portuguese consul, in his letter of complaint to Provincial President Chichorro da Gama, reported the seriousness of the event—one of the victims was in danger of losing his sight in one eye as a result of the attack. The consul also reported other incidents in which Portuguese had been insulted and threatened. He attributed these events to the electoral season and warned that one might expect more such incidents.[65]

The chief of police, of course, was a partisan political appointee of the provincial president and a Praieiro. In commenting on the consul's letter, he left little doubt of his party's view of Portuguese influence on local politics. He played down the seriousness of the attacks and affirmed that the most important incidents were purely personal, one of which had been prompted by the victim's own behavior when he slapped a prostitute in public. However, the police chief then went on to criticize Portuguese attitudes and behavior, asserting that many Portuguese were impudent and ungrateful for the hospitality with which they were received.[66] He argued, "Any time a group of people gather, to exercise their right assured by the constitution, some Portuguese immediately say, 'There's looting!' If one did not know Pernambucans, one would think they were given to pillage. This is a provocation."[67]

The police chief leveled his most important charge when he declared that the consul's real motivation was to assist the Conservative opposition in the elections. He lamented such Portuguese involvement in domestic politics, noting the fact that electoral activity was only appropriate for Brazilian citizens.[68] The chief of police passed on to the provincial president a report from a deputy police commissioner that named six Portuguese involved in the recent elections, one of whom even attended Conservative meetings.[69]

Several months later the police chief had to deal with far more serious disturbances. On Saturday, December 4, 1847, in the charged political atmosphere just four days before Recife's electoral college was to meet to select representatives to the national Chamber of Deputies in Rio and the local provincial assembly, the mostly Portuguese membership of the Philo-Terpsichore dancing society on the Rua da Praia gathered for a dance. Throughout the night there were several bouts of stone throwing by a crowd that had gathered at the building. When the members tried to leave, they were attacked by the crowd.[70]

Isolated attacks on Portuguese men also occurred on December 6 and 7. On December 8, the final day of festivities that the Nossa Senhora da Conceição do Arco brotherhood celebrated in the Bairro do Recife (the main commercial area, in which the Portuguese presence was considerable), as a fireworks display began, some in the crowd began shouting, inciting people against the Portuguese. A group charged the fireworks, setting them all off. Confusion reigned as those taken for Portuguese or other foreigners were beaten. The Conservative paper the *Lidador* reported that the cavalry soon dispersed the crowd, but foreigners' houses on nearby streets were stoned, windows and verandas were broken, and two hundred illumination posts set up for the festivities were destroyed. The rioters coursed through the streets, beating the Portuguese they found and stoning foreigners' houses.[71]

Seven months later, while Praieiro representatives in the court called for nationalization of retail commerce, a far larger outbreak shook Recife and surrounding towns. On the morning of June 26, 1848, a student entered one of the many meat warehouses on the Rua da Praia and insulted a Portuguese clerk. The clerk responded with words of his own, the student hit him with his cane, and the clerk struck him with an iron weight, rendering him unconscious. The fallen student's friends incited passersby against the clerk, a crowd gathered, and the accumulated hostility against the Portuguese soon overflowed. Chilling cries of "Mata marinheiros!" and "Morra marinheiros!" (Kill the Portuguese! and Death to the Portuguese!) pierced the air. The city streets were soon abandoned to rioters, and the authorities were charged with putting down the disturbances.[72]

Partisan journalistic accounts concurred in the description of heterogeneous mobs, emphasizing the lower classes, the *plebe* and slaves, yet also noting upper-class students (and even police wielding bayonets, according to the *Diário Novo*). The mobs broke down doors, looted stores, and dragged the Portuguese they found into the streets and beat them. Word of the riots spread quickly; on the evening of the December 26, in neighboring Olinda, rioters attacked Portuguese bakeries and taverns and beat foreigners. Reports of the death toll varied; the *Lidador* claimed eight Portuguese deaths, with several of the corpses dragged through the streets, while the Praieiros' *Diário Novo* initially claimed only three or four deaths.[73]

On June 27, the second day of the disturbances, there were new rounds of beatings and looting. At one school a group gathered and, following the example of a crowd that had converged on the government palace the day before to insist on actions against foreigners massacring starving Brazilians, wrote a petition to the provincial assembly. A crowd, described by the Conservative *Diário de Pernambuco* as a great multitude of barefoot people and slaves, marched to the assembly, entered the galleries, and forced its petition on the body.[74]

The nine-point petition raised issues similar to those raised by the Praia leadership in the court. The document called for a monopoly of retail commerce by native-born Brazilians and limits on the number of foreign-owned, large-scale commercial houses engaged in international commerce. It also sought protection for textile production and agriculture and help for the lower classes to earn an honest living. Standard Liberal issues were raised, demonstrating again the conflation of ethnic hatred and liberal ideology. These included greater power for provincial assemblies and local use of tax revenues collected locally, at the expense of the national government.[75]

Liberal appeals to Lusophobia, and the dangers it entailed, were not exclusive to Pernambuco. National leaders, faced with a weakening political position, cooperated with Praieiro Joaquim Nunes Machado's reviving the politics of Lusophobia in the court. Liberals emphasized Lusophobia in an effort to defeat José Clemente Pereira, the Conservative, Portuguese-born statesman who had close links to the *saquaremas* and was a candidate for an open seat on the court's municipal council in September 1848. Lusophobic appeals and the tense electoral atmosphere led to violent confrontations, beatings, and crowds in the streets of the court screaming, "Death to the Portuguese!"[76]

The Praieiros' mobilization of the urban lower classes clearly set them apart from the Conservatives. Yet Lusophobia had proved dangerous; its appeal was potent, at times too potent for moderate Praieiros to control, even if they wished to do so. Here was an essential dilemma of the party. The Praieiro tactics and their willingness to use violence against the Portuguese handed Conservatives an opening to attack the Praia as a dangerous party of the lower classes. Because of the dominant political culture, Praia leaders could not openly defend the political violence with which their appeals were identified. They had to defend their policies in terms of that political culture—in terms of legitimate authority and the virtue of order, which often implied a status quo inimical to their aspirations and appeals.

The Praia, Its Ideology, and Legitimate Authority

The appeal to legitimate authority and order was crucial in the political discourse of the day; unhappily for the Praia, by 1842 the Party of Order (the soon-to-be Conservative Party) had defined both and conflated them with an established system over which they presided. The Conservative press used the same arguments in blaming the Praieiros for the events of June 1848 that it had used for the Lusophobic attacks of December 1847. Conservatives argued that Praia doctrines incited the lowest classes of society against the men of order and orderly liberty.[77] The *Lidador* denounced nocturnal electoral meetings in which the ignorant masses heard stories that presented Portuguese stores "like a Potosí to be conquered."[78] The paper charged that the Praieiros sought to inspire the masses with subversive doctrines and mobilize them for electoral purposes. In so doing, they created volatile mobs that were vulnerable to manipulation. Invoking the violent intimidation that Juan Manuel de Rosas (with whom Brazil was in conflict at the time and whom Brazilian newspapers were denouncing as a demagogic dictator) inflicted on his opponents, the Conservative newspaper charged that some sought to harness these mobs as a *mashorca*, an instrument of vengeance. Others sought to terrorize the vice-president of the province; republicans sought to exterminate foreigners and usher in a Constituent Assembly.[79]

A Conservative sympathizer portrayed a similar picture in his diary. "New newspapers appeared advising the people to demand their rights. They were Brazilians: they should react against foreigners. Every night there were popular meetings, in which they tried to excite further the people's spirit. That exaltation grew until it touched delirium."[80]

The Liberals could not accept such accusations and retain political viability. Their response perforce appealed to the same value of legitimate authority held by the Conservatives; indeed, like the Conservatives, the Liberals blamed their opponents for the riots. Each side denounced the behavior of prominent individuals among their rivals. The *Diário Novo* charged that Conservative police authorities had encouraged the rioters in June, that the Conservative-dominated national guard battalion in the Recife suburb of Afogados had goaded people on to commit further acts of violence, and that by midday on December 26, only Conservatives were rioting.[81]

The *Diário Novo* charged that the Conservative papers *Lidador*, *Carranca*, and *Esqueleto* had "incessantly attempted to undermine the emperor's delegate (the provincial president)."[82] The Praieiro paper also blamed the doctrines of these Conservative journals for sowing insubordination and disobedience. It argued that Conservative resistance to police authorities earlier that year, when Conservative planters in the south of the province had taken up arms to challenge Praieiro-appointed authorities, seemed to imply a right of armed rebellion. Conservatives had resisted the police, assaulted political opponents, and demoralized the national guard when Liberals held state power; all of this helped justify insubordination to established authority.[83] Throughout, the emphasis on order and the inappropriateness of undermining public authority is noteworthy; it makes clear the common value of legitimate authority to which both Praieiros and Conservatives appealed. Respectable political discourse assumed the fundamental value of a stable, orderly society, and the assumption of legitimate authority derived from, and conflated with, the monarch.

Loyalty to the emperor and the legitimate authority he embodied marked the outer range of respectable dissent. Their acceptance was the sine qua non of participation within the representative institutions established by 1841. It is for this reason that the Praia leadership looked with suspicion on Antônio Borges da Fonseca, the most prominent radical in Pernambuco and a long-time agitator for a republic.[84]

Borges da Fonseca began his long political career at the age of sixteen, with minor participation in the 1824 Confederation of the Equator, the republican rebellion against the first emperor. He was an indefatigable publisher of newspapers, a proponent of a republic, an agitator, a street orator, and an opponent of the Portuguese. What set him apart from other radicals was his insistent republican stance, which led him to oppose whichever of the two main parties of the monarchy was in power. Thus he was brought up on charges of libel by both Conservative and Liberal administrations.

The success of Borges da Fonseca's various newspapers suggests that he had a certain following. There was a wing of the Praia movement open to his more radical political critique. The latter appealed especially to the urban middle and lower classes (known as the Cinco Mil, the Five Thousand).[85] The radicals played a key role in Praia politics because they were active in polemical journalism and in street actions. Yet the party leadership, the representatives in the Chamber of Deputies, and the editors of the main press organ, the *Diário Novo*, were all monarchists and reformists and rejected Borges da Fonseca's extremism.

Borges da Fonseca fought alongside the Praieiros during the Praieira Revolution. Indeed, he rose to a leadership position in the Northern

Army and authored the radical "Manifesto to the World." The Praieiro leadership was seeking deep reforms, but they were unwilling to embrace the more extreme demands and actions of radical republican leaders
like Borges da Fonseca. They denounced the "Manifesto to the World"
as a forgery. Yet the radicals contributed to the useful political unrest
among the urban middle and lower classes. The reformist party leadership's own policies had encouraged such unrest as well, and the moderate leaders were quite willing to seize on this unrest for electoral purposes and to help mobilize supporters during the Praieira Revolution.[86]
Still, the leaders clung to the monarchy in their own pronouncements.
How could they do otherwise and expect to function effectively in the
dominant political system?

Lusophobic disturbances had certain noteworthy characteristics in this
regard. The Praieiro and Conservative press organs sought to outdo each
other in denouncing instances of rioting as anarchic, as did even the *Voz
do Brasil*—a paper whose raison d'être was to denounce Portuguese influence and which had asserted that with canes and knives the Portuguese
presence could be reduced to zero! Yet the shouts of the rioters themselves suggest not a ferocious and uncontrollable mob but people with
a deep sense of grievance over the trampling on their rights and dignity.
During the anti-Portuguese actions of December 8, 1847, for example,
xenophobic cries of "Out with the foreigners, the land is ours, death to
the Portuguese!" were accompanied by vivas to the emperor. When the
police chief tried to calm the crowd, he was met with shouts of "The land
is ours, we are within our rights!"[87] The invocation of the emperor, the
insistence on Brazil being their country, and the affirmation of acting
within their rights all belie the journalistic denunciations of mere anarchy and suggest purposeful action within a coherent worldview, in which
the trampling of perceived rights prompted a legitimate, if violent, response. Thus, for many of the common people, unconstrained by the
need to work within the proprieties of the established representative institutions, there was no necessary conflict between Lusophobic violence
and the values of legitimate authority, nationalism, and monarchy.[88]

The social and economic weight and political influence of the Portuguese and Portuguese-born *adotivos* appeared to frustrate expectations for

change in the decades after independence. Politicians were not exempt from such views; indeed, Liberal championing of Lusophobic, nationalistic development, and the traditional liberal program of decentralized, democratic liberalism, marked clear differences from Conservatives. Liberal Lusophobia likewise corresponded to differing socioeconomic support for the Liberals as well as their willingness to use violence. At the same time, there was an outer limit on the range of party differences, and this was marked by the concept of legitimate authority. Understanding of the latter divided the Praia leadership from some of its followers. However much Praieiros risked violence through their Lusophobic policies, and however much they took advantage of the extremists' work to blatantly encourage violence, they could not expect to maintain their viability within legal, representative institutions if they openly defied the concept of legitimate authority that was associated with the monarch. For some of their followers, however, Lusophobic violence was entirely legitimate and did not contradict their loyalty to the emperor and the nation.

The arguments presented here indicate not only the usefulness of reexamining ideology and formal political institutions in the several decades after Brazil's independence; they also suggest comparative perspectives on the role of xenophobia in state building and on middlemen groups as particular targets of nativist hostility. Resentment directed at holdovers from the colonial regimes is a common phenomenon, and there are clear parallels in Spanish America. In Mexico, for example, there were four major campaigns to expel Iberian-born *peninsulares* between 1827 and 1834, resulting in three-quarters of the Spanish-born citizens of Mexico leaving the country. Two of the groups most affected in Mexico correspond to groups that were particular targets in Brazil—merchants and army officers. In Mexico the popular, nativistic movement was significant, and divisive, at both the state and national levels until the mid-1830s, and the Spanish-born merchant was an unpopular figure for far longer. There was fear of possible re-colonization in both Mexico and Brazil, although the danger seemed greater in Mexico, as the Spanish government did plan for such efforts and even undertook one attempt.[89] Analysis of xenophobia in state building, including hostility toward middleman minority groups, thus suggests comparative perspectives for other postcolonial societies as well.

8

The Praieira Revolution, 1848–50

In 1847 Conservatives in the upper chamber decisively bolstered their Pernambucan allies by nullifying the elections of two Praieiro allies to the Senate. The confrontational May 22, 1847, Liberal ministry of Alves Branco in turn supported the Praieiros. Armed battles in the south of the province and the Praieiros' resort to Lusophobia marked the increasing polarization in Pernambuco by late 1847. The formation of a dissident group, the *Praia nova* (new Praia), added to the troubles of the ruling Praieiro party. These dissenters, notably the first vice-president, Manuel de Sousa Teixeira, and the Machado Rios brothers—Antônio, the commander of the police corps, and Francisco, a deputy police commissioner—were apparently angered over the selection of candidates for the provincial assembly and ran their own slate in the elections, garnering several seats. This split in the party, particularly the loss of Antônio and Francisco Machado Rios and their influence among the military troops and police, prompted further radicalization of the party and greater appeal to Lusophobia.[1]

Armed resistance by Conservative planters, which had begun in 1847, increased in early 1848. The greatest confrontation was the showdown between government and baronist planters at the Lages estate in the south of the province. In April, however, a change of cabinets in the court pulled the ground from under the Praieiros. The March 8, 1848, ministry led by the Viscount of Macaé attempted to broaden political support by carrying out conciliatory policies. A law was passed to end the practice of provincial presidents running for national office from the provinces in which they served. The new measure had a profound impact in Pernambuco. The Praieiro ally Chichorro da Gama stepped down as provincial president and returned to the court to take his seat in the Chamber of Deputies.[2]

The first vice-president, Manuel de Sousa Teixeira, was among those who had recently split from the Praieiros. When he assumed the presidency on a temporary basis, he immediately began a reversal across the province, dismissing five hundred Praieiros from official positions. Amidst widespread Praieiro resistance to the changes, a moderate provincial president was named who attempted to chart a middle-of-the-road course between the contending forces. The conciliatory policies did little to slow the polarization in the province. The centralized system, after all, had been structured to allow the cabinet to secure support across the empire; a provincial president who partially displaced one party from official positions, while not fully embracing the other, only invited more challenges and open hostilities.

In June the court sent news that for the second time Conservatives in the Senate had nullified the election of Praieiro allies to the upper chamber. Radicalization was the order of the day. There were risks, however, as demonstrated by the violent anti-Portuguese riots that rocked Recife in late June. In the court Praieiro leader Joaquim Nunes Machado called for legislative action against the Portuguese. Most importantly, in September Liberal leaders invoked Lusophobia in their campaign against José Clemente Pereira for a seat on the municipal council of Rio de Janeiro. When violent incidents against the Portuguese flared into a general disruption of public order, Conservatives seized the opportunity to denounce the irresponsible and demagogic tactics of the Liberals and the Praieiro leader Nunes Machado in particular.

The emperor soon removed the Liberals from power, calling on the Pernambucan statesman Pedro de Araújo Lima, the Viscount of Olinda, to form a Conservative ministry. National, provincial, and local politics were intimately intertwined after the centralizing legislation of the Regresso. The ruling party in the court as a matter of course named its provincial allies to occupy official posts, and the public resources that such positions afforded, especially armed force, were normally decisive in local struggle. The ramifications of political changes in the court swept across the entire country as new cabinets empowered their provincial partisans.

The Praieiros did not accept being displaced from power. Beginning with individual acts of defiance, they were soon coordinating their resistance. The Praieira Revolution had begun. Party leaders issued a statement explaining their resort to violence as an act of self-defense against abuses of power, not rejections of the legal order. In December a new provincial president instituted hard-line policies, limiting the opposition press, searching the houses of Praieiro sympathizers, and forcing party leaders to flee Recife for fear of arrest. Shortly afterward, party leaders issued "The Banner of the Liberal Movement," a manifesto in which they went far beyond justifying their armed defiance as a simple response to illegal actions of the new officeholders. They railed against the absence of effective constitutional guarantees, denounced the Portuguese for undermining national sovereignty, and called for decentralization of the empire's political institutions as the only way to guard against absolutism. Party leaders invoked the sovereignty of the nation and the right to rebel and called on Pedro to convoke a Constituent Assembly that would carry out the reforms needed to save the monarchy.

The Praieiro Northern Army, with radical republican activist Antônio Borges da Fonseca in a leadership position, issued a "Manifesto to the World," a far more radical document that called for a Constituent Assembly that would establish universal suffrage and federalism, eliminate the moderating power and the current system of military recruitment, and restrict retail commerce to Brazilians. The moderate party leaders who had issued "The Banner of the Liberal Movement" rejected the radical manifesto, at first even denouncing it as a forgery. There had always been differences among the Praieiros. The moderates, under the pressure of warfare, were adopting much more radical positions than they had previously. It is hardly surprising that others might go further in their demands.

The decisive event on the field of battle was the February 2, 1849, Praieiro attack on Recife. When government forces moved south in an effort to inflict a knock-out blow on the rebel forces, the Praieiros bypassed them heading north in a bold attempt to seize the provincial capital. The brief window of opportunity of numerical superiority was lost, however, with the unanticipated arrival of more imperial troops by steamship and the hurried return to Recife once leaders of the government forces realized the capital was in danger. Although some Praieiro forces would continue fighting for a time, their best chance at success was lost. The Praieira Revolution was a test of strength not only between provincial rivals but also for the national political system constructed in the regency and early years of the Second Reign by the future leaders of the Conservative Party. There was no longer any doubt about the outcome.

Conservative Resistance: A March to Civil War?

In January the Praia administration moved to strengthen its position by replacing police authorities in Goiana, north of Recife, and Bonito, Panelas, and Água Preta, south of the capital.[3] Such moves exacerbated conflict. In the district of Quipapá, for example, the dismissal of the Conservative deputy police commissioner Luís Bispo Bizerra Cavalcanti prompted Conservative partisans to post threatening flyers on the new official's door. When ordered to turn over the arms and ammunition he held, the fired official responded by only producing those weapons that were in poor condition. The police chief responded to the deputy police commissioner's fears for his life by sending twelve policemen to be put at his command.[4]

A series of attacks by the bandits known as the Moraes de Alagoas inflamed the south and the interior of the province. Mobility and the element of surprise gave them a decided advantage as they carried out attacks in the districts of Garanhuns and Brejo da Madre de Deus—both located in the *agreste*, the transitional zone between the coastal forest zone and the vast, dry, *sertão* of the interior—and in Pajeú de Flores in the *sertão*. The first attack was carried out by a brother-in-law of Moraes who, along with twenty-seven accomplices, left a man dead in the village of São Benedito, in Garanhuns.[5] The town of Correntes was next, on January 30. Thirty-seven men entered the town and made threats, and when they were unable to locate the individual they sought to murder, they robbed his home and injured a member of his family. In Pa-

pacaça they sought the deputy police commissioner. Facing well-armed opponents, however, they withdrew, but not before killing five people. They reportedly murdered a total of ten people in the district and stole money, gold, silver, slaves, and horses.[6]

Traveling west and apparently joined by new additions as they went, the bandits struck at Pajeú de Flores on the afternoon of February 11. They broke down doors with axes and killed four individuals, including the county judge and a member of the police detachment. They shot at the door of the police commissioner's house, threatening to kill him and Col. Barbosa, the leading Praia ally in the area.[7]

Police authorities in the towns that were victimized by the Moraes gang were clear about the political importance of these events. The police commissioner of Flores, for example, reported that many influential people opposed to the government aided the bandits. The police commissioner of Bonito wrote that the Moraes of Alagoas had apparently been involved in several clandestine meetings with influential opponents of the government, in which a plan for a rebellion had been hatched. Despite such reports, as of late February the police chief was of the opinion that the Moraes were not truly motivated by politics. Rather, these were crimes against personal security and property. He warned, however, that "either of the two opposing parties . . . can make use of those bandits to upset public order."[8]

By March the cooperation of some Conservatives with the Moraes gang was clearer. On March 6 the police in Bonito reported that the previous day's sacking of the town of Panelas was carried out by Moraes, who was accompanied by Conservative planters João Guilherme Azevedo and Luís Bizerra Cavalcanti, the former deputy police commissioner of Quipapá.[9] The provincial president soon received warnings that the southern parishes of Água Preta, Una, Serinhaem, and Escada were in danger.[10] The chief of police implored the president, for the second time, to request a force of six hundred men, as well as significant new supplies of arms and ammunition, from the Liberal administration in the court.[11]

By the end of the month, police were reporting opposition gatherings on the estates of Col. Agostinho Bizerra and João do Rego Barros, the brother of the former provincial president, the Baron of Boa Vista. Both were in Cabo, the center of the older sugar plantations, and long a

Conservative stronghold. Government supporters there feared assaults.[12] There were also reports of opposition gatherings and open conspiracy in Jaboatão and Poço de Panelas, both near Recife, as well as an attack on the police barracks and the home of the deputy police commissioner in the town of Taquaratinga, north of the capital.[13]

Escada, another parish in the southern forest zone, where the baronists were strongest, proved to be the largest center of opposition resistance. In late March, police reports had identified José Pedro Veloso da Silveira and João Guilherme Azevedo as conspiring to repeat the recent violent attacks on government supporters. The chief of police was sufficiently concerned that he requested 150 rifles and 8,000 rounds of ammunition be sent there.[14]

José Pedro's Lages estate became a fortified safe point at which Conservative oppositionists gathered and from which they conducted armed action against government supporters. Powerful Conservatives such as João do Rego Barros brought large numbers of armed followers with them. Fortifications were built, three pieces of artillery were set up, and guards were posted. The chief of police indignantly reported that the bandits were convinced that they were safe in that feudal castle and that they could threaten police authorities and the lives and properties of government supporters.[15]

Police reports linked many of those gathered there, such as Father Joaquim de Pinto Campos, José Severino Cavalcanti de Albuquerque, and João Guilherme Azevedo, to recent incidents of theft, arson, and murder in Panelas, Quipapá, Pajeú de Flores, and Garanhuns. Father Campos called for an uprising against the government in the assault on Panelas, and flyers with the same message were distributed elsewhere. José Pedro's son had been in contact with the rebels in the forests of Panelas and Jacuípe to coordinate activities.[16] The possible reach of the plans is suggested by the discovery of subversive proclamations in the pockets of a worker in the customs house.[17] Indeed, upon receiving news of the imminent linking up of a thousand armed men under José Pedro and João do Rego Barros, the commander feared a possible assault on Recife.[18]

By early April parts of the area were virtually in open civil war. At four o'clock on the morning of April 5, after bribing a soldier on guard, José Pedro led his forces from Lages on a surprise attack that overran government loyalists at his own Cahité estate, which had previously been seized by government forces. José Pedro's attack sent the Praieiro troops into retreat helter-skelter. Government loyalists fared better in battles at the Bamburral estate (belonging to the deputy police commissioner of Escada, Antônio Feijó de Melo) and Aguas Claras, defeating the opposition forces.[19] Police authorities in surrounding areas hurriedly prepared themselves for their own defense, while sending what men they could to Escada to assist in the struggle against the main focus of the opposition movement based at the Lages estate. Significant military, police, and national guard forces gathered for an assault on that stronghold.[20]

Pernambuco's police commander insisted on the need for energetic responses to the crisis, including increasing the numbers of men and the weapons and improving the inadequate rations. Rebel invasions of properties, murders, and theft, he argued, were demoralizing the population. The morale of the local population was also on the mind of the commander of the forces preparing to assault the Conservative stronghold. He declared that he was "rigorous" in explaining to the inhabitants of the region that if they did not take up arms and defeat José Pedro's forces, their hardships would be much worse later.[21] Considering the local strength of the Conservatives, it is not surprising that the commander felt the need to drive the point home. It is easy to imagine some hesitancy on the part of the poor when asked to do battle against powerful *senhores* with a permanent presence in the area.

On April 18 the government forces attacked the Lages estate. Antônio Feijó de Melo, the Praia commander, approached the well-fortified estate with 350 men at six o'clock in the morning. Another force was to initiate the planned combined assault. After an unexpected delay of three hours, some scattered shooting was heard and Feijó de Melo's men advanced. Under heavy fire for two hours, they suffered many casualties. No significant second force arrived, however—only a small guerrilla group at one o'clock in the afternoon. Meanwhile, Conservative reinforcements made their way to Lages. Feijó de Melo was obliged to retreat.[22] Leaders of the assault reported a need for artillery to break through the trenches, food and supplies for the soldiers (many of whom were deserting to return to their families), and a surgeon to aid the wounded.[23] A surgeon, ambulance, medicine, and sixteen thousand rounds of ammunition were sent to aid them the next day, but the twenty guards accompanying them were overpowered by João do Rego Barros's men and the supplies fell into the rebels' hands.[24]

A Conciliatory Liberal Ministry Undermines the Praieiros

The battle against the Conservative *senhores* in the Lages estate was undermined at this point by national events in the court. The May 22, 1847, ministry, which favored the Praieiros' aggressive politics, had been fatally weakened by a split between the cabinet chief, Alves Branco, and Aureliano de Sousa e Oliveira Coutinho, the emperor's most trusted advisor. Alves Branco favored protectionist policies and forceful opposition to Great Britain's assertion of a right to seize Brazilian slave ships and treat them as if they were engaging in piracy. He argued for favorable resolution of these issues prior to negotiations with the British over a new treaty to end the slave trade and a new commercial treaty.[25] Saturnino de Sousa e Oliveira, Aureliano's brother and ally, opposed both of these positions and resigned from the cabinet when the emperor failed to support him. The loss of the support of the *áulicos* (Aureliano's faction) severely weakened Alves Branco's standing. Despite his position as president of the Council of Ministers and his personal appeals to the emperor to permit him to remain, the emperor opted to allow José Carlos Pereira de Almeida Tôrres, the Viscount of Macaé, and Antônio Limpo de Abreu to lead a new ministry.[26]

The March 8, 1848, ministry led by the Viscount of Macaé attempted to replicate the "conciliatory" politics of the May 5, 1846, ministry, which had garnered support from the Conservative leadership, the *saquaremas*. As part of this effort, the ministry proposed a law to end the practice of provincial presidents running for national office from the provinces in which they served (and thus holding both offices). Demonstrating its commitment to this principle, the cabinet dismissed the *saquaremas'* bête noire Aureliano as the president of Rio de Janeiro, as well as his ally, the Praia partisan and provincial president Chichorro da Gama in Pernambuco.[27]

On April 20 Chichorro da Gama embarked for the court to assume his old seat in the Chamber of Deputies, leaving the interim presidency of Pernambuco to the vice-president, Praia dissident Manuel de Sousa Teixeira. This interim president completely reversed course, turning against the Praieiros. He appointed a new commander of arms, who dismissed the Praia leaders involved in the siege of José Pedro's estate. The new commander accepted José Pedro's promises to remove the barricades constructed there and return the armaments and ammunition in his possession that did not belong to him.[28]

In his reports to Rio de Janeiro, the interim president maintained that the conflict was born of private conflicts. He claimed that political manipulation of events might encourage "extreme and dangerous ideas" and that the hostilities might spread. Thus, Manuel de Sousa Teixeira, who as a Praieiro had dismissed Conservative officeholders in June 1845, now argued in opposition to his former party for the need to dismiss Praia loyalists from the same posts. He rationalized this maneuver by arguing that many of those officeholders had become corrupt and were oppressing people through arbitrary and vengeful acts, which led to the current state of civil war. Conciliation and unity for the good of the monarchy, he said, now required responding to the public outcry and carrying out a reversal of fortunes at the local level. In six days he dismissed five hundred Praia officeholders, including key police, national guard, and public administration positions.[29]

The Futility of Moderation

On April 26 the new provincial president, Vicente Pires da Mota, arrived in Recife. He faced a formidable task in trying to calm the province. Not only had the Praieiros been frustrated by the dispersal of their forces surrounding the Lages estate, but the massive dismissals by Manuel de Sousa Teixeira threatened to almost entirely displace them from official positions, leaving them at the mercy of their enemies. Praia Police Chief Antônio Afonso Ferreira responded by calling on police officials not to step down from their posts, despite their dismissals. The police chief and the respected Praia deputy Félix Peixoto de Brito e Melo also led an effort to mobilize Praia forces for possible armed action.[30]

By mid-May an interim chief of police had replaced Antônio Afonso Ferreira. The new officeholder lamented the state of revolt in the province, declaring that all the powerful citizens were arming themselves. He requested 200 to 250 soldiers to be stationed at Cabo, Nazareth, Limoeiro, and other points to impede an outbreak of hostilities.[31] At the same time, a Conservative leader wrote to the old Pernambucan Conservative chieftain in the court, the Viscount of Olinda, "The Praieiros, in their frightful gatherings, have decreed the assassination of a few of their influential adversaries, and for that excursion they have armed themselves publicly." He also reported on a threat in the *Diário Novo* that "once the first drop of blood is spilt, the carnage will be horrible."[32]

By May the eruption of civil war over control of public posts and the coercive potential they offered seemed imminent. Police authorities in Limoeiro and Pau d'Alho, in the northern forest zone, Muribeca in the southern forest zone, and Pajeú de Flores in the *sertão* called for measures to preserve order.[33] On May 9 Praia partisan João Ignácio Ribeiro Roma was reported to be in the forest near the town of Poço de Panelas (three miles northwest of Recife) with armed men, possibly to seek revenge on his adversaries now that he no longer held office. The following day a skirmish between Roma's men and military troops broke out in nearby Apipucos.[34] In Bonito, Conservatives were on the offensive. Possibly related to these tensions was the arrest of an individual for attempting to convince several soldiers guarding the customs house to desert because "the government of Brazil was composed of men who were enemies of Brazil."[35]

Faced with civil war, Provincial President Pires da Mota tried to find a middle road between the contending parties. Ratifying the widespread dismissals of Praia officeholders might trigger open armed resistance by the Praieiros, who, having occupied their positions for several years, were well armed. The president thus reinstated many of the fired officeholders to their posts. However, he chose not to support those who had publicly and forcefully opposed him. Thus, forty-one of the dismissals of police commissioners and deputy police commissioners were ratified. Although he attempted to find individuals distant from both parties to take over these posts, most of the positions were simply not filled. (The substitutes were officially considered to be in office.) The Praieiro officeholders maintained that they still occupied the positions, yet the posts served them little. The value of such offices was based on support from the government (for example, responding positively to requests for troops) that officeholders normally could expect. The state of limbo had a deleterious effect on public order in some places. In Bonito the failure to nominate new police officials prompted complaints about the abandonment of the police, which made it difficult to carry out even such basic functions as guarding the jail.[36]

Conflicts over nominations of police officials were a constant over the subsequent months. President Pires da Mota's reluctance to name Conservative partisans to posts ultimately led Firmino Antônio de Sousa, the interim chief of police who replaced Praia partisan Antônio Affonso Ferreira, to resign.[37] Struggles over who would occupy particular posts more typically emerged at the local level. Joaquim Machado Portella, for example, was named the new deputy police commissioner of Muribeca by the vice-president on July 12, yet the officeholder there refused to recognize him or turn over the documentation pertaining to the deputy police commissioner post. When a new chief of police took office, he backed the old officeholder, prompting a flurry of correspondence with the provincial president.[38]

In Rio Formoso the mutual accusations and recriminations between an interim police commissioner, and a recently nominated deputy police commissioner give some idea of the sorts of partisan struggles that were occurring across the province. The interim police commissioner attempted to block Manuel Fermino de Melo from occupying the position as deputy police commissioner to which he had been nominated, which prompted a number of appeals to the provincial president. Fermino de Melo prevailed, but he was subsequently embroiled in controversy when the same police commissioner reported that Fermino de Melo had dismissed ward inspector Arcanjo Cavalcanti de Albuquerque and replaced him with a long-time ally. On August 19 a subordinate of the new inspector fatally shot Arcanjo Cavalcanti de Albuquerque while the victim was standing in his doorway speaking with the vicar. Indignation was such that at seven o'clock that evening a crowd gathered at the house of the deputy police commissioner, yelling "Fora, fora!" (Out with you!). When they realized he was not at home, they threw stones, breaking a glass lamp shade.[39]

The intensity of the ongoing conflicts helps explain the importance of public offices to each side. On June 4 Manuel Tomás de Jesus arrived in Vitória to begin his appointment as the new police commissioner. He reported that Conservative partisans had been terrorized over the previous year. Six people had taken shelter in his house for three days, fearful of staying in their own homes. Nightly, he reported, gangs of thugs roamed the streets, pounding on the doors of Conservatives' homes and yelling insulting epithets. Police authorities were of no help; they sometimes accompanied the men who were terrorizing Conservative families. The new police commissioner explained that the division of the province into two competing parties was the origin of the problems. Influential people were ashamed to engage in the "despicable behavior" that helped secure political success, such as intimidation of opponents and theft of electoral urns, so they appointed infamous individuals to police positions to carry out the dirty work for them. These authorities, however, proved impossible to control, to the point that even the Liberals who had appointed them were now sometimes fearful of them. The police commissioner declared that João Antônio Miranda—a man who had murdered, committed theft, and dishonored his sisters-in-law—was typical of the caliber of police authorities. Manuel Tomás de Jesus went on to report that he had substituted the deputy commissioners and ward inspectors, and he also requested a new military detachment because many of the soldiers stationed there were from Vitória and were related to the troublemakers.[40]

Although such a report might be exaggerated, it is far from unusual. Private correspondence from early July communicates the desperation of baronist partisans elsewhere. Francisco José de Figueiredo described the anxiety felt by Conservatives in his town, where insults and threats were so serious that he and other baronists felt that if the Praieiros were not removed from office soon, the Conservatives would be forced to leave the area to protect their families. He wrote that flyers had been placed on the doors of all the baronist and Portuguese houses, encouraging "the scum" to beat those residents. The district judge may have been intimidated by the Praieiros' strength; Francisco José wrote that the judge seemed to be a baronist only inside the safety of his house.[41]

On July 5 County Judge José Bandeira de Melo arrived in Nazareth to take up an appointment as a police commissioner. He was met by a Praieiro who had organized armed men to impede him from taking office. The new appointee called on the national guard to counteract the armed gathering, but the request for armed force was met with "inertia." José Bandeira de Melo then asked to step down from his position, citing concern for his family and public order. Meanwhile, fifty troops arrived to support him, but the judge insisted that even with armed force, he lacked the "moral authority" necessary for the position. Praia strength in the district was so great, and any principle of political tolerance so wanting, that both Liberals and Conservatives had informed him that any appointee not endorsed by the Praieiros would be subject to open defiance. To avoid being an object of laughter, the new police commissioner would have to dismiss most of his subordinates, which would provoke much resentment. He saw the position as untenable, urged the vice-president to accept his request for transfer, and advised that any new appointee was likely to fail if he was not respected by the Praieiros. The police commissioner's concern for his family might have been amplified by rumors that Praieiros were operating a laboratory for the production of ammunition.[42]

Tension and emotions were so high that in July even Jerônimo Martiniano Figueira de Melo, who would later play a key role in repressing the Praieira Revolution as chief of police (and would publish a basic account of the struggle), was urged by his brother to find an excuse to leave the province. "If a soulless Praieiro wants, can't he insult you?" he asked, suggesting the Praieiros' willingness to provoke an altercation. "People willing to serve like that are not lacking. . . . You are not cautious, you go out at night."[43]

The tense atmosphere in the province was not relieved by the moderate position taken by President Pires da Mota and his successor Antônio da Costa Pinto. Regresso legislation of the late 1830s and early 1840s had set the framework for authoritarian, centralized rule in which powerful local offices were staffed by men chosen by cabinet appointees; yet now the court's decisive role in local politics was being used ambiguously. The Praieiros had been partially displaced from power, but no general inversion had taken place to confer authority to Conservatives. This made each official post in each community a possible arena for struggle.

Provincial Polarization, National Polarization

The Praieiros no longer controlled the administrative apparatus in the province, so on May 19 they founded the Pernambucan Imperial Society. Members in each district were to be responsible to a local leadership body, composed of a president, secretary, and treasurer, which maintained contact with the organization's directorate in Recife. This group facilitated communication and helped coordinate Praia activities across the province.[44] While the Pernambucan Imperial Society was beginning its efforts, police spies were reporting on secret Praia reunions in Recife and secret societies in the suburbs of Poço de Panelas, Afogados, and São José, as well as open conspiracy elsewhere in the province.[45]

The Praieiros were also stepping up efforts to mobilize support through nationalistic appeals to nativist resentment of the large Portuguese presence. In the court, Praia deputy Joaquim Nunes Machado delivered speeches to the Chamber on June 3, 16, and 28 in which he railed against the harmful effects of unrestricted Portuguese access to Brazil. He called for measures to increase opportunities for Brazilian-born store owners and employees in retail commerce, culminating in the proposal to ban foreign participation in this sector. The Lusophobic riots of June 26 and 27 in Pernambuco did not deter the Praieiros from hammering away at this theme.

Nunes Machado's June speeches came at a time when the Praieiros had taken the lead role among Liberal factions in the Chamber of Deputies. The Macaé cabinet, though Liberal and supported by the *saquarema* minority and Bahia's deputies, proved unable to gather sufficient support in the Chamber to govern. Both the Praieiros and the *áulicos* had been displaced from local and ministerial power and opposed the cabinet. Likewise, Teófilo and Cristiano Otoni and their followers, the most ideologically consistent of the Liberal factions, refused to support Macaé. Their allies from São Paulo and Ceará added to the opposition to the cabinet.[46]

On May 31, 1848, Francisco de Paula Sousa e Melo formed a new cabinet, the sixth since the Liberals established the February 2, 1844, ministry.[47] Paula Sousa made a renewed attempt at the conciliatory politics that Macaé had tried, and Conservative leaders Honório Hermeto Carneiro Leão in the Senate and the *saquarema* Eusébio de Queirós in the Chamber offered cooperation. Praia leader Urbano Sabino Pessoa de Melo took to the floor of the Chamber, however, asserting that neutrality would not be tolerated in Pernambuco and effectively squelched the idea.[48]

Events quickly demonstrated that struggle, not nonpartisan neutrality, was the order of the day. Conflict between the Chamber, controlled by Liberal factions, and the Conservative-dominated Senate, flared up. The dispute over the Senate's right to block the Chamber of Deputies' call for convening a joint body of the Senate and Chamber, by virtue of Article 61 of the 1824 Constitution (which had already provoked the fall of the May 26, 1845, ministry and to which the *paulista* Liberals attached great importance), reemerged in May 1848. In June word arrived that the Senate had annulled the second senatorial election in Pernambuco, once again impeding Praia partisans Chichorro da Gama and Ernesto Ferreira França from occupying the coveted seats. The committed Liberal Cristiano Otoni proffered his formulation that Conservative senators were making inoperative the two justifications of life tenures in the Senate—the Chamber's right to fusion of the two houses and the renewal of membership through new elections subsequent to the death of a member—and were thereby forcing reforms to reduce the Senate's power.[49]

After the first annulment, the Viscount of Olinda had made veiled threats that Conservatives would take up arms to defend the Senate's prerogatives; now it was Honório Hermeto Carneiro Leão's turn. As was his style, he left aside subtlety and nuance, raising the specter of a forceful defense of the state. "If the government feared a violent usurpation by the Chamber of Deputies, public forces would find unanimous and effective support in public opinion across the country to complete its rigorous duty, to maintain the reality of the Constitution."[50]

The annulment of the Praieiro elections to the Senate only spurred the Praia to further radicalization. In the court, Nunes Machado made his calls in June for legal restrictions on the Portuguese. In Pernambuco, in cases such as the posting of flyers calling for the beating of baronists and Portuguese residents, the Praieiros identified Conservatives as accomplices of the Portuguese. The Praieiros soon brought their Lusophobic campaign to the streets of the court.[51]

The Politics of Lusophobia in the Court

The intransigent, even threatening, Conservative stance in the Senate, the weakness of the successive Liberal ministries by mid-1848, and in the Praieiros' case the frustration over the consistent failure of Liberal cabinets to choose their members for cabinet posts all seem to have contributed to the radicalization process. Liberals in the court, including prominent leaders such as Antônio Paulino Limpo de Abreu, joined the Praieiros in appealing to Lusophobia in order to prevail in the September 7 elections for the municipal council of the court. Liberals denounced the Conservative candidate José Clemente Pereira for his Portuguese birth, despite the fact that he, like many other Iberian-born but longtime residents of Brazil, had long ago acquired Brazilian citizenship.[52]

The strident tactic employed by the Liberals was fraught with risk. José Clemente Pereira was a particularly successful example of the phenomenon, especially common in the court, of Portuguese men who had settled in Brazil, become naturalized citizens, and managed to position themselves well within networks of influence. José Clemente, for example, had earlier appointed the Conservative military hero Luís Alves de Lima e Silva (the victor in repressing various rebellions during the regency, as well as the liberal rebellions of 1842 in Minas Gerais and São Paulo; the current commander of arms in the court; a stalwart monarchist; and the Count and future Duke of Caxias) to a command of military forces in the South. Caxias used his influence to secure the presence of several Conservative deputies from Rio Grande do Sul in the Chamber. One of these, Dr. José Martins da Cruz Jobim, also served as the palace physician, a position that allowed him to offer political advice to the emperor. Dr. Jobim, as director of the faculty of medicine in the court, had long-established relations with José Clemente because of the latter's position as director of the Santa Casa da Misericórdia, the court's charity hospital. Dr. Jobim's position also led to considerable contact with Bahian deputies, who by virtue of having a faculty of medicine in their capital were interested in issues concerning medical education. Thus, the appeal to Lusophobia in the municipal elections challenged not only the many *adotivos* in the court but specifically a successful individual with solid support in the palace, the Chamber, and the military.[53]

The Liberal press accused Dr. Jobim of palace conspiracies, of preparing a "Conservative Joana," a reference to Conservative denunciations of Aureliano's influence. The Bahian deputies were supposedly involved in these plans, which led Liberals to call for the dismissal of the president of Bahia, the Baron of Monserrate. The Praieiros, for their part, went further, calling for dismissals of various military leaders, including Caxias, the commander of arms in the court, and the Conservative leader of the First Battalion of Sharpshooters, fearful that they would use force to intervene in the municipal elections in the court beginning on September 7. Nunes Machado played a particularly prominent role, taking to the floor of the Chamber of Deputies to denounce Conservative manipulation of influence within the palace. The cabinet did not yield to the pressure for dismissals, prompting criticism from the Liberal Party organ, the *Corrieo Mercantil*, which asserted that the cabinet could not be charged with attempting to appear "energetic, strong, or violent and capable of committing to an opinion" and went on to lament that the ministry "avoids with extreme care anything that could displease the opposition . . . [and has] carried that goal to the point that it is already accused of being lukewarm and not very diligent in defense of the interests of those whose triumph elevated it to power."[54]

The appeals to Lusophobia by various Liberals heightened the always tense electoral atmosphere in the court. On September 8 a group gathered in the parish of Sacramento, reportedly after hearing of the Conservative opposition's efforts to block Liberals from voting in the parish of Santa Rita. The angry group stormed to Santa Rita, shouting all the way and crying out against the Portuguese. In Santa Rita a confrontation with a butcher who objected to the Lusophobic shouts erupted into violence. The butcher reportedly hurled a cleaver, wounding a man in the arm. The butcher was beaten, as was a man who threw a bottle from a nearby house into the crowd. After this incident, the crowd coursed through nearby streets, screaming "Death to the Portuguese!" and other Lusophobic denunciations. Shops in the area closed as commerce shut down. All available police, military infantry and cavalry, and national guards were soon patrolling the streets, yet further incidents occurred on September 8 and 9.[55]

Conservatives quickly used such destabilizing and shocking events as fodder for partisan attacks in the press and on the floor of the Senate and Chamber of Deputies. The Liberal *Corrieo Mercantil* initially insinuated that Conservatives were fanning the flames of Lusophobia in order to frighten *adotivos* into wholehearted support of their protectors, the Conservatives.[56] As the magnitude of the events became clearer, however, Liberals attempted to play down the size of the disturbances and the Lusophobic elements. The events were depicted as typical of "electoral fever," perhaps amplified by the excitement and celebrations of September 7, the anniversary of Pedro's declaration of independence from Portugal.[57] The Liberal organ declared that Conservatives were greatly exaggerating the magnitude of the events, in part to cover up their electoral defeats but mainly to weaken the Liberal ministry by depicting the imperial court in turmoil.[58] The paper denounced "the comedy acted out in the Parliament to convince the provinces that Rio de Janeiro is swimming in blood."[59] Conservative partisans managed to heighten the sense of turmoil by provoking pandemonium in the Chamber when, in the midst of a speech by a Conservative deputy, a man in the gallery began shouting out against the Liberal ministry. The incident insulted the Liberal ministers and their allies.[60]

Conservative Party stalwarts Bernardo Pereira de Vasconcelos, Honório Hermeto Carneiro Leão, and Joaquim José Rodrigues Tôrres in the Senate and Eusébio de Queirós in the Chamber propagated images of respectable citizens terrorized by anarchy.[61] The danger was so great that the Chamber of Deputies had been unable to meet on September 9 for fear of disturbances in the galleries.[62] They blamed Liberals for inciting Lusophobia. In the course of a two-hour speech, Eusébio de Queirós, a *saquarema*, emphasized the Liberals' implacable opposition to his relative, José Clemente Pereira. In the Senate, Honório denounced the manipulation of Lusophobia, declaring it an electoral tactic that intimidated *adotivos* and dissuaded them from voting. He asserted, "Following the shout of 'Death to the Portuguese, *os Chumbos, os Marinheiros*,' . . . disastrous, lamentable and woeful consequences always follow. Not long ago we had the example of Pernambuco."[63] The Conservative statesman also invoked the terrors of revolutionary France: "In France, the key word is 'down with the aristocrats,' here it is 'down with the Portuguese.'"[64] Conservatives also blamed the Liberal ministry for failing to properly repress the disturbances once they had broken out. The Conservative press, meanwhile, accused Praieiro parliamentarian Joaquim Nunes Machado of personally leading mobs in the streets. *O Brasil*, the leading Conservative paper, asserted that "the movement was entirely Praieiro."[65]

The risks to social stability presented by the Praieiro mobilization of the urban middle and lower classes through Lusophobia had already been demonstrated in Pernambuco. Indeed, the conflictive state of the province even prior to the June 26 and 27 riots had already been a topic of discussion nationally, following the publication of the report written by Vice-President Manuel de Sousa Teixeira when he stepped down as acting president.[66] The Praieiros' use of inflammatory, high-risk tactics in the very seat of the government and the participation of significant Liberal leaders in using such tactics were fatal to an already weak Liberal ministry.

The deep divisions among Liberal factions that undercut the ministry reached the point where the Praieiros opposed the cabinet on budgetary votes in September, apparently in the mistaken belief that a new ministry might favor them. Weakened by a lack of a loyal majority in the Chamber of Deputies, the Liberal ministry also faced the perennial challenge of a Conservative-dominated Senate. The September riots in the streets of Rio de Janeiro proved too much. The decision to resign was finally prompted by a legislative defeat regarding the extremely difficult issue of a new treaty with Great Britain concerning the abolition of the slave trade. The ministers perceived a lack of support from Pedro as a further blow. On September 29 the emperor appointed a Pernambucan enemy of the Praia, the former regent Pedro de Araújo Lima, the Viscount of Olinda, to head a new ministry, one that would hand power back to the Conservatives. Years later, writing on his decision to invite the Conservatives to form a new cabinet, the emperor wrote that "the political atmosphere of the northern provinces" and "the lack of energy against the rioters of September" had contributed to the decision.[67]

A Conservative Ministry: Whither Pernambuco?

Word of the ministerial change reached Pernambuco on October 13, 1848, when Herculano Ferreira Pena, the newly appointed provincial president, disembarked from the steamship Imperatriz along with his new chief of police and commander of arms.[68] Ferreira Pena entered a province racked by conflict. In September a group brandishing swords and firing guns had marched through Afogados, a suburb of the capital, insulting supporters of the government, hurling offensive epithets at the *mulambos* (Liberals), and yelling "Morras!" (Death!) to the government.[69] Nor was the conflict confined to the coast. Partisan struggle and violence were so intense in the *sertão* district of Pajeú de Fores, and the government presence so ineffective, that the chief of police personally traveled to the distant region to restore order.[70]

Joaquim Nabuco later described the state of the province as almost revolutionary. The Praieiros, he wrote, had wanted to rebel, even under a Liberal ministry, when Chichorro da Gama had been relieved of executive authority in the province. The new Conservative ministry apparently feared sending a "strong man," which might have sparked an open rebellion. Nabuco saw this as a fatal mistake. Herculano Ferreira Pena possessed neither special talent nor noteworthy prestige. A powerful figure who could command respect, such as nationally prominent Conservatives like Honório Hermeto Carneiro Leão or the military leader the Count of Caxias, might have been able to contain the situation. Nabuco perceived the failure to dissolve the Chamber of Deputies and call for new elections as further compounding the problem. This step was not taken until February of the following year, leaving some doubt as to whether Conservative control of the ministry was definitive and thus encouraging resistance.[71]

The new president assured the Praieiros that he would not carry out a general inversion of officeholders.[72] Conservatives apparently were slightly suspicious of Ferreira Pena's intentions because he did not pursue an immediate wave of dismissals.[73] Baronists were not long disappointed, however. Nine days after Ferreira Pena took office, dismissals of Praia partisans began. On October 26 Praia partisans in the *sertão* district of Flores and Recife's neighborhood of Boa Vista were dismissed from police posts; by November 7 Praieiros had been relieved in Exú, Pau d'Alho, Recife, Goiana, Nazareth, Cabo, Rio Formoso, Serinhaem, and Santo Antão.[74]

The Praia grip on official positions established under President Chichorro da Gama had been weakened by the presidents (chosen by Liberal cabinets) who succeeded him, but they had not been entirely displaced.[75] Clearly, President Ferreira Pena was now carrying out a vast change in office holding. On November 3 a commission of Praieiro leaders met with the president and warned him that unless he reversed course on the dismissals, they would oppose him and would be unable to ensure public order.[76]

For the Viscount of Olinda, an elder Conservative statesman, a Pernambucan, and the head of the Conservative ministry, the time had come to hand over power to Conservatives in Pernambuco. State resources—above all, the coercive potential of police and national guard posts—were to be controlled by the cabinet chief's Conservative allies. If the transition occurred quickly, it would allow baronists to occupy official positions before the November 19 elections for municipal councils and justices of the peace.

Conservatives had bitterly complained when Praieiros occupied official posts. Their accusations of vengeance and abuse of authority, so common in the discourse of the period, reflected their belief that state power was inappropriately used for personal gain. This argument was even used to justify open armed actions. José Pedro Veloso da Silveira, for example, after the battles at his Lages estate in April 1848, declared that it was not the government that he had opposed but simply the acts of his personal enemy, deputy police commissioner Antônio Feijó de Melo. Now the roles were reversed, and it was the Praieiros who indignantly rejected their enemies' exercise of authority.

Praia deputy Urbano Sabino Pessoa de Melo, in the principal defense of his party's role in the Praieira Revolution, cited infamous crimes, such as the murder at the Genipapo estate and the protection of criminal bands at the Lages estate, and railed against investing the authors of such crimes with police powers. "And the men chosen [to occupy official posts?] Implacable enemies of the Liberal Party, inflamed by the fever for vengeance, . . . many of immoral and ferocious character; a few [were] implicated directly, or indirectly through relatives, in Praia police actions that seized from their house three hundred stolen slaves. Others shortly before had raised the banner of revolt to *resist the king*, burning and sacking towns and murdering defenseless citizens."[77]

President Herculano Ferreira Pena's delay of nine days before beginning the dismissals of officeholders allowed him time to prepare to hand over power to the Conservatives. The secrecy of the preparations and the failure to follow the routine practice of publishing news of the dismissals made for a series of spontaneous confrontations as new authorities attempted to take power across the province. The new officeholders arrived, often backed by armed force, military, or national guard troops as well as their own retainers, with the documents declaring their appointments in hand. Numerous violent confrontations ensued.[78]

Praieiro Resistance to the New Authorities
and the Imminence of Civil War

In Pau d'Alho the dismissed Praieiro commander of the police force, Pedro Bezerra de Menezes, gathered armed men on the night of November 5 at the Lavagem estate belonging to fellow Praieiro Francisco José de Barros e Silva. Shortly thereafter these forces unsuccessfully assaulted the local police force. Soon some families abandoned the area. In Limoeiro the new police commissioner was warned that he would be shot if he tried to enter town. Asserting the need to ensure public order, the Praieiro police commissioner and national guard officer Henrique Pereira de Lucena assembled a group of armed men. In Nazareth, when authorities were unable to put down an uprising, rebels invaded and searched the properties of a district judge and the municipal judge. Other inhabitants fled, and an armed group seized the weapons in the police headquarters. When authorities gathered several hundred armed men, the rebels split into two columns and headed to Pau d'Alho and Igarassu. Similar incidents occurred across the province.[79]

On November 7 national guard Col. José Joaquim de Almeida Guedes, the police commissioner of Olinda, and national guard Lt. Col. João Paulo Ferreira, a deputy police commissioner, sent letters of resignation to the provincial president, gathered the national guard members they commanded, and marched toward Igarassu. They were joined by more national guardsmen in Pau Amarelo and at the Inhamam estate of national guard Col. Manuel Pereira Moraes, a prominent Praieiro. En route to Igarassu, they questioned a fisherman they encountered, and upon hearing of his loyalty to the Conservatives, they killed him.[80]

The following morning, Chief of Police Firmino Antônio de Sousa marched one hundred men to Olinda. They marched through the city to the accompaniment of a beating drum, reading aloud an order to dismiss two rebel officials. After swearing in new officials, the chief of police gathered the available forces and marched toward Igarassu. After hearing reports that the rebels included three to four hundred national guardsmen, the chief of police sent for reinforcements. On November 10, with additional police, military, and national guard troops, the government forces overcame a guerrilla ambush at Maricota and approached Igarassu, ready for battle.[81]

Faced with open warfare, the provincial government immediately moved to strengthen itself. Orders were sent across the province to seize arms that had been distributed by Praieiro officeholders. During Chichorro da Gama's presidency, considerable quantities of arms and ammunition had been distributed to Praia occupants of police and national guard posts.[82] The efficacy of such orders during a state of civil war is doubtful, of course. The provincial government also moved to arm its partisans in their newly occupied posts. The government requested troops, weapons, and ammunition from the court and from the nearby provinces of Bahia, Alagoas, and Ceará.[83] Troops had already arrived from the imperial court before any armed conflict occurred, and more arrived from Ceará on November 11, suggesting that the government anticipated the possibility of a violent response to the political changes in the province.[84] The president also ended *Diário Novo*'s status as the official paper of the government—the one that printed government notices—because "the false news it spread on the state of the province was considered true by the less thinking part of the population."[85]

In late October the district judge of Nazareth had correctly identified Nazareth as a likely point for an uprising to begin, noting the Praieiro strength in the area, the willingness to oppose violently attempts at dismissal, and the fervor of Praia partisans. The first major battle occurred on November 14. After abandoning Igarassu as government forces approached, the rebels, now numbering six hundred, easily overpowered the police detachment of fifty men in Nazareth.[86] They freed the prisoners in jail. They then settled into the Mussopinho estate. The leaders occupied barricaded structures, others dug trenches alongside a fence, and still others hid in the hills alongside the road approaching the estate. With superior numbers, the rebels initially inflicted heavy losses on the attacking forces. The government troops attacked in three columns and, carrying out a flanking maneuver, ultimately sent the rebels fleeing after three hours of intensive gunfire. The government presented the action in the best possible light, claiming only twenty-three losses compared to nearly twice that many for the rebels. The British consul, however, reported to London that government losses totaled 170 men and the entire cavalry. The Praia deputy Felipe Lopes Neto later claimed that the government victory had been achieved only by betraying the flying of a white truce flag by the Praieiros.[87]

In Serinhaem, in the coastal region south of Recife, Lt. Col. Manuel Henrique Wanderley arrived to take over as police commissioner on November 10. Aware that the police detachment was loyal to the dismissed police commissioner and Praia partisan Caetano Francisco de Barros Wanderley, the new appointee came accompanied by a large group of armed men. Many of these men had been supplied by José Pedro Veloso da Silveira, the owner of the Lages estate and a major figure in the armed resistance to the Praia administration of Chichorro da Gama's administration. Various Praia partisans were promptly arrested and others were forced to abandon the area. On the Cachoeira estate, Caetano Francisco de Barros Wanderley gathered two hundred armed men. On November 17 the new police commissioner marshaled fifty military troops and one hundred national guard supplied by José Pedro and attacked the Praia loyalists on the Cachoeira estate. After fifteen minutes the government forces had dislodged their opponents from many of their protected positions, and within an hour they had put them all to flight. Eight rebels were left dead on the battlefield and two more drowned, shot as they tried to escape across a river.[88]

In the *sertão* the locally prominent Conservative Manuel Pereira da Silva was installed as police commissioner of Flores on November 17. On the following day, the Praieiro leader Francisco Barbosa Nogueira Paes entered the village with twenty-eight armed men. In consort with several local allies and their fifty men, they controlled the village, barricading positions in the jail, Nogueira Paes's house, and several other houses. The police commissioner barricaded himself in his house, unable to advance on the Praieiros' superior numbers during a three-hour battle. On November 19 fighting began again and continued until four o'clock the next afternoon, when eighty reinforcements arrived with Lt. Col. Simplício Pereira da Silva. Two and a half hours later, the government forces prevailed. A majority of the Praia forces escaped, but Francisco Barbosa Nogueira Paes and twenty others were arrested and taken to Serra Talhada. Curiously, after discussions with Nogueira Paes's relatives in Piancó, in the neighboring province of Alagoas, and written assurances that the Praieiro would not interfere with the Conservative officials and would in fact stay out of the province, he was released on December 4.[89] Perhaps this flexibility on the part of Pereira da Silva reflected the recognition that in the distant sertão, where news and assistance from the capital was slow in coming, reducing tension with local rivals might avoid attempts at retribution by family members and allies.

By mid-November much of the province was in arms. Although the possibility of resistance when a Conservative ministry handed offices back to the baronists had long been anticipated, the armed responses showed no evidence of coordinated action.[90] Across the province, opposition to the appointees who arrived to occupy official posts erupted spontaneously. The Praieiro leadership hoped to avert armed struggle. Deputies in Recife had earlier written to the popular leader Joaquim Nunes Machado, urging him to return from the court and help avert an outbreak. By the time of his arrival in Recife on November 17, however, violent struggles were well under way.[91]

Praieiro resistance to dismissals in late April and early May had been partially successful. Some dismissed officeholders were returned to office and some nominations were abandoned, leaving interim officeholders officially in the posts. In the changed circumstances of November, however, it was clear that resistance would not prompt the provincial president to yield. On the contrary, President Pena was moving to solidify the Conservatives' ascension. The bloody death toll of the battle at the Mussopinho estate demonstrated that the new administration was committed to crushing Praieiro recalcitrance. Moreover, facing resistance across the province, on November 13 the president postponed until December 17 the elections for municipal councilmen and justices of the peace that were scheduled for November 19. These elections were crucial, as the victors would control the electoral boards that would qualify electors in the next elections for the Provincial Assembly, the Chamber of Deputies, and the imperial Senate.[92]

Nunes Machado disembarked into a province in open conflict, where the blood of his fellow Praieiros had already been spilled, and where a

Conservative administration, backed by a cabinet headed by the Conservative Pernambucan statesmen the Viscount of Olinda, seemed determined to stamp out resistance to its turning over the state apparatus to Conservative opponents of the Praieiros. Nunes Machado's initial conciliatory attitude and his hope of finding grounds for pulling back from armed conflict (such as securing an amnesty from President Pena for acts committed over the previous weeks), led to rumors that the Praieiro leader had betrayed the movement and was switching sides to support the *guabirus*. On November 18, flyers were distributed in which Nunes Machado vehemently denied such rumors and insisted on his adherence to his principles and continued opposition to the *saquaremas*. He denounced President Pena's use of force and declared his willingness to offer his own life, if necessary, to save Pernambuco.[93]

The Praieira Revolution

On November 25 Nunes Machado and the other seven Praieiro deputies to the Chamber of Deputies issued a manifesto in which they railed against the atrocious acts of the new officeholders and denounced the inflexible attitude of the administration, which, instead of listening to their complaints, sent troops to crush them. They insisted that they did not want war and were only motivated by self-defense. The manifesto was emphatic on not rejecting constitutionality. It did not call for broad reforms or radical changes. Rather, it insisted on the illegality of numerous acts by President Pena and his allies. The deputies asserted that they had no choice but to "accompany our fellow citizens in their glorious defense [and] protest in the name of the constitution and the emperor against so many atrocities committed by his delegate [the provincial president]." The term used—"accompany" their fellow citizens—reflects the fact that the revolt was initiated by Praieiros across the province; when party leaders arrived from the court, they were faced with a fait accompli.[94]

One contemporary, the Conservative leader Honório Hermeto Carneiro Leão, interpreted these events in terms of personal loyalty, noting that Nunes Machado had "courage in all matters, save resisting his friends."[95] Without underestimating the importance that personal attachments and loyalties must have had, it also seems clear that failure to accompany their allies would have meant abandoning their leading role in the party at its most critical moment.[96] The polarization of the province over the previous year, with escalating rhetoric, broader and riskier mobilization of allies, and periods of open armed conflict in several regions, must have made it difficult to stop the momentum toward greater armed action. Thus, despite their sober judgment suggesting the difficulty of prevailing, all eight of the Praia deputies to the Chamber agreed on the manifesto.[97] Party leaders in Recife then set out to organize the Praieiro forces throughout the province.[98]

The Conservative administration, meanwhile, was preparing for a lengthy struggle. Volunteer battalions were formed, with the largest headed by Sebastião do Rego Barros, a prominent baronist and brother of the Baron of Boa Vista. While arrangements were being made for men and material from the court, on November 23 the entirety of the military troops previously stationed in Bahia arrived. The troops were accompanied by the commander of arms of Bahia, Brig. Gen. José Joaquim Coelho, a decorated military leader who had served in the independence wars and in suppressing revolts in Pernambuco in 1824, Bahia in 1838, and in Rio Grande do Sul at various times. Orders from the court soon named him supreme commander of the forces suppressing the Praieira as well as commander of arms. Instructions from Rio de Janeiro removed Praia deputies Félix Peixoto de Brito e Melo and José Francisco de Arruda Câmara from posts as district judges and also replaced Praia partisans on the list of vice-presidents for the province.[99]

A series of battles in the coastal forest region north of Recife demonstrated the government's superiority in open battle. In Nazareth three government columns entered the town and within an hour dislodged rebel troops from their defensive positions in houses and the church, inflicting six deaths and capturing thirty-five. The Praieiros, however, made full use of surprise and mobility. They employed guerrilla tactics at times, concentrated their forces for surprise attacks on lightly defended towns, and dug themselves into well-protected positions for larger battles when it suited them. A frustrated Gen. Coelho wrote to the provincial president that the rebels spoke with great bravado and then shamelessly fled when government troops approached, only to claim victory afterward.[100]

A major battle at Maricota on November 30 was typical of the government forces' success in inflicting greater casualties than their opponents, only to see the Praieiros escape worse damage by successfully retreating to regroup elsewhere. The Praieiros massed troops in dug-in positions in the hilly, forested area along the principal road heading north from Recife, aiming for a surprise attack on government troops returning from Goiana. The plan was discovered, however, and four hundred troops were sent from nearby Igarassu to engage the Praieiros. The government forces retreated at nightfall and claimed victory after dislodging their enemy from its positions and inflicting greater casualties.[101]

On December 10 the supreme commander of the government forces, José Joaquim Coelho, personally directed a battle against Praia forces gathered in the Catucá forest north of Recife. The Praieiros used this area as a safe haven for gathering forces, retreating when defeated, and taking advantage, as runaway slaves had long done, of the dense forest and its possibilities for hidden refuge and surprise attacks on the estates of nearby baronists. Rumors of preparations for an attack on Recife, which spread such panic that some families fled to ships in the harbor for safety, might have prompted the general's decision to enter the forest. The Praieiros saw their positions overrun, but they had little difficulty escaping, particularly as the forces of João do Rego Barros did not arrive in time to cut off an escape route.[102]

The Praieiros took advantage of Coelho's massing of troops in the Catucá forest to seize Goiana. On December 13 eight hundred men overpowered the few national guardsmen left there after the gathering of government forces for the attack in the Catucá forest. Although only six national guardsmen were killed in the initial attack, the death toll tripled in the hectic retreat. The Praieiros sacked the houses of their Conservative opponents and then abandoned the town the next day as Coelho's troops approached. They took advantage of the hilly, forest terrain twenty-one miles to the west, at the village of Cruangí, to dig into a strong defensive position. Twelve hundred men settled in to await the government attack, which came on December 20. After eight and a half hours of combat, the defenders were forced to abandon their positions and escape under the cover of darkness; yet they had achieved a victory in an open, large-scale battle.[103]

The Praieiros' use of the Catucá forest presented problems for the government. Praia faithful in nearby parishes, including São Lourenço da Mata to the north of Recife and Muribeca and Jaboatão to the south, funneled men, money, arms, ammunition, and supplies to the rebels. The government strengthened its presence in Casa Forte, Monteiro, and Apipucos, villages just to the north of Recife. The precautions proved wise because rebels attacked the Dois Irmãos estate in Apipucos on November 30. Praieiros were also active proselytizing for the cause in these villages and in parishes such as Afogados and Varzea near the capital. Figueira de Melo, discussing these efforts in the latter two places in his 1850 account of the Praieira, noted the success of national guard Capt. Manuel Romão Correia, who "had achieved a certain ascendancy among the men of color."[104] Police reports show that various individuals were arrested for distributing propaganda and recruiting support for the rebels. Antônio Simfranio Rodrigues de Luna, for example, not only distributed "incendiary proclamations" door to door but also gathered people and read the proclamations aloud for those who could not read.[105]

In the forest zone south of the capital, a similar situation prevailed. Officeholders in Escada and Ipojuca used their national guard and police posts to gather men, then resisted new appointees and refused to hand over their weapons and ammunition. Prominent, wealthy figures such as João do Rego Barros, brother of the Baron of Boa Vista, and Pedro Cavalcanti Wanderley, both familiar enemies of the Praia, were appointed to national guard and police posts, and when combat drew them away from the area, the Praieiro nemesis José Pedro Veloso da Silveira moved in as temporary commander of the forces there. Praieiros attacked at the Gaipió estate on November 30, only to withdraw when large government forces approached. On hearing of a rebel gathering at the Benfica estate, José Pedro led police and national guard forces early in the morning of December 13 on a preemptive strike that seized arms, ammunition, and several prisoners. At three o'clock the next morning 150 Praieiros attacked the São Francisco Convent where the prisoners were held, only to be held off for three hours by thirty-six policemen before abandoning the effort.[106]

In the far south of the province, in Una on the coast and Água Preta inland, Praia officeholders successfully resisted new appointees. They occupied the town of Una, stealing and wrecking the houses of Conservative opponents. The forces they gathered reflected the makeup of the local population, which included many *caboclos* (people of mixed Indian and European ancestry) from Barreiros and men who had escaped defeat at the Cachoeira estate in Serinhaem. Confronted with the prospect of facing more than three hundred national guardsmen and forty-three military troops, they abandoned the area on November 27. The Praieiros split into two forces, one that crossed the border into Alagoas and another that went west to Água Preta. The latter joined up with Praia leaders Pedro Ivo and Caetano Alves and were attacked by government forces on December 8 at the Camorim estate; they lost twelve men and inflicted five deaths on the government forces. The Praieiros nonetheless enjoyed freedom of movement in the forests of the region and sent out patrols that disrupted the government's communications with its southern headquarters in Rio Formoso. An unsuccessful attack at the Almecega estate on the night of December 22 and into the next morning again indicates the makeup of the troops the Praia leaders employed in the south: two hundred Indians from Jacuípe and Água Preta launched the attack for the Praia.[107]

A Hard-Line Provincial President
and the Radicalization of the Praieiros

December proved to be decisive in determining the character of the conflict. In full-scale confrontation, momentum was toward greater radicalization. On December 25, Manuel Vieira Tosta, accompanied by 340 soldiers of an artillery battalion and another 40 cavalry soldiers, arrived to replace Herculano Ferreira Pena as the president of Pernambuco. President Tosta, a prominent Praia opponent when he served in the Chamber of Deputies in Rio de Janeiro, soon named Jerônimo Martiniano Figueira de Melo chief of police. Figueira de Melo was from Ceará but married into the prominent Paes de Andrade family in Pernambuco. He had impeccable credentials as a hard-line Praia opponent, having proved himself an acerbic critic of the Praieiros as an editor of the Conservative newspapers *Lidador* and *União*.[108]

The significance of these appointments was clear. President Pena's strategy of moderation, which had maintained the normal state of legality, respect for the Praieiro deputies' immunity from arrest, and normal operation of the opposition press, would be abandoned. President To- sta would use the full force of his position, including suspending con- stitutional guarantees, to crush the rebel movement. On the day of his appointment, he said, "I will not vacillate before the use of the most en- ergetic measures to extinguish the anarchistic movements, which have already caused so much harm."[109]

President Tosta was true to his word. He quickly moved against the press. On January 4 the *Voz do Brasil* was shut down, and its publisher and its editor, Ignácio Bento de Loyola, were jailed without legal for- malities.[110] In mid-January the printing press of Typographia Nazarena, which published the *Voz do Brazil*, was seized. The principal Praieiro organ, the *Diário Novo*, was repeatedly harassed; the publisher's build- ing and home were searched repeatedly, and employees and distribu- tors were arrested. Ordered not to cover provincial affairs, the paper ran blank columns in place of the stories it could not run. By February it too had been shut down.[111]

Police actions broadened in scope. Praia sympathizers in Recife had their houses searched for weapons. Arrests and recruitment for the mil- itary increased. Facing the prospect of an end to the immunity for Praie- iro deputies, the political leadership, which up to that point had operated freely in Recife, had to flee the city or go into hiding.[112]

The appointment of Manuel Vieira Tosta and his hard-line actions to crush the Praieiro movement forced the Praia deputies not only to flee Recife for fear of imprisonment but also to redefine their party's posi- tion. This they did in late December and early January in a proclama- tion issued by the Praieiro deputies, in which they called on people to take up arms, and in three articles in the *Diário Novo* entitled "The Ban- ner of the Liberal Movement."[113]

The Praieiro leaders mounted a three-fold attack on the status quo, im- plicating the Conservatives in each criticism. First, they denounced the lack of effective constitutional guarantees, demonstrated by the Conser- vatives' trampling on rights, especially through arbitrary imprisonments and paying professional assassins from public funds.[114] Second, they railed against the continued undermining of national sovereignty by the Por- tuguese. Here they returned to a theme the Praia press had been empha- sizing since the beginning of the hostilities, depicting the Conservatives, with labels such as "*luso-guabiru* gang," as allies of the Portuguese in a continuing assault on Brazilian sovereignty.[115] Third, the Praieiros raised the traditional liberal banner of provincial rights, one that had been central to the Liberal revolts of 1842 in São Paulo and Minas Gerais. In doing so, they rejected the achievement of the Regresso that had laid the basis for authoritarian, centralized rule. The Praieiros challenged the Conservatives' claim that they were defenders of the monarchy, asserting, "The throne of Brazil cannot remain unless it is surrounded by liberal institutions; absolutist concentration is the garrote of this monarchy."[116] Denouncing the failure of the government in Rio to name a single Pernambucan to a high position in the current provincial administration, the Praieiros asked, "Does the present state of affairs differ at all from the old colonial regime? Do we, Pernambucans, have the slightest role in governing this province?"[117] The call for autonomy was also an appeal to provincial resentment against remitting taxes to the court; the Praieiros argued that locally collected revenues should be spent locally.[118]

The Praieiro statements constituted a call to arms. The leaders invoked the sovereignty of the nation and the right to rebel and declared, "Since we cannot avoid a conflagration in the province . . . we have to follow the impulse of the movement and give it appropriate direction."[119] The Praieiro leaders also abandoned their earlier position of simple resistance to illegal acts by the Conservative administration in Recife and called for sweeping political reforms.[120] They called on the emperor to convene a Constituent Assembly within six months to carry out the needed constitutional reforms. This was the only path to creating the truly liberal institutions needed to save the throne. Not even bothering to veil the threat, the Praieiros declared that failure to implement reforms would lead to a dissolution of the empire, although they insisted on their desire to maintain the monarchical form of government and the territorial integrity of the nation.[121]

The expansion of goals to embrace more radical positions is not, of course, surprising in the midst of armed struggle.[122] Under physical threat, radical tendencies can more easily come to the fore, overcoming moderate impulses within individuals as well as groups. After all, more extreme positions had long coexisted with reformist ones. The Praieiro paper *A Barca de São Pedro* (The Boat of Saint Peter), for example, in July had declared that revolution was inevitable. "We want a revolution . . . not a revolt, nor a tumult, nor a military sedition. . . . We want a complete reorganization of the country."[123] The radicalization can also be seen in part as an effort to mobilize people for the struggle. Yet there were risks in such an approach. The moderate Praieiro leadership faced the difficulty of mobilizing support for their movement without losing control to the radicals.[124]

The republican activist Antônio Borges da Fonseca had joined the fight in mid-November and, bolstered by his lengthy experience as a polemicist and agitator, quickly attained a leadership position in the Praia's Northern Army. On January 1, 1849, the entire leadership of the Northern Army signed and issued a proclamation entitled "Manifesto to the World."[125] Written by Borges da Fonseca, it was clearly inspired by European liberalism and, in particular, the Revolution of 1848 in France. The document declared that the absolutist ministry of September 29, 1848, "decided to conquer the country, as a reaction to the progressive movements of Europe, that have annihilated tyrants, and achieved the promise of the All Powerful to depose the Kings from their thrones, and raise the people." After denouncing the September 29 ministry, the "conquest" of Pernambuco in support of the centralized political system, and the predominance of the Portuguese, the document called for a Constituent Assembly to achieve ten principles: (1) universal suffrage, (2) liberty of the press, (3) work as a guarantee of life, (4) retail commerce restricted to Brazilians (5) complete independence of the constituted powers, (6) elimination of the moderating power and the right to bestow titles, (7) federalism, (8) reform of the judiciary, to ensure individual rights, (9) elimination of the conventional interest law, and (10) elimination of the current system of military recruitment.

The Praia leadership promptly denounced the document as a forgery that was spread by *guabirus* hoping to stigmatize the Praieiros.[126] References to progressive European movements deposing kings from their thrones, the need to eliminate the moderating power, and the right to work were far too radical for the moderate Praieiro leadership. The moderates themselves were indeed adopting positions that were more extreme than their previous stances, but they were not willing to allow a republican radical like Borges da Fonseca, whose formulations constituted a complete rejection of the imperial regime and included far-reaching, leveling reforms, to define the movement. The Conservative press, of course, pounced on the opportunity and depicted Borges da Fonseca's participation in the struggle and the "Manifesto to the World" as evidence of the real, although previously disguised, republican agenda of the Praieiros.[127]

A New Praieiro Strategy and the Attack on Recife

In the face of President Tosta's hard-line policies, five of the Praieiro deputies left Recife by ship on December 31, disembarking the next day just across the border between Pernambuco and Alagoas, the neighboring province to the south. In Alagoas they met with an ally, the police commissioner José Luiz Beltrão Mavignier. One of the deputies, Félix Peixoto de Brito e Melo, had served as provincial president of Alagoas until May 1848, and with Mavignier's assistance the deputies sought to recruit provincial support for the movement. The president of Alagoas, however, dismissed Mavignier, ordered the Praieiro deputies arrested, sent troops to the area, had a ship patrol the coast to prevent the movement of arms, and sent the chief of police and several other high officeholders to persuade people not to support the movement in Pernambuco. The president's decisive actions effectively dissuaded potential allies from extending support. The Praieiros thus proved no more successful in Alagoas than in their earlier efforts to secure support from Ceará and Paraíba, provinces to the north of Pernambuco.[128]

Despite the inability to obtain assistance from outside Pernambuco, the Praieiros were not faring poorly in battle. The victory at Cruangí on December 20 had demonstrated a newfound willingness to engage the government in large-scale battles. Victory seemed to embolden them; attacks on Conservative estates to seize ammunition increased. In late December and early January Praia forces acquitted themselves well in a series of battles: at Água Preta and Ipojuca in the south of the province; at Bezerros, farther inland and sixty-nine miles southwest of Recife; in a canoe-borne attack on the island of Itamaracá, north of Recife; and at the Utinga estate in Igarassu.[129]

In response to the hard-line policies of the new president, which effectively interrupted communication between Recife and fighters elsewhere in the province, Praieiro leaders adopted a new strategy. Pedro Ivo Veloso da Silveira, a former army captain and a nephew of the Conservative planter and Praia opponent José Pedro Veloso da Silveira, had established a significant armed force in the far south. Several of the Praia deputies who had been compelled to abandon efforts to gather support in Alagoas joined up with him at the Tentugal estate in the parish of Una. From this estate, four to five hundred fighters launched successful attacks on the town of Barreiros and the Camorim estate on January 10 and 12, reportedly killing more than one hundred men in the first attack. Faced with the inability to direct operations from Recife, Praieiro leaders opted to concentrate their forces in the south of the province.[130]

Between forces already in the region and additional ones that came down from the north, the Praieiros had gathered between sixteen hundred and two thousand men, the bulk of them in Água Preta.[131] The effectiveness of these forces was weakened by chronic shortages of ammunition and a lack of discipline. Although the Indian and *caboclo* fighters led by Pedro Ivo and Caetano Alves proved to be disciplined, the majority of the troops, mobilized by planters, were only accustomed to obeying their particular patrons and to action in small-scale battles.[132]

These difficulties were not easily overcome, but the Praieiro leaders did establish a formal leadership structure that was composed of a Liberal directorate and three divisions, each divided into brigades and battalions, to provide clear direction to the movement. Henceforth, conflict over tactical issues, such as whether to attack the numerous government forces in Rio Formoso in pursuit of a major victory or attack the smaller forces in Bonito, was reduced because the decisions fell to those designated to make them. Similarly, leaders were designated to handle political issues, such as Borges da Fonseca's desire to promote far-reaching constitutional reforms rather than focus strictly on military victory. Leaders of the various forces selected Félix Peixoto de Brito e Melo as the commanding general and Antônio Afonso Ferreira, Manuel Pereira de Moraes, and Antônio Borges da Fonseca as the other members of the directorate.[133]

The Praia forces were concentrated in Água Preta, and Gen. José Joaquim Coelho, commander of the government forces, perceived an opportunity to crush them. He gathered three thousand men and marched to Rio Formoso in preparation for a January 30 attack on the enemy at Água Preta. The Liberal directorate, however, having received word from Praia deputy Felipe Lopes Neto that Recife was left only lightly defended after Coelho's departure, decided to attempt to seize the capital by surprise. Marching for Recife on January 26, they escaped the trap being set by Gen. Coelho. They avoided battle en route, rushing as quickly as possible and arriving on the outskirts of the capital on the evening of February 1.[134]

The geography of the capital facilitated its defense; sea and rivers divided the city into three districts—Boa Vista to the east, Santo Antônio in the middle, and the Bairro do Recife on the ocean—with bridges linking the three. Trenches and walls helped defenders control the bridges. The Praieiros had only a few military officers among those leading their troops. They did not possess artillery or cavalry. The success of the assault depended on throwing superior numbers at the defenders in a surprise attack.[135]

At five o'clock on the morning of February 2, the Praieiro forces began their assault. They split into three forces. Pedro Ivo Veloso da Silveira led a group of eight hundred men, along with Borges da Fonseca, Henrique Pereira de Lucena, and Leandro César Paes Barreto, which attacked from the south, seized the suburb of Afogados, and then invaded Santo Antônio. For some time they controlled the bridge to Boa Vista from nearby houses, but by half past ten they were dislodged. They attacked the government palace but could not seize it. Likewise, efforts to capture the arsenal and the arms and ammunition stocked there failed. Throughout the day, the Praieiros took advantage of the shelter offered by the houses of supporters and the barricades constructed by the troops. The Praieiros inflicted heavy losses on the national guard defending the Cinco Pontas fort, attacking from neighboring houses and dug-in positions. Gen. Coelho's arrival at three o'clock that afternoon proved decisive; although tired from the long, forced march, the reinforcements he brought significantly increased the government forces and boosted morale. Escape proved difficult and Praieiro losses were heavy, because government forces were controlling the two bridges connecting Santo Antônio to Boa Vista and the Bairro do Recife. In the disorderly attempt to flee, many Praieiros were shot or bayoneted, some drowned while trying to swim to safety, and others were taken prisoner, but some managed to hide in the houses of supporters.[136]

Manuel Pereira de Moraes's men approached the city from the north. When they found the Brum and Buraco forts heavily manned and ships ready to add their fire to the defense of the city, however, they returned to Olinda. The largest force, directed by João Ignácio Ribeiro Roma to the west of the city, divided into two groups, one that Roma led to Olinda to join up with Moraes's troops and another group of five hundred men led by Joaquim Nunes Machado that attacked Boa Vista at Soledad.[137]

The Praieiros who attacked Boa Vista at five o'clock in the morning were initially blocked at the Olho do Boi bridge, but eventually they passed through, overrunning the military barracks at Soledad. Both sides made ample use of houses, firing from the safety offered by the buildings. Gen. Coelho gave instructions to use artillery to dislodge the rebels if necessary, but reinforcements from Nazareth, northwest of Recife, arrived at eleven o'clock and proved sufficient. The Praieiros suffered heavy losses, including their popular leader Joaquim Nunes Machado, who fell dead when he was struck by a bullet to his head while battling government troops retaking the Soledad barracks.[138]

By nine o'clock that night the fighting in Recife was over. The Praieiros were in a hasty retreat, fleeing the city toward Nazareth. They had lost two hundred men; another four hundred were captured, including various leaders.[139] One Praia partisan maintained that the failure to take Boa Vista had been crucial; victory here, combined with the initial successes in Santo Antônio, might have led to a Praieiro victory.[140] The larger issue, though, was the size of the forces that each side could marshal. The bold move of an attack on Recife had depended on the element of surprise. With Gen. Coelho preparing for battle in the south of the province, the capital had far fewer defenders than normally was the case. Praia victory depended on seizing this momentary advantage and then taking advantage of the geography, which favored the defense of the city. However, reinforcements arrived before the attack. On February 1 some five hundred sailors and naval sharpshooters arrived by steam packet, unexpected even by the government. Crucially, Gen. Coelho perceived the Praieiros' plan in time to rush his troops back to the capital and enter the fray in the afternoon. The numerical superiority the Praieiro leaders counted on dissipated; in fact, the defenders of the city ultimately out-numbered the attackers.[141]

The failed attempt to seize the provincial capital was the turning point of the struggle. The Praieiros suffered large losses, both in deaths and prisoners seized. House-to-house searches of Recife in the days following the attack compounded the losses, as government forces arrested large numbers of Praieiro combatants and supporters, and shot some of those they found. Searches of houses in Recife throughout the month turned up weapons and ammunition. The authorities sent lower-class prisoners to Rio de Janeiro for forced military service, banished others to the is-land of Fernando de Noronha, and housed others awaiting trial on ships in the harbor.[142] Although armed Praieiros remained in the field, they never again posed a significant threat to the government.

Gen. Coelho's decision to rest his troops instead of immediately pur-suing the Liberal forces allowed the Praieiros to regroup north of the capital. Some six hundred to eight hundred men seized Goiana on Feb-ruary 11, acquiring twenty-five thousand much-needed rounds of am-munition. Pursued by a government column, these forces suffered some losses at the Pau Amarelo estate, including the mortal wounding of the Praieiro leader João Roma, and then headed north to the neighboring province of Paraíba. On February 18 an ally in Paraíba, County Judge Maximiliano Lopes Machado, welcomed them, but his support could not prevent the pursuing government column from inflicting serious losses in a battle at Brejo da Areia.[143]

After the setback in Paraíba, the Praieiro forces returned to the Ca-tucá forest north of Recife. A plan was made to regroup with the remain-ing Praia forces in the south of the province. After the debacle of the at-tack on the capital, Pedro Ivo and Caetano Alves had led their largely Indian and *caboclo* troops back to the south of the province, easily cap-turing Água Preta.[144]

The End Nears
By this time, however, the inevitability of the Praieiros' defeat was clear. Losses had been heavy and were mounting, chronic ammunition short-ages were only getting worse, the party's newspapers had been shut down, and many leaders were dead or imprisoned. The dissolution of the Cham-

ber of Deputies in Rio was the final blow. With the end of immunity for Praia deputies and without the deputies to argue for the legitimacy of the struggle, leaders began looking for ways out. Government offers of amnesty were now appealing. The troops faced no punishment, and more important figures might obtain amnesty or a safe passage to exile. The principal leaders, however, received no offers of protection.[145]

Félix Peixoto de Brito e Melo, the commander in chief of the Liberal army, sailed a *jangada* to Alagoas and, hearing of the dissolution of the Chamber of Deputies, boarded a ship for Portugal. Moraes and João Paulo Ferreira made their way to the United States and later to Portugal. Borges da Fonseca, when denied amnesty, continued fighting and was captured on March 30. By early April most leaders of the forces remaining in the field were either planning their flight to exile, deciding where to hide if they chose to take their chances in Brazil, or negotiating the terms of their surrender. The most significant exception was Pedro Ivo Veloso da Silveira, who remained in the field, retreating to the forests in the south of the province. On April 10 President Tosta declared to the newly convened Provincial Assembly that the civil war had been won.[146]

The Aftermath

In August nine men—Dr. Felipe Lopes Neto, Dr. Jerônimo Vilela de Castro Tavares, Gen. José Ignácio de Abreu Lima, Antônio Correia Pessoa de Melo, Henrique Pereira de Lucena, Leandro César Paes Barreto, Feliciano Joaquim dos Santos, Antônio Feitosa de Melo, and Antônio Borges da Fonseca—were brought to trial on charges of the political crime of rebellion. Praieiro partisans were indignant at the proceeding. José Tomás Nabuco de Araújo presided over the hearings, and Jerônimo Martiniano Figueira de Melo served as prosecuting attorney. Both men were prominent Praia opponents. Both served as editors of partisan Conservative newspapers. Figueira de Melo, of course, was the chief of police brought in by President Tosta to implement hard-line policies for repressing the revolt. Likewise, the president of the jury was a Conservative partisan. Not surprisingly, the nine defendants were found guilty as heads of the rebellion and condemned to life in prison and hard labor.[147]

Despite President Tosta's declaration to the Provincial Assembly and the judgment against the nine Praieiro leaders, the province was not entirely pacified. Moreover, the president was alienating people with his hard-line tactics. In March he had instructed all estate owners within 120 kilometers of Água Preta to abandon their estates, as a means of eliminating support for Pedro Ivo's rebels. When Miguel Afonso Ferreira joined Pedro Ivo, the president ordered his crops burned and his slaves and sugar processing machinery seized and brought to Recife. The president warned that all political opponents in the area would be treated similarly, because even unarmed opponents provided valuable information to the rebels. Tosta also offended foreign consuls, invading their residences in search of Praieiros and even bringing criminal charges against the British consul after a conflict over an arrested British officer. The opening of the Provincial Assembly also occasioned controversy; hostile groups of spectators in the galleries shouted down Praia speakers and the police arrested Praieiro deputies.[148]

The Conservative ministry in the court sent Honório Hermeto Carneiro Leão to replace President Tosta. Honório was one of the principal leaders of the Conservative Party, and the ministry could not have found a stronger figure. Yet he was not sent to crush the Praieiros; that had been Tosta's assignment. Honório was sent to promote reconciliation in the province and to ensure a legitimate victory in the elections scheduled for August. When he arrived on July 2, he immediately took steps to bind the wounds opened by the revolt. Prisoners held on ships were transferred to prisons on land; thirty-seven men banished to the island of Fernando de Noronha were freed; various prisoners in Recife were released. Military recruiting was ended temporarily. Opposition journals were allowed to publish again.[149]

The president's conciliatory approach was met by two principal difficulties. One was the renewed fighting by the remaining praieira troops in the field. The other, which only worsened as fighting expanded, was opposition to Honório's moderate approach by leading Pernambucan Conservatives. As early as the August elections, Conservatives demonstrated their resistance to the president's approach by disregarding his clear instructions to avoid the excesses of intimidation tactics and egregious abuse of public authority that so often characterized elections. Honório incensed Conservatives when he undermined their tactics in the war effort. Presi-

dent Tosta had made a valuable alliance with Vicente de Paula, the charismatic guerrilla leader sought by the authorities since the Guerra dos
Cabanos of the 1830s. Vicente and his experienced fighters had contributed much to the war against the Praieiros, yet the new president arrested
him when he showed up for a meeting to receive a payment promised by
President Tosta. Likewise, the president grossly insulted Conservative
leaders early in 1850 when he sent government troops to the residence
of Francisco do Rego Barros and attempted to seize Pedro Ivo while he
was in a secret meeting with leading Conservatives, during which he had
agreed to leave the province and await amnesty.[150]

Embroiled in conflicts with the president, Conservative planters did
not throw their full support behind the effort to finish the pacification
of the province. In mid-October 1849, rumors surfaced that the Praieiros would attack the lightly defended capital from the Catucá forest. In
mid-December Praia forces were sighted within twenty-one kilometers
of the capital, raising fears of an attack. Honório realized that without
the full cooperation of local Conservatives, he could not ensure the success of his mission. In a meeting with Conservative leaders Francisco do
Rego Barros, Francisco de Paula Cavalcanti de Albuquerque, and Sebastião do Rego Barros, he assured them that he would cease his conciliatory policies and vigorously suppress the Praieiros. He promptly had a
number of Praia leaders arrested and banished to the island of Fernando
de Noronha. In return, he secured the full cooperation of the Conservative planters in finishing the war effort. A final offensive was launched in
March 1850, following the completion of the sugar harvest, and the remaining Praia forces put down their arms. The last of the great regional
rebellions of the empire was over.[151]

Late 1847 and early 1848 saw increasing polarization both in the imperial court and in Pernambuco. Senate Conservatives invalidated the
elections of two Praieiro allies to the Senate, and Alves Branco's Liberal
May 22, 1847, ministry steadfastly supported the Praieiros. However, a
split among the Praieiros—especially the loss of Antônio and Francisco
Machado Rios, who had considerable influence on the police and the
military—weakened them. The Praieiros responded to the split in the
party with further radicalization and greater appeal to Lusophobia. In

early 1848 Conservative planters stepped up the armed resistance they had begun the year before.

The Viscount of Macaé's March 8, 1848, ministry initiated conciliatory policies in an effort to broaden political support. The consequences in Pernambuco could hardly have been greater. The practice of provincial presidents running for national office from the provinces in which they served was prohibited, which led the Praieiro ally Chichorro da Gama to step down as provincial president. The first vice-president, Manuel de Sousa Teixeira, was among those who had abandoned the party in the Praia nova split. Upon taking office, he immediately dismissed five hundred Praieiros from official positions. As Praieiros resisted the changes, the newly appointed provincial president, Vicente Pires da Mota, arrived and charted a conciliatory course between the conflicting political groups. It is easy to see why these efforts were futile. The centralized system had been designed to permit the cabinet to secure support across the empire. A provincial president who maintained some of one party's partisans in power, while handing over other offices to the opposition, created a recipe for increasing conflict, not diminishing hostilities.

In June 1848 the news reached Pernambuco that for the second time Conservatives in the Senate had nullified the election of Praieiro allies to the imperial Senate. This dramatic partisan defiance of usual political practice only prompted greater radicalization. In the court, Praieiro leader Joaquim Nunes Machado called for legislative action against the Portuguese. Crucially, Liberal leaders invoked Lusophobia in their campaign for a seat on the municipal council of Rio de Janeiro. As street violence erupted against the Portuguese, Conservatives denounced the Liberals for using demagogic tactics that endangered public order.

The emperor quickly dismissed the Liberal cabinet and called on the Pernambucan Pedro de Araújo Lima, the Viscount of Olinda, to form a Conservative ministry. The ramifications of the change in the cabinet swept across the entire country as the new ministry empowered its provincial partisans.

First with individual acts of defiance and soon after with coordinated efforts, the Praieiros resisted being turned out of power; the Praieira Revolution had begun. Party leaders initially justified their actions as self-defense against abuses of power. When, in late December, new Provincial

President Manuel Vieira Tosta adopted hard-line policies, party leaders fled Recife. They soon issued a manifesto that denounced the absence of effective constitutional guarantees, railed against the Portuguese for undermining national sovereignty, and called for decentralization of the empire's political institutions as the only means of protecting against absolutism. Invoking the right of a sovereign nation to rebel against injustice, they called on Pedro II to convoke a Constitutional Assembly that would carry out the reforms needed to save the monarchy.

Just as moderate party leaders were adopting more extreme positions in the crucible of war, radicals were also taking more extreme positions. The radical republican activist Antônio Borges da Fonseca achieved a leadership position in the Praieiros' Northern Army and issued a manifesto calling for a Constitutional Assembly that would establish universal suffrage and federalism, eliminate the moderating power of the crown and the current system of military recruitment, and restrict retail commerce to Brazilians. Moderate party leaders vehemently rejected such extreme positions, even as they themselves, under the pressure of warfare, were adopting much more radical positions.

The Praieiros gambled everything on a bold attack on Recife on February 2, 1849. The plan to capture the provincial capital depended on seizing a brief numerical advantage in the size of their troops. The unanticipated arrival of imperial troops by steamship and the rapid march of imperial troops to Recife once military leaders grasped the rebels' strategy foiled the Praieiros' plans. The imperial army inflicted a crushing blow on the Praieiro forces that effectively ended any hopes for victory.

The Praieira Revolution was a test of strength, not only between provincial rivals but also for the national political system constructed in the latter years of the regency and early years of the Second Reign by the future leaders of the Conservative Party. The centralized institutions they had helped construct in the Regresso now provided them with valuable military resources too great for provincial Liberal challengers to overcome. The effectiveness of the reactionary institutions of the monarchy was evident to all.

Conclusion

Recent research on state and nation building has yielded a more nuanced understanding and, in particular, has demonstrated the importance of people who were largely left out of traditional narratives. The collapse of the old order in the Portuguese world opened up a fluid period in which diverse social groups struggled and shaped a new order. Conceptualizations of the new state and society were ardently contested in Pernambuco and across Brazil, but they all incorporated notions of popular sovereignty, constitutional rule, and broader political participation. This book examines the active political participation of middling and lower-class groups whose beliefs were informed by such liberal ideas. It shows how their mobilization conflicted with traditional elite concerns about the distribution of power in society.

The appearance of liberal political ideas in the Age of Revolution is a rather familiar topic, even if the circulation of such ideas and how different social groups understood and made use of them is less well analyzed. Such an analysis presents numerous challenges and difficulties. Several topics addressed in this book could be fruitfully explored in future research.

The importance of the Catholic Church in the 1817 revolt in Pernambuco perhaps should not be too surprising in light of the liberal Enlightenment figures among the clergy in Spanish America—most famously, the leaders of the independence movement in Mexico, Miguel Hidalgo and José María Morelos. Yet, in contrast to studies of Spanish America, the role of the church in Brazil in this era has drawn relatively little attention. The institution was traditional but served as a vehicle for new ideas; its priests were respected figures; and many of the conflicts in society undoubtedly were replicated within the church. One might ask many questions about the church in this period; among them should be queries about the institution's role in establishing, maintaining, and challenging social and political authority.

The weight and circulation of republican ideas also cries out for research.[1] Republican ideas normally were marginalized by the political system, yet during times of crisis they could emerge with some force. During armed conflicts in Pernambuco and nearby captaincies and provinces in 1817, 1824, and 1848, some individuals openly called for a republic. This likely was in part a practical tactic that was used to challenge a monarchy unlikely to make significant concessions. The published rhetoric of the period was generally dismissive of republicanism, presenting it as dangerously radical and demonstrably a failure in Spanish America. Yet there was clearly an audience for republican, radical liberal agitators like Borges da Fonseca in Pernambuco and in the court, as sales of his newspapers and success in agitation in the army barracks demonstrate. Moreover, we know that in 1889 a republic would be declared. It seems improbable that republican perspectives were wholly inspired from new sources later in the century. In all likelihood, republican ideas survived beneath the level of formal institutions and sprang forth anew under different circumstances after 1870. Exploration of this topic might reveal much about the movement of political ideas more generally.

The focus of this book is not on the emergence of a national identity but on the more easily observable play of competing political projects and the construction of an effective state. In 1817 and 1824, movements in Pernambuco and surrounding captaincies and provinces that were in part secessionist efforts were defeated; and in 1845 in Rio Grande do Sul the last secessionist movement, the Farroupilha Revolt, came to an end. Yet what we can say about national identity is limited. In 1817 there were multiple identities that might draw communities together—for example, belonging to a *pátria* such as Pernambuco or being Portuguese. How strong various identities were among different social groups and how attachment to different communities changed over time are less clear. From the beginning, slaves were excluded from citizenship. After Brazil's political separation from Portugal, many viewed the Portuguese—even *adotivos*, Portuguese-born Brazilian citizens—with hostility. This sharp demarcation of outsiders, this negative identity, no doubt contributed to a sense of national identity. Yet the various means by which a strong, inclusive sense of national identity was formed are unclear, as is the point at which most inhabitants of Brazil came to see Brazilian national identity as fundamental to who they were.

Both Brazilian identity and the survival of Brazil itself were at play. Throwing off absolutism and Iberian rule and struggling to establish a new political system opened up unprecedented possibilities for broader political participation, both among the elite and among groups traditionally marginalized in governing institutions. The nature of such participation had unforeseen consequences. Without firmly established rules of the game, the ability to mobilize armed men was crucial. However, the outcome of such mobilization might be not inclusion, but implosion. Conflicts among the elite might be decided by force, but armed conflicts could easily escape elite control. Although what was probably the most dramatic example of this occurred in Pará, with the drawn-out strife of the Cabanagem leading to an immense death toll, Pernambuco was also the site of significant conflicts, including the Guerra dos Cabanos, in which a rural insurgency dragged on for three years.

The tenuous state presence in much of the country meant that the army would play the key role in suppressing serious armed challenges to social stability. Yet the army itself was a site of considerable struggle. An obvious example was the important role of the military in the imperial court in prompting Pedro I's abdication (not to mention the similar fate that awaited Pedro II some fifty-eight years later). The barracks revolts and officers' revolts in Pernambuco in 1831 also come to mind as examples, and they were typical of experiences elsewhere in Brazil. Although mainstream discourse commonly dismissed enlisted men's actions as mindless violence, the shouts of Setembrizada rebels in Pernambuco against presumed restorationist officers and corporal punishment are indicative of the rebels' purposefulness and political perspectives rather than simple "anarchic" violence.

Officers and enlisted men also played a role in some of the street actions of radical liberals. Although these were usually rather limited, the extreme cases, such as the Pedrosada in Pernambuco in 1823, provoked considerable consternation. For some, these events seemed to raise the dreaded prospect of a "race war" reminiscent of the Haitian Revolution. In hindsight, we can say that the Pedrosada appears to have been less a serious threat to the entire social order and more an extreme extension of conventional political conflict. Nonetheless, it raised sufficient fear that many *pardos* and blacks backed down from challenging public authorities, suggesting that such individuals had significant vested interests in the existing social order. These events raise questions for any simplistic reading of racial identity that might assume that most people of color were potential rebels or that only the elites were threatened by instability.

The armed movement in 1817 in Pernambuco and surrounding captaincies demonstrated the high value that the elite placed on regional autonomy. During the struggles that culminated in political separation from Portugal and throughout the 1820s, the elite in Pernambuco, as in many parts of the country that were distant from the court, maneuvered to protect their freedom of action. Yet a part of the elite—the wealthy, sugar-producing elite based south of Recife—soon realized the advantages of allying with Pedro's government in the court when confronted with provincial challengers. They relied on the imperial government to defeat the 1824 Confederation of the Equator, yet when secure in the province, they pressed for greater autonomy from the central government. The Pernambucan statesman Holanda Cavalcanti, for example, was prominent in the First Reign opposition to Pedro's expansive view of his role. In this, the southern elite of Pernambuco appear to have been at the extreme end of a continuum of regional elites who were allied with the emperor but were nonetheless willing to challenge intrusive imperial power under some conditions. This dynamic is closely related to the widespread phenomenon of the large numbers of the elite across Brazil who embraced the Regresso and the construction of a strong central state and thus acquiesced in the reduction of local and provincial autonomy in the face of the upheavals of the regency.

The Regresso centralization accelerated party formation and polarization at the local level. The newly interwoven local, provincial, and national institutions of the Regresso created a system in which the party in power in the court could empower its partisans across the entire country. With so much at stake, Liberal revolts erupted in São Paulo and Minas Gerais in 1842. In Pernambuco the response was even more dire. With Liberals in power in the mid- to late 1840s, Conservatives in Pernambuco forcibly resisted the police (or, as they would have put it, their partisan enemies wielding police authority). Polarization led to political "meetings" in which partisan speakers whipped up enthusiasm with denunciations of their political opponents. This resistance and radicalization is a sure indicator of the unusually high level of rancor and hostility in the political struggle in Pernambuco, a conflict that would lead in 1848 to the last of the great regional rebellions of the empire.

Although scholars have long examined "high politics," much work remains to be done for a broader understanding of the emergence of a party system. The experience in Pernambuco suggests that the parties were more than simple vehicles for seizing government spoils; they exhibited important differences in composition, ideology, and willingness to mobilize the middling and lower classes. In proposing a more nationalistic economic program, Liberals in Pernambuco embraced Lusophobia and proposed restrictions on Portuguese access to the domestic market. Liberals also consistently promoted the traditional issue of decentralization. Clearly, scholars must take political ideas seriously as they reconstruct the functioning of political parties in this period.

Lusophobia is only beginning to draw sustained attention from scholars. In many respects, what we have seen in Pernambuco can also be seen in other parts of Brazil. Enlisted army men were angry at Portuguese-born officers for poor treatment, and Brazilian-born officers resented the strong presence of *adotivos* who blocked their upward mobility. Economic resentments and racial tensions contributed to outbreaks in the streets in which the Portuguese became targets of popular hostility and violence. In both Pernambuco and the imperial court, political mobilization on the basis of Lusophobia led partisans to commit acts of violence, going further than party leaders could have imagined, perhaps partly in an effort to pressure party leaders for more decisive action. Such Lusophobic outbursts offer important glimpses of the values and norms of groups who turned violent when their "moral economy" was violated. The prevalence and political importance of anti-Portuguese sentiments in Pernambuco are clear; only by comparison with research elsewhere will we be able to determine if Pernambuco was unusual (for example, in the degree of political mobilization on the basis of such sentiments).

With the defeat of the Praieira Revolution, Brazil's imperial system was thoroughly consolidated. The government's strength was clear in its successful shutting down of the trans-Atlantic slave trade between 1850 and 1853, despite the damage this represented to various slaveholding interests. The Conciliação of 1853–56, in which moderate Liberal and Conservative statesmen worked together in bipartisan cabinets, perfectly showed that the era of ideological struggle over the nature of the state had ended. New challenges would emerge by 1868, and the foundations of the empire would be rocked again in the 1880s, when the empire would be overthrown in favor of a republic. But that is another story.

Notes

Introducton

1. Rodrigues, *Independencia*, 4:124.

2. On the Historical and Geographical Institute, see Wehling, *Origens do Instituto Histórico e Geográfico Brasileiro*; Sandes, *A invenção da nação*; and Schwarcz, *Spectacle of the Races*. Also see Holanda, "A Herança Colonial" and "A Interiorização da Metrópole."

3. Barman, *Brazil*, 25–30, 39–41. See p. 26 for the quotation and the map on p. 40 for an illustration of possible alternatives to a unified nation-state of Brazil. Also see Jancsó and Pimenta, "Peças de um mosaico." For Pernambuco, see Berbel, "Pátria."

4. Good entry points for this extensive literature are Hobsbawm, *Nations and Nationalism*, and Anthony D. Smith, "State-Making and Nation-Building."

5. Schultz, *Tropical*; Malerba, *A corte no exílio*; Maria Lyra, *A utopia do poderoso império*; Iara Lis Carvalho Souza, *Pátria*; Oliveira, *A astúcia liberal*; Renato Leite, *Republicanos e libertários*; and Lustosa, *Insultos impressos*.

6. Cohen, Brown, and Organski, "The Paradoxical Nature of Statemaking."

7. Among Charles Tilly's works, see especially *Contentious French*; *Coercion, Capital, and European States*; and the influential volume he edited, *The Formation of National States in Western Europe*. Similar assumptions operate in the distinction between despotic and infrastructural power in Michael Mann's theory of the modern state. Mann sees despotic power in the range of actions that the state elite are empowered to undertake without need for routine negotiations with civil society. Infrastructural power is conceptualized as the capacity to penetrate civil society and implement political decisions throughout the realm. Mann, "The Autonomous Power of the State" and *Sources of Social Power*.

8. See Nugent, "Building the States, Making the Nation" and chap. 1 of *Modernity* for discussions of what he terms an "oppositional model" of state-society relations. For examples of recent regional studies that deal with issues of center and periphery and incorporate the lower classes, see Bieber, *Power*, which examines the relationship between state centralization and municipal politics in the interior of Minas Gerais; Kraay, *Race*, which works both as a social history of the military in Bahia and

as a study of state building on the periphery; Fuente, *Children of Facundo*; Guardino, *Peasants*; and Walker, *Smoldering Ashes*.

9. In addition to chapter 8 of the standard work of José Murilo de Carvalho, *A construção*, see the more recent advances by Barman, *Brazil*, chap. 8; Bieber, *Power*, chaps. 3 and 7; Needell, "Provincial Origins" and "Party Formation."

10. Despite the recent renaissance in studies of nineteenth-century Brazil, there are still few works that systematically link provincial and national political concerns. In addition to Bieber, *Power*, see, for an earlier period, Marcus Carvalho, "Hegemony."

11. Barman, *Brazil*; José Murilo de Carvalho, *A construção* and *Teatro*; Costa, *Brazilian Empire*; Flory, *Judge and Jury*; Mattos, *O tempo saquarema*.

12. Balmori, Voss, and Wortman, *Notable Family*, 10, 23. For a later period in Brazil, see Lewin, *Politics and Parentela*, and Borges on family strategies in Bahia, in *Family in Bahia*, chap. 7. Also see Viana, *Populações meridionais*.

13. Emília Viotti da Costa, *Brazilian Empire*, 72; Prado Júnior, *Evolução política*, 81; and Richard Graham, *Patronage and Politics*, 4–5, 71–100.

14. For seminal work that explores the state's power to influence the discursive frameworks within which people conceptualize the world, see Joseph and Nugent, *Everyday Forms of State Formation*; and Mallon, *Peasant and Nation*. Also see Mallon, "Promise and Dilemma." Two key works that influenced these authors are Corrigan and Sayer, *The Great Arch*, and Anderson, *Imagined Communities*. On historiographical trends and the increasing emphasis on the cultural construction of meaning, see Stern, "Between Tragedy and Promise."

15. Marcus Carvalho goes furthest in showing connections over time; see "Hegemony." For recent work on events in 1817 and 1824, see Glacyra Leite, *Pernambuco 1817*; Mota, *Nordeste 1817*; Glacyra Leite, *Pernambuco 1824*; and Cabral de Mello, *A outra independência*. On the formation of the elites in this period, see Marcus Carvalho, "Cavalcantis." On collective identities, see Berbel, "Pátria," and Bernardes, "Pernambuco e o império." On the regency revolts, see Marcus Carvalho, "O encontro"; Andrade, *Guerra dos Cabanos*; Mosher, "Challenging Authority"; Luiz Sávio de Almeida, "Memorial biográphico"; and Lindoso, *A utopia armada*. On the Praieira Revolution, see Marcus Carvalho, "A guerra do moraes"; Marson, *O império*; Mosher, "Political Mobilization"; and Naro, "Brazil's 1848." On slavery in Pernambuco, see Marcus Carvalho, *Liberdade*.

1. Portuguese Empire in the Age of Revolution

1. Manuel Correia de Andrade, *Land*, chap. 2, and pp. 73 and 76; Marcus Carvalho, "Hegemony," 22; Eisenberg, *Sugar*, 36, 121–23; Naro, "Brazil's 1848," 11–12, 14–15n4.

2. Andrade, *Land*, 18, 224n16, 118; Marcus Carvalho, "Hegemony," 21; Koster, *Travels*, 98, 169–70.

3. On the approximate nature of measurements and boundaries, see Koster's observation that *sertanejos* speak of large leagues, small leagues, and nothing leagues,

all of varying and approximate size, although none smaller than four miles. Koster, *Travels*, 42.

4. Andrade, *Land*, 144–47, 157–59; Koster, *Travels*, 65, 69, 72.

5. Andrade, *Land*, 149–53.

6. Eisenberg, *Sugar*, 14–16.

7. Eisenberg, *Sugar*, 6–7, 126–27, 129–31; Naro, "Brazil's 1848," 18; T. Lynn Smith, *Brazil*, 257–82.

8. Pang, *In Pursuit*, 78–80. For basic biographical information on prominent Pernambucans, see Francisco Augusto Pereira da Costa, *Dicionário*.

9. Eisenberg, *Sugar*, 34–36; p. 146 cites averages of fifty-five, twenty, and seventy slaves from surveys in 1842, 1854, and 1857. The second figure, being so far out of line with the others, seems questionable. Koster, *Travels*, 161–63.

10. Eisenberg, *Sugar*, 37–39; on being slower to adopt innovation than counterparts elsewhere, see 41–48; for publications on sugar in various other provinces, see xiiin2. Koster, *Travels*, 164–66. The classic work on sugar is Deerr, *History of Sugar*. For colonial Brazil, see Schwartz, *Sugar Plantations*. For comparison, Moreno Fraginals, *Sugarmill*; Galloway, *Sugar Cane Industry*; and Mintz, *Sweetness*.

11. On *jangadas*, see Koster, *Travels*, and Tollenare, *Notas*, 17–18.

12. Maria Dundas Graham, *Journal*, 99.

13. Eisenberg, *Sugar*, 50–52; Koster, *Travels*, 28.

14. Tollenare, *Notas*, 20, including the second quotation. On the natural breakwater, see Maria Dundas Graham, *Journal*, 101.

15. On the canoe traffic, see Marcus Carvalho, *Liberdade*, 29–40. Koster, *Travels*, 6–7; Tollenare, *Notas*, 18–19, 21–23; Figueiredo, "O Recife," 179–92; and Kidder, *Brazil and the Brazilians*, 154–55.

16. Population estimates vary greatly. See Figueira de Mello, *Ensaio sobre a estatística*, 265–83, and statistical tables 5 and 6 in the appendixes. See Marcus Carvalho's *Liberdade*, chap. 2, for his reflections on the difficulties of using census data from this period. Also see Kraay's discussion of the problematic use of racial terminology in this period, in Kraay, *Race*, 20–23, 89.

17. Russell-Wood, "The gold cycle." Lima Júnior, *Historia*. Mansuy-Diniz Silva, "Imperial re-organization"; Maxwell, *Pombal* and chaps. 1–3 of *Conflicts*; and Russell-Wood, "Preconditions and Precipitants." On the expansion of agriculture, see Alden, "Late Colonial Brazil."

18. On the conspiracies, see chaps. 4–8 of Maxwell, *Conflicts*; Jancsó, *Na Bahia*; and Muniz Tavares, *História*. On rumors of conspiracy in Rio de Janeiro in 1793 and 1794, see Higgs, "Unbelief and Belief." On ideas, see Burns, "Intellectuals as Agents," which also treats the rumored conspiracy in Pernambuco. On this conspiracy, also see Neves, "A suposta conspiração," and DHI 10. Schwartz, "Formation of a Colonial Identity." On independence as a consequence of the rupture of the colonial pact with the emergence of industrial capitalism, see Novais, *Brasil e Portugal*, and Emília Viotti da Costa, "Political Emancipation." The key chapter of Novais's

work is available in English translation in Richard Graham, *Brazil and the World System*. For a reconsideration of these issues, see Alexandre, *Os sentidos*, and the debate in Pedreira, "From Growth to Collapse," and Arruda, "Decadence or Crisis." For a brief statement critical of Novais and Emília Viotti da Costa, see Barman, *Brazil*, 38–39. On the notion of an age of revolution, see especially Palmer, *Age of the Democratic Revolution*; Godechot, *France and the Atlantic Revolution*; and, more recently, Langley, *The Americas*.

19. Schultz, *Tropical*; Malerba, *A corte no exílio*. The classic study is Oliveira Lima, *Dom João VI*.

20. Emília Viotti da Costa, "The Political Emancipation," 52–57; Glacyra Leite, *Pernambuco 1817*, 60–62, 81–82; and Mota, *Nordeste 1817*, 22–23.

21. On the construction of the royal court, see chap. 4 of Schultz, *Tropical*. For a detailed discussion of the increased tax burden on Pernambuco and Caetano Pinto's concerns, see Glacyra Leite, *Pernambuco 1817*, 55, 92–93, 136–45. Also see Mota, *Nordeste 1817*, 20, 27. For broader discussions of taxation, see Wilma Peres Costa, "Do domínio 'a nação"; and Maria Lyra, "Centralisation."

22. Muniz Tavares, *História*, 30–31, and annotation 10 on p. 252–56 (hereafter annotations appear in the format 252n10); Emília Viotti da Costa, "The Political Emancipation," 58–61; Mota, *Nordeste 1817*, 31–32; Prado Júnior, *Colonial Background*, 437–39. For the impact of enlightened ideas and French thought on conspirators in Minas Gerais and Bahia, see Freire, *O diabo*, and Mattoso, *A presença francesa*. On the founder of the Seminary of Olinda, see Burns, "Role of Azeredo Coutinho."

23. Muniz Tavares, *História*, 36–37, 274–83n23, and 282–83n27; Barman, *Brazil*, 56–57; Bethell, "Independence," 20; Mota, *Nordeste 1817*, 19, 30, 34–35; Glacyra Leite, *Pernambuco 1817*, 194–97.

24. Muniz Tavares, *História*, 37, 274–83n23, and 282–83n27; Prado Júnior, *Colonial Background*, 431–37; Célia de Barros Barreto, "Ação das sociedades secretas"; Barman, *Brazil*, 57; Mota, *Nordeste 1817*, 29; Emília Viotti da Costa, "The Political Emancipation," 61–63.

25. For an accusation made after the 1817 revolt that Arruda Câmara came to Pernambuco to spread republican ideas, see *Documentos Históricos* vol. 104, doc. 80: p. 154, letter to Tomás Antônio de Vila Nova Portugal, April 30, 1818. (Hereafter, *Documentos Históricos* are cited as DH; volume, document, and page numbers will follow [e.g., DH104, 80:154].) For a report on masonry, following a long list of prisoners taken during the revolt, many of whom were cited as having attended meetings, see DH104, 83:167. Muniz Tavares, *História*, 37, 274–83n23, and 282–83n27. On the banquets, see Tollenare, *Notas*, 137. Mélo, *A maçonaria*; Célia de Barros Barreto, "Ação das Sociedades Secretas," 200–203. José Antônio Gonsalves de Melo has raised doubts about the existence of the Areópago Lodge and has speculated that the key evidence may even be apocryphal. See Andrade, *Brasil*, 89. For a rebuttal of the argument that Masonic clubs had long prepared for revolution, see the argument

that secrets are too hard to keep, in DH109, 7:77–78, Defesa de Manuel do Nascimento da Costa Monteiro.

26. Tollenare, *Notas*, 147–48, 150, 153, 156–57, 176.

27. Muniz Tavares, *História*, 37–39 (the order of the day is reprinted on p. 38); 137–39. Cabral de Mello, *Rubro veio*. On the Henriques, see Silva, "Negros."

28. For a summary of the revolt, see DH102, 1:5–14, letter from João Lopes Cardoso Machado, June 15, 1817; DH107, 88:201–4, 214, Testimony of José Carlos Mairink da Silva Ferrão; DH107, 22:60, trial records of Domingos Teotônio Jorge, José de Barros Lima, and Father Pedro de Souza Tenório, second witness. Muniz Tavares, *História*, 39–43 (quote, 43). Tollenare, *Notas*, 138–39. For a summary of Pedroso's career, see Silva, "Negros," 515–20. Among those whose arrests were ordered were several who would play prominent roles in the revolt: the civilians Domingos José Martins, Father João Ribeiro, Antônio Gonçalves da Cruz, and artillery officers Domingos Teotônio Jorge and Pedro da Silva Pedroso.

29. DH107, 88:204, Testimony of José Carlos Mairink da Silva Ferrão. DH102, 1:5–14, letter from João Lopes Cardoso Machado. Muniz Tavares, *História*, 44–48, and 289–91n33. Tollenare, *Notas*, 139–41, 163. DH101, 30:38, letter from Luis Malheiro de Melo.

30. Consul Joseph Ray to Secretary of State John Quincy Adams, July 20, 1817, Dispatches from the U.S. Consuls in Pernambuco, 1817–1906, T-344, roll 1. DH107, 88:204–6, 215–16, Testimony of José Carlos Mairink da Silva Ferrão. Muniz Tavares, *História*, 50–54. Tollenare, *Notas*, 139–42.

31. DH107, 88:206–7, Testimony of José Carlos Mairink da Silva Ferrão. Muniz Tavares, *História*, 56–58; Tollenare, *Notas*, 145. DH109, 6:61, Defesa de Luís Francisco de Paula Cavalcanti. DH101, 30:38, letter from Luis Malheiro de Melo.

32. Muniz Tavares, *História*, 60–64, and 317–22n51. DH101, 89:128.

33. Muniz Tavares, *História*, 56. The first manifesto from the rebels, the "Preciso" by José Luiz de Mendonça, in DH105, 47:97–99. Tollenare, *Notas*, 146. DH103, 53:127, twentieth letter, letter to Tomás Antônio Vila Nova Portugal. The first five witnesses' testimony in DH102, 78:182–86. DH101, 25:34, Proclamation, March 18, 1817. DH102, 1:8, letter from João Lopes Cardoso Machado. Berbel, "Pátria," 347–52; Bernardes, "Pernamubco e o imperio," 222–23, 228–33; Cabral de Mello, *A outra independência*, 40–41, 45–46, and *Rubro veio*, chap. 3; Iara Lis Carvalho Souza, *Pátria*, 70–73. DH103, 5:110. Conference papers published in Andrade and Fernandes, *O nordeste brasileiro*. DH101, 26:25, Proclamation, March 18, 1817. DH107, 88:218–19, Testimony of José Carlos Mayrink da Silva Ferrão.

34. The first two quotations are from proclamations reprinted in DH101, 6:15, and DH105, 47:97–100, Preciso. The fourth quotation is from Muniz Tavares, *História*, 32; on heavy taxation and the waste of revenue in the court, see p. 112. DH101, 30:38, letter from Luis Malheiro de Melo. DH107, 88:207, Testimony of José Carlos Mairink da Silva Ferrão, and pp. 67–69. For the third quotation, see Maria Dundas Graham,

Journal, 58. Tollenare, *Notas*, 142, 145. DHIOI, 5:13, Decreto reduzindo o imposto, Casa do Govêrno, March 9, 1817. Bernardes, "Pernamubco e o imperio," 228–30, especially the list of new taxes on 228–29. Maria Lyra, "Centralisation." On taxation prompting revolts, see Gabriel Ardant's incisive analysis of financial policy and state-making, in Ardant, "Financial Policy and Economic Infrastructure." Muniz Tavares, *História*, 113–15. Carreira, *As companhias pombalinas*, and José Ribeiro Júnior, *Colonização e monopólio*. DHIOI, 3:11–12, "Ordem do Govêrno Provisório," Casa do Govêrno Provisório, March 8, 1817.

35. Muniz Tavares, *História*, 65, and Oliveira Lima's annotations, 327–32nn54–57, in which he emphasizes the equivocal positions of some of these advisors, or at least the equivocal positions they emphasized when they were brought to trial. DHIOI, 55:68–69, letter from Antônio Carlos Ribeiro de Andrada Machado e Silva to Martim Francisco Ribeiro de Andrada.

36. Tollenare, *Notas*, 145. DHIOI, 4:12–13, Proclamação do Bispado de Olinda, March March 9, 1817, and DHIOI, 2:10–11, Proclamação do Govêrno do Bispado, Olinda, March 8, 1817. Muniz Tavares, *História*, 69–72. For a brief description of the religious festivities celebrating the new regime, see DHIO2, 1:9, letter from João Lopes Cardoso Machado. For a list of the forty-four priests charged with treason, see DHIO4, 34:50–65. For a statement justifying the revolt in religious terms, see the proclamation, signed by the General Vicar and Father João Ribeiro among others, see DHIOI, 17:25–27, Proclamation. For evidence that General Vicar Bernardo Luiz Ferriera Portugal intended to ask the king for a constitution, see DHIO4, 80:154, letter to Tomás Antônio de Vila Nova Portugal. DHIO3, 63:160–200. Barman, *Brazil*, 58; Gilberto Vilar de Carvalho, *A liderança do clero*.

37. Muniz Tavares, *História*, 60, and 316–17n50. For the first quotation, see Oliveira Lima's annotation, 316–17n50, in Muniz Tavares, *História*. For the second, see DHIOI, 1:9–10, Proclamação assinada pelos Governadores do Bispado de Pernambuco, March 8, 1817.

38. Muniz Tavares, *História*, 66, 75–83, 87–91, and 340–44nn71–72. Tollenare, *Notas*, 143, 145. DHIO9, 5:46–54. DHIO2, 1:8, letter from João Lopes Cardoso Machado. DHIOI, 14:22–23, 15:24, 22:30–32. DHIO2, 17:42, letter to the Count of Barca; also DHIO2, 59:146–47.

39. Consul Joseph Ray to Secretary of State John Quincy Admas, July 20, 1817, Dispatches from the U.S. Consuls in Pernambuco, 1817–1906, T-344, roll 1. DHIO7, 88:208, Testimony of José Carlos Mairink da Silva Ferrão. Muniz Tavares, *História*, 91–97 (the March 21 proclamation from the Count of Arcos is on pp. 94–95). Also in Muniz Tavares, *História*, see Oliveira Lima's annotations, 344–49nn73–77. And see DHIOI, 31:39–40. Pagano, *O conde dos Arcos*. On José Inácio de Abreu e Lima, see Oliveira Lima's note 80, in Muniz Tavares, *História*, 352–53; and Chacon, *Abreu e Lima*. Morel, *Cipriano*, 94–95. Kraay, *Race*, 48–49, 54, alludes to rumors of sympathy for the 1817 rebels in the military in Bahia.

40. DHIOI, 10:18, letter from Provisional Government of Pernambuco to the Pres-

ident of the United States, March 12, 1817. For a letter from Provisional Government of Pernambuco to Hípolito José da Costa, requesting his help in securing the support, or at least abstaining from supporting the Portuguese monarchy, see DH101, 11:19–20, March 12, 1817, and the attached letter to be forwarded to the British government, DH101, 12:20–21. On efforts to buy arms in the United States, see DH102, 77:181–82 and DH102, 1:9, letter from João Lopes Cardoso Machado. Muniz Tavares, *História*, 104–5, and 353–58n80, 366–68n88, and 358–59n83. Tollenare, *Notas*, 154. Kahler, "Relations between Brazil and the United States." Mourão, *Revolução de 1817*. See Barman's careful discussion of Hipólito José da Costa's views, in *Brazil*, 50–53, 60–61.

41. Muniz Tavares, *História*, 152–54, 156, 390n114, and 396–97n117. Tollenare, *Notas*, 145. DH101, 34:45–46, letter from Antônio Galdino Alves da Silva, on a landowner donating forty slaves to the war effort; DH101, 89:128, on Francisco de Paula Cavalcanti de Albuquerque (Suassuna) leading armed blacks in the streets; and DH101, 147:226, letter to the Counde de Arcos, on Domingo José Martins leading a large number of slaves. See DH101, 121:190, letter from Paulo Fernandes Viana on fear that freeing slaves might augment the patriot forces. See DH101, 53:66, letter from André Dias, on an individual appealing to slaves with a flag and shout of "Long Live Liberty."

42. DH104, 52:99–100, Proclamation, March 10, 1817. Muniz Tavares, *História*, 65–66, 116–19. Tollenare, *Notas*, 161, 177.

43. On Alagoas, DH101, 61:75–78, letter from Antônio David e Souza Coutinho, March 31, 1817; and DH107, 88:209, Testimony of José Carlos Mairink da Silva Ferrão. Muniz Tavares, *História*, 121–29, 139–40.

44. DH101, 31:39–42, Three Proclamations. DH107, 88: 209, Testimony of José Carlos Mairink da Silva Ferrão. On food shortages that resulted form the blockade, see DH102, 1:9–10, letter from João Lopes Cardoso Machado. Muniz Tavares, *História*, 123, 131–35, 149; Tollenare, *Notas*, 161–62, 164. DH101, 146:222–25, letter to José Maria Monteiro, Commander of the Frigate Pérola, May, 20, 1817.

45. Muniz Tavares, *História*, 135–38, 141–43. Tollenare, *Notas*, 162, 168. On Paraíba, DH101, 127:195–98, letter setting terms for surrender, May 6, 1817.

46. DH107 88:209, Testimony of José Carlos Mairink da Silva Ferrão. Muniz Tavares, *História*, 159–68.

47. DH101, 31:42, Published Notice, May, 29, 1817. Muniz Tavares, *História*, 169–77. Tollenare, *Notas*, 169.

48. Muniz Tavares, *História*, 180–83. Rodrigo Lobo's response is reprinted on pp. 182–83.

49. DH101, 149:228–29, letter to Tomás Antônio de Vila Nova Portugal, May 26, 1817. DH102, 1:11, letter from João Lopes Cardoso Machado. DH107, 74:177–78, letter from three officers of ships, and 88:210–11, 220, Testimony of José Carlos Mairink da Silva Ferrão. Muniz Tavares, *História*, 183–92. Domingos Teotônio's letter is on pp. 183–84. Also see Oliveira Lima's annotation, 393–94n116, in Mu-

niz Tavares, *História*. Tollenare, *Notas*, 173–75. DH109, 6:57, Defesa de Luís Francisco de Paula Cavalcanti.

50. Tollenare, *Notas*, 174–79 (quote, 176). Muniz Tavares, *História*, 194. DH102, 1:11, letter from João Lopes Cardoso Machado.

51. Tollenare, *Notas*, 176, 180–81. DH102, 1:12–13, letter from João Lopes Cardoso Machado. Muniz Tavares, *História*, 195, 393–94n116, and 418n126. The quote of Luiz do Rego is from Oliveira Lima, 418n126.

52. DH101, 158:255–57, letter from Joaquim Caetano Santos, June 13, 1817, Bahia. Muniz Tavares, *História*, 196–97, 199–202. Kraay, *Race*, 115, notes that the prisoners in Bahia would influence their supporters in constitutionalist clubs.

53. Consul Joseph Ray to Secretary of State John Quincy Admas, July 20, 1817, Dispatches from the U.S. Consuls in Pernambuco, 1817–1906, T-344, roll 1. Muniz Tavares, *História*, 205–8, and 400–416nn120–24. DH102, 22:77, Trial Records for Domingos Teotônio Jorge, José de Barros Lima, and Father Pedro de Sousa Tenório.

54. For a description of the ritual prior to executions, see DH102, 23:79–80; and Tollenare, *Notas*, 195–97. Readers may notice similarities to the processions Michel Foucault describes in his analysis of torture and execution in *Discipline and Punish*. See especially pp. 48–50. The spectacular torture of those cases is, of course, absent here. The logic of the processions and the public display of severed body parts seem analogous.

55. Muniz Tavares, *História*, 209–18, and 416–22n125 and nn128–30.

56. For a reference to Francisco Paes Barreto's "enormous crimes," along with an acknowledgement that he did turn himself in to the authorities, see DH101, 150:231, letter to the king.

57. DH104, 80:154, letter to Tomás Antônio de Vila Nova Portugal, April 30, 1818. DH104, 48:95–96, letter from Antônio Carlos Ribeiro Nadrada Machado e Silva, March 29, 1817. DH104, 12:16–23.

58. Recall Roderick Barman's important discussion of the concept of the *pátria* in *Brazil*, especially pp. 26–27.

59. DH105, 48:104, "Proclamation", March 7, 1817.

60. Tollenare, *Notas*, 142.

61. Luiz do Rego Barreto, *Memória*, 4–7 (quotes, 4 and 6). This work reveals repeated expressions of frustration with being labeled arbitrary and tyrannical; see, for example, pp. 23–24 and 35. For the last quotation, see DH103, 53:82, Luiz do Rego to Tomás Antônio Vila Nova Portugal, April 23, 1818. The U.S. Consul used this exact terminology, labeling the repression "arbitrary" and "sanguinary," and stating that the approach taken was that anyone who disagreed with Luiz do Rego Barreto should be "unrelentingly persecuted." Consul Joseph Ray to Secretary of State John Quincy Admas, October 15, 1817, Dispatches from the U.S. Consuls in Pernambuco, 1817–1906, T-344, roll 1. Barman, *Brazil*, 61–63; Bethell, "Independence," 176–77; see Bethell's evaluation of Tomás Antônio de Vilanova Portugal on p. 177. For another example of Luiz do Rego criticizing Bernardo Teixeira and the military

commission, see DH103, twelfth letter grouped under 53:112, letter to Tomás Antônio de Vila Nova Portugal, in which he wrote that the inquiry "is perhaps the most irregular that has ever been conducted," and that "some witnesses were mistreated and threatened for not testifying as the judge wanted."

2. Independence, Rebellion, and the Struggle over the State

1. Barman, *Brazil*, 64–65, 67–68; Márcia Regina Berbel, *A nação como artefato*, chap. 1; José Honório Rodrigues, *Independência*, 69–74; Iara Lis Carvalho Souza, *Pátria*, 78–83; Alexandre, *Os sentidos*, pt. 5, chap. 1.

2. Schultz, *Tropical*, chap. 7, and Iara Lis Carvalho Souza, *Pátria*, chaps. 2–4, especially pp. 94–106 on the events described. Barman, *Brazil*, 67–72 (quote, 72); Bethell, "Independence," 177–80; Kraay, *Race*, 108; Oliveira Lima, *O movimento*, 123–24; and Rodrigues, *Independência*, 169–70.

3. Luiz do Rego Barreto, *Memória*, 24–27, 33–34; Barman, *Brazil*, 63, 71; Manuel Emilio Gomes de Carvalho, *Os deputados*, 103–4; Oliveira Lima, *O movimento*, 123–24, 127–28; Mota, "O processo," 228–29; Rodrigues, *Independência*, 174–79. Marco Morel argues that Cipriano Barata was a conspirator in 1817, but the evidence is not convincing. See Morel, *Cipriano*, 95–97.

4. Luiz do Rego Barreto, *Memória*, 4–7, 22–23, 36–37 (quote, 33). Luiz do Rego's June 14, 1821, letter to the *juiz de fora* of Goiana, reproduced in Teobaldo Machado, *As insurreições*, 136–38. Oliveira Lima, *O movimento*, 124–26, 129; Quintas, "A agitação republicana," 224–25.

5. Luiz do Rego Barreto, *Memória*, 39–40; Maria Dundas Graham, *Journal*, 103; Oliveira Lima, *O Movimento*, 129; Francisco Augusto Pereira da Costa, *Anais pernambucanos*, 8:151–56; Quintas, "A agitação republicana," 225.

6. Luiz do Rego Barreto, *Memória*, 42–51; Maria Dundas Graham, *Journal*, 104. See Marcus Carvalho, "Hegemony," 35, on the support of the northern planters; Oliveira Lima, *O movimento*, 129–30; Teobaldo Machado, *As insurreições*, 134, 138. Antônio Joaquim de Melo, *Biografia*, 28; for Gervásio Pires's proclamation to reassure European merchants, 28–30.

7. Luiz do Rego Barreto, *Memória*, 53, 56, 58, 67; Consul James H. Bennett to Secretary of State John Quincy Admas, Sept. 15, 1821, T-344, roll 1; Oliveira Lima, *O movimento*, 130–33; Marcus Carvalho, "Hegemony," 35; Teobaldo Machado, *As insurreições*, 157–58.

8. Maria Dundas Graham, *Journal*, 107–8, 112; Luiz do Rego Barreto, *Memória*, 58–62, 69–70, 72; Oliveira Lima, *O movimento*, 130–34, 136–37; Teobaldo Machado, *As insurreições*, 159–64.

9. Luiz do Rego Barreto, *Memória*, 76–78; Consul James H. Bennett to Secretary of State John Quincy Adams, Nov. 4, 1821, Dispatches from the U.S. Consuls in Pernambuco, 1817–1906, T-344, roll 1. Antônio Joaquim de Melo, *Biografia*, 30, 37–52; for the junta's document explaining its refusal to allow the soldiers to dis-

embark, 43–52. Oliveira Lima, *O movimento*, 137–40; Teobaldo Machado, *As insurreições*, 164–65. For Maria Graham's quotation, see *Journal*, 131.

10. Marcus Carvalho's pioneering work, "Hegemony," incisively identifies this split among the elites as a key to understanding politics in Pernambuco in this period. See chap. 1, especially pp. 32–35, 56–61, 72–73. Also see Marcus Carvalho, "Cavalcantis." On the cotton boom of the late eighteenth century, see Alden, "Late Colonial Brazil," especially pp. 318–22.

11. Barman, *Brazil*, 26–27, 66–71; Bethell, "Independence," 178, 180; Manuel Carvalho, *Os deputados*; Rodrigues, *Independência*, 183–84; Macaulay, *Dom Pedro*, 128; Iara Lis Carvalho Souza, *Pátria*, 112–15. For Pernambuco, see Marcus Carvalho, "Cavalcantis," 333–34, 345–46, 359.

12. Barman, *Brazil*, 69, 71–72, 76, 81–84; Bethell, "Independence," 179–83; Dias, "A interiorização"; Florentino, *Em costas negras*; Fragoso, *Homens*; Lenharo, *As tropas da moderação*; Oliveira, *A astúcia*, chap. 2; Rodrigues, *Independência*, 188, 202–11; Iara Lis Carvalho Souza, *Pátria*, 44–50, 134–35.

13. Barman, *Brazil*, 85–87, 91, 93; Bethell, "Independence," 183–84; Marcus Carvalho, "Cavalcantis," 333–34; Rodrigues, *Independência*, 214–18; "José Bonifácio de Andrada e Silva: A Brazilian Founding Father," chap. 2 of Emilia Viotti da Costa, *Brazilian Empire*.

14. Barman, *Brazil*, 74, 93; Marcus Carvalho, "Hegemony," 37; Marcus Carvalho, "Cavalcantis," 333–34; Oliveira Lima, *O movimento*, 286–90.

15. Oliveira Lima, *O movimento*, 286–92. The church's representative on the junta is quoted by Oliveria Lima on p. 290. Barman, *Brazil*, 88. Iara Lis Carvalho Souza, *Pátria*, 143–50.

16. Barman, *Brazil*, 93; Marcus Carvalho, "Hegemony," 38–40; Oliveira Lima, *O movimento*, 286, 288–89, 291–93. Iara Lis Carvalho Souza, *Pátria*, 119.

17. Barman, *Brazil*, 93–94. Rodrigues, *Independência*, 234–38.

18. Barman, *Brazil*, 96, 104–7; Bethell, "Independence," 184–89; Oliveira Lima, *O movimento*, 294, 397. Rodrigues, *Independência*, 249–51 (quote, 250–51); on the reliability of the account of Pedro's dramatic gesture, see 295–96n172.

19. In Ouvidoria Geral do Crime de Pernambuco, "A Sedição," the testimony of nearly all thirty witnesses indicates Pedroso's support among blacks and mulattoes. Anonymous, "A Pedrosada: 1823," 578–79; this anonymous account of the revolt was signed "Seu Amigo da Coração" (Your Heart-felt Friend). A handwritten copy of the original, of which the published piece is a transcription, is available in the Instituto Arqueológico, Histórico, e Geográfico Pernambucano. Francisco Augusto Pereira da Costa, *Anais pernambucanos*, 8:403. Marcus Carvalho, "Hegemony," 41.

20. Most of the witnesses cited in Ouvidoria Geral do Crime de Pernambuco, "A Sedição," provide testimony on the events of the first day. See especially Taveira's own account (witness nine, pp. 418–22, and witness five, p. 408) in Ouvidoria Geral do Crime de Pernambudo, "A Sedição." Anonymous, "A Pedrosada: 1823," 579. Marcus Carvalho, "Hegemony," 42.

21. Ouvidoria Geral do Crime de Pernambuco, "A Sedição"; see especially witness two, p. 403, witness three, p. 405, witness five, pp. 408–9, witness eight, p. 417, witness nine, p. 420, witness ten, p. 423, and witness seventeen, p. 444. For shouts that they only wanted Pedroso as military governor, see witness eight, p. 417, and witness seventeen, p. 444; for Pedroso as the 'Father of the *Pátria*,' see witness nine, p. 420. Anonymous, "A Pedrosada: 1823," 579–81; Marcus Carvalho, "Hegemony," 42. On the uprising in the Brum Fort, see Ouvidoria Geral do Crime de Pernambuco, "A Sedição," witness one, p. 400, witness two, p. 403, and especially witnesses six and fourteen, p. 411 and p. 438.

22. Anonymous, "A Pedrosada: 1823," 578–79. This piece cites 162 arrests, while Marcus Carvalho, "Hegemony," 42, cites a source that claims 180 arrests. For the quotation that begins "The riff raff," see Anonymous, "A Pedrosada: 1823," 579. For the ditty,

> Marinheiros e caiados
> Todos devem se acabar,
> Porque só pardos e pretos
> O país hão de habitar

see Fernando Augusto Pereira da Costa, *Anais pernambucanos*, 9:63, and Correa, "Margem da revolução," 336. On these verses, see especially Marcus Carvalho, "Hegemony," 43–44. I have used Carvalho's translation. Witness three in Ouvidoria Geral do Crime de Pernambuco, "A Sedição," p. 406, alludes to the ditty. A majority of the witnesses cite the insulting use of the term *caiados*. See witness twelve on supporters of Pedroso being released from jail. On the arrests of Portuguese, see witness one, p. 401, witness seven, pp. 415–16, witness eight, p. 418, and witness thirteen, p. 436. On the insults to white women see witness two, p. 402, and for the quotation, witness six, p. 412. Recreating the scenes of Saint Domingue appears in much of the testimony; see witness one, p. 402, witness three, p. 406, witness four, p. 407, and witness six, p. 411.

23. Anonymous, "A Pedrosada: 1823," 582–84. Ouvidoria Geral do Crime de Pernambuco, "A Sedição," see especially witness seven, a member of the forces coming from Cabo, p. 414, as well as witness two, pp. 403–4, witness five, pp. 409–10, witness eight, p. 417, witness ten, p. 423, witness twelve, p. 431, and witness thirteen, p. 435. Francisco Augusto Pereira da Costa, *Anais pernambucanos*, 9:405–6. Marcus Carvalho, "Hegemony," 44.

24. On challenges to the racial order, both insults to whites and allusions to Saint Domingue and the possibility of a race war, see Ouvidoria Geral do Crime de Pernambuco, "A Sedição," n107. On the idea that the Portuguese government released Pedroso with the understanding that he would then pave the way for their reconquest of Pernambuco, see witness two, p. 402, witness seven, p. 416, witness eight, p. 428, witness eleven, p. 429, witness twelve, p. 433, and witness sixteen, p. 442, who

attempted to reconcile some of the contradictory evidence in arguing that Pedroso began with the intention of facilitating a Portuguese reconquest but switched to promoting a movement like that in Saint Domingue when he saw the effective mobilization of the Afro-Brazilian lower classes. On the movement as an effort to keep Captain Pedroso in power as the military governor, see witness six, p. 412, witness seven, p. 416, witness eight, p. 417, witness eight, p. 418, witness nine, p. 420, witness eleven, p. 429, witness thirteen, p. 437, and witness sixteen, p. 442.

25. Marcus Carvalho observes that Friar Caneca, a radical liberal priest who opposed the movement, noted that there was no looting or theft. See Marcus Carvalho, "Hegemony," 42.

26. On the involvement of Francisco de Paula Gomes dos Santos and Jozé Fernandes da Gama, see Ouvidoria Geral do Crime de Pernambuco, "A Sedição," witness five, p. 404, witness seven, p. 415, witness ten, p. 424, witness eleven, p. 428, witness twelve, p. 432, witness thirteen, p. 436, and witness sixteen, p. 442. Witness seventeen, p. 446, notes that *Desembargador* Bernardo José da Gama (a nephew of Jozé Fernandes (da) Gama) was a key leader in the plot and had been instrumental in having Pedroso selected as military governor.

27. For the relevant section of Taveira's testimony, see Ouvidoria Geral do Crime de Pernambuco, "A Sedição," witness nine, pp. 419–20. The witness cited who summed up the attitudes of the rebels was witness five, p. 410. Pedroso's comments were reported by Taveira, witness nine, p. 422.

28. I would like to acknowledge Jeffrey Needell for drawing my attention to this last point in a private communication.

29. Barman, *Brazil*, 97–98, 108; Faoro, *Os donos*, 1:282–85; Macaulay, *Dom Pedro*, 145.

30. On Pedro's 1831 abdication as the completion of independence, see "Comunicado," *Diário de Pernambuco* (Recife), Oct. 6, 1831, 860–61, especially, "If the independence of Brazil was a vain title . . . it became a reality on April 7 of the current year 1831."

31. Macaulay, *Dom Pedro*, 153–14, 243–44, and 333n56; Barman, *Brazil*, 110, 112 (quote), 115–16, 120, 135, 158.

32. *Falas do Trono: Desde o ano de 1823 até 1889* (São Paulo: Melhoramentos, 1977), 37.

33. Barman, *Brazil*, 109, 115–18; Macaulay, *Dom Pedro*, 128–29, 135, 146–47, 153–56; Faoro, *Os donos*, 1:283–84. On Lusophobia in the Constituent Assembly, see Barman, *Brazil*, 107–18, and Macaulay, *Dom Pedro*, 145–58.

34. Barman, *Brazil*, 119–22; Bethell and Carvalho, "1822–1850," 51. On events in Bahia, see Reis, *Slave Rebellion*, 24–25 (quote, 25); and Kraay, *Race*, 110.

35. "Têrmo de convocação desta Câmara pela Tropa e Povo desta Capital para o que o abaixo se declara," in Francisco Augusto Pereira da Costa, *Anais pernambucanos*, 8:471–73; Marcus Carvalho, "Hegemony," 48; Glacyra Leite, *Pernambuco 1824*, 94.

36. Marcus Carvalho, "Hegemony," 47–48; Glacyra Leite, *Pernambuco 1824*, 94–95; Lima Sobrinho, *Pernambuco*, 158–59. For a study of Barata, see Morel, *Cipriano*.

37. Pereira da Costa, *Anais pernambucanos*, 8:489–92; Marcus Carvalho, "Hegemony," 46, 49–50; Glacyra Leite, *Pernambuco 1824*, 96.

38. "Sessão extraordinária e Grande Conselho de 13 de dezembro de 1823," in Francisco Augusto Pereira da Costa, *Anais pernambucanos*, 8:323–24; also see the account by the Colonel José de Barros Falcão, reprinted in Lima Sobrinho, *Pernambuco*, 179–80. See also Lima Sobrinho, *Pernambuco*, 159–60; Marcus Carvalho, "Hegemony," 50; Glacyra Leite, *Pernambuco 1824*, 95.

39. "Habitantes de Pernambuco," proclamation by Manuel de Carvalho, in Francisco Augusto Pereira da Costa, *Anais pernambucanos*, 8:492–93; the letter to the emperor is printed in Fernando Augusto Pereira da Costa, *Anais pernambucanos*, vol. 9; the quotation is on p. 4. Barros Falcão's account in Lima Sobrinho, *Pernambuco*, 179–80. Francisco Augusto Pereira da Costa, *Anais pernambucanos*, 8:493–94; Marcus Carvalho, "Hegemony," 50–52; Glacyra Leite, *Pernambuco 1824*, 95–97; Lima Sobrinho, *Pernambuco*, 160–62. On the October 11 law, see Barman, *Brazil*, 110–12.

40. Lima Sobrinho, *Pernambuco*, 162–69; Glacyra Leite, *Pernambuco 1824*, 97–98; Francisco Augusto Pereira da Costa, *Anais pernambucanos*, 9:11–15.

41. Lima Sobrinho, *Pernambuco*, 171–72.

42. "Ofício do coronel José de Barros de Lacerda, comandante de armas dirigido à câmara municipal do Recife sôbre—o horroroso atentado do dia 20," in Francisco Augusto Pereira da Costa, *Anais pernambucanos*, 9:20; "Orden do dia de 22, assinada por Manuel Silvestre da Fonseca Silva, ajundante-de-ordens do commando das armas," in Francisco Augusto Pereira da Costa, *Anais pernambucanos*, 9:21–22. Also in Francisco Augusto Pereira da Costa, *Anais pernambucanos*, 9:18–20; Consul James H. Bennett to Secretary of State John Quincy Adams, April 3, 1824, Dispatches from the U.S. Consuls in Pernambuco, 1817–1906, T-344, roll 1; Lima Sobrinho, *Pernambuco*, 173–76; Glacyra Leite, *Pernambuco 1824*, 97–98.

43. "Proclamação do presidente Manuel de Carvalho, Palácio do Governo de Pernambuco, March 22," in Francisco Augusto Pereira da Costa, *Anais pernambucanos*, 9:22–23; see the letter from Dr. Tomás Xavier Garcia de Almeida to Manuel de Carvalho, in Francisco Augusto Pereira da Costa, *Anais pernambucanos*, 9:27–28. Also Francisco Augusto Pereira da Costa, *Anais pernambucanos*, 9:22, 23–25. Marcus Carvalho, "Hegemony," 55.

44. Glacyra Leite, *Pernambuco 1824*, 99; Lima Sobrinho, *Pernambuco*, 177–82; Francisco Augusto Pereira da Costa, *Anais pernambucanos*, 9:4–6.

45. "Instructions," PPE, Manuel de Carvalho Paes de Andrade, Recife, to Colonel and Governor of Fernando de Noronha, Luís de Moura Acióli, February 5, 1824, reprinted in Francisco Augusto Pereira da Costa, *Anais pernambucanos*, 9:8–9; on Manuel de Carvalho's measures that targeted the Portuguese, see Francisco Augusto Pereira da Costa, *Anais pernambucanos*, 9:28, and see pp. 40–41 for the proclamation in June; on the attacks on the Portuguese and the near uprising, see Francisco Au-

gusto Pereira da Costa, *Anais pernambucanos*, 9:41–43 and 59–92; Lima Sobrinho, *Pernambuco*, 173; and Glacyra Leite, *Pernambuco 1824*, 101–2.

46. Francisco Augusto Pereira da Costa, *Anais pernambucanos*, 9:46–47; for a fascinating account of the political atmosphere in the court, see the account by Bazilio Quaresma Torreão, one of the three Pernambucans who traveled there to explain the political situation to the emperor, reproduced on pages 33–39 (quote, 37). Lima Sobrinho, *Pernambuco*, 185–95; and Glacyra Leite, *Pernambuco 1824*, 100.

47. Barman, *Brazil*, 119–21 (quote, 120). Glacyra Leite, *Pernambuco 1824*, 100. Ferraz, *Liberaes & liberaes*, 80–98; and Maria Lyra, "Pátria."

48. Glacyra Leite, *Pernambuco 1824*, 100–101. Francisco Augusto Pereira da Costa, *Anais pernambucanos*, 9:126.

49. For the June 10 proclamation, Francisco Augusto Pereira da Costa, *Anais pernambucanos*, 9:51–53. Lima Sobrinho, *Pernambuco*, 195–98; the June 11 proclamation is on pp. 196–97, as well as in Francisco Augusto Pereira da Costa, *Anais pernambucanos*, 9:67–68. Barman, *Brazil*, 100, 127.

50. "Proclamation of the Confederation of the Equator," July, 2, 1824, President Manuel de Carvalho Paes de Andrade, and "Manifesto. Brasileiros," Manuel de Carvalho Paes de Andrade, in Francisco Augusto Pereira da Costa, *Anais pernambucanos*, 9:64–67. Brandão, *Pernambuco de outr'óra*, reproduces much documentation.

51. Barman, *Brazil*, 123. Francisco Augusto Pereira da Costa, *Anais pernambucanos*, 9:68, states that six provinces joined with Pernambuco in the Confederation of the Equator, adding Piauí, Maranhão, and Pará, but the author acknowledges that many writings only recognize the first three.

52. Glacyra Leite, *Pernambuco 1824*, 105–7, 109–16; Francisco Augusto Pereira da Costa, *Anais pernambucanos*, 9:71–73. Ceará selected nine representatives to the Great Council, including four priests and two military officers, who left for Pernambuco on September 3. The proposed Constituent Assembly never gathered. On the mission to the south, see Francisco Augusto Pereira da Costa, *Anais pernambucanos*, 9:77–80.

53. Glacyra Leite, *Pernambuco 1824*, 113–14, 116–23 (quote, 113). Francisco Augusto Pereira da Costa, *Anais pernambucanos*, 9:71–72, 91, 99.

54. Francisco Augusto Pereira da Costa, *Anais pernambucanos*, 9:99–102.

55. Glacyra Leite, *Pernambuco 1824*, 123. Francisco Augusto Pereira da Costa, *Anais pernambucanos*, 9:8–87.

56. Consul James H. Bennett to Secretary of State John Quincy Admas, Sept. 24, 1824, Dispatches from the U.S. Consuls in Pernambuco, 1817–1906, T-344, roll 1. Glacyra Leite, *Pernambuco 1824*, 91–96, 99–104, 109–12, 123–28. Friar Caneca wrote a detailed account of his experiences in fleeing with the troops to the north. See "Itinerário do Frei Caneca" in Ferraz, *Frei Caneca*.

57. "Proclamation of the Emperor to the troops, on the Manifesto proclaiming the Confederation of the Equator," in Francisco Augusto Pereira da Costa, *Anais pernambucanos*, 9:89–90 (quote, 89); the orders for the investigations and military com-

mission are reprinted on pp. 116–17. Much of Friar Caneca's journalistic production has been reprinted in Chacon and Neto, *O typhis Pernambucano*.

58. Francisco Augusto Pereira da Costa, *Anais pernambucanos*, 9:87–89. For the trial proceedings, see Ferraz, *Frei Caneca*. Glacyra Leite, *Pernambuco 1824*, 129–36, discusses Friar Caneca's trial. Monteiro, *História do império*, 154–56, 158, 160–61. Barman, *Brazil*, 122, notes the creation of martyrs.

59. Marcus Carvalho, "Hegemony," 65; and Glacyra Leite, *Pernambuco 1824*, 110. For the text of Manuel de Carvalho's announcement, see Brandão, *Pernambuco de outr'óra*, 215. The proclamation outlawed the slave trade to the port of Recife and stated that the final resolution of the issue will be determined by the Sovereign Constituent and Legislative Assembly.

60. Francisco Augusto Pereira da Costa, *Anais pernambucanos*, 9:127–28. The text that was sworn to is on p. 128.

61. On the key features of the constitution, see Barman, *Brazil*, 123–26. I have followed his presentation closely in this and the succeeding paragraph. Also see Faoro, *Os donos*, 1:289–92. Bueno, *Direito público*, is the standard work on the constitution. Also see two other nineteenth-century works: Soares de Souza, *Ensaio sôbre*; and Rodrigues de Sousa, *Analyse e commentario*. Richard Graham emphasizes the comparatively broad suffrage under the empire; see Richard Graham, *Patronage and Politics*.

62. Barman, *Brazil*, 124–26. I have drawn the quotations from the constitution from Barman, *Brazil*, 125. The notion of the "moderating power" (*o poder moderador*) was developed by the French jurist Benjamin Constant. See Fontana, *Political Writings of Benjamin Constant*, especially p. 184, from the chapter "The Nature of Royal Power in a Constitutional Monarchy" in *Principles of Politics Applicable to All Representative Governments*, where he develops the notion that "you need a power that can restore them [the executive, legislative, and judicial powers] to their proper place." Welch, *Liberty and Utility*, establishes the context for Constant. Also see Faoro, *Os donos*, 1:290–92. On the Council of State, see José Murilo de Carvalho, *Teatro*, 107–38; Garner, "In Pursuit of Order"; and Rodrigues, *O conselho*. On the Council of State, remember Frei Caneca's objection to it as an instrument of absolutism, pointing out that the men Pedro selected for it had all long served Portuguese absolutist monarchs.

63. Bethell, *Abolition*. Also see Barman, *Brazil*, 126–29, 141; Bethell and Carvalho, "1822–1850," 52–53.

64. Barman, *Brazil*, 141, 147; Bethell and Carvalho, "1822–1850," 52–53. The standard work on the ending of the trade is Bethell, *Abolition*.

65. Barman, *Brazil*, 141, 146–48.

66. On Pedro's involvement in Portuguese dynastic struggles, see Barman, *Brazil*, 131, 142–43, 148–49.

67. Barman, *Brazil*, 128, 130–31, 139–40, 146, 150–51. On the conflict, see Seckinger, *Brazilian Monarchy*. Marcus Carvalho, "Hegemony," 77, offers the figure of eight thousand deaths.

68. Barman, *Brazil*, 132–33, 140–41, 147–48; Marcus Carvalho, "Hegemony" 78; Kraay, *Race*, 153.

69. Barman, *Brazil*, 135–38, 141–44, 146–50, 152. The standard work on the judicial reforms is Flory, *Judge and Jury*. On the judicial reforms in Pernambuco, see Marcus Carvalho, "Hegemony," 75–77, 79, 91–94; for a discussion of the emperor selecting a Senate of reliable supporters, and examples from Pernambuco, see 148–50.

70. Barman, *Brazil*, 153, on radical liberals nationally; Marcus Carvalho, "Hegemony," 162–63. On Antônio Borges da Fonseca, see his own *Manifesto politico*. Ricci, *A atuação*, focuses on Borges da Fonseca's activism in the First Reign. Mário Márcio de Almeida Santos, *Um homem*. Gladys Ribeiro, *A liberade em construção*. Also see Vianna, "'O Repúblico'"; chap. 5 of Chacon, *História das ideias socialistas*.

71. Marcus Carvalho, "Hegemony," 70–72, 77–79, 83–86. Francisco Paes Barreto was later elevated to the Marquis of Recife; see Pang, *In Pursuit*, 77.

72. Marcus Carvalho, "Hegemony," 164–67. On the reemergence of the press nationally in this period, see Barman, *Brazil*, 152.

73. PPE to Military Governor, Feb. 3, 1829, APEJE/SM, OG 30, fol. 278; PPE to Commander of *Ordenanças* of Villa de Santo Antão, Feb. 5, 1829, APEJE/SM, OG 30, fol. 282r; *Circular* to Captain Majors of the *Ordenanças* of Recife and Olinda, Feb. 7, 1829, APEJE/SM, OG 30, fol. 286; PPE to Presidents of Alagôas, Parahiba, Rio Grande do Norte, and Ceará, Feb. 9, 1829, APEJE/SM, OG 30, fol. 291; PPE to MI, Recife, Feb. 12, 1829, APEJE/SM, CC 31, fol. 201. Marcus Carvalho, "Hegemony," 167–69. Sousa, *Bernardo*, 83, 85, 90.

74. Sousa, *Bernardo*, 83–93; for the quotation from Minister of Justice Lucio Soares Teixeira de Gouvea, see p. 85; for Vasconcellos's quote, see p. 90; for Feijo's quote, see p. 91. Marcus Carvalho, "Hegemony," 152–53; Ricci, *A atuação*, 107–10; José Honório Rodrigues, *O parlamento*, 64–65.

75. I am following Marcus Carvalho's excellent analysis of the logic of Holanda Cavalcanti's position. See "Hegemony," 148, 150–56.

76. Barman, *Brazil*, 154–56; Sousa, *Bernardo*, 78–82. In this special session, Vasconcelos also criticized the government for continued (and expensive) involvement in the dynastic struggles in Portugal; see p. 79.

77. Barman, *Brazil*, 156–58; Marcus Carvalho, "Hegemony," 174–75. See Barman on the increasing political mobilization of the period (actually this period and the following few years) in *Brazil*, 65–67. Chasteen, "Cabanos and Farrapos," 34–36, and Flory, *Judge and Jury*, 181–89, agree on the importance of the expansion of press activity. For Pernambuco, see Marcus Carvalho, "Hegemony," 177, 181, 184. See Sodré, *História da imprensa*, 130–38, on the press and the abdication, and 179–200, on the characteristics of the press in a slightly broader period.

78. Silverio Candido Faria, "Breve história dos felizes acontecimentos politicos no Rio de Janeiro nos dias 6 e 7 de abril de 1831," Biblioteca Nacional/Seção de Manuscritos (hereafter referred to as BN/SM) I:32, 6, 24, fol. 26–79; Barman, *Brazil*, 158–59; Bethell and Carvalho, "1822–1850," 56–58; Macaulay, *Dom Pedro*, 246–52, and Nabuco, *Estadista*, 23–32; Gladys Ribeiro, "As noites das garrafadas."

3. Liberal Reforms and the Resort to Arms

1. Nabuco, *Estadista*, 29–30.

2. On the disillusionment of the radicals, see Nabuco, *Estadista*, 27–28, and Ottoni, *Circular dedicada*, 19. Not all radical liberals sought a republic, but federalism was a universal position among them. Radical liberals, unlike most other politically active groups, often resorted to action in the streets. Their nativism was especially appealing to artisans. Antônio Borges da Fonseca was a leading *exaltado* in Pernambuco. On radical liberal publications, see Nascimento, *História da imprensa de Pernambuco*; Vianna, *Contribuição*; Sodré, *História da imprensa*.

3. Barman, *Brazil*, 160–62; Pereira de Castro, "A experiência republicana," 11–13.

4. Ottoni, *Circular dedicada*, 40–41, asserted that without fear of restoration, the key liberal reform, the Additional Act, would not have passed. Nabuco, *Estadista*, 31, and Barman, *Brazil*, 175–78, agree. Flory, *Judge and Jury*, 66, makes the same argument for the passage of the 1832 Criminal Procedure Code. Although the term *coluna* explicitly referred to members of the restorationist society Coluna do Trono e Altar (Column of the Throne and the Altar), by implication it could refer to restorationists (partisans of Pedro's return to the Brazilian throne) more broadly and even to the Portuguese in general.

5. For a comparative perspective and a small sample of the vast literature that deals with federalism, utilitarianism, and liberalism in Spanish America, see Adelman, *Republic of Capital*; Bushnell, *Santander Regime*; Chambers, *From Subjects to Citizens*; Chiaramonte, *Ciudades, Provincias, Estados*; Simon Collier, *Ideas and Politics*; Gootenberg, *Imaging Development*; Guardino, *Peasants*; Gudmundson and Lindos-Fuents, *Central America*; Hale, *Mexican Liberalism*; Halperín Donhi, *Sarmiento*; Love and Jacobsen, *Guiding the Invisible*; Mallon, *Peasant and Nation*; Peloso and Tenenbaum, *Liberals, Politics, and Power*; Shumway, *Invention of Argentina*; Thurner, *From Two Republics*; Walker, *Smoldering Ashes*.

6. On the judiciary in the colonial period, see Schwartz, *Sovereignty*, and Flory, *Judge and Jury*, 31–34.

7. Flory, *Judge and Jury*, 31–43, 49–63, 109–11.

8. For the classic account, see Sousa, *História de dois golpes*. Leal, *Do ato adicional*, 16–23. Also see Faoro, *Os donos*, 1:304–5; Barman, *Brazil*, 172–75.

9. Faoro, *Os donos*, 1:305–7; Flory, *Judge and Jury*, 33–34, on localism and the contrast to the Portuguese colonial system's attempts to isolate judges from local influences. On this latter subject, also see Schwartz, *Sovereignty*.

10. Minister of Justice, "Relatório apresentado á Assembleia Geral Legislativa," AN/SPE, 1840, 14; Minister of Justice, "Relatório apresentado á Assembleia Geral Legislativa," AN/SPE, 1838, 14–15; Flory, *Judge and Jury*, 49–68; Faoro, *Os donos*, 1:306–7.

11. Bethell and Carvalho, "1822–1850," 64; Faoro, *Os donos*, 1:306; Emilia Viotti da Costa, *Brazilian Empire*, 67.

12. Bethell and Carvalho, "1822–1850," 64; Flory, *Judge and Jury*, 112, 115–19; Faoro, *Os donos*, 1:306.

13. Castro, *A milicia cidadã*; Fernando Uricoechea, *Patrimonial Foundations*; Bieber, *Power*, 114–18; Holloway, *Policing*, especially 82–85; Kraay, *Race*, chap. 8; Meznar, "Ranks of the Poor," 337–40. For data on the military budget and criticism of its size, see McBeth, "Politicians," 166–74. In theory, the national guard were to replace the previous militia and the Corpos de Ordenanças, yet in practice in Pernambuco they all continued to exist for some time, resulting in confused, parallel hierarchies, a theme that Carvalho emphasizes. See Marcus "Hegemony," 216–19.

14. Ottoni, *Circular dedicada*, 40–41. Barman, *Brazil*, 175–78; Faoro, *Os donos*, 1:22–23; Nabuco, *Estadista*, 31.

15. Friar Caneca is cited in Faoro, *Os donos*, 1:305. See Article 98 of the constitution in Bueno, *Direto público*, 492.

16. Soares de Souza, *Estudos práticos*. Leal provides a detailed study of the Additional Act in "História Constitucional," part 1 of *Do ato adicional*, 23–40. Barman, *Brazil*, 177–78; Faoro, *Os donos*, 1:306–10; Flory, *Judge and Jury*, 90, 158–59; Needell, "Brasilien 1830–1889"; Torres, *A democracia coroada*, 435–40.

17. For the text of the Additional Act, see Bueno's classic commentary on the constitution, *Direito público*, 506–12, especially 507–9; or Torres, *A democracia coroada*, 497–501, especially 498–99. Barman, *Brazil*, 177–78. For the presidential speech on the opening of the Legislative Assembly, see *Diário de Pernambuco*, 51, April 6, 1835.

18. Flory has argued that since some of the powers granted to the provincial assemblies had previously been located not in the court but in municipalities, the Act was actually the first hesitant step away from decentralization; Flory, *Judge and Jury*, 158–59. Bieber has similarly argued that even the decentralizing reforms of the 1830s did not stop the longer-run trend toward the loss of municipal authority. "Although provinces gained autonomy with respect to the nation in the 1830s . . . municipal polities experienced a steady loss of political autonomy and self-determination with respect to both provincial and national governments"; Bieber, *Power*, 47–49 (quote, 47).

19. Flory, *Judge and Jury*, 17–30.

20. Silverio Candido Faria, "Breve noticia dos felizes acontecimentos políticos no Rio de Janeiro nos dias 6 e 7 de abril de 1831," bn/sm I:32, 6, 24, fol. 26–79; Macaulay, *Dom Pedro*, 250–51; Bethell and Carvalho, "1822–1850," 58–59.

21. bn/sm II:32, 44, 47, for the petition demanding dismissal of Portuguese-born officers and names of those to be dismissed.

22. "Acta da sessão extraordinaria do Conselho Geral do Governo de 6 de Maio de 1831, presidida pelo excelentisimo senhor. Presidente Joaquim José Pinheiro de Vasconcelos," in Francisco Augusto Pereira da Costa, *Anais pernambucanos*, 9:392; bn/sm II:32, 44, 47; Marcus Carvalho, "Hegemony," 192–94; Andrade, *Movimentos nativistas*, 54–60.

23. Kraay, "Reconsidering Recruitment"; Kraay, *Race*, chap. 3, 183–203; McBeth, "Politicians"; Richard Graham, *Patronage and Politics*, 27–31; Andrade, *Movimentos*

nativistas, 75–77. For a later period, but quite germane for issues of recruitment in this period as well, see Beattie, *Tribute of Blood*.

24. Andrade, *Movimentos nativistas*, 77. Official correspondence of the period is full of requests to pay back salaries; McBeth, "Politicians," 68, places salaries even lower, at sixty to seventy réis a day. "Correspondencia," signed Caheté, *Diário de Pernambuco*, October 4, 1831, 854–55; Mário Márcio de Almeida Santos, "A Setembrizada," 177.

25. *Diário de Pernambuco*, September 30, 1831. On corporal punishment, see "Narração official," 79, and McBeth, "Politicians" 71–75. On the slave curfew, see Marcus Carvalho, "Hegemony," 204–5. Holloway, *Policing*, 67, notes that whipping was reserved solely for slaves, chain gang prisoners, and soldiers. For the quotation from Cunha Mattos, see McBeth, "Politicians," 60. On the weakening of the distinction between soldiers and slaves in Bahia, see Kraay, *Race*, 75–76, 126, 129–30, 133, 204–6; and on efforts to reform the practice of corporal punishment, 203–12.

26. PPE to Minister of Empire, Recife, Sept. 20, 1831, BN/SM II:32, 34, 51, no. 1, fol. 1–6; CA to PPE, Recife, Sept. 20, 1831, printed in the *Diário de Pernambuco*, Sept. 23, 1831; Commander of the Thirteenth Battalion to CA, Sept. 23, 1831, printed in *Diário de Pernambuco*, Oct. 12, 1831; Captain in Charge (capitão mandante) of the Fourth Artillery Corps to CA, Sept. 22, 1831, printed in *Diário de Pernambuco*, Oct. 1, 1831, and Oct. 3, 1831; *Bússola da Liberdade* (Recife), Sept. 21, 1831, provides a narrative that follows closely the Sept. 20 report of the Commander of Arms to the President of the Province; "Narração official," 80, refers to "scum and slaves" joining in the looting.

27. Recall that members of the restorationist society Coluna do Trono e Altar (Column of the Throne and Altar) were referred to as colunas.

28. CA to PPE, Sept. 20, 1831, *Diário de Pernambuco*, Nov. 8, 1831.

29. Intendant of the Navy to PPE, Sept. 20, 1831, printed in *Diário de Pernambuco*, Sept. 28, 1831.

30. Intendant of the Navy to PPE, Sept. 20, 1831, printed in *Diário de Pernambuco*, Sept. 28, 1831; PPE to Minister of Empire, Recife, Sept. 20, 1831, BN/SM II:32, 34, 51, no. 1, fol. 1–6; Captain in Charge of the Fourth Artillery Corps to PPE, Sept. 22, 1831, printed in *Diário de Pernambuco*, Oct. 1, 1831, 845–48, and Oct. 3, 1831.

31. PPE to MI, Recife, Sept. 20, 1831, BN/SM II 32, 34, 51, no. 1, fols. 1–6; "Narração official," 80; *Olindense*, Sept. 20, 1831, lengthy excerpts of which appear in Vianna, *Contribuição*, 52.

32. Sociedade Patriótica Harmonizadora to PPE, Sept.22, 1831, printed in *Diário de Pernambuco*, Oct. 5, 1831. This organization, like the Sociedade Defensora da Liberdade e Independencia Nacional (Society in Defense of Liberty and National Independence) in other provinces, was an instrument of moderate liberals, opposed to both restorationism and radicalism, and supportive of constitutional legality as the surest means to maintain order. Such organizations doubtless helped coordinate

support for the moderate majority in the Chamber of Deputies and the cabinet associated with that majority, a cabinet led by Minister of Justice Feijó.

33. *Diário de Pernambuco*, Sept. 30, 1831. Similar criticisms, equating low-quality Brazilian soldiers with a propensity to rebel, were also made elsewhere. See McBeth, "Politicians," 76–78.

34. Octávio, "Setembrizada e Novembrada," 54, on troops from Ceará manning prisons in Recife. See the letter of Sept. 19, 1831, signed by 193 law students, offering to serve to help keep order, in *Diário de Pernambuco*, Sept. 26, 1831. Marcus Carvalho, "Hegemony," 213.

35. Edict from the Justice of the Peace of Santo Antônio, Oct. 1, 1831, printed in *Diário de Pernambuco*, Oct. 3, 1831; "Circular: Instruçoes para os Delegados do Bairro de S. Antônio do Recife," Oct. 1,1831, printed in *Diário de Pernambuco*.

36. Edict from the President of Pernambuco Oct. 3, 1831, printed in *Diário de Pernambuco*, Oct. 5, 1831.

37. *Diário de Pernambuco*, Sept. 26, 1831. For data on the military budget and criticism of its size, see McBeth, "Politicians," 166–74.

38. The U.S. Consul dissented from this view, reporting that the insurrection was premeditated but that its goals were unknown. Consul John Mansfield to Secretary of State, Oct. 2, 1831, Dispatches from the U.S. Consuls in Pernambuco, 1817–1906, T-344 roll 1.

39. PPE to MI, Recife, Sept. 20, 1831, BN/SM II:32, 34, 51, no. 1, fols. 1–6; Commander of Thirteenth Battalion to CA, Sept. 23, 1831, printed in *Diário de Pernambuco*, Oct. 12, 1831; "Narração official," 79; CA to PPE, Sept. 20, 1831.

40. Mário Márcio de Almeida Santos, "A Setembrizada," 170, 183.

41. "Olindense," Sept. 26, 1831 [published in Olinda], in Vianna, *Contribuição*, 52.

42. Commander of the Thirteenth Battalion to CA, Sept. 23, 1831, printed in *Diário de Pernambuco*, Oct. 12, 1831; PPE to MI, Sept.20, 1831 BN/SM II:32, 34, 51 no. 1, fols. 1–6; CA to PPE, Sept. 20, 1831, printed in *Diário de Pernambuco*, Sept. 23, 1831; Marcus Carvalho, "Hegemony," 205.

43. *Diário de Pernambuco*, Sept. 28, 1831. Also *Diário de Pernambuco*, Oct. 4, 1831, and Oct. 17, 1831, for similar charges.

44. BN/SM II:32 34, 51 no. 1, fols. 1–6, PPE to MI, Sept. 20, 1831. Also see the section on the shouts of the rebels, which contradicts the notion of the rebellion being the work of restorationists.

45. On this so-called color intrigue (*intriga de cores*), see correspondence critical of it in *Bússola da Liberdade*, Oct. 9, 1831; *Diário de Pernambuco*, Oct. 13, 1831, disputes the praise offered by the *Echo d'Olinda* of some of their partisans' roles in the repression. The *Bússola da Liberdade* complained on Sept. 21 that liberals did much to restore order, but that others tried to deny this.

46. This included the radical liberals. Note, for example, the editor of the *Bússola da Liberdade*, a radical liberal newspaper, volunteering to assist in putting down the

rebellion. See Coronel Comandante Militar de Olinda to Interim Director of Law Faculty, Sept. 17, 1831, and the Sept. 19 letter signed by 193 law students ensuring their continued willingness to help maintain order, printed in the *Diário de Pernambuco*, Sept. 26, 1831; Intendant of the Navy to PPE Sept. 20, 1831, printed in *Diário de Pernambuco*, Sept 28, 1831. Students continued to help man forts for some time afterward. In mid-October there were seventy students helping at the Brum and Buraco forts. Francisco Augusto Pereira da Costa, *Anais pernambucanos*, 9:432.

47. Abreu e Lima, a contemporary of the events, stated that three hundred rebels were killed, according to Francisco Augusto Pereira da Costa, *Anais pernambucanos*, 9:428. Presumably the figure comes from Abreu e Lima, *Synopsis*. See Marcus Carvalho, "Hegemony," 206.

48. Mário Márcio de Almeida Santos, "A Setembrizada," 185. This author gives the number killed as five hundred, citing Milton Mello, *A Setembrizada*; "Narração official," 80–81; "Bando," 81.

49. Captain of Fourth Artillery Corp to CA, *Diário de Pernambuco*, Oct. 1, 1831.

50. Marcus Carvalho, in "O encontro," makes a similar point, incisively arguing that these soldiers had a political vision, as a consequence, in part, of some of them having, for example, fought in the Rio de la Plata, participated in the actions in the court that led to Pedro's abdication, and seen and interacted with people in different parts of Brazil.

51. See chap. 2 of McBeth, "Politicians." See p. 30 for the figure of fifty-one Portuguese-born and forty-six Brazilian-born generals in 1831. Freitas, *Os guerrilheiros*, 79, also notes that at the time of the abdication, more than half of the brigadier generals and generals were Portuguese-born.

52. *Bússola da Liberdade*, Sept. 21, 1831. Another was "Death to the Commander of Arms and long live our liberty!" Thirteenth Battalion Commander to CA, *Diário de Pernambuco*, Sept. 23, 1831.

53. *Bússola da Liberdade*, Nov. 2, 1831, referred to Vasconcelos as "the hero of April 7 (whose only crime in this province was to join the Pernambucan liberals)." Andrade affirms that Vasconcelos was the first high-ranking officer to lead his troops to fraternize with civilians in the court demanding the resignation of the ministry, which culminated in Pedro's abdication. See Andrade, *Movimentos nativistas*, 65.

54. Andrade, *Movimentos nativistas*, 67–68.

55. *Bússola da liberdade*, Oct. 19, 1831.

56. *Diário de Pernambuco*, Oct. 4, 1831.

57. For a fuller development of Lusophobia, see chapter 7. below.

58. BN/SM II:32, 34, 4, "Representação da gente reunida em Cinco Pontas"; *Diário de Pernambuco*, Nov. 25, 1831.

59. Minister of War to the PPE, Oct. 20, 1831, informed the provincial president that the commander of arms was being dismissed for having allowed the Setembrizada, reprinted in *Diário de Pernambuco*, Nov. 4, 1831.

60. *Diário de Pernambuco*, Nov. 14, 1831; *Bússola da Liberdade*, Nov. 2, 1831.

61. *Diário de Pernambuco*, Nov. 5, 1831, for the petition.

62. The absence of a demand for the reinstatement of the commander of arms leaves a degree of ambiguity on the point. Marcus Carvalho, "Hegemony," 234, has argued for this link, asserting that those who signed the petition were the same people who staged the revolt.

63. See *Diário de Pernambuco*, Nov. 29, 1831, for the Nov. 16 message from the rebels to the provincial president.

64. "Olindense," Nov. 28, 1831, reprinted in Vianna, *Contribuição*, 59–61.

65. "Olindense," Nov. 28, 1831, in Vianna, *Contribuição*, 61.

66. *Diário de Pernambuco*, Dec. 7, 1831.

67. BN/SM II:32, 34, 4, no. 3, fol. 5–7.

68. For the quotation, see the president's Nov. 19 instructions to the commander of arms printed in the *Diário de Pernambuco*, Dec. 1, 1831. Also see the president's Nov. 16 instructions to the commander of arms and intendant of the Navy in *Diário de Pernambuco*, Nov. 29, 1831, and other similar instructions printed in the *Diário de Pernambuco*, Dec. 1, 1831.

69. Nov. 18, 1831, statement from the Federal Society Commission to the Provincial President, printed in *Diário de Pernambuco*, Dec. 1, 1831.

70. Andrade, *Movimentos nativistas*, 122–123.

71. "Olindense," Nov. 28, 1831, reprinted in Vianna, *Contribuição*, 64.

72. Marcus Carvalho, "Hegemony," 234–35.

73. Andrade, *Movimentos nativistas*, 124–25; Marcus Carvalho, "Hegemony," 235.

74. Justice of the Peace of Flores to PPE, Flores, Feb. 8, 1836, BN/SM II:33, 6, 41, and accompanying documents; Brito, "A Rebelião de Joaquim Pinto Madeira."

75. Andrade, *Guerra dos Cabanos*, 32–34; *Diário de Pernambuco*, April 28, 1832, and May 4, 1832. Note that a restorationist uprising also erupted in the court on April 14 in an effort to seize the capital. Barman links Minister of Justice Feijó's frustration over the failure to remove José Bonifácio, whom Feijó believed was implicated in the uprising, from his position as the young emperor's guardian with the resignation of the minister of justice and the rest of the cabinet and also with the subsequent attempted coup on July 30 in an effort to install a new constitution. See Barman, *Brazil*, 173–74.

76. Compare the names of men implicated in the Abrilada, "Relação dos cumplices na revolta apparecida nesta Provincia na noite de 14 do corrente," BN/SM II:33, 6, 33, with names of individuals whose dismissal was demanded in May of 1831, BN/SM II:32, 34, 47, and with a similar list prepared during the Novembrada, "Relação para fora da Provincia," BN/SM II:32, 34, 4 no. 3, fols. 6–7.

77. Marcus Carvalho, "Hegemony," 239–47; Freitas, *Os guerrilheiros*, 77–81.

78. Marcus Carvalho, "Hegemony," 238–39.

79. Andrade, *Guerra dos Cabanos*, 31–32.

80. PPE to President of Paraíba, April 15, 1832, in *Diário de Pernambuco*, April 26,

1832, 14–34; *Bússola da Liberdade,* April 14, 1832; CA to PPE, "Exposição dos acontecimentos, que tiverão lugar nesta Provincia nos dias 14, 15, e 16 d'Abril do corrente anno," April 17, 1832, in *Diário de Pernambuco,* April 26, 1434–36, and April 27, 1832, 1437–38; "Circular da Sociedade Patriótica Harmonizadora," May 6, 1832, in Francisco Augusto Pereira da Costa, *Anais pernambucanos,* 9:484–86; M. Lopes Machado, "O 14 de Abril," 55; Andrade, *Guerra dos Cabanos,* 34–35; Portella, "A Setembrisada," 429.

81. Portella, "A Setembrizada," 430; M. Lopes Machado, "O 14 de Abril," 57; Andrade, *Guerra dos Cabanos,* 35. Years later Coelho led the military forces that put down the Praieira Revolution.

82. Portella, "A Setembrizada," 430–31; M. Lopes Machado, "O 14 de Abril," 56–58; Andrade, *Guerra dos Cabanos,* 34–36; CA to PPE, April 17, 1832, in *Diário de Pernambuco,* April 26, 1832, 1434–36, and April 27, 1832, 1437–38; *Bússola da Liberdade,* April 19, 1832.

83. Portella, "A Setembrizada," 431–32; M. Lopes Machado, "O 14 de Abril," 58–59. Both sources note that cadavers were dragged to the cemetery of the convent. Machado gives sixty as the number of bodies brought there.

84. Note that Tôrres Galindo also was on the Novembrada rebels' list of people to be expelled from the province. "Relação para fora da Provincia," BN/SM II:32, 34, 4, no. 3, fols. 6–7. Marcus Carvalho, "Hegemony," 243–48; Andrade, *Guerra dos Cabanos,* 38–39. For a meticulously documented study of the Guerra dos Cabanos, see Luiz Sávio de Almeida, "Memorial biográphico."

85. Marcus Carvalho, "Hegemony," 249–51; Andrade, *Guerra dos Cabanos,* 51–55, 59.

86. Marcus Carvalho, "Hegemony," 261–64. Carvalho emphasizes the significance of clientelism in mobilizing the Indians of Jacuípe. Also see his "Os Índios de Pernambuco." On clientelism, patronage, and access to land, see Richard Graham, *Patronage and Politics,* 20–23; Freitas, *Os guerrilheiros,* 37–39. For a study of the war, focusing on the Indian communities in the south of the province, see Lindoso, *A utopia armada.*

87. Marcus Carvalho, "Hegemony," 262–70; Freitas, *Os guerrilheiros,* 94–95.

88. Vicente de Paula's raids with his armed bands in the 1830s and 1840s continued to preoccupy political leaders long after the Guerra dos Cabanos was over. In the 1840s various Conservative and Liberal leaders even attempted to attract him to their side in armed struggles.

89. Andrade, *Guerra dos Cabanos,* 63, 205–9; Freitas, *Os guerrilheiros,* 106–9, 116. The name was later changed to Restorationist Forces.

90. Nov. 16, 1833, proclamation by Vicente de Paula, reprinted in Francisco Augusto Pereira da Costa, *Anais pernambucanos,* 9:535–36; Freitas, *Os guerrilheiros,* 53–63; Andrade, *Guerra dos Cabanos,* 205–9. The rural poor making common cause with Conservatives was not unprecedented at this time in Latin America. On support for Rafael Carrera, see Woodward, *Rafael Carrera;* and Wortman, *Government and So-*

ciety, 261–68. For Venezuela, see Carrera Damas, *Boves*. For a later period in Brazil, see Cunha, *Os sertões*, and Levine, *Vale of Tears*.

91. Andrade, *Guerra dos Cabanos*, 211.

92. Quote from a Nov. 29, 1833, letter printed in *Diário de Pernambuco*, Jan. 12, 1834, reprinted in Andrade, *Guerra dos Cabanos*, 227–29; Andrade, *Guerra dos Cabanos*, 209–13.

93. Consul John Mansfield to Secretary of State Louis McLane, Feb. 7, 1834, Dispatches from the U.S. Consuls in Pernambuco, 1817–1906, T-344, roll 1. Consular Agent L. G. Ferreira to Secretary of State John Forsyth, Dec. 11, 1834, and Jan. 27, 1835, Dispatches from the U.S. Consuls in Pernambuco, 1817–1906, T-344, roll 1. Alfredo de Carvalho, "As carneiradas." The quotation from the speech of Antônio Carneiro Machado de Rios was printed in the *Diário de Pernambuco* on Jan. 27 and reproduced by Alfredo de Carvalho in 605–6n16.

94. Andrade, *Guerra dos Cabanos*, 127–54, 175–85; Freitas, *Os guerrilheiros*, 151–55.

95. Marcus Carvalho, "Hegemony," 265–66.

96. Barman, *Brazil*, 170, presents maps that locate the revolts; chap. 6 includes summaries of them; Bethell and Carvalho, "1822–1850," 68–75; Flory, "Race and Social Control"; Francisco Augusto Pereira de Castro, "A 'Experiencia,'" 14–19. On individual revolts, see Flores, *A revolução farroupilha*; Spalding, *A revolução farroupilha*; Reis, *Slave Rebellion*; Assunção, "Elite Politics"; Silveira, *Cabanagem*; Chiavento, *Cabanagem*; David Cleary, "'Lost Altogether'"; Paolo, *Cabanagem*; Kraay, "'As Terrifying'"; Kraay, *Race*, 141, 146–51, 181, 235–39, 256; Paulo César Souza, *Sabinada*; Janotti, *Balaiada*; Maria Januária Vilelea Santos, *Balaiada e a insurreição*.

4. Social Control and Construction of a Centralized State

1. Nabuco, *Estadista*, 33.

2. Provincial President of Pernambuco, "Relatório que á Assembleia Legislativa de Pernambuco," AN/SPE, 1839; see p. 15 on widespread use of arms. On institutional limitations in repressing crime in the interior of Minas Gerais, see Bieber, *Power*, 111–19.

3. Province of Pernambuco, *Falla*, 16, 21.

4. Minister of Justice, "Relatório apresentado á Assembleia Geral Legislativa," AN/SPE, 1838, 8.

5. Minister of Justice, "Relatório apresentado á Assembleia Geral Legislativa," AN/SPE, 1838, 10–12. The minister of justice lamented, "It is not possible, senhores, for the police, as it is currently organized, to carry out the important functions of this ministry" (11). On the police in the court, see Holloway, *Policing*, and Brandão, Mattos, and Carvalho, *A polícia*.

6. Provincial President of Pernambuco, "Relatório que á Assembleia Legislativa de Pernambuco," AN/SPE, 1843, 5.

7. Minister of Justice, "Relatório apresentado á Assembleia Geral Legislativa," AN/SPE, 1838, 11, and 1840, 22.

8. See Province of Pernambuco, *Falla,* 18–19, which contained a call for salaries under the earlier system; and ANRJ IJ¹322, PPE to MJ, Recife, April 8, 1843, for the suggestion that police commissioners and deputy police commissioners earn a salary to allow them to devote more time and vigor to their duties.

9. On the national guard, see Castro, *A milicia cidadã,* and Uricoechea, *Patrimonial Foundations.*

10. Province of Pernambuco, *Falla,* 21.

11. Minister of Justice, "Relatório apresentado á Assembleia Geral Legislativa," AN/SPE, 1841, 30; Province of Pernambuco, *Falla que,* 22. On Recife and Olinda, see Provincial President of Pernambuco, "Relatório que á Assembleia Legislativa de Pernambuco," AN/SPE, 1839, 20.

12. Minister of Justice, "Relatório apresentado á Assembleia Geral Legislativa," AN/SPE, 1841, 30.

13. Province of Pernambuco, *Falla,* 22; "Relatório que á Assembleia Legislativa de Pernambuco," AN/SPE, 1843, 5–6.

14. Province of Pernambuco, *Falla,* 22.

15. Minister of Justice, "Relatório apresentado á Assembleia Geral Legislativa," AN/SPE, 1841, 30–31.

16. Richard Graham, *Patronage and Politics,* 27–31.

17. Richard Graham, *Patronage and Politics,* 20–23.

18. Minister of Justice, "Relatório apresentado á Assembleia Geral Legislativa," AN/SPE, 1841, 26.

19. The minister clearly differentiated himself and his audience from this culture and people by referring to the contrast with "our littoral." Minister of Justice, "Relatório apresentado á Assembleia Geral Legislativa," AN/SPE, 1841, 19. Sarmiento advanced a similar argument for Argentina, although his argument is ambiguous about how much weight is assigned to the isolation of the interior and how much to the influence of what he saw as the backward civilization of Spain, symbolized by Córdoba, in explaining the barbarous backlands of Argentina. Domingo Faustino Sarmiento, *Facundo.* For consideration of coastal images of the Brazilian interior as retrograde, and reflections on the continuing vestigial impact such attitudes have had on historical research, see Bieber, *Power,* 7–9.

20. Minister of Justice, "Relatório apresentado á Assembleia Geral Legislativa," AN/SPE, 1841, 19.

21. Minister of Justice, "Relatório apresentado á Assembleia Geral Legislativa," AN/SPE, 1839, 15, Provincial President Francisco do Rego Barros expressed his frustration with "professional criminals" who worsened the effects of impunity. He suggested adopting a law similar to one passed in Maranhão in 1830 that punished property owners who allowed people without honest occupation to reside on their lands as *agregados* or for other specious reasons. This seems as unrealistic as the minister of justice's 1841 comments, given that the practice was so widespread.

22. Provincial President of Pernambuco, "Relatório que á Assembleia Legislativa

de Pernambuco," AN/SPE, 1839, 3–4. For a twentieth-century novel revolving around this incident, see José Lins do Rego, *Pedra Bonita*.

23. Minister of Justice, "Relatório apresentado á Assembleia Geral Legislativa," AN/SPE, 1841, 18–19, and 1843, 4.

24. Provincial President of Pernambuco, "Relatório que á Assembleia Legislativa de Pernambuco," AN/SPE, 1842, 4.

25. Provincial President of Pernambuco, "Relatório que á Assembleia Legislativa de Pernambuco," AN/SPE, 1842, 3–4; PPE to MJ, Recife, Feb. 12, 1842, and the appended letters, Prefeito of Recife to PPE, Feb. 5, 1842, and Juiz de Direito Primeira Vara do Crime to PPE, Feb. 11, 1842, AN/SPE, IJ¹322.

26. Provincial President of Pernambuco, "Relatório que á Assembleia Legislativa de Pernambuco," AN/SPE, 1843, 4–6; Minister of Justice, "Relatório apresentado á Assembleia Geral Legislativa," AN/SPE, 1843, 6. On Antônio Francisco's murder, see *Diário Novo*, Jan. 13, 1843 (including the reprinting of CP to PPE, Jan. 8, 1843, and First Police Commander to PPE, Jan. 8, 1843); also *Diário Novo*, Jan. 18, 1843, and Jan. 27, 1843. On the absolving of the police officials involved, see the various documents in PPE to MJ, May 10, 1843 and Oct. 27, 1843, AN/SPE, IJ¹322.

27. PPE to MJ, Recife, April 8, 1843, AN/SPE, IJ¹322.

28. PPE to MJ, July 11, 1843, AN/SPE, IJ¹322. Isabel was subsequently executed, and the slave José who assisted her was condemned to life in prison.

29. Minister of Justice, "Relatório apresentado á Assembleia Geral Legislativa," AN/SPE, 1838, 0–18, especially 12–13; Minister of Justice, "Relatório apresentado á Assembleia Geral Legislativa," AN/SPE, 1841, 18–30, especially 18–19. On the important roles of Vasconcelos and Paulino, as they were often called, see Needell, "Party Formation," and Barman, *Brazil*, chap. 7.

30. Minister of Justice, "Relatório apresentado á Assembleia Geral Legislativa," AN/SPE, 1841, 20, and 1838, 8. For a discussion of the idea of "elite impunity" in the interior of Minas Gerais, see Bieber, *Power*, 119–28.

31. Minister of Justice, "Relatório apresentado á Assembleia Geral Legislativa," AN/SPE, 1838, 10–18 (quote, 10–11), and 1840, 14.

32. Minister of Justice, "Relatório apresentado á Assembleia Geral Legislativa," AN/SPE, 1838, 15; Provincial President of Pernambuco, "Relatório que á Assembleia Legislativa de Pernambuco," AN/SPE, 1839, 14; Minister of Justice, "Relatório apresentado á Assembleia Geral Legislativa," AN/SPE, 1841, 22–23; PPE to MJ, June 10, 1843, and the appended CP to PPE, May 11, 1843, AN/SPE, IJ¹322.

33. Province of Pernambuco, *Falla*, 14.

34. PPE to MJ, April 8, 1843, AN/SPE, IJ¹322.

35. PPE to MJ, Feb. 12, 1842, and the appended Prefeito Interino to PPE, Feb. 5, 1842, AN/SPE, IJ¹322.

36. Minister of Justice, "Relatório apresentado á Assembleia Geral Legislativa," AN/SPE, 1843, 25.

37. Minister of Justice, "Relatório apresentado á Assembleia Geral Legislativa," AN/SPE, 1843, 6.

38. See any *falla* or *relatório* of the provincal president of Pernambuco to the provincial assembly in this period. Also see "Ouvidor da Comarca do Sertão to PPE," Aug. 22, 1831, reprinted in *Diário de Pernambuco*, Sept. 26, 1831. After the Setembrizada, prisoners were kept on ships in the harbor because the prisons were under repair. See PPE to MI, Sept. 20, 1831, BN/SM II:32, 34, 51, no. 1, fol. 1–6. In 1841 the minister of justice also asserted the need to build better prisons to reduce the likelihood of escape. Minister of Justice, "Relatório apresentado á Assembleia Geral Legislativa," AN/SPE, 1841, 24.

39. Flory, *Judge and Jury*, 134–39, 142–44, and especially Feijó's article in the *Aurora Fluminense* (Rio de Janeiro) on Jan. 26, 1835.

40. See the quotations from ministers of justice Vasconcelos, in 1838, and Paulino Soares de Sousa, in 1841, four paragraphs below; Flory, *Judge and Jury*, 144–48. As an example of this argument's durability, consider Oliveira Viana. This influential conservative thinker of the early twentieth century explicitly used the experience of the First Reign and regency as evidence for his reactionary critique of democracy in Brazil. He also made a parallel argument against the "liberal" restructuring of power in the old republic. See Viana, *Populações meridionais*. On Viana, see Needell, "History, Race, and the State," 1–30. Similar critiques of liberalism could also be found elsewhere in Latin America at this time. See, for example, Vallenilla Lanz, *Cesarismo democrático*.

41. For a detailed reconstruction and analysis of the emergence of this opposition group, see Needell, "Party Formation." Note that Needell dates its beginning at 1835, slightly earlier than is usual (1837) in the historiography. Also see Mattos, *O tempo saquarema*.

42. Nabuco, *Estadista*, 41. For an analysis of Vasconcelos's shift, see Leal, *Do ato adicional*, 77–82. José Murilo de Carvalho has noted the lack of documentation to prove the authenticity of this quotation, although he also judges that it is "one of the most famous, and certainly the best-written, professions of faith in the political history of Brazil," José Murilo de Carvalho, *Bernardo Pereira de Vasconcelos*, 9.

43. Leal, *Do ato adicional*, 72–76; Needell, "Party Formation," 274–75, 280–82, 298–99, 302, 304; Flory, *Judge and Jury*, 132. Barman, *Brazil*, 187, emphasizes the importance of failure against the *farrapos* and takes the split with Evaristo da Veiga, just before his death in May, as a sure sign of the near moribund state of the *moderados*.

44. Minister of Justice, "Relatório apresentado á Assembleia Geral Legislativa," AN/SPE, 1838, 12.

45. Minister of Justice, "Relatório apresentado á Assembleia Geral Legislativa," AN/SPE, 1841, 18–19.

46. Minister of Justice, "Relatório apresentado á Assembleia Geral Legislativa," AN/SPE, 1841, 18, and 1843, 18.

47. Minister of Justice, "Relatório apresentado á Assembleia Geral Legislativa," AN/SPE, 1843, 1.

48. For a revisionist interpretation of the Regresso, which emphasizes the conti-

nuity of provincial legislative powers in arguing that the institutional structure continued to be characterized by federalism, see Dolhnikoff, "Elites Regionais."

49. Bastos, *A Provincia*, 166–72, 181–83; Flory, *Judge and Jury*, 159–64, 171–77 (quote, 177).

50. See Bagehot, *English Constitution*. Bagehot saw an evolution from a time when the dignified and efficient elements were united in an absolute monarch to a period (Bagehot published his work in 1867) in which the efficient aspect of government was directed by the cabinet in parliament. In the Brazilian constitution the monarch possessed a significant portion of the efficient aspect of government.

51. Cited by Carvalho in *Teatro*, 16.

52. Barman, *Brazil*, 197, 202, 296n64; Vauthier, *Diário íntimo*, 646–47. On court ritual, see Schwarcz, *As barbas do imperador*; Maria Eurydice de Barros Ribeiro, *Os símbolos do poder*.

53. Needell, "Party Formation," especially 297–98, also 261–62, 286–87. Also see Needell, "Provincial Origins." Barman, *Brazil*, 196–97; Flory, *Judge and Jury*, 133. For a broad ranging, yet detailed, local study of *fluminense* coffee, see Stanley Stein's classic work, *Vassouras*. For more recent work, see Nancy Priscilla Naro, *A Slave's Place*.

54. Needell, "Party Formation," 268–71, 284, 288; Flory, *Judge and Jury*, 134; Barman, *Brazil*, 192.

55. Needell, "Party Formation," 289–94.

56. Nabuco, *Estadista*, 32.

5. Political Organization

1. Barman, *Brazil*, 189, 196, 224; Needell, "Party Formation," 304–5; also see Needell, "Provincial Origins," 133–34, 141, 144. For a contrasting view, a more inclusive understanding of what constitutes a party, see Morel, "Restaurar."

2. For the quotation, see Nabuco, *Estadista*, 37; Pang, *In Pursuit*, 76–80; Naro, "Brazil's 1848," 79. Nabuco's statement on diverse circles parallels a comment in a newspaper edited by the subject of the biography, his father, José Tomás Nabuco de Araújo. It was in response to denunciations of the Cavalcantis, whose target included a broader group of families allied with the Cavalcantis. Joaquim Nabuco was himself quite familiar with the Pernambucan elite. His mother was a niece of Francisco Paes Barreto (the Marquis of Recife and a leader of the 1817 bid for regional independence). See Nabuco, *Estadista*, 46–47. The Cavalcanti de Albuquerque brothers were cousins of Francisco do Rego Barros by virtue of marriage between a paternal aunt and the Baron of Boa Vista's father.

3. Recall from chapter 2 that Manuel de Carvalho had led the 1824 Confederation of the Equator, against which the Cavalcantis and their southern allies had struggled. Sentenced in absentia after the defeat, he went into exile, returning only after Pedro's abdication.

4. Barman, "Brazilians in France"; Safford, "Politics, Ideology, and Society." In

Argentina, for example, Sarmiento's depiction of New World barbarism is one in which retrograde Spanish influence, symbolized in Córdoba, is partly responsible. Sarmiento, *Facundo*.

5. *Diário de Pernambuco*, Feb. 21, 1840.

6. *Diário de Pernambuco*, Nov. 17, 1842. The same paper later explained that many of the ideas and phrases in one of its articles were derived from a recent article on events in France. *Diário de Pernambuco*, Jan. 5, 1843.

7. Nabuco, *Estadista*, 48.

8. Province of Pernambuco, *Falla que*, 48–50 (quote, 49). Guerra, *O conde*, 87–88, 91–93; Freyre, *Um engenheiro*, 291–93; Provincial President of Pernambuco, "Relatório que á Assembleia Legislativa de Pernambuco," AN/SPE, 1840, 12; Auler, *A companhia de operários*.

9. Provincial President of Pernambuco, "Relatório que á Assembleia Legislativa de Pernambuco," AN/SPE, 1841, 8–9; Freyre, *Um engenheiro*, 312–15.

10. Freyre, *Um engenheiro*, 285–90, 292. Under João VI (initially as the prince regent and then as king), the prefect of Rio de Janeiro, Paulo Fernandes Viana, had undertaken similar reforms. See Schultz, *Tropical*, chap. 4, especially 105–13. Also see Needell, *Tropical Belle Epoque*, 24–25.

11. Provincial President of Pernambuco, "Relatório que á Assembleia Legislativa de Pernambuco," AN/SPE, 1839, 36 (quote).

12. Provincial President of Pernambuco, "Relatório que á Assembleia Legislativa de Pernambuco," AN/SPE, 1839; Francisco Augusto Pereira da Costa, *Anais pernambucanos*, 10:173–75; Freyre, *Um engenheiro*, on the first meeting; Guerra, *O conde*, 78, 80, 82. Funding cuts under the Liberals delayed its opening until 1850. It was named after the heir to the Brazilian throne, Princess Isabel.

13. Province of Pernambuco, *Falla que*, 35.

14. Freyre, *Um engenheiro*, 307–10; Province of Pernambuco, 33–53; Provincial President of Pernambuco, "Relatório que á Assembleia Legislativa de Pernambuco," AN/SPE, 1839, 28–36; Provincial President of Pernambuco, "Relatório que á Assembleia Legislativa de Pernambuco," AN/SPE, 1840, 10–13; Provincial President of Pernambuco, "Relatório que á Assembleia Legislativa de Pernambuco," AN/SPE, 1841, 7–10; Provincial President of Pernambuco, "Relatório que á Assembleia Legislativa de Pernambuco," AN/SPE, 1842, 17–19; Provincial President of Pernambuco, "Relatório que á Assembleia Legislativa de Pernambuco," AN/SPE, 1843, 20–24; Provincial President of Pernambuco, "Relatório que á Assembleia Legislativa de Pernambuco," AN/SPE, 1844, 14–17. For roads, see all the presidential reports to the provincial assembly of the period, and Naro, "Brazil's 1848," 88–92; for iron bridges, see Province of Pernambuco, *Falla*, 41–42, and Provincial President of Pernambuco, "Relatório que á Assembleia Legislativa de Pernambuco," AN/SPE, 1841, 8. On the Caxangá suspension bridge, see Provincial President of Pernambuco, "Relatório que á Assembleia Legislativa de Pernambuco," AN/SPE, 1843, 21; and Guerra, *O conde*, 90–93.

15., "Prefácio," 330–31; Marson, *O império*, 191–92. Joaquim Nunes Machado

(1808–1848) and Urbano Sabino Pessoa de Melo (1811–1870) became parliamentary leaders of the Praia Party.

16. *Diário Novo*, Feb. 6, 1843.

17. Coronel Chefe da Legião to PPE, Jan. 15, 1840; Lieutenant Colonel of the Second Battalion to Chefe da Legião, Jan. 2, 1840; Major Comandante of the Cavalry Squadron to the Coronel Chefe, Jan. 9, 1840; Lieutenant of the First Company of the Cavalry Squadron to Chefe Coronel Jan. 4, 1840; all printed in *Diário de Pernambuco*, Jan. 17, 1841.

18. "Correspondencias," signed Henrique Pereira de Lucena, *Diário de Pernambuco*, Feb. 1, 1840.

19. *Diário de Pernambuco*, July 14, 1840.

20. PPE to MJ, Jan. 20, 1841, and five appended letters, AN/SPE, IJ^{1}322.

21. See *Diário de Pernambuco*, July 15, 1842, and July 30, 1840, alternately praising and criticizing the performance of Nogueira Paz in office.

22. Lopes Neto to Peretti, July 9, 1838, in Instituto Arqueológico, Histórico e Geográfico Pernambucano, "Notícia breve," 32.

23. Lopes Neto to Peretti, June 18, 1838, in Instituto Arqueológico, Histórico e Geográfico Pernambucano, "Notícia breve," 31.

24. Lopes Neto to Peretti, August 14, 1838, in Instituto Arqueológico, Histórico e Geográfico Pernambucano, "Notícia breve," 36.

25. Lopes Neto to Peretti, July, 9, 1838, and August 14, 1838, in Instituto Arqueológico, Histórico e Geográfico Pernambucano, "Notícia breve," 32 and 36.

26. Lopes Neto to Peretii, Feb. 29, 1839, in Instituto Arqueológico, Histórico e Geográfico Pernambucano, "Notícia breve," 46.

27. Herculano Alves da Silva to Peretti, May 11, 1839, in Instituto Arqueológico, Histórico e Geográfico Pernambucano, "Notícia breve," 78.

28. Joaquim Nabuco wrote that by 1844, Pedro was surpassing Rego Barros among Conservatives. Nabuco, *Estadista*, 76; Naro, "Brazil's 1848," 98, alludes to a split among the Conservatives in 1842, in part because of rivalry between Pedro Francisco and the Baron of Boa Vista.

29. For Camaragibe's comment, see Nabuco, *Estadista*, 102n.

30. Nabuco, *Estadista*, 102–3.

31. *Diário Novo* (Recife), Aug. 1, 1842.

32. *Diário Novo*, Jan. 13, 1843; CP to the PPE, Jan. 8, 1843, in *Diário Novo*, Jan. 18, 1843; First Commander to the PPE, Jan. 8, 1843, in *Diário Novo*, Jan. 27, 1843.

33. *Diário Novo*, Jan. 13, 1843.

34. *Diário Novo*, Jan. 13, 1843. "Os assassinatos em Pernambuco, e os homens do punhal e bacamarte," *Diário Novo*, Nov. 23, 1842, 1–3, lists four residents of Recife and thirteen of the interior.

35. *Diário Novo*, Nov. 23, 1842, 1–3; *Diário Novo*, Jan. 13, 1843; *Diário Novo*, Jan. 2, 1843.

36. *Diário Novo*, April 22, 1844, 2.

37. *Diário Novo*, April 22, 1844, 2. Note that, in speaking of of "your fellow party members" in other states, the critic is assuming a sufficient degree of homogeneity among those he is attacking.

38. *Diário Novo*, Oct. 27, 1842; *Diário Novo*, Oct. 31, 1842, reprinted from *Diário do Rio*; *Diário Novo*, Nov. 11, 1842; *Diário Novo*, Nov. 28, 1842; *Diário Novo*, Dec. 15, 1842.

39. *Diário Novo*, May 31, 1844.

40. *Diário Novo*, April 27, 1844; *Diário Novo*, May 11, 1844.

41. *Diário Novo*, March 3, 1843.

42. *Diário Novo*, Nov. 21, 1842.

43. Among many examples, see *Diário Novo*, Dec. 10, 1842, and *Diário Novo*, April 17, 1844.

44. *Diário Novo*, Nov. 22, 1842; *Diário Novo*, Dec. 10, 1842; *Diário Novo*, Dec. 20, 1842; *Diário Novo*, Jan. 5, 1843.

45. On isolation and lack of support for the provincial president, *Diário Novo*, Dec. 20, 1842.

46. *Diário Novo*, Jan. 3, 1843, develops the theme extensively.

47. Freyre, *Um engenheiro*, 323–24, citing *Sete de Setembro*, Nov. 18, 1845.

48. Freyre, *Um engenheiro*, 293–95; *Diário Novo*, Feb. 6, 1843, 1.

49. Freyre, *Um engenheiro*, 305. Freyre cites *Diário Novo*, Nov. 16, 1841.

50. For both quotes, *Diário Novo*, Dec. 25, 1842.

51. Freyre, *Um engenheiro*, 304, citing *Diário Novo*, Apr. 27, 1844.

52. "Communicado," *Diário Novo*, Dec. 25, 1842. 1.

53. *Diário Novo*, Jan. 9, 1843; *Diário Novo*, Dec. 19, 1842; *Diário Novo*, Dec. 25, 1842; on wrong priorities, see *Diário Novo*, Jan. 9, 1843.

54. *Diário Novo*, Jan. 9, 1843. For an attack on the fiscal policies of the Conservatives' allies at the national level, see *Diário Novo*, April 20, 1844.

55. Freyre, *Um engenheiro*, 298; *Diário Novo*, Jan. 9, 1843; *Diário Novo*, Dec. 25, 1842.

56. *Diário Novo*, Aug. 1, 1842.

57. *Diário Novo*, Sept. 12, 1842; *Diário Novo*, Dec. 10, 1842.

58. *Diário Novo*, Aug. 1, 1842.

59. Nabuco, *Estadista*, 49; Beiguelman, *Formação política*, 64–65. Beiguelman cites only Nabuco for this argument.

60. Lima Sobrinho, "Urbano Sabino Pessoa de Melo."

61. *Diário de Pernambuco*, March 14, 1842; *Diário Novo*, March 15, 1842; *Diário de Pernambuco*, March 17, 1842.

62. *Diário de Pernambuco*, April 1, 1842.

63. *Jornal do comercio* (Rio de Janeiro), May 8, 1840, reporting on the session of May 7.

64. Again, see Marcus Carvalho's careful discussion in "Hegemony," 148, 150–56.

6. The Centralized State and Political Polarization

1. Almeida, *O conselheiro*, 32–33 (quote 33), on the change of ministry. The emperor wrote marginalia in this celebrated contemporary biography, and his writings appeared in subsequent editions as footnotes. This quote is from one such note.

2. Almeida, *O conselheiro*, 32–33; Pereira de Castro, "Política e administração," 509–11, 517, 519–21; Vianna, *Da maioridade*, 13–14, 16–20; Nabuco, *Estadista*, 57; Beiguelman, *Formação política*, 65, 70–71. For the most comprehensive explanation of Aureliano's role, see chaps. 3 and 4 of Barman, *Citizen Emperor*. The significance of the emperor's role in politics continues to be disputed. Compare Richard Graham, *Patronage and Politics*, and Emilia Viotti da Costa, *Brazilian Empire*, who downplay his role, with Barman, *Brazil* and *Citizen Emperor*.

3. Pereira de Castro, "Política e administração," 522–23; Vianna, *Da maioridade*, 21; Nabuco, *Estadista* 75–76.

4. *Diário Novo*, May 7, 1844, reprinted from the *Pharol constitucional*.

5. *Diário Novo*, May 8, 1844, reprinted from *Pharol constitucional*.

6. Barman, *Brazil*, 220.

7. *Diário de Pernambuco*, March 7, 1844.

8. Nabuco, *Estadista*, 76.

9. *Diário Novo*, April 17, 1844; Barman, *Brazil*, 220.

10. *Diário Novo*, April 18, 1844, reprinted from *Pharol constitucional*; *Diário Novo*, May 4, 1844, reprinted from *O nacional*.

11. *Diário Novo*, April 30, 1844, reprinted from *O nacional*. Note that Liberals labeled the Conservative leadership "the oligarchy."

12. For charges of electoral abuse, *Diário Novo*, April 19, 1844; *Diário Novo*, April 20, 1844. On the alleged falsification of electoral documents in Igarassu, *Diário Novo*, May 13, 1844.

13. *Diário Novo*, April 27, 1844; *Diário Novo*, April 27, 1844.

14. *Diário Novo*, May 2, 1844; *Diário Novo*, May 4, 1844, rejoices in Ribeiro Roma's being absolved of all charges.

15. Pereira de Castro, "Política e administração," 523–524.

16. Nabuco, *Estadista*, 56–57.

17. Vianna, *Da maioridade*, 24.

18. Nabuco wrote that "where he went he carried with him political fortune." *Estadista*, 56.

19. The emperor's moderating power allowed him to dissolve the Chamber of Deputies and call for new elections at any time. As the emperor chose the individual who would select a cabinet, and as the advantages of incumbency always allowed the ruling party to prevail at the national level in general elections, the emperor's actions were decisive. See Bueno, *Direito público*, and Richard Graham, *Patronage and Politics*, 97.

20. Nabuco, *Estadista*, 56–57; Pereira de Castro, "Política e administração," 509–13, 517–22; Vianna, *Da maioridade*, 11–28.

21. Vianna, *Da maioridade*, 24, citing the Feb. 16, 1844, edition.

22. *Diário de Pernambuco*, March 25, 1844. The term used was *trinidade negrejão*.

23. Vianna, *Da maioridade*, 11, 13–28, 21–28; Pereira de Castro, "Política e administração," 517, 519–21, 523; Nabuco, *Estadista*, 56,75, 77; Beiguelman, *Formação política*, 70–71.

24. Pereira de Castro, "Política e administração," 523–24; Nabuco, *Estadista*, 75–77.

25. Beiguelman, *Formação política*, 64, 70 71; Nabuco, *Estadista*, 76.

26. *Diário Novo*, May 8, 1844. The article preceded Marcelino de Brito's June 6 arrival and informed of his coming appointment.

27. *Diário Novo*, May 23, 1844.

28. *Diário Novo*, June 7, 1844.

29. Marson, *O império*, 235.

30. "Justa apreciação do predominio do partido Praieiro," *Diário Novo*, May 6, 1847, 1–3. This document is a party history and statement of aims. The Conservative press published lengthy responses to this piece. These articles, written by Nabuco de Araújo (although the author was not specified at the time), were subsequently released in book form with a title that played on the Praieiros' original title, *Justa apreciação do predominio do Partido praiero ou historia da dominação do praia*. They are cited elsewhere in this work, with Nabuco de Araújo as the author. Marson, *O império*, 235, gives the figures of eight police commissioners and ten deputy commissioners replaced.

31. Marson, *O império*.

32. *Diário Novo*, Aug. 26, 1844, and Sept. 7, 1844.

33. Consul G. T. Snow to Secretary of State John C. Calhoun, Sept. 6, 1844, Dispatches from the U.S. Consuls in Pernambuco, 1817–1906, T-344, roll 3.

34. Richard Graham emphasizes that violence was a normal and essential part of elections. See *Patronage and Politics*, 102–7, 122–23, 134–35, 139–40. *Diário Novo*, Sept. 26, 1844. On the intimidation tactics by the justice of the peace, see Subdel. of Affogados to cp, Sept. 23, 1847, apeje/sm, pc-17, fol. 156.

35. *Diário de Pernambuco*, Sept. 10, 1844; *Diário de Pernambuco*, Sept. 12, 1844, 1–2; *Diário de Pernambuco*, Sept. 16, 1844.

36. The reader will recall the Guerra dos Cabanos, the restorationist peasant rebellion of the 1830s, as well as the term "Baronist" to refer to Conservative supporters of the Baron of Boa Vista. Thus, "cabano Baronist" invoked two associations to attack Manuel Joaquim.

37. *Diário de Pernambuco*, Sept. 10, 1844; *Diário de Pernambuco*, Sept. 12, 1844; *Diário de Pernambuco*, Sept. 17, 1844; *Diário Novo*, Sept. 19, 1844; *Diário Novo*, Sept. 30, 1844.

38. *Diário Novo*, Sept. 13, 1844.

39. *Diário Novo*, Sept. 16, 1844.

40. *Diário Novo*, Sept. 12, 1844, including p. 2, "Correspondencia," signed Joa-

quim Nunes Machado, and pp. 2–3, "Correspondencia," signed Francisco Carneiro Machado Rios; *Diário Novo*, Sept. 26, 1844; *Diário Novo*, Oct. 1, 1844.

41. Consul G. T. Snow to Secretary of State John C. Calhoun, Oct. 8, 1844, Dispatches from the U.S. Consuls in Pernambuco, 1817–1906, T-344 roll 3.

42. Nabuco, *Estadista*, 77, and Naro, "Brazil's 1848," 106.

43. *Lidador*, Aug. 6, 1845.

44. *Diário Novo*, Feb. 13, 1845, 2, cited by Naro, "Brazil's 1848," 106.

45. "Justa apreciação," *Diário Novo*, May 6, 1847, 1–3; Marson, *O império*, 247. She has followed Pereira de Castro's analysis, "Política e administração."

46. *Diário de Pernambuco*, Oct. 7, 1844.

47. Nabuco, *Estadista*, 77.

48. *Diário de Pernambuco*, June 5, 1845.

49. In September 1845 the *Lidador* published lists of all those dismissed, in a series of articles entitled "O lidador monstro." José Tomás Nabuco de Araújo, a leading Conservative politician and an editor of the *Lidador*, also published the list in *Justa apreciação*, 64–71.

50. Araújo, *Justa apreciação*, 71–73.

51. For the quotation, see Consul Snow to Commanding Officer of the U.S. Brig. of War Bainbridge, July 30, 1845, Dispatches from the U.S. Consuls in Pernambuco, 1817–1906, T-344, roll 3.

52. *Lidador*, July 9, 1845, 1–2.

53. *Lidador*, June 7, 1845.

54. *Lidador*, July 2, 1845. These charges were reprinted each day for several weeks. For a more extensive development of the charge that the Praieiros were hostile to the monarchy, see *Lidador*, July 9, 1845.

55. *Lidador*, June 9, 1845 (first quote); *Lidador*, June 7, 1845 (second quote). For the third quote, see the Consul G. T. Snow to Secretary of State James Buchanan, June 9, 1845, Dispatches from the U.S. Consuls in Pernambuco, 1817–1906, T-344, roll 3.

56. *Diário Novo*, June 5, 1845.

57. *Diário Novo*, July 11, 1845.

58. *Diário Novo*, Sept. 19, 1845, 2–3, offers a detailed rebuttal of the defense of Conservatives dismissed from office in "O *Lidador* Monstro."

59. *Diário Novo*, June 6, 1845.

60. See the discussion of police searches of plantations in Marcus Carvalho, "A guerra do moraes," 42–44.

61. Among the articles and testimony of the slaves, see "De bom a melhor," *Diário Novo*, Jan. 7, 1846; "Os salteadores em debanada em todas as comarcas da provincia e acastellados na freguezia do Cabo!" *Diário Novo*, Jan. 14, 1846; "Não merecia resposta; porém vá que seja," Jan. 27, 1846; "Não ha remedio; assim o querem, assim o tenhão," *Diário Novo*, Jan. 28, 1846; "A isso somos obrigados: queixme-se de si," *Diário Novo*, Jan. 30, 1846; "Estamos promptos, não recuamos," *Diário Novo*, Jan. 31, 1846.

62. Part of the purification process to produce sugar in a crystalline form was carried out in a "purging house." See chapter 1.

63. *Diário Novo*, Oct. 15, 1846.

64. *Diário Novo*, Sept. 28, 1846.

65. Richard Graham, *Patronage and Politics*, 22. Marson, *O império*, 258.

66. See Araújo, *Justa apreciação*, 42, for an example of his denunciation of the searches.

67. Araújo, *Justa apreciação*, 10.

68. Araújo, *Justa apreciação*, 10. Nabuco de Araújo's biographer, his son, Joaquim Nabuco, followed this line of argument when he wrote that "the Praieira invasion was a necessary imposition; afterwards would come a democratic reconstruction, or perhaps not; the essential point, of course, was the conquest of the interior by the law." Nabuco, *Estadista*, 85.

69. Nabuco, *Estadista*, 10.

70. *Diário Novo*, Sept. 28, 1846.

71. On the police, see Holloway, *Policing*. Richard Graham, *Patronage and Politics*, 122–45, on elections keeping the court in touch with the balance of power in far-flung communities.

72. Flory, *Judge and Jury*, chap. 10, especially 189–94; José Murilo de Carvalho, *A construção*. On marriage, see Flory, *Judge and Jury*, 193–94. On Nabuco de Araújo's marriage, see Nabuco, *Estadista*, 46–47.

73. On intimidation, violence, and fraud in elections, see Richard Graham, *Patronage and Politics*, chap. 5. The U.S. Consul cast doubt on charges of unusual election irregularities in the first Senate elections, reporting that they had "been conducted with the greatest order." Consul George Manouvier to Secretary of State James Buchanan, July 7, 1846, Dispatches from the U.S. Consuls in Pernambuco, 1817–1906, T-344, roll 3. Also see the May 14, 1846 correspondence. Mutual accusations were routine following elections. Praieiro police authorities, for example, charged that Conservatives had tried to disrupt voting at two polling places. At one church, they reportedly stole the ballot box and at another the justice of the peace arbitrarily tried to postpone the election. See Subdel. of First District of S. Amaro, Jaboatão to Police Chief, Sept. 25, 1847, APEJE/SM, PC-17, fol. 168, on the first incident and Subdel. of Escada to CP Sept., 22, 1847, APEJE/SM, PC-17, fol. 161, on the second.

74. Pereira de Castro, "Política e administração," 534–37 (quote, 537).

75. Vianna, *Da maioridade*, 27–28.

76. Both quotations are from Paulino José Soares de Sousa to Figueira de Mello, Nov. 29, 1846, BN/SM, Figueira de Mello Collection. Alencar was José Martiniano de Alencar (1798–1860), a Liberal senator from Ceará (and father of the celebrated author and politician of the same name).

77. *Lidador*, June 16, 1847.

78. Nabuco, *Estadista*, 79–81; Beiguelman, *Formação política*, 74–75; Marson, *O império*, 337. For the fullest explanation of Aureliano's role, see chaps. 3 and 4 of Barman, *Citizen Emperor*.

79. For Conservatives, the term "republican" was immensely pejorative.

80. *Lidador*, June 13, 1847 (first and third quotes); *Lidador*, June 16, 1847 (second quote).

81. *Diário Novo*, July 12, 1847, 2, reprinted from *Diário do Rio de Janeiro*.

82. "A corôa e a facção," *Diário Novo*, Aug. 4, 1847, reprinted from *Conservador* in Rio de Janeiro. Liberal papers ran a series of articles developing the theme under this title.

83. Nabuco, *Estadista*, 81–84.

84. Cited in Pereira de Castro, "Política e administração," 537. After the second annulment, Honório Hermeto Carneiro Leão even implied a willingness to use armed force to defend the Senate's prerogatives. On the viscount and future marquis of Olinda, see Cascudo, *O Marquez de Olinda*.

85. Beiguelman, *Formação política*, 75, offers this interpretation, based on a reading of Nabuco. See Nabuco, *Estadista*, 84–85.

86. CP to PPE, July 3, 1847, APEJE/SM, PC-17, fol. 3, and PPE to MJ, July 14, 1847, AN/SPE, IJ¹324. See Carvalho's meticulous study "A guerra do moraes," especially chap. 3, on the Conservatives' armed resistance of Praia police authorities.

87. PPE to MJ, March 23, 1847, AN/SPE, IJ¹324.

88. PPE to MI, Aug. 4, 1846, AN/SPE, IJJ⁹253, and the enclosed letters from Municipal Judge of Limoeiro to PPE, July 7, 1846, Del. of Limoeiro to CP, July 21, 1846, and the Subdel. of Limoeiro to the CP, July 7, 1846.

89. See PPE to the MJ, Dec. 30, 1846, AN/SPE, IJJ⁹324, and the enclosed document, Subdel. of Taquaratinga to CP, Dec. 27, 1846; see the list of recent crimes in CP to the PPE, Jan. 12, 1847. For more details on the Natuba estate and the complicity of local police officials who allowed gatherings of armed men there, see Subdel. of Freguesia of Taquaratinga to Del. of Limoeiro Aug. 5, 1847, APEJE/SM, PC-17, fol. 122, and Del. of Limoeiro to CP, Sept. 2, 1847, APEJE/SM, PC-17, fol. 125.

90. See CP to PPE, July 3, 1847, APEJE/SM, PC-17; Del. of Limoeiro to CP, Aug. 28, 1847, APEJE/SM, PC-17, fol. 121; Subdel. of Taquaratinga to Del. of Limoeiro, Aug. 5, 1847, APEJE/SM, PC-17; CP to PPE, Sept. 2, 1847, APEJE/SM, PC-17, fol. 124; Del. of Limoeiro to CP, Sept. 2, 1847, APEJE/SM, PC-17.

91. Del. of Victoria to CP, June 21, 1847, APEJE/SM, PC-17, fol. 73, and Subdel. of Uma to CP, July 16, 1847, APEJE/SM, PC-17, fol. 71. Del. of Água Preta to the CP, June 19, 1847, and Subdel. of Una to CP, June 19, 1847, both archived in the Casa da Cultura. In Feb. 1847 Francisco da Cunha Machado Pedroza had reported a Conservative gathering of ninety men at one estate and raised the possibility of an assassination attempt against himself, the subdelegado, or the vicar. He stated that if things did not improve soon, he (Francisco) would move with his family to Recife. See Francisco da Cunha Machado Pedroza to Subdel. of Una, Feb. 24, 1847, APEJE/SM, PC-18, fol. 14.

92. CP to PPE, July 3, 1847, APEJE/SM, PC-17, fol. 3; CP to PPE, July 14, 1847, APEJE/SM, fol. 26. Subdel. of the District of Capoeira to CP, (Reserved) May 28, 1847, APEJE/SM, PC-17, fol. 61; Subdel. of Bonito to Del. of Bonito, May 25, 1847, APEJE/SM, PC-

17, fol. 62; Subdel. of Panellas to Del. of Bonito, July 16, 1847, APEJE/SM, PC-17, fol. 67. See PPE to MJ, July 7, 1847, AN/SPE, and enclosed letter from Francisco Vasco de Araújo to PPE, which claim that the Baronistas paid Vicente fourteen *contos de réis*.

93. Del. of Agua Preta to CP, July 16, 1847, APEJE/SM, PC-17, fol. 70. The police commissioner did not specify what these government orders were.

94. CP to PPE, Nov. 5, 1847, APEJE/SM, PC-17, fol. 260 and the enclosed documents; Inspeitor de quarteirão to Subdel. Cabo, Nov. 2, 1847, APEJE/SM, PC-17, fol. 261; and Subdel. Cabo to CP, Nov. 22, 1847, APEJE/SM, PC-17, fol. 263; CP to PPE, Nov. 12, 1847, APEJE/SM, PC-17, fol. 270. For a summary of the events, see PPE to MJ, AN/SPE, IJ¹324, Nov. 12, 1847, as well as the CP to PPE correspondence of Nov. 27, 1847, that follows.

95. Del. of Flores to CP, Oct. 28, 1847, APEJE/SM, PC-17, fol. 275, and PPE to MJ, AN/SPE, IJ¹324, Nov. 12, 1847.

96. "Para os Exms. Srs. Vasconcelos e Hollanda Cavalcanti verem," *Diário Novo*, Oct. 6, 1847, reprinted from *Diário do Rio*. Marson, *O império*, 339–40.

97. Quintas, *O sentido social*, 25.

98. *Lidador*, Dec. 4, 1847, and similarly, *Lidador*, July 11, 1848.

99. See Richard Graham, *Patronage and Politics*, 154–55. Of course, the marshaling of supporters to vote, intimidate, and sometimes fight on election day, which Graham illustrates, was far from merely a gentlemen's game. It had little to do with campaigning, however.

7. Political Parties, Popular Mobilization, and the Portuguese

1. See Prado Júnior, *Evolução política*, 81. Likewise, Emília Viotti da Costa has written that "political struggle was really little else than a struggle for power between factions under the leadership of prestigious families." See *Brazilian Empire*, 72. Richard Graham believes that emphasizing struggles over ideology and policies is to misunderstand nineteenth-century politics; politicians were concerned, above all, with patronage. In its focus on patronage, he concludes, politics was, first and foremost, about reinforcing values that undergirded stability. See *Patronage and Politics*.

2. José Murilo de Carvalho has analyzed the composition of the political parties of the empire with data on the occupations and provinces represented by those who served as government ministers. The author himself, of course, suggested the limitations of his pioneering attempt to address the issue. Indeed, without a larger documentary base that explores the rank and file of the parties, his findings remain preliminary—unless one makes the problematic assumption that the parties' leadership accurately reflected the composition of the parties. See chapter 8 of his seminal work on state making in Brazil, *A construção*. Also see his appendix, "Algumas observações sobre fontes de dados biográficas," on data available for such studies. A recent exception to this generalization is Bieber, *Power*, which carefully analyzes the operation and meaning of political parties in three *municipios* of the interior of Minas Gerais during the empire. See especially chapters 3 and 7.

3. For works that address Lusophobia, see Bieber, "Postmodern Ethnographer" and *Power*; Marcus Carvalho, "O antilusitanismo"; John Charles Chasteen, "Cabanos and Farrapos"; Gladys Ribeiro, *A liberdade em construção*; Rowland, "Patriotismo"; and Seckinger, "Politics of Nativism."

4. I understand ideology as operating on two levels. First, in a formal sense, it is a well-developed and explicit understanding of the way the world is or ought to be. In the latter case it may entail a call to change it. Second, ideology can also operate unselfconsciously through assumptions about how the world is or should be. My use of the term in this work refers to the first level, that of a well-developed and explicit understanding of the way the world is or ought to be. For a brief statement on ideology, see Williams, *Keywords*, 153–57. For a fuller treatment by Williams, see *Marxism and Literature*, 55–71. On the multiple ways in which the concept has been used, see Eagleton, *Ideology: An Introduction* (London: Verso, 1991). Also see his anthology, Terry Eagleton, *Ideology*. Conversations with Jeffrey Needell have very much influenced my thinking on the topic.

5. The Lusophobic discourse of the period often conflated the two—Portuguese citizens and Portuguese-born individuals who had acquired Brazilian citizenship after independence (*adotivos*). There is inherently a degree of ambiguity, as complaints against *adotivos* were in part based on the notion that they had dual loyalties and exercised undue power in Brazil by virtue of advantages that Portuguese birth allowed them.

6. This is not to deny that for some there was no forgetting the seemingly sordid story of Portuguese offenses. Colonial restrictions had stifled the Brazilian colony; fabulous quantities of gold had been sent to Portugal with little benefit to Brazil; the Portuguese government acted unscrupulously, ridding itself, for example, of shiploads of prostitutes and criminals by sending them to Brazil. See the excerpts of *Memórias históricas de Pernambuco* published in *Voz do Brasil*, Feb. 19, Feb. 26, March 4, and March 11, 1848.

7. Reis, *Slave Rebellion*, 14.

8. The Portuguese domination of trans-Atlantic trade seems a given in the period and was not contested by Conservatives responding to anti-Portuguese arguments. Nonetheless, in the 1840s the Portuguese never comprised a majority of the import/export merchants listed in trade almanacs; there were typically as many British merchant houses listed as Portuguese. See Naro, "Brazil's 1848," 56, and Quintas, *O sentido social*, 24. Eugene Ridings notes that in Brazil generally the number of Portuguese merchants was greater than that of all other foreign merchants combined, although the same did not hold for the quantities and values of the goods they handled. See Ridings, *Business Interest Groups*, 33, 35, 80–81. On the British role in the trade, see chap. 3 of Richard Graham, *Britain*, and Manchester, *British Preeminence*.

9. Joaquim Nunes Machado in a speech in the Chamber of Deputies; see *Diário Novo*, July 17, 1848. Nunes Machado and similar speeches are discussed later in this chapter.

10. On Portuguese immigration and employment practices see Carvalho, "O antilusitanismo," 149–55, and Jorge Fernandes Alves, *Os brasileiros*, 61–65, 77–78.

11. Thomas Flory notes a Portuguese author's comments that "Brazil was a land of 'monkeys, Negroes, and snakes,' settled by people 'netted on the coast of Africa.'" See Flory, "Race and Social Control," 205–6. Hendrik Kraay has pointed out to me that the author was a Portuguese representative to the Lisbon Cortes. Also see Kraay's discussion of Lusophobia and racial antagonism in Salvador, Bahia, in *Race*, 113–14.

12. For a summary of the anti-Portuguese disturbances in various provinces following Pedro's abdication, see Bethell and Carvalho, "1822–1850," 56, 58–61; for a summary of the regency rebellions mentioned here, 68–70, 72–75. On Lusophobia in Bahia, see Reis, *Slave Rebellion*, 14, 18, 22–28, and Kraay, "'As Terrifying,'" especially 507–8, 519. On Minas Gerais, see Beiber, "Postmodern Ethnographer." On Mato Grosso, see Seckinger, "Politics of Nativism," especially 410–12. Chasteen, "Cabanos and Farrapos"; Chiavento, *Cabanagem*; Paolo, *Cabanagem*; Silveira, *Cabanagem*. Janotti, *Balaiada*; Maria Januária Vilelea Santos, *Balaiada e a insurreição*; for an account by a contemporary of the events, see Magalhães, "Memória histórica."

13. On the importance of the press in spreading nativistic discourse, see Chasteen, "Cabanos and Farrapos," 34–35.

14. "Prospecto," *A Voz do Brasil*, Oct. 27, 1847.

15. Nonetheless, hostility toward other foreigners for occupying jobs that Brazilians might otherwise hold also existed. In chapter 5 we saw complaints about German and French engineers, technicians, and artisans employed on public works projects.

16. Portuguese Consul in Pernambuco to Minister of State for Foreign Affairs, Recife, June 28, 1848, ANTT/NE, caixa 310, no. 2266, fol. 1.

17. *A Voz do Brasil*, Nov. 24, 1847. On Portuguese domination of commerce more generally, see *A Voz do Brasil*, Oct. 27, 1847.

18. *O Regenerador Brazileiro*, June 15, 1844. The figure of eighteen thousand jobs lost is from *Regenerador Brazileiro*, June 22, 1844.

19. For the quotation, *Sete de Setembro*, Oct. 31, 1845, cited by Freyre in *Um engenheiro*, 284; *O Regenerador Brazilero*, June 15, 1844; *A Voz do Brasil*, April 5, 1848.

20. On the disputes over hiring foreign artisans and engineers, see chapter 5. At the "Jornadas de 1848: 150 Anos da Revolução Praieira" conference at UFPE in Recife in December 1998, Izabel Andrade Marson emphasized the importance of competition for state contracts as an element of Lusophobia.

21. See Eisenberg, *Sugar*, 63–73. This author claims that rates might reach as high as 6 percent a month, which seems extraordinarily elevated for a business with a relatively low profit rate. Freyre gives the figure of 9 percent a year; see Freyre, *Mansions and Shanties*, 18. Citing a report from a later period (1878), Ridings offers a range of from 18 percent to 24 percent annually; see Ridings, *Business Interest Groups*, 133.

22. Freyre, *Mansions and Shanties*, 15.

23. See Eisenberg, *Sugar*, 72–73, and Ridings, *Business Interest Groups*, 144–45, on laws regarding collecting bad debts. Foreclosures on mortgages, prohibited in

the colonial period, were allowed in the nineteenth century but on very unfavorable terms for the *correspondente*. Also see Freyre, *Mansions and Shanties*, 18, and Stein, *Vassouras*, 18–19.

24. *A Voz do Brasil*, Nov. 2, 1847; *A Voz do Brasil*, Nov. 24, 1847; *O Regenerador Brazileiro*, June 22, 1844; *O Regenerador Brazileiro*, July 11, 1844.

25. *O Liberal*, Sept. 10, 1847; *O Regenerador Brazileiro*, July 17, 1844, and Aug. 22, 1844.

26. *A Voz do Bebiribi*, March 16, 1835.

27. *O Regenerado Brazileiro*, May 25, 1844 (quote, 1); *O Liberal*, Sept. 7, 1847; *O Foguete*, June 29, 1844. For the constitutional text that granted Brazilian citizenship to the Portuguese-born (as long as they had not taken up arms against independence), see Bueno, *Direito público*, 482.

28. *A Voz do Brasil*, Oct. 27, 1847.

29. *Voz do Brasil*, Nov. 10, 1847; *O Regenerador Brazileiro*, June 22, 1844.

30. *A Voz do Brasil*, May 10, 1848. For the quote, *A Voz do Brasil*, May 2, 1848.

31. *A Voz do Brasil*, Nov. 2, 1847; *A Voz do Brasil*, Nov. 24, 1847; *A Voz do Brasil*, Feb. 19, 1848.

32. *A Voz do Brasil*, Nov. 10, 1847; *A Voz do Brasil*, March 22, 1848; *A Voz do Brasil*, March 28, 1848.

33. *A Voz do Brasil*, Oct. 27, 1847, and Nov. 2, 1847; *O Regenerador Brazileiro*, June 22, 1844.

34. *A Voz do Brasil*, Feb. 19, 1848.

35. *A Voz do Brasil*, March 28, 1848. Heavy recruitment in the northern provinces for the war in the Banda Oriental was ascribed to Portuguese influence in the court; *A Voz do Brasil*, Oct. 27, 1847. This war against the United Provinces of the Plate River (the future Argentina), from 1825 to 1828, over territory long disputed by Spain and Portugal, led to the creation of Uruguay. See Seckinger, *Brazilian Monarchy*.

36. The same charge was sometimes made without the racial angle; see *O Regenerador Brazileiro*, July 17, 1844.

37. *O Liberal*, Sept. 10, 1847.

38. *A Voz do Brasil*, June 9, 1848.

39. *A Voz do Brasil*, April 19, 1848.

40. *A Voz do Brasil*, May 2, 1848.

41. I have closely followed Edna Bonich and John Modell's work on middleman minorities. See chapter 2 of Bonich and Modell, *Economic Basis of Ethnic Solidarity*, and Bonich, "Theory of Middleman Minorities." For a review of the literature, see chapter 1 of Walter Zenner's comparative work, *Minorities in the Middle*. For a selection of recent studies employing the concept, see Chirot and Reid, *Essential Outsiders*. Also see Horowitz, *Deadly Ethnic Riot*.

42. "Câmara dos Srs. Deputados. Sessão em 28 de junho de 1848," *Diário Novo*, July 17, 1848, 1–2. See praise for this speech in *Diário Novo*, July 20, 1848, 1.

43. "Câmara dos Srs. Deputados. Sessão em 28 de junho de 1848," *Diário Novo*, July 17, 1848 (quotes), and July 18, 1848.

44. "Câmara dos Srs. Deputados. Sessão em 28 de junho de 1848," *Diário Novo*, July 17, 1848, and July 18, 1848.

45. *Diário Novo*, July 20, 1848, for text of the June 28 proposal. On June 16, 1848, Nunes Machado had offered a less radical proposal for discussion; it recommended that all commercial houses be obligated to employ at least one Brazilian clerk, and that Brazilian clerks be exempted from national guard duty, placing them on more equal footing with Portuguese clerks. See "Câmara dos Senhores Deputados. Sessão em 16 de junho," *Diário Novo*, June 28, 1848.

46. "Câmara dos Srs. Deputados. Sessão em 28 de junho de 1848," *Diário Novo*, July 17, 1848, 2. See Sales Torres Homen's defense of Nunes Machado's call for restrictions on the Portuguese, in "O libelo do povo," in Magalhães Júnior, *Três Panfletários*, 111–14.

47. On the strong Portuguese presence in the court, in Rio de Janeiro province, and among the politically connected, see Needell, "Party Formation," 262–65, 283, 285–86, 289–94.

48. See Freyre, *O velho Félix*, 12. The author of these memoirs was Félix Cavalcanti de Albuquerque Melo. (The work is generally catalogued under Freyre's name; Freyre edited and introduced it.)

49. *Lidador*, July 6, 1848 (quote). *Lidador*, Dec. 14, 1847.

50. The *Lidador* legitimized its stance by pointing to the successful United States, declaring its envy of "the enlightened policy . . . that has received all people with open arms." *Lidador*, Dec. 14, 1847.

51. On order as a fundamental value, see Richard Graham, *Patronage and Politics*, 39–42, 51, 74, 77.

52. On order under the presidency of Francisco do Rego Barros, see Naro, "Brazil's 1848," 55. Also see chapter 5.

53. *Diário de Pernambuco*, Sept. 10, 1844.

54. The quotation is from a letter signed "O inimigo da anarchia," in *Diário de Pernambuco*, Sept. 12, 1844.

55. *Diário de Pernambuco*, Sept. 10, 1844.

56. *Diário Novo*, Sept. 13, 1844.

57. *Lidador*, Dec. 4, 1847, 2.

58. *Lidador*, Dec. 4, 1847, 2.

59. *Lidador*, Dec. 14, 1847, 1–2.

60. Nabuco, *Estadista*, 102. Nabuco, who had rejected the republican coup of 1889, wrote this as a monarchist and in the aftermath of the popular, demagogic dictatorship of Floriano Peixoto in the early 1890s. See Needell, "A Liberal," 159–80. Note that Nabuco's father, José Tomás Nabuco de Araújo, shifted from the Conservative to the Liberal Party by the late 1860s. By then, of course, the Praia tradition of violent radicalism was moribund.

61. The pioneering article with respect to the diversity of the Praia's composition, and particularly the important presence of planters, is Lima Sobrinho, "A Rev-

olução Praieira." Also see Carvalho, "A guerra do moraes," chap. 3; Marson, *O império*, 272–74; Naro, "Brazil's 1848," chap. 5.

62. Portuguese Consul in Pernambuco to Minister of State for Foreign Affairs, Recife, Sept. 13, 1844, ANTT/NE, caixa 310, no. 639, fol. 1r.

63. After the Lusophobic riots of June 1848, for example, the U.S. Consul reported that "according to the general opinion, there is every possibility of a new disturbance taking place on or about the seventh September next, at the time of the elections." Consul Salinas to Secretary of State Buchanon, Aug. 14, 1848, Dispatches from the U.S. Consuls in Pernambuco, 1817–1906, T-344, roll 3. Amaro Quintas relates the disturbances in the electoral seasons of September of 1844 and 1845 to Lusophobia, in Quintas, *O sentido social*, 25.

64. Recall from chapter 6 that Conservatives in the imperial Senate in Rio had nullified Praieiro electoral victories in Senate elections, going so far as to clash with the emperor over the issue. Victory would have consolidated the Praieiro presence in national politics and strengthened the Liberal party in the Conservative-dominated Senate.

65. Portuguese Consul to PPE, September 28, 1847, APEJE/SM, DC-5, fol. 130.

66. CP to PPE, APEJE/SM, DC-5, fol. 131.

67. CP to PPE, APEJE/SM, DC-5, fol. 131. A report from a subdelegado to the PPE provides the information on the incident with the prostitute, Oct. 2, 1847, APEJE/SM, DC-5, fol. 134.

68. CP to PPE, APEJE/SM, DC-5, fol. 131.

69. Subdel. to PPE, Oct. 2, 1847, APEJE/SM, DC-5, fol. 136. The Portuguese Consul denied charges of his involvement with the opposition. Portuguese Consul to PPE, Oct. 7, 1847, APEJE/SM, DC-5, fol. 143.

70. *Diário de Pernambuco*, Dec. 8, 1847; *Lidador*, Dec. 11, 1847; also see the five documents on the incident reprinted in the *Diário Novo*, Dec. 18, 1847.

71. Instituto Arqueológico, Histórico e Geográfico Pernambucano, Actas da Irmandade da Nossa Senhora da Conceição da Congregação, livro 1, fol. 51; Portuguese Consul to PPE, Dec. 7, 1847, APEJE/SM, DC-5, fol. 157; *Diário de Pernambuco*, Dec. 10, 1847, 1; *Lidador*, Dec. 11, 1847. The U.S. Consul's report on this "riotous mob" claimed that not only were Portuguese beaten, but an English merchant and a Frenchman were beaten as well; see U.S. Consul Salinas to Secretary of State Buchanan, Jan. 20, 1848, Dispatches from the U.S. Consuls in Pernambuco, 1817–1906, T-344, roll 3. The chief of police played down the scale of the incidents. He noted, though, that they seemed not to be spontaneous, but incidents that were planned in advance. See CP to PPE, Dec. 11, 1847, APEJE/SM, PC-17, fol. 313. Also see Portuguese Consul in Pernambuco to Minister of State for Foreign Affairs, Recife, Dec. 10, 1847, ANTT/NE, caixa 310, Oficio N26, and December 18, 1847, Oficio N27.

72. *Lidador*, June 30, 1848; *Lidador*, July 4, 1848; *Diário Novo*, July 1, 1848; *Diário de Pernambuco, Supplemento*, June 28, 1848. Portuguese Consul to PPE, June 26, 1848, APEJE/SM, DC-5, fol. 199, and Portuguese Consul to PPE July 3, 1848, APEJE/SM, DC-

5, fol. 201. Also see the detailed account in Portuguese Consul to Minister of Foreign Affairs, Recife, July 12, 1848, ANTT/NE, caixa 310, no. 2809, and the eleven attached letters, as well as his first report on June 28, no. 2266. Naro, "Brazil's 1848," 53–55.

73. *Diário de Pernambuco*, June 28, 1848, *Supplemento*, 1; *Diário Novo*, July 1, 1848, 1; *Lidador*, June 28, 1848; June 30, 1848. On events in Olinda, see *Lidador*, July 11, 1848, 2. Five weeks later the Portuguese consul called for an investigation into the fatal shooting of a Portuguese merchant while he was standing in the doorway to his house. The consul reported that there continued to be beatings of Portuguese in various towns and villages, such as Abreu and Rio Formoso. Portuguese Consul to PPE, August 7, 1848, APEJE/SM, DC-5, fol. 213.

74. *Diário de Pernambuco*, Supplemento, June 28, 1848.

75. *Diário Novo*, July 11, 1848.

76. On the events in the court, see chapter 8.

77. *Lidador*, June 30, 1848; *Lidador*, July 11, 1848.

78. *Lidador*, July 11, 1848, 2. The reference to Potosí is to the immense silver deposits the Spanish mined in the colonial period in what is present-day Bolivia.

79. *Lidador*, June 30, 1848, 2–3. On Rosas as symptomatic of a strain of New World barbarism, see the celebrated polemic by the Argentine statesman Domingo Faustino Sarmiento, *Facundo*. Also see Lynch, *Argentine Dictator*.

80. Freyre, *O velho Félix*, 12–13.

81. *Diário Novo*, July 8, 1848, 1–2. The presence of Conservative authorities under a Liberal provincial administration is only apparently contradictory. In late April the Liberal cabinet had replaced the Praieiro provincial president, Antônio Chichorro da Gama, with Vicente Pires da Mota, who dismissed many, although not all, Praia officeholders, allowing the return of many local Conservatives to state power. See chapter 8 for an explanation of this apparent political incoherence.

82. *Diário Novo*, July 5, 1848.

83. *Diário Novo*, July 7, 1848. Also see *Diário Novo*, July 11, 1848.

84. For works on Borges da Fonseca, see chap. 2, note 70.

85. Izabel Andrade Marson identifies the origin of the term "the Five Thousand" as an allusion to classical Athens, referring to the citizens in general, in contrast to the oligarchical regime of "the Four Hundred." See Marson, *O império*, 229–30.

86. During the Praieira Revolution, moderate Praieiro newspapers insistently reiterated charges that their Conservative opponents were allied with the Portuguese in oppressing Pernambucans. See chapter 8.

87. *Lidador*, Dec. 11, 1847.

88. Likewise, in Olinda, during the June 26 and 27 events the group of rioters referred to themselves as "police patrols," again suggesting the legitimacy of their activities; see *Lidador*, July 11, 1848, 2. For classic statements on deciphering the actors' sense of legitimacy in certain types of violent crowds, see Thompson, "Moral Economy," and Davis, "Rites of Violence."

89. On the Mexican case, see Sims, *Expulsion of Mexico's Spaniards*, especially 207–20; Caballero, *Counterrevolution*; Anna, *Forging Mexico*, 196–98, 201–4; Green, *Mexican Republic*, 140–48, 165–66. On Spain's efforts to reconquer Mexico, also see Delgado, *España y México*; José L. Franco, "Política continental americana"; and Lamego, *La invasión española de 1829*.

8. The Praieira Revolution

1. A series of politicians was designated vice-president. The first vice-president was to assume the presidency on an interim basis when needed. If he was unable to carry out the presidential duties, the second was called on, and so forth. Joaquim Nabuco wrote that the inclusion of Provincial President Chichorro da Gama on electoral lists led to defections from the party—during the Senate elections, Francisco Muniz Tavares, the veteran of the 1817 struggle, defected; and during elections to the Chamber of Deputies in 1847, Manuel de Sousa Teixeira defected. The latter, who had initiated the period of Praia ascendancy by beginning the dismissals of Conservative officeholders in June of 1845, was potentially very serious because he had been selected as the first vice-president and therefore was first in line to step in as interim president, if needed. Nabuco, *Estadista*, 89; Marson, *O império*, 352–56; Naro, "Brazil's 1848," 139–40.

2. Pereira de Castro, "Política de administração," 533; Nabuco, *Estadista*, 89–90. Nabuco refers to "the scandal of presidents electing themselves."

3. APEJE/SM, PC-18, fols. 86–94.

4. Del. of Bonito to CP, Feb. 10, 1848, APEJE/SM, PC-18, fol. 136.

5. Del. of Bonito to CP, Feb. 10, 1848, APEJE/SM, PC-18, fol. 136.

6. CP to PPE, Feb. 22, 1848, APEJE/SM, PC-18, fol. 160; Del. of Bonito to CP, Feb. 22, 1848, APEJE/SM, PC-18, fol. 175.

7. Del. of Flores to CP, Feb. 19, 1848, APEJE/SM, PC-18, fol. 147; CP to PPE, Feb. 22, APEJE/SM, PC-18, 1848, fol. 160; "Relatório apresentado pelo ex-Presidente de Província Chichorro da Gama ao 1º Vice-Presidente Manuel de Sousa Teixeira," PPE to MI, AN/SPE, IJJ⁹253, fol. 99.

8. For the chief of police's view, and the quote, see CP to PPE, Feb. 22, 1848, APEJE/SM, PC-18, fol. 160; for the others, see Del. of Flores to CP, Feb. 19, 1848, APEJE/SM, PC-18, fol. 147, and Del. of Bonito to CP, Feb. 22, 1848, APEJE/SM, PC-18, fol. 175.

9. Del. of Bonito to CP, March 5 and March 6, 1848, APEJE/SM, PC-18, fol. 191; CP to PPE, March 17, 1848, APEJE/SM, PC-18, fol. 219.

10. CP to PPE, March 11, 1848, APEJE/SM, PC-18, fol. 200.

11. CP to PPE, March 17, 1848, APEJE/SM, PC-18, fol. 219; CP to PPE, Feb. 22, 1848, APEJE/SM, PC-18, fol. 219.

12. Del. of Cabo to CP, March 27, 1848, APEJE/SM, PC-18, fol. 258.

13. Subdel. of First District of Jaboatão to CP, March 23, 1848, APEJE/SM, PC-18, fol. 247. Subdel. Poço de Panellas to CP, April 4, 1848, APEJE/SM, PC-18, fol. 296. "Relatório apresentado pelo ex-Presidente Chichorro da Gama ao 1º Vice-Presidente Manuel de Sousa Teixeira," PPE to MI, AN/SPE, IJJ⁹253, fol. 99.

14. CP to PPE, March 20, 1848, APEJE/SM, PC-18, fol. 228.

15. CP to PPE, April 10, 1848, APEJE/SM, PC-18, fol. 277.

16. CP to PPE, April 10, 1848, APEJE/SM, PC-18, fol. 277.

17. "Relatório apresentado pelo ex-Presidente da Provincia de Pernambuco Chichorro da Gama ao 1o Vice-Presidente Manuel de Sousa Teixeira," PPE to MI, AN/SPE, IJJ⁹253, fol 99.

18. CA to PPE, April 9, 1848, in Arquivo Público, "Comandante das Armas," 56.

19. Subdel. Second District of Escada to Del. of Vitoria, April 5, 1848, APEJE/SM, PC-18, fol. 273; Subdel. Second District of Escada to General Commander of Police, April 5, 1848, APEJE/SM, PC-18, fol. 324; Lieutenant Colonel Commander of Second Battalion to Del. of Bonito, April 6, 1848, APEJE/SM, PC-18, fol. 323; CP to PPE, April 10, 1848, APEJE/SM, PC-18, fol. 277. Carvalho, "A guerra do moraes," 76; chapter 3 of Carvalho's work provides considerable detail on the Conservative armed mobilization.

20. General Commander of the Police Corps to CP, April 9, 1848, APEJE/SM, PC-18, fol. 318, and April 7, 1848, fol. 321. Commanding Colonel of Forces (in charge of battling the rebels in Escada) to CP, April 12, 1848, APEJE/SM, PC-18, fol. 326.

21. General Commander of the Police Corps to CP, April 7, 1848, APEJE/SM, PC-18, fol. 321.

22. Commander of the Forces (in charge of battling the rebels in Escada) to CP, April 18, 1848, APEJE/SM, PC-18, fol. 335.

23. Commander of the Forces (in charge of battling the rebels in Escada) to CP, April 18, 1848, APEJE/SM, PC-18, fol. 335. Subdel. Second District of Serinhaem to CP, April 18, 1848, APEJE/SM, PC-18, fol. 389 and appended Commander of the Forces (in charge of battling the rebels in Escada) to Subdel. Second District of Serinhaem.

24. CA to PPE, April 21, 1848, reprinted in *Revista do Arquivo Público* 2 no. 4 (2nd semestre 1948): 63–64; João Lucio [da Morrti?], Second Commander to Coronel do Estado Maior Joaquim José Lins de Sousa, April 21, 1848, APEJE/SM, OE-12, fol. 34.

25. On the Aberdeen Bill, as it was called in Brazil, see Bethell, *Abolition*.

26. Pereira de Castro, "Política e administração," 530–33. On the fall of the ministry, also see the letter from Eusébio de Queirós quoted extensively by Nelson Lage Mascarenhas, in *Um jornalista*, 154.

27. Pereira de Castro, "Política de administração," 533; Nabuco, *Estadista*, 89–90.

28. PPE to MI, April 26, 1848, "Relatório apresentado pelo ex-Presidente de Provincia Chichorro da Gama ao 1o Vice-Presidente Manuel de Sousa Teixeira," PPE to MI, AN/SPE, IJJ⁹253, fol. 98; CA to Vice PPE, April 25, 1848, in Arquivo Público, "Comandante das Armas," 66–68. Colonel of the Estado Maior Joaquim José Lins de Sousa to PPE Vicente Pires da Mota, Bamburral Estate, April 29, 1848, APEJE/SM, OE-12, fol. 33.

29. For lists of police commissioners, deputy commissioners, officers of the police corps, national guard officers, and public employees dismissed, see PPE to MI, April 26,

1848, "Relatório apresentado pelo ex-Presidente de Provincia Chichorro da Gama ao 10 Vice-Presidente Manuel de Sousa Teixeira," PPE to MI, AN/SPE, IJJ⁹253, fols. 87–96. Marson, *O império*, 366, places the total number of dismissals at five hundred.

30. Marson, *O império*, 367; Nabuco, *Estadista*, 90; for the text of the chief of police's letter, see Marson, *O império*, 49. CP to PPE, May 1, 1848, APEJE/SM, PC-19, fol. 1. Colonel of the Estado Maior Joaquim José Lins de Sousa to PPE, May 4, 1848, APEJE/SM, OE-12, fol. 39, and Jusice of the Peace, Rio Formoso, to Colonel of the Estado Maior Joaquim José Lins de Sousa, fol. 42.

31. CP to PPE, May 16, 1848, APEJE/SM, PC-19, fol. 46.

32. Maciel Monteiro to Marquis of Olinda, May 22, 1848, Instituto Histórico e Geográfico Brasileiro, Marquis of Olinda Collection, lata 219, doc. 52.

33. On Limoeiro, see CP to PPE, May 10, 1848, APEJE/SM, PC-19, fol. 33, and May 11, 1848, fol. 36; on Pau d'Alho, see CP to PPE, May 15, 1848, APEJE/SM, PC-19, fol. 54; on Pajeú de Flores, see CP to PPE, May 10, 1845, APEJE/SM, PC-19, fol. 34; on Muribeca, see CP to PPE, May 11, 1848, APEJE/SM, PC-19, fol. 36.

34. CP to PPE, May 9, 1848, APEJE/SM, PC-19, fol. 31. Interim CA to PPE, May 11, 1848, in "Arquivo Público, Comandante das Armas," 73–74. Marson, *O império*, 368.

35. Interim Captain Commandant to CA, May 19, 1848, in Arquivo Público, "Comandante das Armas," 80–81.

36. Marson, *O império*, 367–68; Carvalho, "A guerra do moraes," 82–84; on Bonito, see CP to PPE, Aug. 18, 1848, APEJE/SM, PC-19, fol. 343.

37. Marson, *O império*, 368.

38. Antônio Henriques de Miranda was the new chief of police, taking office on July 19. Subdel. of Muribeca to PPE, July 20, 1848, APEJE/SM, PC-19, fol. 349; Subdel. of Muribeca to CP, July 16, APEJE/SM, PC-19, fol. 350; CP to PPE, Aug. 28, 1848, APEJE/SM, PC-19, fol. 375, and the four appended letters on the same case.

39. CP to PPE, Aug. 12, 1848, APEJE/SM, PC-19, fol. 313; Del. to CP, August 8, 1848, APEJE/SM, PC-19, fol. 315; Del. to Manoel Fermino de Melo, APEJE/SM, PC-19, fol. 316; Del. Rio Formoso to CP, August 20, 1848, APEJE/SM, PC-19, fol. 355; Subdel. Rio Formoso to CP, Aug. 10, 1848, APEJE/SM, PC-19, fol. 320. Fols. 321–26 also treat the same case.

40. PPE to MJ, June 15, 1848, AN/SPE, IJ¹324, and the appended letter from the delegado of Vitória to the PPE, June 5, 1848.

41. Francisco José de Figueiredo to José Maria Freire Gameiro, July 2, 1848, BN/SM, Figueira de Mello Collection I:29, 21, no. 70. The town is not identified.

42. Municipal Judge of Nazareth to Vice-President of Pernambuco, July 15, 1848, APEJE/SM, PC-19, fol. 215–18.

43. João Pedro de Bandeira de Mello to Figueira de Mello, July 20, 1848, BN/SM, Figueira de Mello Collection I:29, 21, no. 62. Also see a similar message in another letter from his brother, dated July 28, 1848, BN/SM, Figueira de Mello Collection I:29, 21, no. 63.

44. On the Sociedade Imperial Pernambucana, see Marson, *O império*, 369–70.

45. Del. First District of Recife to CP, August 26, 1848, APEJE/SM, PC-19, fol. 369, for a summary of a May 26 meeting with President Pires da Mota. The president sought the printing press that had recently printed a republican proclamation. He authorized the use of spies and assured the delegado that he could "count on all the necessary money, even from my own pocket if necessary."

46. Pereira de Castro, "Política e administração," 533–34; Nabuco, *Estadista*, 90.

47. He was generally referred to as Paula Sousa.

48. Pereira de Castro, "Política e administração," 537–38.

49. Pereira de Castro, "Política e administração," 535–37. On the Senate election, see chapter 4.

50. Pereira de Castro, "Política e administração," 537.

51. On the proposals by Nunes Machado, see chapter 7. The threatening flyers are discussed earlier in this chapter.

52. Pereira de Castro, "Política e administração," 538. See Sales Torres Homem's partisan attack on José Clemente Perreira in "O Libelo do Povo," 71–75. See, for example, the characterization of José Clemente as "tenacious in his Lusitanism, and through whose thick skin sentiments of the country that has adopted him have never been able to penetrate (71)." Note that Pereira's change in politics, from radical liberal to conservative, may help explain the vehemence of his liberal critics.

53. Pereira de Castro, "Política e administração." On José Clemente's political career, see Augusto Tavares de Lyra, *Instituições políticas*, 297–98. On Caxias's extraordinary military career, see Sisson, *Galeria dos brasileiros*. I would like to acknowledge Jeffrey Needell for pointing out some of these connections.

54. Pereira de Castro, "Política e administração," 539; *Corrieo Mercantil* (Rio de Janeiro), Sept. 32, 1848.

55. *Correio Mercantil*, Sept. 9, 1848. *Correio Mercantil*, Sept. 11, 1848, published official correspondence regarding the events; see especially the description in the fourth document, from the Court police to the minister of justice, Sept. 9, 1848.

56. *Correio Mercantil*, Sept. 9, 1848.

57. *Correio Mercantil*, Sept. 11, 1848.

58. *Correio Mercantil*, Sept. 11, 1848, Sept. 12, 1848, Sept. 13, 1848, Sept. 14, 1848, and Sept. 20, 1848.

59. *Correio Mercantil*, Sept. 14, 1848. The paper also had made the same charge on Sept. 12 and Sept. 13.

60. *Correio Mercantil*, Sept. 12, 1848.

61. For the transcriptions of key speeches in the Chamber on September 11, see the *Correio Mercantil*, Sept. 17, 1848; for the Senate, see the speeches of Sept. 9, published in the *Jornal do Commercio*, Sept. 10 and 11, 1848.

62. See the Senate speeches on Sept. 9, 1848, published the following day in the *Jornal do Commercio*. For the *Correio Mercantil*'s rejection of these assertions, see Sept. 11, 1848.

63. See the speeches in both the Senate and the Chamber cited above; for the quote, see Sept. 10, 1848, 2. Also see the response in the *Correio Mercantil* on, Sept. 12, 1848.

64. Cited in Calmon, *História de Dom Pedro II*, 358.

65. *Correio Mercantil*'s responded to this charge, Sept. 20, 1848.

66. Nabuco, *Estadista*, 90.

67. For the quotes, see footnote 25, written by Pedro, in Almeida, *O conselheiro*, 39. In the first quotation I have rendered *estado dos espíritos* as "political atmosphere." Pereira de Castro, "Política e administração," 540; Calmon, *História de Dom Pedro II*, 358–59; Nabuco, *Estadista*, 91–92; Vianna, *Da maioridade*, 31–34. See Sales Torres Homem on the role of violence in September in the fall of the ministry in "O Libelo do Povo," 114–16.

68. Jerônimo Martiniano Figueira de Mello, *Crônica*, 15.

69. Subdel. of Affogados to Del. of First Termo of Recife, Sept. 9, 1848, APEJE/SM, PC-20, fol. 22, and Sept. 11, 1848, fol. 23.

70. PPE to MJ, Oct. 16, 1848, AN/SPE, IJ¹324, and the appended document, PPE to CP, Oct. 10, 1848. On events here, also see CP to PPE, Sept. 14, 1848, APEJE/SM, PC-20, fol. 32, and especially, CP to PPE, Sept. 23, 1848, APEJE/SM, PC-20, fol. 65, and the appended documents, as well as the chief of police's letters of Oct. 2, fol. 97 and 100, and the appended documents. Also General Commander of the Police Corps to PPE, APEJE/SM, PC-19, fol. 80.

71. Nabuco, *Estadista*, 94. Nabuco might have been overly optimistic about the possibility of anyone successfully containing an upheaval.

72. Urbano Sabino Pessoa de Mello, *Apreciação*, 55.

73. Jerônimo Martiniano Figueira de Mello, *Crônica*, 17.

74. Jerônimo Martiniano Figueira de Mello, *Crônica*, 19–24, lists those dismissed and their replacements.

75. For a description of this policy, see the report to the new president by the outgoing president, Antônio da Costa Pinto, PPE to MI, Oct. 17, 1848, AN/SPE, IJJ⁹253, fol. 155.

76. Jerônimo Martiniano Figueira de Mello, *Crônica*, 25–26.

77. Urbano Sabino Pessoa de Mello, *Apreciação*, 57 (quote), 65–67.

78. Urbano Sabino Pessoa de Mello, *Apreciação*, 57, 61–62; Jerônimo Martiniano Figueira de Mello, *Crônica*, 21; Marson, *O império*, 39.

79. First Commander, Pau d'Alho to General Commander of Police Corps, Pau d'Alho, APEJE/SM, PC-19, fol 222. CP to PPE, Nov. 4, 1848, APEJE/SM, PC-20, fol. 218, and appended letter from Del. Pau d'Alho to CP, Nov. 3, 1848, fol. 219. JD Pão d'Alho to President of Pernambuco, Nov. 7, 1848, APEJE/SM, JD-6, fol. 264. Commander of Detachment in Limoeiro to PPE, Limoeiro, Nov. 6, 1848, APEJE/SM, PC-19, fol. 214, and appended Secretary of the Municipal Council to Commander of Detachment in Limoeiro, fol. 216, and from the same commander again, Nov. 20, 1848 fol. 240. Sergeant Commander of Detachment of Nazareth to General Commander of

the Police Corps, Nazareth, Nov. 6, 1848, APEJE/SM, PC-19, fol. 223. Subdel., First District of Nazareth to CP, Nov. 6, 1848, APEJE/SM, PC-20, fol. 235. District Judge, Nazareth to PPE, Nov. 6, 1848, APEJE/SM, JD-6, fol. 257, and Nov. 9, 1848, fol. 265. Jerônimo Martiniano Figueira de Mello, *Crônica*, 27–28; Urbano Sabino Pessoa de Mello, *Apreciação*, 57–61.

80. Del., Goiana to CP, Nov. 8, 1848, APEJE/SM, PC-20, fol. 257. José Roxa do [Baril?] Cajo to PPE, Nov. 9, 1848, APEJE/SM, OE-12, fol. 86. Jerônimo Martiniano Figueira de Mello, *Crônica*, 28–29.

81. Jerônimo Martiniano Figueira de Mello, *Crônica*, 29–30.

82. According to Jerônimo Martiniano Figueira de Mello, the chief of police during much of the repression of the rebellion, 5,000 arms and 350,000 cartridges of ammunition were distributed. See his *Crônica*, 26. Naro, "Brazil's 1848," 150, has calculated that a little more than 255,000 cartridges were distributed, more than half of them between January and April 1848.

83. Jerônimo Martiniano Figueira de Mello, *Crônica*, 32.

84. Urbano Sabino Pessoa de Mello, *Apreciação*, 55; Marson, *O império*, 39.

85. Jerônimo Martiniano Figueira de Mello, *Crônica*, 30.

86. District Judge to PPE, Oct. 26, 1848, APEJE/SM, JD-6, fol. 244, and appended document, Municipal Judge to District Judge, fol. 246. On events around Nazareth from late October through November 1848, see Subdel., Second District of Tracunhaém to Del. of Tracunhaém, April 25, 1849, APEJE/SM, PC-23, fol. 19.

87. Commander of the Northern Forces to PPE, Nov. 14, 1848, and the same Commander's Ordem do Dia, Nov. 15, 1848, printed in Jerônimo Martiniano Figueira de Mello, *Crônica*, 38–42; also see Figueira de Mello's comments on the battle, *Crônica*, 36–38, 43. British Consul Cowper to Lord Viscount Palmerston, Nov. 20, 1848 FO 13/260, fol. 293, British Consul Secretary of State for Foreign Affairs. On Lopes Neto's claim, see Jerônimo Martiniano Figueira de Mello, *Crônica*, 48–49.

88. District Judge Rio Formoso to PPE, Nov. 19, 1848, APEJE/SM, JD-6, fol. 281. District Attorney, Rio Formoso to PPE, Nov. 23, 1848, APEJE/SM, JD-6, fol. 283. Urbano Sabino Pessoa de Mello, *Apreciação*, 58; Ordem do Dia, Nov. 17, 1848, Major Comandante General Ignácio de Siqueira Leão e Cruz, reprinted in Jerônimo Martiniano Figueira de Mello, *Crônica*, 86–88; as also see Figueira de Mello's account, *Crônica*, 85–86.

89. Delegado of Flores to PPE, Nov. 26, 1848, reprinted in Jerônimo Martiniano Figueira de Mello, *Crônica*, 100–102; also Figueira de Mello, *Crônica*, 99 and 102.

90. This despite Figueira de Mello's subsequent partisan efforts in *Crônica* to depict the Praieira Revolution as a plan preconceived in the court. Urbano Sabino Pessoa de Mello, in *Apreciação*, contests this argument.

91. Urbano Sabino Pessoa de Mello, *Apreciação*, 38–39; Nabuco, *Estadista*, 96–97.

92. On the electoral postponement, see "Transferencia das eleições," *Diário Novo*, Nov. 15, 1848, 1; Marson, *O império*, 51–52, 64.

93. The flyer was subsequently published in the Praieiro press; see *Diário Novo*, November 20, 1848, 1. Jerônimo Martiniano Figueira de Mello, *Crônica*, 50–51; Nabuco, *Estadista*, 97; Lima Sobrinho, "Urbano Sabino Pessoa de Mello," 22. Figueira de Mello conceded that Nunes Machado intended to restrain his allies, but he criticized what he described as Nunes Machado's weakness of character for abandoning his principles and accepting armed struggle once he saw that he was unable to prevail. See Jerônimo Martiniano Figueira de Mello, *Crônica*, 50–51.

94. "Aos Pernambucanos," reprinted in Urbano Sabino Pessoa de Mello, *Apreciação*, 197–202 (quote, 202). Lima Sobrinho, "Urbano Sabino Pessoa de Mello," 22.

95. Quoted in Nabuco, *Estadista*, 97.

96. Figueira de Melo put this in terms of vanity—that is, that Nunes Machado did not want to lose the adulation of his followers; Jerônimo Martiniano Figueira de Mello, *Crônica*, 50–51.

97. On the difficulties facing the deputies trying to contain their Praia allies, and on Nunes Machado's fatalism concerning the likely outcome of armed struggle, see Nabuco, *Estadista*, 97, 105.

98. Jerônimo Martiniano Figueira de Mello, *Crônica*, 53; Naro, "Brazil's 1848," 161.

99. Jerônimo Martiniano Figueira de Mello, *Crônica*, 55–57.

100. On Nazareth, see Lieutenant Colonel Jose and Commander of the Center Forces Maria Idelfonço da Veiga to José Joaquim Coelho, Commander of the Forces in Operation in the Province, Encampment at Cursahi Estate, Nov. 30, 1848, APEJE/SM, CA-11, fol. 442. On rebel forces retreating to the forest when outnumbered, see Colonel and Commander Jozé Vicente de Amorim Bezerra to General in Chief José Joaquim Coelho, Igarassu, Nov. 28, 1848, in Arquivo Público, "Comandante das Armas," 120–21. For an expression of frustration with the rebels' guerrilla tactics, see the first paragraph of General José Joaquim Coelho to PPE, Nazareth, Dec. 26, 1848, reprinted in Arquivo Público, "Comandante das Armas," 162–64. On fleeing, only to claim victory afterward, see General José Joaquim Coelho to PPE, Nazareth, Dec. 29, 1848, APEJE/SM, CA-11, fol. 493.

101. "Ordem do Dia no. 3," Cruangi, Dec. 21, 1848, in Arquivo Público, "Comandante das Armas," 151–54. Jerônimo Martiniano Figueira de Mello, *Crônica*, 64.

102. General José Joaquim Coelho to PPE, Dec. 11, 1848, in Arquivo Público, "Comandante das Armas," 136–37. Jerônimo Martiniano Figueira de Mello, *Crônica*, 61–62, 70–73.

103. Jerônimo Martiniano Figueira de Mello, *Crônica*, 74–75, on the taking of Goiana and 78–81 for the Cruangí battle. General José Joaquim Coelho to PPE, Goiana, Dec. 16, 1848, APEJE/SM, CA-11, fol. 471, and General José Joaquim Coelho to PPE, Cruangi, Dec. 21, 1848, APEJE/SM, CA-11, fol. 475. "Ordem do Dia," Cruangi, Dec. 21, APEJE/SM, CA-11, fol. 485. *Revista do Arquivo Público* 2, no. 4 (2nd semestre 1948): 146–47, and APEJE/SM, CA-11, fol. 487.

104. CP to PPE, Dec. 4, 1848, APEJE/SM, PC-20, fol. 339. On the arrest of a slave with

seven horses and supplies for the rebels, see CP to PPE, Dec. 11, 1848, APEJE/SM, PC-20, fol. 359; also see Jerônimo Martiniano Figueira de Mello, *Crônica*, 96–97, and the quote on p. 97 on the same topic as well as on recruiting support. On the Apipucos attack, see "ORDEM DO DIA," Nov. 30, 1848, from Major Comandante João Guilherme de Bruce, reprinted in Jerônimo Martiniano Figueira de Mello, *Crônica* 62–63; see Figueira de Melo's comments, 62.

105. On Antonio, see Del. (Supp) of Olinda to CP, Dec. 12, 1848, APEJE/SM, PC-20, fol. 372. For arrests of others, see CP to PPE, Dec. 12, 1848, fol. 361, and Dec. 19, 1848, fol. 395. Subdel. of Olinda (supp) to CP, Olinda, Dec. 12, 1848, fol. 375, Del. (Supp) of Cimbres to CP, Dec. 391, 1848, fol. 391.

106. For the attack on Gaipió estate, see CP to PPE, Dec. 4, 1848, APEJE/SM, PC-20, fol. 338. Jerônimo Martiniano Figueira de Mello, *Crônica*, 93–95.

107. Jerônimo Martiniano Figueira de Mello, *Crônica*, 88–93.

108. Jerônimo Martiniano Figueira de Mello, *Crônica*, 88–93.

109. For the quote, see the proclamation dated Dec. 25, 1848, by Manoel Vieira Tosta, reprinted in Jerônimo Martiniano Figueira de Mello, *Crônica* 108–9; Urbano Sabino Pessoa de Mello, *Apreciação*, 75–76; Naro, "Brazil's 1848," 165, 167; Lima Sobrinho, "Urbano Sabino Pessoa de Mello," 22–23.

110. *Diário* de Pernambuco, Jan. 5, 1849. CP to PPE, Jan. 4, 1849, APEJE/SM, PC-21, fol. 7. CP to PPE, Jan. 19, 1849, APEJE/SM, PC-21.

111. CP to PPE, Jan, 19 1849, APEJE/SM, PC-21, fol 77, and the attached letter from the Subdel. of Santo Antonio to CP, Jan. 18, 1849, fol. 78. Urbano Sabino Pessoa de Mello, *Apreciação*, 77–78. Jerônimo Martiniano Figueira de Mello, *Crônica*, 136–39.

112. Jerônimo Martiniano Figueira de Mello, *Crônica*, 135–40; Urbano Sabino Pessoa de Mello, *Apreciação*, 75–76; Naro, "Brazil's 1848," 171–72.

113. For the Proclamação dos Deputados, see Urbano Sabino Pessoa de Mello, *Apreciação*, 203–4, and Jerônimo Martiniano Figueira de Mello, *Crônica*, 125–27. "The Banner of the Liberal Movement" ran in the *Diário Novo* on Dec. 30, 1848, and Jan. 1 and 2, 1849. The articles are also available in Urbano Sabino Pessoa de Mello, *Apreciação*, 204–13. The author of the articles was Felipe Lopes Neto. See Marson, *O império*, 77.

114. See Proclamação dos Deputados, reprinted in Urbano Sabino Pessoa de Mello, *Apreciação*, 203–4.

115. Typical of the charges in the *Diário Novo* and the *Guarda Nacional* was the accusation in *Diário Novo*, Nov. 14, 1848, that President Pena was using the army "to sustain the influence of family (i.e., the Cavalcantis) and of foreigners." The Proclamação dos Deputados declared that President Manoel Vieira Tosta was "completely dedicated to the Portuguese cause." See the reprint in Urbano Sabino Pessoa de Mello, *Apreciação*, 203.

116. See the third of the "A bandeira do movimento liberal" articles, reprinted in Urbano Sabino Pessoa de Mello, *Apreciação*, 211.

117. See the second of the three articles titled "A bandeira do movimento lib-

eral," reprinted in Urbano Sabino Pessoa de Mello, *Apreciação*, especially 208–9 (quote, 209).

118. See the first of the three articles of "A bandeira do movimento liberal," 205, 207.

119. On sovereignty and the right to rebel, see the first of the "A bandeira do movimento liberal" articles, in Urbano Sabino Pessoa de Mello, *Apreciação*, 207; for the quote, see the second of the articles, 208.

120. For a statement on the earlier position, see Urbano Sabino Pessoa de Mello, *Apreciação*, 76.

121. See the second and third articles of the "A bandeira do movimento liberal" series. These articles also specified that the Constituent Assembly would be composed only of Brazilian-born citizens, with each province represented by the number of deputies and senators that each province currently sent to the Chamber of Deputies and Senate.

122. Likewise, remember the initial embrace of armed resistance by Nunes Machado, shortly after he arrived in Recife with the explicit intention of averting armed action. Once blood had been spilled, it proved impossible for him to restrain his fellow party members.

123. Chacon, *História das idéias socialistas*, 114, citing *A Barca de São Pedro*, July 11, 1848. "The Boat of Saint Peter" can refer to the Catholic Church.

124. Joaquim Nabuco later commented on their dilemma, writing, "Each palm the Jacobins conquered at the expense of conservative liberalism . . . produced a defection (to the Conservatives)." Nabuco, *Estadista*, 105.

125. For the text, see *União* (Recife), Jan. 13, 1849, 2, or Jerônimo Martiniano Figueira de Mello, *Crônica*, 116–18.

126. *Diário Novo*, Dec. 13, 1849.

127. See *União*, Dec. 14, 1848, Jan. 9, 1849, Jan. 18, 1849, and Jan. 25, 1849. On the deputies distancing themselves from Borges da Fonseca, see Marson, *O império*, 81–82.

128. CP of Alagoas to PPE, Porto Calvo, Jan. 7, 1849, APEJE/SM, PC-21, fol. 18. Jerônimo Martiniano Figueira de Mello, *Crônica*, 127–32; both the author's narrative and the documents reproduced there and in the appendix for chapter 4. Marson, *O império*, 84–85; Naro, "Brazil's 1848," 169–70. Mavignier was soon arrested. See CP of Alagoas to PPE, Porto Calvo, Jan. 10, 1849, APEJE/SM, PC-21, fol. 35.

129. CP of Alagoas to PPE, Porto Calvo, Jan. 10, 1849, APEJE/SM, PC-21, fol. 35, provides a narrative of battles in the south. Jerônimo Martiniano Figueira de Mello, *Crônica*, 112–15, 140–44, 149–53; Marson, *O império*, 86–87.

130. Jerônimo Martiniano Figueira de Mello, *Crônica*, 132–35, 144–46, 148–49.

131. Jerônimo Martiniano Figueira de Mello, *Crônica*, 159, 168, estimates at least sixteen hundred men initially and two thousand by the time of preparations for the attack on Recife. General Coelho likewise estimates two thousand men. See "Commando das Armas. Ordem do Dia," signed by José Joaquim Coelho, *União*, Feb. 10, 1849, 1.

132. Marson, *O império*, 92–93.

133. Jerônimo Martiniano Figueira de Mello, *Crônica*, 161–66; on conflicts among the Praia leadership, see Marson, *O império*, 91, 93–94, and 481 for an organizational chart of the Liberal army.

134. Jerônimo Martiniano Figueira de Mello, *Crônica*, 159–60, 166–69; "Commando das Armas. Ordem do Dia," signed by José Joaquim Coelho, *União*, Feb. 10, 1849, 1; *União*, Feb. 8, 1849, 1; British Consul Cowper to Secretary of State for Foreign Affairs Lord Palmerston, Feb. 6, 1849, FO 13/269, no. 11, fol. 83–88, British Consul Secretary of State for Foreign Affairs. Naro estimates the government forces at three thousand men; see Naro, "Brazil's 1848," 173–74.

135. Urbano Sabino Pessoa de Mello, *Apreciação*, 87; British Consul Cowper to Secretary of State for Foreign Affairs Lord Palmerston, Feb. 6, 1849, FO 13/269, N⁰ 11, fol. 83–88, British Consul Secretary of State for Foreign Affairs.

136. British Consul British Consul Cowper to Secretary of State for Foreign Affairs Lord Palmerston, Feb. 6, 1849, FO 13/269, N⁰ 11, fol. 83–88, British Consul Secretary of State for Foreign Affairs, gives an overview; for a detailed general account, see *Diário de Pernambuco*, Feb. 5, 1849. For reports on events in particular areas, see "Commando das Armas. Ordem do Dia," signed by José Joaquim Coelho, *União*, Feb. 10, 1849; *União*, Feb. 8, 1849; "Corpo de Voluntarios," a report from the Lieutenant Colonel, Commander of the Corp of Volunteers to Superior Commander, Feb. 6, 1849, printed in *União*, Feb. 10, 1849; and Subdel. Suplente of First District of Affogados to CP, Feb. 21, 1849, fol. 263, appended to CP to PPE, April 2, 1849, APEJE/SM, PC-22, fol. 262.

137. British Consul Cowper to Secretary of State for Foreign Affairs Lord Palmerston, Feb. 6, 1849, FO 13/269, N⁰ 11, fol. 83–88, British Consul Secretary of State for Foreign Affairs.

138. Jerônimo Martiniano Figueira de Mello, *Crônica*, 179–81, 189; "Commando das Armas. Ordem do Dia . . . 10 de fevereiro de 1849," signed by José Joaquim Coelho, *União*, Feb. 15, 1849; Urbano Sabino Pessoa de Mello, *Apreciação*, 85–86; British Consul Cowper to Secretary of State for Foreign Affairs Lord Palmerston, Feb. 6, 1849, FO 13/269, N⁰ 11, fol. 83–88, British Consul Secretary of State for Foreign Affairs.

139. *Diário de Pernambuco*, Feb. 13, 1849; Jerônimo Martiniano Figueira de Mello, *Crônica*, 182; Urbano Sabino Pessoa de Mello, *Apreciação*, 87.

140. Urbano Sabino Pessoa de Mello, *Apreciação*, 85.

141. For the plan to defend the city, see "Defesa da capital. Quartel do commando da praça na cidade do Recife, 31 de janeiro de 1849. Ordem reservada," *Diário de Pernambuco*, Feb. 5, 1849, 1–2. Estimates of the numbers involved vary; most sources put the number of defenders around sixteen hundred to eighteen hundred, with a somewhat smaller number, although still well over a thousand men, attacking the city. Only the British Consul differed markedly, reporting the figure of twenty-five hundred attackers; see British Consul Cowper to Secretary of State for Foreign Af-

fairs Lord Palmerston, Feb. 6, 1849, FO 13/269, no. 11, fol. 83–88, British Consul Secretary of State for Foreign Affairs. See the document in the *Diário de Pernambuco*, Feb. 5, cited above, as well as "O dia 2 de fevereiro," *União*, Feb. 8, 1849, 1–2; Jerônimo Martiniano Figueira de Mello, *Crônica*, 170–74; Urbano Sabino Pessoa de Mello, *Apreciação*, 89–90. Marson lists defenders at sixteen hundred and Praieiros at twelve hundred but does not give the source for those figures; *O império*, 97. On the arrival of forces by steam packet, see Barman, *Brazil*, 232.

142. Urbano Sabino Pessoa de Mello, *Apreciação*; see pp. 98–99 on assassinations by government forces, p. 103 on wholesale arrests of suspected sympathizers, and p. 109 on the banishment of Fernando de Noronha. On the fate of the prisoners, and for a list of significant Praieiros captured, see Jerônimo Martiniano Figueira de Mello, *Crônica*, 191–93. On seizures of weapons and ammunition, see CP to PPE, APEJE/SM, PC-21, fol. 171 (Feb. 17, 1849), fol. 202 (Feb. 18, 1849), fol. 213 (Feb. 19, 1849), fol. 214 (Feb. 20, 1849), and fol. 249 (Feb. 26, 1849).

143. Jerônimo Martiniano Figueira de Mello, *Crônica*, 201–15; British Consul Cowper to Secretary of State for Foreign Affairs Lord Palmerston, Feb. 20, 1849, FO 13/269, no. 15, fol. 99–100, and March 2, 1849, no. 17, fol. 103–5, British Consul Secretary of State for Foreign Affairs; Carneiro, *A insurreição*, 128–37. On actions around Nazareth, see Del. of Nazareth to CP, Feb. 10, 1849, APEJE/SM, PC-21, fol. 179 and Interim Subdel. of Nazareth to CP, Feb. 12, 1849, APEJE/SM, PC-21, fol. 180.

144. Jerônimo Martiniano Figueira de Mello, *Crônica*, 214–15, 218–19; Carneiro, *A insurreição*, 136–38; Marson, O *império*, 99–101.

145. Jerônimo Martiniano Figueira de Mello, *Crônica*, 219–224; Marson, *O império*, 104–5; British Consul Cowper to Secretary of State for Foreign Affairs Lord Palmerston, March 24, 1849, FO 13/269, no. 19, fol. 109–11, British Consul Secretary of State for Foreign Affairs; Carneiro, *A insurreição*, 140–41.

146. Jerônimo Martiniano Figueira de Mello, *Crônica*, 219, 227–31, 234–35, 241; Naro, "Brazil's 1848," 180–82; Carneiro, *A insurreição*, 141. For Borges da Fonseca's lengthy responses to questions during interrogation, see CP to PPE, April 2, 1849, APEJE/SM, PC-22, fol. 256.

147. Urbano Sabino Pessoa de Mello, *Apreciação*, 150–51, 168. See Nabuco, *Estadista*, 108–11, on Nabuco de Araújo as judge. Praieiros objected to various elements of the trial. See Urbano Sabino Pessoa de Mello, *Apreciação*, chaps. 12 and 13. None of the defendants actually served out their entire life sentences; all were amnestied a few years later. For the documents on the trial, see Jerônimo Martiniano Figueira de Mello, *Autos do inquérito*.

148. Naro, "Brazil's 1848," 182–84; Urbano Sabino Pessoa de Mello, *Apreciação*, 143–47; British Consul Cowper to Secretary of State for Foreign Affairs Lord Palmerston, May 29, 1849, FO 13/269, N⁰ 31, fol. 169–70, British Consul Secretary of State for Foreign Affairs.

149. Urbano Sabino Pessoa de Mello, *Apreciação*, 175–80; Naro, "Brazil's 1848," 141.

150. Naro, "Brazil's 1848," 192–94; Urbano Sabino Pessoa de Mello, *Apreciação*, 181–85; Carneiro, *A insurreição*, 167–68.

151. Naro, "Brazil's 1848," 193–94; Pedro Ivo secured a safe pass to leave Pernambuco but was seized in Rio de Janeiro. He was imprisoned and tried in a military court, and his sentence to hang was commuted to life in prison. Liberal leaders in the court conspired to smuggle him out of prison and onto a ship bound for Europe. He died en route. See Carneiro, *A insurreição*, 165–66.

Conclusion

1. See the pioneering work of Renato Leite, *Republicanos e libertários*.

Bibliography

Orthography here reflects the usage in the works cited, which does not always correspond to the modern usage found in the text.

Abbreviations

APEJE/SM: Arquivo Público Estadual Jordão Emerenciano/Seção de Manuscritos

AN/SPE: Arquivo Nacional/Seção do Poder Executivo, Rio de Janeiro

ANT/NE: Arquivo Nacional Torre do Tombo, Negócios Estrangeiros, Portugal

BN/SM: Biblioteca Nacional/Seção de Manuscritos, Rio de Janeiro

CP: chief of police

CA: commander of arms

DEL: delegado (police commissioner)

JD: juiz de direito (district judge)

DH: *Documentos Históricos*

FO: foreign office

MI: minister of the empire

MJ: minister of justice

OE: oficios do exército

OG: oficios do governo

PM: policia military

PPE: president of Pernambuco

Subdel.: subdelegado (deputy police commissioner)

Archives and Manuscript Collections

Arquivo Nacional/Seção do Poder Executivo (AN/SPE), Rio de Janeiro

President of Pernambuco to Minister of Justice (PPE to MJ), IJ^{1}322, IJ^{1}324.

President of Pernambuco to Minister of the Empire (PPE to MI), IJJ^{9}253.

Minister of Justice to the General Legislative Assembly, Rio de Janeiro. "Relatório apresentado á Assembleia Geral Legislativa na Sessão Ordinaria pelo Ministro e Secretario de Estado dos Negocios da Justiça," 1838; 1840; 1841; 1843; 1843 1a Sessão; 1843 2a Sessão.

Provincial President of Pernambuco to the Legislative Assembly, Pernambuco.

"Relatório que á Assembleia Legislativa de Pernambuco apresentou na Sessão Ordinaria o Exmo. Presidente da mesma Provincia," 1838, 1839, 1841, 1842, 1843.

Arquivo Nacional Torre do Tombo, Negócios Estrangeiros (ANTT/NE), Lisbon, Portugal. Caixa 310.

Arquivo Público Estadual Jordão Emerenciano/Seção de Manuscritos (APEJE/SM), Recife, Brazil. CA-11, DC-5, JD-5–6, OE-12, and PC-17–23.

Biblioteca Nacional/Seção de Manuscritos (BN/SM), Rio de Janeiro. I:32, 6, 24, fol. 26–79; II:32, 44, 47; II:32, 34, 51, no. 1; II:32, 34, 51, no. 1; II:32, 34, 51, no. 1; II:32, 34, 4; II:32, 34, 4, no. 3; II:33, 6, 41; II:33, 6, 33; II:32, 34, 47; II:32, 34, 4, no. 3.

Figueira de Mello Collection. I:29, 21, no. 70; I:29, 21, no. 62; I:29, 21, no. 63.

British Consul Secretary of State for Foreign Affairs. Public Record Office, Foreign Office, Great Britain. FO 13/260, 13/269.

Casa da Cultura, Recife, Brazil. Del. of Água Preta to Chief of Police and Subdel. of Una to the Chief of Police.

Dispatches from the U.S. Consuls in Pernambuco, Brazil, 1817–1906. General Records of the Department of State—Record Group 59. U.S. National Archives. Washington, DC. T-344, rolls 1, 3.

Documentos Históricos (DH). Biblioteca Nacional, Divisão de Obraras Raras e Publições, 1953–55. Rio de Janeiro. Vols. 101–5, 107, 109, 110.

Instituto Arqueológico, Histórico e Geográfico Pernambucano, Recife, Brazil. Actas da Irmandade da Nossa Senhora da Conceição da Congregação, livro 1, fol. 51.

Instituto Histórico e Geográfico Brasileiro, Rio de Janeiro. Marquis of Olinda Collection, lata 219, doc. 52.

Published Works

Abreu e Lima, Ignácio. *Synopsis ou deducção chronológica dos factos mais notáveis da história do Brasil.* Recife: M. F. de Faria, 1845.

Adelman, Jeremy. *Republic of Capital: Buenos Aires and the Legal Transformation of the Atlantic World.* Stanford: Stanford University Press, 1999.

Alden, Dauril. "Late Colonial Brazil, 1750–1808." In Bethell, *Colonial Brazil.*

Alexandre, Valentim. *Os sentidos do império: Questão nacional e questão colonial na crise do antigo regime português.* Porto, Portugal: Edições Afrontamento, 1993.

Almeida, Luiz Sávio de. "Memorial biográphico do capitão de todas as matas." PhD diss., Universidade Federal de Pernambuco, 1995.

Almeida, Tito Franco de. *O conselheiro Francisco José Furtado: Biografia e estudo de história política contemporanea.* São Paulo: Companhia Editora Nacional, 1944.

Alves, Jorge Fernandes. *Os brasileiros: Emigração e retorno no Porto oitocentista.* Porto, Portugal: 1994.

Anderson, Benedict. *Imagined Communities: Reflections on the Origin and Spread of Nationalsim.* London: Verso, 1991.

Andrade, Manuel Correia de. *A guerra dos cabanos.* Rio de Janeiro: Conquista, 1965.

———. *Brasil: Realidade e utopia*. Recife: Editora Universidade/UFPE, 2000).

———. *The Land and People of Northeast Brazil*. Albuquerque: University of New Mexico Press, 1980.

———. *Movimentos nativistas em Pernambuco: Setembrizada e Novembrada*. Recife: Universidade Federal de Pernambuco, 1971.

Andrade, Manuel Correia de, and Eliane Moury Fernandes, eds. *O nordeste brasileiro e a Revolução Francesa*. Recife: FUNDAJ, Editora Massangana, 1992.

Andrews, George Reid. *Blacks and Whites in São Paulo, Brazil, 1888–1988*. Madison: University of Wisconsin Press, 1991.

Anna, Timothy E. *Forging Mexico: 1821–1835*. Lincoln: University of Nebraska Press, 1998.

Anonymous. "A Pedrosada: 1823." *Revista do Instituto Archeológico e Geográphico Pernambucano* 13, no. 74 (1908): 577–85.

Araújo, José Thomaz Nabuco de. *Justa apreciação do predominio do partido Praieiro ou historia da dominação da praia*. Recife: União, 1847.

Ardant, Gabriel. "Financial Policy and Economic Infrastructure of Modern States and Nations." In *The Formation of National States in Western Europe*, edited by Charles Tilly. Princeton NJ: Princeton University Press, 1975.

Arquivo Público Estadual Pernambuco. "Comandante das armas ao Presidente de Provincia de Pernambuco (1848)," reprinted in *Revista do Arquivo Público* 2, no. 4 (2nd semestre 1948).

Arruda, José Jobson de Andrade. "Decadence or Crisis in the Luso-Brazilian Empire: A New Model of Colonization in the Eighteenth Century," *Hispanic American Historical Review* 80, no. 4 (November 2000): 865–78.

Assunção, Matthias Röhrig. "Elite Politics and Popular Rebellion in the Construction of Post-colonial Order: The Case of Maranhão, Brazil (1820–1841)." *Journal of Latin American Studies* 31 (February 1999): 1–38.

Auler, Guilherme. *A companhia de operarios, 1839–1843: Subsídios para o estudo da emigração germánica no Brasil*. Recife, Brazil: Arquivo Público Estadual, 1959.

Bagehot, Walter. *The English Constitution*. Ithaca NY: Cornell University Press, 1986.

Balmori, Diana, Stuart F. Voss, and Miles Wortman. *Notable Family Networks in Latin America*. Chicago: University of Chicago Press, 1984.

"Bando." *Revista do Instituto Archeológico e Geográphico Pernambucano* 10, no. 56 (1902): 81.

Barbalho, Nelson. *1710: Recife versus Olinda. A guerra municipal de Açucar. Nobres x mascates*. Recife: Centro de Estudos de História Municipal/FIAM, 1986.

Barman, Roderick. *Brazil: The Forging of a Nation, 1798–1852*. Stanford: Stanford University Press, 1988.

———. "Brazilians in France, 1822–1872: Doubly Outsiders." In *Strange Pilgrimages: Exile, Travel, and National Identity in Latin America, 1800–1990s*, edited by Ingrid E. Frey and Karen Racine. Wilmington DE: Scholarly Resources, 2000.

———. *Citizen Emperor: Pedro II and the Making of Brazil, 1825–91*. Stanford: Stanford University Press, 1999.

Barreto, Célia de Barros. "Ação das xociedades xecretas." In *História geral da civilização Brasileira*. Tomo 2, vol. 1, *O processo de emancipação*, edited by Sérgio Buarque de Holanda and Pedro Moacyr Campos. São Paulo, Brazil: DIFEL, 1985.

Barreto, Luiz do Rego. *Memória justificativa sobre a conducta do Marechal do Campo Luiz do Rego Barreto durante o tempo em que foi governador de Pernambuco e Presidente da Junta Constitucional da mesma provincial*. Recife: FUNDARPE, 1991.

Bastos, Aureliano Cândido Tavares. *A provincia: Estudo sobre a descentralizacão no Brazil*. São Paulo: Editora Nacional, 1937.

Beattie, Peter M. *The Tribute of Blood: Army, Honor, Race, and Nation in Brazil, 1864–1945*. Durham: Duke University Press, 2001.

Beiguelman, Paula. *Formação política do Brasil*. São Paulo: Livraria Pioneira, 1976.

Berbel, Márcia Regina. *A nação como artefato: Deputados do Brasil nas cortes portuguesas (1821–1822)*. São Paulo: Hucitec, Fapesp, 1999.

———. "Pátria e patriotas em Pernambuco (1817–1822) nação, identidade e vacabulário politico." In Jancsó, *Brasil: Formação do estado e da nação*.

Bernardes, Denis Antônio de Mendonça. "Pernambuco e o Império: Sem constituição soberana não há união." In Jancsó, *Brasil: Formação do estado e da nação*.

Bethell, Leslie. The Abolition of the Brazilian Slave Trade: Britain, Brazil and the Slave Trade Question, 1807–1869. Cambridge: Cambridge University Press, 1970.

———, ed. *Colonial Brazil*. Cambridge: Cambridge University Press, 1987.

———. "The Independence of Brazil." In *The Independence of Latin America*, edited by Leslie Bethell. Cambridge: Cambridge University Press, 1987.

Bethell, Leslie, and José Murilo de Carvalho. "1822–1850." In *Brazil: Empire and Republic, 1822–1930*, edited by Leslie Bethell. Cambridge University Press, 1989.

Bieber, Judy. "Postmodern Ethnographer in the Backlands: An Imperial Bureaucrat's Perceptions of Post-Independence Brazil." *Latin American Research Review* 33, no. 2 (1998): 37–72.

———. *Power, Patronage, and Political Violence: State Building on a Brazilian Frontier, 1822–1889*. Lincoln: University of Nebraska Press, 1999.

Bonich, Edna. "A Theory of Middleman Minorities." *American Sociology Review* 38 (October 1973): 583–94.

Bonich, Edna, and John Modell. *The Economic Basis of Ethnic Solidarity: Small Business in the Japanese American Community*. Berkeley: University of California Press, 1980.

Borges, Dain. *The Family in Bahia, Brazil, 1870–1945*. Stanford CA: Stanford University Press, 1992.

Boxer, C. R. *The Golden Age of Brazil. 1695–1750: Growing Pains of a Colonial Society*. Berkeley: University of California Press, 1962.

Brandão, Bernice Cavalcanti, Ilmar Rohlof de Mattos, and Maria Alice Rezende de Carvalho. *A polícia e a força policial no Rio de Janeiro*. Série Estudos, no. 4. Rio de Janeiro: PUC/RJ, 1981.

Brandão, Ulysses de Carvalho Soares. *Pernambuco de out'ora: A confederação do Equador*. Recife: Officinas Graphicas da Repartição de Publicações Officiais, 1924.

Brito, Sócrates Quintino da Fonseca e. "A rebelião de Joaquim Pinto Madeira: Fatores políticos e sociaes." Master's thesis, Universidade Federal de Santa Catarina, Brazil.

Bueno, José Antônio Pimenta. *Direito público brasileiro e análise da Constituição do Império*. Rio de Janeiro: Ministro da Justiça e Negocios Interiores, 1958.

Burns, E. Bradford. "The Intellectuals as Agents of Change and the Independence of Brazil, 1724–1822." In *From Colony to Nation: Essays on the Independence of Brazil*, edited by A. J. R. Russell-Wood. Baltimore: Johns Hopkins University Press, 1975.

———."The Role of Azeredo Coutinho in the Enlightenment of Brazil." *Hispanic American Historical Review* 44, no. 2 (1964): 145–60.

Bushnell, David. *The Santander Regime in Gran Colombia*. Newark: University of Delaware Press, 1954.

Caballero, Romeo Flores. *Counterrevolution: The Role of the Spaniards in the Independence of Mexico, 1804–1838*. Lincoln: University of Nebraska Press, 1974.

Cabral de Mello, Evaldo. *A outra independência: O federalismo pernambucano de 1817 e 1824*. São Paulo: Editora 34, 2004.

———. *Rubro veio: O imaginário da restauração pernambucana*. Rio de Janeiro: Nova Fronteira, 1986.

Calmon, Pedro. *História de Dom Pedro II: Tomo primeiro: Infância e Juventude, 1825–1853*. Rio de Janeiro: José Olympio, Instituto Nacional de Livro, 1975.

Carneiro, Edison. *A insurreição Praieira (1848–49)*. Rio de Janeiro: Conquista, 1960.

Carreira, António. *As companhias pombalinas de Grão Pará e Maranhão e Pernambuco e Paraíba*. Lisbon: Editorial Presença, 1983.

Carrera Damas, Germán. *Boves: Aspectos socioeconomicos de la guerra de independencia*. Caracas: Ediciones de la Biblioteca, Universdad Central de Venezuela, 1972.

Carvalho, Alfredo de. "As carneiradas: Episodios da guerra dos cabanos, 1834–1835." *Revista do Instituto Archeológico e Geográphico de Pernambuco* 13 (December 1908): 591–617.

Carvalho, Gilberto Vilar de. *A liderança do clero nas revoluções republicanas (1817 a 1824)*. Petrópolis, Brazil: Vozes, 1980.

Carvalho, José Murilo de, ed. *Bernardo Pereira de Vasconcelos*. São Paulo: Editora 34, 1999.

———. *A construção da ordem: A elite política imperial*. Rio de Janeiro: Editora Campus, 1980.

———. *Teatro de sombras: A política imperial*. Rio de Janeiro: Instituto Universitário de Pesquisa do Rio de Janeiro, 1988.

Carvalho, Manuel Emilio Gomes de. *Os deputados brasileiros nas cortes gerais de 1821*. Porto, Portugal: Livraria Chardron, 1912.

Carvalho, Marcus Joaquim Maciel de. "O antilusitanismo e a questão social em Pernambuco, 1822–1848." In *Emigração em Portugal: Actas do colóquio internacional sobre emigração e imigração em Portugal (séc. XIX-XX)*, edited by Maria Beatriz Nizza da Silva, Maria Ioannis Baganha, Maria José Maranhâo, and Miraim Halpern Pereira. Algés, Portugal: Fragmentos, 1993.

———. "Cavalcantis e cavalgados: A formação das alianças políticas em Pernambuco, 1817–1824." *Revista Brasileira de História* 18, no. 36 (1998): 331–66.

———. "O encontro da 'soldadesca desenfreada' com os 'Cicadãos de cor mais levianos' no Recife em 1831," *Clio* 1, no. 18 (1998): 109–37.

———. "A guerra do moraes: A luta dos senhores de engenho na Praieira." Master's thesis, Universidade Federal de Pernambuco, Recife, 1986.

———. "Hegemony and Rebellion in Pernambuco (Brazil), 1821–1835." PhD diss., University of Illinois, Urbana–Champaign, 1989.

———. "Os índios de Pernambuco no ciclo das insurreições liberais, 1817/1848: Ideologias e resistência." *Revista da Sociedade Brasileira de Pesquisa Histórica* 1, no. 11 (1996): 51–69.

———. *Liberdade: Rotinas e rupturas do escravismo, Recife, 1822–1850*. Recife: UFPE, 1998.

Carvalho Soares Brandão, Ulysses de. *Pernambuco de outr'óra: A confederação do equador*. Recife: Officinas Graphicas da Repartição de Publicações Officiaes, 1924.

Cascudo, Luis da Camara. *O marquez de Olinda e seu tempo (1783–1870)*. São Paulo: Companhia Editora Nacional, 1938.

Castro, Jeanne Berrance de. *A milicia cidadã: A guarda nacional de 1831 a 1850*. São Paulo: Companhia Editora Nacional, 1977.

Chacon, Vamireh. *Abreu e Lima: General de Bolívar*. Rio de Janeiro: Paz e Terra, 1983.

———. *História das idéias socialistas no Brasil*. Fortaleza and Rio de Janeiro: Edições UFC and Civilização Brasileira, 1981.

Chacon, Vamireh, and Leonardo Leite Neto, eds. *O typhis pernambucano*. Brasília: Senado Federal, Centro Gráfico, 1984.

Chambers, Sarah C. *From Subjects to Citizens: Honor, Gender, and Politics in Arequipa, Peru, 1780–1854*. University Park: Pennsylvania State University Press, 1999.

Chasteen, John Charles. "Cabanos and Farrapos: Brazilian Nativism in Regional Perspective, 1822–1850." *Locus* 7:1 (Fall 1994): 31–46.

Chiaramonte, José Carlos. *Ciudades, provincias, estados: Los orígenes de la nación Argentina, 1800–1846*. Buenos Aires: Ariel, 1997.

Chiavento, Júlio José. *Cabanagem: O povo no poder*. São Paulo: Brasiliense, 1984.

Chirot, Daniel, and Anthony Reid, eds. *Essential Outsiders: Chinese and Jews in the Modern Transformation of Southeast Asia and Central Europe*. Seattle: University of Washington Press, 1997.

Cleary, David. "'Lost Altogether to the Civilized World': Race and the *Cabanagem* in Northern Brazil, 1750 to 1850." *Comparative Studies in Society and History* 40, no. 1 (January 1998): 681–711.

Cohen, Youssef, Brian Brown, and A. F. K. Organski. "The Paradoxical Nature of Statemaking: The Violent Creation of Order." *American Political Science Review* 75, no. 4 (December 1981): 901–20.

Collier, Simon. *Ideas and Politics of Chilean Independence, 1808–1833.* Cambridge: Cambridge University Press, 1967.

Correa, Viriato. "A margem da revolução de 1824." *Revista do Instituto Archeológico e Geográphico Pernambucano* 27 (January 1925): 334–42.

Corrigan, Philip, and Derek Sayer. *The Great Arch: English State Formation as Cultural Revolution.* Oxford: Basil Blackwell, 1985.

Costa, Emília Viotti da. *The Brazilian Empire: Myths and Histories.* Chicago: University of Chicago Press, 1985.

———. "The Political Emancipation of Brazil." In *From Colony to Nation: Essays on the Independence of Brazil,* edited by A. J. R. Russell-Wood. Baltimore: Johns Hopkins University Press, 1975.

Costa, Francisco Augusto Pereira da. *Anais pernambucanos.* Vol. 8, *1818–1823.* Recife: Arquivo Público Estadual, 1962.

———. *Anais pernambucanos.* Vol. 9, *1824–1833.* Recife: FUNDARPE, 1983.

———. *Anais pernambucanos.* Vol 10, *1834–1850.* Recife: FUNDARPE, 1985.

———. *Dicionário de pernambucanos célebres.* Recife: Fundação de Cultura Cidade do Recife, 1981.

Costa, Wilma Peres. "Do domínio à nação: Os impasses da fiscalidade no processo de Independência." In Jancsó, *Brasil: Formação do estado e da nação.*

Cunha, Euclides da. *Os sertões (campanha de canudos).* Rio de Janeiro: F. Alves, 1914.

Davis, Natalie Zemon. "The Rites of Violence: Religious Riot in Sixteenth-Century France." *Past and Present* 59 (May 1973): 51–91.

Dean, Warren. *Rio Claro: A Brazilian Plantation System, 1820–1920.* Stanford: Stanford University Press, 1976.

Deerr, Noel. *The History of Sugar.* 2 vols. London: Chapman and Hall, 1949–50.

Delgado, Jaime. *España y México en el siglo XIX.* Vol. 1, *1820–1830.* Madrid: Consejo Superior de Investigaciones Científicas and Instituto Gonzalo Fernández de Oviedo, 1950.

Dias, Maria Odila Silva. "A interiorização da metrópole (1808–1853)." In *1822: Dimensões.* Carlos Guilherme Mota, ed. São Paulo: Editora Perspectiva, 1972.

Dolhnikoff, Miriam. "Elites regionais e a construção do estado nacional." In Jancsó, *Brasil: Formação do estado e da nação.*

Eagleton, Terry, ed. *Ideology.* London: Longman, 1994.

———. *Ideology: An Introduction.* London: Verso, 1991.

Eisenberg, Peter L. *The Sugar Industry in Pernambuco: Modernization without Change, 1840–1910.* Berkeley: University of California Press, 1974.

Evans, Peter. *Dependent Development: The Alliance of Multinational, State, and Local Capital in Brazil.* Princeton: Princeton University Press, 1979.

Falas do Trono: Desde ao ano de 1823 até 1889. São Paulo: Melhoramentos, 1977.

Faoro, Raymundo. *Os donos do poder: Formação do patronato político brasileiro*. 2 vols. Rio de Janeiro: Globo, 1987.

Ferraz, Socorro, ed. *Frei Caneca: Acusação e defesa*. Recife: Editora Universitária da Universidade Federal de Pernambuco, 2000.

————. *Liberaes & liberaes: Guerras civis em Pernambuco no século XIX*. Recife: Editora Universitária da Universidade Federal de Pernambuco, 1996.

Figueiredo, Antônio Pedro de. "O Recife." Excerpt in *O Recife: Quatro séculos de sua paisagem*, edited by Mário Souto Maior and Leonardo Dantas Silva. Recife: Fundação Joaquim Nabuco, Editora Massangana, Prefeitura da Cidade do Recife, Secretaria de Educação e Cultura, 1992.

Florentino, Manolo. *Em costas negras: Uma história do tráfico atlântico de escravos entre a Africa e o Rio de Janeiro, séculos XVIII e XIX*. Rio de Janeiro: Arquivo Nacional, 1995.

Flores, Moacyr. *A revolução farroupilha*. Porto Alegre, Brazil: University Federal do Rio Grande do Sul, 1990.

Flory, Thomas. *Judge and Jury in Imperial Brazil, 1808–1871: Social Control and Political Stability in the New State*. Austin: University of Texas Press, 1981.

————. "Race and Social Control in Independent Brazil," *Journal of Latin American Studies* 9 (November 1977): 199–224.

Fonseca, Antônio Borges da. *Manifesto politico: Apontamentos da minha vida politica e da vida politica do Dr. Urbano Sabino Pessoa de Mello*. Recife, 1867.

Fontana, Biancamaria, ed. *The Political Writings of Benjamin Constant*. Cambridge: Cambridge University Press, 1988.

Foucault, Michel. *Discipline and Punish: The Birth of the Prison*. New York: Vintage Books, 1995.

Fragoso, João Luís Ribeiro. *Homens da grossa ventura: Acumulação e hierarquia na praça mercantil do Rio de Janeiro, 1790–1830*. Rio de Janeiro: Arquivo Nacional, 1992.

Franco, Afonso Arinos Melo. "História e teoria do partido político no direito constitucional brasileiro." Rio de Janeiro, 1948.

Franco, José L. *Política continental americana de España en Cuba, 1812–1830*. Havana: Archivo Nacional, 1947.

Freire, Eduardo. *O diabo na livraria do conêgo: Como era Gonzaga? E outros temas mineiros*. Belo Horizonte, Brazil: Itatiaia, 1981.

Freitas, Décio. *Os guerrilheiros do imperador*. Rio de Janeiro: Graal, 1978.

Freyre, Gilberto. *Um engenheiro francês no Brasil*. Vol. 2. Rio de Janeiro: José Olympio, 1960.

————. *The Mansions and the Shanties: The Making of Modern Brazil*. Berkeley: University of California Press, 1986.

————, ed. *O Velho Félix e suas "Memórias de um Cavalcanti."* Recife: FUNDAJ, Editora Massangana, 1989.

Fuente, Ariel de la. *Children of Facundo: Caudillo and Gaucho Insurgency during the Ar-*

gentine State-Formation Process (La Rioja, 1853–1870). Durham: Duke University Press, 2000.

Galloway, J. H. *The Sugar Cane Industry: An Historical Geography from Its Origin to 1914*. Cambridge: Cambridge University Press, 1989.

Garcia, Paulo. *Cipriano Barata, ou, A liberdade acima de tudo*. Rio de Janeiro: Topbooks, 1997.

Garner, Lydia Magalhães Nunes. "In Pursuit of Order: A Study in Brazilian Centralization, the Section of Empire of the Council of State, 1842–1889." PhD diss., Johns Hopkins University, 1988.

Godechot, Jacques León. *France and the Atlantic Revolution of the Eighteenth-Century, 1770–1779*. 2 vols. New York: Free Press, 1959–64.

Gootenberg, Paul. *Imaging Development: Economic Ideas in Peru's "Fictitious Prosperity" of Guano, 1840–1880*. Berkeley: University of California Press, 1993.

Graham, Maria Dundas (Lady Maria Callcott). *Journal of a Voyage to Brazil, and Residence There, during Part of the Years 1821, 1822, 1823*. New York: Praeger, 1969.

Graham, Richard, ed. *Brazil and the World System*. Austin: University of Texas Press, 1991.

———. *Britain and the Onset of Modernization in Brazil, 1850–1914*. Cambridge: Cambridge University Press, 1972.

———. *Patronage and Politics in Nineteenth-Century Brazil*. Stanford: Stanford University Press, 1990.

Green, Stanley C. *The Mexican Republic: The First Decade, 1823–1832*. Pittsburgh: University Of Pittsburgh Press, 1987.

Guardino, Peter F. *Peasants, Politics, and the Formation of Mexico's National State: Guerrero, 1808–1857*. Stanford: Stanford University Press, 1996.

Gudmundson, Lowell, and Hector Lindos-Fuents. *Central America, 1821–1871: Liberalism before Liberal Reform*. Tuscaloosa: University of Alabama Press, 1995.

Guerra, Flávio. *O conde da Boa Vista e o Recife*. Recife: Fundação Guararapes, 1973.

Hale, Charles. *Mexican Liberalism in the Age of Mora, 1821–1853*. New Haven: Yale University Press, 1968.

Hall, John. "Introduction." In *States in History*, edited by John Hall. Oxford: Basil Blackwell, 1986.

———. "Introduction: The State and Social Theory." In *The State*, edited by John Hall and G. John Ikenberry. Minneapolis: University of Minnesota Press, 1989.

Halperín Donhi, Tulio, ed. *Sarmiento: Author of a Nation*. Berkeley: University of California Press, 1994.

Higgs, David. "Unbelief and Politics in Rio de Janeiro during the 1790s." *Luso-Brazilian Review* 12 (Summer 1984): 13–31.

Hobsbawm, Eric. *Nations and Nationalism since 1780: Programme, Myth, Realtiy*. Cambridge: Cambridge University Press, 1991.

Holanda, Sérgio Buarque de. "A Herança Colonial—Sua Desagregação." In *História geral da civilização brasileira*. Tomo 2, vol. 1, *O processo de emancipação*, edited by Sérgio Buarque de Holanda and Pedro Moacyr Campos. São Paulo: DIFEL, 1985.

Holloway, Thomas. *Policing Rio de Janeiro: Repression and Resistance in a 19th-Century City*. Stanford: Stanford University Press, 1993.

Homem, Francisco de Sales Torres. "O Libelo do povo." In Raymundo Magalhães Júnior, ed. *Três Panfletários do Segundo Reinado*. São Paulo: Companhia Editoria Nacional, 1956.

Horowitz, Donald L. *The Deadly Ethnic Riot*. Berkeley: University of California Press, 2001.

Instituto Arqueológico, Histórico, Geográfico Pernambucano. "Notícia breve do 2° reinado NUMA TROCA DE CORRESPONDENCIA." *Revista do Instituto Arqueológico, Histórico e Geográfico Pernambucano* 43 (1950–1953): 13–17.

Jancsó, István, ed. *Brasil: Formação do estado e da nação*. São Paulo: Hucitec, Editora Unijuí, and Fapesp, 2003.

———. *Na Bahia, contra o império: História do ensaio de sedição de 1798*. São Paulo and Salvador: Hucitec and EDUFBA, 1996.

Jancsó, István, and João Paulo G. Pimenta. "Peças de um mosaico (ou apontamentos para o estudo da emergência da identidade nacional brasileira)." In *Viagem incomplete. A experiência brasileira (1500–2000). Formação: histórias*, edited by Carlos Guilherme Mota. São Paulo: Editora SENAC São Paulo, 2000.

Janotti, Maria de Lourdes Mônaco. *A balaiada*. São Paulo: Brasiliense, 1987.

Joseph, Gilbert M., and Daniel Nugent, eds. *Everyday Forms of State Formation: Revolution and the Negotiation of Rule in Modern Mexico*. Durham: Duke University Press, 1994.

Kahler, Mary Ellis. "Relations between Brazil and the United States, 1815–1825, with Special Reference to the Revolutions of 1817 and 1824." PhD diss., American University, 1968.

Kidder, Daniel Parrish. *Brazil and the Brazilians Portrayed in Historical and Descriptive Sketches*. Excerpt in *O Recife: Quatro séculos de sua paisagem*, edited by Mário Souto Maior and Leonardo Dantas Silva. Recife: Fundação Joaquim Nabuco, Editora Massangana, Prefeitura da Cidade do Recife, Secretaria de Educação e Cultura, 1992.

Koster, Henry. *Travels in Brazil*. Carbondale: Southern Illinois University Press, 1966.

Kraay, Hendrik. "'As Terrifying as Unexpected': The Bahian Sabinada, 1837–1838." *Hispanic American Historical Review* 72 (November 1992): 501–28.

———. *Race, State, and Armed Forces in Independence-Era Brazil: Bahia, 1790s-1840s*. Stanford: Stanford University Press, 2001.

———. "Reconsidering Recruitment in Imperial Brazil." *The Americas* 55 (July 1998): 1–33.

Lamego, Miguel A. Sánchez. *La invasión española de 1829*. Mexico City: Editorial Jus, 1971.

Langley, Lester D. *The Americas in the Age of Revolution, 1750–1850*. New Haven: Yale University Press, 1996.

Leal, Aurelino. *Do ato adicional a maioridade*. Brasília: Senado Federal, 1978.

Leite, Glacyra Lazzari. *Pernambuco 1817: Estrutura e comportamentos sociais*. Recife: Fundação Joaquim Nabuco, Massangana, 1988.

———. *Pernambuco 1824: A confederação do Equador*. Recife: Fundação Joaquim Nabuco, Massangana, 1989.

Leite, Renato Lopes. *Republicanos e libertários: Pensadores radicais no Rio de Janeiro (1822)*. Rio de Janeiro: Civilização Brasileira, 2000.

Lenharo, Alcir. *As tropas da moderação: O abastecimento da corte na formação política do Brasil, 1808–1842*. São Paulo: Edições Símbolo, 1979.

Levine, Robert. *Vale of Tears: Revisiting the Canudos Massacre in Northeastern Brazil, 1893–1897*. Berkeley: University of California Press, 1992.

Lewin, Linda. *Politics and Parentela in Paraíba: A Case Study of Family-Based Oligarchy in Brazil*. Princeton: Princeton University Press, 1987.

Lima Júnior, Augusto de. *Historia dos diamantes nas Minas Gerais, século XVIII*. Lisbon: Dois Mundos, 1945.

Lima Sobrinho, Barbosa. *Pernambuco: Da independência à confereação do Equador*. Recife: Conselho Estadual de Cultura, 1979.

———. "A Revolução Praieira." *Revista do Arquivo Público* 5 (1949).

———. "Urbano Sabino Pessôa de Melo." *Revista do Instituto Archeológico, Histórico e Geográfico Pernambucano* 47 (1975): 329–69.

Lindoso, Dirceu. *A utopia armada: Rebeliões de pobres nas matas do tombo real*. Rio de Janeiro: Paz e Terra, 1983.

Love, Joseph, and Nils Jacobsen, eds. *Guiding the Invisible Hand: Economic Liberalism and the State in Latin America*. New York: Praeger, 1988.

Lustosa, Isabel. *Insultos impressos: A guerra dos jornalistas na independência (1821–1823)*. São Paulo: Companhia das Letras, 2000.

Lynch, John. *Argentine Dictator, Juan Manuel de Rosas, 1829–1852*. Oxford: Oxford University Press, 1981.

Lyra, Augusto Tavares de. *Instituições políticas do império*. Brasília: Senado Federal, 1978.

Lyra, Maria de Lourdes Viana. "Pátria do cidadão: A concepção de pátria/nação em Frei Caneca." *Revista Brasileira de História* 18, no. 36 (1998), http://www.scielo.br/scielo.php?script=sci_arttext&pid=S0102-01881998000200016.

———. "Centralisation, systhème fiscal et autonomie provinciale dans l'empire brésilien: La province de Pernambuco, 1808–1835." PhD diss., Université Paris-X, Paris, 1985.

———. *A utopia do poderoso império—Portugal e Brasil: Bastidores da política, 1798–1822*. Rio de Janeiro: Sette Letras, 1994.

Macaulay, Neill. *Dom Pedro: The Struggle for Liberty in Brazil and Portugal, 1798–1834*. Durham: Duke University Press, 1986.

Machado, M. Lopes. "O 14 de Abril de 1832, em Pernambuco." *Revista do Instituto Archeológico e Geográphico Pernambucano* 6, no. 38 (1890): 37–66.

Machado, Teobaldo. *As insurreições liberais em Goiana, 1817–1824*. Recife: FUNDARPE, 1990.

Magalhães, Domingos José Gonçalves de. "Memória histórica e documentada da revolução da província do Maranhão desde 1839 até 1840." *Novos Estudos CEBRAP* 23 (March 1989): 7–66.

Magalhães Júnior, Raymundo, ed. *Três panfletários do segundo reinado*. São Paulo: Companhia Editora Nacional, 1956.

Malerba, Jurandir. *A corte no exílio: Civilização e poder no Brasil às vésperas da independênica*. São Paulo: Companhia das Letras, 2000.

Mallon, Florencia. *Peasant and Nation: The Making of Postcolonial Mexico and Peru*. Berkeley: University of California Press, 1995.

———. "The Promise and Dilemma of Subaltern Studies: Perspectives from Latin American History." *American Historical Review* 99 (December 1994): 1491–1515.

Manchester, Alan. *British Preëminence in Brazil: Its Rise and Decline—A Study in European Expansion*. Chapel Hill: University of North Carolina Press, 1933.

Mann, Michael. "The Autonomous Power of the State: Its Origins, Mechanisms, and Results." In *States in History*, edited by John Hall. Oxford: Basil Blackwell, 1986.

———. *The Sources of Social Power*. Vol 2, *The Rise of Classes and Nation-States, 1760–1914*. Cambridge: Cambridge University Press, 1993.

Mansuy-Diniz Silva, Andrée. "Imperial Re-organization, 1750–1808." In Bethell, *Colonial Brazil*.

Marson, Izabel Andrade. *O Império do progresso: A revolução Praieira em Pernambuco (1842–1855)*. São Paulo: Editora Brasiliense, 1987.

Mascarenhas, Nelson Lage. *Um jornalista do imperio (Firmino Rodrigues Silva)*. São Paulo: Companhia Editora Nacional, 1961.

Mattos, Ilmar Rohloff de. *O tempo saquarema: A formação do estado imperial*. São Paulo: Editora Hucitec, 1990.

Mattoso, Kátia M. de. *A presença francesa no movimento democrático baiano de 1798*. Salvador, Brazil: Itapuã, 1969.

Maxwell, Kenneth R. *Conflicts and Conspiracies: Brazil and Portugal 1750–1808*. Cambridge: Cambridge University Press, 1973.

———. *Pombal: Paradox of the Enlightenment*. Cambridge: Cambridge University Press, 1995.

McBeth, Michael. "The Brazilian Recruit during the First Empire: Slave or Soldier?" In *Essays Concerning the Socioeconomic History of Brazil and Portuguese India*, edited by Dauril Alden. Gainesville: Florida International University, 1977.

———. "The Politicians vs. the Generals: The Decline of the Brazilian Army During the First Empire, 1822–1831." PhD diss., University of Washington, 1972.

Mello, Jerônimo Martiniano Figueira de, ed. *Autos do inquérito da Revolução Praieira*. Brasília: Senado Federal and Editora da Universidade de Brasília, 1979.

———. *Crônica da Rebelião Praieira, 1848 e 1849*. Brasília: Senado Federal, Editora Universidade de Brasília, 1978.

———. *Ensaio sobre a estatística civil e política da provincia de Pernambuco*. Recife: M. F. de Faria, 1852.

Mello, Milton. *A Setembrizada*. Recife: Directoria de Documentação e Cultura, 1951.

Mello, Urbano Sabino Pessoa de. *Apreciação da Revolta Praieira em Pernambuco*. Brasília: Senado Federal, Editora Universidade de Brasília, 1978.

Melo, Antônio Joaquim de. *Biografia de Gervásio Pires Ferreira*. Recife: Editora Universitária da Universidade Federal de Pernambuco, 1973.

Mélo, Mário Carneiro do Rego. *A maçonaria e a revolução republicana de 1817*. Recife: Imprensa Industrial, 1912.

Meznar, Joan E. "The Ranks of the Poor: Military Service and Social Differentiation in Northeast Brazil, 1830–1875." *Hispanic American Historical Review* 72 (August 1992): 335–51.

Mintz, Sidney. *Sweetness and Power: The Place of Sugar in Modern History*. New York: Penguin Books, 1986.

Monteiro, Tobias. *História do império: O primeiro reinado*. Vol. 1. Belo Horizonte and São Paulo: Editora Itatiaia and Editora da Universidade de São Paulo, 1982.

Morel, Marco. *Cipriano Barata na sentinella da liberdade*. Salvador, Brazil: Academia das Letras da Bahia, Assembleia Legislativa do Estado da Bahia, 2001.

———. "Restaurar, fracionar e regenerar a nação: O partido caramuru nos anos 1830." In Jancsó, *Brasil: Formação do estado e da nação*.

Moreno Fraginals, Manuel. *The Sugarmill: The Socio-Economic Complex of Sugar in Cuba, 1760–1860*. New York: Monthly Review Press, 1976.

Mosher, Jeffrey C. "Challenging Authority: Political Violence and the Regency in Pernambuco, Brazil, 1831–1835." *Luso-Brazilian Review* 37 (Winter 2000): 33–57.

———. "Political Moblization, Party Ideology, and Lusophobia in Nineteenth-Century Brazil: Pernambuco, 1822–1850." *Hispanic American Historical Review* 80 (November 2000): 881–912.

Mota, Carlos Guilherme. *Idéia da revolução no Brasil: Estudo das formas do pensamento*. Petrópolis, Brazil: Vozes, 1979.

———. *Nordeste 1817: Estruturas e argumentos*. São Paulo: Perspectiva, 1972.

———. "O processo de independência no nordeste." In *1822: Dimensões*, ed. Carlos Guilherem Mota. São Paulo: Editora Perspectiva, 1972.

Mourão, Gonçalo de Barros Carvalho e Mello. *A revolução de 1817 e a história do Brasil: Um estudo de história diplomática*. Belo Horizonte, Brazil: Editora Itatiaia Limitada, 1996.

Muniz Tavares, Francisco. *História da revolução de Pernambuco de 1817*, annotated by Manuel de Oliviera Lima. Recife: Govêrno do Estado, Casa Civil de Pernambuco, 1969 (1840).

Nabuco, Joaquim. *Um estadista do imperio: Nabuco de Araújo, sua vida, suas opiniões, sua época*. Tomo 1, *1813–1857*. Rio de Janerio: H. Garnier, 1900.

Naro, Nancy Priscilla. "Brazil's 1848: The Praieira Revolt." PhD diss., University of Chicago, 1980.

———. *A Slave's Place, A Master's World: Fashioning Dependency in Rural Brazil*. London: Continuum, 2000.

"Narração official dos acontecimentos da provincia de Pernambuco nos dias 14, 15, e 16 de Setembro." *Revista do Instituto Archeológico e Geográphico Pernambucano* 10, no. 56 (1902): 79–81.

Nascimento, Luís de. *História da imprensa de Pernambuco, 1821–1954.* Vol. 2, *Diários do Recife, 1828–1900,* and vol. 4, *Periódicos do Recife, 1821–1850.* Recife: Imprensa Universitária Federal de Pernambuco, 1968.

Needell, Jeffrey D. "A Liberal Embraces Monarchy: Joaquim Nabuco and Conservative Historiography." *Americas* 48 (October 1991): 159–80.

———. *A Tropical Belle Epoque: Elite Culture and Society in Turn-of-the-Century Rio de Janeiro.* Cambridge: Cambridge University Press, 1987.

———. "Brasilien, 1830–1889." In *Handbuch der Geschichte Lateinamerikas,* edited by Raymond Buve and John Fisher. 3 vols. Stuttgart: Klett-Cotta, 1992.

———. "History, Race, and the State, in the Thought of Oliveira Viana." *Hispanic American Historical Review* 75 (February 1995): 1–30.

———. "Identity, Race, Gender, and Modernity in the Origins of Gilberto Freyre's 'Oeuvre.'" *American Historical Review* 100 (February 1995): 51–77.

———. "Party Formation and State-Making: The Conservative Party and the Reconstruction of the Brazilian State, 1831–1840." *Hispanic American Historical Review* 81, no. 2(2001): 259–308.

———. "Provincial Origins of the Brazilian State: Rio de Janeiro, the Monarchy, and National Political Organization, 1808–1853." *Latin American Research Review* 36, no. 3 (2001): 132–53.

Neves, Guilherme Pereira das. "A suposta conspiração de 1801 em Pernambuco: Idéias ilustradas ou conflitos tradicionais?" *Revista Portuguesa de História* 33, no. 2 (1999): 439–91.

Novais, Fernando A. *Brasil e Portugal na crise do antigo sistema colonial (1777–1808).* São Paulo: Hucitec, 1979.

Nugent, David. "Building the States, Making the Nation: The Bases and Limits of State Centralization in 'Modern' Peru." *American Anthropologist* 96, no. 2 (1994): 333–69.

———. *Modernity at the Edge of Empire: State, Individual, and Nation in the Northern Peruvian Andes, 1885–1935.* Stanford: Stanford University Press, 1997.

Octávio, José. "Setembrizada e Novembrada—Fontes de irradiação nordestina." In *Movimentos populares no nordeste no periodo regencial,* edited by Manuel Correia de Andrade. Recife: Massangana, 1989.

Oliveira, Cecília Helena L. de Salles. *A astúcia liberal: Relações de mercado e projetos políticos no Rio de Janeiro (1820–1824).* Bragança Paulista, Brazil: EDUSF e ÍCONE, 1999.

Oliveira Lima, Manuel de. *Dom João VI no Brasil (1808–1821).* Rio de Janeiro: Topbooks, 1996.

———. *O movimento da independência, 1821–1822.* Rio de Janeiro: Topbooks, 1997.

Ottoni, Theópilo. *Circular dedicada aos Srs. eleitores pela provincia de Minas Gerais.* São Paulo: Establecimento Graphico Irmãos Ferraz, 1930.

Ouvidoria Geral do Crime de Pernambudo. "A sedição de fevereiro de 1823: Traslado do Auto da Devassa que procedeu o Dr. Dezembargador e Ouvidor Geral do Crime da Relação Antonio José Osorio e Pina Leitão, pela sedição, tumultos, mortes e ferimentos praticadaos nesta villa, desde o dia vinte e um até o de vinte e oito de fevereiro do anno passado de mil oitocentos e vinte tres," *Revista do Instituto Archeológico e Geográphico Pernambucano* 14, no. 77 (1909): 379–494.

Pagano, Sebastião. *O conde dos arcos e a revolução de 1817*. São Paulo: Companhia Editora Nacional, 1938.

Palmer, R. R. *The Age of the Democratic Revolution: A Political History of Europe and America, 1760–1800*. 2 vols. Princeton: Princeton University Press, 1959–1964.

Pang, Eul-Soo. *In Pursuit of Honor and Power: Noblemen of the Southern Cross in Nineteenth-Century Brazil*. Tuscaloosa: University of Alabama, 1988.

Paolo, Pasquale di. *Cabanagem: A revolução popular da Amazônia*. Belem, Brazil: Centro de Estudos Jurídicos do Pará, 1986.

Pedreira, Jorge M. "From Growth to Collapse: Portugal, Brazil, and the Breakdown of the Old Colonial System (1750–1830)." *Hispanic American Historical Review* 80 (November 2000): 839–64.

Peloso, Vincent C., and Barbara A. Tenenbaum, eds. *Liberals, Politics, and Power: State Formation in Ninetenth-Century Latin America*. Athens: University of Georgia Press, 1996.

Pereira de Castro, Paulo. "'A experiência republicana,' 1831–1840." In *História geral da civilização brasileira*. Tomo 2, vol. 2, *Dispersão e unidade*, edited by Sérgio Buarque de Holanda and Pedro Moacyr Campos. São Paulo: DIFEL, 1985.

———. "Política e administração de 1840 a 1848." In *História geral da civilização Brasileira*. Tomo 2, vol. 2, *Dispersão e unidade*, edited by Sérgio Buarque de Holanda and Pedro Moacyr Campos. São Paulo: DIFEL, 1985.

Pimenta Bueno, José Antônio. *Direito público brasileiro e analise da constituição do Império*. Rio de Janeiro: Ministro da Justiça e Negocios Interiores, 1958.

Portella, Felix Fernandes. "A Setembrisada, a Abrilada, e a Guerra dos Cabanos: Apontametos para a história pátria." *Revista do Instituto Archeológico e Geográphico Pernambucano* 10, no. 58 (1903).

Porto, José de Costa. "Prefácio." In *Apreciação da Revolta Praieira em Pernambuco*, by Urbano Sabino Pessoa de Mello. Brasília: Senado Federal, Editora Universidade de Brasília, 1978.

Prado Júnior, Caio. *The Colonial Background of Modern Brazil*. Berkeley: University of California Press, 1971.

———. *Evolução política do Brasil e outros estudos*. São Paulo: Editora Brasiliense, 1963.

Province of Pernambuco. *Falla que, na occaziào da abertura da Assembleia Legislativa Provincial de Pernambuco recitou o Presidente da mesma Provincia*. Government of the Province of Pernambuco, Brazil: 1838.

Quintas, Amaro. "A agitação republicana no Nordeste." In *História geral da civilização brasileira*. Vol 2., *O Brasil monárquico*. No. 1., *O processo de emancipação*. São Paulo: DIFEL, 1985.

———. *O sentido social da Revolução Praieira.* Rio de Janeiro: Civilização Brasileira, 1967.

Rego, José Lins do. *Pedra Bonita.* Rio de Janeiro: José Olympio, 1961.

Reis, João José. *Slave Rebellion in Brazil: The Muslim Uprising of 1835 in Bahia.* Baltimore: Johns Hopkins University Press, 1993.

Ribeiro, Gladys Sabina. *A liberade em construção: Identidade nacional e conflitos antilusitanos no primeiro reinado.* Rio de Janeiro: Relume Dumará, 2002.

———. "As noites das garrafadas: Uma história entre outras de conflitos antilusitanos e raciais na Corte do Rio de Janeiro." *Luso-Brazilian Review* 37 (Winter 2000): 59–74.

Ribeiro, Maria Eurydice de Barros. *Os símbolos do poder: Cerimônias e imagenes do estado monárquico no Brasil.* Brasília: Editora UnB, 1995.

Ribeiro Júnior, José. *Colonização e monopólio no nordeste brasileiro: A companhia geral de Pernambuco e Paraíba, 1759–1780.* São Paulo: Hucitec, 1976.

Ricci, Maria Lúcia de Souza Rangel. *A atuação de um publicista: Antônio Borges da Fonseca.* Campinas, Brazil: Pontífica Universidade Católica de Campinas, 1995.

Ridings, Eugene. *Business Interest Groups in Nineteenth-Century Brazil.* Cambridge: Cambridge University Press, 1994.

Rodrigues, José Honório. *O conselho do estado, o quinto poder?* Brasília: Centro Gráfico do Senado Federal, 1978.

———. *Independência: Revolução e contra-revolução: A evolução política.* Rio de Janeiro: F. Alves, 1975.

———. *O parlamento e a evolução nacional: Introdução histórica.* Vol. 1. Brasília: Senado Federal, 1979.

Rodrigues de Sousa, Joaquim. *Analyse e commentario da Constituição politica do Imperio do Brazil, ou, Theoria e pratica do governo constitucional brazilero.* 2 vols. São Luiz do Maranhão, Brazil: B. de Mattos, 1867–1870.

Rowland, Robert. "Patriotismo, povo, e ódio aos portugueses: Notas sobre a construção da identidade nacional no Brasil independente." In Jancsó, *Brasil: Formação do estado e da nação.*

Russell-Wood, A. J. R. "The gold cycle, c. 1690–1750." In Bethell, *Colonial Brazil.*

———. "Preconditions and Precipitants of the Independence Movement in Portuguese America." In *From Colony to Nation: Essays on the Independence of Brazil,* edited by A. J. R. Russell-Wood. Baltimore: Johns Hopkins University Press, 1975.

Safford, Frank. "Bases of Political Alignment in Early Republican Spanish America." In *New Approaches to Latin American History,* edited by Richard Graham and Peter H. Smith. Austin: University of Texas Press, 1974.

———. "Politics, Ideology, and Society." In *Spanish America After Independence, c. 1820–c.1870,* edited by Leslie Bethell. Cambridge: Cambridge University Press, 1987.

Sandes, Noé Freire. *A invenção da nação: Entre a monarquia e a república.* Goiânia, Brazil: Editora UFG and Agência Goiana de Cultura Pedro Ludovico Teixeira, 2000.

Santos, Maria Januária Vilelea. *A balaiada e a insurreição de escravos no Maranhão.* São Paulo: Ática, 1983.

Santos, Mário Márcio de Almeida. *Um homen contra o império: Vida e lutas de Antônio Borges da Fonseca*. Recife: Fundação do Patrimônio Histórico e Artístico de Pernambuco, 1995.

———. "A Setembrizada." *Clio* 5 (1982).

Sarmiento, Domingo Faustino. *Facundo: Civilización y barbarie*. Madrid: Editora Nacional, 1975.

Schultz, Kirsten. *Tropical Versailles: Empire, Monarchy, and the Portuguese Royal Court in Rio de Janeiro, 1808–1821*. New York: Routledge, 2001.

Shumway, Nicolas. *The Invention of Argentina*. Berkeley: University of California Press, 1991.

Schwarcz, Lilia Moritz. *As barbas do imperador: D. Pedro II, um monarca nos trópicos*. São Paulo: Companhia das Letras, 1998.

———. *The Spectacle of the Races: Scientists, Institutions, and the Race Question in Brazil, 1870–1930*. New York: Hill and Wang, 1999.

Schwartz, Stuart. "The Formation of a Colonial Identity in Brazil." In *Colonial Identity in the Atlantic World, 1500–1800*, edited by Nicholas Canny and Anthony Pagden. Princeton: Princeton University Press, 1987.

———. *Sovereignty and Society in Colonial Brazil: The High Court of Bahia and Its Judges, 1609–1751*. Berkeley: University of California Press, 1971.

———. *Sugar Plantations in the Formation of Brazilian Society: Bahia, 1550–1835*. Cambridge: Cambridge University Press, 1985.

Seckinger, Ron. *The Brazilian Monarchy and the South American Republics, 1822–1831: Diplomacy and State Building*. Baton Rouge: Louisiana State University Press, 1984.

———. "The Politics of Nativism: Ethnic Prejudice and Political Power in Mato Grosso, 1831–1834." *The Americas* 32 (April 1975): 393–416.

"A sediçao militar de Setembro de 1831." *Revista do Instituto Archeológico e Geográphico de Pernambuco* 10, no. 56 (1902): 79–86.

Silva, Luiz Geraldo. "Negros patriotas: Raça e identidade social na formação do estado nação (Pernambuco, 1770–1830)." In Jancsó, *Brasil: Formação do estado e da nação*.

Silveira, Itala Bizerra da. *Cabanagem: Uma luta perdida*. Belém, Brazil: Secretaria de Estado da Cultura, 1984.

Sims, Harold. *The Expulsion of Mexico's Spaniards, 1821–1836*. Pittsburgh: University of Pittsburgh Press, 1990.

Sisson, S. A. *Galeria dos brasileiros ilustres (Os contemporâneos)*. 2 vols. São Paulo: Martins, 1948.

Smith, Anthony D. "State-Making and Nation-Building." In *States in History*, ed. John A. Hall. Oxford: Basil Blackwell, 1986.

Smith, T. Lynn. *Brazil: People and Institutions*. Baton Rouge: Louisiana State University Press, 1972.

Soares de Souza, José Paulino. *Ensaio sôbre o direito administrativo*. Rio de Janeiro, 1960.

————. *Estudos práticos sobre a administração das provincias no Brasil, pelo Visconde do Uruguay. Primeira parte: Ato Adicional.* Rio de Janeiro: B. L. Garnier, 1865.

Sodré, Nelson Werneck. *História da imprensa no Brasil.* Rio de Janeiro: Civilização Brasileira, 1966.

Sousa, Octavio Tarquinio de. *Bernardo Pereira de Vasconcellos e seu tempo.* Rio de Janeiro: José Olympio, 1937.

————. *História de dois golpes de estado.* Rio de Janerio: José Olympio, 1939.

Souto Maior, Mário, and Leonardo Dantas Silva, eds. *O Recife: Quatro séculos de sua paisagem.* Recife: Fundação Joaquim Nabuco, Editora Massangana, Prefeitura da Cidade do Recife, Secretaria de Educação e Cultura, 1992.

Souza, Iara Lis Carvalho. *Pátria coroada: O Brasil como corpo politico autônomo—1783–1831.* São Paulo: Fundção Editora da UNESP, 1999.

Souza, Paulo César. *A sabinada: A revolta separatista da Bahia, 1837.* São Paulo: Brasiliense, 1987.

Spalding, Walter. *A revolução farroupilha.* Porto Alegre, Brazil: Petroquímica Triunfo, 1987.

Stein, Stanley. *Vassouras: A Brazilian Coffee County, 1850–1900.* Cambridge: Harvard University Press, 1957.

Stern, J. Steve. "Between Tragedy and Promise: The Politics of Writing Latin American History in the Late Twentieth Century." In *Reclaiming the Political in Latin American History,* edited by Gilbert Joseph. Durham: Duke University Press, 2001.

Tavares, Luís Henrique Dias. *História da sedição intentada na Bahia em 1798: "A conspiração dos alfaiates."* São Paulo: Livraria Pioneira, 1975.

Taylor, William. "Between Global Process and Local Knowledge: An Enquiry into Early Latin American Social History, 1500–1900." In *Reliving the Past: The Worlds of Social History,* ed. Olivier Zunz. Chapel Hill: University of North Carolina Press, 1985.

Thompson, E. P. "The Moral Economy of the English Crowd in the Eighteenth Century." *Past and Present* 50 (1971): 76–136.

Thurner, Mark. *From Two Republics to One Divided: Contradictions of Postcolonial Nationmaking in Andean Peru.* Durham: Duke University Press, 1997.

Tilly, Charles. *Coercion, Capital, and European States, A.D. 990–1990.* Cambridge: Cambridge University Press, 1990.

————. *The Contentious French.* Cambridge: Cambridge University Press, 1986.

————, ed. *The Formation of National States in Western Europe.* Princeton: Princeton University Press, 1975.

Tollenare, L. F. *Notas dominicais.* Recife: Estado de Pernambuco, Secretaria de Educação e Cultura, Departamento de Cultura, 1978.

Torres, João Camillo de Oliveira. *A democrácia coroada: Teoria política do Império do Brasil.* Petrópolis, Brazil: Editora Vozes Limitada, 1964.

Uricoechea, Fernando. *Patrimonial Foundations of the Brazilian Bureaucratic State.* Berkeley: University of California Press, 1980.

Vallenilla Lanz, Laureano. *Cesarismo democrático: Estudios sobre las bases sociológicas da la constitución effectiva de Venezuela.* Caracas: Empresa El Cojo, 1919.

Vauthier, Louis Léger. *Diário íntimo de Louis Léger Vauthier.* Reprinted in Gilberto Freyre, *Um engenheiro francês no Brasil.* Tomo 2. Rio de Janeiro: José Olympio, 1960.

Viana, Oliveira. *Populações meridionais do Brasil: História, organização, psychologia.* São Paulo: Monteiro Lobato, 1922.

Vianna, Hélio. *Contribuição à história da imprensa Brasileira (1812–1869).* Rio de Janeiro: Imprensa Nacional, 1945.

———. *Da maioridade à Conciliação: Síntese de história, política, e bibliografia do período 1840–1857.* Rio de Janeiro: Universidade, 1945.

———. "'O Repúblico' Antônio Borges da Fonseca (1808–1872)." *Cultura política* 40 (May 1944): 151–90.

Walker, Charles F. *Smoldering Ashes: Cuzco and the Creation of Republican Peru, 1780–1840.* Durham: Duke University Press, 1999.

Wehling, Arno, ed. *Origens do Instituto Histórico e Geográfico Brasileiro: Idéias filosóficas e sociais e estruturas do poder no segundo reinado.* Rio de Janeiro: Instituto Histórico e Geográfico Brasileiro, 1989.

Welch, Cheryl. *Liberty and Utility, the French Idéologues and the Transformation of Liberalism.* New York: Columbia University Press, 1984.

Williams, Raymond. *Keywords: A Vocabulary of Culture and Society.* Rev. ed. New York: Oxford University Press, 1985.

———. *Marxism and Literature.* Oxford: Oxford University Press, 1977.

Woodward, Ralph Lee. *Rafael Carrera and the Emergence of the Republic of Guatemala, 1821–1871.* Athens: University of Georgia Press, 1993.

Wortman, Miles. *Government and Society in Central America, 1680–1840.* New York: Columbia University Press, 1982.

Zenner, Walter P. *Minorities in the Middle: A Cross-Cultural Analysis.* Albany: State University of New York Press, 1991.

Index

trade. *See* commerce
Tweed (ship), 75
two-party system, 138, 158, 168, 253

Uchoa, Pedro Cavalcanti de Albuquerque, murder of, 126, 149
Una, PE, 234–35, 240
União (newspaper), 235
United Provinces of the Rio de la Plata, 79
United States: anticommunism in, 194; approached for aid, 29; as source of republican model, 21
United States consul, 169, 173; on 1848 elections, 296n63; on Luiz do Rego Barreto, 262n61; on Setembrizada, 274n38
Uruguay, 81, 294n35. *See also* Cisplatine province
Utinga estate, battle of, 239

Vasconcelos, Bernardo Pereira de, 85, 127, 147, 223; criticism of justices of the peace, 128; named minster of justice, 131; Regresso and, 130, 281n42
Vasconcelos, Francisco de Paula, 99–100, 105–6, 108, 275n52–53, 276n62
Vasconcelos, Manuel Xavier de, murder of, 127
Vasconcelos, Pedro Francisco de, 147
Vauthier, Louis Léger, 143–44, 152
Veiga, Evaristo da, 130, 131, 281n43
Vergueiro, Nicoláu de Campos, 178
Viscount of Albuquerque. *See* Albuquerque, Antônio Francisco de Paula de Holanda Cavalcanti de, Viscount of Albuquerque
Viscount of Camaragibe. *See* Albuquerque,

Pedro Francisco de Paula Cavalcanti de, Viscount of Camaragibe
Viscount of Macaé. *See* Torres, José Carlos Pereira de Almeida, Viscount of Macaé
Viscount of Monte Alegre. *See* Carvalho, José da Costa
Viscount of Recife. *See* Barreto, Francisco Paes
Viscount of Sepetiba. *See* Coutinho, Aureliano de Sousa e Oliveira, Viscount of Sepetiba
Viscount of Suassuna. *See* Albuquerque, Francisco de Paula Cavalcanti de, Viscount of Suassuna
Viscount of Uruguai. *See* Sousa, Paulino José Soares de
Vitória de Santo Antão, PE, 85, 144, 216–17
voting franchise, 30; call for universal suffrage, 238, 248; qualifications for, 78
A Voz do Beberibi (Beberibe), 190
Voz do Brasil (Recife), 187, 204; closed, 236; Lusophobia and, 190–91

Wanderley, Caetano Francisco de Barros, 229
Wanderley, João Maurício Cavalcanti da Rocha, 145–46, 181
Wanderley, Manuel Henrique, 229
Wanderley, Pedro Cavalcanti, 234
Wanderley family, 140

xenophobia, 191, 293n15; state formation and, 205. *See also* estrangerismo (preference for foreigners)

zona de mata (forest area), 11, 122, 125, 158, 182